ARCO

Master the

GED

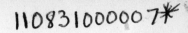

W9-AAC-536

2007

Ronald M. Kaprov, Ed.D.

Steffi R. Kaprov, M.A.

THOMSON

PETERSON'S

Australia • Canada • Mexico • Singapore • Spain • United Kingdom • United States

THOMSON

PETERSON'S

ISBN 13: 978-0-7689-2315-5 (Book only)
ISBN 10: 0-7689-2315-8 (Book only)
ISBN 13: 978-0-7689-2316-2 (Book with CD)
ISBN 10: 0-7689-2316-6 (Book with CD)

Printed in the United States of America

10 9 8 7 6 5 4 3 2 1   08 07 06

Twenty-first Edition

Other Recommended Titles:

ARCO 30 Days to the GED

ARCO Master the GED: Language Arts, Reading

ARCO Master the GED: Language Arts, Writing

ARCO Master the GED: Mathematics

ARCO Master the GED: Social Studies

ARCO Master the GED: Science

Peterson's GED Success

Contents

PART VIII: TWO PRACTICE TESTS

Preface

Congratulations! You made the decision to get your high school diploma by preparing to take the GED high school equivalency diploma test. The high school diploma is an important document to have. With a diploma, you can take advantage of education and training opportunities beyond the high school level and increase your earning potential by as much as 50 percent.

Since 1942, the GED Testing Program has enabled more than 14 million adults to obtain high school credentials. By following the advice in this book, you, too, can earn a high school equivalency diploma and increase your chances of professional and personal success.

ARCO Master the GED is an attempt to help you gain a clear idea of what to expect and how to prepare for the GED examination. It will give you a fair and reasonable explanation of testing procedures, scoring information, and useful test-taking hints. It will not give you any questions or answers from an actual examination. However, the three full-length Practice Tests, and the practice questions for each subject area will give you an understanding of the kinds of questions you may expect. You will find that this book is a useful guide for taking and passing the GED exam with the least possible heartache and headache.

The writers, Ronald M. Kaprov and Steffi R. Kaprov, each have many years of experience in the field of education, with Dr. Kaprov having worked on this highly successful book during the last twenty years.

Their unique qualifications include experience as master teachers, knowledge of curriculum and test preparation, and expertise in educational psychology and learning styles. They have had successful careers in allied fields, such as educational and test-preparation writing, engineering, and school psychology.

Each author has had a lifelong rapport with young people and an eagerness to help prepare them successfully for the GED and subsequent educational or work requirements. The authors and Thomson Peterson's wish you the best of luck earning your GED.

Credits

Before You Begin

HOW THIS BOOK IS ORGANIZED

You want to do your best on this test, and that's why you bought this book. Used correctly, this self-tutor will show you what to expect while giving you the most effective practice with subjects you can expect to see on the actual exam. *ARCO Master the GED 2007* provides you with the necessary tools to make the most of the study time you have, including:

- **"Top 10 Strategies to Raise Your Score"** gives you test-taking strategies.
- **Part I** provides the basics of the GED.
- **Part II** includes the Diagnostic Test.
- **Part III** reviews the Language Arts, Writing Test.
- **Part IV** reviews the Social Studies Test.
- **Part V** reviews the Science Test.
- **Part VI** reviews the Language Arts, Reading Test.
- **Part VII** reviews the Mathematics Test.
- **Part VIII** includes two complete practice tests.

THE DIAGNOSTIC PRACTICE TEST AND PROCESS

The diagnostic practice test does more than give you testing experience. The easy-to-use error analysis helps you track your performance, identify your strengths, and pinpoint areas for improvement. No other book helps you identify your areas for improvement as painlessly and completely. By understanding your "testing profile," you can immediately address your weak areas by working through the relevant review chapters, learning the relevant test-taking tips, and completing the additional practice exercises.

The Review Sections

1. The Mathematics Section provides user-friendly explanations of math processes in recognition of the particular difficulty many students have in this area. The answer explanations are written with care, taking you "by the hand" to coach you, and enable you to comprehend difficult concepts that might have been previously elusive in the classroom. There is also a

clearly presented step-by-step section on using the special scientific calculator effectively, as this instrument is utilized in part of the GED Mathematics Test.

2 The Language Arts, Reading Section provides an opportunity for improving these skills, which are necessary for good performance in reading as well as in all the other academic areas. The selections include a wide range of reading matter.

3 The Language Arts, Writing Section and the Social Studies Section include graphic illustrations in response to contemporary trends and current changes in curriculum and the demands of the GED.

4 The extensive Business Reading Section will help you become familiar with selections of a business, practical, or work-related nature. This enables you to deal more easily with readings of this kind throughout the GED.

THE PRACTICE TESTS

When you have completed your reviews, take the practice tests under simulated test conditions to sharpen your skills further. Find a quiet place where you won't be interrupted, set a timer for the required time, and work through each test as though it were test day.

SPECIAL STUDY FEATURES

Overview

Each chapter begins with a bulleted overview listing the topics that will be covered in the chapter. You know immediately where to look for a topic that you need to work on.

Summing it up

Each review chapter ends with a point-by-point summary that captures the most important points. The summaries are a convenient way to review the content of the chapters.

Bonus Information

QUICK TIPS!

Quick Tips! are brief, but broad-based suggestions that are helpful, proven aids in improving performance in the specific areas tested on the GED test.

NOTE

Notes highlight critical information about the GED format.

ALERT!

Alerts do just what they say—alert you to common pitfalls or misconceptions.

ABOUT THE CD

If you have the CD edition of this book, you have additional GED test preparation available to you. The CD contains 2 practice tests. We suggest that you begin by taking the diagnostic test at the beginning of the book. Once you have an idea of how you did and where to focus your preparation, review the material in the book. As the final part of your preparation, take the other tests in the book and on the CD.

YOU'RE WELL ON YOUR WAY TO SUCCESS

Remember that knowledge is power. By using *ARCO Master the GED 2007,* you will be studying the most comprehensive GED preparation guide available, and you will become extremely knowledgeable about the GED. We look forward to helping you obtain your GED. Good luck!

GIVE US YOUR FEEDBACK

We welcome any comments or suggestions you may have about this publication and invite you to complete our online survey at www.petersons.com/booksurvey or complete the survey at the back of his book, tear it out, and mail it to us at:

Publishing Department
Thomson Peterson's
2000 Lenox Drive
Lawrenceville, NJ 08648

Your feedback will help us to provide personalized solutions for your educational advancement.

TOP 10 STRATEGIES TO RAISE YOUR SCORE

When it comes to taking the GED, some test-taking skills will do you more good than others. Here are our picks for the top 10 ways to raise your score.

1. **Get to the test center early.** Make sure you give yourself plenty of extra time to get there.

2. **Listen to the test monitors and follow their instructions carefully.**

3. **Read every word of the instructions. Read every word of every question.**

4. **Mark your answers by completely darkening the answer space of your choice.**

5. **Mark only ONE answer for each question, even if you think that more than one answer is correct.** You must choose only one. If you mark more than one answer, the scoring machine will consider you wrong.

6. **If you change your mind, completely erase your initial choice.** Leave no doubt as to which answer you intend.

7. **Check often to be sure that the question number matches the answer space, that you haven't skipped a space by mistake.**

8. **Stay alert.** Be careful not to mark a wrong answer just because you weren't concentrating.

9. **Don't panic.** If you cannot finish a part before time is up, don't worry. Do not let your performance on any one part affect your performance on any other part.

10. **Check and recheck, time permitting.** If you finish a part before time is up, use the remaining time to check that each question is answered in the right space and that there is only one answer for each question. Return to the questions you found difficult and rethink them.

PART I

GED BASICS

All About the GED

WHAT IS THE GED?

The General Educational Development (GED) tests are a series of examinations that are designed to determine whether a person has the literacy and computational skills equivalent to those of the upper two thirds of the students currently graduating from high schools in the United States. The tests are sponsored by the American Council on Education, a nonprofit educational organization located in Washington, D.C. The tests are designed and developed by the GED Testing Service.

Since 1942, millions of adults have earned their high school credentials by passing the GED tests. Approximately 900,000 adults take the GED test each year, and more than 600,000 of them are awarded high school equivalency diplomas. Although passing rates vary widely from state to state, about 70 percent of all test-takers pass the five-part exam. All fifty states, the District of Columbia, nine United States territories and possessions, and ten Canadian provinces use GED results as the basis for issuing high school equivalency diplomas. The tests are administered under the supervision of state or provincial (in Canada) offices at designated GED testing centers (there are about 3,000 such centers), and the standards for a passing grade are set by each state or province. In addition, federal and state correctional and health institutions and the military services also administer the tests to persons under their jurisdictions.

What do the tests measure? According to the American Council on Education, the tests measure "broad concepts and general knowledge, not how well they

chapter 1

(test-takers) remember details, precise definitions, or historical facts. Thus, the tests do not penalize candidates who lack recent academic or classroom experience or who have acquired their education informally.

The GED Test

The current edition of this book represents a broadly updated version, to fully prepare you for the GED. The book was revised, after numerous consultations with the GED Testing Service of the American Council on Education, to comply with the changes made in the test as well as with national standards in the different academic areas.

These changes include:

- a greater emphasis on business-related skills broadly applied to all academic areas, and the potential needs of the third-millennium workplace
- an expanded use of graphics and other visual modes of presenting information
- more emphasis on practical, commonsense approaches and skills as related to academic subjects
- a greater recognition of the increasing impact of technology on daily life

WHERE CAN I TAKE THE GED TEST?

By contacting one of the telephone numbers listed below, you can receive information concerning the location of the testing center closest to you, the qualifications for taking the GED test in your particular state or area, and the fees involved.

UNITED STATES

Alabama
(334) 353-4889 or
(334) 353-4886

Alaska
(907) 465-8714

Arizona
(602) 258-2410

Arkansas
(501) 682-1978

California
(916) 445-9405 or
(800) 331-6316 (in-state only)

Colorado
(303) 866-6613 or
(303) 866-6743

Connecticut
(860) 807-2110

Delaware
(302) 739-3743

District of Columbia
(202) 274-7173

Florida
(800) 237-5113

Georgia
(404) 679-1621

Hawaii
(808) 594-0170 or
(808) 586-3124

Idaho
(208) 332-6980

Illinois
(217) 782-0083

Indiana
(317) 232-0522

Iowa
(515) 281-3636

Kansas
(785) 296-3191

Kentucky
(502) 573-5114

Louisiana
(225) 342-0444 or
(225) 226-7631

Maine
(207) 624-6754

Maryland
(410) 767-0538

Massachusetts
(800) 447-8844 or
(781) 388-3300

Michigan
(517) 373-1692

Minnesota
(651) 582-8437

Mississippi
(888) 4 ABE GED or
(601) 432-6481

Missouri
(573) 751-3504

Montana
(406) 444-4438

Nebraska
(402) 471-2475 or
(402) 471-4830

Nevada
(775) 687-9104 or
(775) 687-9167

New Hampshire
(603) 271-6698

New Jersey
(609) 777-1050 or
(609) 777-0577

New Mexico
(505) 827-6507

New York
(518) 474-5906 (Upstate Hotline)
(212) 803-3333 (NYC Hotline)

North Carolina
(919) 807-7137 or
(919) 807-7138 or
contact your local
    community college

North Dakota
(701) 328-2393

Ohio
(614) 466-1577

Oklahoma
(405) 521-3321 or
(800) 405-0355

Oregon
(503) 378-8648 ext. 369 or ext. 373

Pennsylvania
(717) 787-6747 or
(717) 783-6871

Rhode Island
(401) 222-4600

South Carolina
(803) 734-8347

South Dakota
(605) 773-3101

Tennessee
(615) 741-7054

Texas
(512) 463-9292

Utah
(801) 538-7870 (testing information)
(801) 538-7921 (test scores and
    records)

Vermont (800) 322-4004 or
(802) 828-5161

Virginia
(800) 237-0178 or
(804) 786-4642

Washington
(360) 704-4321

West Virginia
(304) 558-6315 or
(800) 642-2670 (Hotline)

Wisconsin
(608) 267-2275

Wyoming
(307) 777-6911 or
(307) 777-5396

U.S. TERRITORIES AND OTHER JURISDICTIONS

American Samoa
011 (684) 633-5237

Guam
011 (671) 735-5611 or
011 (671) 735-5566

Marshall Islands
011 (692) 625-3394 or
011 (692) 625-3236

Micronesia
011 (691) 320-2647

Northern Mariana Islands
(670) 234-5498

Palau
011 (680) 488-5452

Puerto Rico
(787) 759-2000

Virgin Islands
(340) 776-3484

CANADA

Alberta
(780) 427-0010

British Columbia
(250) 356-8133
(250) 356-2451

Manitoba
(877) 716-3889

New Brunswick
(506) 453-8251

Newfoundland
(709) 729-2405 or
(709) 729-4310

Northwest Territories
(867) 920-8939

Nova Scotia
(902) 424-4227 or
(902) 424-5162

Ontario
(416) 484-2737 or
(416) 484-2600

Prince Edward Island
(902) 368-5988 or
(902) 368-5978

Quebec
(418) 646-8363

Saskatchewan
(306) 787-5597

Yukon
(867) 668-8740

WHAT SUBJECTS ARE TESTED IN THE GED BATTERY?

The English-language GED battery consists of five individual tests:

1. *Language Arts, Writing*, contains two subsections: Part 1, Multiple-Choice Section, consists of 50 questions that ask you to identify errors in sentence structure, usage, mechanics (of writing), and organization; Part 2, Essay Test, is a writing exercise to determine how well you write.

2. *Social Studies* contains 50 questions drawn from history, economics, geography, and civics and government. The questions are designed to test your understanding of the basic principles in each area by asking you to interpret reading passages, cartoons, graphs, and charts. You should be able to draw conclusions and identify cause-and-effect relationships based on the material presented. Although some factual knowledge is necessary to answer certain questions, most questions require only a wide general knowledge. The student who habitually reads a newspaper or one of the major weekly news magazines should not have too much difficulty with this segment.

3. *Science* is probably the most difficult of the five segments. The 50 questions are drawn from the areas of life science, earth and space science, and physical science (chemistry and physics). Most questions test for an understanding of basic scientific principles and ideas. Answering the questions requires a combination of excellent reading skills and the ability to interpret scientific data.

4. *Language Arts, Reading,* contains 40 questions based on approximately seven excerpts from literature and nonfiction. The passages may be drawn from newspapers, magazines, novels, short stories, poetry, drama, and business or legal documents. The literary prose readings consists of representative selections written before 1920, the period between 1920 and 1960, and post 1960.

5. *Mathematics* is the part of the exam most universally feared by GED candidates. It really shouldn't be. Most of the 50 questions can be solved using the basic arithmetic operations of addition, subtraction, multiplication, and division.

There are a substantial number of algebra, measurement, and geometry questions on the test, as well as some number theory, data analysis, and probability. Most questions are presented as word problems. You will see questions that involve real-life situations or ask you to interpret information presented in graphs, charts, tables, or diagrams.

Part 1 of the Mathematics Test will allow you to use a calculator, and Part 2 will not. When you take the actual test, you will be given a chance to do some practice examples to get accustomed to using the calculator. You will also be given a sheet of important formulas to help you solve some of the problems on the exam. All scrap paper will be collected with your test.

You must pass both parts in order to get credit for the Mathematics GED Test. In other words, if you fail either Part 1 or Part 2, you will need to take the entire math test again.

NOTE

You must pass both parts of the writing test in order to receive credit for this test. In other words, if you fail either the Essay Test or the Multiple-Choice Section, you must take the entire Language Arts, Writing Test again.

NOTE

You must pass both parts in order to get credit for the Mathematics GED Test. In other words, if you fail either Part 1 or Part 2, you will need to take the entire math test again.

PREPARING TO TAKE THE TEST

There are two kinds of tests. The most widespread is called a *power* test, and it measures what you know, not how fast you can produce an answer. In a power test, you are generally given a liberal amount of time to complete a specific number of tasks or to answer a specific number of questions. The second kind of test is called a *time* test. In a time test, you are competing with the other candidates to see who can give the greatest number of correct answers within a very limited amount of time. The SAT is an example of a rigidly enforced time test, because it is essentially a competition among prospective college entrants to determine who will achieve the highest marks and be rewarded with admission to desired colleges.

The GED battery of tests is a blend of a power test and a time test, with greater emphasis on what you know than on how fast you can work out the correct answers. In the GED, you are in competition only with yourself. Of course, you should aim at getting the highest scores you can, but remember that you are not competing with anyone else.

Although the GED is not precisely a time test, there are time limits. Therefore, it is important that you learn to pace yourself. The time allowed for each test is always announced or written on the chalkboard by the exam proctor so that you can tell how much time you have. If possible, bring a watch to the exam so that you can keep track of your progress.

In most of the tests, the easiest questions come first, and you should be able to answer them quickly. The later questions are apt to be more complex and difficult; therefore, greater effort—and time—will be needed to solve them. Always answer the questions you are sure of first, then go back and spend additional time on the ones that you find more difficult.

Each of the questions on the GED includes five possible answers, and only one of the five is correct. If you're sure of the correct answer, don't waste time working through the other possibilities. Go on to the next question.

The new GED exam contains a total of 240 multiple-choice questions and 1 essay to be answered in 7 hours, 15 minutes. The following chart indicates the makeup of a typical GED Test Battery.

Format of the GED Test Battery

SUBJECT	NUMBER OF QUESTIONS	TIME ALLOWED
Test 1: Language Arts, Writing	50	75 minutes
Part I. Multiple Choice		
Sentence Structure (30%)		
Usage (30%)		
Mechanics (25%)		
Organization (15%)		
Part II. Essay	1	45 minutes
Test 2: Social Studies	50	70 minutes
History (40%)		
Economics (20%)		
Geography (15%)		
Civics and Gov't (25%)		
Test 3: Science	50	80 minutes
Life Science (45%)		
Physical Science (Physics and Chemistry) (35%)		
Earth and Space Science (20%)		
Test 4: Language Arts, Reading	40	65 minutes
Literary (75%)		
Prose, Poetry, and Drama		
Nonfiction (25%)		
Reviews, Business, Biography		
Test 5: Mathematics	50	90 minutes
Measurement and Geometry (20% to 30%)	• 25 questions with calculator use	
Algebra (20% to 30%)	• 25 questions without calculator use	
Number Standards and Operations (20% to 30%)		
Data Analysis (20% to 30%)		

NATURE OF THE QUESTIONS

Test 1: Language Arts, Writing

The Language Arts, Writing Test consists of two basic parts: Part I, the Multiple-Choice Section, and Part II, the Essay Test.

Part I. **Multiple-Choice Section**—Items here are based on paragraphs of about 12–18 sentences in length. The questions are of three types: sentence corrections, sentence revisions, and construction shifts. Some of the sentences are correct. Others contain errors. The errors will be of the following types:

1 Sentence Structure—will test your ability to recognize such errors as sentence fragments, run-on sentences, comma splices, incorrect subordination, or misplaced modification. There will be approximately 15 questions of this type.

2 Usage—will cover possible errors in subject-verb agreement, verb tense, and pronoun reference. This area will be represented by about 15 questions of this type.

3 Mechanics—will include questions testing rules of capitalization, punctuation, and the proper use of homonyms, possessives, and contractions. Mechanics will be tested by 12 to 13 questions.

4 Organization—will include questions about clarity of transition within paragraphs, text divisions, topic sentences, and general unity and coherence of written text. There will be about 7 to 8 questions in this area.

Part II. **The Essay**—You will have 45 minutes to write an essay on a single topic. In your essay, you will be required to present an opinion or an explanation regarding a situation about which adults would be expected to have some general knowledge. You will be told to draw upon your own personal observations, knowledge, and experience in writing your composition.

The essay will be graded on a four-point scale. Two judges will evaluate each essay for its overall effectiveness. A score of "4" will be given to a paper that is effectively written, well organized, and contains few writing errors; a score of "1" will be given to an essay that has not answered the question, is poorly organized, and is full of grammatical errors. (A score of "1" will result in a failing grade.)

Test 2: Social Studies

The subject matter for the Social Studies Test is drawn from topics in history (both American and world), geography, economics, civics, and government.

Questions may often combine more than one subject area. For example, a question about legislation to limit acid rain might combine the concepts of government, economics, and geography. When considering an answer, you should think of it as relating to an individual or to a member of a social group, such as a family, local community, a nation, or the global community.

Social Studies questions will not be solely based on memory but will challenge you to make use of everyday decision-making skills. Often they will include a short reading passage or a picture such as a map, a cartoon, or a graph. Problems will measure your ability to understand the questions, to apply them to other situations, to analyze specific parts of them, and to evaluate their accuracy.

If you have difficulty reading graphs, maps, or charts correctly, study the section entitled "Reading Charts, Maps, Graphs, and Illustrations," which you will find in the Language Arts, Reading Review Section of this book.

Test 3: Science

The subject matter for science items is drawn from life science, earth and space science, and physical science (physics and chemistry). Major themes include change, conservation of mass and energy, interactions, relationships, time and space, environmental and health topics, and science as it relates to everyday life.

Questions of the Science Test are divided among life science (45%), physical science (35%), and earth and space science (20%). Most questions require thinking rather than memory skills, with an emphasis on common, everyday decision-making skills.

The questions are designed to evaluate the following:

1 Did you understand the idea presented?

2 Can you apply something you just learned to an altogether different use?

3 How does something work? Can you analyze the steps?

4 Can you judge whether a statement is correct?

Most questions will require you to read graphs or charts of different kinds. If you have difficulty in this area, you can study the section entitled "Reading Charts, Maps, Graphs, and Illustrations," which you will find in the Language Arts, Reading Review Section of this book.

Test 4: Language Arts, Reading

The reading material in this test is chosen from one of the following:

1 Literary (75%)—good examples of contemporary fiction, classical literature, poetry, and drama that will probably be read for many years to come. The prose passages will consist of pieces written before 1920, between 1920 and 1960, and after 1960.

2 Nonfiction (25%)—examples of business documents (such as business forms or directions, legal agreements, employee directives or instructions, etc.); articles or reviews of films, theater, television, music, dance, or sports events; and passages from biographies.

Approximately six questions are asked after each of the seven reading passages. These questions test just how well you have understood the passages, can apply the knowledge to other situations, and are able to analyze the elements of style and structure in the reading passages.

Test 5: Mathematics

The mathematics section consists of problems in the following areas:

1 Measurement—perimeter, area, volume, rate of motion, rate of interest, time, and money

2 Geometry—parallel and perpendicular lines; triangle theory; slope; Pythagorean theorem; and congruent, similar, isosceles, and right triangles. There will also be problems in trigonometry.

3 Algebra—translating word problems, setting up equations, solving equations, inequalities, quadratic equations, linear functions, factoring, and algebraic fractions

4 Number Standards and Operations—sequences with fractions and decimals, comparing data, exponents, and scientific notation

5 Data Analysis—calculating mean, median, ratio, and simple probability; and interpreting graphs and tables

Thinking skills are stressed. To limit the amount of memorizing required, a page of mathematical formulas is provided on the test for reference. Also, you will be given a calculator to use for Part I of the test. Part II will require that you answer the questions without the use of a calculator.

HOW TO TAKE THE GED TEST

It is not unusual to dislike the concept of tests. Most adults fear tests because they evoke bad memories from childhood when tests given by teachers were always a chore and often a punishment. Therefore, it is important to understand that tests are essentially ways of measuring what you have learned and are not punishments. If you are afraid of tests, the best way to combat that fear is to take them as frequently as possible. In this case, familiarity breeds a healthy contempt and can reduce anxiety. Practice tests, such as the ones in this book, give you a chance to simulate in private what you will confront when you actually take the GED battery.

When you are satisfied that you are prepared to take the GED, consider the following test-taking tips:

1. Read every question carefully before attempting to answer it. If you don't understand what is required, ask the proctor for help.

2. Answer the easiest questions first. If you have absolutely no idea about how to answer a particular question, go on to the next one and come back to it later.

3. Leave no questions unanswered. Since you are not penalized for an incorrect answer on the GED, answer every question. Even when you do not have the vaguest notion about the correct answer, you have a 20 percent chance of being right. By eliminating obviously silly answers, you raise your chances of choosing the right answer.

4. Try to avoid careless errors, which may occur when you misunderstand what is requested. Do not do more than is required and do not assume that the test is trying to trick you. It probably isn't.

5. Bring chewing gum or hard candy with you to the test. Believe it or not, quietly chewing gum or sucking on hard candy tends to relieve nervousness, according to several prominent psychologists.

6. Make sure you hand in all your papers and that they all include your name and/or your identifying number and other requested information. Your answers cannot be marked unless your properly identified answer sheet is given to the proctor at the end of the test.

7. Be careful. Make certain that you fill in the blank spaces exactly as you had intended. For example, did you answer question 5 by marking the box reserved for question 6? Did you choose a "correct" answer when the "wrong" answer was requested? Did you answer every question (even those you may have skipped at first)?

WHAT IS A PASSING SCORE?

GED scores are reported as standard scores for each test. The raw score (or number of questions answered correctly) is converted to a standard score so that all tests and all forms of the GED battery may be evaluated similarly. Standard scores are based on the performance of high school seniors on these tests.

To be successful in passing the GED, a candidate must get a certain minimum score on each of the five tests. In general, that means that the person who answers just over half of the questions in each test correctly will probably get a passing score.

To be certain of earning a GED certificate or diploma, candidates should aim to score substantially above the minimum score on as many tests as possible. However, those who fall short of passing a single test or several tests can retake only those sections they failed to attain a minimum passing score. Information on retaking the GED test is available from the Department of Education of each state or province. (See the list of telephone numbers for each state or province on pages 4–6.)

TIPS FOR THE TEACHER

The *ARCO Master the GED Teacher's Manual* has been designed to enhance your students' learning opportunities. It presents teaching strategies designed to increase your students' comprehension of the skills and content found in this book. You can download a free copy of the manual at www.petersons.com/ged/teachers_manual.

More often than not, GED teachers get little or no orientation on the nature of the actual tests their students must eventually face. It would be enlightening, of course, if GED teachers were able to see or to take the actual examination in order to know specifically the kinds of questions their students must face. Unfortunately, current GED regulations do not allow this. If you, as a teacher, were to take the test, you would be violating the policies of the GED Testing Service and the laws of the state where you teach.

To obtain resources for educators teaching GED preparation courses, contact the American Council on Education's GED Testing Program at www.acenet.edu and choose Programs and Services.

Another source of information is *The GED Testing Program, Policies & Centers*, which is published by the GED Testing Service. It breaks down the policies and require-ments for issuance of GED diplomas on a state-by-state basis (there are no absolute or uniform requirements nationwide) and gives the methods and costs of applying to take the tests in each state. This source also lists the locations of test centers where the GED exam battery is given.

HOW TO TAKE THE PRACTICE TESTS

The Practice Tests in this book are as much like the actual GED test as possible. They cover each of the five subject areas using the same kinds of questions, the same directions, and the same time limits as the actual test. Taking these Practice Tests will show you what you know (and do not know) about the GED test, so you can direct your study to the areas that are most important for you.

As mentioned before, you will need a calculator for the first half of the GED Mathematics Test. While you will be given the Casio fx-260 Solar model at the test site itself, it would be helpful to have access to one while you are studying for the GED. The model mentioned above may be purchased at many large retail stores or by mail from: ACE Fulfillment Center, Department 191, Washington, D.C. 20055.

Start by taking the Practice Test 1: Diagnostic, and follow the step-by-step procedures below.

1. Read all directions carefully and follow them exactly.

2. Stick to the time limits given for each test.

3. Enter your answers on the tear-out answer sheet provided for the test.

4. When you have completed the entire exam, compare your answers with the correct answers given at the end of the test battery.

5. Count the total number of correct answers for each of the five tests and enter this number in the box provided on your answer sheet.

6. Add the five subtotals to obtain your total score for the test battery.

7. Use the Error Analysis Chart following the Diagnostic Exam to see where you are strong and where you are weak. This chart breaks down each test in the Diagnostic GED test battery into content areas. In the column headed "Questions," circle the number of every question you answered incorrectly. Count the number of circles in each content area and write the total number missed in the column headed "Number Incorrect." A large number of incorrect responses in a particular area indicates the need for further study in that area.

8. Start your review by consulting the Answer Explanations to all questions that you missed.

9. Turn next to the Skills Reviews provided in Parts III through VII of this book. Pay particular attention to the areas in which your Error Analysis showed you to be weak.

10. Take the two complete Practice Tests at the end of this book, following the procedures outlined in Steps 1 through 8.

STUDY TIPS FOR ADULT LEARNERS

These tips were written for you. Some time ago you dropped out of high school and now you realize that you need a high school diploma to do what you want to do with your life. You're intelligent enough to pass the GED, but you'll probably have to study well in order to do so.

These tips can help you become a winner. Follow the advice they give.

To help you use them, the tips have these features:

- They are written in language that is as clear as possible.
- Each tip begins with an action word to aid understanding.
- Similar ideas are repeated in different tips, worded a bit differently each time. This kind of repetition will help you learn these ideas.
- Most tips are easy to understand, but some are harder than others. If you don't immediately understand a tip, don't give up. Return to it at another time. The idea will become clear to you if you keep trying.

How to Use the Tips to Help You Pass the GED

Don't expect to learn all these tips at once. Focus on only one or two at a time. You can't learn all these tips at once because there are so many of them. If you don't have much time:

- Pick the tips that mean something special to you.
- Pick the tips that you feel will be most helpful.

Once you've mastered a tip, you may not need to refer to it again.

Write any tip that you think is especially important on a 3×5 inch index card or small piece of paper. Look at it often. Then you'll remember it.

- Put the card in your purse or pocket and look at it any time (while walking, or riding a bus, or dressing, or eating breakfast).
- If you write tips on several cards, put the cards in an envelope or file box. As you learn each one, throw it away. You'll soon have an empty envelope or box, and then you'll feel good about that.

Main Ideas to Look for in the Tips

You'll find these ideas throughout the tips.

TAKE RESPONSIBILITY FOR YOUR OWN LIFE AND LEARNING

- You're taking the GED not because someone is forcing you to, but because you want to. You're an adult—which means you have the power to make your own decisions and choose the patterns of your present and future life.
- Use that power to decide what's right for you. Choose to study and to be confident in your ability to succeed.

KNOW YOURSELF

- In school and afterward, you've developed many habits of learning and studying. Build on these.

ASK YOURSELF QUESTIONS SUCH AS THESE

- Did I enjoy something about school? If so, why? If not, why not?
- Did I get good grades in some subjects? If so, how?
- Do I remember very much of what I learned? If so, why? If not, why not?

- How well do I really know myself? How well do I want to know myself? What can I do to get to know me better?

BUILD YOUR CONFIDENCE

- Keep reviewing the confidence-building tips in the pages that follow. Those tips may be the most important ones of all.

BECOME VERY COMFORTABLE WITH THE GED EXAM

- Learn all you can about it and ways to take it well.

Build Your Confidence. Remind Yourself of Your Strengths. Know That You Can Do It

Developing confidence in your ability to pass the GED may be the most important part of your study program.

Remember: If you say to yourself, "I can't," then, indeed, you can't. If you say to yourself, "I can," then you probably can.

You must say to yourself, "I can do this," and then you will do it! You'll succeed!

TIP **Learn to say good things about yourself.**

- Do you hear yourself saying good things about yourself (like "I can do it!" and "I'm OK")?

- If you hear yourself thinking, "I can learn this. I feel good about learning this," listen closely. Be happy about what you're hearing.

- Do you hear yourself saying bad things about yourself?

- If you hear yourself thinking, "I can't learn this. I hate learning this. I'm not good enough to learn this," change the message. Make it positive. Remind yourself of what you do right.

SOME MESSAGES TO CHANGE

If you say:	*Instead say:*
I never do anything right.	I will do it right!
I never get any breaks.	I'll make my own breaks and I'll succeed.
Why should I try? It won't work out anyway.	I'll do my best, and I'll make it happen!
I tried and it didn't work.	I tried, but this time I'll try harder.
I'm no good at . . .	I am good at . . .

TIP **Remind yourself of your successes.**

Write something you've done well. _____

TIP **Remind yourself of how you felt after you succeeded.**

Write how you felt. _____

_____

TIP **Count your strengths. Remind yourself of the good things you recognize about yourself.**

The strengths listed below show a person's ability to think and take control of his or her life. They're ordinary things that you probably already do and never think about.

Check the items that apply to you. The more of these strengths you have, the more confident you should be.

_____ I am curious.

_____ I enjoy thinking about things.

_____ I wonder why things happen as they do.

_____ I remember things I thought about yesterday and important things I did last week.

_____ I speak easily to my friends and family.

_____ I am impressed with the amount of information people have learned about our world.

_____ I really enjoy what's beautiful in our world.

_____ I can recognize what's truly important in life and distinguish it from what's trivial.

_____ I write and use lists (like grocery and shopping lists).

TIP **Collect successes.**

Do one or two jobs that you consider tough—any kind of jobs. Say "I can do it," and then DO IT.

List these jobs when you complete them. Eventually, you'll have a list of successes. Read your list often.

TIP **See yourself as successful.**

Create that vision by closing your eyes and concentrating on seeing these pictures of yourself:

• Feeling confident as you work at the job you have in mind.

• Doing it.

• Feeling good afterward because you succeeded.

• Holding your head high when you take the GED.

TIP **Read the following messages and repeat one of them at least three times a day, before each meal.**

• I like who I am. I'm happy to be me!

• I'm going to be the best "me" I can be!

- I can do whatever I want to do if I want to do it badly enough.
- I'm happy to be alive. I'm going to make my life as good as it can be.
- Today is a good day. I'm going to make it even better by doing something that I'll be happy about tomorrow.

TIP **Remind yourself of the good feeling you get when you learn something new. Think of what you say to yourself when you get that feeling.**

- Hurray! I found it! I did it!
- Terrific! The problem came out right!
- Great! I never did that before, and I did it by myself—really well!
- Right on! I'm ready to try a new project!

TIP **Notice and be glad about what you learn. Ask yourself:**

- What did I know yesterday?
- What do I know now?
- How much did I learn in one day?

Feel good about knowing so much more now than you did. Think about how much better you'll feel when you know even more.

TIP **Recognize the power that comes from knowing a lot. Learn in order to gain that power. The power of knowledge can:**

- Win you the respect of friends and family
- Give you control over yourself (the most important power)
- Give you control over others
- Focus and drive your energy and excitement
- Give meaning to your life
- Direct your need to be useful
- Prevent tiredness and boredom

TIP **Stimulate your curiosity about your world.**

- Think of questions to which you'd like to know the answers. Then think of where you might find the answers or who might know them.
- Collect questions you want to know.

TIP **Do not be discouraged if you don't understand something at first. Learning new things is not always easy.**

- Be good to yourself! Give yourself a break.

TIP **Reward yourself when you've succeeded in learning something new.**

- Everybody loves a pat on the back.

TIP **Take one thing at a time.**

- Don't let yourself get swamped by trying to do everything at once.

TIP **Judge yourself by achieving success in your own goals and completing tasks you want to complete.**

- Don't judge yourself by your grades in school.
- If you have good grades, then enjoy that.

TIP **Accept help from those who offer help. Let them know that you appreciate their help.**

- Build your own strength and courage.

TIP **Be courageous: Ask questions, even if you think they're dumb.**

- You may be surprised how many people wanted to ask the same question but were afraid to do so.

TIP **Avoid griping and complaining. That only makes learning more difficult.**

- Instead, try to think positively about problems. Know that you can solve them. (It may take a while and some effort.)

TRY THESE FOUR STEPS:

1. Ask yourself, "What's the problem?" Answer the question.

2. Ask yourself, "What can I do about it?" Answer with as many possibilities as you can think of.

3. Ask yourself, "Which of the possibilities am I willing to try?" Answer by choosing the one possibility you like best.

4. Ask yourself, "What do I need to do to make it work?" Answer by writing a plan that includes:

   - All of the materials you'll need

   - When you want to complete it

   - People you'll need to tell about it

   - Exactly what you'll need to do in order to complete it

   - Anything else that will help you succeed in completing the job

Know Yourself So You Can Study in the Way That's Best for You

These tips should help you look at yourself (really look at yourself) and understand yourself. Then you can choose the study methods that work best for you.

TIP **Know what you know (and whether you know it correctly).**

- Say it in your own words.

    —Say it in several ways.

    —Invite someone you trust to check your accuracy.

- Write it in your own words.

    —Check your version with the original. (Just write it, don't worry about how it is written.)

- Speak into a tape recorder. Listen to what you've taped and check the accuracy:

    —With the book

    —With someone you trust

TIP **Take study breaks from time to time to record your progress.**

- Ask:

    —What did I know when I started?

    —What do I know now?

    —How much more do I want (or need) to learn?

    —Remind yourself that you now know much more than you did before. (And feel good about that!)

- Feel good about:

    —How much you've learned.

    —How much you've improved your skills (thinking, writing, reading, learning).

TIP **Find your own best way to concentrate. Solid concentration is necessary for good study.**

- Experiment with time, place, atmosphere (music?).

TIP **Figure out why some information is especially hard to learn. (Then do something to help yourself.)**

Don't feel as if you're stupid if you ask for help! You'll be stupid if you *don't* ask for help.

- Is there a special vocabulary that's difficult?

Then ask someone to help you understand those words.

- Is the organization of the information confusing?

Then ask someone to help you to outline it.

- Are there too many details?

Then organize the details in a way that means something to you.

- Is the logic (as in math or science) hard to follow?

Then ask for help!

- Do you feel bored with the material? Does it seem to be repetitive? Confusing?

Then *find* something to like about it.

- Should you have more background information in order to learn it?

Then explain the problem to your teacher or tutor and find material that will help.

TIP **Discover your learning strengths and use them.**

Do you:

- Memorize details easily?
- Learn best from listening, reading, or talking about ideas?

Then use that method when you study.

TIP **Discover your own pleasures in learning and enjoy those pleasures.**

- The joy of thinking up an idea by yourself
- Enthusiasm and excitement for a new project
- The satisfaction of fulfilling your own goals
- The challenge of a tough mental workout
- The good fellowship of sharing ideas
- The good fellowship of sharing the hardship and pain of tough work

TIP **Motivate yourself.**

Which works better for you?

- Fear of failure? (Remind yourself of that fear.)
- Desire for success? (Drive yourself with that desire.)

TIP **Know the senses through which you learn best—and use them.**

- Seeing? Then draw pictures or make graphs.
- Hearing? Then say ideas aloud and use a tape recorder.

TIP **Know how to reward yourself when you study well.**

- Pizza and soda?
- Jogging or swimming?
- Goofing off with friends?
- TV?

TIP **Recognize mental fatigue when it sets in.**

You'll know you're tired when you look at a page without seeing it or when you forget what you thought a minute earlier.

- Take a nap.

- Exercise.
- Take a shower.

TIP **Know when you study best—usually early in the morning or late at night.**

- Use that time well.

TIP **Know where you study best.**

- At the library?
- In your favorite chair?
- Outside?
- At a desk?

Most people study best when they find a place well suited to them and go there regularly.

TIP **Set realistic goals for yourself.**

- Determine what you're likely to be able to do.

  —If your goals are too high, you'll be discouraged.

  —If they're too low, you'll stop short of your ability.

- Set your goals for:

  —Today

  —This week

  —This month

- Check off the goals you've fulfilled. Reward yourself for your success.

Make Use of Your Community Resources

There are many resources available in your community to help you prepare for the GED. Two of the best are your local school and your library. Give both of them a call!

TIP **Call any nearby school district office and ask for information about the GED.**

- Someone should be able to direct you to the people who provide books, tutors, classes, and other aids for people who are studying for the GED.

TIP **Call your local library and ask for information about the GED.**

- Find someone—possibly in the reference department—who can tell you about books and equipment to help you study for the GED.

TIP **Learn to use all library services relating to the GED.**

- Books and magazines
- Microfilm and microfiche
- Videotapes
- Computer programs
- Audiotapes

Remember: Ask library personnel for help. They're there to help you.

TIP **Look in your TV guide for programs geared to helping you pass the GED.**

The two channels most likely to have programs that can help you are:

- PBS (Public Broadcasting)
- TLC (The Learning Channel)

If you have no program guide, call these stations or call the TV cable company. Ask them for information.

TIP **Call your local community college.**

Ask about available resources to help you study for the GED.

- You may need to be patient while someone figures out with whom you should talk.
- Someone there is likely to be able to guide you and suggest sources of information.

TIP **Look for special community services that may be available for people who have difficulty learning.**

These special services may be available in:

- Libraries

    —Audiotapes that you can listen to

    —Reading machines to help you read better (Some of them even talk to you or read a book aloud.)

    —Literacy programs

- Schools

    —Remedial programs in which you might still be eligible to enroll

    —Tutors who have been trained in how to help you with your special difficulty

- Private and government agencies (like the Bureau of Vocational Rehabilitation) with training programs

TIP **Seek on-the-job programs to help you read and learn better.** Tell the personnel director of your company (if there is one) that you want to take the GED and ask for information about:

- Literacy or GED training programs

- Bureau of Vocational Rehabilitation (BVR) programs
- Computer programs that might be helpful
- Any other options?

If there is no personnel director, ask your boss.

Discover How Ideas Are Organized So You Can Understand Them

The ideas in this section are not easy. Read them and try to understand them now. If you don't understand them at first, come back to this section at another time and try again.

If you can discover how information is organized:

- You'll learn information more efficiently and remember it better
- You'll read with more understanding
- You'll organize your own ideas better when you write

Ideas follow each other in logical order. That means that like the cars of a train, ideas are attached, one to the other, and they follow one another in a way that must make sense. In addition, the whole train of ideas must be going somewhere, saying something as a whole.

To organize their ideas, all writers follow a basic pattern. The tips that follow will help you understand this pattern.

Key Words

To determine how ideas are organized, there are certain key words you must know. These words are defined below.

MAIN IDEA

Every paragraph, chapter, paper, or book develops one main idea. It's the idea that all the writing focuses on. The main idea is the destination or goal of the whole train of thought.

GENERALIZATION

A generalization states an idea that is true for all the details that follow it. Main ideas are usually generalizations.

> **Rivers provide many advantages for the people who live near them.** You can develop this idea by writing about how different rivers help people in different ways:
> - The Nile River and how it overflows each year to provide water for farming
> - The Mississippi and how it provides a "highway" for ships carrying cargo
> - The Amazon River and how its waters provide fish for people to eat

DETAILS

Details fill in information to make generalizations clear, meaningful, and acceptable. They support the main idea. Details make up most of what's written.

Good families are affectionate. Affection, of course, takes many forms. In some families, members greet each other with polite handshakes. In others, people show affection with hugs and warm kisses.

The first sentence in this example states the generalization. The second sentence introduces supporting details. The last two sentences provide the details, naming "handshakes," "hugs," and "kisses."

OUTLINING

Outlining is a way of showing visually the relationship among the ideas in a written or spoken passage.

Outlines take a form that may be familiar to you:

```
I. . . . . . . .
    A. . . . . . . .
    B. . . . . . . .
        1. . . . . . . .
        2. . . . . . . .
II. . . . . . . .
    A. . . . . . . .
        1. . . . . . . .
        2. . . . . . . .
    B. . . . . . . .
        etc.
```

I and II are the highest levels of generalization within the book or chapter or essay. "A" and "B" give details on I or II, and 1 and 2 give details on the capital letter they follow. Each lower level develops information that is closer and closer to what we can see or smell or count. When we can see or count precisely, then we call the information "a fact." Facts mean the same thing to everyone who reads them.

LISTS AND PARALLEL FORMS

When you create a list, you are grouping things that are related. You write them in parallel (that is, similar) form.

Here is a list of things to do, all written in parallel or similar form (one word):
- Shopping
- Driving
- Cooking

The following is a different list of things to do, also written in parallel form (word groups that start with an action word):

- Fix broken lock
- Mail phone bill
- Walk the dog

Note that all of these study tips are written in parallel form.

In an outline, all Roman numbers form a list, all capital letters form a list, and so on.

SUBORDINATE IDEA

A detail that describes a main idea is called a "subordinate" idea.

You are writing a paragraph with the main idea, "Apples appeal to us through several senses." That's your topic sentence. You plan to discuss the texture, taste, and smell of apples. You start with texture. You write, "They are smooth and cool to touch." This is your subordinate idea. Then you might continue by writing, "They taste sweet and tangy." This is another subordinate idea. These details both support the idea that "Apples appeal to us."

INFERENCE

An inference is a conclusion that you draw from information you hear or see.

You may read, "All acorns come from oak trees," and "The tree in my yard produces acorns." The inference you would draw is that the tree in the yard is an oak tree.

Be aware that not all inferences are correct. For example, suppose you read:

"Colonel Jones had a long nose. Colonel Ericson had a long nose. Colonel Zanofesky had a long nose."

The inference you might draw from this information is "All Colonels have long noses." This inference is not only incorrect, it's foolish.

Tips to Help You Understand

TIP **Find the main idea.**

- Try to answer the question "What is this about?"
- State the idea in your own words.
- Relate it to things you know.

If you understand the main idea, you won't have to work hard to remember it. You'll know it! Also, the details that support the main idea will be easier to recognize.

TIP **Define key words precisely and meaningfully for yourself.**

- Say and write these definitions in your own words.
- Ask a reliable person whether your definition is correct.

TIP **Relate details to the main idea.**

Details that relate to the main idea can be found in:

- Examples
- Explanations
- Descriptions

TIP **Outline everything so you can:**

- See how information is organized
- See how main ideas relate to details

TIP **Write and rewrite all your notes in outline form.**

- This way you can remember easily.

TIP **Outline chapters in your books.**

- Studying the information will be easier.

TIP **Relate what you're learning to what you know.**

- Ask yourself: What do I know (from experience, from other reading, from my own thinking) that relates to this new idea?
- Think up a mental picture to help you remember the new idea.

TIP **Know when you've fully understood a new idea.**

When you understand a new idea, you'll be able to:

- Think up your own examples of it
- Recognize other examples of it in what you read or hear
- Draw it—as a map
- Use arguments to agree or disagree with it

TIP **Ask questions about what you read and hear.**

- Ask yourself after reading or hearing information:

  —What should I know about this information?

—What more can I know about it?

—What are some examples?

—How does this work?

—What's the point?

—What does this mean?

—How is this made?

- Improve your questioning skills.

TIP **Look for what's interesting in what you're learning.**

- Seek more reasons for learning this than passing an exam.

- Think of how your new knowledge can help you in your daily life.

Understand What You Read in Texts and Study Guides

This section probably won't help you read more quickly, but it can suggest techniques that will help you read with more understanding.

TIP **Use "OK4R."**

If you learned a reading technique like this one while you were in school, review what you learned. (It might have been one called SQ3R or REAP.) If you never learned such a technique, try this one.

❶ Overview: Scan the title, headings, words in bold type, first and last paragraphs, table of contents, bulleted lists, and picture captions—everything that stands out in the text.

❷ Key Ideas: Skim the text to get a sense of the main ideas. Look for key words, which will probably be highlighted and repeated. Make sure you understand them.

❸ Read: Read the information quickly. Pay close attention to what you read.

❹ (W)Rite: Write down the main ideas in your own words as you understand them. Check your words to make sure that you caught the author's meanings. (Note: Do not write the author's words. That's not very helpful.)

❺ Relate: Connect the information with what you already know. Remember a personal experience or a meaningful picture, and relate this new idea to that.

❻ Review: Go over the information again and again, not necessarily immediately, but soon.

TIP **Know how to "skim" a text well.**

Look it over quickly but pause to read more completely:

- Title

- First paragraph or two and last paragraph

- First sentence in each paragraph

- Headings and subheadings

- Pictures (and captions), maps, graphs, and the like
- End-of-chapter questions
- Boldface terms and phrases

When you skim a text, keep your eyes moving quickly over the words. Don't stop moving your eyes. Skip unimportant words. Work to improve your skimming skill. It will be very helpful during the exam.

TIP **Know how to "scan" a text well.**

- Scanning means looking for one or two specific words, often words that answer a question on a test. Work to improve your scanning skills. It will be very helpful during the exam.

TIP **Read for the main idea.**

Each paragraph and each essay must have only one main idea. You can usually find it in the first sentence or the final one.

- To find the main idea, ask yourself, "What is the writer saying?" Then answer your own question with one sentence.
- State that main idea in your own words.

Work to improve this skill of finding the main idea. It will be very helpful during the exam.

TIP **Avoid trying to remember all details.**

- Choose only those that seem important to the author.

TIP **Learn to tell facts from opinions.**

- Recognize the difference between statements of fact and statements of opinion.

> She has black hair and green eyes. (fact)
> She is the best-looking woman in the room. (opinion)

TIP **Ask yourself questions as you read. Try to predict what the author will say.**

- You'll focus your attention more keenly and read more actively.

TIP **Read actively. Add your thinking to that of the author.**

In other words, as you read:

- Make connections between what you're reading and something you already know.
- Hear your own disagreements and disputes.
- Think about the importance of these ideas in your life.

TIP **Talk to others about the information, especially if it doesn't mean much to you.**

- Ask friends and teachers what they think about it.
- Look up the ideas in other books.

TIP **Read aloud something you particularly want to remember.**

- Think of people with whom you want to share these ideas.

TIP **Talk to yourself—aloud if possible—about the information.**

- Talk as if you're telling a young child about it. (In fact, if you have a young child, tell him or her about it. Find something to make it fascinating!)

TIP **Put the book aside from time to time and outline the main ideas.**

- If you can do this, you'll remember what you read.

Learn How to Get the Most from Your Teachers and Classes

- Many of you are preparing for the GED by taking a special class or by using a tutor or private teacher. These tips should help you get the most from teachers and classes.

- You can find out about GED classes by calling your high school or your GED testing center in your community. The testing centers exist to help you pass the GED.

Take an Active Part in Your Classes

TIP **Don't be afraid to ask questions when you need help.**

- Tell your teacher if you don't understand a lesson. When you say you don't understand, your teacher will be happy to help you. Your teacher is trained to give information in a way that you will understand.

- Best idea of all: Ask questions and ask the teacher exactly what you need to know.

TIP **Take a tape recorder to your class/tutoring session.**

- Ask permission to record the session, and then you can listen to it later. This can be especially helpful if you have trouble reading your own notes.

TIP **Know what skills or information you hope to learn in each class session.**

For example, you might expect to:

- Sharpen multiplication and division skills.
- Practice writing essays.
- Learn how to read a map or a political cartoon.

If you don't know what goals to set for these classes, ask your teacher/tutor. After class, review what you've learned.

Enjoy the Class and Your Classmates

[TIP] **Look for moments of excitement in class.**

- This excitement can happen when any one of you learns something new or solves a difficult problem.

[TIP] **Learn to like and trust the other students.**

Other students can help you in these ways:

- Encouraging you when you need it
- Sharing their worries—which are probably the same as yours
- Listening to you when you need to talk to someone
- Giving you their opinions of your ideas
- Studying with you

[TIP] **Offer to help other students.**

- You'll feel good about yourself if you can help someone who needs help.
- You'll learn the information better if you explain it to someone else.

[TIP] **Avoid people who have a negative attitude.**

- Some people in your class might make negative comments that discourage you. Just avoid them. Ignore them. Don't let them get you down, and don't let them think they have the power to get you down.

[TIP] **Go to class well rested if possible so that you can pay attention.**

- You'll get more out of your classes if you are wide awake and ready to learn.

Use Class Time Well to Listen and Learn

[TIP] **Sit in the seat that's best for you, perhaps near the front or beside a special person or near the chalkboard. Try different seats.**

- See where you learn best.
- Try sitting in the front row. Your teacher will know that you want to learn and will respond to you better.
- Sit where you can see movies and videos best.

[TIP] **Listen for the main idea.**

- Always ask yourself, "What's the big idea here? What does my teacher really want me to learn?"
- Recognize some ways that teachers introduce a main idea:

  —They may say, "This is the main point," or "I want to be sure that you know this point."

  —They say the main idea with a strong voice and body language.

  —They spend a lot of time making the idea clear.

—They introduce a special word, a "key word," and define it. They reuse that word often.

TIP **Listen to what your teacher says about the main idea.**

Does the teacher:

- Give examples (saying "for example")?
- Describe how something works (saying "this is step 1, step 2, step 3," and so on)?
- Compare the idea with other ideas (saying "in comparison" or "in contrast")?
- Restate the idea (saying "in other words")?
- Give facts that support the idea (saying "these are the facts" or "this is how we know this is true")?
- Define words (saying "this means")?

TIP **Be willing to accept new information.**

Don't assume that what your teacher says is true.

- If you think there is something wrong, ask your teacher.
- Don't fight against learning the information because you disagree.

TIP **Listen very carefully to the first 5 minutes and last 5 minutes of a class.**

- That's when your teacher will state or restate the main ideas of the class.

Take Notes Well in Class

TIP **Write your notes so you can read them later.**

- Write in your best handwriting.
- Ask your teacher to speak more slowly if you're having trouble taking good notes.

TIP **Write down only what's important.**

- Don't try to write down everything the teacher says. If you do, you might miss something important.

TIP **Leave a lot of white space in your notebook. Your writing will be easier to read and you will have space to add things later.**

- Write large and skip lines.
- Write on only one side of the paper.

TIP **Leave wide margins all around the paper.**

- Leave two inches on the left side of the paper. Use this space to write:

  —One or two key words

  —Your thoughts: doubts, questions, and what you already know that relates to what you're learning

- Leave 2 inches at the top of the page so you can add headings to tell you what's on the page. (Heading are titles for the information that follows.)

TIP **Use headings frequently in your notes.**

- Write each heading on a line by itself.

TIP **Copy all board work—words and drawings—exactly.**

- If you're not sure how correct your notes are (words or drawings), mark your page somehow, perhaps with question marks. Then later, ask other students or the teacher.

TIP **Create your own shorthand so you can write quickly.**

- Abbreviate common words.
- Use simple symbols that are meaningful to you. For example:
    < less than
    > more than
    = the same as

TIP **Mark important points clearly.**

- <u>Underline</u>
- Star**
- CAPITAL LETTERS
- Different colored pens and pencils

TIP **Relate one idea in your notes to other ideas written earlier.**

- Draw arrows to connect ideas.

TIP **Recopy your notes after class.**

- Squeeze your notes into fewer words.
- Outline your notes to highlight main ideas.

TIP **Don't take notes at all if you take poor notes or if you can't read what you write.**

- Use your class time just to listen and try to remember.
- Tape recording the lecture or conversation might help.

Learn How to Memorize What You Need to Know for the Test

So much information exists that no one can memorize it all. But you need to know some information about history, geography, science, literature, and so on. You need to memorize some of it so you can find it in your mind when you need to know it.

Here is some useful information about memory:

- You will remember information best if you link new information with something you already know.
- No memory will be reliable if you don't understand what you're trying to remember.
- Tension, stress, and anxiety confuse memory and prevent you from remembering clearly.

TIP **Link what you're learning to what you already know.**

- Make connections between the new information and:

    —Familiar images

    —Familiar experiences

    —Familiar information (for example, what you've learned in earlier classes)

TIP **Write down key ideas.**

- Head blank sheets of paper with an important date or key word.
- Fill in supporting details (in your own words).
- Study the main ideas and details together so you will remember how they relate to each other.

TIP **Use all your senses when memorizing.**

- Hear it: say it aloud.
- Touch it: use your fingers and skin.
- Feel it: alert yourself to your gut feelings.
- Taste or smell it if you can.

TIP **Review your notes as soon as possible after your class or tutoring session.**

- Highlight the information you *most* want to remember.
- Ask the teacher or your classmates for correct information if you think your notes may not be right.
- Seek main ideas and key words. Review them again and again.

TIP **Make up your own memory aids or use ones suggested by your teacher.**

- Make up acronyms—words composed of the first letters of names or ideas to be remembered.

HOMES is composed of the first letters of the names of the Great Lakes: Huron, Ontario, Michigan, Erie, and Superior.

- Create a jingle with rhyme and rhythm (the sillier, the better).

"i" before "e" except after "c"

Columbus sailed the ocean blue in fourteen hundred ninety-two.

The number you are dividing by turn, upside down and multiply. (rule for dividing fractions)

- Create images you can see or feel.

If you're learning places on a map, imagine traveling from place to place.

- Make up sentences (again, the sillier, the better) in which the first letters of each word remind you of something you want to remember.

Please excuse my dear aunt Sally.
(This is the order for solving algebraic equations: parenthesis, exponents, multiplication, division, addition, and subtraction.)

TIP **Focus on the main idea of a lesson or reading passage just before you go to sleep.**

- That idea will come to you immediately the next morning when you wake up.

TIP **Repeat information to be memorized at odd moments—not just when you're sitting at your desk "studying" but when you're eating or waiting for the bus or walking home.**

TIP **Use index cards to write down questions and answers that you want to remember.**

- Write the questions on one side and the answers on the other.

   —Test yourself.

   —Reshuffle cards with questions you can't answer, then test yourself again on those questions.

   —Exchange cards with classmates who have also written questions.

- Use index cards to learn new words. Write the word on the front of the card and definition on the back.

TIP **Repeat information aloud. Hearing the words will help you remember.**

- If you study better alone, say the information you're learning aloud to yourself. If you study better with others, repeat the information aloud to each other.

TIP **Write down everything you learn.**

- Write it all in your own words so you're sure to understand what you've written.
- Write as if you are writing for a reader who doesn't know anything about this information.
- Write as if you're keeping a journal of your learning. Indeed, keep your notes as a journal.

TIP **Write down what you've learned in as few words as you can.**

- Rewrite your class notes in short sentences or groups of words.
- Rewrite your reading assignments in short sentences, mentioning only the main idea.

`TIP` **Vary the order in which you repeat items in a list.**

- You'll remember listed items better if you say the list:

  —From start to finish

  —Backward

  —In mixed up order

`TIP` **Be confident that you'll remember what you've studied.**

- If you've studied well, the information is there in your mind, ready for you to use.
- If you feel swamped, remind yourself of how much information you've already learned.
- If you've made a checklist, check off your accomplishments so you can see how far you've come.

`TIP` **Don't let your emotions prevent you from learning.**

- If you're having trouble remembering what you're studying, ask yourself if it's because you're feeling:

  —Nervous

  —Anxious and tense

  —Afraid

  —Sad

  —Depressed

  —Angry

  —Very happy

- Recognizing your emotions will help reduce their power over you.

`TIP` **Learn why an idea is important so you can better remember it.**

- If you consider the idea trivial or useless, you'll have a harder time memorizing it.

`TIP` **Use audiotapes to help you memorize.**

- Make your own tapes. Read or say the information you want to learn. Then play back your taped message. You'll memorize the information in two ways:

  —By saying it

  —By listening to it

- Listen to your tapes when you're walking or driving—any place you have a tape player handy.

`TIP` **Associate a list you're learning with a list that you already know well, like the days of the week, the months of the year, or the alphabet.**

- Link each item in the new list with an item in the list you know.
- Associate items from the two lists that start with the same letter.
- Use your imagination to picture items on a list as people sitting together around a table.

Arrange Your Study Space and Materials Well

You know best how to make yourself comfortable when you study. Here are some suggestions to consider:

TIP **Unclutter the area.**

- Bring only what you need to your study area—papers, books, pencils, etc.

TIP **Get rid of all distractions.**

- For example, music

    —Does it distract you? If so, don't play it.

    —Does it help you concentrate (possibly by drowning out other sounds)? Then let it play.

TIP **Sit comfortably.**

- Don't get so comfortable that you feel dull or sleepy.

TIP **Arrange lighting so you can see without strain.**

- Keep a lamp slightly behind or beside your left shoulder.
- Avoid glaring lights and ceiling lights.

TIP **Check your study preference:**

- When it's quiet
- By yourself
- In the morning
- At a desk
- When it's noisy
- With others
- In a special area at home
- At night
- In a chair

TIP **Always study in the same place.**

TIP **Keep your calendar handy.**

- Write all deadlines on it so you won't worry about forgetting something.

Manage Your Time Well

Clearly, you have a lot to do when you're handling adult responsibilities and at the same time studying for the GED. These TIPS should help you manage your time successfully.

TIP **Make a personal calendar well before the test. Write down deadlines for all the work you need to complete.**

- Include all deadlines. Check with teachers, advisers, tutors—everyone—so you can be realistic about how much you have to do and how much time you need to do it. Set deadlines early.

TIP Don't put off studying. Just do it.

- Know and avoid these excuses:

  —Not in the mood

  —Don't feel good

  —Swamped by the amount to be learned

  —Unsure of what to do when . . .

- Break large tasks into several small tasks and get started.

- Recognize that the worst part of studying is thinking about studying.

- Feel the wonderful feeling that comes with finishing a task successfully.

TIP Figure out what time of day you work best.

- Do you work best in the early morning? In the late evening? At that time, study:

  —What's most important

  —What's most difficult

  —What will help you feel successful so that you'll go on to study well

TIP Create your own list of things to do.

- List the tasks you want to complete:

  —Daily

  —Weekly

  —From now until the day of the test

- Include: Task deadline, date completed, and suggested reward.

- Use a red pen to check off each task you finish. (You'll be pleased with yourself.)

TIP Reward yourself when you complete tasks.

- Pizza? Exercise? TV?

TIP Tell friends and relatives about your schedule.

- Let them know that you expect them to respect it.

TIP Break up your study time.

- Study for three 1-hour periods rather than one 3-hour period.

TIP Know when taking a break will help you to study better.

- Recognize when you need a break:

  —Your eyes glaze over.

  —You read without understanding.

  —You read the same words over and over again.

TIP Plan your social time as well as your study time.

TIP Say "no" to time-consuming requests from others.

• Studying for the GED is your most important task.

Remember: You Can Do It!

Last year, more than 700,000 people in the United States and Canada passed the test and received their GED diplomas. You can do it, too!

SUMMING IT UP

- The GED is administered throughout the United States and Canada; the standards for a passing grade are set by each state or province.

- The tests that make up the GED battery are Language Arts, Writing; Social Studies; Science; Language Arts, Reading; and Mathematics.

- You must pass all five tests of the GED battery to earn your GED.

- Learning the question types in advance is one of the best ways to prepare for the GED.

- Developing confidence in your ability to pass the GED may be the most important part of your study program.

- Arrange your study space and materials well.

- Manage your time well. It is important that you learn to pace yourself.

PART II

DIAGNOSING STRENGTHS AND WEAKNESSES

CHAPTER 2   Practice Test 1: Diagnostic

Practice Test 1: Diagnostic

DIRECTIONS FOR TAKING THE DIAGNOSTIC TEST

There are five tests in the Diagnostic Test: Test 1—Language Arts, Writing; Test 2—Social Studies; Test 3—Science; Test 4—Language Arts, Reading; Test 5—Mathematics. Each test has a different time limit and a different set of directions.

Plan to take an entire test at one time. Follow the directions given at the start of each test.

Tear out the answer sheet found on pages 45–49 and use it to mark your answers to all questions.

As you complete each test, check your answers with the Answer Key that starts on page 135. On your answer sheet, mark an X through each incorrect answer. Then, turn to the Error Analysis chart on page 159 and circle the number of each question you answered incorrectly.

The Error Analysis shows you the subject area of each test question. Once you have circled all your incorrect answers, count the number of circles in each subject area and write that number in the column marked "Number Incorrect."

Use your Error Analysis to determine which content areas you need to study most in order to raise your GED score. Parts III through VII of this book provide skill reviews and practice questions for each GED subject area. Read the review and answer the practice questions to help strengthen the areas where you are weak.

At the end of this book are two more Practice GED Tests. Take these exams just as you took the Diagnostic Test. They will provide valuable practice for the GED test, and they will help you to decide whether you are ready for the "real thing."

SCORING THE DIAGNOSTIC TEST

When you have completed the Diagnostic Test, score yourself and write the total number of your correct answers at the corner of each test's answer sheet. Then compare your number of correct answers with the numbers in the table below. Of course, you cannot score your own essay. Ask a person whose judgment you respect to read, criticize, and score your essay. Let your reader study the scoring guidelines on page 220 of this book before that person assigns a number to your essay. If your reader needs more guidance, the sample scored essays on pages 221–224 should prove helpful.

	Ready	Probably Ready	Possibly Ready	Not Yet Ready
Language Arts, Writing	38–50	26–37	18–25	0–17
Essay	4	3	2	1
Social Studies	38–50	26–37	18–25	0–17
Science	38–50	26–37	18–25	0–17
Language Arts, Reading	30–40	21–29	14–20	0–13
Mathematics	38–50	26–37	18–25	0–17

The pattern of your scores on the table above should readily suggest a study plan. Allot most of your time to the "Not Yet Ready" and "Possibly Ready" categories. Each topic is represented by a part in this book. Read the text. Study the examples. Try the practice questions. Study the explanatory answers. Go over the entire part again and again. If you have left yourself ample study time, turn next to the parts related to your "Probably Ready" scores. You might check now to see how your errors on the Diagnostic Test were distributed on the Error Analysis table on page 159. If time begins to get tight, concentrate on your weakest areas. If you have the luxury of time, read through your "Ready" areas for extra insurance and confidence-building.

When you feel satisfied that you have mastered the subjects to be tested on the GED examination, try the first of the complete sample tests in Part VIII.

ANSWER SHEET PRACTICE TEST 1: DIAGNOSTIC

Test 1. Language Arts, Writing—Part 1

1. ①②③④⑤   11. ①②③④⑤   21. ①②③④⑤   31. ①②③④⑤   41. ①②③④⑤
2. ①②③④⑤   12. ①②③④⑤   22. ①②③④⑤   32. ①②③④⑤   42. ①②③④⑤
3. ①②③④⑤   13. ①②③④⑤   23. ①②③④⑤   33. ①②③④⑤   43. ①②③④⑤
4. ①②③④⑤   14. ①②③④⑤   24. ①②③④⑤   34. ①②③④⑤   44. ①②③④⑤
5. ①②③④⑤   15. ①②③④⑤   25. ①②③④⑤   35. ①②③④⑤   45. ①②③④⑤
6. ①②③④⑤   16. ①②③④⑤   26. ①②③④⑤   36. ①②③④⑤   46. ①②③④⑤
7. ①②③④⑤   17. ①②③④⑤   27. ①②③④⑤   37. ①②③④⑤   47. ①②③④⑤
8. ①②③④⑤   18. ①②③④⑤   28. ①②③④⑤   38. ①②③④⑤   48. ①②③④⑤
9. ①②③④⑤   19. ①②③④⑤   29. ①②③④⑤   39. ①②③④⑤   49. ①②③④⑤
10. ①②③④⑤   20. ①②③④⑤   30. ①②③④⑤   40. ①②③④⑤   50. ①②③④⑤

Test 2. Social Studies

1. ①②③④⑤   11. ①②③④⑤   21. ①②③④⑤   31. ①②③④⑤   41. ①②③④⑤
2. ①②③④⑤   12. ①②③④⑤   22. ①②③④⑤   32. ①②③④⑤   42. ①②③④⑤
3. ①②③④⑤   13. ①②③④⑤   23. ①②③④⑤   33. ①②③④⑤   43. ①②③④⑤
4. ①②③④⑤   14. ①②③④⑤   24. ①②③④⑤   34. ①②③④⑤   44. ①②③④⑤
5. ①②③④⑤   15. ①②③④⑤   25. ①②③④⑤   35. ①②③④⑤   45. ①②③④⑤
6. ①②③④⑤   16. ①②③④⑤   26. ①②③④⑤   36. ①②③④⑤   46. ①②③④⑤
7. ①②③④⑤   17. ①②③④⑤   27. ①②③④⑤   37. ①②③④⑤   47. ①②③④⑤
8. ①②③④⑤   18. ①②③④⑤   28. ①②③④⑤   38. ①②③④⑤   48. ①②③④⑤
9. ①②③④⑤   19. ①②③④⑤   29. ①②③④⑤   39. ①②③④⑤   49. ①②③④⑤
10. ①②③④⑤   20. ①②③④⑤   30. ①②③④⑤   40. ①②③④⑤   50. ①②③④⑤

Test 3. Science

1. ①②③④⑤   11. ①②③④⑤   21. ①②③④⑤   31. ①②③④⑤   41. ①②③④⑤
2. ①②③④⑤   12. ①②③④⑤   22. ①②③④⑤   32. ①②③④⑤   42. ①②③④⑤
3. ①②③④⑤   13. ①②③④⑤   23. ①②③④⑤   33. ①②③④⑤   43. ①②③④⑤
4. ①②③④⑤   14. ①②③④⑤   24. ①②③④⑤   34. ①②③④⑤   44. ①②③④⑤
5. ①②③④⑤   15. ①②③④⑤   25. ①②③④⑤   35. ①②③④⑤   45. ①②③④⑤
6. ①②③④⑤   16. ①②③④⑤   26. ①②③④⑤   36. ①②③④⑤   46. ①②③④⑤
7. ①②③④⑤   17. ①②③④⑤   27. ①②③④⑤   37. ①②③④⑤   47. ①②③④⑤
8. ①②③④⑤   18. ①②③④⑤   28. ①②③④⑤   38. ①②③④⑤   48. ①②③④⑤
9. ①②③④⑤   19. ①②③④⑤   29. ①②③④⑤   39. ①②③④⑤   49. ①②③④⑤
10. ①②③④⑤   20. ①②③④⑤   30. ①②③④⑤   40. ①②③④⑤   50. ①②③④⑤

answer sheet

Test 4. Language Arts, Reading

1. ①②③④⑤	11. ①②③④⑤	21. ①②③④⑤	31. ①②③④⑤
2. ①②③④⑤	12. ①②③④⑤	22. ①②③④⑤	32. ①②③④⑤
3. ①②③④⑤	13. ①②③④⑤	23. ①②③④⑤	33. ①②③④⑤
4. ①②③④⑤	14. ①②③④⑤	24. ①②③④⑤	34. ①②③④⑤
5. ①②③④⑤	15. ①②③④⑤	25. ①②③④⑤	35. ①②③④⑤
6. ①②③④⑤	16. ①②③④⑤	26. ①②③④⑤	36. ①②③④⑤
7. ①②③④⑤	17. ①②③④⑤	27. ①②③④⑤	37. ①②③④⑤
8. ①②③④⑤	18. ①②③④⑤	28. ①②③④⑤	38. ①②③④⑤
9. ①②③④⑤	19. ①②③④⑤	29. ①②③④⑤	39. ①②③④⑤
10. ①②③④⑤	20. ①②③④⑤	30. ①②③④⑤	40. ①②③④⑤

Test 5. Mathematics—Part 1

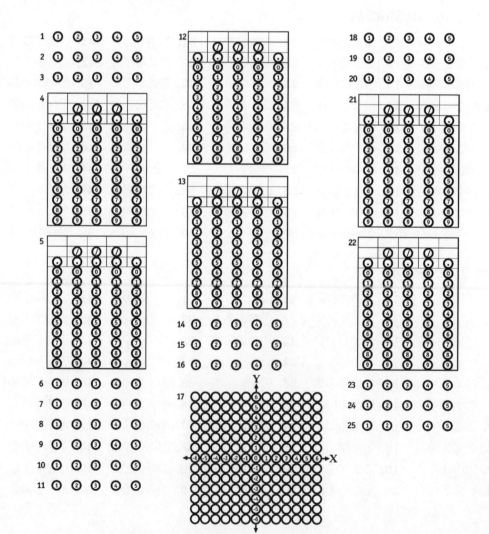

Test 5. Mathematics—Part 2

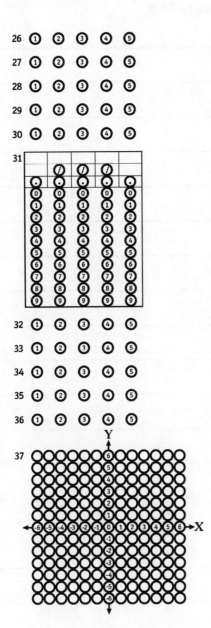

26 ① ② ③ ④ ⑤
27 ① ② ③ ④ ⑤
28 ① ② ③ ④ ⑤
29 ① ② ③ ④ ⑤
30 ① ② ③ ④ ⑤

31

32 ① ② ③ ④ ⑤
33 ① ② ③ ④ ⑤
34 ① ② ③ ④ ⑤
35 ① ② ③ ④ ⑤
36 ① ② ③ ④ ⑤

37

38 ① ② ③ ④ ⑤
39 ① ② ③ ④ ⑤
40 ① ② ③ ④ ⑤
41 ① ② ③ ④ ⑤
42 ① ② ③ ④ ⑤

43

44 ① ② ③ ④ ⑤
45 ① ② ③ ④ ⑤
46 ① ② ③ ④ ⑤
47 ① ② ③ ④ ⑤
48 ① ② ③ ④ ⑤
49 ① ② ③ ④ ⑤
50 ① ② ③ ④ ⑤

answer sheet

ANSWER SHEET PRACTICE TEST 1: DIAGNOSTIC

Language Arts, Writing—Part 2 Essay Test

_____

_____

_____

_____

_____

_____

_____

_____

_____

_____

_____

_____

_____

_____

_____

_____

_____

_____

_____

Language Arts, Writing—Part 2 Essay Test (continued)

_____

_____

_____

_____

_____

_____

_____

_____

_____

_____

_____

_____

_____

_____

_____

_____

_____

answer sheet

TEST 1. LANGUAGE ARTS, WRITING

This test has two parts. Part 1 measures your ability to recognize errors in written material. Part 2 tests your ability to write a short essay.

Part 1. Recognizing and Correcting Errors

75 Minutes • 50 Questions

Directions: This test consists of several written passages with numbered sentences and lettered paragraphs. Some of the sentences contain errors in sentence structure, usage, or mechanics. There are also a few errors of organization that require moving a sentence or paragraph or deleting or replacing a sentence. First read each sentence carefully, then answer the questions that follow. For each item, choose the answer that will correct an error and result in the most effective writing. The best answer must be consistent with the meaning and tone of the passage. Record your answers in the Language Arts, Writing section of the answer sheet.

Q   Often their are two equally effective ways to solve a problem.
What correction should be made to this sentence?

    (1) Replace <u>their</u> with <u>there</u>
    (2) Change <u>are</u> to <u>is</u>
    (3) Change <u>two</u> to <u>too</u>
    (4) Insert a comma after <u>equally</u>
    (5) No change is necessary   ● ② ③ ④ ⑤

A   In this example, the word *their*, which means "belonging to them," is incorrectly substituted for the word *there*. To indicate this correction, mark answer space (1) on your answer sheet.

How Do You Prepare Before Taking a Trip?

A

(1) It is necessary to take care of some practical details as well as to plan ahead when you are going to take a trip. (2) Aside from planning the trip itself, like the destination, means of travel, hotels, and packing, it is important to thinking of what you are leaving behind. (3) If you doesn't, you will find a mess upon returning.

B

(4) For example, what will happen to your mail? (5) You can have the post office hold the mail for you and deliver it all at once the day after you return. (6) If you are going to be away for any length of time, say three or more weeks, you might think of prepaying some of your bills. (7) Otherwise, you might be charged finance fees before you get around to paying the bills. (8) You can call up your telephone and charge card companies, and prepay the balances. (9) You should send in the rent or mortgage payment, the electric bill, the car payment, and any other expected bills. (10) Remember, not having a mountain of bills to face when you return.

C

(11) How about you're pets or plants, and have you arranged for their watering or care? (12) Will someone be available to keep an eye on your home or apartment? (13) Have that person pick up advertisements that get put on your doorstep to keep from informing strangers that you're away.

D

(14) Take care of all these details and you would have a carefree and pleasant time, and get the very most you can out of your trip.

1. Sentence (1): **It is necessary to take care of some practical details as well as to plan ahead when you are going to take a trip.**

   If you began this sentence with When you are going to take a trip, the next word(s) should be:

   (1) to plan ahead

   (2) it is

   (3) as well as

   (4) to take care

   (5) some practical details

2. Sentence (2): **Aside from planning the trip itself, like the destination, means of travel, hotels, and packing, it is important to thinking of what you are leaving behind.**

   What correction should be made to sentence (2)?

   (1) remove the comma after itself

   (2) change like the destination, to as the destination,

   (3) change thinking to think

   (4) remove the last two commas

   (5) change packing to packs

3. Sentence (3): **If you doesn't, you will find a mess upon returning.**

   What correction needs to be made to this sentence?

   (1) change upon to on

   (2) remove the comma

   (3) change doesn't to does not

   (4) change find to finds

   (5) change doesn't to don't

4. Sentence (7): **Otherwise, you might be charged finance fees before you get around to paying the bills.**

Which revision should be made to sentence (7) to make paragraph B more effective?

(1) move sentence (7) to follow sentence (9)

(2) begin a new paragraph with sentence (7)

(3) delete sentence (7)

(4) move sentence (7) to the end of paragraph B

(5) no revision is necessary

5. Sentence (10): **Remember, not having a mountain of bills to face when you return.**

What correction should be made to this sentence?

(1) change <u>having</u> to <u>have</u>

(2) remove the comma

(3) insert <u>this,</u> after <u>Remember</u>

(4) insert <u>it will be nice</u> before <u>not</u>

(5) no correction is needed

6. Sentence (11): **How about you're pets or plants, and have you arranged for their watering or care?**

What correction would improve this sentence?

(1) change <u>arranged</u> to <u>arranging</u>

(2) change <u>watering or care</u> to <u>watering care</u>

(3) change <u>you're</u> to <u>your</u>

(4) change <u>their</u> to <u>they're</u>

(5) remove <u>and</u>

7. Sentence (14): **Take care of all these details <u>and you would have</u> a carefree and pleasant time, and get the very most you can out of your trip.**

What correction should be made to the underlined portion of this sentence? If you think it's correct as written, choose option (1).

(1) and you would have

(2) and you will have

(3) and you have

(4) or you wouldn't have

(5) and, you would having

ITEMS 8 TO 15 REFER TO THE FOLLOWING BUSINESS COMMUNICATION.

Searington Computer Consultants
Mason Shores
Searington, MA 01272

Mr. Jeffrey Karl
Lakeside Parkway East
Lestone, MA 01240

January 25, 2005

Dear Mr. Karl:

A

(1) It was a pleasure meeting with you last Friday. (2) Our staff was impressed with your credentials and interested in the ideas you presented; which would certainly be an asset to our firm if you choose to join us.

B

(3) While your making a decision concerning your future, we would like you to consider the many advantages to you if you were to work for us. (4) In addition to the direct benefits of working for Searington Computer Consultants, which were discussed at length during the interview, we also want to stress the potential advantages of life in Searington for you and your family.

C

(5) The beautiful historic town of Searington is well located in western Massachusetts, just a couple of hours from Boston and New York and 1 hour from Albany. (6) The lovely Berkshire mountains surround Searington, which has its own sparkling lake for summer swimming and boating and winter skating and ice fishing. (7) Each season have its own special scenic beauty, festivals, and events. (8) The Josh Billings Triathlon, the Tanglewood Summer Music Festival, and the Berkshire Theater Festival are only some of the yearly, world-renowned events. (9) Nearby, Berkshire Community College and Williams College offer first-rate program of study. (10) There are houses of worship in the area, they serve all denominations. (11) The finest retail stores and businesses are represented in nearby malls, making the Berkshires a shopper's mecca. (12) We regard Searington and the surrounding area as an ideal place to live, work, and raise a family. (13) We do hope that we will hear from you soon, and that the above has been helpful toward enabling you to come to a decision regarding your future.

(14) Very truly yours
Ronald M. Myron
Director of Personnel Services

8. Sentence (3): **While your making a decision concerning your future, we would like you to consider the many advantages to you if you were to work for us.**

What correction should be made to this sentence?

(1) change <u>concerning</u> to <u>concern</u>

(2) change <u>future, we</u> to <u>future. We</u>

(3) change <u>if you were</u> to <u>if you was</u>

(4) change <u>While your</u> to <u>While you're</u>

(5) no correction is necessary

9. Sentence (5): **The beautiful historic town of Searington is well located in western Massachusetts, just a couple of hours from Boston and New York and 1 hour from Albany.**

If you rewrite this sentence beginning with <u>Just a couple of hours from Boston and New York and 1 hour from Albany</u>, the next word is

(1) the

(2) beautiful

(3) of

(4) located

(5) in

10. Sentence (6): **The lovely Berkshire mountains surround Searington, which has its own sparkling lake for summer swimming and boating and winter skating and ice fishing.**

What correction should be made to this sentence?

(1) change <u>surround</u> to <u>surrounding</u>

(2) change the comma after <u>Searington</u> to a period

(3) change <u>Berkshire mountains</u> to <u>Berkshire Mountains</u>

(4) change <u>which has</u> to <u>which have</u>

(5) change <u>ice fishing</u> to <u>ice-fishing</u>

11. Sentence (7): **Each season have its own special scenic beauty, festivals, and events.**

Which of the following choices is the best way to write the underlined portion of this sentence? If you think the original is best, choose option (1).

(1) Each season have its

(2) Each season, have its

(3) Each season have it's

(4) Each Season have its

(5) Each season has its

12. Sentence (9): **Nearby, Berkshire Community College and Williams College offer first-rate program of study.**

What correction should be made to sentence (9)?

(1) remove the comma after <u>Nearby</u>

(2) change <u>first-rate</u> to <u>first rate</u>

(3) change <u>program of study</u> to <u>programs of study</u>

(4) change <u>offer</u> to <u>offers</u>

(5) change <u>and</u> to <u>or</u>

13. Sentence (10): **There are houses of worship in the <u>area, they serve all</u> denominations.**

    Which of the following choices is the best way to write the underlined portion of this sentence? If you think the original is the best, choose option (1).

    (1) area, they serve all
    (2) area, they serving all
    (3) area, and serve all
    (4) area. They serve every
    (5) area. They serve all

14. Sentence (13): **We do hope that we will hear from you soon, and that the above has been helpful toward enabling you to come to a decision regarding your future.**

    What revision should be made to sentence (13) to improve the organization of the text of this business letter?

    (1) move sentence (13) before sentence (5)
    (2) begin a new paragraph with sentence (13)
    (3) move sentence (13) before sentence (12)
    (4) delete sentence (13)
    (5) no revision is necessary

15. Sentence (14):

    Very truly yours
    Ronald M. Myron
    Director of Personnel Services

    What correction should be made to this closing?

    (1) change <u>Very truly yours</u> to <u>Very Truly Yours</u>
    (2) change <u>Director of Personnel Services</u> to <u>Director: Personnel Services</u>
    (3) insert a period after <u>Very truly yours</u>
    (4) insert a comma after <u>Very truly yours</u>
    (5) change <u>Very truly yours</u> to <u>Sincerely</u>

ITEMS 16 TO 22 REFER TO THE FOLLOWING SELECTION.

Traveling to Australia

A

(1) Have you ever thought of traveling to Australia? (2) The land "down under" is idyllic, with great whether all year round, friendly people, and surrounded by the ocean for lovers of water sports.

B

(3) Visiting Australia is easy to arrange, provided you've got the money for the plane fare. (4) If you're a U.S. citizen, a simple phone call, with valid passport and credit card in hand, can secure an E.T.A., or an Electronic Travel Authority. (5) An E.T.A. is a tourist visa, and that's the only permission required to enter the country. (6) A tourist visa is valid for a three-month stay, but it's fairly easy to have them extended for an additional three months (or even longer) when you're already there.

C

(7) The most popular way to explore Australia is to buy an inexpensive bus pass, which allowing you to visit some of the most wonderful sites for no additional cost. (8) In most well-visited places, it's easy to arrange to stay in a youth hostel. (9) These are friendly, youth-oriented communal hotels with many practical facilities that provide inexpensive lodging and cater to visitors from many countries.

D

(10) Some visitors prefer to rent a car, but this is costly unless the expense can be shared by a group traveling together. (11) The advantage of driving yourself is the total independence, gotten from bus schedules and routes.

E

(12) A visit to Australia will provide you with gorgeous modern cities and beautiful ocean scenery as well as a taste of the "outback," which refers to the flat, untamed land inland from the ocean. (13) You will encounter great places to hike,

surf, scuba dive, snorkel, and enjoy the sun. (14) If you go, don't fail to explore the Great Barrier Reef, which lies along the coast of Queensland and is well known for its incredible supply of colorful coral and tropical fish.

16. Sentence (2): **The land "down under" is idyllic, with great whether all year round, friendly people, and surrounded by the ocean for lovers of water sports.**

    What correction should be made to this sentence?

    (1) change "down under" to <u>down under</u>
    (2) change <u>is idyllic, with</u> to <u>is idyllic. With</u>
    (3) change <u>great whether</u> to <u>great weather</u>
    (4) remove the comma after <u>all year round,</u>
    (5) no correction is necessary

17. Sentence (3): **Visiting Australia is easy to arrange, provided you've got the money for the plane fare.**

    If you rewrote this sentence, beginning with <u>Provided you've got the money for the plane fare</u>, the next word will be

    (1) is
    (2) to
    (3) easy
    (4) arrange
    (5) visiting

18. Sentence (6): **A tourist visa is valid for a three-month stay, but it's fairly easy to have them extended for an additional three months (or even longer) when you're already there.**

    What correction should be made to this sentence?

    (1) change <u>to have them extended</u> to <u>to have it extended</u>
    (2) change <u>three-month stay</u> to <u>three-month staying</u>
    (3) change <u>easy</u> to <u>easier</u>
    (4) change <u>you're already there</u> to <u>you're already going there</u>
    (5) change the comma to a period

19. Sentence (7): **The most popular way to explore Australia is to buy an inexpensive bus pass, which allowing you to visit some of the most wonderful sites for no additional cost.**

    Which of the following is the best way to write the underlined portion of this sentence? If you think that the original way is best, then choose option (1).

    (1) pass, which allowing you
    (2) pass. Which allowing you
    (3) pass, which allow you
    (4) pass, which allows you
    (5) pass which allowing you

20. What revision can be made to paragraph D to improve the organization of this piece?

    (1) move paragraph D after paragraph A
    (2) move paragraph D after sentence (7)
    (3) combine paragraph D with paragraph C
    (4) move paragraph D after paragraph E
    (5) delete paragraph D

21. Sentence (11): **The advantage of driving yourself is the total independence, gotten from bus schedules and routes.**

    Which of the following is the best way to write the underlined portion of this sentence? If you think the original way is best, then choose option (1).

    (1) total independence, gotten from
    (2) total independence. Gotten from
    (3) total independence gotten from
    (4) total independence, from getting
    (5) totally independent, gotten from

22. Sentence (14): **If you go, don't fail to explore the Great Barrier Reef, which lies along the coast of Queensland and is well known for its incredible supply of colorful coral and tropical fish.**

    What correction should be made to this sentence?

    (1) put a comma after <u>incredible supply</u>
    (2) change <u>Great Barrier Reef</u> to <u>great barrier reef</u>
    (3) change <u>lies</u> to <u>lyes</u>
    (4) change <u>coast of Queensland</u> to <u>Coast of Queensland</u>
    (5) no correction is needed

ITEMS 23 TO 29 REFER TO THE ARTICLE BELOW.

Volunteerism

A

(1) Volunteers' are people who reach out beyond paid employment and the usual responsibilities of life to help their fellow man. (2) Volunteerism has always played a role in American life, but more than ever, there opportunities to get involved in the life of your community, your country, and even the world. (3) Even in these prosperous times, there are many people in dire need of assistance and many ways to give back something to society. (4) Whether you are young or not so young, your energy, ability, and interest are much in demand.

B

(5) On an international level, the Peace Corps has more than 7,300 volunteers serving in seventy-seven different countries. (6) These volunteers work with people in developing countries to help them be "independent" and take charge of their own lives. (7) Projects include furthering educational opportunities for children, improving health care for families, growing more food, doing environmental protection work, and creating greater economic opportunities. (8) Being in the Peace Corps is a great way to see the world, learn about other cultures, and make a difference in other people's life.

C

(9) On a more local level, many young people are increasingly getting involved in a variety of services. (10) Food pantries, homeless shelters, latchkey programs for children, "friendly neighbor" visits, *Teach for America*, nursing home work, car rides for the elderly and handicapped, home-delivered meals, recreational and tutoring centers, transitional housing, and many more programs for would-be volunteers to participate in.

D

(11) Aside from the personal satisfaction gotten from helping others and the opportunity for growth and learning, volunteering gives the chance to gain experience, knowledge, and leadership skills. (12) This can certainly be an important factor when applying for employment, or even college.

23. Sentence (1): **Volunteers' are people who reach out beyond paid employment and the usual responsibilities of life to help their fellow man.**

    What correction should be made to sentence (1)?

    (1) change their fellow man to they're fellow man

    (2) change paid employment and to paid employment, and

    (3) change people to peoples

    (4) change reach out to reaching out

    (5) change Volunteers' to Volunteers

24. Sentence (2): **Volunteerism has always played a role in American life, but more than ever, there opportunities to get involved in the life of your community, your country, and even the world.**

    Which of the following is the best way to write the underlined portion of this sentence? If you think that the original way is best, choose option (1).

    (1) than ever, there opportunities

    (2) than ever, their opportunities

    (3) than ever, opportunities

    (4) than ever, there are opportunities

    (5) than ever: there opportunities

25. Sentence (6): **These volunteers work with people in developing countries to help them be "independent" and take charge of their own lives.**

    What correction should be made to this sentence?

    (1) change volunteers work to volunteers' work

    (2) put a comma after with people

    (3) change "independent" to independent

    (4) change to help to too help

    (5) change their to there

26. Sentence (8): **Being in the Peace Corps is a great way to see the world, learn about other cultures, and make a difference in other people's life.**

    Which of the following choices is the best way to write the underlined portion of this sentence? If you think that the original way is best, choose option (1).

    (1) in other people's life.

    (2) in other people's lifes.

    (3) in other peoples life.

    (4) in other person's life.

    (5) in other people's lives.

27. Sentence (10): **Food pantries, homeless shelters, latchkey programs for children, "friendly neighbor" visits, *Teach for America*, nursing home work, car rides for the elderly and handicapped, home-delivered meals, recreational and tutoring centers, transitional housing, and many more programs for would-be volunteers to participate in.**

Which of the following is the best way to write the underlined portion of the above sentence? If you feel the original way is best, pick option (1).

   (1) programs for would-be volunteers

   (2) programs are available for would-be volunteers

   (3) programs for "would-be volunteers"

   (4) programs would be volunteers

   (5) programs—for would-be volunteers

28. If inserted before sentence (11), which of the following would be the best sentence to improve the clarity of paragraph D?

   (1) Volunteers must be kind and giving people.

   (2) Not everyone can get into the Peace Corps, which wants to recruit people with special skills.

   (3) Not only does the recipient of aid benefit, but so does the volunteer.

   (4) Some volunteers participate in building houses for people in need.

   (5) *Teach for America* is a program where college graduates from top colleges and universities are trained to teach in needy schools.

29. Sentence (11): **Aside from the personal satisfaction gotten from helping others, and the opportunity for growth and learning, volunteering gives the chance to gain experience, knowledge, and leadership skills.**

If you rewrote this sentence beginning with the words <u>Volunteering gives the chance to gain experience, knowledge, and leadership skills</u>, the next words would be:

   (1) aside from

   (2) from helping

   (3) growth and learning

   (4) satisfaction gained

   (5) the personal

ITEMS 30 TO 36 REFER TO THE ARTICLE BELOW.

The World of the Smithsonian

A

(1) One of the wonderful places to see when visiting our nation's capital is the Smithsonian, which is off the national mall in Washington, D.C. (2) The red sandstone building, designed in a twelfth-century Norman style and built in the mid-nineteenth century, resembles a castle and symbolizes the museum for many people, but there is much more to the Smithsonian.

B

(3) The Smithsonian is the largest museum complex in the world, containing more than 140 million different items. (4) They range from Judy Garland's red shoes from *The Wizard of Oz* to fossils that are over 3 billion years old. (5) There are items from the Apollo lunar landing module, the blue 45-carat Hope diamond and a red 138-carat ruby, and ancient Chinese bronzes. (6) The collections cover many areas of interest: and help us understand the past and preserve its history. (7) All these are now housed not in the castle anymore but in a complex of sixteen different museums.

C

(8) The Smithsonian is also one of the lead research centers of the world. (9) The National Zoological Park conducts a breeding preserve and study center for rare and endangered animals in the Blue Ridge Mountains in Front Royal, Virginia. (10) At the Marine Station at Link Port, in Fort Pierce, Florida, scientists study marine life and environmental changes. (11) Physical characteristic of the universe are researched at the Whipple Observatory on Mount Hopkins, in Tucson, Arizona. (12) Tropical organisms at the Tropical Research Institute in Panama. (13) On expeditions to many parts of the world, scientists make new discoveries, publish their findings, and increase scientific understanding.

D

(14) The fun part of all this research can be enjoyed at the Smithsonian. (15) The National Air and Space Museum, the National Museum of Natural History, the National Museum of American History, the National Museum of African Art, and the National Postal Museum, all part of the Smithsonian, are only some of the places awaiting your visit.

30. Sentence (1): **One of the wonderful places to see when visiting our nation's capital is the Smithsonian, which is off the national mall in Washington, D.C.**

Which of the following is the best way to write the underlined portion of this sentence? If you think the original way is correct, choose option (1).

(1) national mall in Washington, D.C.

(2) National Mall in Washington, D.C.

(3) national mall, Washington, D.C.

(4) Washington, D.C. national mall

(5) national mall in Washington, d.c.

31. Sentence (6): **The collections cover many areas of interest: and help us understand the past and preserve its history.**

What correction should be made in this sentence?

(1) remove the colon after of interest:

(2) change collections cover to collections covering

(3) change of interest: to for interest:

(4) change help us understand to helped us understand

(5) change preserve its history to preserve its histories

32. Sentence (8): **The Smithsonian is also one of the lead research centers of the world.**

What correction should be made to sentence (8)?

(1) put a comma after also

(2) change research centers to Research Centers

(3) change of the world to for the world

(4) change lead to leading

(5) change research centers to researching centers

33. Sentence (9): **The National Zoological Park conducts a breeding preserve and study center for rare and endangered animals in the Blue Ridge Mountains in Front Royal, Virginia.**

If you rewrote this sentence beginning with the words In the Blue Ridge Mountains in Front Royal, Virginia, the next words would be

(1) a breeding preserve

(2) study center

(3) the National

(4) for rare

(5) conducts a

34. Sentence (11): **Physical characteristic of the universe are researched at the Whipple Observatory on Mount Hopkins, in Tucson, Arizona.**

    What correction should be made to this sentence?

    (1) change <u>universe</u> to <u>Universe</u>
    (2) remove the comma after <u>Mount Hopkins</u>
    (3) change <u>are researched</u> to <u>is researched</u>
    (4) change <u>Physical</u> to <u>Physically</u>
    (5) change <u>characteristic</u> to <u>characteristics</u>

35. Sentence (12): **Tropical organisms at the Tropical Research Institute in Panama.**

    Which of the following is the best way to write the underlined portion of the sentence above? If you feel the original is best, then pick option (1).

    (1) Tropical organisms at the
    (2) Tropical organisms are studied at the
    (3) Tropical organisms were studied at the
    (4) Tropical organisms' at the
    (5) Tropical organisms, at the

36. Sentence (14): **The fun part of all this research can be enjoyed at the Smithsonian.**

    In order to improve the organization and clarity of this article, what is the best place to move sentence (14)?

    (1) to the beginning of paragraph A
    (2) to the end of paragraph B
    (3) before sentence (7)
    (4) delete sentence (14)
    (5) leave sentence (14) where it is

ITEMS 37 TO 43 REFER TO THE SELECTION BELOW.

Suzuki Violin

A

(1) Most people who start playing a musical instrument begin taking lessons when they are 7, 8, or 9 years' old. (2) However, there is a method of instruction that begins teaching children at a far younger age. (3) It is called the "Suzuki" method, and it was invented by a violin teacher in Japan more than fifty years ago. (4) While he initially only taught children the violin because it could be miniaturized, the method is now also used with other instruments, like the cello.

B

(5) Mr Suzuki's theory was that a young child can begin to learn a musical instrument in the same way that he learns language and everything else—by listening, watching, and imitating. (6) The child learns naturally and with little conscious effort by responding to his mother, who encourages the child by repetition, demonstration, singing, and playing. (7) In the same way, the child can learn a musical instrument as early as 3 years of age from a music teacher. (8) He first begins to play "Twinkle, Twinkle Little Star" on a tiny violin by copying the teacher, surrounded by other little pupils in a class. (9) He's having fun and is not aware that he's doing anything hard. (10) He learns from the teacher, from watching the other children, and from his mother, who also must participate in classes and learn to play. (11) Before long, the child tackle harder and harder pieces, and eventually learns to read music, often before he's learned to read books in school.

C

(12) Mr. Suzuki feels that no special talent is necessary and that all children can play if exposed to music and encouraged. (13) Of course, some children progress faster than others, not every child enjoys playing classical music. (14) However, this method of teaching is enormously popular all over the

world and is responsible for having produced a large number of high proficient players of music.

37. Sentence (1): **Most people who start playing a musical instrument begin taking lessons when they <u>are 7, 8, or 9 years' old.</u>**

Which of the following is the correct way of writing the underlined portion of this sentence? If you think the original way is best, choose option (1).

(1) are 7, 8, or 9 years' old.

(2) are 7, 8, or 9 year old.

(3) are 7, 8, or 9 years old.

(4) were 7, 8, or 9 years' old.

(5) are 7, 8, or 9 years'.

38. Sentence (5): **Mr Suzuki's theory was that a young child can begin to learn a musical instrument in the same way that he learns language and everything else—by listening, watching, and imitating.**

What correction should be made to this sentence?

(1) change <u>begin to learn</u> to <u>beginning to learn</u>

(2) change <u>Mr Suzuki</u> to <u>Mr. Suzuki</u>

(3) change <u>musical instrument</u> to <u>music instrument</u>

(4) change <u>everything else—by</u> to <u>everything else. By</u>

(5) put a comma after <u>a young child</u>

39. Sentence (7): **In the same way, the child can learn a musical instrument as early as 3 years of age from a music teacher.**

What revision to sentence (7) would improve the organization of *Suzuki Violin*?

(1) move sentence (7) to the end of paragraph A

(2) move sentence (7) to the end of paragraph B

(3) start a new paragraph with sentence (7)

(4) move sentence (7) after sentence (8)

(5) delete sentence (7)

40. Sentence (8): **He first begins to play "Twinkle, Twinkle Little Star" on a tiny violin by copying the teacher, surrounded by other little pupils in a class.**

If you rewrote this sentence beginning with the words <u>Surrounded by other pupils in a class</u>, the next words would be

(1) on a

(2) "Twinkle, Twinkle . . ."

(3) the teacher

(4) he first

(5) tiny violin

41. Sentence (11): **Before long, the child tackle harder and harder pieces, and eventually learns to read music, often before he's learned to read books in school.**

What correction should be made to this sentence?

(1) remove the comma after <u>read music</u>

(2) change <u>before he's learned</u> to before he learnt

(3) change <u>read music, often</u> to <u>read music. Often</u>

(4) change <u>Before long,</u> to <u>Before it's longer,</u>

(5) change <u>the child tackle</u> to <u>the child tackles</u>

42. Sentence (13): **Of course, some children progress faster <u>than others, not every</u> child enjoys playing classical music.**

Which of the following choices is the best way to write the underlined portion of this sentence? If you think the original way is best, choose option (1).

(1) than others, not every

(2) than others not every

(3) than others. Not every

(4) than other, not every

(5) than others, not each

43. Sentence (14): **However, this method of teaching is enormously popular all over the world and is responsible for having produced a large number of <u>high proficient players of</u> music.**

Which of the following choices is the best way to write the underlined portion of this sentence? If you think the original way is best, choose option (1).

(1) high proficient players of

(2) highest proficient players of

(3) high proficient playing of

(4) highly proficient players of

(5) high proficient players for

ITEMS 44 TO 50 REFER TO THE FOLLOWING ARTICLE.

"Skeleton Flats," Montana

A

(1) Residents of Montana laughingly refer to the small, windblown settlement of Ekalaka in the eastern badlands as "Skeleton Flats;" but as curious as it may sound, the name is appropriate. (2) So many fossils have been dug up in this otherwise unremarkable town that it has become a paradise for *paleontologists*, name of scientists who use fossils to study prehistoric life forms. (3) In fact, dinosaur bones are plentiful in this area, ranchers have been known to use them as doorstops!

B

(4) The entire population soon took up Peck's pastime, and a lot of people began digging for dinosaur bones. (5) Ekalaka's fame began to grow more than eighty years ago when Walter H. Peck, whose hobby was geology, found the bones of a *stegosaurus*, a huge, plant-eating dinosaur. (6) Led by the local science teacher, new bones were hunted, and they rarely returned empty-handed. (7) It would seem there is no end to the fossil riches founded in Ekalaka. (8) Among the most valuable finds were the remains of a *brontosaurus*, an 80-foot-long monster that probably weighed 40 tons. (9) The skeleton of a *triceratops* was also found the head alone of this prehistoric giant weighed more than 1,000 pounds. (10) Careful searching also yields small fossilized fishes, complete with stony scales, and the remains of a huge sea reptile.

C

(11) Today, Ekalaka celebrates its prehistoric heritage through the Carter County Museum. (12) The Museum displays both artifacts and actual prehistoric specimens. (13) *Anatosaurus* is their most impressive "resident" in the form of a nearly complete skeleton of this duck-billed dinosaur.

44. Sentence (2): **So many fossils have been dug up in this otherwise unremarkable town that it has become a paradise for *paleontologists,* name of scientists who use fossils to study prehistoric life forms.**

Which of the following is the best way to write the underlined portion of this sentence? If you think the original is the best way to write the sentence, choose option (1).

  (1) paleontologists, name of scientists

  (2) paleontologists, or scientists

  (3) paleontologists. Because scientists

  (4) paleontologists or name of scientists

  (5) paleontologists—name of scientists

45. Sentence (3): **In fact, dinosaur bones are plentiful in this area, ranchers have been known to use them as doorstops!**

Which of the following is the best way to write the underlined portion of this sentence? If you think the original is the best way to write the sentence, choose option (1).

  (1) area, ranchers have

  (2) area, even though ranchers

  (3) area despite ranchers

  (4) area ranchers have

  (5) area. Ranchers have

46. Sentence (4): **The entire population soon took up Peck's pastime, and a lot of people began digging for dinosaur bones.**

What revision should be made to sentence (4)?

  (1) move sentence (4) to follow sentence (5)

  (2) move sentence (4) to the end of paragraph A

  (3) move sentence (4) to follow sentence (7)

  (4) delete sentence (4)

  (5) no revision is necessary

47. Sentence (6): **Led by the local science teacher, new bones were hunted, and they rarely returned empty-handed.**

What correction should be made to this sentence?

  (1) change science teacher to Science teacher

  (2) remove the first comma

  (3) change were hunted to was hunted

  (4) change they to people

  (5) no correction is necessary

48. Sentence (7): **It would seem there is no end to the fossil riches founded in Ekalaka.**

Which of the following is the best way to write the underlined portion of this sentence? If you think the original is best, choose option (1).

  (1) riches founded in Ekalaka.

  (2) riches, founded in Ekalaka.

  (3) riches to be found in Ekalaka.

  (4) and Ekalaka.

  (5) riches founding in Ekalaka.

49. Sentence (9): **The skeleton of a *triceratops* was <u>also found the head</u> alone of this prehistoric giant weighed more than 1,000 pounds.**

Which of the following is the best way to write the underlined portion of this sentence? If you think that the original is the best, then choose option (1).

(1) also found the head

(2) also found. The head

(3) also found, the head

(4) also finding the head

(5) found also, the head

50. Sentence (10): **Careful searching also yields small fossilized fishes, complete with stony scales, and the remains of a huge sea reptile.**

What correction should be made to this sentence?

(1) change <u>careful</u> to <u>carefully</u>

(2) insert a comma after <u>searching</u>

(3) change <u>yields</u> to <u>yielded</u>

(4) change <u>complete</u> to <u>completing</u>

(5) no correction is necessary

Part 2. Essay Test

45 Minutes • 1 Essay

Directions: This part of the GED is designed to find out how well you write. You will be given one question that asks you to either explain something or present an opinion on an issue. In constructing your answer for this part of the exam, you should include your own observations and experiences and take the following steps:

1 Before you begin to write your answer, read the directions and the question carefully.

2 Think of what you wish to say and plan your essay in detail before you begin to write.

3 Use the blank pages in the test booklet (or scrap paper provided for you) to make notes for planning your essay.

4 Write your essay neatly on the separate answer sheet.

5 Carefully read over what you have written and make any changes that will improve your work.

6 Check your paragraphing, sentence structure, spelling, punctuation, capitalization, and language usage, and correct any errors.

You will have 45 minutes to write a response to the question you are given. Write clearly with a ballpoint pen so the evaluators can read what you have written. Any notes you make on the blank pages or scratch paper will not be included in your evaluation.

Your essay will be scored by at least 2 trained readers who will evaluate the paper according to its overall impact. They will be concerned with how clearly you make your main points, how thoroughly your ideas are supported, and how effective and correct your writing is throughout the entire composition. You will receive no credit for writing on a topic other than the one assigned.

Sample Topic

Some people think that a vegetarian diet is good for you. Others believe that this is an unnatural diet for human beings. What do you think? Write a composition of about 250 words in which you give your opinion on this issue. Be specific, and use examples from your own experience and knowledge to support your views.

Use this page for notes.

diagnostic test

TEST 2. SOCIAL STUDIES

70 Minutes • 50 Questions

Directions: The Social Studies Test consists of multiple-choice questions intended to measure your knowledge of general concepts in history, economics, geography, and civics and government. The questions are based on reading passages, maps, graphs, charts, and cartoons. For each question, first study the information given and then answer the questions about it. You may refer to the readings or graphs as often as necessary in order to answer the questions. Record your answers in the Social Studies section of your answer sheet.

Q Which medium most regularly presents opinions and interpretations of the news?

(1) National television news programs
(2) Local television news programs
(3) Newspaper editorial pages
(4) Teletype news agency reports
(5) Radio news broadcasts   ① ② ● ④ ⑤

A The correct answer is "newspaper editorial pages." Therefore, you should mark answer space (3) on your answer sheet.

ITEMS 1 TO 4 REFER TO THE FOLLOWING SELECTION.

Modern cartography was born in royal France during the latter part of the seventeenth century when King Louis XIV offered a handsome prize for anyone who could devise a method for accurately determining longitude. For 2,000 years, sailors had been trying to find an exact way to locate different places on Earth. The circumference of the earth had been calculated by the Greek Eratosthenes 400 years before the birth of Christ, but as late as 1650, it was still difficult to exactly locate any single position on a map, and particularly difficult to determine longitude on land or sea. Longitude is used to determine the distance of a place east or west of a point of reference. By the end of the seventeenth century, two instruments had been invented that would provide greater accuracy in calculating longitude. The two new instruments were the telescope and the accurate clock. One final instrument remained to be devised. It was perfected by John Harrison in the latter part of the eighteenth century. It was called a chronometer.

1. Which of the following was the main benefit of the birth of modern cartography?

    (1) More accurate clocks
    (2) The determination of the exact location of the North Pole
    (3) Newer and better maps
    (4) The introduction of excellent telescopes
    (5) The invention of the chronometer

2. Which of the following statements can be inferred from this paragraph?

    (1) John Harrison was a Frenchman.
    (2) The French government was interested in accurate maps.
    (3) The clock was invented in the seventeenth century.
    (4) Because maps were inaccurate, people rarely traveled on land or sea.
    (5) The telescope and the accurate clock were invented around 1780.

3. Which of the following was adopted as a direct result of modern cartography?

    (1) Radar as a time measurement
    (2) Plutonium temperature recording devices
    (3) Pollution control devices
    (4) Armaments by France
    (5) Universally accepted time zones

4. Which of the following statements is best supported by the information presented in this paragraph?

    (1) Sailors and members of King Louis XIV's court were the only ones concerned with accurately determining longitude.
    (2) King Louis XIV frequently offered large prizes for new discoveries, but this was the largest yet.
    (3) Relatively little was discovered during King Louis XIV's reign.
    (4) Everyone in the society was aware of these new instruments, and the general public began to travel a great deal.
    (5) King Louis XIV had an interest in worldwide exploration.

ITEMS 5 TO 8 REFER TO THE FOLLOWING CARTOON.

THE MELTING POT

Pizza	Hamburgers
Frankfurters	Sushi
Egg rolls	French fries
Tacos	Belgian waffles
Knish	Scones
Bagel	Blintzes
Swedish meatballs	English muffins
Fish n' chips	Greek salad
Fried chicken	Pita bread

5. Which of the following groups or situations does the restaurant in the cartoon represent?

   (1) The fast-food industry

   (2) Worldwide poverty and hunger

   (3) The oil crisis

   (4) The American people

   (5) Workers and employees

6. Which of the following is a hypothesis suggested by this cartoon?

   (1) Americans eat out a great deal, especially at inexpensive fast-food restaurants.

   (2) Americans are unwilling to accept newcomers easily. As a result, immigrants tend to live in isolated groups.

   (3) Americans dislike foods that are popular in other nations.

   (4) Americans have a tendency to eat too much convenience and snack food.

   (5) A wide variety of nationalities make up American culture.

7. What would someone who disagrees with the cartoonist's view call this restaurant?

   (1) "The Stew Pot"

   (2) "The Salad Bowl"

   (3) "Goulash to Go"

   (4) "The Soup Bowl"

   (5) "Sauce Supreme"

8. Which of the following statements is best supported by evidence presented in this cartoon?

   (1) There is a wide variety of foods offered at fast-food restaurants.

   (2) The United States is made up of immigrants from many nations.

   (3) The cost of food keeps rising.

   (4) American food is imported from Europe.

   (5) A balanced diet is very important to good health.

ITEM 9 REFERS TO THE FOLLOWING STATEMENT.

Nations sent early explorers for three reasons: gold, glory, and God. Later explorers were sent out for raw materials, trading posts, and places to colonize.

9. According to this passage, which of the following motivated early explorers?

   (1) Hopes of fame and fortune

   (2) A desire for better living conditions

   (3) A search for raw materials

   (4) A belief that the monarchy was always right

   (5) A search for spices to preserve meats

ITEMS 10 TO 13 REFER TO THE STOCK MARKET REPORT BELOW.

YTD % Chg	52-week Hi	52-week Lo	Stock (SYM)	Div	YLD %	Vol PE	Net 100s	Close	Change
–14.9	39.15	22.50	ChrlsRvrLab **CRL**	...	...	31	3274	28.5	–0.43
–6.4	5.15	1.80	Chartlnd **CTI**	...	...	dd	82	2.20	–0.05
29.4	35.40	23.40	ChrtrOneFnl **CFs**	88f	2.5	15	10623	35.12	0.53
38.8	13.65	8.25	Chaselnd **CSI**	...	...	21	72	12.70	–0.05
–1.7	32.18	28.3	ChateuCmnty **CPJ**	2.20f	7.5	23	734	29.38	–0.23
25.4	19.15	8.76	CheckptSys **CKP**	...	...	80	1770	16.80	–0.29
17.1	58.30	42.52	ChelseaProp **CPG**	3.24f	5.6	21	1450	57.51	1.14
12.0	39.25	26.50	Chemed **CHE**	44	1.2	33	310	37.98	–0.14
12.3	27.90	19.60	ChemFst **CEM**	.40	1.5	dd	153	26.92	0.26
–3.5	30.80	21.90	ChespkeCp **CSK**	.88	3.3	3	712	26.85	–1.00
21.8	9.45	4.50	ChespkeEngy **CHK**	...	...	5	21244	8.05	–0.13
–0.8	19.99	17.75	ChespkeUtil **CPK**	1.10	5.6	16	30	19.65	0.15
–5.1	98.49	78.60	ChevronTex **CVX**	2.80	3.3	21	21737	85	–1.98
14.3	38.75	19.05	ChicagoB & 1 **CBI**	24	.8	34	131	30.53	0.27
34.9	37.25	13.67	Chicos **CHS s**	...	...	35	7042	35.70	–0.26
10.7	15.95	8.60	ChileTel ADS **CTC**	.01e	.1	...	3359	14.9	0.31
28.8	18.10	8.40	ChinaEstrnAir **CEA**	48e	3.1	...	1	15.35	...
39.2	2.15	0.70	ChinaEnt **CSH**	.08	5.6	...	50	1.42	–0.13
–7.8	27.60	13.09	ChinaMobile **CHL**	...	...	...	6782	16.11	0.26
28.9	21.25	12.54	ChinaPete ADS **SNP**	e		...	114	17.35	–0.54
12.6	18.10	8	ChinaAir ADS **ZNH**	...	...	...	31	16.10	–0.20
–11.7	18.02	8.92	ChinaUnicom **CHU**	...	...	...	2027	9.86	0.12
129.2	2.20	0.25	ChinaYuchai **CYD**	.21e	9.5	...	265	2.20	0.05
23.7	39.06	8.66	ChiquitaBrd **CQB s**	j	...	dd	5858	16.71	0.44
24.7	6.24	3.25	Chiquita wt n	...	...	...	405	6.05	0.23
15.9	31.85	21.75	Chittden **CHZ s**	.80f	2.5	18	413	32	0.23
15.1	27	11.90	ChoiceHtl **CHH**	...	...	85	331	25.50	–0.37
10.5	61.80	34.16	ChoicePt **CPS**	...	...	73	2371	56	–0.85
21.1	13.40	8	Chromcrft **CRC**	...	...	...	5	13.05	...
9.4	79.50	55.54	Chubb **CB**	1.40f	1.9	cc	11353	75.51	–0.91
8.4	31.80	23.52	Church&Dwt **CHD**	.30	1.0	25	1191	28.86	–1.08
21.5	38.35	24	CibaSpctyChem **CSB**	.59e	1.6	...	137	37.78	–0.12
–24.9	11.70	4.50	CIBER **CBR**	...	...	cc	2722	7.10	0.23
1.2	26.35	24.80	CincGE deb **JRL**	2.07	8.1	...	38	25.70	–0.04
9.1	37.17	28	CINergyCp **CIN**	1.80	4.9	13	6087	36.48	–0.15
16.6	24.10	13.65	Circorlnt **CIR**	.15	.7	21	89	21.51	–0.04
–17.0	31	9.55	CircCty **CC**	.07	.3	24	11970	21.53	–0.67

10. Which stock showed the greatest change in price from the day before?

  (1) ChespkeUtil

  (2) Chicos

  (3) ChicagoB & I

  (4) ChevronTex

  (5) ChileTel ADS

11. Which stock is selling closest to its highest selling price for the entire year?

  (1) ChespkeCp

  (2) ChespkeEngy

  (3) ChespkeUtil

  (4) ChevronTex

  (5) ChicagoB&I

12. If John wanted to buy 100 shares of Chubb, about how much would he spend?

   (1) $91
   (2) $1,000
   (3) $7,551
   (4) $10,000
   (5) $11,353

13. Which stock pays the highest dividend?

   (1) ChelseaProp
   (2) Chemed
   (3) ChemFst
   (4) ChespkeCp
   (5) ChespkeUtil

ITEMS 14 TO 18 REFER TO THE FOLLOWING INFORMATION.

Throughout American history, people have been selected for positions within the government and in private companies in several ways. Some of these ways are still used today; others have fallen into disfavor. Listed below are five methods that have been used for candidate evaluation and promotion:

   a. **The "spoils system"**—candidates are selected for positions based on their membership in a political party and/or for supporting their candidate's election bid

   b. **The merit system**—an impartial body tests and evaluates job applicants

   c. **The "Old Boy" network**—people are placed in high-status jobs because they are members of the upper-middle or upper classes

   d. **Nepotism**—positions are awarded based on a candidate's relationship to a person within the company

   e. **Networking**—people look for positions through social contacts

Each of the following statements describes an aspect of the application review process. Choose the system in which the process would most likely occur. The categories may be used more than once in the set of items, but no one question has more than one best answer.

14. Brian Parker's mother is the assistant vice president of the Amalgamated Tool Company. Rather than being given the expected entry-level position in the stock room, Brian starts work as a floor manager. Which of the following systems was used to evaluate Brian's qualifications?

   (1) The spoils system
   (2) The merit system
   (3) The "Old Boy" network
   (4) Nepotism
   (5) Networking

15. In 1883 Congress passed the Pendleton Act, setting up the Civil Service Commission. This impartial body was to test and rate applicants for federal jobs. Which system did this Act establish?

   (1) The spoils system
   (2) The merit system
   (3) The "Old Boy" network
   (4) Nepotism
   (5) Networking

16. Somerset St. Pierre's father is the president of a major oil company. His mother is active in many charitable organizations. In addition, his parents are friends with many socially important people. Somerset, like his father and grandfather, attended the exclusive and expensive preparatory high school, Wooded Hills. When Somerset graduated from an Ivy League college, his father's friend told him about an excellent position in an investment banking firm. Under which system did Somerset receive his job?

   (1) The spoils system
   (2) The merit system
   (3) The "Old Boy" network
   (4) Nepotism
   (5) Networking

17. In 1939 Congress passed the Hatch Act, providing that federal employees may not be asked for political contributions and may not actively participate in political affairs. The Act was passed to lessen the influence of

(1) the spoils system.

(2) the merit system.

(3) the "Old Boy" network.

(4) nepotism.

(5) networking.

18. Meredith Jones met Nancy Grant at a party. They had lunch twice, and through Nancy, Meredith became acquainted with a handful of people in real estate, a field she had tried hard to break into. She invited several of these people to a barbecue and carefully kept in touch with them all. Several months later, one of them offered Meredith a job in a newly opened real estate office. Under which system did Meredith get her job offer?

(1) The spoils system

(2) The merit system

(3) The "Old Boy" network

(4) Nepotism

(5) Networking

ITEMS 19 AND 20 REFER TO THE GRAPH BELOW.

PROPORTIONS OF WOMEN IN DIFFERENT CATEGORIES

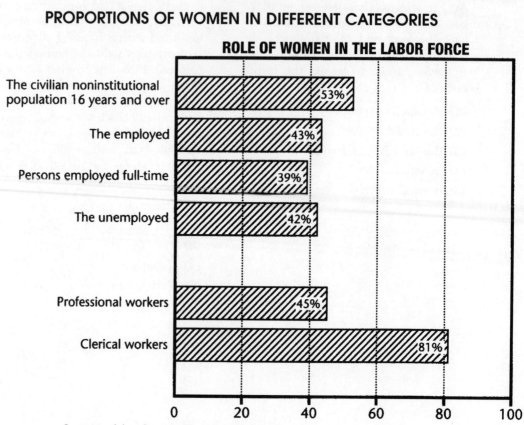

ROLE OF WOMEN IN THE LABOR FORCE

The civilian noninstitutional population 16 years and over — 53%

The employed — 43%

Persons employed full-time — 39%

The unemployed — 42%

Professional workers — 45%

Clerical workers — 81%

0   20   40   60   80   100

Summary labor force indicators for women

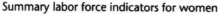

19. According to the graph above, which of the following statements may be supported as accurate?

  I. 45% of employed women are professional workers.

  II. 43% of women are unemployed.

  III. Women are not a minority in the labor market.

  IV. Four out of five clerical workers are women.

  (1) I, II, and III only

  (2) I, II, and IV only

  (3) I and II only

  (4) II and IV only

  (5) III and IV only

20. Which of the following statements is supported by the information depicted in the graph above?

  (1) Women are a minority group.

  (2) Women will never achieve economic equality with men.

  (3) The U.S. economy would be seriously damaged if women were not available to the labor force.

  (4) A high proportion of women will continue to be unemployed.

  (5) Fewer women are likely to be trained as professional workers.

ITEM 21 REFERS TO THE FOLLOWING GRAPHS.

Cable TV—Basic Subscribers, Average Monthly Rate, and Revenue: 1980 to 1995

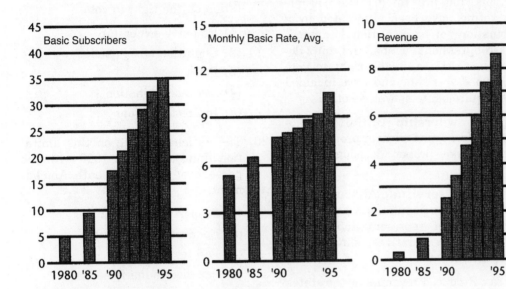

21. Based on the graphs shown above, which of the following statements could you most strongly support?

   (1) The number of cable television subscribers will continue to grow.

   (2) The average monthly fee is unlikely to increase much beyond the year 2000.

   (3) The cable television industry enjoyed huge growth in total revenue and number of subscribers between 1985 and 1995.

   (4) Cable television has become a less profitable business than network television.

   (5) Revenue from cable is likely to drop after 2000.

ITEMS 22 TO 25 REFER TO THE INFORMATION BELOW.

In the time of George Washington perhaps 1 in 15 Americans was entitled to vote. Since then, many of the various restrictions that prevented certain people from voting have been eliminated by a combination of constitutional amendment, congressional action, and court decision. Restrictions on the right to vote have varied over time and have included these requirements as well as others:

Property ownership All thirteen colonies considered men without property unable to make proper decisions about government.

Condition of servitude Although three fifths of the slave population was counted for purposes of representation in the House of Representatives, slaves were not entitled to vote.

Poll tax Produced revenue for the states but effectively barred poor people from exercising the franchise.

Sex discrimination Women were allowed to vote in 1869, but only in Wyoming. Popular opinion viewed women as uninterested, incapable, or likely to obey their husbands.

Indirect elections The Founders of the United States felt full democracy would lead to rash and unhealthy decisions about government.

Identify the voting restriction that was removed by each of the following constitutional amendments:

22. In 1964, the Twenty-Fourth Amendment effectively outlawed this limitation on the right to vote.

    (1) Property ownership
    (2) Condition of servitude
    (3) Poll tax
    (4) Sex discrimination
    (5) Indirect elections

23. The national debate on this limitation finally ended in 1920 with the passage of the Nineteenth Amendment.

    (1) Property ownership
    (2) Condition of servitude
    (3) Poll tax
    (4) Sex discrimination
    (5) Indirect elections

24. The passage of the Fourteenth and Fifteenth Amendments removed this limitation to the right to vote.

    (1) Property ownership
    (2) Condition of servitude
    (3) Poll tax
    (4) Sex discrimination
    (5) Indirect elections

25. After the Seventeenth Amendment was ratified in 1913, senators were no longer elected by each state legislature.

    (1) Property ownership
    (2) Condition of servitude
    (3) Poll tax
    (4) Sex discrimination
    (5) Indirect elections

ITEM 26 REFERS TO THE MAP SHOWN BELOW.

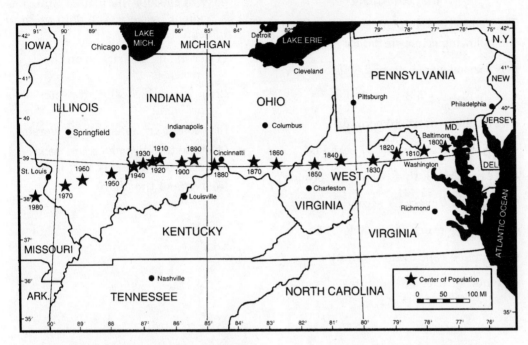

26. The center of population is defined as that point at which an imaginary flat, weightless, and rigid map of the U.S. would balance if weights of identical value were placed on it so that each weight represented the location of one person on the date of the census. What is the best conclusion that can be drawn by studying the map above?

(1) Ohio, Indiana, and Illinois were not part of the original thirteen colonies.

(2) Cities on the Mississippi River had a greater opportunity for growth.

(3) People moved from more sparsely populated areas to more crowded ones.

(4) The American population has experienced the greatest growth in the western portion of the country.

(5) The American population has experienced the greatest growth in the eastern half of the country.

ITEM 27 REFERS TO THE FOLLOWING INFORMATION.

The Federal Bureau of Investigation reports the following crime statistics:

- A serious crime every 2.6 seconds

- A theft every 4.8 seconds

- A burglary every 10 seconds

- A violent crime every 27 seconds

- A car or truck theft every 29 seconds

- An assault every 51 seconds

- A robbery every 68 seconds

- A forcible rape every 7 minutes

- A murder every 24 minutes

27. From the data here, it would be very easy to classify the United States as a "violent" society. The data seem to indicate that

   (1) crime in America is on the increase.
   (2) crime is basically an urban problem.
   (3) violent crime is getting worse.
   (4) the statistics given are debatable and probably unreliable.
   (5) None of the above

ITEM 28 REFERS TO THE FOLLOWING GRAPH.

Federal and State Prisoners—Number: 1950–1985

(Thousands of Prisoners)

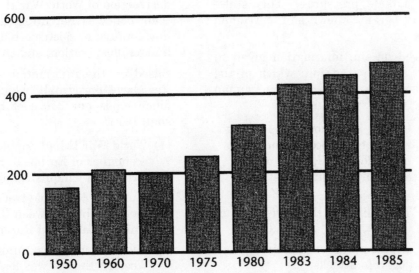

28. Assuming that the expenditure for prison construction generally followed the number of prisoners, choose the line graph that would most nearly describe the outlay for construction of prisons and rehabilitation centers.

(1)

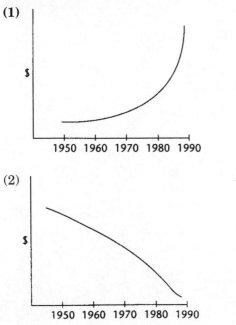

(2)

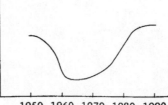

(3)

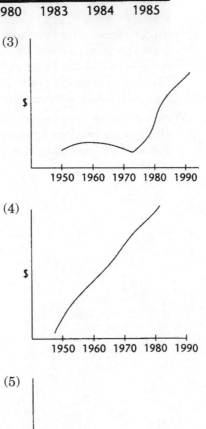

(4)

(5)

29. In 1947, President Truman announced that "it must be the policy of the United States to support free peoples who are resisting attempted subjugation by named minorities or by outside pressures." This statement became known as the Truman Doctrine.

Based on the information given in the above paragraph, which of the following is one *effect* of the Truman Doctrine?

(1) Greece, in economic chaos as a result of Axis occupation there in World War II, came under attack from Communist guerrillas.

(2) Tito split from the Soviet Union.

(3) With American military aid, Greece put down Communist guerrilla attacks.

(4) Turkey was under pressure from the Soviet Union for concessions in the Dardanelles, the straits connecting the Black Sea and the Mediterranean.

(5) Soviet troops suppressed the Hungarian freedom fighters, successfully smashing the revolution.

30. In 1947, Secretary of State George C. Marshall offered economic aid to all European nations (including the Soviet Union and its satellites) to enable them to recover from the destruction of World War II. He said, "Our policy is not directed against any country or doctrine but against hunger, desperation, and chaos."

Based on the information given in the above paragraph, which of the following is one *cause* of the Marshall Plan?

(1) World War II had crippled the economies of European nations, victor and vanquished alike.

(2) Mutually profitable trade was reestablished between the United States and Europe.

(3) The danger of Communism in Western Europe was lessened.

(4) Western European countries moved toward economic unity.

(5) The Soviet Union condemned the Marshall Plan as a scheme of American capitalists to gain economic and political control over Europe.

ITEM 31 REFERS TO THE FOLLOWING GRAPHS.

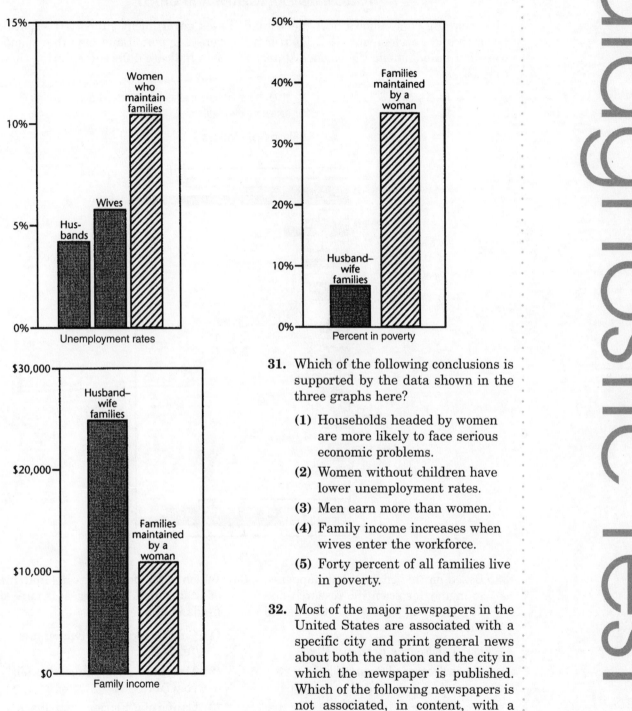

31. Which of the following conclusions is supported by the data shown in the three graphs here?

(1) Households headed by women are more likely to face serious economic problems.

(2) Women without children have lower unemployment rates.

(3) Men earn more than women.

(4) Family income increases when wives enter the workforce.

(5) Forty percent of all families live in poverty.

32. Most of the major newspapers in the United States are associated with a specific city and print general news about both the nation and the city in which the newspaper is published. Which of the following newspapers is not associated, in content, with a particular city?

(1) *New York Times*

(2) *Washington Post*

(3) *Boston Globe*

(4) *St. Louis Post-Dispatch*

(5) *Wall Street Journal*

ITEMS 33 TO 35 REFER TO THE
FOLLOWING PARAGRAPH AND CHART.

The following chart shows how the United States government supported scientific research and development (R & D) over an eleven-year period and how that money was distributed among the various states. The bars indicate differences during three time periods.

Federal R & D support to the 10 states leading in such support
for selected years

Billions of dollars

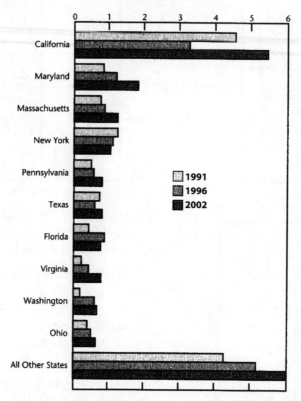

33. Based on this chart, what happened to money for scientific research and development over the time period shown?

(1) It increased dramatically.

(2) It decreased dramatically.

(3) It probably just kept up with inflation.

(4) It enabled dramatic scientific breakthroughs.

(5) It helped the Defense Department increase its effectiveness.

34. Which of the following combinations of states had the largest share of funds in 1996?

(1) California, Pennsylvania, and Texas

(2) Maryland, Massachusetts, and New York

(3) California, Florida, and Texas

(4) Pennsylvania, Texas, and Florida

(5) New York, Pennsylvania, and Virginia

35. Which state had the largest percentage decline in funds over the time period of the chart?

(1) Florida

(2) New York

(3) California

(4) Texas

(5) Virginia

ITEMS 36 TO 40 REFER TO THE INFORMATION BELOW.

As part of its regulatory and educational activities, the federal government has established agencies that issue a wide variety of consumer information publications. These publications are available free or for a small cost. Listed below are five such agencies and the topics of the consumer material they publish.

1. Department of Agriculture discusses food, clothing, and housing.

2. National Bureau of Standards translates technical research findings by the government into terms that will be useful to consumers.

3. National Highway Safety Bureau provides information on safety aspects of automobile performance.

4. Federal Trade Commission alerts consumers to common types of fraudulent claims and deceptive practices.

5. Cooperative Extension Service is administered by state universities and issues bulletins on homemaking, gardening, and farming.

Each of the following statements describes a topic that would be of concern to one of the agencies listed above. Choose the agency that would be most likely to publish material on this topic. The categories may be used more than once in the set of items, but no question has more than one best answer.

36. Provides information about acceleration, passing times, and distances on tire reserve loads (the capacity of tires to bear additional weight) and on stopping distances.

(1) Department of Agriculture

(2) National Bureau of Standards

(3) National Highway Safety Bureau

(4) Federal Trade Commission

(5) Cooperative Extension Service

37. Advises that ads recruiting prospects to breed chinchillas for profit "present a glowing picture of large sums of money easily made through the breeding of chinchillas at home. Most such ads have one serious flaw. They are false."

(1) Department of Agriculture

(2) National Bureau of Standards

(3) National Highway Safety Bureau

(4) Federal Trade Commission

(5) Cooperative Extension Service

38. Advises that a certain vegetable glue "paste" is suitable for use only with paper and has "poor moisture resistance and low strength."

(1) Department of Agriculture

(2) National Bureau of Standards

(3) National Highway Safety Bureau

(4) Federal Trade Commission

(5) Cooperative Extension Service

39. Provides information on consumer problems with lawn grubs and spider mites.

(1) Department of Agriculture

(2) National Bureau of Standards

(3) National Highway Safety Bureau

(4) Federal Trade Commission

(5) Cooperative Extension Service

40. Provides information on the movement of food from the farm to the market and offers tips about its preparation. Also provides a handy way to figure nutritional value.

(1) Department of Agriculture

(2) National Bureau of Standards

(3) National Highway Safety Bureau

(4) Federal Trade Commission

(5) Cooperative Extension Service

41. Where is the nation's capital located?

(1) Maryland

(2) Virginia

(3) Pennsylvania

(4) Washington

(5) None of the above

42. Which of the following was a weakness of the agreements made at the conclusion of World War I?

A. Russia was not represented.

B. Germany was humiliated.

C. The League of Nations was too weak.

D. The U.S. didn't ratify the treaty.

(1) A only

(2) B only

(3) C only

(4) D only

(5) All of the above

ITEM 43 REFERS TO THE FOLLOWING STATEMENTS MADE BY WINSTON CHURCHILL IN 1940 TO THE BRITISH PEOPLE.

"We shall fight on the beaches, we shall fight on the landing grounds, we shall fight in the hills; we shall never surrender . . ."

"I have nothing to offer but blood, toil, tears, and sweat."

43. What trait of Churchill's was most clearly evident in these statements?

(1) Military strategy

(2) Leadership

(3) Historical knowledge

(4) Economic planning

(5) Courage

44. In 1789, the French people revolted against the aristocratic government because of its unfair treatment of the masses who lived in poverty and had few voting rights but were taxed heavily. How did the people punish the aristocratic leaders?

(1) Jailing them

(2) Flogging them

(3) Guillotining them

(4) Hanging them

(5) Exiling them

45. The Monroe Doctrine was aimed at the European powers that existed in 1823. What was its intent?

(1) To warn them not to interfere with Latin America

(2) To warn them not to intercept our shipping

(3) To warn them not to attack the United States

(4) To protest taxation by foreign powers

(5) To remove any rights given to foreign aliens

> ### COME AND HELP THE STUDENTS OF YOUR COMMUNITY!
>
> Clara Barton Elementary School
> Newark, Florida
>
> NEEDED: We are looking for men and women to be tutors to our children, grades 1 through 5. You must be a high school graduate and have a minimum of 4 hours a week to spend with a student after school, from 3 to 4 p.m. No experience is necessary—we will train and supervise the right person! Good verbal communication skills and an ability to relate to young children are a plus. Please call: 222-1234 after 4 p.m. for an interview.
>
> February 2005

46. The above announcement is an example of which one of the following?

    (1) Faulty advertising

    (2) Volunteerism

    (3) Patriotism

    (4) Religious zeal

    (5) Preschool education

"When in the course of human events, it becomes necessary for one people to dissolve the political bands that have connected them with another, and to assume among the Powers of the earth, the separate and equal station to which the laws of Nature and of Nature's God entitle them, a decent respect to the opinion of mankind requires that they should declare the causes that impel them to the separation."

47. Which famous person's ideas inspired the reference to "the laws of Nature" mentioned above?

    (1) Plato

    (2) Aristotle

    (3) Newton

    (4) Galileo

    (5) Washington

48. There are major differences between Ireland and Great Britain over Northern Ireland. Which of the following statements is true?

    (1) Northern Ireland belongs to Scotland.

    (2) Ireland and Wales are economic partners.

    (3) Northern Ireland is officially under the control of Great Britain.

    (4) Ireland has never had an interest in Northern Ireland.

    (5) None of the above

diagnostic test

49. What was meant by the term "Cold War"?

  (1) A war fought in northern regions

  (2) A political battle between Russian and the United States after WWII

  (3) Disagreements between the Allies and the Axis powers

  (4) Economic battles stemming from excessive reparations

  (5) The bitterness of the Japanese after the bombing of Hiroshima

50. Gutenberg was responsible for revolutionizing the dissemination of information. What did he invent?

  (1) The printing press

  (2) Eye glasses

  (3) Papyrus for writing

  (4) The fountain pen

  (5) Book binding

Use this page for notes.

diagnostic test

TEST 3. SCIENCE

80 Minutes • 50 Questions

Directions: The Science Test consists of multiple-choice questions intended to measure general concepts in life science, earth and space science, physics, and chemistry. Some of the questions are based on short readings. Others are based on graphs, charts, tables, or diagrams. For each question, study the information given and then answer the question or questions based upon it. Refer to the information as often as necessary in answering the questions. Record your answer in the Science section of your answer sheet.

Q A physical change may alter the state of matter but does not change its chemical composition. Which of the following is NOT a physical change?

(1) Boiling water
(2) Dissolving salt in water
(3) Shaving wood
(4) Rusting metal
(5) Breaking glass

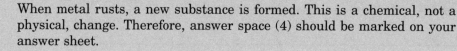

A When metal rusts, a new substance is formed. This is a chemical, not a physical, change. Therefore, answer space (4) should be marked on your answer sheet.

ITEMS 1 TO 4 REFER TO THE FOLLOWING ARTICLE.

For breakfast aboard Spacelab, the Blue Shift enjoys orange drink, peaches, scrambled eggs, sausages, cocoa, and sweet rolls. The food as well as the food preparation facilities could easily be the envy of many earthbound chefs, homemakers, and diners. Crew members can select from a menu almost as varied and certainly as tasty and nutritious as in most homes or restaurants. One crew member can prepare meals for his shift in about 5 minutes. Members of the Blue and Red Shifts may eat breakfast and dinner together on some missions if schedules permit.

In a galley to the left of the bunks are an oven, hot and cold water dispensers, and a pantry stocked with seventy-four kinds of food and twenty different beverages. There are drinking cups and eating utensils.

There is no refrigerator and none is needed. To save weight and space, most onboard foods are dehydrated by a freeze-drying process developed especially for space use. Ample water for reconstituting these foods is provided by the fuel cells, which deliver clean water as a by-product of their electricity-generating chemical processes.

Some foods are stored in conventional sealed, heat-sterilized cans or plastic pouches. A few foods, such as cookies and nuts, are in ready-to-eat form. Meals provide for an average of 2,700 calories daily.

1. According to the article, which of the following choices best describes the difference between the food eaten on Earth and the food eaten in space?

   (1) Food eaten in space is more fattening.
   (2) Food eaten in space can be prepared more quickly.
   (3) Food eaten on Earth is saltier.
   (4) People on Earth eat food higher in carbohydrates.
   (5) Astronauts are better cooks than earthbound people.

2. Which of the following best defines the word "reconstituting"?

   (1) Bring back to original form
   (2) Recooking to change the shape
   (3) Refining into a purer substance
   (4) Scrambling up the contents
   (5) Chopping into smaller pieces

3. What can be inferred from the fact that the astronauts consume 2,700 calories daily?

   (1) Astronauts are large-framed people who tend to overeat.
   (2) People need additional calories in space.
   (3) Astronauts eat less than people on Earth.
   (4) Space flight makes people hungry.
   (5) 2,700 calories represent the recommended daily allowance.

4. Based on the information given, which of the following statements is/are statements of fact, rather than opinion?

   A. Food served in space has been dehydrated to save space.

   B. Food served on Earth has a better appearance than food served in space.

   C. It takes just a few minutes to prepare a meal in space.

   D. Food just tastes better in space!

   (1) A only
   (2) A and B only
   (3) A and C only
   (4) C only
   (5) A, B, and D only

ITEMS 5 TO 8 REFER TO THE CHART BELOW.

MATURATION OF FRUIT FLIES

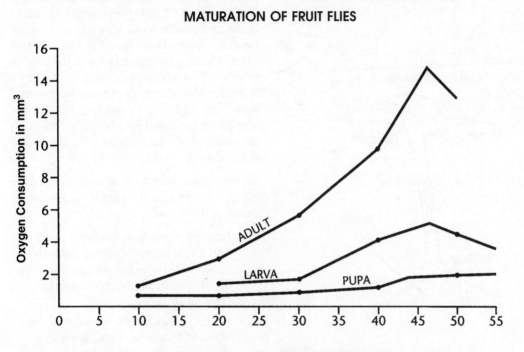

Temperature—Degrees Centigrade

5. According to the chart, when is the greatest amount of oxygen consumed during each stage?

(1) Between 10° and 20°
(2) Between 20° and 30°
(3) Between 30° and 40°
(4) Between 40° and 50°
(5) Between 50° and 55°

6. According to the chart, what was the highest stage of oxygen consumption in the adult?

(1) 2 to 6 mm^3
(2) 4 to 6 mm^3
(3) 6 to 8 mm^3
(4) 8 to 10 mm^3
(5) 10 to 14 mm^3

7. Which of the following can be inferred from the information on the chart?

(1) Fruit flies can reach maturity without oxygen.
(2) Adult fruit flies need more oxygen than pupae.
(3) Larvae do well in temperatures between 5° and 15°.
(4) The oxygen consumption of pupae greatly increases as they grow.
(5) Larvae grow faster than pupae.

8. We can infer that this information can be used for which of the following reasons?

(1) To increase growth in seasonal plants
(2) To inhibit growth in roaches
(3) To increase lab production of fruit flies
(4) To test new instruments
(5) To test new hormone therapies

ITEMS 9 REFERS TO THE DIAGRAM BELOW.

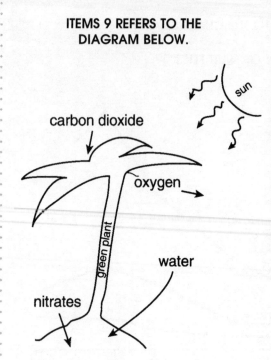

9. As illustrated in the diagram above, when green plants carry out photosynthesis, they take carbon dioxide and water and, in the presence of sunlight, change the raw materials into sugar and oxygen. Which of the following is the chemical formula for photosynthesis?

(1) $C_6H_{12}O_6+C_6H_{12}O_6{\rightarrow}C_{12}H_{22}O_{11}+H_2O$

(2) $CO_2+12H_2O{\rightarrow}C_6H_{12}O_6+6H_2O+6O_2$

(3) $NaOH+HCl{\rightarrow}NaCl+H_2O$

(4) $C_6H_{12}O_6{\rightarrow}2C_2H_5OH+2CO_2+H_2O$

(5) $2H_2O{\rightarrow}2H_2+O_2$

ITEMS 10 TO 14 REFER TO THE FOLLOWING PASSAGE.

Laser surgery has been going on for about thirty years. Lasers used for surgery do their work by destroying tissue, or cells, in a process called photocoagulation necrosis. The heat, or energy, from the laser is absorbed by the cell's moisture, which thus is turned into vapor and dissipated. Solids that remain when all moisture has been removed are ash and may be disposed of by suction, sponging, or brushing away. Often tissue is not completely turned to ash, but is no longer living, and eventually sloughs away from adjacent living tissue. Tumors, including cancerous cells, can be destroyed with a laser such as the CO_2 if they can be identified and reached. To make a cut or incision, a narrow laser beam is focused and played along the path where the cut is desired. Tissue destruction is limited to a specific width and depth with minimal injury to adjacent or underlying tissue. The beam is played into the same incision as many times as needed to achieve the desired length and depth of cut.

Lasers have certain advantages over more conventional surgical methods. Principally, these:

- Laser surgery's employment of heat and the minimal contact with tissue make for sterile conditions that are highly desirable for reducing the risks of infection.

- With certain lasers, a surgeon can work in the nose, ears, mouth, throat, vagina, and other close areas. In conventional surgery, extra cutting may be required to open up such areas enough to use a scalpel or other conventional surgical instrument.

- Advocates claim that because lasers operate by vaporization of and destruction of tissues, healing is usually prompt and there is a minimum of scarring and swelling.

10. According to the passage, which of the following choices best defines a laser?

(1) A beam of light rays

(2) A metal cutting tool

(3) A diamond-tipped drill

(4) A tool that has yet to be invented

(5) A tool that will someday replace doctors

11. As used in this passage, the word "vaporization" is best defined in which of the following choices?

- **(1)** Exploding a cancer cell
- **(2)** Removing moisture from a cell
- **(3)** Melting ice to form water
- **(4)** Sponging away dead cells
- **(5)** Slicing cancer cells into small sections

12. Which of the following is NOT an advantage of laser surgery, according to the passage?

- **(1)** Reduces scarring and swelling
- **(2)** Reduces amount of cutting necessary
- **(3)** Reduces risk of infection
- **(4)** Reduces risk of cancer
- **(5)** Reduces risk of harm to adjacent tissues

13. According to this passage, what may happen to dead cancer cells that are not completely removed by the laser?

- **(1)** They will reinfect the body.
- **(2)** They can still be brushed or sponged away.
- **(3)** They may be changed into healthy cells.
- **(4)** They may be shed away from healthy cells.
- **(5)** They will be attacked by white blood cells.

14. Which of the following statements is most likely based on opinion rather than fact?

- **(1)** Lasers have been used in surgery for about thirty years.
- **(2)** Lasers destroy healthy as well as infected tissue.
- **(3)** Laser surgery lessens pressure to adjacent areas.
- **(4)** Laser surgery usually heals promptly.
- **(5)** Lasers are the best tools to use in surgery.

diagnostic test

ITEMS 15 TO 17 REFER TO THE FOLLOWING CHART.

INCIDENCE OF HEMOPHILIA IN QUEEN VICTORIA'S DESCENDANTS

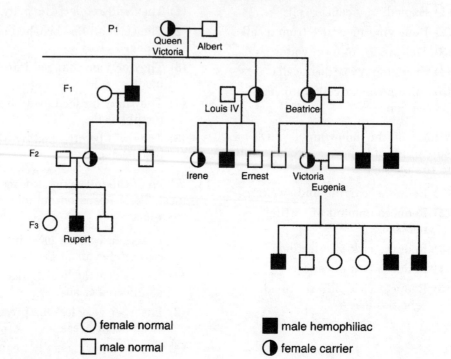

○ female normal   ■ male hemophiliac

□ male normal   ◐ female carrier

The accompanying pedigree chart shows only a part of Queen Victoria's descendants. The family tree indicates no history of hemophilia (a disease in which the blood fails to clot properly) for either parent prior to the P1 generation.

15. Which assumption about the P1 generation is true?

(1) Albert did not carry the gene for hemophilia.

(2) Queen Victoria had two X chromosomes, each with a gene for hemophilia.

(3) Neither Albert nor Victoria had a gene for hemophilia.

(4) Albert was probably a carrier of the gene for hemophilia.

(5) Albert had hemophilia.

16. If Beatrice had married a hemophiliac, what is the probability that her daughters would have been afflicted with the disease?

(1) 0%

(2) 25%

(3) 50%

(4) 75%

(5) 100%

17. From the information on the chart, what is the most reasonable explanation that Rupert exhibits hemophilia?

(1) A mutation occurred on the Y chromosome, which he received from his father.

(2) His mother suffered from the disease and transmitted it to him.

(3) His father was a carrier.

(4) His maternal grandfather had the disease.

(5) His father had the disease.

18. Stephen Hawking is world-renowned for his contributions to the "unified-field theory." He is a(n)

    (1) physicist.

    (2) biologist.

    (3) chemist.

    (4) astronaut.

    (5) doctor.

19. Precipitation refers to the forms of condensation that fall to Earth. Which of the following is NOT a form of precipitation?

    (1) Dust

    (2) Rain

    (3) Sleet

    (4) Hail

    (5) Snow

ITEM 20 REFERS TO THE FOLLOWING PASSAGE.

About ten million years ago, in what is now Nebraska and the Great Plains, there was a major volcanic eruption that created an enormous volume of a powdery substance. This blew and eventually settled on the ground of these areas. Lots of powdery ash settled over many hundreds of square miles. This was very similar to what happened in the 1980s, when Mount St. Helens erupted in the Cascade Range of Washington, but it was much more serious. Many animals that lived in these areas at that time, including camels, rhinoceroses, and strange looking sabertoothed deer, suffocated and died in the blowing dust.

20. Which of the following overwhelmed the animals?

    (1) Hot lava

    (2) Volcanic dust

    (3) Earthquakes

    (4) Loud sounds

    (5) A violent storm

ITEMS 21 TO 24 REFER TO THE GRAPH BELOW.

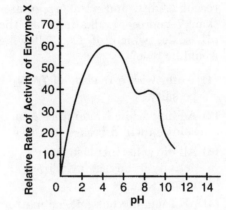

21. Which of the following conclusions is supported by the graph?

    (1) pH has no effect on enzyme action.

    (2) The relative rate of enzyme X is constant.

    (3) The rate of enzyme action varies with the pH.

    (4) Plants grow best in strong sunlight.

    (5) Enzyme X increases in volume as the pH increases.

22. According to the graph, between which pH values does the rate of activity of enzyme X increase most?

    (1) 0 and 2

    (2) 2 and 4

    (3) 4 and 6

    (4) 6 and 8

    (5) 8 and 10

23. Which of the following processes could be the subject of this graph?

    (1) Digestion

    (2) Evaporation

    (3) Photosynthesis

    (4) Sleep

    (5) Respiration

24. Based on the information in the graph and the fact that 7 represents neutrality, numbers less than 7 represent acidity, and numbers greater than 7 represent alkalinity on the pH scale, which of the following would be true?

(1) Water with a reading of 7 would be salty.

(2) Adding acidic lemon juice to a solution will decrease its pH.

(3) All enzymes increase their activity in an acidic environment.

(4) pH remains constant, no matter what is added.

(5) Some enzymes react to differences in pH.

25. A scientist did the following experiment: He covered two petri dishes with the same type of bacteria. Then he put a drop of penicillin on one dish and a drop of chemical "X" on the other. Several hours later he saw the results as shown in the diagram below. What can you infer from looking at the diagram?

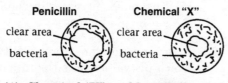

(1) Chemical "X" could not kill any bacteria.

(2) Chemical "X" is a stronger antibiotic than penicillin.

(3) Chemical "X" is penicillin because penicillin kills germs.

(4) Nothing can be determined by looking at the diagram.

(5) Chemical "X" is a weaker antibiotic than penicillin.

ITEM 26 REFERS TO THE FOLLOWING SELECTION.

Biofeedback is a treatment technique in which people are trained to improve their health by using signals from their own bodies. People learn, for example, to read devices that "feed back" information about their body's condition. Physical therapists use biofeedback to help stroke victims regain movement in paralyzed muscles. Psychologists use it to help tense and anxious clients learn to relax. Specialists in many different fields use biofeedback to help their patients cope with pain.

26. Which of the following is NOT an example of the use of biofeedback?

(1) Measuring electrical impulses

(2) Stepping on a scale

(3) Jumping rope

(4) Taking your temperature

(5) Making blood pressure measurements

ITEM 27 REFERS TO THE FOLLOWING INFORMATION.

Instincts are involuntary actions that are inborn. Some scientists believe that human beings possess no instincts. Everything they do has to be learned. You are observing examples of instincts when you watch a spider spinning a web, a bird building a nest, or a beaver building a dam. Humans learn habits. A habit is an action that is repeated so often that it can be done without a second thought. Typing without looking at the keys or biting one's nails are examples of habits.

27. Which of the following is properly matched?

(1) Habit—an ant builds a colony

(2) Instinct—a baby rolls a ball

(3) Habit—a prairie dog digs a tunnel

(4) Instinct—a child runs for the school bus

(5) Habit—a driver stops at a red light

ITEMS 28 TO 32 REFER TO THE FOLLOWING GRAPH.

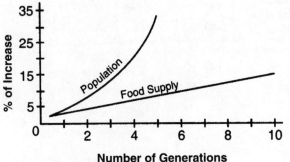

Darwin got some of his ideas for the Theory of Natural Selection from Malthus's *An Essay on the Principle of Population.* Malthus's ideas are represented on the graph above.

28. According to the information on the graph, what was Malthus's theory?

    (1) Population increases arithmetically; food increases geometrically.
    (2) There will always be sufficient food for the population.
    (3) Eventually, food production will outstrip population increases.
    (4) Population increases faster than food supply.
    (5) The fittest will survive.

29. Specifically, Malthus's ideas most directly lent support to which of Darwin's ideas?

    (1) Variation
    (2) Overproduction
    (3) Adaptation
    (4) Inheritance of variations
    (5) Survival of the fittest

30. If the food-supply trend line continues as indicated on the graph, what will probably eventually happen to the population curve?

    (1) It will reach a peak and then drop downward until it again meets the food supply trend line.
    (2) It will level off at about the 45% point on the graph and continue indefinitely at this level.
    (3) The slope of the curve will decrease.
    (4) It will always run parallel to the food supply line.
    (5) It will level off at about the 75% point on the graph and continue at this point until the year 2000.

31. A group of nations are trying to change the outcome of Malthus's theory. Which of the following factors do they have to take into consideration to do so?

    A. War
    B. Famine
    C. Improved agriculture
    D. Medical advances

    (1) A only
    (2) A and B
    (3) A and C
    (4) A and D
    (5) A, B, C, and D

32. Which of the following is/are likely to be first to feel the effect of Malthus's theory?

    A. China
    B. America
    C. Africa
    D. Canada

    (1) A and B
    (2) A and C
    (3) C
    (4) A and D
    (5) A, B, and C

diagnostic test

33. Sublimation is the process of changing a substance directly from a solid to a gaseous state. Since most substances first become a liquid, sublimation is an unusual event. Which of the following elements could sublime when heated?

(1) Br_2 (liquid)

(2) I_2 (solid)

(3) H_2 (gas)

(4) F_2 (gas)

(5) Cl_2 (gas)

ITEMS 34 AND 35 REFER TO THE FOLLOWING INFORMATION.

When an object moves at a constant speed, the distance it travels is equal to the rate it travels times the total time it travels:

R(rate) $\times T$(time) $= D$(distance)

34. The average speed of a runner in a 400-meter race is 8.0 meters per second. How long, in seconds, did it take this runner to complete the race?

(1) 80

(2) 50

(3) 40

(4) 32

(5) 10

35. Sharon finished the 20-mile race in 2.5 hours. What was her rate of speed in miles per hour?

(1) 1

(2) 5

(3) 8

(4) 10

(5) 15

ITEMS 36 TO 38 REFER TO THE FOLLOWING TABLE.

TABLE OF PERIODIC ELEMENTS

Atomic number → 1 H 1.0079 ← Atomic mass

Representative elements (s block)

Transition elements (d block)

Representative elements (p block)

Inner transition elements (f block)

1A	2A	3B	4B	5B	6B	7B	8B	8B	8B	1B	2B	3A	4A	5A	6A	7A	8A
1 H 1.0080																	2 He 4.0026
3 Li 6.941	4 Be 9.0122											5 B 10.81	6 C 12.011	7 N 14.007	8 O 15.9994	9 F 19.00	10 Ne 20.183
11 Na 22.9898	12 Mg 24.305											13 Al 26.98	14 Si 28.09	15 P 30.974	16 S 32.064	17 Cl 35.453	18 Ar 39.95
19 K 39.102	20 Ca 40.08	21 Sc 44.96	22 Ti 47.90	23 V 50.94	24 Cr 51.996	25 Mn 54.94	26 Fe 55.85	27 Co 58.93	28 Ni 58.71	29 Cu 63.55	30 Zn 65.37	31 Ga 69.72	32 Ge 72.59	33 As 74.92	34 Se 78.96	35 Br 79.9	36 Kr 83.8
37 Rb 85.468	38 Sr 87.62	39 Y 88.91	40 Zr 91.22	41 Nb 92.91	42 Mo 95.94	43 Tc 98.91	44 Ru 101.07	45 Rh 102.91	46 Pd 106.4	47 Ag 107.87	48 Cd 112.4	49 In 114.82	50 Sn 118.69	51 Sb 121.75	52 Te 127.6	53 I 126.9	54 Xe 131.3
55 Cs 132.91	56 Ba 137.34	57 La 138.91	72 Hf 178.49	73 Ta 180.95	74 W 183.85	75 Re 186.2	76 Os 190.2	77 Ir 192.2	78 Pt 195.1	79 Au 196.97	80 Hg 200.59	81 Tl 204.37	82 Pb 207.2	83 Bi 208.98	84 Po (210)	85 At (210)	86 At (222)
87 Fr (223)	88 Ra (226)	89 Ac (227)															

58 Ce 140.12	59 Pr 140.91	60 Nd 144.24	61 Pm (147)	62 Sm 150.4	63 Eu 151.96	64 Gd 157.25	65 Tb 158.93	66 Dy 162.5	67 Ho 164.93	68 Er 167.26	69 Tm 168.93	70 Yb 173.04	71 Lu 174.97
90 Th 232.04	91 Pa 231.04	92 U 238.03	93 Np 237.05	94 Pu (242)	95 Am (243)	96 Cm (247)	97 Bk (247)	98 Cf (247)	99 Es (254)	100 Fm (253)	101 Md (256)	102 No (254)	103 Lw (257)

diagnostic test

36. There was no potassium left in the chemical storeroom. Which atom is most similar in properties to potassium (K)?

(1) P

(2) Al

(3) Na

(4) Ca

(5) Mg

37. The elements in the periodic table are arranged according to their

(1) atomic numbers.

(2) atomic masses.

(3) conductivity.

(4) mass number.

(5) oxidation states.

38. Most elements are found to occur naturally. However, some have been created by scientists and engineers in laboratories with the use of nuclear technology. What atomic numbers would these man-made elements have?

(1) 92–103

(2) 93–103

(3) 89–103

(4) 57–71; 89–103

(5) 1–10

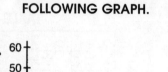

ITEM 39 REFERS TO THE FOLLOWING GRAPH.

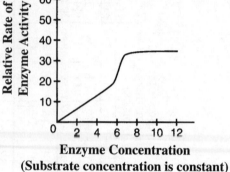

Enzyme Concentration
(Substrate concentration is constant)

39. What is indicated by the information on this graph?

(1) The rate of enzyme action is directly dependent upon the substrate concentration.

(2) The rate of enzyme action becomes stabilized when a certain enzyme concentration is reached.

(3) Enzyme concentration has no effect upon the rate of enzyme action.

(4) When the substrate concentration is increased, the enzyme action is decreased.

(5) Enzyme activity is affected by temperature.

ITEMS 40 TO 42 ARE BASED ON THE FOOD PYRAMID BELOW.

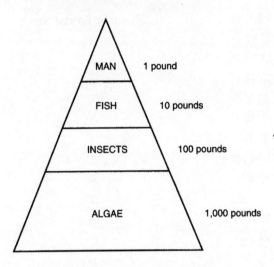

The diagram above represents a food pyramid. It shows how many pounds of food are needed to sustain the animal above it.

40. According to this food pyramid, how many pounds of fish would it take to sustain a 100-pound man?

   (1) 10
   (2) 100
   (3) 1,000
   (4) More than 1,000
   (5) More than 10,000

41. From the information provided by this pyramid, how do insects get their energy?

   (1) They swim in the water.
   (2) They are eaten by fish.
   (3) They are eaten by algae.
   (4) They eat algae.
   (5) They feed on human blood.

42. Which of the following would result if the fish were removed from this pyramid?

   (1) The number of insects would increase.
   (2) The number of insects would decrease.
   (3) The amount of algae would increase.
   (4) The number of men would increase.
   (5) The insects would starve.

ITEMS 43 TO 46 REFER TO THE CHART BELOW.

SELECTED RADIOISOTOPES

Nuclide	Half-Life	Particle Emission
^{14}C	5730 y	$\beta-$
^{60}Co	5.3 y	$\beta-$
^{147}Cs	30.23 y	$\beta-$
^{220}Fr	27.5 s	α
^{3}H	12.26 y	$\beta-$
^{131}I	8.07 d	$\beta-$
^{10}K	1.28×10^9 y	$\beta+$
^{42}K	12.4 h	$\beta-$
^{32}P	14.3 d	$\beta-$
^{226}Ra	1600 y	α
^{90}Sr	28.1 y	$\beta-$
^{235}U	7.1×10^4 y	α
^{238}U	4.51×10^9 y	α

y = years; d = days; h = hours; s = seconds

Half-life is the period of time required for the disintegration of one half of the atoms in a sample of some specific radioactive substance.

43. Suppose you have 100 grams of each of the following radioisotopes. Which will have the most atoms remaining after 1 year?

(1) ^{32}P

(2) ^{226}Ra

(3) ^{90}Sr

(4) ^{235}U

(5) ^{238}U

44. How many grams of ^{220}Fr will remain if you hold 100 grams for 110 seconds?

(1) 62.50

(2) 50.00

(3) 12.50

(4) 6.25

(5) 1.00

45. According to the chart, what portion of the original quantity of ^{60}Co will remain at the end of 10.6 years?

(1) $\dfrac{1}{2}$

(2) $\dfrac{1}{4}$

(3) $\dfrac{1}{8}$

(4) $\dfrac{1}{16}$

(5) $\dfrac{1}{32}$

46. Based on the chart, which of the following radioisotopes will disintegrate most rapidly?

(1) ^{60}Co

(2) ^{42}K

(3) ^{3}H

(4) ^{131}I

(5) ^{32}P

ITEMS 47 TO 50 REFER TO THE FOLLOWING SELECTION.

GALE WARNING: When winds of 38–55 miles per hour (33–48 knots) are expected, a gale warning is added to the advisory message.

STORM WARNING: When winds of 55–74 miles per hour (48–64 knots) are expected, a storm warning is added to the advisory message.

When gale or storm warnings are part of a tropical cyclone advisory, they may change to a hurricane warning if the storm continues along the coast.

HURRICANE WATCH: If the hurricane continues its advance and threatens coastal and inland regions, a hurricane watch is added to the advisory, covering a specified area and duration. A hurricane watch means that hurricane conditions are a real possibility; it does not mean they are imminent. When a hurricane watch is issued, everyone in the area covered by the watch should listen for further advisories and be prepared to act quickly if hurricane warnings are issued.

HURRICANE WARNING: When hurricane conditions are expected within 24 hours, a hurricane warning is added to the advisory. Hurricane warnings identify coastal areas where winds of at least 74 miles per hour are expected to occur. A warning may also describe coastal areas where dangerously high water or exceptionally high waves are forecast, even though winds may be less than hurricane force.

When the hurricane warning is issued, all precautions should be taken immediately. Hurricane warnings are seldom issued more than 24 hours in advance. If the hurricane's path is unusual or erratic, the warnings may be issued only a few hours before the beginning of hurricane conditions.

47. At which of the following wind speeds are gale warnings issued?

(1) 20 mph

(2) 30 mph

(3) 40 mph

(4) 60 mph

(5) 80 mph

48. "Citizens, store your food and water. Board up your windows and move to your storm cellars."

Which of the following would this message be issued for?

(1) Weather report

(2) Gale warning

(3) Storm warning

(4) Hurricane watch

(5) Hurricane warning

49. According to the passage, hurricanes are especially dangerous in which of the following areas?

(1) Major cities

(2) Prairies

(3) Near high buildings

(4) Coastal areas

(5) The ocean

50. We can infer from the passage that hurricanes are dangerous for which of the following reasons?

(1) Flooding

(2) Electrical shocks

(3) Power loss

(4) Food spoilage

(5) Disruption of services

Use this page for notes.

_____

_____

_____

_____

_____

_____

_____

_____

_____

_____

_____

_____

_____

_____

_____

_____

_____

_____

_____

diagnostic test

TEST 4. LANGUAGE ARTS, READING

65 Minutes • 40 Questions

> **Directions:** The Language Arts, Reading Test consists of multiple-choice questions based on a variety of excerpts from literary and nonfiction writings. Read each selection carefully and then answer the questions based upon it. You may refer to the selection as often as necessary to answer the questions. However, do not spend more time than necessary on any one item. Record your answers on the Language Arts, Reading section of your answer sheet.

> He died at eventide . . . I saw his breath beat quicker and quicker, pause, and then his little soul leapt like a star that travels in the night and left a world of darkness in its train. The day changed not . . . Only in the chamber of death writhed the world's most piteous thing—a childless mother.
>
> The reader can infer that death has come to a(n)
>
> **(1)** old man.
> **(2)** favorite dog.
> **(3)** child.
> **(4)** mother.
> **(5)** soldier.
>
> ① ② ● ④ ⑤
>
> **A** The correct answer is "child"; therefore, you should blacken answer space (3) on your answer sheet.

ITEMS 1 TO 6 REFER TO THE FOLLOWING EXCERPT.

Can a Brave Man Be Afraid?

Line "Could you see the whites of their eyes?" said the man who was seated on a soapbox.

"Nothing of the kind," replied old
(5) Henry warmly. "Just a lot of flitting figures, and I let go at where they 'peared to be the thickest. Bang!"

"Mr. Fleming," said the grocer—his deferential voice expressed somehow
(10) the old man's exact social weight— "Mr. Fleming, you never was frightened much in them battles, was you?"

The veteran looked down and grinned. Observing his manner, the
(15) entire group tittered. "Well, I guess I was," he answered finally. "Pretty well scared, sometimes. Why, in my first battle I thought the sky was falling down. I thought the world was coming
(20) to an end. You bet I was scared."

Everyone laughed. Perhaps it seemed strange and rather wonderful to them that a man should admit the thing, and in the tone of their laughter
(25) was probably more admiration than if old Fleming had declared that he had always been a lion. Moreover, they knew that he had ranked as an orderly sergeant, and so their opinion of
(30) his heroism was fixed. None, to be sure, knew how an orderly sergeant ranked, but then it was understood to be somewhere just shy of a major general's stars. So when old Henry admit-
(35) ted that he had been frightened, there was a laugh.

"The trouble was," said the old man, "I thought they were all shooting at me. Yes, sir, I thought every man in
(40) the other army was aiming at me in particular, and only me. And it seemed so darned unreasonable, you know. I wanted to explain to 'em what an almighty good fellow I was, because I
(45) thought then they might quit all trying to hit me. But I couldn't explain,

and they kept on being unreasonable—blim-blam!-bang! So I run!" Two little triangles of wrinkles appeared at
(50) the corners of his eyes. Evidently he appreciated some comedy in this recital. Down near his feet, however, little Jim, his grandson, was visibly horror-stricken. His hands were
(55) clasped nervously, and his eyes were wide with astonishment at this terrible scandal, his most magnificent grandfather telling such a thing.

When little Jim walked with his
(60) grandfather he was in the habit of skipping along on the stone pavement in front of the three stores and the hotel of the town and betting that he could avoid the cracks. But upon this
(65) day he walked soberly, with his hand gripping two of his grandfather's fingers.

Then finally he ventured: "Grandpa—now—was that true what
(70) you was telling those men?"

"What?" asked the grandfather. "What was I telling them?"

"Oh, about your running."

"Why, yes, that was true enough,
(75) Jimmie. It was my first fight, and there was an awful lot of noise, you know."

Jimmie seemed dazed that this idol, of its own will, should so totter. His
(80) stout boyish idealism was injured.

From Stephen Crane,
"The Veteran."

1. The reader quickly learns that Henry is

   (1) a storekeeper.
   (2) owner of a tannery.
   (3) an ex-soldier.
   (4) a major general.
   (5) a grocer.

2. What is the old man's leading characteristic?

   (1) Hypocrisy
   (2) Pride
   (3) Honesty
   (4) Unfriendliness
   (5) Idealism

3. When Mr. Fleming admitted that he had been afraid in battle, what was the adult listeners' attitude toward him?

   (1) It turned to amusement, because they knew he had never been to war.
   (2) It turned to bitterness.
   (3) It changed to disgust.
   (4) It remained one of admiration.
   (5) It changed to horror.

4. The old man does not seem to be aware that

   (1) his grandson is horrified by his admission of fear.
   (2) little Jim never knew he had fought in a war.
   (3) the listeners think he is a fool.
   (4) his grandson is listening.
   (5) war can be a terrifying experience.

5. What is the most important point that the author wishes the reader to understand?

   (1) That the boy doesn't like his grandfather.
   (2) That Henry was afraid in battle.
   (3) That the boy's image of his grandfather as a hero has been damaged.
   (4) That Henry is highly regarded by his town's people.
   (5) That the boy enjoys the company of the older men.

6. From their reactions, what can we assume about Henry's audience?

   (1) They are other veterans like Henry.
   (2) They are old men.
   (3) They are strangers.
   (4) They seem to be skeptics.
   (5) They are probably younger men who have never been to war.

ITEMS 7 TO 11 REFER TO THE FOLLOWING BUSINESS DOCUMENT.

How Should an Employee Behave?

Guidelines for Employees

1. Welcome to Riverdale Graphics! We are happy you came to work for us and wish you many happy and productive years.

2. You will be paid on a bi-weekly basis on Fridays. Paychecks will reflect necessary deductions for taxes, social security, the company health plan, and retirement benefits. Vacation days will be negotiated at the end of six months of successful employment.

3. Our hours are from 8:30 a.m. until 5:30 p.m., Monday to Friday. Lateness to work is not acceptable. In case of bad weather, please give yourself extra time to get here. If you are late by more than 20 minutes, a deduction will be made from your paycheck. Too much lateness will necessitate our reviewing whether this is the right company for you.

4. We expect you to come to work each and every day. If you are ill or an emergency comes up, please call us as soon as possible so that we can make arrangements to cover your assignment. If you are returning from an illness that kept you home more than two days, you must bring in a doctor's note explaining the reason for your absence.

5. We expect you to dress suitably for your position. If you meet the public as part of your job, a jacket and tie

are necessary for men, and women must wear an appropriate dress or pants suit. If you are working in the shop, work uniforms will be provided, but it will be the responsibility of the employee to launder these at least weekly. Each employee will be assigned a locker.

6. Your lunch must be eaten in the lunchroom only. Lunch is from 12 noon until 1 p.m. for some employees and from 1 p.m. to 2 p.m. for others. You will be assigned one of these lunch hours according to the needs of the company.

7. You may not have snacks or beverages at your desk or other worksites, and personal telephone conversations are to be brief and limited in number. We expect you to behave professionally at all times.

8. Your immediate supervisor will explain your exact duties to you. If you have any questions or concerns please discuss them with him (or her).

9. We expect each employee to be an enthusiastic member of our team. We want you to be creative, energetic, helpful, and alert. We all try to treat one another and our customers with courtesy and respect. Again, if you have a problem or are not quite certain how to handle something, please feel free to ask your supervisor. He (or she) is here to help you.

An excerpt from Riverdale Graphics Training Manual. *5/01*

7. John arrived at work at 8:45 a.m., then telephoned his girlfriend as well as his mother and another friend. Which of the company rules has he broken?

   (1) 4
   (2) 3 and 7
   (3) 6
   (4) None of the above
   (5) All of the above

8. Susie is asked to put some computer files on floppy disks. She has no idea how to do this. What should she do?

   (1) Take a computer course on Saturdays.
   (2) Ask to be given another job to do.
   (3) Susie needs to read the manual.
   (4) She should talk to her supervisor.
   (5) Look for another job, since the demands of this one are clearly too much for her.

9. The Guidelines suggest that Riverdale Graphics

   (1) is a well-run company that makes a lot of money.
   (2) is not fair to its employees.
   (3) is trying to maximize production.
   (4) expects mature, responsible behavior from its employees.
   (5) is not a good place to work.

10. If Freddie wakes up 20 minutes late in the morning, what do the Guidelines suggest that he do?

    (1) Turn over and go back to sleep.
    (2) Skip breakfast and get a move on.
    (3) Call his supervisor.
    (4) Panic.
    (5) Look for another job.

11. The saying "The customer is always right" relates to the following rule of Riverdale Graphics:

    (1) 9
    (2) 8
    (3) 9 and 5
    (4) All the rules
    (5) None of the above

**ITEMS 12 TO 17 REFER TO THE
FOLLOWING STORY.**

Why Was the Beggar Blind?

Line "Listen, guv'nor.[1] Just a minute of your time. I ain't no beggar, guv'nor. I got a handy little article here"—he fumbled until he could press a small
(5) object in Mr. Parsons' hand—" that I sell. One buck. Best cigarette lighter ever made."

Mr. Parsons stood there, somewhat annoyed and embarrassed. He was a
(10) handsome figure in his immaculate gray suit and gray hat and Malacca stick.[2] Of course the man with the cigarette lighters could not see him . . . "But I don't smoke," he said.
(15) "Listen, I bet you know plenty people who smoke. And, mister, you wouldn't mind helping a poor guy out?"

Mr. Parsons sighed and felt in his pocket. He brought out the two half
(20) dollars and pressed them into the man's hands. He hesitated, not wanting to be boorish and inquisitive, even with a blind peddler. "Have you lost your sight entirely?"
(25) "Fourteen years, guv'nor." Then he added with an insane sort of pride: "Westbury, sir. I was one of 'em."

"Westbury," repeated Mr. Parsons. "Ah, yes. The chemical explosion
(30) . . . The papers haven't mentioned it for years."

"You want to know how I lost my eyes?" cried the man. "Well, here it is!" His words fell with the bitter and
(35) studied drama of a story often told, and told for money. "I was there in C shop, last of all the folks rushing out. Out in the air there was a chance, even with the buildings exploding
(40) right and left. And just as I was about there, crawling along between those big vats, a guy behind me grabs my legs. He says, 'Let me past, you—!' Maybe he was nuts. I dunno. I try to
(45) forgive him in my heart, guv'nor. But he was bigger than me. He hauls me back and climbs right over me. And he gets out, and I lie there with all that poison gas pouring down on all sides
(50) of me, and flame and stuff . . ." He swallowed—a studied sob—and stood dumbly expectant. "That's the story, guv'nor."

"Not quite," said Mr. Parsons.
(55) The blind peddler shivered crazily. "Not quite, what do you mean, you—?"

"The story is true," Mr. Parsons said, "except that it is the other way around."
(60) "Other way around?" he croaked un-amiably. "Say, guv'nor—"

"I was in C shop," said Mr. Parsons. "It was the other way. You were the fellow who hauled back on me and
(65) climbed over me. You were bigger than I was, Markwardt."

The blind man stood for a long time, swallowing hoarsely. He gulped: "Parsons. By God. I thought you—." And
(70) then he screamed fiendishly: "Yes. Maybe so. Maybe so. But I'm blind! You got away, but I'm blind'."

"Well," said Mr. Parsons, "don't make such a row about it, Markwardt,
(75) . . . So am I."

Adapted from "A Man Who Had No Eyes" *by Mackinlay Kantor.*

---

[1]guv'nor—a slang term of address used to a stranger or one's superior or employer.
[2]Malacca stick—a light walking stick made from rattan.

12. What can be inferred about the narrator of the story from the information given?

   (1) He worked with Markwardt and Parsons.
   (2) He is blind.
   (3) He is a young boy.
   (4) He has befriended Parsons.
   (5) He has eyesight.

13. The title of this story is "A Man Who Had No Eyes." What does this title refer to?

   (1) The people who lost their eyesight in the Westbury explosion
   (2) Markwardt's inability to admit the truth
   (3) The supervisor at C shop
   (4) A person in Parsons' hotel who develops chemicals
   (5) Both Parsons' and Markwardt's blindness

14. The reader can infer that Markwardt has repeated his story many times when the author says,

   (1) "His words fell with the bitter and studied drama of a story often told, and told for money."
   (2) "The blind man stood for a long time, swallowing hoarsely."
   (3) "He brought out the two half dollars and pressed them into the man's hands."
   (4) "The blind peddler shivered crazily."
   (5) "Westbury, sir. I was one of 'em."

15. How does the author establish a contrast between Parsons and Markwardt?

   (1) Different disabilities
   (2) Levels of diction
   (3) Their marriages
   (4) Opposing political views
   (5) Their destinations

16. How do we know that Mr. Parsons has done better economically than Markwardt since the time of the accident?

   (1) He is well dressed and stylish.
   (2) We don't really know if he's better off or not.
   (3) We're told he now owns Westbury.
   (4) He is now the boss of the company.
   (5) He has money in his pocket.

17. At what point in the story does Mr. Parsons recognize Markwardt?

   (1) When he is initially approached by him
   (2) When he realizes the peddler is blind
   (3) When Markwardt tells of his escape from the chemical plant
   (4) When he first hears his voice
   (5) When he reads about him in the newspapers

ITEMS 18 TO 23 REFER TO THE FOLLOWING POEM.

Where Is the Highwayman Headed?

The Highwayman

Line The wind was a torrent of darkness among the gusty trees,
The moon was a ghostly galleon tossed upon cloudy seas,
(5) The road was a ribbon of moonlight over the purple moor,
And the highwayman came riding—
Riding—riding—
The highwayman came riding, up to
(10) the old inn-door.
He'd a French cocked-hat on his forehead, a bunch of lace at his chin,
A coat of the claret velvet, and breeches of brown doeskin;
(15) They fitted with never a wrinkle: his boots were up to the thigh!
And he rode with a jewelled twinkle, His pistol butts a-twinkle,
His rapier hilt a-twinkle, under the
(20) jewelled sky.
Over the cobbles he clattered and clashed in the dark inn-yard,
And he tapped with his whip on the shutters, but all was locked and
(25) barred;
He whistled a tune to the window, and who should be waiting there
But the landlord's black-eyed daughter, Bess, the landlord's daughter,
(30) Plaiting a dark red love-knot into her long black hair.
And dark in the dark old inn-yard a stable-wicket creaked
Where Tim, the ostler, listened; his
(35) face was white and peaked;
His eyes were hollows of madness, his hair like mouldy hay,
But he loved the landlord's daughter, The landlord's red-lipped daughter,
(40) Dumb as a dog he listened, and he heard the robber say—
"One kiss, my bonny sweetheart, I'm after a prize tonight,

But I shall be back with the yellow
(45) gold before the morning light;
Yet, if they press me sharply, and harry me through the day,
Then look for me by moonlight, Watch for me by moonlight,
(50) I'll come to thee by moonlight, though hell should bar the way."

by Alfred Noyes

18. The first ten lines are an example of which of the following?

   (1) Personification
   (2) A haiku
   (3) A sonnet
   (4) An extended metaphor
   (5) A stanza

19. How does the highwayman appear to be dressed?

   (1) To conceal his identity
   (2) In dull, dark clothing
   (3) In loose-fitting clothes
   (4) As a resplendent gentleman
   (5) Without frills

20. Another term for a *highwayman* would be a

   (1) toll collector.
   (2) robber.
   (3) model for men's clothing.
   (4) bridegroom.
   (5) stable hand.

21. It may be inferred from the poem that the highwayman was in danger because

   (1) Bess did not like him.
   (2) his horse was lame and he would be thrown.
   (3) Tim was jealous of him.
   (4) he owed the landlord back rent.
   (5) he was as "Dumb as a dog."

22. Why can we assume that the high-wayman was not expected when he arrived at the inn?

(1) All the doors and shutters were closed.

(2) Because it was late at night.

(3) There was a storm raging.

(4) (1) and (2) are correct.

(5) We're told he was a stranger to Bess.

23. The highwayman in this poem went off to

(1) find an inn that was open.

(2) France.

(3) see Tim.

(4) prospect for gold.

(5) commit a robbery.

ITEMS 24 TO 28 REFER TO THE FOLLOWING PASSAGE.

How Did the Fresh Legs Dance?

Line This year, the **School of American Ballet's** Annual Showcase of its students infused new life into two staples of the academy's parent company, the
(5) New York City Ballet—Balanchine's *Tombeau de Couperin* and Robbins' *Fanfare. Tombeau,* created in 1975 to the Ravel score, is an exquisite ensemble piece for eight couples—no
(10) stars, no soloists, every dancer equal. Its magically shifting patterns reflect both the court dancing of Couperin's time and the related configurations and communal interplay of American
(15) square dancing. Richard Tanner, assisted by Susan Pilarre, captured the delicately filigreed style of the piece that the music dictates. Their proteges moved through the lovely configu-
(20) rations of the dance with luminous pleasure, apparently realizing themselves to be links in the chain of beauty (in the words of the great Danish ballet master August Bournon-

(25) ville), no less wonderful or important for being anonymous.

As danced by preprofessionals rather than their often more condescending elders, the 1953 *Fanfare,* staged by
(30) Christine Redpath, assisted by Pilarre, overcame the onus of being a ballet one is embarrassed to watch without the excuse of accompanying a child. The choreography fulfills the in-
(35) structive chore of the music—both the stuff of Family Matinees—which is to deconstruct the orchestra to its component instruments, then reunite them via a fugue. The SAB performers
(40) entered into the occasion joyously, relishing their mini-solo or small-group bits, the frequent wit of Robbins' invention, and the empathy involved in the instruments' uniting to create
(45) something larger than themselves. Carla Korbes, a petite, juicy dancer, was as dulcet a Harp—the role is a tiny star turn—as anyone could wish.

Christopher Wheeldon, NYCB's fair-
(50) haired boy, contributed the latest entry in a choreographic career that is being ardently supported by dance observers desperate for emergent choreographic genius. (I'm desperate
(55) right along with them, but I find Wheeldon's work to date dully conventional and intolerably sentimental.) The new piece, *Scenes de Ballet,* set to the Stravinsky score of that name, is a
(60) showcase for 62 SAB pupils, ranging from tiny accomplished female sprites and grave little boys pushed beyond their powers through the adolescents whom Balanchine, in his day, wisely
(65) cloistered until they matured as professionals. The proceedings Wheeldon has devised are overbusy and, where not pointless, banal (little moppet gazing wistfully at the near adults' love
(70) duet, etc.).

From Fresh Legs,
a review by Tobi Tobias,
New York *Magazine, 6/21/99.*
Used by permission.

24. What is the author's main purpose in writing this article?

(1) She wants to make suggestions to Balanchine and Robbins.

(2) She wants to display her knowledge of dance.

(3) She is a dance teacher looking for more pupils.

(4) She wants people to see professional dancers rather than just students.

(5) She wants to give her impressions of the dance performance in terms of the quality of the dancing and the pieces performed.

25. The "fresh-legged" dancers mentioned in this review are

(1) members of the New York City Ballet.

(2) young preprofessionals.

(3) soloists.

(4) choreographers.

(5) all girls.

26. Balanchine, Robbins, and Christopher Wheeldon are

(1) well-known choreographers.

(2) parents of the dancers.

(3) Danish soloists.

(4) French musicians.

(5) producers of SAB.

27. Which of the three pieces discussed does the reviewer seem to like?

(1) *Tombeau* but not *Fanfare*

(2) Only *Fanfare*

(3) *Scenes de Ballet*

(4) *Tombeau* and *Fanfare*

(5) All the pieces

28. What did the reviewer think of Wheeldon's *Scenes de Ballet*?

(1) She loved it.

(2) She thought it was conventional and too sentimental.

(3) She described it as overly busy and pointless.

(4) She thought it was too difficult for the young dancers.

(5) She felt it gave the dancers good opportunities to learn difficult steps.

ITEMS 29 TO 34 REFER TO THE FOLLOWING EXCERPT FROM A CLASSICAL PLAY.

Who Will Miss Neville Marry?

Line MISS NEVILLE: He's a very singular character, I assure you. Among women of reputation and virtue, he is the modestest man alive; but his acquain-

(5) tance gives him a very different character among creatures of a different stamp: you understand me.

MISS HARDCASTLE: An odd character, indeed. I shall never be able to man-

(10) age him. What shall I do? Pshaw, think no more of him, but trust to occurrences for success. But how goes on your own affair, my dear? Has my mother been courting you for my

(15) brother Tony, as usual?

MISS NEVILLE: I have just come from one of our agreeable *tête-à-têtes*. She has been saying a hundred tender things, and setting off her

(20) pretty monster as the very pink of perfection.

MISS HARDCASTLE: And her partiality is such, that she actually thinks him so. A fortune like yours is no small temp-

(25) tation. Besides, as she has the sole management of it, I'm not surprised to see her unwilling to let it go out of the family.

MISS NEVILLE: A fortune like mine,

(30) which chiefly consists in jewels, is no

such mighty temptation. But, at any rate, if my dear Hastings be but constant, I make no doubt to be too hard for her at last. However, I let her sup-
(35) pose that I am in love with her son; and she never once dreams that my affections are fixed upon another.

MISS HARDCASTLE: My good brother holds out stoutly. I could almost love
(40) him for hating you so.

MISS NEVILLE: It is a good-natured creature at bottom, and I'm sure would wish to see me married to anyone but himself. But my aunt's
(45) bell rings for our afternoon's walk round the improvements. *Allons!* Courage is necessary, as our affairs are critical.

MISS HARDCASTLE: Would it were bed-
(50) time, and all were well.

From She Stoops to Conquer
by Oliver Goldsmith

29. Which of the following statements most accurately describes the main theme of this selection?

(1) It's hard to be a rich girl.

(2) With friends like these, who needs enemies?

(3) It's sometimes difficult to marry the person you love, especially if you're wealthy.

(4) All men are fortune hunters.

(5) There are few people in life who can be trusted.

30. What is the problem faced by Miss Neville?

(1) Her guardian wants to marry her to Tony, but she loves another.

(2) Tony no longer loves her.

(3) Her fortune is dwindling day by day.

(4) The man she loves is unfaithful to her.

(5) Tony is managing her fortune against her will.

31. How would you describe Miss Hardcastle's attitude toward Miss Neville's dilemma?

(1) Mournful

(2) Aghast

(3) Repulsed

(4) Scornful

(5) Sympathetic

32. What is Miss Neville's opinion of Tony Hardcastle?

(1) He is a horrible monster.

(2) He is good-natured but not for her.

(3) He is cruel and money-hungry.

(4) He is modest and virtuous.

(5) He is the only man she could love.

33. Which of the following words best describes the tone of Miss Hardcastle's statement, "I could almost love him for hating you so"?

(1) Hypocritical

(2) Bitter

(3) Affectionate

(4) Sarcastic

(5) Pretentious

34. From the young women's remarks, what can the reader infer about the character of Mrs. Hardcastle?

(1) She is lazy and dull.

(2) She is greedy and nosy.

(3) She is straightforward and kind.

(4) She is affectionate and pleasant.

(5) She is creative and artistic.

ITEMS 35 TO 40 REFER TO THE STORY BELOW.

What Will the Young Man Do with His Life?

Line In the spring of 1926 I resigned from my job.

The first days following such a decision are like the release from a hospi-
(5) tal after a protracted illness. One slowly learns how to walk again; slowly and wonderingly one raises one's head.

I was in the best of health, but I was
(10) innerly exhausted. I had been teach-ing for four and a half years in a boys' preparatory school in New Jersey and tutoring three summers at a camp connected with the school. I was to all
(15) appearance cheerful and dutiful, but within I was cynical and almost to-tally bereft of sympathy for any other human being except the members of my family. I was 29 years old, about to
(20) turn 30. I had saved two thousand dol-lars—set aside, not to be touched—for either a return to Europe (I had spent a year in Italy and France in 1920–1921) or for my expenses as a gradu-
(25) ate student in some university. It was not clear to me what I wanted to do in life. I did not want to teach, though I knew I had a talent for it; the teaching profession is often a safety-net for just
(30) such indeterminate natures. I did not want to be a writer in the sense of one who earns his living by his pen; I wanted to be far more immersed in life than that. If I were to do any so-called
(35) "writing," it would not be before I had reached the age of 50. If I were des-tined to die before that, I wanted to be sure that I had encompassed as varied a range of experience as I could—that
(40) I had not narrowed my focus to that noble but largely sedentary pursuit that is covered by the word "art."

Professions. Life careers. It is well to be attentive to successive ambitions
(45) that flood the growing boy's and girl's imagination. They leave profound traces behind them. During those years when the first sap is rising the future tree is foreshadowing its con-
(50) tour. We are shaped by the promises of the imagination.

> *From* Theophilus North,
> *by Thornton Wilder.*
> *Used by permission.*

35. The author of this piece

  (1) is starting to teach.

  (2) was just released from the hospital.

  (3) has just quit a job.

  (4) is having a mental breakdown.

  (5) is an old man writing his autobiography.

36. How does the writer describe the teaching profession?

  (1) He implies that it is exhausting work.

  (2) He indicates that people often teach when they are indecisive about their lives.

  (3) He is clear that it is not some-thing he wishes to do any longer.

  (4) All of the above

  (5) None of the above

37. What does the narrator mean by the following sentence? "During those years when the first sap is rising the future tree is foreshadowing its contour."

    (1) He means that early youthful experiences shape the development of the mature adult.

    (2) He is saying that sap must rise before the tree can fall.

    (3) He means that people need to collect the sap coming from trees while they're young.

    (4) The author is telling people not to be saps.

    (5) He is saying that every person is confused at some point in his life.

38. What does the writer intend to do with his savings?

    (1) He doesn't have any idea.

    (2) He is going to use the money to become a teacher.

    (3) He wants to live on it while he writes about his adventures.

    (4) His medical bills will be paid off with this money.

    (5) He wants to eventually return to Europe or go to graduate school.

39. Which of the following statements would the author of this piece be most likely to agree with?

    (1) Better to be safe than sorry.

    (2) It is important for a young person to actively experience life to its fullest.

    (3) It is preferable to be a writer than an artist.

    (4) Young people need clear guidance and structure.

    (5) To be a success in life, be clear as to where you are headed.

40. What is the mood expressed in this piece?

    (1) Dreary and sad

    (2) Seriously confused

    (3) Generally cheerful and optimistic

    (4) Sarcastic and bitter

    (5) Loving and sympathetic

TEST 5. MATHEMATICS

90 Minutes • 50 Questions

PART 1—25 QUESTIONS (A CALCULATOR IS PERMITTED): 45 MINUTES
PART 2—25 QUESTIONS (A CALCULATOR IS NOT PERMITTED): 45 MINUTES

Directions: The Mathematics Test consists of questions intended to measure general mathematics skills and problem-solving ability. The questions are based on short readings that often include a graph, chart, or figure. Work carefully, but do not spend too much time on any one question. Be sure you answer every question. You will not be penalized for incorrect answers.

Formulas you may need are given on page 120. Only some of the questions will require you to use a formula. Record your answers on the separate answer sheet. Be sure that all information is properly recorded.

There are three types of answers found on the answer sheet:

Type 1 is a regular format answer that is the solution to a multiple-choice–type question. It requires shading in 1 of 5 bubble choices.

Type 2 is an alternate format answer that is the solution to the Standard Grid "fill-in" type question. It requires shading in bubbles representing the actual numbers, including a decimal or division sign where applicable.

Type 3 is an alternate format answer that is the solution to a Coordinate Plane Grid problem. It requires shading in the bubble representing the correct coordinate of a graph.

Type 1: Regular Format, Multiple-Choice Question

To record your answers for multiple-choice questions, fill in the numbered circle on the answer sheet that corresponds to the answer you select for each question in the test booklet.

Q Jill's drug store bill totals $8.68. How much change should she get if she pays with a $10.00 bill?

(1) $2.32
(2) $1.42
(3) $1.32
(4) $1.28
(5) $1.22   ① ② ● ④ ⑤

A **The correct answer is (3).** Therefore, you should mark answer space (3) on your answer sheet.

Type 2: Alternate Format, Standard Grid Question

To record the answer to the previous example, "1.32," using the Alternate Format, Standard Grid, see below:

Standard Grid

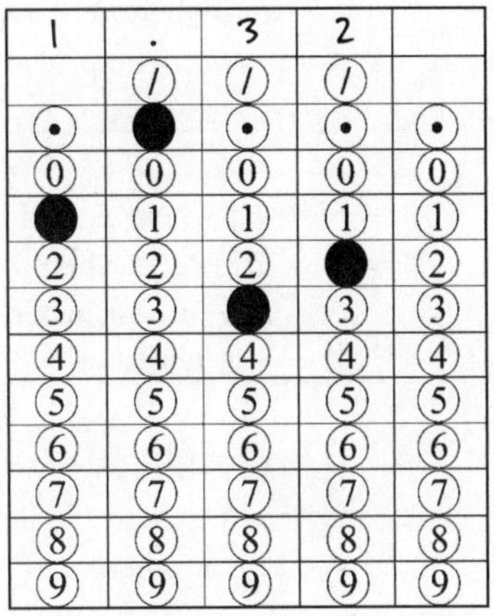

Type 3: Alternate Format, Coordinate Plane Grid Question

To record your answer, fill in the numbered circle on the answer sheet that corresponds to the correct coordinate in the graph. For example:

Q A system of two linear equations is given below.

$$x = -3y$$

$$x + y = 4$$

What point represents the common solution for the system of equations?

A **The correct answer is (6, −2).** The answer should be gridded as shown below.

Coordinate Plane Grid

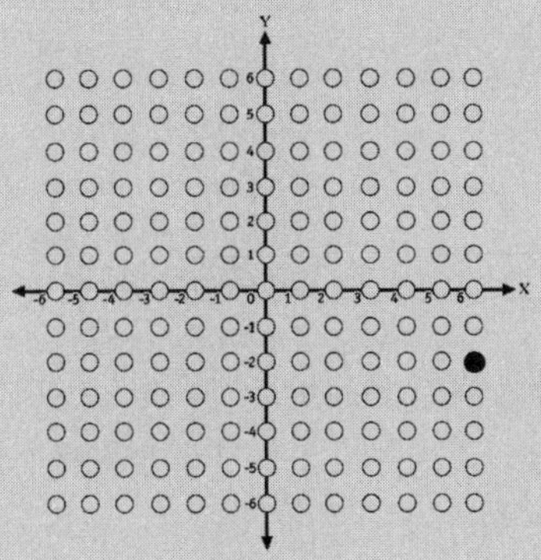

FORMULAS

Description	Formula
AREA (A) of a:	
square	$A = s^2$; where s = side
rectangle	$A = lw$; where l = length, w = width
parallelogram	$A = bh$; where b = base, h = height
triangle	$A = \frac{1}{2}bh$; where b = base, h = height
circle	$A = \pi r^2$; where π = 3.14, r = radius
PERIMETER (P) of a:	
square	$P = 4s$; where s = side
rectangle	$P = 2l + 2w$; where l = length, w = width
triangle	$P = a + b + c$; where a, b, and c are the sides
Circumference (C) of a circle	$C = \pi d$; where π = 3.14, d = diameter
VOLUME (V) of a:	
cube	$V = s^3$; where s = side
rectangular container	$V = lwh$; where l = length, w = width, h = height
cylinder	$V = \pi r^2 h$; where π = 3.14, r = radius, h = height
square pyramid	Volume $= \frac{1}{3} \times$ (base edge)$^2 \times$ height
cone	Volume $= \frac{1}{3} \times \pi \times$ radius$^2 \times$ height; π is approximately equal to 3.14.
Pythagorean theorem	$c^2 = a^2 + b^2$; where c = hypotenuse, a and b are legs of a right triangle
distance (d) between two points in a plane	$d = \sqrt{(x_2 - x_1)^2 + (y_2 - y_1)^2}$; where (x_1, y_1) and (x_2, y_2) are two points in a plane
slope of a line (m)	$m = \dfrac{y_2 - y_1}{x_2 - x_1}$ where (x_1, y_1) and (x_2, y_2) are two points in a plane
trigonometric ratios	given an acute angle with measure x of a right triangle, $\sin x = \dfrac{\text{opposite}}{\text{hypotenuse}}$, $\cos x = \dfrac{\text{adjacent}}{\text{hypotenuse}}$, $\tan x = \dfrac{\text{opposite}}{\text{adjacent}}$
mean	mean $= \dfrac{x_1 + x_2 + \cdots + x_n}{n}$; where the x's are the values for which a mean is desired, and n = number of values in the series
median	median = the point in an ordered set of numbers at which half of the numbers are above and half of the numbers are below this value
simple interest (i)	$i = prt$; where p = principal, r = rate, t = time
distance (d) as function of rate and time	$d = rt$; where r = rate, t = time
total cost (c)	$c = nr$; where n = number of units, r = cost per unit

You may use a scientific calculator for Part 1. (A Casio FX-260 Scientific Calculator will be provided at your Official GED Testing Center.)

CALCULATOR DIRECTIONS

You may practice with your calculator, using the following directions.

CALCULATOR DIRECTIONS

To prepare the calculator for use the *first* time, press the [ON] (upper-rightmost) key. "DEG" will appear at the top-center of the screen and "O" at the right. This indicates the calculator is in the proper format for all your claculations.

To prepare the calculator for *another* question, press the [ON] or the red [AC] key. This clears any entries made previously.

To do any arithmetic, enter the expression as it is written. Press [ON] (equals sign) when finished.

EXAMPLE A: 8 – 3 + 9

First press [ON] or [AC].
Enter the following:

[8] [–] [3] [+] [9] [=]

The correct answer is 14.

If an expression in parentheses is to be multiplied by a number, press [x] (multiplication sign) between the number and the parenthesis sign.

EXAMPLE B: 6(8 + 5)

First press [ON] or [AC].
Enter the following:

[6] [x] [( ] [8] [+] [5] [ )] [=]

The correct answer is 78.

To find the square root of a number
  • enter the number;
  • press the [SHIFT] (upper-leftmost) key ("SHIFT" appears at top-left of the screen);
  • press [x^2] (third from the left on top row) to access its second function: square root.
  DO NOT press [SHIFT] and [x^2] at the same time.

EXAMPLE C: $\sqrt{64}$

First press [ON] or [AC].
Enter the following:

[6] [4] [SHIFT] [x^2] [=]

The correct answer is 8.

To enter a negative number such as -8,
  • enter the number without the negative sign (enter 8);
  • press the "change sign" ([+/-]) key which is directly above the [7] key.
All arithmetic can be done with positive and/or negative numbers.

EXAMPLE D: -8 – -5

First press [ON] or [AC].
Enter the following:

[8] [+/-] [–] [5] [+/-] [=]

The correct answer is -3.

Part 1

You may now begin Part 1 of the Mathematics Test. You may use your calculator for this part. Bubble in the correct response to each question on Part 1 of your answer sheet.

1. The area of a square stamp is .60 square inches. What is the length of one of its sides in inches?

   (1) .33
   (2) .36
   (3) .69
   (4) .77
   (5) 1.20

2. Taking inventory of the stock in the notions department, a clerk finds that she has only 3 partial spools of blue ribbon left. The first spool has $10\frac{2}{3}$ yards of ribbon, the second spool has $5\frac{3}{4}$ yards, and the third spool has $2\frac{1}{6}$ yards. How many yards of blue ribbon are available for sale?

   (1) 17.00
   (2) 17.42
   (3) 18.00
   (4) 18.58
   (5) 51.45

3. A 234-foot wire is attached to the top of a TV tower (*D*) and is anchored on the ground (*A*) (see diagram). Angle *A* is 70°. Find the height of the tower (*BD*) in feet.

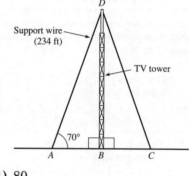

   (1) 80
   (2) 85
   (3) 220
   (4) 249
   (5) 643

ITEM 4 REFERS TO THE FOLLOWING TABLE OF TRANSACTIONS THAT CARLOS MADE IN HIS CHECKING ACCOUNT DURING APRIL 2000.

TRANSACTIONS IN CARLOS'S CHECKING ACCOUNT (APRIL 2000)

Date	Transaction
5	wrote check for $15.75
7	deposited $25.00
19	deposited $18.00
26	wrote check for $36.19

4. Carlos wanted to balance his checking account for the month of April. He began the month with $100.00 in his account. How many dollars did he have left at the end of April?

   Mark your answer in the circles in the grid on your answer sheet.

ITEM 5 REFERS TO THE FOLLOWING INFORMATION.

REVENUES FOR ABC ANTIQUES: JANUARY 17, 2002

Time of Day	Sales (dollars)	Number of Customers
9 a.m. – 12 p.m.	$ 87	1
12 – 3	138	1
3 – 6	239	3
6 – 9 p.m.	492	4

5. Find the ratio of total sales, in dollars, to the total number of customers.

   Mark your answer in the circles in the grid on your answer sheet.

6. Elaine bought 1.85 pounds of vegetables to put into a homemade vegetable soup for 8 people. But 6 more people were invited at the last minute. How many *more* pounds of vegetables should be bought?

   (1) 0.23
   (2) 1.39
   (3) 2.23
   (4) 3.24
   (5) 5.09

7. In 1 hour and 25 minutes, the minute hand of a clock rotates through an angle equivalent to

   (1) 170°
   (2) 255°
   (3) 330°
   (4) 510°
   (5) 540°

8. Sam wants to have a cushion made for his favorite lounge chair. The information he has is shown in the diagram below. Find the number of degrees in angle DAB if line ABC is a straight line and angle DBC equals 128°.

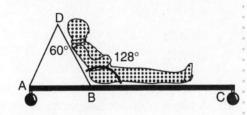

   (1) 60°
   (2) 64°
   (3) 68°
   (4) 72°
   (5) Insufficient data are given to solve the problem.

ITEMS 9 AND 10 REFER TO THE FOLLOWING SEWAGE TREATMENT PLANT PROBLEM.

A cone-shaped Sewage Treatment Plant container receives raw sewage at a rate of 10 gallons per minute (see diagram below.)

radius = 6 feet
height = 12 feet

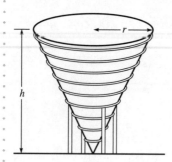

9. Find the volume of the container in cubic feet.

   (1) 25
   (2) 75
   (3) 452
   (4) 512
   (5) 600

10. A larger container, capacity 1,000 ft^3, was needed. How many minutes would it take to fill this one? [0.13 ft^3 = 1 gallon]

    (1) 100
    (2) 130
    (3) 348
    (4) 548
    (5) 769

11. Solve the following equation for the value of x.

    $0.12 - 0.34X = 0.56$

    (1) 1.29
    (2) 0.17
    (3) −0.48
    (4) −1.29
    (5) −2.09

ITEMS 12 AND 13 REFER TO THE FOLLOWING INFORMATION.

Finishing time for the three runners in the mini-marathon

Runner	Hours	Minutes
#1	2	15
#2	2	14
#3	1	55

12. What was the average finishing time in hours for the three runners? Give your answer to two decimal places.

    Mark your answers in the circles in the grid on your answer sheet.

13. How fast, in hours, would #3 have had to run for the average to be 2 hours? Give your answer to two decimal places.

    Mark your answers in the circles in the grid on your answer sheet.

ITEMS 14 TO 16 REFER TO THE FOLLOWING CHART THAT COMPARES THE COST OF DIFFERENT BRANDS OF FACIAL TISSUES.

Brand	Cost ($ per box)	Count (number per box)	Quality (S = soft; R = normal)
A. Softez (regular)	$1.69	100	S
B. Softez (large)	3.09	200	S
C. Blowez (regular)	1.49	100	R
D. Blowez (large)	2.69	200	R
E. Store Brand	1.39	100	R

14. How many cents per tissue are saved by buying a large rather than a regular box of Softez?

   (1) $1.70

   (2) $1.29

   (3) $0.31

   (4) $0.18

   (5) $0.15

15. If the quality does not matter, what is the best buy?

   (1) A

   (2) B

   (3) C

   (4) D

   (5) E

16. Debbie had a discount coupon for 50 cents off on two large-size Softez. How much would she spend, per 100 tissues?

   (1) $0.26

   (2) $1.00

   (3) $1.10

   (4) $1.30

   (5) $1.42

17. Barry developed a fever and had to recuperate for 5 days. He recorded the following data: on Day 1 his fever was 2°F above normal; on Day 2 it went up 4°F. He then saw a doctor and began taking a prescribed medication to lower the fever. On Day 3 his fever went down 1°F. If the day before he became sick is at (0,0) on the graph shown below, find the coordinates on Day 3.

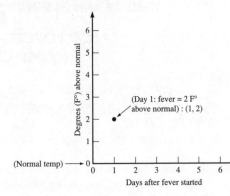

DO NOT MARK THE POINT ON THE GRAPH ABOVE.

Mark your answer on the Coordinate Plane Grid on your answer sheet.

18. The bottom (*B*) of an 18-foot ladder leaned on the side of the house at the bottom edge of window (*W*) makes a 37° angle with the ground (see diagram below). How many feet was the window from the ground (*G*)?

(1) 11
(2) 12
(3) 14
(4) 15
(5) 17

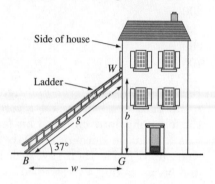

ITEMS 19 AND 20 REFER TO THE FOLLOWING INFORMATION.

LABOR FORCE—% Distribution by Age
(SOURCE: U.S. CENSUS BUREAU)

Year	Civilian Labor Force	16–19 years	20–24 years	25–34 years	35–44 years	45–54 years	55–64 years	65 yrs and older
1970	82,771,000	8.8	12.8	20.6	19.9	20.5	13.6	3.9
1999	139,368,000	6.0	10.0	23.1	27.2	21.1	9.8	2.9

19. In 1999, how many people (in millions) between the ages of 25 and 54 had jobs?

(1) 32.1
(2) 68.6
(3) 71.4
(4) 99.5
(5) 132.1

20. The percentage of young people (from 16 to 24 years of age) who worked declined for the last 30 years. What was the decline in the percent of young people who worked in 1999 as compared to 1970?

(1) 2.8
(2) 4.7
(3) 5.6
(4) 10.4
(5) 15.6

21. To plan a diagonal flower design for his rectagular garden, Wayne uses the graph below. How long should he make the "flower design"? Round off the answer to the nearest inch.

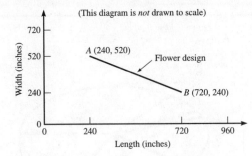

(This diagram is *not* drawn to scale)

Mark your answer in the circles in the grid on your answer sheet.

22. A hole whose circumference was 3 feet long was cut in the ice with a saw. What would be the radius of the hole in feet?

Round off the answer to two decimal places.

Mark your answer in the circles in the grid on your answer sheet.

ITEMS 23 TO 25 REFER TO THE TWO PIE CHARTS BELOW. THE CHARTS DESCRIBE HOW THE UNITED STATES RECEIVED AND SPENT ITS BUDGET FOR 1999.

MAJOR CATEGORIES OF FEDERAL INCOME AND OUTLAYS FOR FISCAL YEAR 1999

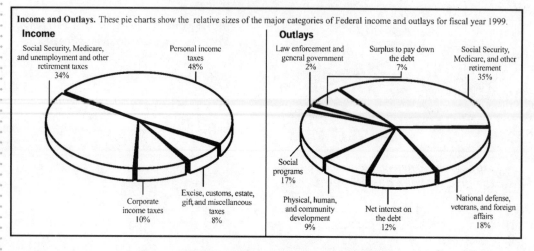

Source: Office of Management and Budget

23. In fiscal year 1999, the federal income (where the money came from) was $1,827 billion, and outlays (how it was spent) were $1,703 billion. Which of the following statements is true?

(1) It receives $12.4 billion more than it spends.

(2) It receives $124 billion more than it spends.

(3) It spends $1.24 billion more than it receives.

(4) It spends $12.4 billion more than it receives.

(5) It spends $124 billion more than it receives.

24. How much is spent on "social programs" and on "Social Security, Medicare, and other retirement" in billions of dollars?

(1) 124

(2) 442

(3) 596

(4) 886

(5) 1444

25. If "personal income taxes" are reduced to 41% and all other items remain the same, then the loss in income is

(1) $128 billion.

(2) $147 billion.

(3) $192 billion.

(4) $749 billion.

(5) $876 billion.

Part 2

You may not return to Part 1 of the Mathematics Test or use your calculator for this part. Bubble in the correct response to each question on Part 2 of your answer sheet.

26. Julia made a 43.1-minute long distance telephone call at 7 cents per minute for a total cost of

(1) $ .30
(2) $2.73
(3) $3.02
(4) $30.10
(5) $36.00

27. If girls were $\frac{5}{9}$ of the class and $\frac{2}{3}$ of the girls passed the math test, then the girls who passed the test represented what fraction of the entire class?

(1) $\frac{10}{27}$

(2) $\frac{5}{9}$

(3) $\frac{2}{3}$

(4) $\frac{5}{12}$

(5) $\frac{33}{27}$

28. Ted went shopping and gave the cashier $50.00. He spent $28.06 for meat, $2.25 for potatoes, and 15 cents for the plastic bag to carry it all home in. How much change (in dollars) should he have gotten?

(1) $4.66
(2) $19.54
(3) $24.04
(4) $25.96
(5) $45.34

29. The sum of 2 coins of value x and 3 coins of value y is 50 cents. If the value of y is 10 cents, which of the following equations can be used to solve for the value of x?

(1) $x + y = 5$
(2) $x + 3y = 50$
(3) $2x = 50 - 3y$
(4) $x = 50 - y$
(5) $2x + y = 10$

30. Simplify the equation:

$3x + 3y + x + 4y - 4x = 5$

(1) $6x = 5$
(2) $7x + 7y = 5$
(3) $-x + 7y = 5$
(4) $7x - y = 5$
(5) $7y = 5$

ITEM 31 REFERS TO THE DIAGRAM BELOW.

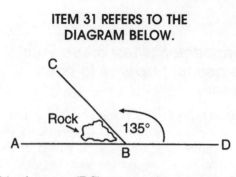

31. A gate, (BC), can swing open only 135 degrees because of a rock that is wedged behind it. Without the rock, the gate could swing all the way back against the fence, (AD), to form a straight angle. Find the number of degrees that the gate is prevented from opening (Angle ABC in the diagram above).

Mark your answer in the circles in the grid on your answer sheet.

32. Mrs. Smith plans to have a table pad made to fit her new round table. The price of table pads varies according to the area of the pad. If Mrs. Smith's table has a radius of 2 feet, in which of the following size ranges will she find the price for the pad she needs?

(1) More than 2 square feet but less than 4 square feet

(2) More than 4 square feet but less than 6 square feet

(3) More than 6 square feet but less than 8 square feet

(4) More than 8 square feet but less than 10 square feet

(5) More than 12 square feet but less than 14 square feet

33. In which of the following equations is 4 the value of x?

(1) $x^2 + x = 12$

(2) $4x - 1 = 7$

(3) $2x - 3 = 5$

(4) $5x = 25$

(5) $\dfrac{3x}{2} + 5 = 17$

34. A part-time worker at a fast-food restaurant is paid \$3.65 per hour. If he works 4 hours on Monday, 3 hours on Tuesday, 5 hours on Wednesday, 4 hours on Thursday, and 4 hours on Saturday, his income could be expressed algebraically as $x =$

(1) $(4 + 3 + 5 + 4 + 6) + 3.65$

(2) $(3.65) (4 \times 3 \times 5 \times 4 \times 6)$

(3) $(3.65) (24)$

(4) $(4 + 3 + 5 + 4 + 4) (3.65)$

(5) y

35. Find the value of $3x^2 - 4x + 3$ if x is equal to 5.

(1) 2

(2) 38

(3) 54

(4) 58

(5) 98

36. In the diagram below, a domino cube is drawn next to a domino box. At most, how many dominoes can fit into the box? (Ignore the thickness of the box.)

DOMINO BOX

1 foot

2 inches

1 inch

DOMINO

2 inches

.25 inch

1 inch

(1) 20
(2) 25
(3) 36
(4) 48
(5) 60

37. Shown below are the three vertices of a parallelogram.

What point on the graph could be the fourth vertex of the parallelogram?

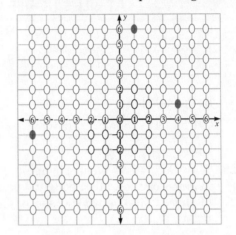

DO NOT MARK THE POINT ON THE GRAPH ABOVE.

Mark your answer on the coordinate plane grid on your answer sheet.

ITEMS 38 TO 40 REFER TO THE FOLLOWING ADVERTISEMENT IN THE
OLD YORK GAZETTE:

SPECIAL 1-DAY-ONLY SALE BONANZA
AT BILL'S HOUSE OF CLOTHES (1/15/06)

Item	Regular Price	Sales Price
A. Polo shirt	$25	Pay the regular price for the first shirt and save $5 for each additional shirt
B. Casual shorts	$25	Save 50% on each
C. Comfort sandals	$40	Save $10 on each

38. Max and Mitzi went shopping for summer clothes. Mitzi bought 3 pairs of shorts. How much did she pay in dollars?

(1) $12.50

(2) $25.00

(3) $37.50

(4) $75.00

(5) $90.00

39. Max bought 7 shirts and 2 pairs of sandals. How much did he pay in dollars?

(1) $205.00

(2) $220.00

(3) $225.00

(4) $230.00

(5) $235.00

40. How much did Max *save* on his purchase, in dollars?

(1) $15.00

(2) $50.00

(3) $55.00

(4) $85.00

(5) $105.00

41. The circumference of the wheel on Tim's tricycle is $\frac{1}{4}$ the circumference of the wheel on his father's car. If the diameter of his father's wheel is 16π, what is the radius of Tim's wheel?

(1) 1

(2) 2

(3) 4

(4) 16

(5) 64

ITEM 42 REFERS TO THE FOLLOWING INFORMATION.

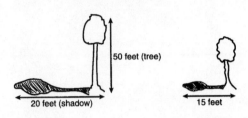

50 feet (tree)

20 feet (shadow)

15 feet

42. Two trees are 10 feet apart. The taller tree, which measures 50 feet in height, casts a shadow of 20 feet, while the shorter tree casts a shadow of 15 feet. How tall is the shorter tree?

   (1) 25 feet

   (2) 30 feet

   (3) 32.5 feet

   (4) 35 feet

   (5) 37.5 feet

ITEMS 43 TO 44 REFER TO THE FOLLOWING INFORMATION.

A family has a monthly income of $3,600. Their monthly expenditures are as shown in the graph below.

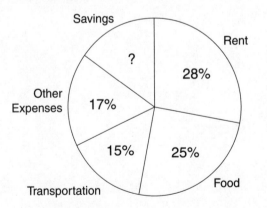

Savings

Rent

?

28%

Other Expenses

17%

15%

25%

Transportation

Food

43. How much money does the family save in a month? (Give the answer as a whole number.)

Mark your answer in the circles in the grid on your answer sheet.

44. What is the cost of rent each month?

   (1) $612

   (2) $750

   (3) $1,000

   (4) $1,008

   (5) $1,200

ITEM 45 REFERS TO THE FOLLOWING INFORMATION.

The chart below shows the gender of the children in the families living on our street.

FAMILY:	1	2	3	4	5
# BOYS:	2	0	1	2	5
# GIRLS:	3	0	2	1	4

45. Compare the average number of girls to boys per family.

   (1) $\frac{1}{2}$ more girls

   (2) 1 more girl

   (3) $\frac{1}{2}$ fewer girls

   (4) 1 fewer girl

   (5) They are the same.

46. Aunt Millie wants to boil water for tea. If the temperature of the water leaving the tap is 10°C, how long will it take for the water to boil? (Answer in seconds.)

   (1) 10

   (2) 90

   (3) 100

   (4) 212

   (5) Insufficient data are given to solve the problem.

47. During a sale, an item's selling price was reduced by 50 cents. If 50 items were sold on the first day of the sale, and X items were sold on the second day, then how many dollars did the store lose by not selling at the original price?

(1) $50

(2) $40

(3) $30

(4) $20

(5) Insufficient data are given to solve the problem.

ITEMS 48 TO 50 REFER TO THE FOLLOWING INFORMATION.

Jim and Jack were curious about the number of red cars they saw each day. One Saturday, they decided to keep track of the red cars that passed their house each hour. They recorded their findings in the table below.

Hour	1	2	3	4	5
Number of Red Cars	5	4	8	0	8

48. What was the mode?

(1) 0

(2) 4

(3) 5

(4) 8

(5) 25

49. What was the average number of red cars that they saw each hour?

(1) 1

(2) 2

(3) 3

(4) 4

(5) 5

50. How many red cars would have to pass the house in the sixth hour to make the mean equivalent to 7?

(1) 5

(2) 7

(3) 9

(4) 15

(5) 17

ANSWER KEY AND EXPLANATIONS

Test 1. Language Arts, Writing—Part 1

1. (2)	11. (5)	21. (3)	31. (1)	41. (5)
2. (3)	12. (3)	22. (5)	32. (4)	42. (3)
3. (5)	13. (5)	23. (5)	33. (3)	43. (4)
4. (1)	14. (2)	24. (4)	34. (5)	44. (2)
5. (4)	15. (4)	25. (3)	35. (2)	45. (5)
6. (3)	16. (3)	26. (5)	36. (5)	46. (1)
7. (2)	17. (5)	27. (2)	37. (3)	47. (4)
8. (4)	18. (1)	28. (3)	38. (2)	48. (3)
9. (1)	19. (4)	29. (1)	39. (3)	49. (2)
10. (3)	20. (2)	30. (2)	40. (4)	50. (3)

1. **The correct answer is (2).** The newly rewritten sentence would read, *When you are going to take a trip it is necessary to take care of some practical details, as well as to plan ahead.*

2. **The correct answer is (3).** The correct form of the verb is *think,* as in *it is important to think.*

3. **The correct answer is (5).** The word *don't* goes with *you,* as in *you don't. Doesn't* would be correct with *he,* as in *he doesn't.*

4. **The correct answer is (1).** Sentence (7), *Otherwise, you might be charged finance fees before you get around to paying the bills,* tells what might happen if you don't do what the writer suggests. Therefore, it should go after sentence (9), which is the last of these suggestions.

5. **The correct answer is (4).** This is a sentence fragment, meaning it's not a complete sentence. By inserting *it will be nice* before *not having a mountain of bills to face when you return,* this becomes a complete sentence that makes sense in the context of the paragraph.

6. **The correct answer is (3).** The word *your* is a possessive and is needed in this sentence. *You're* is a contraction for *you are,* which does not make sense here.

7. **The correct answer is (2).** The conditional *would* needs to be changed to the future form, *will,* as in *you will have a carefree and pleasant time.*

8. **The correct answer is (4).** The word is *you're,* which completes the verb *making,* as in *While you're making. You're* is a contraction for *you are.*

9. **The correct answer is (1).** The newly rewritten sentence reads *Just a couple of hours from Boston and New York and 1 hour from Albany, the beautiful historic town of Searington is well located in western Massachusetts.*

10. **The correct answer is (3).** Because the word *Mountains* is part of a proper noun, *Berkshire Mountains,* it must be capitalized.

11. **The correct answer is (5).** The proper form of the verb is *has,* as in *Each season has its.*

12. **The correct answer is (3).** The sentence speaks of two colleges, so the word *program* needs to be changed to its plural form, *programs.*

13. The correct answer is (5). This is a run-on sentence, meaning it expresses two complete thoughts instead of one. Separating them with a period and capital letter after *area* will work well to clarify the meaning and create two correct sentences.

14. The correct answer is (2). Sentence (13) begins the closing salutation, or greeting, of this letter. Therefore, it should begin a new paragraph.

15. The correct answer is (4). A sign-off to a letter, such as *Very truly yours* or *Sincerely,* always requires a comma, with the signature of the writer inserted on the next line.

16. The correct answer is (3). The correct spelling here is *weather,* which refers to the climate, temperature, etc.

17. The correct answer is (5). The newly rewritten sentence reads *Provided you've got the money for the plane fare, visiting Australia is easy to arrange.*

18. The correct answer is (1). The word *them* needs to be changed to *it* because it refers to the *visa,* which is singular.

19. The correct answer is (4). The correct expression is *which allows you,* not *which allowing you.*

20. The correct answer is (2). Since sentence (7) and paragraph D both deal with possible means of transportation for getting around Australia, they belong together in this article.

21. The correct answer is (3). The comma after *total independence* is confusing because it breaks up the thought, which is *total independence gotten from bus schedules and routes.* It should therefore be dropped.

22. The correct answer is (5). No correction is needed in this sentence.

23. The correct answer is (5). The meaning of the sentence calls for the plural of *Volunteer,* which is *Volunteers.*

24. The correct answer is (4). The correct words here are *there are opportunities.* The verb *are* is needed.

25. The correct answer is (3). No quotation marks are required around *independent.*

26. The correct answer is (5). The plural form of *life* is *lives,* which should be used because the sentence talks of more than one person.

27. The correct answer is (2). This is a sentence fragment even though it seems like a long sentence. It needs *are available* to be inserted to make sense and to turn it into a full sentence.

28. The correct answer is (3). Paragraph D, which is the last paragraph of this piece, talks about the benefits to the giver, the volunteer. Choice (3), which is *Not only does the recipient of aid benefit, but so does the volunteer,* clarifies this idea and is a good choice to introduce this paragraph.

29. The correct answer is (1). The rewritten sentence reads *Volunteering gives the chance to gain experience, knowledge and leadership skills, as well as the personal satisfaction gotten from helping others, and the opportunity for growth and learning.*

30. The correct answer is (2). The *National Mall* is the name of an actual place in our nation's capital, and therefore it needs to be written with capitals.

31. The correct answer is (1). The colon serves no purpose in this sentence and should be removed.

32. **The correct answer is (4).** The adjective form of *lead,* as in *leading research centers,* should be used here.

33. **The correct answer is (3).** The newly rewritten sentence now reads *In the Blue Ridge Mountains in Front Royal, Virginia, the National Zoological Park conducts a breeding preserve and study center for rare and endangered animals.*

34. **The correct answer is (5).** The words *are researched* in this sentence tell us that the plural form of *characteristic,* or *characteristics,* should be used.

35. **The correct answer is (2).** This is a sentence fragment that needs a verb. Adding *are studied* after *Tropical organisms* corrects this error.

36. **The correct answer is (5).** This sentence is in its proper place and should not be moved or deleted.

37. **The correct answer is (3).** The word *years* is the plural of *year,* which is correct here.

38. **The correct answer is (2).** Titles such as *Mr.* or *Mrs.* are always written with a period.

39. **The correct answer is (3).** Sentence (7) begins a discussion about how this method works, and therefore it could start a new paragraph to add clarity to this section of the article.

40. **The correct answer is (4).** The newly rewritten sentence now reads *Surrounded by other little pupils in a class, he first begins to play "Twinkle, Twinkle Little Star" on a tiny violin by copying the teacher.*

41. **The correct answer is (5).** The present tense singular of this verb is *tackles,* as in *the child tackles.*

42. **The correct answer is (3).** This is a run-on sentence that needs

correction. By putting a period after *others* and starting the next sentence with *Not every,* you have created two complete, correct, and clear sentences.

43. **The correct answer is (4).** The correct adverb here is *highly,* as in *highly proficient players of music.*

44. **The correct answer is (2).** The word *or* inserted after the comma clarifies that what follows explains what *paleontologists* are. *Names of scientists* is incorrect.

45. **The correct answer is (5).** This is a run-on sentence that needs to be divided with a period and capitalized first word after *area.*

46. **The correct answer is (1).** Sentence (5) makes no sense unless it has sentence (4) to introduce and clarify it. This change makes the narration flow more logically and improves the organization of the paragraph.

47. **The correct answer is (4).** Unless *they* is changed to *people,* it is unclear who *rarely returning empty-handed* is referring to. Is it the bones or the people?

48. **The correct answer is (3).** The correct expression is *to be found in Ekalaka.* This is the only response that provides coordination of sentence structure.

49. **The correct answer is (2).** This is a run-on sentence that needs to be divided into two sentences after the words *was also found.*

50. **The correct answer is (3).** While the sentence when looked at alone is correct, it needs to be changed to the past tense when taken in context with the sentence before it. Since sentence (9) was written in the past tense, it makes sense that this sentence should be also. Therefore, *yields* needs to be changed to its past tense form, which is *yielded.*

Language Arts, Writing—Part 2

SAMPLE ESSAY RESPONSE

Judging by the large variety of vegetarian dishes that are now available in most restaurants, it seems that vegetarian diets are getting very popular. Usually, these dishes are presented as "healthy" alternatives to foods that are often rich in animal protein and fat. They appeal to many people because of health concerns about the bad effects of fats and cholesterol, as well as a reluctance to eat the flesh of a once-living being.

However, it seems doubtful to me that strictly vegetarian dishes are really sufficient if they are the only basis of a person's diet. I think that it is almost impossible to get all the nutrients that are necessary for good health from a non-meat or fish vegetarian diet. For example, the need for protein is about 45 grams per day at a minimum. This is difficult to get from meals that exclude meats, fish, eggs, and dairy products. Another important nutrient is calcium, which is easily gotten from dairy products, but hard to get enough of in a vegetarian diet. There are many more examples like this. A person would have to be very knowledgeable in nutrition to get all the necessary ingredients for good health from this limited diet. For that reason alone it is safest to eat a full range of foods instead of being a vegetarian.

People have been hunter-gatherers since prehistoric times, meaning that foods like meat and fish form a natural part of their diet. Our digestive systems are built for this kind of food. Therefore, these foods should be included in everyone's diet in order to ensure good health.

Test 2. Social Studies

1. (3)	11. (3)	21. (3)	31. (1)	41. (5)
2. (2)	12. (3)	22. (3)	32. (5)	42. (5)
3. (5)	13. (1)	23. (4)	33. (3)	43. (2)
4. (5)	14. (4)	24. (2)	34. (3)	44. (3)
5. (4)	15. (2)	25. (5)	35. (2)	45. (1)
6. (5)	16. (3)	26. (4)	36. (3)	46. (2)
7. (2)	17. (1)	27. (5)	37. (4)	47. (3)
8. (2)	18. (5)	28. (3)	38. (2)	48. (3)
9. (1)	19. (5)	29. (3)	39. (5)	49. (2)
10. (4)	20. (3)	30. (1)	40. (1)	50. (1)

1. **The correct answer is (3).** Cartography is the science of making maps. Being able to accurately determine longitude results in newer and better maps.

2. **The correct answer is (2).** Offering a "handsome"—meaning large—prize for better maps suggests the French government's interest in accuracy.

3. **The correct answer is (5).** The only direct consequence of improved maps was the ability of nations to agree on clearly defined time zones, since it was then possible to locate a single position on a map and determine longitude.

4. **The correct answer is (5).** King Louis XIV offered the prize because he was especially interested in expanding exploration.

5. **The correct answer is (4).** The restaurant represents the American population with its many different kinds of people.

6. **The correct answer is (5).** The cartoon suggests America is made up of a number of different nationalities, as indicated by foods representative of each culture.

7. **The correct answer is (2).** "The Melting Pot" suggests the different cultures that have formed America have "melted" together, obscuring individual cultural differences. Only "The Salad Bowl" disagrees with this view, suggesting that the cultures have been "tossed" together but have not blended.

8. **The correct answer is (2).** The different foods indicate the United States has been settled by people from many other countries.

9. **The correct answer is (1).** "Glory" is fame and fortune.

10. **The correct answer is (4).** ChevronTex went down $1.98 a share from its closing price the day before, the largest jump.

11. **The correct answer is (3).** ChespkeUtil closed at $19.65, which is almost at its 52-week highest selling price of $19.99.

12. **The correct answer is (3).** 100 shares times $75.51 a share equals $7,551.

13. **The correct answer is (1).** ChelseaProp pays $3.24, the highest amount here.

14. **The correct answer is (4).** The preferential treatment shown to Brian because of his mother's position in the company is an example of nepotism.

15. **The correct answer is (2).** The Pendleton Act established the merit system.

16. **The correct answer is (3).** Awarding a job to a candidate because of social standing is an example of the "Old Boy" network in action.

17. **The correct answer is (1).** The Hatch Act greatly decreased the effects of the spoils system.

18. **The correct answer is (5).** Meredith made good use of networking when she cultivated the acquaintance of people in the field in which she wished to be employed.

19. **The correct answer is (5).** III and IV only. Women are not a minority if they comprise 53% of the population under scrutiny. If 81% of all clerical workers are women, it is accurate to say that four out of five clerical workers are women. I and II are inaccurate because the graph depicts something different. It shows that 45% of all professional workers are women (*not* that 45% of employed women are professional workers) and that 43% of all the unemployed are women (*not* that 43% of women are unemployed). Neither I nor II is defensible since the total number of categories of women depicted would have to add up to 100%.

20. **The correct answer is (3).** The U.S. economy would be seriously damaged if women were not available to the labor force. If women comprise nearly half of all employed workers (43%), nearly half of the professional workers (45%), and an overwhelming percentage of the clerical workers (81%), who could possibly replace them if they all left the job market at once? (1) is inaccurate as compared to the chart, while (2), (4), and (5) are unsupported, since the chart offers no comparisons with men or future or past activity in the labor force.

21. **The correct answer is (3).** During the time period shown in the chart, cable television experienced a huge increase in the number of

basic subscribers and the total amount of revenue. The average monthly basic rate rose from less than six dollars to more than ten. The statement "The cable television industry enjoyed huge growth in total revenue and number of subscribers between 1985 and 1995" can be supported. There is also some support for choices (1) and (2) since the trend shown for fifteen years is likely to continue; however, the support offered for choice (3) is stronger. The graphs offer no comparisons with network television nor any indication that revenue is likely to drop, which eliminates (4) and (5).

22. **The correct answer is (3).** The poll tax was outlawed in federal elections by the Twenty-Fourth Amendment, and Supreme Court decisions outlawed it in state and local elections.

23. **The correct answer is (4).** The Nineteenth Amendment entitled women to vote.

24. **The correct answer is (2).** The Fourteenth Amendment (ratified 1868) defined slaves as citizens and the Fifteenth (1870) gave them the right to vote.

25. **The correct answer is (5).** When the Seventeenth Amendment was ratified, it provided for the direct election of senators but left the Electoral College in place.

26. **The correct answer is (4).** If the "center" of the U.S. has shifted to the west, it is because the western portion of the country has added more "weight"; that is, population. Choice (1) is irrelevant; choice (2) is not supportable since the center of population has jumped west of the Mississippi. Choice (3) may be accurate with respect to certain periods of American history, but all the major cities are no longer concentrated on the eastern seaboard. Choice (5) is inaccurate, since if

this were true, the center would shift to the east.

27. **The correct answer is (5).** You cannot make a comparison without data from previous years.

28. **The correct answer is (3).** The number of prisoners has increased quite sharply from 1975 on. The comparison between 1980 and 1985 suggests that the number of prisoners will continue to increase, and since the allocation of public monies for major problems usually suffers a considerable time lag, it is likely that there will be considerable public expenditures for prisons through the 1990s.

29. **The correct answer is (3).** Choice (3) is the only *effect* of the Truman Doctrine. Choices (1) and (4) are *causes*, not effects. Choices (2) and (5) do not directly address the question.

30. **The correct answer is (1).** This is the only cause; all the rest are effects.

31. **The correct answer is (1).** All three charts support the fact that female heads of households suffer economically: they have higher unemployment rates, their total income is lower, and a larger percentage are likely to fall below the definition of the poverty line. Choice (2) is not addressed since we have no direct comparison for women with and without children; choice (3) is incorrect since we do not know who works in husband-wife families; choices (4) and (5) are not supported by the information supplied.

32. **The correct answer is (5).** The *Wall Street Journal* covers national and international events that affect all aspects of economic life. All the other newspapers have the name of a city in their title.

33. **The correct answer is (3).** By observation we can see that there

was probably less than a 50 percent increase in available funds over the eleven years. The only possible option among all the answer choices is (3).

34. **The correct answer is (3).** The 1996 bar shows us that Florida and Texas combined had more funding than Pennsylvania and Texas combined. Add California and you have the largest combination.

35. **The correct answer is (2).** Only New York showed a consistent decline over the eleven-year period.

36. **The correct answer is (3).** National Highway Safety Bureau

37. **The correct answer is (4).** Federal Trade Commission

38. **The correct answer is (2).** National Bureau of Standards

39. **The correct answer is (5).** Cooperative Extension Service

40. **The correct answer is (1).** Department of Agriculture

41. **The correct answer is (5).** The nation's capital, Washington, is not located in any state so as not to give special preference to any particular state. Instead, it is located in the District of Columbia, which borders on the states of Maryland and Virginia.

42. **The correct answer is (5).** Because of all the weaknesses in the peace treaties that ended World War I, unstable conditions unfortunately led to a second world war in 1939.

43. **The correct answer is (2).** These statements, made at Britain's "darkest hour" when Germany was threatening invasion and all of Europe had collapsed, worked to lead the British people, after much bloodshed, into ultimate victory.

44. **The correct answer is (3).** Many of the so-called "enemies of the people" were guillotined—having

their heads cut off in public. This led, for a while, to a violent bloodbath. These unfortunate people included King Louis XVI and his wife, Marie Antoinette.

45. **The correct answer is (1).** The Monroe Doctrine's main intent was to protect the newly formed independent states of Latin America from foreign intervention.

46. **The correct answer is (2).** This is an example of "volunteerism," or working for the good of your fellow citizens and community. "Faulty advertising" involves selling something for profit in a misleading way. "Patriotism" involves working for one's country in relation to the rest of the world. The other choices do not apply here.

47. **The correct answer is (3).** Sir Isaac Newton (1642–1726) was a prolific scientist whose thoughts were respected in the colonies. His *Principia Mathematica* (1687) described the relationship of science and nature.

48. **The correct answer is (3).** This has been a major cause of long-standing problems between Great Britain and Ireland, which feels it should be united with Northern Ireland.

49. **The correct answer is (2).** A political stalemate existed between the U.S. and Russia beginning in 1949 when each possessed atomic weapons, but using them would have been unimaginable. This period was referred to as the "Cold War," meaning that there wasn't any outright fighting, but there were feelings of mutual hostility and suspicion.

50. **The correct answer is (1).** Johann Gutenberg (1397–1488) developed the printing press, reducing the cost of printing books and thus allowing ordinary people to have access to previously expensive books.

Test 3. Science

1. (2)	11. (2)	21. (3)	31. (5)	41. (4)
2. (1)	12. (4)	22. (1)	32. (2)	42. (1)
3. (5)	13. (4)	23. (1)	33. (2)	43. (5)
4. (3)	14. (5)	24. (5)	34. (2)	44. (4)
5. (4)	15. (1)	25. (5)	35. (3)	45. (2)
6. (5)	16. (3)	26. (3)	36. (3)	46. (2)
7. (2)	17. (4)	27. (5)	37. (1)	47. (3)
8. (3)	18. (1)	28. (4)	38. (2)	48. (5)
9. (2)	19. (1)	29. (2)	39. (2)	49. (4)
10. (1)	20. (2)	30. (3)	40. (3)	50. (1)

1. **The correct answer is (2).** The passage states that it takes about 5 minutes to prepare a meal in space. It takes more time to prepare a meal in a conventional kitchen with conventional foods.

2. **The correct answer is (1).** The foods are "reconstituted" with the "ample water" provided by the fuel cells.

3. **The correct answer is (5).** Since the astronauts are given 2,700 calories daily and we are not told that they are in any way different from earthbound people, the only choice we can infer is that these calories represent a recommended daily allowance.

4. **The correct answer is (3).** Both A and C are facts; B and D are opinions, open to discussion and question.

5. **The correct answer is (4).** Between 40° and 50° the oxygen consumption of the three stages was at its highest.

6. **The correct answer is (5).** The highest stage of oxygen production in the adult was 10 to 14 mm^3, indicated by the sharp upturn in the line.

7. **The correct answer is (2).** Adult fruit flies need more oxygen than pupae, as indicated by the sharply rising line.

8. **The correct answer is (3).** Of the choices, the only one that the information applies to is choice (3). The experiment would be useful to increase lab production of fruit flies.

9. **The correct answer is (2).** During photosynthesis, carbon dioxide and water are changed to sugar and oxygen as indicated by formula (2). Choice (1) is the formula of dehydration synthesis. Choice (3) is the formula for combining sodium hydroxide and hydrochloric acid to form salt and water. Choice (4) is fermentation, changing sugar to alcohol. Choice (5) is electrolysis.

10. **The correct answer is (1).** In the first paragraph the laser is called a "beam." From this we can infer that a laser is a "beam of light rays."

11. **The correct answer is (2).** Paragraph 2 explains how lasers destroy cells by removing water from them.

12. **The correct answer is (4).** Laser surgery can be used to destroy cancerous cells, but it does not reduce the risk of cancer. All of the other choices are specifically mentioned as advantages of laser surgery.

13. **The correct answer is (4).** The first paragraph states that dead cells that are not completely removed by the laser are sloughed off (cast off, discarded) from adjacent living tissue.

14. **The correct answer is (5).** The article does not state that lasers are the best tools, only that they are useful in certain situations. We have no way of knowing if other articles agree with this one. Choice (5), therefore, is opinion, not fact.

15. **The correct answer is (1).** According to the key, Albert was a normal male. Although hemophilia is a recessive trait, it is also sex-linked, according to the chart. A male would therefore need only one gene for hemophilia for the trait to appear. Since Albert was normal, it is evident that he had no gene for the disease.

16. **The correct answer is (3).** Beatrice was a carrier. Her marriage to a hemophiliac could be analyzed as follows:

    Key: XX—normal female; X̲X—female carrier; X̲X̲—female hemophiliac; XY—normal male; X̲Y—male hemophiliac.

    Beatrice: X̲ X
    her husband: X̲ X̲X̲ XX
                  _____
                  Y   X̲Y XY

    50% of Beatrice's daughters would have inherited the disease for hemophilia: X̲X̲. The other 50% would have been carriers: X̲X.

17. **The correct answer is (4).** Rupert's maternal grandfather was shown to have hemophilia (X̲Y). He transmitted the trait to his daughter, who was a carrier (X̲X). When this female married a normal male (XY), she transmitted the condition to her son, Rupert (X̲Y).

18. **The correct answer is (1).** Perhaps the most famous physicist since Albert Einstein, Stephen Hawkings has been trying to figure out the laws that govern the origins of the universe.

19. **The correct answer is (1).** Dust does not fit the definition; it is not condensation that falls to earth.

20. **The correct answer is (2).** The paragraph states that the animals "died in the blowing dust."

21. **The correct answer is (3).** The graph shows the relative activity of enzyme X at various pH levels.

22. **The correct answer is (1).** At pH 4, relative rate of activity peaks at 60. However, the greatest *increase* in rate of activity is between pH 0 and 2 when activity increases from 0 to almost 50.

23. **The correct answer is (1).** Enzymes are used in digestion.

24. **The correct answer is (5).** Based on the graph and additional information, only choice (5) can be inferred. The graph indicates only that enzyme X reacts to pH differences; therefore it can be said that some enzymes react to differences in pH.

25. **The correct answer is (5).** The smaller clear area shows there are more bacteria growing. Thus, chemical "X" is a weaker antibiotic than penicillin.

26. **The correct answer is (3).** Jumping rope is not mentioned in the article as affecting biofeedback.

27. **The correct answer is (5).** A driver stopping at a red light is an example of a habit. All the other choices are incorrectly matched.

28. **The correct answer is (4).** According to the graph, Malthus stated that living things multiply in geometric ratio, while the food supply only increases in arithmetic ratio. In other words, population increases faster than food supply.

29. The correct answer is (2). According to the graph, the population is increasing faster than the food supply. Darwin stated that species tend to overproduce; that is, to produce more individuals than are needed for the species to survive.

30. The correct answer is (3). Since the slope of the population curve is increasing more than that of the food curve, starvation will probably occur, reducing the rate of population increase and the slope of the curve, choice (3).

31. The correct answer is (5). All the choices listed have to be taken into consideration if the theory is to be affected.

32. The correct answer is (2). China and Africa have the greatest population density and the least arable land, efficient agriculture, and transportation. They are already feeling the effects of the theory; China is trying to curb population growth and Africa has experienced severe famines.

33. The correct answer is (2). Iodine is the only element listed in its solid state, so it is the only one that could sublime.

34. The correct answer is (2). From the equation, $R \times T = D$, the question asks for the time ("how long") to complete the race. Thus, the time must be found. Dividing both sides of the equation by

R(rate) we get: $R \times \dfrac{T}{R} = \dfrac{D}{R}$ or $T = \dfrac{D}{R}$. Substituting, we get $T = \dfrac{400}{8} = 50$ seconds.

35. The correct answer is (3). Substituting into the formula $D = R \times T$, or solving for rate, $R = \dfrac{D}{R}$, we get $R = \dfrac{20(\text{miles})}{2.5(\text{miles})} = 8$ miles/hour.

36. The correct answer is (3). Atoms in the same groups (columns in the periodic table) behave similarly. K and Na are both in group 1.

37. The correct answer is (1). The first atom, hydrogen, has an atomic number 1 with 1 proton. Each larger atom gains 1 more proton as its atomic number increases.

38. The correct answer is (2). The first 92 elements are the only ones found in nature. The others (above 92) occur through nuclear reactions initiated by scientists and engineers.

39. The correct answer is (2). The relative rate of enzyme activity rises as the enzyme concentration increases until the concentration is about 7. At that point, the relative rate of enzyme activity levels off at about 35, and remains the same.

40. The correct answer is (3). The ratio is 1 to 10. A 100-pound man would need 1,000 pounds of fish.

41. The correct answer is (4). The insects get their energy by eating the organisms directly below them in the pyramid. That means the insects eat algae.

42. The correct answer is (1). The number of insects would increase because without the fish there would be nothing to kill them.

43. The correct answer is (5). ^{238}U has the longest half-life and therefore decays the slowest.

44. The correct answer is (4). Since the half-life for Fr is 27.5 seconds, then $\dfrac{100}{27.5} = 4 = 4$ half-lifes, therefore:

(1) 100 grams → 50 grams

(2) 50 grams → 25 grams

(3) 25 grams → 12.5 grams

(4) 12.5 grams → 6.25 grams

(Note that each half-life causes $\frac{1}{2}$ of the sample to be used up.)

45. **The correct answer is (2).** The table shows that Co has a half-life of 5.3 years. At the end of 5.3 years of the original quantity of Co will remain. At the end of 10.6 years $\frac{1}{2}$ of $\frac{1}{2}$, or $\frac{1}{4}$, of the original quantity of Co will remain. If you started with 100 grams of Co, at the end of 5.3 years you would have 50 grams of Co. In another 5.3 years you would have 25 grams of Co. $\frac{25}{100} = \frac{1}{4}$.

46. **The correct answer is (2).** ^{42}K has a half-life of 12.4 hours. This is the shortest half-life of the choices offered and, therefore, ^{42}K decays most rapidly.

47. **The correct answer is (3).** Winds of 38–55 miles per hour are expected during a gale warning.

48. **The correct answer is (5).** Hurricane warnings require an immediate response to precautions, since such precautions are often issued with less than 24 hours' notice.

49. **The correct answer is (4).** According to the passage, coastal areas are especially dangerous during a hurricane, because of the danger of flooding and high waves.

50. **The correct answer is (1).** Even though all the choices can be the result of a hurricane, the passage suggests that the most dangerous effect is flooding.

Test 4. Language Arts, Reading

1. (3)	11. (1)	21. (3)	31. (5)
2. (3)	12. (5)	22. (4)	32. (2)
3. (4)	13. (2)	23. (5)	33. (4)
4. (1)	14. (1)	24. (5)	34. (2)
5. (3)	15. (2)	25. (2)	35. (3)
6. (5)	16. (1)	26. (1)	36. (4)
7. (2)	17. (3)	27. (4)	37. (1)
8. (4)	18. (5)	28. (3)	38. (5)
9. (4)	19. (4)	29. (3)	39. (2)
10. (2)	20. (2)	30. (1)	40. (3)

1. **The correct answer is (3).** Henry is talking about a battle and war in general. We are not told what job he has in civilian life. We are specifically told that Henry was an "orderly sergeant."

2. **The correct answer is (3).** The old man is honest in the description of his fears; therefore, he is no hypocrite. He does not seem to have undue pride in himself and is certainly not unfriendly.

3. **The correct answer is (4).** His fellow townsmen just won't believe that Henry is anything less than a hero. There is no indication that they believe him a liar or that they are bitter or disgusted. Jim is the one who is horrified.

4. **The correct answer is (1).** Jim, we are told, is "horror-stricken" at

his grandfather's admission that he was afraid in battle. Perhaps Jim didn't know the old man was a soldier, but we are not told so. The probability is that he did know, since his grandfather is his hero. As they walked home together, they probably also came to the store together, and so Henry knew little Jim was present and listening. The listeners don't regard Henry as a fool; that is obvious from their respectful attitude toward him. Henry is well aware of the terror of war.

5. **The correct answer is (3).** We can eliminate choice (1), for it is apparent that little Jim worships his grandfather. Choices (2) and (4) are true statements. Henry was afraid in battle and admitted it, and he is highly regarded by the townspeople. But the author focuses his—and our—attention upon Jim's reaction to what his grandfather said.

6. **The correct answer is (5).** If they had been veterans, or of the same age as Henry, they would have known more about war, such as understanding rank and the experience of normal fear during battle. Their deferential behavior suggests that they were probably younger than Henry and inexperienced with war.

7. **The correct answer is (2).** Rule number 3 states that John is expected at work at 8:30, not 8:45. Rule number 7 says that he is not supposed to make so many personal telephone calls. Therefore, since he has broken both these rules, choice (2) is the correct answer.

8. **The correct answer is (4).** Rule number 8 clearly states that "any questions or concerns should be brought up to the supervisor." This is repeated in rule number 9, so this is all she needs to do.

9. **The correct answer is (4).** This seems to be the only reasonable choice. We don't know if the company is well run generally, whether it makes a lot of money, or anything about its production practices. The rules seem to be fair, and the mention of health and possible vacation benefits imply that it may be a very good place to work.

10. **The correct answer is (2).** If Freddie skips breakfast and moves quickly, he can probably make up for his late start and get to work on time. Calling in will only delay him even further.

11. **The correct answer is (1).** This rule, which instructs workers to treat customers and each other with "courtesy and respect," is related to this saying.

12. **The correct answer is (5).** The narrator sees all characters in the story. He describes the clothing of the two main characters. Don't confuse the narrator with Parsons, a character in the story.

13. **The correct answer is (2).** Markwardt has lied to himself and to others about the accident in C shop and thereby has handicapped himself from improving his situation.

14. **The correct answer is (1).** From this statement, the reader can infer that Markwardt told the C shop story often to obtain a few dollars from sympathetic listeners.

15. **The correct answer is (2).** The characters speak differently. Parsons uses the sentence structure and vocabulary associated with the upper middle class, while Markwardt uses the slang expressions typical of the lower class.

16. **The correct answer is (1).** We are told in the second paragraph that Mr. Parsons is dressed "in his immaculate gray suit and gray hat and Malacca stick," which suggests that he is more prosperous than

Markwardt, who is a peddler in the streets.

17. **The correct answer is (3).** It is likely that hearing the story of the accident is what gave Mr. Parsons the clue. There is no indication that he knew who he was speaking to before this.

18. **The correct answer is (5).** The first ten lines form an organized unit that is set apart from the following lines. This is an example of a stanza.

19. **The correct answer is (4).** In stanza two, the highwayman is described as wearing lace, a red velvet coat, doeskin pants, and high boots. This is resplendent attire.

20. **The correct answer is (2).** The last line of the fourth stanza refers to the highwayman as a "robber."

21. **The correct answer is (3).** The fourth stanza reveals that Tim also loved the landlord's daughter and states that his eyes "were hollows of madness . . ."

22. **The correct answer is (4).** Lines 24–25 states that "all was locked and barred," and the scene takes place at night. Therefore, we can assume that the highwayman was not expected.

23. **The correct answer is (5).** The last stanza states the highwayman's plans for the night: ". . . I'm after a prize tonight, But I shall be back with the yellow gold before the morning light." You can assume that he is going to commit a robbery.

24. **The correct answer is (5).** Her purpose in writing this piece is to evaluate the performance. She is a dance reviewer, a writer who is knowledgeable about dance. In order to do this she speaks of the dancers and the pieces performed.

25. **The correct answer is (2).** The article states at the beginning of the second paragraph that these dancers are preprofessionals, meaning they are young dancers who are not yet earning their living at dance, but are on their way there.

26. **The correct answer is (1).** The author speaks of the dances created by these people and danced in this performance. They are, therefore, choreographers.

27. **The correct answer is (4).** The reviewer describes *Tombeau* as an "exquisite ensemble piece" with "lovely configurations," and *Fanfare* is said to have "wit." She clearly doesn't speak well of Wheeldon and his choreography. Therefore, choice (4) is the correct answer.

28. **The correct answer is (3).** In the last sentence of the review, the words "overbusy and pointless" are used to describe the writer's opinion about the Wheeldon piece. This indicates that she does not admire this dance piece.

29. **The correct answer is (3).** Although there seems to be a grain of truth in all the choices, the best answer is choice (3), which describes the whole point of the scene. Miss Neville has to use all her cunning and intelligence to get what she wants, which is to marry the man she really loves in spite of her guardian's wishes.

30. **The correct answer is (1).** The problem is stated in Miss Hardcastle's first speech and further explained in Miss Neville's third.

31. **The correct answer is (5).** Miss Hardcastle's joking manner makes "sympathetic" the only possible choice.

32. **The correct answer is (2).** "It is a good-natured creature at bottom," says Miss Neville of Tony Hardcastle.

33. The correct answer is (4). The sentence implies first that Miss Hardcastle does not love her brother, but that his dislike for Miss Neville makes him more appealing to her (since it paves the way for Miss Neville to marry the man of her choice).

34. The correct answer is (2). Mrs. Hardcastle is trying to get Miss Neville's fortune by meddling in her private life.

35. The correct answer is (3). He states in the first sentence that he has just resigned from a job.

36. The correct answer is (4). All these choices reflect statements made in the second paragraph. The writer states that he is exhausted and that he doesn't want to continue teaching, and he describes the profession as a "safety net for just such indeterminate natures."

37. The correct answer is (1). By comparing a small tree to a developing young person, the author emphasizes the importance of early experiences in influencing the future of the young man. He also broadens this point by relating it to youthful imagination, and subsequent career choices.

38. The correct answer is (5). In the middle of the second paragraph, he states that these savings are being kept only for a possible return to Europe or for graduate school.

39. The correct answer is (2). The author suggests that he is open to life, that he isn't at all clear what will happen to him and that he wants to do all he can and see what life has to offer while he's young. He's not looking for structure or help, and he's not worried about being safe.

40. The correct answer is (3). While he states at the beginning that he is "innerly exhausted," the speaker is actually very cheerful and optimistic and is enjoying thoughts about his adventurous life to come.

Test 5. Mathematics

1. (4)	11. (4)	21. 556	31. 45	41. (2)
2. (4)	12. 2.13	22. 0.48	32. (5)	42. (5)
3. (3)	13. 1.52	23. (2)	33. (3)	43. 540
4. 91.06	14. (5)	24. (4)	34. (4)	44. (4)
5. 956/9	15. (4)	25. (1)	35. (4)	45. (5)
6. (2)	16. (5)	26. (3)	36. (4)	46. (5)
7. (4)	17. (3,5)	27. (1)	37. (−3,−6)	47. (5)
8. (3)	18. (1)	28. (2)	38. (3)	48. (4)
9. (3)	19. (4)	29. (3)	39. (1)	49. (5)
10. (5)	20. (3)	30. (5)	40. (2)	50. (5)

Part 1

Note: The word CALCULATOR **indicates that you should enter the following on your calculator.**

1. **The correct answer is (4).** From the Formula page, the Area of a square is, Area = side^2 :

$$A = s^2 \ or \ s = \sqrt{0.60}$$

CALCULATOR 0.60 SHIFT x^2 = [Answer: $s = 0.7745$; rounded to **0.77** inches]

Hint: When working on your scrap paper, SHORTEN THE NUMBER OF DIGITS DISPLAYED ON YOUR CALCULATOR TO FOUR DECIMAL PLACES.

In the display window of your calculator, you will often see decimal numbers with as many as nine decimals places! Shortening (truncating) the number of digits to four decimal places makes it easier to write since rarely are more than four decimals needed in a problem. _Then_ round off your answer to the correct number of decimal places that are required in the answer. In this case, the required number of decimal places is two since all choices are given to two decimal places. Here, the answer, 0.7745 is rounded to **0.77** inches.

2. **The correct answer is (4).** Add the 3 fractions on the calculator:

$$10\frac{2}{3}+5\frac{3}{4}+2\frac{1}{6}$$

CALCULATOR $10 + 2 \div 3 + 5 + 3 \div 4 + 2 + 1 \div 6 =$

[Answer: 18.5833; rounded to **18.58** yards of blue ribbon]

3. **The correct answer is (3).** Use Formula page (Trigonometry Ratios) to find _BD_, using _AD_ (234) and angle _A_ (70°);

$$\sin = \frac{opposite}{hypotenuse}$$

$$\sin A = \frac{BD}{AD}; \sin 70° = \frac{BD}{234}$$

Solving for _BD_, by multiplying both sides by 234, $BD = 234 \times \sin 70°$

CALCULATOR $234 \times 70\sin =$ [Answer: BD = 219.8880; rounded to

220 feet]

4. Alternate form: 9 1 . 0 6

Add the signed numbers on the calculator to find the final balance:

$\boxed{\text{C A L C U L A T O R}}$ 100 − 15.75 + 25 + 18 − 36.19 = [Answer: **$91.06**]

Or, using the ± key, the same result can be found.

$\boxed{\text{C A L C U L A T O R}}$ 100 + 15.75 ± 25 + 18 + 36.19 ± = [Answer: $91.06]

5. Alternate form: 9 5 6 / 9

$$\text{The Ratio} = \frac{\text{sum of sales}}{\text{sum of customers}} = \frac{87+138+239+492}{1+1+3+4} = \frac{956}{9}$$

6. **The correct answer is (2).** Set up a ratio. Let X = amount of vegetables needed for 14 people. Then, $\dfrac{1.85}{8} = \dfrac{X}{14}$

Solving for X by multiplying both sides by 14,

$\boxed{\text{C A L C U L A T O R}}$ 1.85 ÷ 8 × 14 = [Answer: $X = 3.2375$]

But the problem asks for how many *more* pounds are required, so 3.2375 − 1.85 = 1.3875 rounded to **1.39** pounds more are needed.

An alternative approach is:

If the recipe requires 1.85 pounds *per* 8 people, then for 6 more, add:

$$6 \cancel{\text{people}} \times \frac{1.85 \text{ pounds}}{8 \cancel{\text{people}}} = \frac{6 \times 1.85}{8} \text{ pounds}$$

$\boxed{\text{C A L C U L A T O R}}$ 6 × 1.85 ÷ 8 = [Answer: 1.3875, rounded to **1.39** pounds]

7. **The correct answer is (4).** Add the number of degrees that the minute hand moves. Begin at an easy place, say 12:00. Make a sketch of the clock:

In the first hour it moves completely around the clock or 360°. Add this to what it moves in the next 25 minutes (5/12th of the clock): $360 + \dfrac{5}{12} \times 360$

CALCULATOR $360 + 5 \div 12 \times 360 =$ [Answer: **510°**]

8. **The correct answer is (3).** The sum of the angles of a triangle = 180°. Therefore, if two angles of a triangle are known, you can find the third angle:

DBA = 180° − 128° = 52°

ADB + DBA = 60° + 52° = 112°

DAB = 180° − 112° = 68°

9. **The correct answer is (3).** See the Formula page for <u>Volume of a cone</u>:

$V = \dfrac{1}{3} \times \pi \times radius^2 \times height$, where radius = 6 and height = 12

$V = \dfrac{1}{3} \times \pi \times 6^2 \times 12$

CALCULATOR $= 1 \div 3 \times EXP \times 36 \times 12 =$

[Answer: 452.3893 ft^3 rounded to **452 ft^3**]

Note: When you hit **EXP** on the calculator you get the value of π.

10. **The correct answer is (5).** Convert the units from [ft^3] to [gallons] by canceling like terms. Recall that, $\dfrac{1\,\text{minute}}{10\,\text{gallons}}$ is equivalent to $\dfrac{10\,\text{gallons}}{1\,\text{minute}}$

The time in [minutes] needed to fill the container is,

$\dfrac{1\,\text{min}}{10\,\cancel{\text{gal}}} \times \dfrac{1\,\cancel{\text{gal}}}{0.13\,\cancel{\text{ft}^3}} \times 1000\,\cancel{\text{ft}^3} =$

$\dfrac{1 \times 1 \times 100\,\cancel{0}}{1\cancel{0} \times .13} = \dfrac{100}{.13}$

CALCULATOR $100 \div .13 =$ [Answer: 769.2307; rounded to **769** minutes]

11. **The correct answer is (4).** Solve for X.

Subtract 0.12 from both sides: $-0.34X = 0.44$

Divide both sides by -0.34: $X = \dfrac{0.44}{-0.34}$

⌨️ CALCULATOR $0.44 \div 0.34 \pm =$ [Answer: $x = -1.294117$; rounded to **−1.29**]

12. Alternate form: <u>2</u> . <u>1</u> <u>3</u> – Find the average. To give your answer as a *decimal*, change minutes to hours by dividing by 60. Add a "new" column to the chart of running times:

Runner	Hours	Minutes	Minutes as decimal
#1	2	15	= 2 + 15/60 = 2.25
#2	2	14	= 2 + 14/60 = 2.2333
#3	1	55	= 1 + 55/60 = <u>1.9166</u>
TOTAL			6.3999

Average = 6.3999 ÷ 3 = 2.1333; rounded to 2.13 hours

13. Alternate form: <u>1</u> . <u>5</u> <u>2</u> – Find the AVERAGE using algebra. Let T = time of runner #3.

$$Average = \frac{2.25 + 2.23 + T}{3} = 2$$

Solve for T, by multiplying both sides; by 3 and then by subtracting 2.25 and 2.23 from both sides; therefore, Average = 6 − 2.25 − 2.23 = **1.52** hours

14. **The correct answer is (5).** For Softex (large), the cost per tissue $= \dfrac{\$3.09}{200} =$ $.01545. For Softex (regular) the cost per tissue $= \dfrac{\$1.69}{100} = \$.0169$.

$$\text{Savings per tissue} = \$.0169 - \$.01545$$
$$= \$.00145$$
$$\approx .15¢$$

15. **The correct answer is (4).** Find the cost per tissue for each brand type. Then, find the *cheapest* one.

(Hint: Write your answer next to the corresponding line on the chart.)

Brand	Cost	Count	Cost/tissue	
A	1.69	100	1.69/100 =	*0.0169*
B	3.09	200		*0.01545*
C	1.49	100		*0.0149*
D	2.69	200		*0.01345 (cheapest)*
E	1.39	100		*0.0139*

16. **The correct answer is (5).** Discount cost is $0.50 for two boxes, but 0.25 for *one* box.

$$\frac{3.09 - 0.25[\$]}{200[\text{tissue}]} = 0.0142 \left[\frac{\$}{\text{tissue}}\right] = 1.42/\text{tissue}$$

An alternative method to solve this problem:
If Debbie bought 2 large boxes of Softez, she'd pay 2 × $3.09 = $6.18 − $.50 = $5.68 for 200 × 2 = 400 tissues.

Dividing $5.68 by 400 = .0142 dollars per tissue or 1.42/100 tissues

17. Alternate form: Coordinate Grid (3,5)

Follow the information in the question carefully.

If his initial Temperature is normal, *initially* (on day "0"), then on the:

1st day it is 2°F above normal ("up 2")

2nd day it is 6°F "   " ("up 4")

3rd day it is **5**°F "   " ("down 1")

So, the coordinates of the Temperature on Day 3 are **(3, 5)**.

A sketch of this information may look like the following:

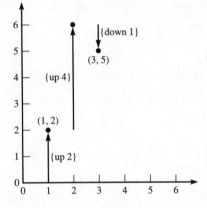

18. **The correct answer is (1).** Construct triangle *BGW*.
    Label it: side opposite *B* = *b*
    side opposite *G* = *g*
    side opposite *W* = *w*

From the Formula page, the <u>Trigonometric Ratio</u> that relates the known and unknown quantities in the question is

$$\sin B = \frac{opposite}{hypotenuse} = \sin 37° = \frac{b}{g} = \frac{b}{18}$$

Multiply both sides by 18 to find $b = 18 \times \sin 37°$

Make sure that the "mode" says DEG (degrees): If not, then on the top of your calculator, *printed* just above the top keys find: "· *4 DEG.*" Press the following:

⌨ CALCULATOR MODE 4   Then press,

⌨ CALCULATOR 18 × 37 sin = [Answer is 10.8327; rounded to **11** feet]

19. **The correct answer is (4).** Find the total percentage of people between 25 and 54. Divide by 100 to change the percent to a fraction. Multiply by the total civilian labor force in 1999.

CALCULATOR $(23.1 + 27.2 + 21.1) \div 100 \times 139,368,000 =$
[Answer: 99,508,752; rounded to **99.5** million]

20. **The correct answer is (3).** Find the difference between % of young workers in 1970 and 1999.

    % of young workers in 1970 = 8.8 {16 to 19} + 12.8 {20 to 24} = 21.6%

    % of young workers in 1999 = 6.0 + 10.0 = 16.0%

    The decline in % from 1970 to 1999 = 21.6 − 16.0 = **5.6%**

21. Alternate form: $\underline{5}\quad\underline{5}\quad\underline{6}\quad\underline{}\quad\underline{}$

    Refer to the Formula page for <u>distance between points</u>, where,

    $A(x_1, y_1) = (240, 520)$; and $B(x_2, y_2) = (720, 240)$

    $distance = \sqrt{\left(x_2 - x_1\right)^2 + \left(y_2 - y_1\right)^2}$, and substituting :

    CALCULATOR $[((720 - 240)\, x^2 + (240 - 520)\, x^2)]$ shift $x^2 =$
    [Answer: 555.6977; rounded to **556** inches]

22. Alternate form: $(\underline{0}\quad.\quad\underline{4}\quad\underline{8}\quad\underline{}\quad\underline{}\quad)$

    Refer to the Formula page: <u>Circumference (C) of a circle</u> = $\pi \times$ diameter.

    Since $d = 2r$, $C = \pi \times 2 \times$ radius (r) and substituting: $3 = \pi \times 2 \times r$

    Solving for r: $r = \dfrac{3}{\pi \times 2}$

    CALCULATOR $r = 3 \div (EXP \times 2) =$

    [Answer: $r = .4774$; rounded to **0.48** feet]

23. **The correct answer is (2).** The {income > outlay}, therefore there is a *surplus*.
    The U.S. took in more taxes (Income) than it spent (Outlay).
    Surplus = 1827 − 1703 = $124 billion
    It receives $124 billion more than it spends.

24. **The correct answer is (4).** Plan: Let A = Outlays for Social programs;

    Let B = Outlays for Social Security, medicine, and retirement
    (Hint: Write "A" and "B" on the *question sheet*.)

    The total spent = $A + B$

    $= 1703 \times$ (fraction spent on A + fraction spent on B)

    $= 1703 \times (0.17 + 0.35) = 1703 \times 0.52$

    $= 885.56$ (rounded to $886 billion spent)

25. **The correct answer is (1).** The reduction in Income = $(0.48 - 0.41) \times 1827 =$
    $0.07 \times 1827 = 127.89$ (rounded to $128 billion)

Mathematics—Part 2

26. **The correct answer is (3).** Multiply. The choices are in *dollars* so change 7¢ to $0.07

$$43.1 \quad \text{(1 decimal)}$$
$$\underline{\times \$0.07} \quad (+ 2 \text{ decimals})$$
$$3.017 \quad \text{(3 decimals in answers)}$$

(Three decimals in answer; rounded to $3.02)

27. **The correct answer is (1).** *Multiply* since, $\frac{2}{3}$ "of" $\frac{5}{9}$ is the same as $\frac{2}{3} \times \frac{5}{9}$

$\frac{2}{3} \times \frac{5}{9} = \frac{2 \times 5}{3 \times 9} = \frac{10}{27}$ of the class were girls who passed.

28. **The correct answer is (2).** Add the three items and subtract the sum from $50.00. Be sure to line up all decimals.

$$
\begin{array}{ll}
28.06 & 50.00 \\
2.25 & -30.46 \\
\underline{.15} & 19.54 \\
30.46 &
\end{array}
$$

The change was **$19.54.**

29. **The correct answer is (3).** Write the equation for the information given:

2 coins of value $x = 2x$

3 coins of value $y = 3y$

$$2x + 3y = 50 \text{ cents}$$

Therefore, $2x = 50 - 3y$

30. **The correct answer is (5).** Add like terms on the left. Remember to add signed numbers correctly.

$$3x + 3y + x + 4y - 4x = 5$$
$$3x + x - 4x + 3y + 4y = 5$$
$$7y = 5$$

31. Alternate form: $\underline{4} \ \underline{5} \ \underline{} \ \underline{}$, angle ABC + 135° = 180° (a straight angle); angle ABC = [Answer: $180 - 135 = \mathbf{45°}$]

32. **The correct answer is (5).** Find the formula for area of a circle on the Formula page. Using $A = \pi r^2$, solve for A:

$A = 3.14 \times (2)^2$

$A = 3.14 \times 4$

$A = \text{More than 12 square feet}$

33. The correct answer is (3). Substitute 4 for x in each equation until you find one that is true:

(1) $(4)^2 + 4 = 16 + 4 \neq 12$

(2) $4(4) - 1 = 16 - 1 \neq 7$

(3) $2(4) - 3 = 8 - 3 = 5$ (This is the correct answer.)

34. The correct answer is (4). Organize your work carefully.

Hourly Wage × Hours Worked = Total Income

($3.65) (4 + 3 + 5 + 4 + 4) = Total Income

The actual numerical solution is not asked for; just the equation you would use to solve the problem, which is choice (4).

35. The correct answer is (4). Substitute 5 for x in the quadratic equation:

$3(5^2) - 4(5) + 3 =$

$3(25) - 20 + 3 =$

$75 - 20 + 3 = 58$

36. The correct answer is (4). Both length and width are the same for the dominos and the box. Can you see how the dominoes will stack inside the box? Determine how many .25 inch-high dominoes can fit into 1 foot:

1 foot = 12 inches

$12 \div .25 = 48$

37. Alternate form, Coordinate Plane Grid (–3, –6)

Locate the point that, when connected to the others, makes a symmetric parallelogram. The point is (–3, –6)

The answer is as follows:

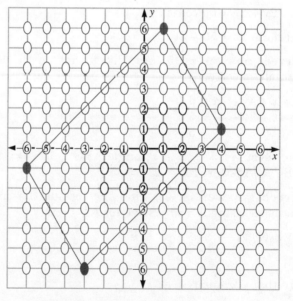

(–3, –6)

38. **The correct answer is (3).** She saved 50% or $\frac{1}{2}$ of $25 for each pair of shorts.

    $\frac{1}{2}$ of 25 = $12.50

    Total : 3 × 12.50 = 37.50

39. **The correct answer is (1).** <u>Shirts</u>: $25 (for the first), and 6 × $20 ("5 dollars off" for the remaining 6 shirts):

    25 + 6 × 20 = $145 <u>Sandals</u>: $30 for each: 2 × 30 = 60
    Total: 145 + 60 = $205

40. **The correct answer is (2).** The total regular price was:

    Shirts + Sandals = (7 × 25) + (2 × 40) = 255

    The Savings:

    Regular Price – Sales Price = 255 – 205 = $50

41. **The correct answer is (2).** From the Formula page, the circumference of Dad's car wheel is C = πd = π × 16. If Tim's tricycle wheel is $\frac{1}{4}$ of this, Tim's wheel is $\frac{1}{4}$ of 16π or 4π. Since 2 × r = d, we can write about Tim's bike: C = π × (2 × r) = 4π. Divide both sides by 2 and then by π.

    $$\frac{\cancel{2} \times \pi \times r}{\cancel{2}} = \frac{\cancel{4}^2 \times \pi}{\cancel{2}}$$
    $$\pi \times r = 2 \times \pi$$
    $$r = 2$$

42. **The correct answer is (5).** These trees and their shadows form similar triangles. Their corresponding sides and angles are proportional, so: Big Tree Parts are proportional to the Small Tree Parts.

    $$\frac{\text{height of big tree}}{\text{length of shadow}} = \frac{\text{height of small tree}}{\text{length of shadow}}$$

    $$\frac{50}{20} = \frac{h}{15}$$

    $$20h = 750$$

    $$h = 37.5$$

    Solving the proportion, we find that h = 37.5 feet.

43. Alternate form: <u>5</u> <u>4</u> <u>0</u> _ _
    Let S = % Savings
    The sum of items = 100%
    S + 17 + 15 + 25 + 28 = 100
    S + 85 = 100
    100 − 85 = 15
    Savings (in dollars) = 15% of 3600
    = .15 × 3600 = $540

44. **The correct answer is (4).** Since 28% is spent on rent, the cost of rent each month is .28 × $3600 = $1008.

45. The correct answer is (5). Find the mean number of boys and the mean number of girls using the formula for the mean from the Formula page:

$$\text{mean (boys)} = \frac{2+0+1+2+5}{5} = \frac{10}{5} = 2$$

$$\text{mean (girls)} = \frac{3+0+2+1+4}{5} = \frac{10}{5} = 2$$

The average number of boys and girls is the same.

46. The correct answer is (5). The time needed to boil water depends on several factors, namely, initial temperature, total amount of water, and the amount of heat supplied. Insufficient data is given, so the problem cannot be solved.

47. The correct answer is (5). If the number of items sold were 50 (on first day) and x (on the second day), the amount lost is $.50 \times (50 + x) = 25 + .50x$. But since x is unknown, no numerical value can be determined; insufficient data is given, choice (5).

48. The correct answer is (4). The mode is the highest frequency observation. Here it is 8 cars, which appeared twice, in hour 3 and hour 5.

49. The correct answer is (5). Using the mean formula from the Formula page we find

$$\text{mean} = \frac{\text{sum of observations}}{\text{\# hours}}$$

$$\text{mean} = \frac{5+4+8+0+8}{5}$$

$$\text{mean} = \frac{25}{5} = 5 \text{ red cars/hour}$$

50. The correct answer is (5). Use the mean formula. However, the number in the 6$^\text{th}$ hour is unknown. Let R = number seen in 6th hour.

$$\text{Mean} = \frac{(\text{sum of observations in 5 hours}) + R}{6} = 7$$

From question 49, we know that the sum of observations in 5 hours = 25

Therefore, $\dfrac{25 + R}{6} = 7$

Multiply both sides of equation by 6: $25 + R = 42$

Subtract 25 from each side of equation: $R = 17$

ERROR ANALYSIS FOR DIAGNOSTIC TEST

Circle the number of each question you answered incorrectly. Count the number of circles in each content area and write the total number missed in the column headed "Number Incorrect." A large number of incorrect responses in a particular area indicates the need for further study in that area.

SUBJECT AREA	QUESTIONS	NUMBER INCORRECT
TEST 1. LANGUAGE ARTS, WRITING	50	
Sentence Structure	1, 5, 9, 13, 17, 21, 27, 29, 33, 35, 37, 40, 42, 45, 47, 49	
Usage	2, 7, 11, 12, 18, 19, 24, 26, 32, 34, 41, 43, 44, 48, 50	
Mechanics	3, 6, 8, 10, 15, 16, 22, 23, 25, 30, 31, 38	
Organization	4, 14, 20, 28, 36, 39, 46	
TEST 2. SOCIAL STUDIES	50	
History	9, 22, 23, 24, 25, 27, 28, 29, 30, 42, 43, 44, 45, 48, 49, 50	
Economics	10, 11, 12, 13, 19, 20, 21, 31, 33, 34, 35	
Geography	1, 2, 3, 4, 26, 41	
Civics and Government	5, 6, 7, 8, 14, 15, 16, 17, 18, 32, 36, 37, 38, 39, 40, 46, 47	
TEST 3. SCIENCE	50	
Life Science	5, 6, 7, 8, 9, 12, 13, 14, 15, 16, 17, 25, 26, 27, 28, 29, 30, 31, 32, 39, 40, 41, 42	
Chemistry	21, 22, 23, 24, 33, 36, 37, 38	
Physics	10, 11, 18, 34, 35, 43, 44, 45, 46	
Earth and Space Science	1, 2, 3, 4, 19, 20, 47, 48, 49, 50	
TEST 4. LANGUAGE ARTS, READING	40	
Drama and Poetry	18, 19, 20, 21, 22, 23, 29, 30, 31, 32, 33, 34	
Literary Readings	1, 2, 3, 4, 5, 6, 12, 13, 14, 15, 16, 17, 35, 36, 37, 38, 39, 40	
Nonfiction	24, 25, 26, 27, 28	
Business Readings	7, 8, 9, 10, 11	
TEST 5. MATHEMATICS	50	
Measurement and Geometry	1, 3, 7, 8, 9, 10, 19, 21, 22, 25, 31, 32, 36, 41	
Algebra	6, 11, 18, 24, 29, 30, 33, 34, 35, 37, 47, 50	
Number Standards and Operations	2, 4, 5, 14, 16, 23, 26, 27, 28, 42	
Data Analysis	12, 13, 15, 17, 20, 38, 39, 40, 43, 44, 45, 46, 48, 49	

PART III
LANGUAGE ARTS, WRITING REVIEW

All About the GED Language Arts, Writing Test

chapter 3

OVERVIEW

- Quick Tips!
- Taking the GED Language Arts, Writing test
- Spelling
- 320 frequently misspelled words
- Punctuation and capitalization
- The essentials of English grammar
- Correct English usage
- Summing it up

QUICK TIPS!

Writing easily and correctly is really just a matter of practice. Try doing word games, such as crossword puzzles. These games are present in most newspapers and many magazines, or you can buy crossword and other word-game magazines. These will help increase your vocabulary, improve spelling, and give you greater verbal fluency.

Give yourself little writing assignments, such as writing letters to friends or relatives, writing lists of things you like to do, and, best of all, keeping an informal journal or diary to record your daily thoughts, wishes, worries, plans, and dreams. **If you do this routinely, with some attention to spelling and correct language usage, you will increase your self-confidence and improve your writing skills enormously.**

TAKING THE GED LANGUAGE ARTS, WRITING TEST

The Language Arts, Writing Test measures your ability to recognize and correct errors in four areas:

- Sentence Structure (30%)
- Usage (30%)
- Mechanics (25%)
- Organization (15%)

The following are some examples of the kinds of errors you will be expected to recognize.

Sentence Structure Errors

Sentence fragments:
Susan bringing her books to the library.
Mr. Smith having taken his daughter home.

Run-on sentences:
Jimmy watched the World Cup race his team lost.
Marie enjoyed the movie her sister came.

Improper coordination:
Jeannie flies often and lives in Nashville.

Improper subordination:
We will continue to depend on local sales taxes even whenever the income tax is passed.

Lack of clarity due to misplaced modifiers or lack of parallelism:
Riding in the car, the light turned red.
Betty likes skiing and to play tennis.

Usage Errors

Lack of agreement between subject and verb:
Sam and Fred is here.
Ron, like his two brothers, are short and muscular.
It are very hot in here.

Incorrect verb tense:
When the teacher walks in, I sat down. (sequence of tenses)
Tomorrow, Sandy went to work. (word clue to tense in the sentence)
Bernie done the job. (verb form)

Incorrect pronouns:
Jimmy is a man which I love. (wrong relative pronoun)
If one wants to earn money, you must get a job. (pronoun shift)
He tried to plead his case to his children and his friends, but they wouldn't listen. (vague reference)
The carpenter followed the plumber into his shop. (ambiguous reference)
Russia was offered help, but they curtly rejected the assistance. (lack of agreement with antecedent)

Mechanics Errors

Capitalization:
They planned to cook a chinese dinner. (proper adjectives)
She booked a tour to italy. (proper nouns)
Susan works for mayor Haley. (titles)
Her birthday falls on memorial day. (holidays)

She lives at 893 Stone avenue. (addresses)

He quit his job last Summer. (seasons)

Punctuation:

I need forks cups and paper plates. (comma between items in a series)

Don wanted to stop for a drink but Janet wanted to finish shopping. (comma between two independent clauses)

When Marta arrived at her brother's house she could not believe the appearance of the basement. (comma after introductory dependent clauses)

He looked, and decided to run. (overuse of commas)

He dislikes sports for example and never watches baseball or football. (comma with appositives)

Spelling (possessives and contractions):

Her mothers old recipe made a delicious soup. (possessives)

Your the tallest man on the team. (troublesome contractions)

Multiple-choice Language Arts, Writing questions are always presented within a passage that averages twelve or more sentences and several paragraphs. When corrected, each reading passage becomes an example of good writing. Most questions contain an error that must be identified and corrected. Some questions contain no error at all. At least a few contain errors in clarity or logic, the sorts of mistakes that often hamper employees and students in everyday writing on the job or in school.

Organization Errors

There are errors in writing that make a piece confusing, hard to follow, and sometimes even illogical. Organization involves developing an idea in an article in a clearly thought-out way so that it can be easily understood by the reader.

You will be presented with questions that ask you to revise the piece you are reading in one of the following ways:

- Adding a sentence, in order to help clarify the passage

- Deleting a sentence in the text, because it isn't part of the idea being discussed and just creates confusion

- Rearranging a sentence, which means putting the sentence in a more logical place in the article

- Substituting a sentence, meaning that you will delete the sentence in the text and substitute another one in its place that is better

You will also be asked a few questions about organizing a passage better by moving a paragraph to a different place in the selection. Here, you will be asked to judge whether the idea presented will be clearer if a whole paragraph is moved elsewhere. In order to do this successfully, you will need to read the passage very carefully and really understand it. These questions will often require more thought, time, and effort on your part.

Writing Skills Questions May Be Asked in One of Three Ways

 Sentence Correction Questions (45% of the Test)

This type of question may test your knowledge in any area of sentence structure, usage, or mechanics. The question is always written with the following cue: WHAT CORRECTION SHOULD BE MADE TO THIS SENTENCE? Since no portion of the sentence is underlined, it is up to you to look at the entire sentence for any possible error in any of the three skills areas.

> **Q**   **When tickets went on sale for the rock concert, young people from miles around lining up at the box office.**
>
> What correction should be made to this sentence?
>
> (1) change <u>went</u> to <u>go</u>
> (2) remove the comma after <u>concert</u>
> (3) change the spelling of <u>people</u> to <u>poeple</u>
> (4) change <u>lining</u> to <u>lined</u>
> (5) no correction is necessary
>
> **A**   **The correct answer is (4).** As it stands, this is a sentence fragment, not a complete sentence. To make it complete you must change *lining* to *lined*, thus giving the sentence the verb it lacks.

② **Sentence Revision Questions (35% of the Test)**

This type of question may test your skills in sentence structure, usage, or punctuation. It will always consist of a sentence with some portion underlined. The underlined portion may or may not contain an error, but you are being asked to look at that part of the sentence, and no other, in order to answer the question. A sentence revision question is always written with the cue: *Which of the following is the best way to write the underlined portion of this sentence? If you think the original is the best way to write the sentence, choose option (1).* Option 1 will *always* be a restatement of the sentence as it appears in the paragraph and in the separate question.

> **Q**   **Education is a life-long <u>process, at</u> every age we learn from family, friends, and associates.** Which of the following is the best way to write the underlined portion of this sentence? If you think the original is the best way to write the sentence, choose option (1).
>
> (1) process, at
> (2) process at
> (3) process. At
> (4) process: at
> (5) process of
>
> **A**   **The correct answer is (3).** This sentence is an example of a comma splice (two complete sentences joined by a comma). To correct the error, separate the two sentences by changing <u>process, at</u> to <u>process. At</u>.

3 Construction Shift Questions (20% of the Test)

This type of question will test your skills in sentence structure, usage, or punctuation. Construction shift questions ask you to rewrite a sentence according to directions given to you. Your new sentence must be clearly and correctly stated, and it must have the same meaning as the original sentence.

> **Q**   **It is more rewarding to make friends than it is to be antisocial. If you rewrote this sentence beginning with <u>Making friends</u>, the next word should be**
>
> (1) Than
> (2) It
> (3) is
> (4) rewarding
> (5) to
>
> **A**   **The correct answer is (3).** The rewritten sentence will be: *Making friends is more rewarding than being antisocial.* Therefore, the word that follows *making friends* is *is*.

SPELLING

Part 1 of the Language Arts, Writing Section of the GED test no longer tests spelling, except for homonyms, possessives, and contractions. The following rules, however, will improve your general spelling ability and improve your score on Part 2—Essay Test. Learn the nine rules that follow and work your way systematically through the list of commonly misspelled words.

Rule 1

For one-syllable words,

- DOUBLE THE FINAL CONSONANT before adding a y or a suffix that begins with a vowel if the word has a single vowel (not including the "u" in *qu*) and ends with one consonant.

- DO NOT DOUBLE THE FINAL CONSONANT before adding a suffix if the word has two vowels before the final consonant (not including the "u" in *qu*) or ends with two consonants.

DOUBLE THE FINAL CONSONANT

-er	-er, -est	-y	-en	-ing	-ed
blotter	biggest	baggy	bitten	budding	nodded
chopper	dimmer	blurry	fatten	clipping	plotted
clipper	fattest	funny	flatten	dropping	rubbed
fitter	flatter	furry	gladden	fanning	scarred
hopper	gladdest	muddy	hidden	fretting	skinned
plotter	grimmer	sloppy	madden	grinning	stabbed
quitter	hottest	starry	sadden	gripping	stepped
shipper	madder	stubby		hopping	stopped
shopper	reddest	sunny		quitting	tanned

DO NOT DOUBLE THE FINAL CONSONANT

-ing, -ed, -er	-ly	-ness	-ful	-y
acting	badly	baseness	boastful	dirty
burned	dimly	bigness	fitful	dusky
cooker	gladly	coldness	fretful	fishy
climber	madly	dimness	masterful	frosty
coasting	manly	fatness	sinful	leafy
farmer	nearly	grimness		misty
feared	sadly	redness		rainy
feasting	thinly	sadness		soapy
quoted	trimly	wetness		weedy

Rule 2

If a word has more than one syllable,

- DOUBLE THE FINAL CONSONANT before adding a suffix that begins with a vowel IF the accent is on the last syllable.

- DO NOT DOUBLE THE FINAL CONSONANT if the accent is not on the last syllable or the suffix begins with a consonant.

DOUBLE THE FINAL CONSONANT

-ing, -ed	-ence, -ent	-ance	-al
befitting	abhorrence	acquittance	acquittal
befogged	concurrent	admittance	transmittal
committing	excellence	remittance	noncommittal
compelled	intermittent	transmittance	
controlling	occurrence		
disbarred	recurrent		
impelling			
incurred			

-ing, -ed	-er	-en	-able
omitting			
permitted			
propelling	beginner	forbidden	controllable
regretted	propeller	forgotten	forgettable
submitting	transmitter		regrettable

DO NOT DOUBLE THE FINAL CONSONANT

Accent Not on the Final Syllable	Suffix Begins with a Consonant
-ing, -ed	-ment
benefiting	allotment
blossomed	annulment
differed	commitment
gathered	deferment
limiting	equipment
profited	interment
quarreling	preferment
soliciting	
summoned	

EXCEPTIONS

programmed	programming	handicapped	backlogged

Rule 3

If a word ends with a silent *e*,

- DROP THE *E* before adding a suffix that begins with a vowel.

- DO NOT DROP THE *E* before a suffix that begins with a consonant.

DROP THE SILENT *E*

-ing, -ed	-able	-ation	-ive
achieving	believable	admiration	abusive
balanced	debatable	continuation	appreciative
believing	desirable	declaration	creative
capsized	endurable	derivation	decorative
relieved	excitable	duplication	expensive
revolving	imaginable	exhalation	exclusive
telephoned	measurable	inclination	illustrative
trembled	observable	inhalation	intensive
trembling	pleasurable	quotation	repulsive

DO NOT DROP THE SILENT *E*

-ful	-ment	-ly	-ness
careful	achievement	accurately	completeness
disgraceful	amusement	affectionately	cuteness
distasteful	announcement	bravely	fineness
fateful	engagement	extremely	genuineness
hopeful	enlargement	genuinely	lameness
prideful	enslavement	immediately	lateness
tasteful	entanglement	intensely	likeness
vengeful	management	intimately	ripeness
wasteful	replacement	sincerely	wideness

EXCEPTIONS

acknowledgment	changeable	judgment	peaceable
acreage	chargeable	manageable	pronounceable
advantageous	dyeing	noticeable	replaceable
argument	exchanging	outrageous	serviceable

Rule 4

To make a word plural,

- ADD -*ES* to words ending in *s*, *x*, *z*, *ch*, or *sh*.

- ADD -*S* to all other words.

ADD -*S*		ADD -*ES*	
advantages	croutons	annexes	fizzes
angles	distances	birches	hoaxes
beacons	effects	brushes	marshes
briquets	rings	caresses	witnesses
candles	coaches		

Rule 5

If a word ends with a *y* that has a vowel sound,

- CHANGE THE *Y* TO *I* if it is preceded by a consonant before adding any suffix except one that begins with the letter *i*.

- DO NOT CHANGE THE *Y* if it is preceded by another vowel or if the suffix begins with *i*.

CHANGE THE *Y* TO *I*

-er, -est, -ly, -ness	-ous	-ance, -ant	-able, -ful
craftier	ceremonious	alliance	beautiful
daintiest	harmonious	compliant	fanciful
healthier	industrious	defiant	justifiable
heavily	injurious	reliance	merciful
moldiness	luxurious		pitiable
moodiest	melodious		
murkiness	mysterious		
steadily	studious		
sleepiness	victorious		

DO NOT CHANGE THE *Y*   **EXCEPTIONS**

-ing	-ly, -ness	-ous
allying	dryly	beauteous
applying	dryness	bounteous
complying	shyly	duteous
defying	shyness	miscellaneous
fortifying	slyly	piteous
justifying	slyness	plenteous
pitying	spryly	
multiplying	wryly	
supplying		

Rule 6

Put *i* before *e*,

Except after *c*,

Or when sounded like *a*,

As in *neighbor* or *weigh*.

I before E	except after C	or sounds like A	EXCEPTIONS
achieve	conceit	deign	ancient
believe	conceive	eight	conscience
fiend	ceiling	freight	deficient
fierce	deceit	inveigh	efficient
grief	deceive	neighbor	foreign
relieve	perceive	reign	glacier
reprieve	receipt	skein	heifer
retrieve	receive	vein	leisure
sieve		weigh	proficient
			weird

Rule 7

The suffix *-ful* never has two *l*'s. When *-ful* is added to a word, the spelling of the base word does not change.

EXAMPLES

careful	disdainful	distasteful
forceful	grateful	hopeful
masterful	powerful	sorrowful

Rule 8

When the suffix *-ly* is added to a word, the spelling of the base word does not change.

EXAMPLES

coyly	frankly	swiftly
forcefully	quickly	

EXCEPTIONS

When *-ly* is added to a word ending with *le*, the *e* is replaced by a *y*.

despicably	forcibly	illegibly
indelibly	probably	suitably

When the base word ends with *y* following a consonant, the *y* is changed to *i* before *-ly*.

busily	daintily	heavily
luckily	merrily	sleepily

Rule 9

When a syllable ends in a long vowel sound, that sound is made by the vowel alone: *open syllable*.

A long vowel sound occurring in a one-syllable word, or in a syllable that ends with a consonant, is usually spelled by a vowel team: *closed syllable*.

Open Syllable	Closed Syllable
recent	sublime
premium	infantile
sequence	crayon
stationary	attainment
fatality	cavalcade
abrasion	genteel
motivate	intercede
custodian	sincere
component	ridicule
proprietor	vestibule
microbe	clapboard
cyclone	disclose
cucumber	telescope
humane	growth

320 FREQUENTLY MISSPELLED WORDS

A poor speller can, in almost every case, become an excellent speller with perseverance and practice. The first step in spelling improvement is to find out which words are troublesome for you. The list that follows contains some of the most frequently misspelled words. Ask a friend to dictate this list to you. Write each word as it is read to you, then compare what you have written with the printed list. Place an X next to each word that you spelled incorrectly (and next to each word that you spelled correctly but were not sure of). For every word you misspelled:

1 LOOK at the word carefully.

2 PRONOUNCE each syllable clearly.

3 PICTURE the word in your mind.

4 WRITE the word correctly at least three times.

Test yourself again—and again—until you have mastered this entire list.

A

a lot	adequate	analysis	arctic
ability	advantageous	analyze	argue
absence	advantage	ancestor	arguing
absent	advertise	angel	argument
across	advertisement	angle	arouse
abundance	advice	annual	arrange
accept	advisable	another	arrangement
acceptable	advise	answer	article
accident	advisor	antarctic	artificial
accidental	aerial	anticipate	ascend
accommodate	affect	antiseptic	asparagus
accompanied	affectionate	anxious	assistance
accomplish	again	apologize	assistant
accumulation	against	apparatus	associate
accurately	aggravate	apparent	association
accuse	aggressive	apparently	attempt
accustomed	agree	appear	attendance
ache	aisle	appearance	attention
achieve	all right	appetite	audience
achievement	almost	application	August
acknowledge	already	apply	author
acknowledgment	although	appreciate	automobile
acquaintance	altogether	appreciation	autumn
acquainted	always	approach	auxiliary
acquire	amateur	appropriate	available
across	American	approval	avenue
address	among	approve	awful
addressed	amount	approximate	awkward

B

bachelor	before	bicycle	breathe
balance	beggar	board	brilliant
balloon	beginning	bored	building
bankruptcy	begun	borrow	bulletin
bargain	being	bottle	bureau
barren	believe	bottom	burial
basic	benefit	boundary	buried
basically	benefited	brake	bury
beautiful	between	breadth	bushes
because	bewilder	breath	business
become			

C

cabinet	choose	competitor	controversy
cafeteria	chose	compliment	convenience
caffeine	cigarette	conceal	convenient
calculator	circumstance	conceit	conversation
calendar	congratulate	conceivable	corporal
campaign	citizen	conceive	corroborate
capital	clothes	concentration	council
capitol	clothing	conception	councilor
captain	coarse	condition	counsel
career	coffee	conference	counselor
careful	collect	confident	courage
careless	college	conquer	courageous
carriage	column	conscience	course
carrying	comedy	conscientious	courteous
category	comfortable	conscious	courtesy
ceiling	commitment	consequence	criticism
cemetery	committed	consequently	criticize
cereal	committee	considerable	crucial
certain	communicate	consistency	crystal
changeable	company	consistent	curiosity
characteristic	comparative	consul	curtain
charity	compel	continual	customer
chief	competent	continuous	cylinder
chimney	competition	controlled	

D

daily	dependent	device	disastrous
dairy	deposit	diary	discipline
daughter	derelict	dictator	discover
daybreak	descend	dictatorship	discriminate
dearth	descent	died	disease
death	descendant	difference	dismal
deceit	describe	different	dissatisfied
deceive	description	difficulty	dissection
December	desert	dilapidated	dissipate
deception	desirable	dilemma	distance
decide	despair	dinner	distinction
decision	desperate	direction	division
decisive	dessert	disappear	doctor
deed	destruction	disappoint	dollar
definite	determine	disappointment	doubt
delicious	develop	disapproval	dozen
demur	development	disapprove	dying

E

earnest	emergency	equipment	exhausted
easy	eminent	equipped	exhaustion
ecstasy	emphasis	especially	exhibition
ecstatic	emphasize	essential	exhilaration
education	enclosure	evening	existence
effect	encouraging	evident	exorbitant
efficiency	endeavor	exaggerate	expense
efficient	engineer	exaggeration	experience
eight	English	examine	experiment
either	enormous	exceed	explain
eligibility	enough	excellent	explanation
eligible	entrance	except	extraordinary
eliminate	envelope	exceptional	extension
embarrass	environment	exercise	extreme
embarrassment			

F

facility	fierce	forfeit	freight
factory	financial	formal	Friday
familiar	financier	former	friend
fascinate	flourish	fortunate	frightening
fascinating	forcibly	forward	fundamental
fatigue	forehead	fourteen	furniture
February	foreign	fourth	further
fiend	foreword	frequent	

G

gallon	ghost	grain	grievous
garden	glacier	grammar	grocery
gardener	glandular	grandeur	guarantee
gaseous	gnash	grateful	guard
general	government	great	guess
genius	governor	grievance	guidance
geography			

H

half	heathen	hideous	humorous
hallelujah	heavily	himself	hundredth
hammer	heavy	hoarse	hurried
handkerchief	height	holiday	hurrying
happiness	heretic	hopeless	hygiene
harassed	heroes	horrify	hymn
healthy	heroine	hospital	hypocrisy
heard			

I

ignorance	indispensable	instead	interruption
imaginary	inevitable	instinct	introduce
imbecile	influence	integrity	invitation
imitation	influential	intellectual	irrelevant
immediately	initiate	intelligence	irresistible
immigrant	innocence	intercede	irritable
incidental	inoculate	interest	island
increase	inquiry	interfere	its
incumbent	insistent	interference	it's
independence	instantaneous	interpreted	itself
independent			

J

January	jewelry	judgment	justice
jealous	journal	judicial	justification
jeopardy			

K

kernel	kilowatt	knee	knot
kiln	kindergarten	knew	know
kilometer	kitchen	knock	knowledge

L

labor	legible	lightening	loneliness
laboratory	leisure	lightning	loose
lacquer	length	likelihood	lose
laid	lesson	likely	losing
language	library	literal	lovable
later	license	literature	loyal
latter	lieutenant	livelihood	loyalty
laugh	light	loaf	

M

magazine	mathematics	mischief	moral
maintenance	measure	mischievous	morale
maneuver	medicine	misspell	mortgage
marriage	memoir	misspelled	mountain
married	million	mistake	mournful
marry	miniature	momentous	muscle
match	minimum	monkey	mysterious
material	miracle	monotonous	mystery
materialize	miscellaneous		

N

narrative	negligence	newspaper	niece
naturally	negligible	newsstand	ninth
necessary	neighbor	nickel	noticeable
needle	neither		

O

o'clock	occurred	omitted	origin
oasis	occurrence	once	original
obedient	ocean	operate	ornamental
obligatory	offer	opinion	oscillate
obsolescence	official	opportune	ought
obstacle	often	opportunity	ounce
occasion	omission	optimist	outrageous
occasional	omit	ordinance	overcoat
occur			

P

paid	perpendicular	positive	primitive
pamphlet	perseverance	possess	principal
panicky	persevere	possession	principle
parallel	persistent	possessive	privilege
parallelism	personality	possible	probably
particular	personal	post office	procedure
partner	personnel	potatoes	proceed
pastime	persuade	practical	produce
patience	persuasion	prairie	professional
peace	pertain	precede	professor
peaceable	physician	preceding	profitable
pear	picture	precise	prominent
peculiar	piece	predictable	promise
pencil	plain	prefer	pronounce
people	playwright	preference	pronunciation
perceive	pleasant	preferential	propaganda
perception	please	preferred	propellor
perfect	pleasure	prejudice	prophecy
perform	pocket	preparation	prophet
performance	poison	prepare	prospect
perhaps	policeman	prescription	psychology
period	political	presence	pursue
permanence	population	president	pursuit
permanent	portrayal	prevalent	

Q

quality	quart	quiet	quite
quantity	quarter	quintuple	quotient
quarreling			

R

raise	recuperate	repeat	respectability
realistic	reference	repetition	restaurant
realize	referred	repetitious	rhythm
reason	rehearsal	representative	rhythmical
rebellion	reign	requirements	ridiculous
recede	relevant	resemblance	right
receipt	relieve	reservoir	role
receive	religious	resistance	roll
recipe	remedy	resources	roommate
recognize	renovate	responsibility	routine
recommend			

S

sandwich	shepherd	source	substantial
Saturday	sheriff	souvenir	succeed
scarcely	shining	special	successful
scene	shoulder	specified	sudden
scenery	shriek	specimen	sufficient
schedule	siege	speech	superintendent
science	sight	stationary	suppress
scientific	signal	stationery	surely
scissors	significance	statue	surgical
season	significant	statute	surprise
secretary	similar	stockings	suspense
seize	similarity	stomach	sweat
seizure	sincerely	straight	sweet
seminar	site	strength	syllable
sense	soldier	strenuous	symmetrical
separate	solemn	stretch	sympathetic
service	sophomore	striking	sympathy
several	soul	studying	synonym
severely			

T

technical	therefore	toward	truculent
telegram	thorough	tragedy	truly
telephone	through	transferred	Tuesday
temperament	title	transient	twelfth
temperature	together	treasury	twelve
tenant	tomorrow	tremendous	typical
tendency	tongue	tries	tyranny
tenement			

U

umbrella	United States	unusual	useful
undoubtedly	university	usage	usual
unique	unnecessary		

V

vacuum	veil	vicinity	villain
valley	vein	vicious	visitor
valuable	vengeance	view	voice
variety	versatile	village	volume
vegetable			

W

waist	week	which	whose
weak	weigh	while	wield
wear	weight	whole	wouldn't
weather	weird	wholesome	wretched
Wednesday	whether	wholly	written

X-Y-Z

xylophone	yacht	zombie
	yield	

PUNCTUATION AND CAPITALIZATION

Without punctuation, writing would be merely a jumble of words, difficult if not impossible to understand and open to all sorts of misinterpretation. Punctuation and capitalization are like signs along an unfamiliar road. They indicate when to stop, when to go, and when to slow down for a detour or a curve. You can master the mechanics of punctuation and capitalization by learning the simple rules that follow.

Punctuation Rules

USE AN APOSTROPHE (')

To indicate possession

Bob's hat; Alan's poems

Note: Use *apostrophe only* (without the *s*) for certain words that end

in *s*:

- When *s* or *z* sound comes before the final *s*
  Moses' journey
  Cassius' plan

- After a plural noun
  girls' shoes
  horses' reins

Where to place the apostrophe

- The apostrophe means *belonging to everything to the* left *of the apostrophe.*
  These (ladie's, ladies') blouses are on sale.
  ladie's means *belonging to ladie* (no such word)
  ladies' means *belonging to ladies* (this is correct)
  These (childrens', children's) coats are a good buy.
  childrens' means *belonging to childrens* (no such word)
  children's means *belonging to children* (this is correct)

- When one firm comprises two or more names, possession is indicated in the last name.
  Lansdale, Jackson, and Roosevelt's law firm
  Sacks and Company's sale

- In a compound noun separated by hyphens, the apostrophe belongs in the last syllable.
  father-in-law's
    Note: The plurals of compound nouns are formed by adding the *s*
    (no apostrophe, of course) to the *first* syllable: I have three *brothers-in-law*.

For plurals of letters and figures
  three *d*'s; five 6's

To show that a letter has been left out
   let's (for let us)
     Note A: ours, yours, his, hers, its, theirs, and whose are possessive but
     have no apostrophe.
     Note B: The apostrophe is omitted occasionally in titles: Teachers College,
     Actors Equity Association.

USE A COLON (:)

After such expressions as "the following," "as follows," and their equivalents
   The sciences studied in high schools are as follows: biology, chemistry, and physics.

After the salutation in a business letter
   Gentlemen:
   Dear Mr. Jones:
     Note: A comma (see below) is used after the salutation in a friendly letter:
   Dear Ted,

Between the figures for hours and minutes when expressing time
   We set the alarm for 6:15, but we did not get up until 9:30.

USE A COMMA (,)

To set off the name of the person being addressed
   Mr. Adams, has the report come in yet?
   Are you sure, Betty, that this is the street?

To set off appositives—words that follow a noun or pronoun and mean the same as the noun or pronoun.
   Mr. Burke, our lawyer, gave us some good advice.

To set off parenthetical expressions—words that interrupt the flow of the sentence, such as *however, though, for instance, by the way.* If you would pause before and after saying such expressions, then they should be set off by commas.
   We could not, however, get him to agree.
   This book, I believe, is the best of its kind.

After the closing of a letter
   Sincerely,
   Truly yours,

In dates and addresses
   November 11, 1918
   Cleveland, Ohio

Between the items in a series
   We had soup, salad, ice cream, and milk for lunch.
     Note: You may omit the comma before the "and" in a series.

After a phrase or clause at the beginning of a sentence (if the phrase or clause is long)
   As I ran from the house on my way to work, my mother called me back to hand me my umbrella.

To separate clauses in a long sentence
We traveled miles out of our way to visit Aunt Mary, but she was not at home when we arrived.

To separate two words or figures that might otherwise be misunderstood.
Two weeks before, Jim had applied for a part-time job.
On January 10, 23 workers were absent.

Before a direct quotation
Mr. Arnold blurted out, "This is a fine mess!"

To set off nonessential phrases and clauses—phrases or clauses that do not restrict the meaning of the thought that is modified
Air travel, *which may or may not be safe*, is an essential part of our way of life. (Nonessential clause—needs commas)
Travel *that is on the ground* is safer than air travel. (Essential clause—no commas)

To set off adjectives that follow the nouns they modify
The dog, frightened and hungry, ran home.

To set off contrasting expressions that start with not *or* though
The girls, not the boys, started the fight.
That car, though too expensive for me, is a very good buy.

To set off introductory expressions such as yes, no, well, *and* why
No, I don't like asparagus.
Well, have you decided which one to buy?

USE A DASH (—)

To break up a thought
There are five—remember I said five—good reasons to refuse their demands.

Instead of parentheses
A beautiful horse—Black Beauty is its name—is the hero of the book.

USE AN EXCLAMATION MARK (!)

After an expression of strong feeling
Ouch! I hurt my thumb.

USE A HYPHEN (-)

To divide a word
mother-in-law
Note: When written out, numbers from twenty-one through ninety-nine are hyphenated.

USE PARENTHESES ( )

To set off that part of the sentence that is not absolutely necessary to the completeness of the sentence
I was about to remark (this may be repetition) that we must arrive there early.

To enclose figures, letters, signs, and dates in a sentence
Shakespeare (1564–1616) was a great dramatist.
The four forms of discourse are (a) narration, (b) description, (c) exposition, (d) argument.

USE A PERIOD (.)

After a complete sentence
The section manager will return shortly.

After an abbreviation
Los Angeles, Calif.
Dr. James E. Brown

USE A QUESTION MARK (?)

After a request for information
When do you leave for lunch?

USE QUOTATION MARKS ("")

To enclose what a person says directly
"No one could tell," she said, "that it would occur."
He exclaimed, "This is the end!"

To enclose the title of a short story, essay, short poem, song, or article (but not a book or play)
The song "Tradition" is from *Fiddler on the Roof*.

USE A SEMICOLON (;)

To avoid confusion with numbers
Add the following: $1.25; $7.50; and $12.89.

Before explanatory words or abbreviations—namely, e.g., etc.
We are able to supply you with two different types of paper; namely, lined and unlined.
    Note: The semicolon goes before the expression "namely." A comma follows the expression.

To separate short statements of contrast
War is destructive; peace is constructive.

Capitalization Rules

Capitalize the first word of a sentence.
With cooperation, a depression can be avoided.

Capitalize all proper names.
America, General Motors, Abraham Lincoln, First Congregational Church

Capitalize days of the week, months of the year, and holidays.
The check was mailed on Thursday, the day before Christmas.

Note: The seasons are not capitalized.
In Florida, winter is mild.

Capitalize the first word and all nouns in the salutation of a letter.
Dear Mr. Jones:
(*but*—My dear Mr. Jones:)

Capitalize the first word of the complimentary close of a letter.
Truly yours,
(*but*—Very truly yours,)

Capitalize the first and all other important words in a title.
The Art of Salesmanship

Capitalize a word used as part of a proper name.
William Street (*but*—That street is narrow.)
Morningside Terrace (*but*—We have a terrace apartment.)

Capitalize titles when they refer to a particular official or family member
The report was read by Secretary Marshall.
(*but*—Miss Shaw, our secretary, is ill.)
Let's visit Uncle Harry.
(*but*—I have three uncles.)

Capitalize points of a compass when they refer to particular regions of a country.
We're going South next week. (*but*—New York is south of Albany.)
　Note: Write: the Far West, the Pacific Coast, the Middle East, etc.

Capitalize the first word of a direct quotation.
It was Alexander Pope who wrote, "A little learning is a dangerous thing."
　Note: When a direct quotation sentence is broken, the *first* word of the *second half* of the sentence is not capitalized.
"Don't phone," Lilly told me, "because it will be too late."

THE ESSENTIALS OF ENGLISH GRAMMAR

Parts of Speech

A **noun** is the name of a person, place, thing, or idea:

| teacher | city | desk | democracy |

Pronouns substitute for nouns:

| he | they | ours | those |

An **adjective** describes a noun:

| warm | quick | tall | blue |

A **verb** expresses action or state of being:

| yell | interpret | feel | are |

An **adverb** modifies a verb, an adjective, or another adverb:

| fast | slowly | friendly | well |

Conjunctions join words, sentences, and phrases:

and   but   or

A **preposition** shows position in time or space:

in   during   after   behind

NOUNS

There are different kinds of nouns.

Common nouns are general:

house   girl   street   city

Proper nouns are specific:

White House   Jane   Main Street   New York

Collective nouns name groups:

team   crowd   organization   Congress

Nouns have *cases*:

   Nominative—the subject, noun of address, or predicate noun

   Objective—the direct object, indirect object, or object of the preposition

   Possessive—the form that shows possession

PRONOUNS

Antecedent of the pronoun—the noun to which a pronoun refers. A pronoun must agree with its antecedent in gender, person, and number.

There are several kinds of pronouns. (Pronouns also have cases.)

   Demonstrative pronouns: this, that, these, those

   Indefinite pronouns: all, any, nobody

   Interrogative pronouns: who, which, what

Personal pronouns:

		Nominative Case	Objective Case	Possessive Case
Singular	1st person	I	me	mine
	2nd person	you	you	yours
	3rd person	he, she, it	him, her, it	his, hers
Plural	1st person	we	us	ours
	2nd person	you	you	yours
	3rd person	they	them	theirs

ADJECTIVES

Adjectives answer the questions "Which one?", "What kind?", and "How many?"

   There are three uses of adjectives:

A **noun modifier** is usually placed directly before the noun it describes:

   He is a *tall* man.

A **predicate adjective** follows an inactive verb and modifies the subject:

> He is *happy*. I feel *terrible*.

An **article** or **noun marker** are other names for these adjectives: *the, a, an*

ADVERBS

Adverbs answer the questions "Why?", "How?", "Where?", "When?", and "To what degree?"

> Adverbs should not be used to modify nouns.

Grammar Rules

1 The subject of a verb is in the nominative case even if the verb is understood and not expressed.
> They are as old as *we*. (As we are.)

2 The word *who* is in the nominative case. *Whom* is in the objective case.
> The trapeze artist who ran away with the clown broke the lion tamer's heart.
> (*Who* is the subject of the verb *ran*.)
> The trapeze artist whom he loved ran away with the circus clown.
> (*Whom* is the object of the verb *loved*.)

3 The word *whoever* is in the nominative ease. *Whomever* is in the objective case.
> Whoever comes to the door is welcome to join the party.
> (*Whoever* is the subject of the verb *comes*.)
> Invite whomever you wish to accompany you.
> (*Whomever* is the object of the verb *invite*.)

4 Nouns or pronouns connected by a form of the verb *to be* should always be in the nominative case.
> It is I. (Not me!)

5 The object of a preposition or of a transitive verb should use a pronoun in the objective case.
> It would be impossible for you and *me* to do that job alone.
> (Use *me*, not *I*, because it is an object of the preposition *for*.)
> The attendant gave Tom and me keys to the locker.
> (Use *me*, not *I*, because it is an object of the verb *gave*.)

6 Do not use the possessive case when referring to an inanimate object.
> He had difficulty with the management of the store.
> (Not—He had difficulty with the *store's* management.)

7 A pronoun agrees with its antecedent in person, number, gender, and case.
> Since you were absent on Tuesday, you will have to ask Mary or Beth for her notes on the lecture.
> (Use *her*, not *their*, because two singular antecedents joined by *or* take a singular pronoun.)

8 A noun or pronoun modifying a gerund should be in the possessive case.

 Is there any criticism of Arthur's going?

 (*Going* is a gerund. Therefore, it must be modified by *Arthur's*, not by Arthur.)

9 *Each, every, everyone, everybody, anybody, either, neither, no one, nobody,* and similar words are singular and require the use of singular verbs and pronouns.

 Each of the men in this class hopes to earn his high school diploma.

 (Use the singular verb form *hopes* and the singular pronoun *his* to agree with the singular subject *each*.)

 Neither of the women has completed her assignment.

 (Use the singular verb form *has completed* and the singular pronoun *her* to agree with the singular subject *neither*.)

10 When modifying the words *kind* and *sort* the words *this* and *that* always remain in the singular.

 This kind of apple makes the best pie.

 That sort of behavior will result in severe punishment.

11 The word *don't* is never used with third-person singular pronouns or nouns.

 She doesn't like classical music.

 It doesn't matter to me.

 (Not—*She don't* or *It don't.*)

12 A verb agrees in number with its subject. A verb should not be made to agree with a noun that is part of a phrase following the subject.

 Mount Snow, one of my favorite ski areas, is in Vermont.

 (The singular subject *Mount Snow* takes the singular verb *is*.)

 The mountains of Colorado, like those of Switzerland, offer excellent skiing.

 (The plural subject *mountains* takes the plural verb *offer*.)

13 The number of the verb is not affected by the addition to the subject of words introduced by *with, together with, no less than, as well as,* etc.

 The captain, together with the rest of the team, was delighted by the victory celebration.

 (The addition of the phrase *together with the rest of the team* does not change the fact that the subject of this sentence is the singular noun *captain,* which requires the singular verb form *was delighted*.)

14 Singular subjects joined by the words *nor* and *or* take a singular verb.

 Neither Adam nor Alex is able to come.

 Either Eric or Mark has the key.

15 A subject consisting of two or more nouns joined by the word *and* takes a plural verb.

 Paul and Sue were the last to arrive.

16 A verb should agree in number with the subject, not with the predicate noun or pronoun.

 Poor study habits are the leading cause of unsatisfactory achievement in school.

 (The plural subject *habits* takes the plural verb *are*.)

The leading cause of unsatisfactory achievement in school is poor study habits.

(The singular subject *cause* takes the singular verb *is*.)

17 In sentences beginning with *there is* and *there are*, the verb should agree in number with the noun that follows it.

There isn't an unbroken bone in her body.

(The singular subject *bone* takes the singular verb *is*.)

There are many choices to be made.

(The plural subject *choices* takes the plural verb *are*.)

18 An adjective should not be used to modify a verb.

He spoke slowly and carefully.

(Not—He spoke *slow* and *careful*.)

19 Statements equally true in the past and in the present are usually expressed in the present tense.

He said that Venus is a planet.

(Not—He said that Venus *was* a planet.)

20 The word *were* is used to express a condition contrary to fact or a wish.

I wish I were a movie star.

(Not—I wish I *was* a movie star.)

CORRECT ENGLISH USAGE

The ability to choose and use the right word is an important part of the GED Language Arts, Writing Test. The list that follows presents some of the most commonly misused words in the English language. Study it well and you will be rewarded with higher test scores.

accede—means to *agree with*.

concede—means *to yield*, but not necessarily in agreement.

exceed—means to *be more than*.
We shall *accede* to your request for more evidence.
To avoid delay, we shall *concede* that more evidence is necessary.
Federal expenditures now *exceed* federal income.

accept—means *to take when offered*.

except—means *excluding*. (preposition)

except—means *to leave out*. (verb)
The draft board will *accept* all seniors as volunteers before graduation.
All 18-year-olds *except* seniors will be called.
The draft board will *except* all seniors until after graduation.

access—means *availability*.

excess—means *too much*.
The lawyer was given *access* to the grand jury records.
The expenditures this month are far in *excess* of income.

adapt—means *to adjust to change*.

adopt—means *to take as one's own*.

adept—means *skillful*.
Children can *adapt* to changing conditions very easily.
The war orphan was *adopted* by the general and his wife.
Proper instruction makes children *adept* in various games.
NOTE: adapt *to*, adopt *by*, adept *in* or *at*.

adapted to—implies *original or natural suitability*.
The gills of the fish are *adapted to* underwater breathing.

adapted for—implies *created suitability*.
Atomic energy is constantly being *adapted for* new uses.

adapted from—implies *changes to be made suitable*.
Many of Richard Wagner's opera librettos were *adapted from* old Norse sagas.

addition—means *the act or process of adding*.

edition—means *a printing of a publication*.
In *addition* to a dictionary, he always used a thesaurus.
The first *edition* of Shakespeare's play appeared in 1623.

advantage—means a *superior position*.

benefit—means *a favor conferred* or *earned* (as a profit).
He had an *advantage* in experience over his opponent.
The rules were changed for his *benefit*.
NOTE: to *take* advantage *of*, to *have* an advantage *over*.

adverse—(AD-verse) means *unfavorable*.

averse—(a-VERSE) means *disliking*.
He took the *adverse* decision in poor taste.
Many students are *averse* to criticism by their classmates.

advise—means *to give advice.*
Advise is losing favor as a synonym for notify.
> *Acceptable:* The teacher will *advise* the student in habits of study.
> *Unacceptable:* We are *advising* you of a delivery under separate cover. (SAY: *notifying*)

affect—means *to influence.* (verb)

effect—means *an influence.* (noun)

effect—means *to bring about.* (verb)
> Your education must *affect* your future.
> The *effect* of the last war is still being felt.
> A diploma *effected* a tremendous change in his attitude.
> NOTE: *Affect* also has a meaning of *pretend.*
> She had an *affected* manner.

after—is unnecessary with the *past* participle.
> SAY: *After* checking the timetable, I left for the station.
> DON'T SAY: *After having checked* (omit *after*) the timetable, I left for the station.

ain't—is an *unacceptable* contraction for *am not, are not,* or *is not.*

aisle—is a *passageway* between seats.

isle—is a *small island.* (Both words rhyme with *pile.*)
> The bride walked down the *aisle.*
> They went on vacation to the *isle* of Bahamas.

all ready—means *everybody* or *everything ready.*

already—means *previously.*
> They were *all ready* to write when the teacher arrived.
> They had *already* begun writing when the teacher arrived.

alright—is *unacceptable.*

all right—is *acceptable.*

all together—means *everybody or everything together.*

altogether—means *completely.*
> The boys and girls sang *all together.*
> This was *altogether* strange for a person of his type.

all ways—means *in every possible way.*

always—means *at all times.*
> He was in *all ways* acceptable to the voters.
> His reputation had *always* been spotless.

allude—means *to make a reference to.*

elude—means *to escape from.*
> Only incidentally does Coleridge *allude* to Shakespeare's puns.
> It is almost impossible for one to *elude* tax collectors.

allusion—means *a reference.*

illusion—means *a deception of the eye or mind.*
> The student made *allusions* to his teacher's habits.
> *Illusions* of the mind, unlike those of the eye, cannot be corrected with glasses.

alongside of—means *side by side with.*
> Bill stood *alongside* of Henry.

alongside—means *parallel to the side.*
> Park the car *alongside* the curb.

alot—is *unacceptable.* It is two words: *a lot.*

among—is used with *more than two persons or things.*
> NOTE: *Amongst* should be avoided.

between—is used with *two persons or things.*
> The inheritance was equally divided *among* the four children.
> The business, however, was divided *between* the oldest and the youngest one.

amount—applies to quantities *that cannot be counted one by one.*

number—applies to quantities *that can be counted one by one.*

A large *amount* of grain was delivered to the storehouse.

A large *number* of bags of grain was delivered.

annual—means *yearly.*

biannual—means *twice a year. (Semiannual* means the same.)

biennial—means *once in two years* or *every two years.*

anywheres—is *unacceptable.*

anywhere—is *acceptable.*

SAY: We can't find it *anywhere.*

ALSO SAY: *nowhere* (NOT nowheres), *somewhere* (NOT somewheres)

aren't I—is colloquial. Its use is to be discouraged.

SAY: *Am I not* entitled to an explanation?

(preferred to *Aren't I* . . .)

as—(used as a conjunction) is followed by a verb.

like—(used as a preposition) is NOT followed by a verb.

Do *as* I do, not *as* I say.

Try not to behave *like* a child.

Unacceptable: He acts *like* I do.

as far as—expresses distance.

so far as—indicates a *limitation.*

We hiked *as far as* the next guest house.

So far as we know, the barn was adequate for a night's stay.

as good as—should be used *for comparisons only.*

This motel is *as good as* the next one.

NOTE: *As good as* does NOT mean *practically.*

Unacceptable: They *as good as* promised us a place in the hall.

Acceptable: They *practically* promised us a place in the hall.

as if—is correctly used in the expression, "He talked *as if* his jaw hurt him."

Unacceptable: He talked *like* his jaw hurt him.

ascared—no such word. It is *unacceptable* for *scared.*

The child was *scared* of ghosts. (NOT *ascared.*)

ascent—is *the act of rising.*

assent—means *approval.*

The *ascent* to the top of the mountain was perilous.

Congress gave its *assent* to the President's emergency directive.

assay—means *to try or experiment.* (verb)

essay—means *an intellectual effort.* (noun)

We shall *assay* the ascent of the mountain tomorrow.

The candidate's views were expressed in a well-written *essay.*

attend to—means *to take care of.*

tend to—means *to be inclined to.*

One of the clerks *will attend to* mail in my absence.

Older people *tend to* gain weight.

back—should NOT be used with such words as *refer* and *return* since the prefix *re-* means *back.*

Unacceptable: Refer *back* to the text if you have difficulty recalling the facts.

backward/backwards—Both are *acceptable* and may be used interchangeably as an adverb.

We tried to run *backward.* (or *backwards*)

Backward as an adjective means *slow in learning.* (DON'T say *backwards* in this case)

A *backward* pupil should be given every encouragement.

berth—is *a resting place*.

birth—means *the beginning of life*.

> The new liner was given a wide *berth* in the harbor.
>
> He was a fortunate man from *birth*.

beside—means *close to*.

besides—refers *to something that has been added*.

> He lived *beside* the stream.
>
> He found wild flowers and weeds *besides*.

better—means *recovering*.

well—means *completely recovered*.

> He is *better* now than he was a week ago.
>
> In a few more weeks, he will be *well*.

both—means *two considered together*.

each—means *one of two or more*.

> *Both* of the applicants qualified for the position.
>
> *Each* applicant was given a generous reference.
>
> NOTE: Avoid using these expressions:
>
> *Both* girls had a new typewriter. (Use *each girl* instead.)
>
> *Both* girls tried to outdo the other. (Use *each girl* instead).
>
> They are *both* alike (Omit *both*).

breath—means *an intake of air*.

breathe—means *to draw air in and give it out*.

breadth—means *width*.

> Before you dive in, take a very deep *breath*.
>
> It is difficult to *breathe* under water.
>
> In a square, the *breadth* should be equal to the length.

bring—means *to carry toward the person who is speaking*.

take—means *to carry away from the speaker*.

> *Bring* the books here.
>
> *Take* your raincoat with you when you go out.

broke—is the past tense of *break*.

broke—is *unacceptable* for *without money*.

> He *broke* his arm.
>
> "Go for *broke*" is a slang expression widely used in gambling circles.

bunch—refers to *things*.

group—refers to *persons* or *things*.

> This looks like a delicious *bunch* of bananas.
>
> What a well-behaved *group* of children!
>
> NOTE: The colloquial use of bunch applied to *persons* is to be discouraged.
>
> A *bunch* of the boys were whooping it up. (*Number* is preferable.)

certainly—(and *surely*) is an *adverb*.

sure—is an *adjective*.

> He was *certainly* learning fast.
>
> *Unacceptable:* He *sure* was learning fast.

cite—means *to quote*.

sight—means *seeing*.

site—means *a place for a building*.

> He was fond of *citing* from the Scriptures.
>
> The *sight* of the wreck was appalling.
>
> The Board of Education is seeking a *site* for the new school.

coarse—means *vulgar* or *harsh*.

course—means *a path* or *a study*.

> He was shunned because of his *coarse* behavior.
>
> The ship took its usual *course*.
>
> Which *course* in English are you taking?

come to be—should NOT be replaced with the expression *become to be*, since *become* means *come to be*.

> True freedom will *come to be* when all tyrants have been overthrown.

comic—means *intentionally funny*.

comical—means *unintentionally funny*.
   A clown is a *comic* figure.
   The peculiar hat she wore gave her a *comical* appearance.

conscience—means *sense of right*.

conscientious—means *faithful*.

conscious—means *aware of one's self*.
   Man's *conscience* prevents him from becoming completely selfish.
   We all depend on him because he is *conscientious*.
   The injured man was completely *conscious*.

considerable—is properly used only as an *adjective*, NOT as a noun.
   He spent a *considerable* amount of time studing for the Spanish test.

cease—means *to end*.

seize—means *to take hold of*.
   Will you please *cease* making those sounds?
   Seize him by the collar as he comes around the corner.

cent—means *a coin*.

scent—means *an odor*.

sent—is the past tense of *send*.
   The one-*cent* postal card is a thing of the past.
   The *scent* of roses is pleasing.
   We were *sent* to the rear of the balcony.

calendar—is a *system of time*.

calender—is a *smoothing and glazing machine*.

colander—is a *kind of sieve*.
   In this part of the world, most people prefer the twelve-month *calendar*.
   In ceramic work, the potting wheel and the *calender* are indispensable.
   Garden-picked vegetables should be washed in a *colander* before cooking.

can—means *physically able*.

may—implies *permission*.
   I *can* lift this chair over my head.
   You *may* leave after you finish your work.

cannot help—must be followed by an *-ing* form.
   We *cannot help feeling* (*NOT feel*) distressed about this.
   NOTE: *Cannot help but* is *unacceptable*.

can't hardly—is a *double negative*. It is *unacceptable*.
   SAY: The child *can hardly* walk in those shoes.

capital—is *the city*.

capitol—is *the building*.
   Paris is the *capital* of France.
   The *Capitol* in Washington is occupied by the Congress. (The Washington *Capitol* is capitalized.)
   NOTE: *Capital* also means wealth.

compare to—means *to liken to something that has a different form*.

compare with—means *to compare persons or things with each other when they are of the same kind*.

contrast with—means *to show the difference between two things*.
   A minister is sometimes *compared to* a shepherd.
   Shakespeare's plays are often *compared with* those of Marlowe.
   The writer *contrasted* the sensitivity of the dancer *with* the grossness of the pugilist.

complement—means *a completing part*.

compliment—is *an expression of admiration*.
   His wit was a *complement* to her beauty.
   He *complimented* her attractive hairstyle.

consul—means *a government representative.*

council—means *an assembly that meets for deliberation.*

counsel—means *advice.*

> Americans abroad should keep in touch with their *consuls.*
> The City *Council* enacts local laws and regulations.
> The defendant heeded the *counsel* of his friends.

convenient to—should be followed by a *person.*

convenient for—should be followed by a *purpose.*

> Will these plans be *convenient to* you?
> You must agree that they are *convenient for* the occasion.

copy—is *an imitation of an original work.* (not necessarily an exact imitation)

facsimile—is *an exact imitation of an original work.*

> The counterfeiters made a crude *copy* of the hundred-dollar bill.
> The official government engraver, however, prepared a *facsimile* of the bill.

could of—is *unacceptable.* (*Should of* is also *unacceptable.*)

could have—is *acceptable.* (*Should have* is *acceptable.*)

> *Acceptable:* You *could have* done better with more care.
> *Unacceptable:* I *could of* won.
> ALSO AVOID: *must of, would of.*

decent—means *suitable.*

descent—means *going down.*

dissent—means *disagreement.*

> The *decent* thing to do is to admit your fault.
> The *descent* into the cave was treacherous.
> Two of the nine justices filed a *dissenting* opinion.

deduction—means *reasoning from the general (laws or principles) to the particular (facts).*

induction—means *reasoning from the particular (facts) to the general (laws or principles).*

> All men are mortal. Since John is a man, he is mortal. (*deduction*)
> There are 10,000 oranges in this truckload. I have examined 100 from various parts of the load and find them all of the same quality. I conclude that the 10,000 oranges are of this quality. (*induction*)

delusion—means *a wrong idea* that will probably influence action.

illusion—means *a wrong idea* that will probably *not* influence action.

> People were under the *delusion* that the earth was flat.
> It is just an *illusion* that the earth is flat.

desert—(pronounced DEZZ-ert) means *an arid area.*

desert—(pronounced di-ZERT) means *to abandon;* also *a reward or punishment.*

dessert—(pronounced di-ZERT) means *the final course of a meal.*

> The Sahara is the world's most famous *desert.*
> A husband must not *desert* his wife.
> Execution was a just *desert* for his crime.
> We had chocolate cake for *dessert.*

different from—is *acceptable.*

different than—is *unacceptable.*

> *Acceptable:* Jack is *different from* his brother.
> *Unacceptable:* Florida's climate is *different than* New York's climate.

doubt that—is *acceptable.*

doubt whether—is *unacceptable.*

> *Acceptable:* I *doubt that* you will pass this term.
> *Unacceptable:* We *doubt whether* you will succeed.

dual—means *relating to two*.

duel—means *a contest between two persons*.

> Dr. Jekyl had a *dual* personality.
> Alexander Hamilton was fatally injured in a *duel* with Aaron Burr.

due to—is *unacceptable* at the beginning of a sentence. Use *because of, on account of*, or some similar expression instead.

> *Unacceptable: Due to* the rain, the game was postponed.
> *Acceptable: Because of* the rain, the game was postponed.
> *Acceptable:* The postponement was *due to* the rain.

each other—refers to *two persons*.

one another—refers to *more than two persons*.

> The two girls have known *each other* for many years.
> Several of the girls have known *one another* for many years.

either . . . or—is used when referring to choices.

neither . . . nor—is the *negative form*.

> *Either* you *or* I will win the election.
> *Neither* Bill *nor* Henry is expected to have a chance.

eliminate—means *to get rid of*.

illuminate—means *to supply with light*.

> Let us try to *eliminate* the unnecessary steps.
> Several lamps were needed to *illuminate* the corridor.

emerge—means *to rise out of*.

immerge—means *to sink into* (also immerse).

> The swimmer *emerged* from the pool.
> The laundress *immerged* the dress in the tub of water.

emigrate—means *to leave one's country for another*.

immigrate—means *to enter another country*.

> Many Norwegians *emigrated* from their homeland to America in the mid-1860s.
> Today government restrictions make it more difficult for foreigners to *immigrate* to this country.

everyone—is written as one word when it is a *pronoun*.

every one—(two words) is used when each individual is stressed.

> *Everyone* present voted for the proposal.
> *Every one* of the voters accepted the proposal.
> NOTE: *Everybody* is written as one word.

everywheres—is *unacceptable*.

everywhere—is *acceptable*.

> We searched *everywhere* for the missing book.

feel bad—means *to feel ill*.

feel badly—means *to have a poor sense of touch*.

> I *feel bad* about the accident I saw.
> The numbness in his limbs caused him to *feel badly*.

feel good—means *to be happy*.

feel well—means *to be in good health*.

> I *feel* very *good* about my recent promotion.
> Spring weather always made him *feel well*.

flout—means *to insult*.

flaunt—means *to make a display of*.

> He *flouted* the authority of the principal.
> Hester Prynne *flaunted* her scarlet "A."

formally—means *in a formal way*.

formerly—means *at an earlier time*.
  The letter of reference was *formally* written.
  He was *formerly* a delegate to the convention.

former—means *the first of two*.

latter—means *the second of two*.
  The *former* half of the book was in prose.
  The *latter* half of the book was in poetry.

forth—means *forward*.

fourth—*comes after third*.
  They went *forth* like warriors of old.
  The *Fourth* of July is our Independence Day.
  NOTE: spelling of *forty* (40) and *fourteen* (14).

get—is a verb that strictly means *to obtain*.
  Please *get* my bag.
  There are many slang forms of GET that should be avoided:
  AVOID: Do you *get* me? (SAY: Do you *understand* me?)
  AVOID: We didn't *get* to go. (SAY: We didn't *manage* to go.)

got—means *obtained*.
  He *got* the tickets yesterday.
  AVOID: You've *got* to do it. (SAY: You *have* to do it.)
  AVOID: We *have got* no sympathy for them. (SAY: We *have* no sympathy for them.)

hanged—is used in reference to a *person*.

hung—is used in reference to a *thing*.
  The prisoner was *hanged* at dawn.
  The picture was *hung* above the fireplace.

however—means *nevertheless*.

how ever—means *in what possible way*.
  We are certain, *however*, that you will like this class.
  We are certain that, *how ever* you decide to study, you will succeed.

if—introduces a *condition*.

whether—introduces a *choice*.
  I shall go to Europe *if* I win the prize.
  He asked me *whether* I intended to go to Europe. (not *if*)

if it was—implies that *something might have been true in the past*.

if it were—implies *doubt*, or indicates *something that is contrary to fact*.
  If your book was there last night, it is there now.
  If it were summer now, we would all go swimming.

in—usually refers to *a state of being*. (no motion)

into—is used for *motion from one place to another*.
  The records are *in* that drawer.
  I put the records *into* that drawer.
  NOTE: "We were walking in the room" is correct even though there is motion. The motion is *not* from one place to another.

irregardless—is *unacceptable*.

regardless—is *acceptable*.
  Unacceptable: Irregardless of the weather, I am going to the game.
  Acceptable: Regardless of his ability, he is not likely to win.

its—means *belonging to it*.

it's—means *it is*.
  The house lost *its* roof.
  It's an exposed house, now.

kind of/sort of—are *unacceptable* for *rather*.
  SAY: We are *rather* disappointed in you.

last—refers to *the final member in a series*.

latest—refers to *the most recent in time*.

latter—refers to *the second of two*.
  This is the *last* bulletin. There won't be any other bulletins.
  This is the *latest* bulletin. There will be other bulletins.
  Of the two most recent bulletins, the *latter* is more encouraging.

lay—means *to place*.

lie—means *to recline*.
  Note the forms of each verb:

TENSE	LAY (PLACE)
Present	He *is laying* the book on the desk.
Past	He *laid* the book on the desk.
Pres. Perf.	He *has laid* the book on the desk.

TENSE	LIE (RECLINE)
Present	The child *is lying* down.
Past	The child *lay* down.
Pres. Perf.	The child *has lain* down.

lightening—is the present participle of *to lighten*.

lightning—means *the flashes of light accompanied by thunder*.
  Leaving the extra food behind resulted in *lightening* the pack.
  Summer thunderstorms produce startling *lightning* bolts.

many—refers to *a number*.

much—refers to *a quantity in bulk*.
  How *many* inches of rain fell last night?
  I don't know; but I would say *much* rain fell last night.

may—is used in the *present tense*.

might—is used in the *past tense*.
  We are hoping that he *may* come today.
  He *might* have come if you had encouraged him.

it's I—is always *acceptable*.

it's me—is *acceptable* only in colloquial speech or writing.

It's him This is her It was them	always *unacceptable*
It's he This is she It was they	*always acceptable*

noplace—as a solid word, is *unacceptable* for *no place* or *nowhere*.
  Acceptable: You now have *nowhere* to go.

number—is singular *when the total is intended*.
  The *number* (of pages in the book) is 500.

number—is plural *when the individual units are referred to*.
  A *number of pages* (in the book) were printed in italic type.

of any—(and *of anyone*) is *unacceptable* for *of all*.
  SAY: His was the highest mark *of all*. (NOT *of any* or *of anyone*)

off of—is *unacceptable*.
  SAY: He took the book *off* the table.

out loud—is *unacceptable* for *aloud*.
  SAY: He read *aloud* to his family every evening.

outdoor—(and *out-of-door*) is an adjective.

outdoors—is an adverb.
  We spent most of the summer at an *outdoor* music camp.
  Most of the time we played string quartets *outdoors*.
  NOTE: *Out-of-doors* is *acceptable* in either case.

people—*a united or collective group of individuals.*

persons—*separate and unrelated individuals.*

> The *people* of New York City have enthusiastically accepted "Shakespeare-in-the-Park."
>
> Only five *persons* remained in the theater after the first act.

persecute—means *to make life miserable for someone.* (Persecution is illegal.)

prosecute—means *to conduct a criminal investigation.* (Prosecution *is* legal.)

> Some groups insist upon *persecuting* other groups.
>
> The District Attorney is *prosecuting* the racketeers.

precede—means *to come before.*

proceed—means *to go ahead.* (*Procedure* is the noun.)

supersede—means *to replace.*

> What were the circumstances that *preceded* the attack?
>
> We can then *proceed* with our plan for resisting a second attack.
>
> It is then possible that Plan B will *supersede* Plan A.

principal—means *chief or main* (as an adjective); *a leader* (as a noun).

principle—means a *fundamental truth* or *belief.*

> His *principal* supporters came from among the peasants.
>
> The *principal* of the school asked for cooperation from the staff.
>
> Humility was the guiding *principle* of Buddha's life.
>
> NOTE: *Principal* may also mean *a sum placed at interest.*
>
> Part of his monthly payment was applied as interest on the *principal.*

sit—means *take a seat.* (intransitive verb)

set—means *place.* (transitive verb)

Note the forms of each verb:

TENSE	SIT (TAKE A SEAT)
Present	He *sits* on a chair.
Past	He *sat* on the chair.
Pres. Perf.	He *has sat* on the chair.

TENSE	SET (PLACE)
Present	He *sets* the lamp on the table.
Past	He *set* the lamp on the table.
Pres. Perf.	He *has set* the lamp on the table.

some time—means *a portion of time.*

sometime—means *at an indefinite time in the future.*

sometimes—means *occasionally.*

> I'll need *some time* to make a decision.
>
> Let us meet *sometime* after twelve noon.
>
> *Sometimes* it is better to hesitate before signing a contract.

somewheres—is *unacceptable.*

somewhere—is *acceptable.*

stationary—means *standing still.*

stationery—means *writing materials.*

> In ancient times people thought the earth was *stationary.*
>
> We bought writing paper at the *stationery* store.

stayed—means *remained.*

stood—means *remained upright* or *erect.*

> The army *stayed* in the trenches for five days.
>
> The soldiers *stood* at attention for one hour.

sure—for *surely* is *unacceptable.*

> SAY: You *surely* (NOT *sure*) are not going to write that!

take in—is *unacceptable* in the sense of *deceive* or *attend*.

SAY: We were *deceived* (NOT *taken in*) by his oily manner.

We should like to *attend* (NOT *take in*) a few plays during our vacation.

their—means *belonging to them*.

there—means *in that place*.

they're—means *they are*.

We took *their* books home with us.

You will find your books over *there* on the desk.

They're going to the ballpark with us.

theirselves—is *unacceptable* for *themselves*.

SAY: Most children of school age are able to care of *themselves* in many ways.

these kind—is *unacceptable*.

this kind—is *acceptable*.

I am fond of *this kind* of apples.

NOTE: *These kinds* would be also *acceptable*.

through—meaning *finished* or *completed* is *unacceptable*.

SAY: We'll finish (NOT *be through with*) the work by 5 o'clock.

try to—is *acceptable*.

try and—is *unacceptable*.

Try to come (NOT *try and* come).

NOTE: *plan on going* is *unacceptable*; *plan to go* is *acceptable*.

two—is the *numeral 2*.

to—means *in the direction of*.

too—means *more than* or *also*.

There are *two sides* to every story.

Three *twos* (or 2's) equal six.

We shall go *to school*.

The weather is *too* hot for school.

We shall go, *too*.

was / **were** | If something is contrary to fact (not a fact), use *were* in every instance.

I wish I *were* in Bermuda.

Unacceptable: If he *was* sensible, he wouldn't act like that.

(SAY: If he *were* . . .)

ways—is *unacceptable* for way.

SAY: We climbed a little way (NOT *ways*) up the hill.

went and took—(*went and stole*, etc.) is *unacceptable*.

SAY: They *stole* (NOT *went and stole*) our tools.

when—(and *where*) should NOT be used to introduce a definition of a noun.

SAY: A tornado *is a* twisting, high wind on land (NOT *is when a twisting, high wind is on land*).

A pool *is a place for swimming* (NOT *is where people swim*).

whereabouts—is *unacceptable* for *where*.

SAY: *Where* (NOT *whereabouts*) do you live?

NOTE: *Whereabouts* as a noun meaning a place is *acceptable*.

Do you know his *whereabouts*?

whether—should NOT be preceded by *of* or *as to*.

SAY: The president will consider the question *whether* (NOT *of whether*) it is better to ask for or demand higher taxes now.

He inquired *whether* (NOT *as to whether*) we were going or not.

which—is used *incorrectly* in the following expressions:

He asked me to stay, *which I did*. (CORRECT: He asked me to stay and I did.)

It has been a severe winter, *which* is unfortunate. (CORRECT: Unfortunately, it has been a severe winter.)

You did not write; besides *which* you have not telephoned. (CORRECT: Omit *which*)

while—is *unacceptable* for *and* or *though*.

> SAY: The library is situated on the south side; (OMIT *while*) the laboratory is on the north side.
>
> *Though* (NOT *while*) I disagree with you, I shall not interfere with your right to express your opinion.
>
> *Though* (*NOT while*) I am in my office every day, you do not attempt to see me.

who } The following is a method
whom } (without going into grammar rules) for determining when to use WHO or WHOM.

Tell me (*who, whom*) you think should represent our company?

STEP ONE: Change the who-whom part of the sentence to its natural order.

You think (*who, whom*) should represent our company?

STEP TWO: Substitute HE for WHO, HIM for WHOM.

You think (*he, him*) should represent our company?

You would say *he* in this case.

THEREFORE: Tell me WHO you think should represent our company? is correct.

who is } Note these constructions.
who am }

> It is I who *am* the most experienced.
> It is he who *is* . . .
> It is he or I who *am* . . .
> It is I or he who *is* . . .
> It is he and I who *are* . . .

whose—means *of whom.*

who's—means *who is.*
> *Whose* is this notebook?
> *Who's* in the next office?

EXERCISES: GED-TYPE WRITING SKILLS

The exercises that follow are similar to the questions you will find in Part 1 of the Language Arts, Writing Test. Writing questions are based on passages of twelve or more sentences that are arranged as paragraphs. Each sentence is numbered and each paragraph is lettered so that you can easily find the part referred to in the question. In each passage, some sentences are correct and others contain errors. Also, some sentences or even paragraphs in the passage are in the wrong place with regard to the logical presentation of the information or idea of the piece. Keep this in mind as you read through the selections. The questions test your ability to recognize these kinds of errors, and you will be asked to find the best ways to correct them.

Correct answers and explanations for these exercises are given at the end of this chapter.

> **Directions:** This section consists of practice selections. Some of the sentences in the pieces contain errors in sentence structure, usage, or mechanics. There may also be errors in organization, which need to be corrected by moving a sentence or paragraph, deleting a line, or substituting a new sentence that might improve the clarity and logic of the passage. After reading each selection carefully, answer the questions by choosing the answer that would correct an error and result in the most effective writing. The best answer must be consistent with the meaning and tone of the passage.

ITEMS 1 TO 7 REFER TO THE FOLLOWING ARTICLE.

The Internet

A

(1) The Internet is a worldwide network of computers that allow for easy sharing and transfer of all sorts of information. (2) It's an incredible tool that is useful for many things, including e-mail services, finding news and information, and much more.

B

(3) To access the Internet, you need a computer, phone line, and Internet service provider (ISP). (4) Popular ISP'es include America Online and Earthlink. (5) Once you're connected, a "browser" program allows you to visit Web sites. (6) The world's most popular Web browser is Internet Explorer, and it's probably already on your computer. (7) To use it, simply type the Web address of the Web site you wish to visit, and then look for "links" (usually underlined and in a different color from regular text) to click on for more information. (8) Want to check out the latest news? (9) Typing www.nytimes.com or www.cnn.com will do the job. (10) If you'd like your own free e-mail address, visiting www.hotmail.com will allow you to sign up with the world's most popular e-mail service. (11) For pro and college basketball coverage, www.insidehoops.com is terrific. (12) These are all examples of Web sites that make it possible to find information, but if you need help, try going to www.google.com and typing in a search for the subject you want.

C

(13) The Internet is here to stay because it make communication much quicker and easier. (14) In addition to the uses listed above, you can visit online stores and purchase products right over your computer. (15) And, there's much more! (16) The best way to learn how to use the Internet is to find a friend who already

knows how to do everything; And ask him or her to show you the ropes. (17) Also, find out about laptops. (18) Enjoy!

1. Sentence (1): **The Internet is a worldwide network of computers <u>that allow for</u> easy sharing and transfer of all sorts of information.**

   Which of the following is the best way to write the underlined portion of this sentence? If you think that the original is the best way to write the sentence, choose option (1).

   (1) that allow for
   (2) that allows for
   (3) that allow
   (4) allow for the
   (5) allow

2. Sentence (3): **To access the Internet, you need a computer, phone line, and Internet service provider (ISP).**

   If you rewrote sentence 3 beginning with <u>You need a computer, phone line, and Internet service provide (ISP)</u>, the next words should be

   (1) the Internet
   (2) access the
   (3) to access
   (4) to Internet
   (5) Internet the

3. Sentence (4): **Popular ISP'es include America Online and Earthlink.**

   What correction should be made to this sentence?

   (1) change <u>Popular</u> to <u>Well-known</u>
   (2) change <u>America Online</u> to <u>America online</u>
   (3) put a comma after <u>America Online</u>
   (4) change <u>ISP'es</u> to <u>isp'es</u>
   (5) change <u>ISP'es</u> to <u>ISP's</u>

4. Sentence (9): **Typing www.nytimes.com or www.cnn.com will do the job.**

   What correction should be made to this sentence?

   (1) change <u>Typing</u> to <u>To type</u>
   (2) change <u>will do</u> to <u>were to do</u>
   (3) change <u>com</u> to <u>come</u>
   (4) change the periods to commas
   (5) no change is necessary

5. Sentence (13): **The Internet is here to stay because it make communication much quicker and easier.** What correction should be made to this sentence?

   (1) change <u>much</u> to <u>more</u>
   (2) change <u>stay</u> to <u>staying</u>
   (3) change <u>communication</u> to <u>communications</u>
   (4) change <u>make</u> to <u>makes</u>
   (5) change <u>quicker</u> to <u>quick</u>

6. Sentence (16): **The best way to learn how to use the Internet is to find a friend who already knows how to <u>do everything; And</u> ask him or her to show you the ropes.**

   Which of the following is the best way to write the underlined portion of the sentence? If you think the original is the best way to write the sentence, then choose option (1).

   (1) do everything; And
   (2) do everything, and
   (3) doing everything; And
   (4) do everything, but
   (5) done everything; And

7. Sentence (17): **Also, find out about laptops.**

What revision should be made to this sentence in order to improve the organization of this article?

(1) move it after sentence (8)
(2) remove the comma
(3) change <u>laptops</u> to <u>Laptops</u>
(4) delete it
(5) no revision is necessary

ITEMS 8 TO 14 REFER TO THE FOLLOWING ARTICLE.

Enjoying "Brit Coms"

A

(1) The experience of seeing the shows called "brit coms" is one of the delights of television viewing. (2) These are comedy shows that are produced in Great Britain, usually a half hour in length, and presented on many noncommercial public television stations throughout the United States. (3) Their usually given in series of approximately a dozen or so shows each.

B

(4) These shows appeal to a wide audience and are written for viewers of all ages. (5) The shows touch on many universal aspects of life such as working, interpersonal relationships, growing old, retirement, and family responsibility. (6) While the settings are usually in an English village, home, or office, the themes are interested for all and show that life can be adventurous even after the age of 30.

C

(7) Some shows are whimsical with elements of fantasy, while others make the viewer both laugh and cry. (8) For example, "Faulty Towers" is the story of a country inn owned by eccentric, people-hating Basil Faulty and his frequent mishaps with the assorted characters who stay with him. (9) "Are You Being Served?" deals with a group of six lively coworkers at an English department store, and their comical doings.

(10) "The Vicar of Dibley" presents life in a small village after the arrival of an outspoken woman vicar who brings fun and joy to everyone. (11) "One Foot in the Grave" is about a retired couple and their often hair-raising adventures. (12) "Keeping up Appearances" follows the outrageous antics of a social-climbing suburban matron. (13) Finally, "Chef" is about a harried London restaurant owner, original from Jamaica, and life in his strange kitchen.

D

(14) They are usually presented on weekend evenings. (15) It is definitely worthwhile for to look them up in your area.

8. Sentence (1): **The experience of seeing the shows called "brit coms" is one of the delights of television viewing.**

What correction should be made to this sentence?

(1) change <u>of television</u> to <u>for television</u>
(2) change <u>shows</u> to <u>show</u>
(3) change <u>"brit coms"</u> to <u>"Brit coms"</u>
(4) change <u>experience</u> to <u>experiences</u>
(5) no correction is necessary

9. Sentence (3): **Their usually given in series of approximately a dozen or so shows each.**

What correction should be made to this sentence?

(1) change <u>Their</u> to <u>There</u>
(2) change <u>so</u> to <u>some</u>
(3) change <u>approximately</u> to <u>about</u>
(4) change <u>series</u> to <u>many series</u>
(5) change <u>Their</u> to <u>They're</u>

10. What revision should be made to the text of *Enjoying "Brit Coms"* to improve the organization of the narration?

    (1) move paragraph B to the beginning of paragraph D

    (2) remove sentence (6)

    (3) move paragraph A to the end of paragraph B

    (4) delete paragraph D

    (5) no revision is necessary

11. Sentence (6): **While the settings are usually in an English village, home, or office, the themes are <u>interested for</u> all and show that life can be adventurous even after the age of 30.**

    What is the best way to write the underlined portion of this sentence? If you think the original is the best way to write the sentence, choose option (1).

    (1) interested for

    (2) of interest to

    (3) to interest

    (4) for to interest

    (5) interested to

12. Sentence (7): **Some shows are whimsical with elements of fantasy, while others make the viewer both laugh and cry.**

    If you rewrote sentence (7) beginning with <u>Some shows make the viewer both laugh and cry</u>, the next words should be

    (1) with elements

    (2) are whimsical

    (3) of fantasy

    (4) while others

    (5) and other

13. Sentence (13): **Finally, "Chef" is about a harried London restaurant owner, original from Jamaica, and life in his strange kitchen.** What correction should be made to this sentence?

    (1) change <u>original</u> to <u>originally</u>

    (2) change <u>harried</u> to <u>hurried</u>

    (3) remove the comma after <u>Finally</u>

    (4) change <u>from Jamaica</u> to <u>a Jamaican</u>

    (5) change <u>life</u> to <u>living</u>

14. Sentence (15): **It is definitely worthwhile <u>for to look</u> them up in your area.**

    Which of the following is the best way to write the underlined portion of this sentence? If you think the original is the best way to write the sentence, choose option (1).

    (1) for to look

    (2) for look

    (3) looks

    (4) to look

    (5) look

Savvas Real Estate

11134 Gulfport Drive
Stockton, Florida 20004

Henry's Electric
1027 Elm Street
Stockton, Florida   March 24, 2005

Dear Henry,

A

(1) I would like to congratulate you on a job well done.

B

(2) On February 15th, I hired you to update the original electrical service in our old 1943 building to enable our business to expand its use of electrical office equipment. (3) You had pointed out that our wiring was inadequate from a safety standpoint. (4) Also, it was necessary to bring our electrical service up to code.

C

(5) Last week you completed the job successfully, you were way ahead of schedule. (6) All the new grounded outlets, telephone jacks, dedicated high amp sockets, new switching fuse box, and reconfigured main connections to the outside power source were installed as agreed upon. (7) The outlet for the augmented air-conditioning service were also completed. (8) We having moved back into the offices, and everything appears to be working well. (9) We are thankful, for your workers' neatness and their ability to put all our things back where they had originally been. (10) That has made it possible for our employees to gotten back to work in record time with minimal stress and confusion.

D

(11) We look forward to working with you in the future and would certainly recommended you to other businesses because of your prompt, capable, and courteous service. (12) We will also be replacing our outdated computers.

E

(13) Enclosed please find a check for $12,350, which represents our payment in full.

Very sincerely yours,

John H. Savvas

---

15. Sentence (2): **On February 15ᵗʰ, I hired you to update the original electrical service in our old 1943 building to enable our business to expand its use of electrical office equipment.**

If you rewrote sentence (2) beginning with the words In order to enable our business to expand its use of electrical office equipment, the next words should be

(1) the original

(2) I hired you

(3) on February 15ᵗʰ

(4) electrical service

(5) to update

16. Sentence (5): **Last week you completed the job successfully, you were way ahead of schedule.**

What correction should be made to this sentence?

(1) no correction is necessary

(2) insert a comma after the job

(3) start the sentence with You were

(4) change ahead of to ahead with the

(5) change successfully, you to successfully. You

17. Sentence (7): **The outlet for the augmented air-conditioning service were also completed.**

What correction should be made to this sentence?

(1) change outlet to outfitting

(2) replace were with was

(3) change augmented to augmenting

(4) end the sentence with a question mark

(5) change air-conditioning to air conditioning

18. Sentence (8): **We having moved back into the offices, and everything appears to be working well.**

What correction should be made to this sentence?

(1) change having to have

(2) change moved to moving

(3) change appears to appear

(4) insert a comma after back

(5) change working to work

19. Sentence (9): **We are thankful, for your workers' neatness and their ability to put all our things back where they had originally been.**

What correction should be made to this sentence?

(1) change workers' to worker's

(2) change they to it

(3) insert a comma after and

(4) remove the comma

(5) no correction is necessary

20. Sentence (10): **That has made it possible for our employees to gotten back to work in record time with minimal stress and confusion.**

Which of the following is the best way to write the underlined portion of this sentence? If you think the original is the best way to write the sentence, choose option.

(1) employees to gotten back to work

(2) employee to gotten back to work

(3) employees to gotten back to working

(4) employees to get back to work

(5) employees forgotten back to work

21. Sentence (11): **We look forward to working with you in the future and would certainly recommended you to other businesses because of your prompt, capable, and courteous service.**

Which of the following is the best way to write the underlined portion of this sentence? If you think the original is the best way to write the sentence, choose option.

(1) would certainly recommended you

(2) will certainly recommended you

(3) would certainly recommend you

(4) will recommended you certainly

(5) we would certainly recommended you

22. Which revision would improve the text of this letter?

(1) delete sentence (3)

(2) move paragraph D before paragraph C

(3) delete paragraph B

(4) delete sentence (12)

(5) no revision is necessary

ITEMS 23 TO 30 REFER TO THE FOLLOWING SELECTION.

Overcoming Employment Obstacles

A

(1) Getting a job can be hard at times for everyone. (2) However, certain groups of job seekers may face special obstacles in obtaining suitable employment. (3) All too often, veterans, youth, handicapped persons, minorities, and women experiences difficulty in the labor market.

B

(4) The reasons for this disadvantage in the job market vary, of course. (5) People may have trouble setting career goals and to look for work for reasons as different as a limited command of English, a prison record, or lack of self-confidence. (6) A growing number of communities have career counseling, training, and placement services for people with special needs. (7) Some people held back by having grown up in a setting that provided few role models and little exposure to the wide range of opportunities in the world of work. (8) Other people may have health or mobility problems that reduce their options for employment.

C

(9) Programs sponsored by many organizations, including Churches and Synagogues, nonprofit organizations, social service agencies, the state public Employment Service, and vocational rehabilitation agencies, help many people. (10) Some of the most successful agencies provide the extensive support that disadvantaged job seekers require. (11) They begin by helping clients resolve personal, family, or other fundamental problems' that prevent them from finding or keeping a suitable job. (12) Some agencies that serve special groups also provide a variety of supportive services designed to help people find and kept jobs.

23. Sentence (3): **All too often, veterans, youth, handicapped persons, minorities, and women experiences difficulty in the labor market.**

Which of the following is the best way to write the underlined portion of this sentence? If you think the original is the best way to write the sentence, choose option (1).

(1) women experiences difficulty

(2) women experiences difficulties

(3) men and women experiences difficulty

(4) women experience difficulty

(5) women experiencing difficulty

exercises

24. Sentence (5): **People may have trouble setting career <u>goals and to look for</u> work for reasons as different as a limited command of English, a prison record, or lack of self-confidence.**

Which of the following is the best way to write the underlined portion of this sentence? If you think the original is the best way to write the sentence, choose option (1).

(1) goals and to look for

(2) goals. And to look for

(3) goals or look for

(4) goals and looking for

(5) goals and for to look for

25. What revision should be made to sentence (6)?

(1) move sentence (6) to the beginning of paragraph C

(2) move sentence (6) to follow sentence (1)

(3) move sentence (6) to follow sentence (12)

(4) delete sentence (6)

(5) no revision is necessary

26. Sentence (7): **Some people held back by having grown up in a setting that provided few role models and little exposure to the wide range of opportunities in the world of work.**

What correction should be made to this sentence?

(1) insert <u>are</u> after <u>Some people</u>

(2) put a comma after <u>exposure</u>

(3) change <u>grown up</u> to <u>growed up</u>

(4) change <u>wide range</u> to <u>wider range</u>

(5) change <u>held</u> to <u>holds</u>

27. Sentence (9): **Programs sponsored by many organizations, including Churches and Synagogues, nonprofit organizations, social service agencies, the state public Employment Service, and vocational rehabilitation agencies, help many people.**

What correction should be made to this sentence?

(1) insert <u>are</u> after <u>Programs</u>

(2) change the comma after <u>Synagogues</u> to a colon

(3) change <u>Churches and Synagogues,</u> to <u>churches and synagogues,</u>

(4) change <u>Employment Service</u> to <u>employment service</u>

(5) change <u>help</u> to <u>helps</u>

28. Sentence (11): **They begin by helping clients resolve personal, family, or other fundamental problems' that prevent them from finding or keeping a suitable job.**

What correction should be made to this sentence?

(1) put commas after <u>finding</u> and <u>keeping</u>

(2) change <u>problems'</u> to <u>problems</u>

(3) change <u>clients</u> to <u>clientele</u>

(4) change <u>resolve</u> to <u>resolving</u>

(5) put a comma after <u>problems'</u>

29. Sentence (12): **Some agencies that serve special groups also provide a variety of supportive services designed to help people find and kept jobs.**

What correction should be made to this sentence?

(1) change <u>serve</u> to <u>served</u>

(2) change <u>provide</u> to <u>providing</u>

(3) insert a period after <u>services</u>

(4) change <u>kept</u> to <u>keep</u>

(5) change <u>groups</u> to <u>group</u>

30. Which of the following would be the best choice as a closing sentence for this article?

   (1) Some agencies are huge, while others have only a couple of workers servicing the public.

   (2) Prisons should help by finding employment and giving proper counseling before they discharge prisoners.

   (3) If a person deals with a private employment agency, he needs to make sure that he will not be charged a fee for the services he receives.

   (4) The range of possible employment possibilities is huge.

   (5) Thanks to all these possible sources of help, no one should be discouraged about the prospects of getting help in finding employment.

ITEMS 31 TO 37 REFER TO THE FOLLOWING PIECE.

The Story of Pasta

A

(1) Sophia Loren once confessed to an interviewer that she had always loved pasta and eating it "by the ton." (2) Most women would eat tons, too, if they could end up with a figure like Sophia's, because they think pasta's fattening. (3) Well, good news, ladies! (4) Nutritionists' say that pasta is not as bad as you might think. (5) Two ounces of dry pasta, which is an average dinner portion, contain about 210 calories. (6) Just like a baked potato, its not the pasta that's fattening, but the sauce that makes the calorie count jump. (7) Pasta to hold its own in the nutrition department, too. (8) No one knows who invented pasta, but it is mentioned in Chinese writings from about 5,000 BCE. (9) Marco Polo used to get the credit for introducing pasta to Italy, but that legend was laid to rest when scholars unearthed an Italian cookbook with pasta recipes published in 1290—at least five years before Marco Polo returned from his wanderings through Asia. (10) Now experts believe that Indians, Arabs, or Mongols introduced pasta to Italy, as early as the eleventh century, though some think the Etruscans were using it in pre-Roman days.

B

(11) Though there's no historical documentation, it's not too hard to imagine how pasta was invented. (12) Somewhere, someone must have carelessly or experimentally dropped a blob of paste made from flour and water into a pot of boiling water and, after tasting it, decided the accident was worth repeating. (13) Since then, pasta has remained a favorite food item in many countries the world over.

31. Sentence (1): **Sophia Loren once confessed to an interviewer that she had always loved pasta and eating it "by the ton."**

   Which of the following is the best way to write the underlined portion of this sentence? If you think the original is the best way to write the sentence, choose option (1).

   (1) pasta and eating it
   (2) pasta and ate it
   (3) pasta and eaten it
   (4) pasta or eat it
   (5) pasta by eating it

32. Sentence (2): **Most women would eat tons, too, if they could end up with a figure like Sophia's, because they think pasta's fattening.**

   What correction should be made to this sentence?

   (1) change Sophia's to Sophias
   (2) change a figure to figures
   (3) add but they don't after Sophia's,
   (4) remove the comma after tons
   (5) no correction is necessary

exercises

33. Sentence (4): <u>**Nutritionists' say that pasta**</u> **is not as bad as you might think.**

Which of the following is the best way to write the underlined portion of this sentence? If you think the original is the best way to write the sentence, choose option (1).

(1) Nutritionists' say that pasta
(2) Nutritionists say that pasta
(3) Nutritionists', say that pasta
(4) Nutritionists' said that pasta
(5) Nutritionists' saying pasta

34. Sentence (6): **Just like a baked potato,** <u>**its not the pasta that's fattening,**</u> **but the sauce that makes the calorie count jump.**

Which of the following is the best way to write the underlined portion of this sentence? If you think the original is the best way to write the sentence, choose option (1).

(1) its not the pasta that's fattening
(2) it not the pasta that's fattening
(3) its not the pasta that fattening
(4) it isn't the pasta that fattening
(5) it's not the pasta that's fattening

35. Sentence (7): <u>**Pasta to hold**</u> **its own in the nutrition department, too.**

Which of the following is the best way to write the underlined portion of this sentence? If you think the original is the best way to write the sentence, choose option (1).

(1) Pasta to hold
(2) Pasta holding
(3) Pasta in order to hold
(4) Pasta can hold
(5) Pasta would be held

36. Sentence (10): **Now experts believe that Indians, Arabs, or Mongols introduced pasta to Italy, as early as the eleventh century, though some think the Etruscans were using it in pre-Roman days.**

What correction should be made to this sentence?

(1) insert a comma after <u>that</u>
(2) change <u>believe</u> to <u>believes</u>
(3) remove the comma after <u>Italy</u>
(4) remove the comma after <u>century</u>
(5) no correction is necessary

37. Which revision would improve the overall organization of this article?

Begin a new paragraph

(1) with sentence (5).
(2) with sentence (6).
(3) with sentence (7).
(4) with sentence (8).
(5) with sentence (9).

ITEMS 38 TO 45 REFER TO THE FOLLOWING ARTICLE.

The Working Dog

A

(1) The dog plays an important role in many people's lives today. (2) As a companion to an older person who is living alone, the dog can bring a sense of well being. (3) For people who are ill, the benefits of companionship have been measured as showing an actual strengthening of the immune system.

B

(4) Certain dogs can be trained to give assistants to people who have special needs and who otherwise would not be able to function well in life. (5) For them, a dog gives the gift of independent living versus the need for constant supervision by a caregiver.

C

(6) There are three common disabilities that are well-served by highly trained dogs, that usually receive an intense 50- or 60-hour training course over a period of a year or more. (7) A "guide" dog helps a person avoid obstacles and maneuver through streets this allows the blind to shop, walk around, and even go to work. (8) "Hearing" dogs can alert people to a ringing alarm clock, a telephone, or a baby's cry. (9) "Service" dogs can help a person who can't move around easily to answer doorbells, turn on light switches, or give them support while they slowly walk. (10) Purebred labradors, golden retrievers, and German shepherds the best breeds for helping blind and visually impaired, deaf and hard of hearing, and physically disabled people.

D

(11) We have certainly learned to value dogs and to make them an integral part of our lives today. (12) Without them, many people's lives very different. (13) Perhaps we can truly understanding the truth to the adage that for many people "a dog is a man's best friend."

38. Sentence (2): **As a companion to an older person who is living alone, the dog can bring a sense of well being.**

    If you rewrote this sentence starting with the words <u>The dog can bring a sense of well being</u>, the next words should be

    (1) to an
    (2) as a
    (3) living alone
    (4) who is
    (5) older person

39. Sentence (4): **Certain dogs can be trained to give assistants to people who have special needs and who otherwise would not be able to function well in life.**

    What correction should be made to this sentence?

    (1) change <u>who have</u> to <u>who having</u>
    (2) change <u>function well</u> to <u>functioning well</u>
    (3) change <u>special needs</u> to <u>especial need</u>
    (4) change <u>assistants</u> to <u>assistance</u>
    (5) change <u>can be trained</u> to <u>can be train</u>

40. Sentence (6): **There are three common disabilities that are well-served by highly trained <u>dogs, that usually receive</u> an intense 50- or 60-hour training course over a period of a year or more.**

    Which of the following choices is the best way to write the underlined portion of this sentence? If you think the original is the best way, choose option (1).

    (1) dogs, that usually receive
    (2) dogs, which usually receive
    (3) dogs, who usually receive
    (4) dogs, that usual receive
    (5) dogs. That usually receive

41. Sentence (7): **A "guide" dog helps a person avoid obstacles and maneuver <u>through streets this allows</u> the blind to shop, walk around, and even go to work.**

    Which of the following is the best way to write the underlined part of the above sentence? If the original way is best, pick option (1).

    (1) through streets this allows
    (2) through streets. This allows
    (3) threw streets this allows
    (4) through streets this allowing
    (5) through-streets this allows

42. Sentence (9): **"Service" dogs can help a person who can't move around easily to answer doorbells, turn on light switches, or give them support while they slowly walk.**

What correction should be made to sentence (9)?

(1) change a person to people

(2) change help to helping

(3) change "Service" dogs to "Servicing" dogs

(4) change light switches to lighting switches

(5) change give them support to gives them support

43. Sentence (10): **Purebred labradors, golden retrievers, and German shepherds the best breeds for helping blind and visually impaired, deaf and hard of hearing, and physically disabled people.**

What correction should be made to this sentence?

(1) insert a comma after German shepherds

(2) insert is after German shepherds

(3) change people to persons

(4) change for helping to help

(5) insert make after German shepherds

44. Sentence (12): **Without them, many people's lives very different.**

Which of the following is the best way to write the underlined portion of this sentence? If you think the original way is best, choose option (1).

(1) people's lives very different.

(2) people's lives is very different.

(3) people's lives be very different.

(4) people's lives would be very different.

(5) peoples' lives very different.

45. Sentence (13): **Perhaps we can truly understanding the truth to the adage that for many people "a dog is a man's best friend."**

What correction should be made to this sentence?

(1) change man's to man

(2) change we can to we could

(3) change understanding to understand

(4) put a comma after adage

(5) change many people to much people

ANSWER KEY AND EXPLANATIONS

1. (2)	11. (2)	21. (3)	31. (2)	41. (2)
2. (3)	12. (4)	22. (4)	32. (3)	42. (1)
3. (5)	13. (1)	23. (4)	33. (2)	43. (5)
4. (5)	14. (4)	24. (4)	34. (5)	44. (4)
5. (4)	15. (2)	25. (1)	35. (4)	45. (3)
6. (2)	16. (5)	26. (1)	36. (3)	
7. (4)	17. (2)	27. (3)	37. (4)	
8. (3)	18. (1)	28. (2)	38. (2)	
9. (5)	19. (4)	29. (4)	39. (4)	
10. (1)	20. (4)	30. (5)	40. (3)	

1. **The correct answer is (2).** Change *that allow for* to *that allows for.* Since this refers to *worldwide network,* it has to be singular.

2. **The correct answer is (3).** If you rewrite the sentence, it will read *You need a computer, phone line, and Internet service provider (ISP) to access the Internet.*

3. **The correct answer is (5).** The correct way to indicate the plural for this abbreviation is an apostrophe and an *s*, as in *ISP's.*

4. **The correct answer is (5).** Since this is the way Internet addresses are commonly written, no correction is needed here.

5. **The correct answer is (4).** Since *make* is supposed to refer to the Internet, it has to be singular. Therefore, *makes* is the correct answer, as in *it makes communication much quicker and easier.*

6. **The correct answer is (2).** The best way to correct this sentence is to replace the semicolon with a comma and put a small *a* on *And.* Both semicolons and commas are always followed by lowercase letters, not capitals.

7. **The correct answer is (4).** This sentence has no place in this piece, which is about the Internet, not computers. Therefore, it is best to delete it.

8. **The correct answer is (3).** Since the word *brit* really means *British*, it should be capitalized. *Coms,* which stands for *comedies,* only needs to be capitalized when it's used in the title of the article but not otherwise.

9. **The correct answer is (5).** The word *Their* is a possessive. The correction should be *They're*, or it could be *They are,* as in *They are usually.*

10. **The correct answer is (1).** In order to improve the organization of this short piece, it would be better to combine these two paragraphs. They both deal with generalities about *Brit coms*, and together make a good ending after the paragraph describing the shows.

11. **The correct answer is (2).** The correct phrasing is *of interest to.* The sentence makes little sense otherwise.

12. **The correct answer is (4).** If the sentence is rewritten beginning with these words, it becomes *Some shows make the viewer both laugh and cry, while others are whimsical with elements of fantasy.*

13. **The correct answer is (1).** The correct adverb here is *originally.*

14. **The correct answer is (4).** The word *for* is extraneous and confusing and should be removed. Only the infinitive, *to look,* is needed, as in *to look them up.*

15. **The correct answer is (2).** The rewritten sentence reads *In order to enable our business to expand its use of electrical office equipment, I hired you on February 15th to update the original electrical service in our old 1943 building.*

16. **The correct answer is (5).** This is an example of a *run-on sentence,* meaning that it contains more words, or information, than is needed to complete one thought. It needs to be corrected by changing the comma into a period. This results in two complete and correctly written sentences.

17. **The correct answer is (2).** Since the sentence speaks of *one thing,* i.e., *the* outlet, or *one* outlet, the word *was* should be used rather than *were,* which would be appropriate when used in reference to many or *multiple* outlets. To see this more clearly, you can simplify the sentence to read *The outlet was also completed.*

18. **The correct answer is (1).** The sentence as it stands is a *sentence fragment.* Changing *having* to *have* completes the past tense verb. The sentence thus becomes *We have moved back into the offices, and everything appears to be working well.*

19. **The correct answer is (4).** The comma breaks up the complete thought—*We are thankful for your workers' neatness . . .*—and is confusing and unnecessary in this straightforward sentence. Choice (1) is incorrect because the words *their ability* later in the sentence tells you that we are hearing about *several,* not one worker.

20. **The correct answer is (4).** The word *gotten* is used incorrectly here. The correct verb is *get* as in *get back to work.* The whole sentence then becomes *That has made it possible for our employees to get back to work in record time with minimal stress and confusion.*

21. **The correct answer is (3).** The letter writer is speaking of the *future,* i.e., what he is willing to do in the future for the electrician. He is willing to *recommend* him to *other businesses* because of his good service. The word *recommended* is incorrectly used here because it is in the past tense.

22. **The correct answer is (4).** The letter as written flows logically and explains what happened clearly. Paragraphs A, B, C, D, and E should remain where they are. However, Sentence (12) is out of place. It has nothing to do with the rest of the letter and should be deleted.

23. **The correct answer is (4).** The word *experience* is correct because it refers to a group of people—veterans, youth, handicapped persons, etc., not a single person.

24. **The correct answer is (4).** For the parallel structure of this sentence, you must balance *setting career goals* with *looking for work.*

25. **The correct answer is (1).** Since paragraph C deals with the sources of help, this sentence, which introduces the concept, logically belongs there. This change improves the flow of this piece.

26. **The correct answer is (1).** This sentence needs the word *are* to complete the verb describing what is happening to the people, as in *Some people are held back.*

27. **The correct answer is (3).** These words are just used in a general sense. Therefore, they do not need to be capitalized. If they were part of proper names, they would be capitalized.

28. The correct answer is (2). The word is used as a plural, so it needs to be changed to *problems.* The word *problems'* is a possessive, which doesn't belong in this sentence.

29. The correct answer is (4). The word *keep* is needed to balance *find,* which is in the present tense, as in *find and keep.*

30. The correct answer is (5). This article needs at least one sentence to act as a summary of the ideas presented here. The main idea is that there is help even for people with special difficulties in getting employment, and this sentence expresses this clearly.

31. The correct answer is (2). The sentence is written in the past tense, which means the word should be *ate* rather than *eating.*

32. The correct answer is (3). The sentence, as it stands, is incomplete and makes no sense. Inserting *but they don't* makes it a meaningful sentence and explains *because they think pasta's fattening.*

33. The correct answer is (2). The simple plural form *nutritionists* is needed here, not the possessive.

34. The correct answer is (5). The word *its* in this sentence is supposed to mean *it is,* and *it is* becomes *it's.* The sentence states that *it's* the *sauce* that is fattening, not the pasta.

35. The correct answer is (4). *To hold* is an infinitive that needs to be changed to *can hold* to give the complete verb form and clarify the meaning.

36. The correct answer is (3). The comma needs to be removed here because it breaks up the complete thought, which is *Now experts believe that Indians, Arabs, or Mongols introduced pasta to Italy as early as the eleventh century.* The other commas are needed to separate the list of people mentioned and for clarification purposes.

37. The correct answer is (4). Since sentence (8) begins a series of lines about the history of pasta, which is a different topic from the first seven lines, it is appropriate to start a new paragraph here. Starting a new paragraph alerts the reader that a new topic is being introduced.

38. The correct answer is (2). The newly rewritten sentence would read *The dog can bring a sense of well being as a companion to an older person who is living alone.*

39. The correct answer is (4). The correct spelling here is *assistance,* which means the help or aid given to people. *Assistants* are the persons who give the *assistance.*

40. The correct answer is (3). The word *that* is only used when referring to inanimate things. Since dogs are being referred to, as in *highly trained dogs,* the correct word to use here is *who.*

41. The correct answer is (2). This is a run-on sentence that must be divided into two sentences. By putting a period after *maneuver through streets* and starting the next line with *This allows the blind,* you have written two complete and correct sentences.

42. The correct answer is (1). The last part of the sentence, which reads *gives them support while they slowly walk,* indicates that we are talking about *people,* not *a person.*

43. The correct answer is (5). This is a lengthy sentence fragment that requires the verb *make* as in *German shepherds make the best breeds* for correct meaning and completion.

44. The correct answer is (4). This is a sentence fragment. It needs to be completed by inserting *would be,* as in *many people's lives would be very different.*

45. The correct answer is (3). The word *understanding* is incorrect as a modifier here to *the truth.* The corrected phrase will read *Perhaps we can truly understand the truth.*

ERROR ANALYSIS FOR WRITING SKILLS PRACTICE QUESTIONS

Circle the number of each question you answered incorrectly. Count the number of circles in each content area and write the total number missed in the column headed "No. Incorrect." A large number of incorrect responses in a particular area indicates the need for further study in that area.

BY CONTENT	QUESTIONS	NO. INCORRECT
Sentence Structure	2, 6, 12, 15, 18, 26, 32, 35, 38, 41, 42, 44	
Usage	1, 5, 11, 13, 14, 17, 20, 21, 23, 29, 31, 40, 43, 45	
Mechanics	3, 4, 8, 9, 19, 24, 27, 28, 33, 34, 36, 39	
Organization	7, 10, 22, 25, 30, 37	

SUMMING IT UP

What You Need to Know About the GED Language Arts, Writing Test

- Writing easily and correctly is really just a matter of practice.

- Multiple-choice questions are always presented within a passage that averages 12 or more sentences and several paragraphs.

- Most questions contain an error that must be identified and corrected. Some questions contain no error at all.

All About the GED Essay Test

chapter 4

OVERVIEW

- Quick Tips!
- A sample essay question
- Planning your essay
- Writing your essay
- Summing it up

QUICK TIPS!

The GED test includes an essay segment. The essay test consists of a single topic on which you are expected to write a well-organized, well-stated response in the 45 minutes allowed. GED essay questions fall into two types: Exposition and Persuasion.

What Is Exposition?

Exposition means writing designed to convey information. Expository writing is *informative* writing. It explains or gives directions. Most of the practical writing you will do in the years to come—papers and examinations, job applications, business reports, insurance claims, your last will and testament—are examples of expository writing. That is why it is a part of this test, because it is so important to your life.

What Is Persuasion?

Persuasion is the ability to use language to move an audience to action or belief. There are three main ways to persuade someone:

1 Appeal to his or her emotions

2 Appeal to his or her sense of reason

3 Appeal to his or her ethics—his or her sense of right and wrong

Argumentation is the form of persuasion that appeals to reason. While an argument may be more concerned with following a line of reasoning than making someone act, it must nonetheless convince its audience that what is being said is worthwhile.

Whichever type of question you get, expository or persuasive, you will have to state your case logically, answering the question fully with specific details and examples.

How Is the Essay Scored?

GED essays are read and scored by 2 trained readers. They read the paper as a whole, evaluating its overall effectiveness. Thus, your paper can have a few errors and still get a very good grade; they are looking more for logic and a complete, well-supported answer to the question.

The score used by the GED readers ranges from a 1 (low) to a 4 (high). The 2 readers' scores are then averaged. The essay score is added to your score on the multiple-choice section of the Language Arts, Writing Test to form a total score. You must receive at least a 2 on the Essay Test to pass this portion. Remember, you must pass both the Multiple Choice (Part 1) section and the Essay Test (Part 2) section in order to get credit for the Language Arts, Writing Test; if you fail either one, you must take this entire test over again.

What Each Grade on the Scale of 1 to 4 Means

1 These papers lack a clear plan of action and organization. There is also great weakness in skills such as grammar, usage, punctuation, spelling, and the ability to write correct and logical sentences and paragraphs. The writer of a "1" paper has not proven his or her point, and he or she has very weak details or examples. The level of reasoning is very poor and displays a lack of understanding of the thesis, or main point.

2 These papers are not well organized and simply list details rather than developing supporting examples. While the purpose may be correctly stated in this "2" paper, (unlike the "1" paper, which does not make a point at all), the purpose is still not well supported with details and examples. There is also weakness with writing skills, as in the "1" paper.

3 These papers, which can be rated as "3," show a clear plan and method of organization, although the supporting detail could be stronger. The ideas presented may not always be related to the topic. There are errors in usage and skills, but they are not intrusive enough to distract or confuse the reader or to destroy the plan of action or the point being made.

4 These papers show a very clear organization and enough support for each point being made so that the topic is well proven. The reader is convinced of the logic of the writer's argument. There is a flair or style in word and example choices that clearly demonstrates the writer's ideas and maturity. The supporting details are effective because they are specific and very clearly prove the point under discussion. There may be a few errors, but the writer clearly shows an understanding of the rules of English grammar and usage.

A SAMPLE ESSAY QUESTION

Let's look at a sample GED essay question and the various ways in which different examinees answered. Look carefully at each written response so you may determine how the various scores (range 1–4) were assigned.

There has been a great deal of attention paid recently to the problem of drinking and driving. The laws on DWI have become much stiffer. Discuss the advantages and disadvantages of stiffer penalties for driving while intoxicated. Be specific.

Sample Essay A

Personally, I think the drinking law should be raised, one reason is there would be less people getting in accidents, many accidents are caused by drunk drivers. The people usually involved in DWI's are all young kids who are under pressure try to act cool and instead injure someone's life. Many kids drinking are not responsible enough and take other people's lives in there hands this is ruining many peoples lives and also society is getting worse. The problem would almost be solved if the laws was raised, putting drinking in the hands of youngsters is like giving a baby coffee, there not of right mind to make a decision whether to take it or not. I think that many teens are to young and therefore I think that the laws should be raised if it were lowered it would only be more problems. The lawmakers are making a right move in order to make society better if they keep doing things to prevent teens to drink this country will have a better chance at surviving problems. I'm glad that the law was raised so that my life wasn't taken in the hands of one irresponsible teenager. That's why I think drunk driving laws should be raised.

Evaluation: This essay is poorly organized and fails to prove the point. There are far too many serious writing errors, especially in sentence construction. Some examples of poor sentences include:

> Personally, I think the drinking law should be raised, one reason is there would be less people getting into accidents, many accidents are caused by drunk drivers.

This is called a *run-on*, which means there are several complete sentences tacked together without proper punctuation. The first sentence ends after the word "raised"; the second, after the word "accidents." After each of these words there should be periods or words that serve as *conjunctions*, such as "and," "or," or "for." In addition to the technical writing problems, the groups of words that are linked do not make the author's point.

Another example of a weak sentence would be:

> Many kids drinking are not responsible enough and take other people's lives in there hands this is ruining many peoples lives and also society is getting worse.

This is also a *run-on*, and should properly end after the word "hands." The ideas do not prove the point and show a lack of logic.

Because of errors such as these, this paper would receive a grade in the *1 range* as a very weak essay. Let's see what can be done to improve it. The author's ideas are:

Advantages of stiffer penalties	Disadvantages of stiffer penalties
fewer accidents	?

The author blames most of the DWI problems on teenagers who cause most of the accidents by their irresponsible attitudes. As we can see, there are not enough *advantages* and *disadvantages* here to make the point. Further, the author's logic is weak. It *may* be correct that the DWI situation is mainly the result of irresponsible teenagers, but nowhere does the author provide facts to back up this assertion. Let's look at another response to the same question.

Sample Essay B

I think the drinking age should be raised because most of the accidents caused today are by young teenage kids who are drunk while they are driving. They nearly kill people because they are drunk. I think the age should be raised to 25 years old because by then many people would have their heads together and they would know whether they should drive or not at that time.

However, many teenage kids or older would not listen to the law and they would drink anyway. I think the cops should check people more to see if they are drunk and if they should get a ticket of a certain amount, depending on how drunk they are or how much damage they have done. People should listen and obey the law (if it ever came about) and less people would probably be killed in automobile accidents involving people who are drinking.

Evaluation: Let's see the advantages and disadvantages here.

Advantages to stiffer DWI penalties	Disadvantages to stiffer DWI penalties
would prevent teenagers from DWI fewer accidents	teenagers would not listen

Again we can see that there are not enough advantages and disadvantages here to completely make the point. Teenagers are again blamed, and once again there is no proof to back up the author's belief that teenagers are the cause of most of the accidents involving drugs and/or alcohol. While the point about tickets is a good one, it does not have a place in this essay, which is concerned with the advantages and disadvantages of stiffer penalties for DWI. Remember that you will not get credit for answers that do not pertain to the question. The skills are rather good here, and so this paper would be in the *2 range*, providing a partial answer to the question.

Sample Essay C

Read this essay and see what "grade" you would assign it. How well does it answer the question? Is there enough specific detail to make the point? Are the skills strong? Is there evidence of an individual "style" or "voice" that makes the paper even more persuasive?

Drinking and driving laws need to be stiffer. When a person drinks and drives he or she is not only taking their own lives, but other innocent lives with them. The government should put very strict laws on those who drink and drive because maybe they will have a second thought about stepping into a car while intoxicated.

There are no advantages to drinking and driving. It is a very foolish thing. The disadvantages are that you will be punished if you violate the law, but that is no one else's fault but your own, for you brought it on yourself.

The advantage to stiffer penalties is that maybe people will stay away from alcohol, if they are driving alone. From my own opinion, I think there are no disadvantages to stiffer penalties.

When a person gets behind the wheel of a car, while intoxicated, they are not aware of many things that are going on around them. This causes them to do things that cause accidents, and many times, take people's lives. Drinking and driving is a very serious and foolish thing to do. Intoxicated drivers deserve a harsh penalty so they won't do it again.

Evaluation: You can see that this paper is much better structured than the previous ones. First of all, the paragraphs use the words "advantages" and "disadvantages" and clearly address themselves to the question. Let's take it apart.

Advantages to stiffer DWI laws	Disadvantages to stiffer DWI laws
will prevent deaths ("second thought")	you will be punished
people will stay away from alcohol	

There are clear divisions and a clear reasoning going on here. While there could be far more specific examples, the paper demonstrates control of the subject and a clear understanding of the question. There is also some style, in phrases such as "There are no advantages to drinking and driving," and "It is a very foolish thing." This paper would *rate a 3* on the scale. With more specific examples, it could very easily be a 4.

Let's look at one more essay:

Sample Essay D

While all concerned agree that something has to be done about the problem of driving while intoxicated, there are both advantages and disadvantages to increasing the penalties. The advantages include the obvious saving of lives and property, while the disadvantages include providing incentive for those inclined to break laws to continue to show they can do so. There is little doubt, however, that the advantages vastly outweigh the disadvantages.

The main advantage of tightening the punishment for driving while under the influence of alcohol or drugs would be the protection of lives. There are so many innocent people killed every year by intoxicated drivers that citizens have been moved to take matters in their own hands. Candy Lightner, the mother of a sixteen-year-old daughter killed by a drunken driver, formed an organization called M.A.D.D. (Mothers Against Drunken Drivers) to educate people about the dangers of driving while under the influence. The Scandinavian countries, where alcoholism and driving has long been a problem, have greatly increased penalties for those convicted of driving drunk, and they found that the death rate has dropped significantly. They have mandatory jail sentences and publish the names of offenders. If even one life was saved through stiffer legislation, it would be worth it.

The disadvantages could include the portion of society that feels duty-bound to break rules and might take increased DWI penalties as a sign that they should try to "beat the system." This could actually raise the number of serious accidents. There is also the problem of how to enact the laws. A recent proposal, involving hosts who can be held responsible for allowing drunken guests to leave their parties, has been greeted with a great deal of disapproval. Despite this, many bars are already limiting their "Happy Hours," especially in Connecticut.

Regardless of those who object to a tightening of DWI laws, it seems clear that something has to be done to decrease the number of deaths related to drivers on the roads when they clearly should not be. A series of stiffer laws seems to be the best way to accomplish the saving of lives. It's worked in other countries, and it can work here, too.

<u>Evaluation:</u> The topic sentence clearly states the question and the points to be covered. The points include:

<u>Advantages</u>	<u>Disadvantages</u>
saving of lives and property	providing incentive for people to break the law

In addition, the paragraph concludes with the author's point: The advantages far outweigh the disadvantages.

The second paragraph clearly states that the protection of lives is the main advantage of stiffer DWI laws. There are *two* specific examples to back this up:

❶ Candy Lightner, founder of M.A.D.D.

❷ Result of tighter laws in Scandinavian countries

These are excellent examples because they *specifically* prove the point under discussion.

The third paragraph also has a clear specific example, involving the recent "host law," holding those who let drunken drivers leave their homes responsible for the results. It also discusses the recent change in Connecticut "happy hour" rules. Both of these examples serve to make the point.

The conclusion has a sentence that sums up each major point and clearly states the writer's conviction that stiffer DWI laws would help all of us in preventing unnecessary deaths.

This would be a 4 paper, because it uses clear specific examples and good organization to make the point. It has a clear voice or tone—the author is obviously very concerned about this issue. The word choice is appropriate and the grammar and usage correct.

PLANNING YOUR ESSAY

Getting Started

The first thing you must always do when answering an essay question is look at the question and see what it asks you to do. Ask yourself these questions:

❶ *What* must I prove?

❷ *How many* things am I being asked to do?

❸ *How many paragraphs* will I need for this?

Look at this sample question:

> A generation ago, young people took it for granted that they would marry and, soon after, become parents. Today's young couples seem to be putting off parenthood well into their marriages, and a significant number are not having children at all. Discuss the advantages and disadvantages of having children. Be specific.

Go back to the three questions and answer each one:

1 *What* must I prove?

You are asked to discuss the advantages and disadvantages of having children. Remember, you will receive no credit if you do not answer what is asked of you.

2 *How many things* am I being asked to do?

You are asked to discuss two things: *advantages* and *disadvantages*. You may have as many advantages and disadvantages as you like, but you must represent both sides.

3 *How many paragraphs* will I need for this?

You will need four paragraphs, to be broken down as follows:

1 Introduction

2 One side—either advantages or disadvantages

3 The other side—either advantages or disadvantages

4 Conclusion

Now, rephrase the question so you are sure you've understood what is asked of you. This can be one of the most important steps in any paper you write, for you must answer the question and if you rush in without fully understanding what the question is asking, you may lose all credit.

Rephrasing: _____

_____

_____

Rephrasing: _____

_____

_____

There are few things as frightening as staring at a blank sheet of paper, knowing that you only have a short amount of time in which to write an essay. Where do you start? This can be really upsetting in a pressured exam, for you do not have the time to stop and think for awhile, and you are not allowed to talk to people and get their help. There is no time to revise and rewrite the paper, the first draft will have to stand as the final draft.

How do you begin? Is it best to just take a deep breath and plunge right in? Or are you better off planning for a few moments, even though it seems like everyone around you is already writing?

It Is Always Better to Plan Before You Write

It is ALWAYS worth the time to set up a plan of action, even though it looks as if you might be left behind, since everyone else just seems to start writing. A plan always makes a better finished project, especially in a timed exam, when you will not have the luxury of a revision. The ideas will flow with greater logic and clarity if you have a plan. There are several different ways to plan—select the one that is best for you.

One Way to Plan: The EGO Method

One of the best ways to set up an essay involves the following steps.

Write down all the possible ideas you can think of on the topic. Do not stop and consider your ideas, and try not to even lift your pen off the paper. Just write as many things as you can think of as fast as you can. This should take no more than 1 or 2 minutes. For example, look back to our question:

> A generation ago, young people took it for granted that they would marry and, soon after, become parents. Today's young couples seem to be putting off parenthood well into their marriages, and a significant number are not having children at all. Discuss the advantages and disadvantages of having children. Be specific.

Allowing 1 to 2 minutes, you might write something like this:

money	time	career	jobs	love
housing	travel	friendships	responsibilities	
continuation				
families	fear	divorce	stepchildren	unity
money	material things	schooling	job advancement	purpose

Eliminate all the things you have doubles of, would rather not write about because you're not too well-versed in them, or are too general and vague. So you would cross off:

~~money~~	time	~~career~~	jobs	love
housing	~~travel~~	friendships	responsibilities	
continuation				
families	~~fear~~	divorce	stepchildren	~~unity~~
money	material things	schooling	job advancement	purpose

You have written "money" twice, so one gets crossed off; "career" and "jobs" are the same; "fear" is too general; and so forth. This should take another minute. Now you have a list of possible things to discuss and are no longer staring at a blank sheet of paper.

This whole process should take 1 to 3 minutes—no more!

Now *group* the items into possible paragraphs. Look back at the question to arrange the groups.

Advantages of having children	Disadvantages of having children
love	schooling
families	jobs
friendships	responsibilities
love	money

Finally, *organize* the groups into possible ways to answer the question: Each Roman numeral (I, II, III, IV, etc.) stands for a paragraph. Each capital letter (A, B, C, etc.) stands for a subheading.

I. Introduction—There are advantages and disadvantages of having children

II. Advantages of having children

A. Friendships

B. Love

III. Disadvantages of having children

A. Money

B. Responsibilities

IV. Conclusion—pick a side

OR

I. Introduction—There are advantages and disadvantages of having children

II. Advantages of having children

A. Love

B. Families

III. Disadvantages of having children

A. Schooling

B. Jobs

IV. Conclusion—pick a side

This is called the EGO method:

E Eliminate (as you crossed off items that you did not need)

G Group (as you grouped the items into possible paragraphs)

O Organize (as you organized the items into a possible answer)

Remember, this entire process is designed to be done very quickly. From start to finish, it should only take a few moments. Do not spend more than 5 minutes organizing your answer or you may not have time to complete the essay.

The advantages of this method, or any planning, are that you have organized and arranged your thoughts into a unified whole. Your answer will make a great deal more sense, and you won't find that you complete a paragraph and then exclaim, "Oh! I forgot the point about . . ." and have to insert arrows and various messy signs.

Outlines Are Important

Outlining is one of the most valuable things you can do to ensure a good grade on the essay. It helps you plan and make sure you are really proving your point with good specific details.

There are many ways to do outlines, depending on the amount of time you have and the amount of detail you need. For our purposes here, we will follow a very specific outline, printed below. Do not worry about spelling and punctuation; just concentrate on getting down the most important points in a very brief amount of time. Focus on DETAIL to make sure you have made your point.

Follow this plan:

    I. Topic paragraph

        A. Topic sentence—rephrases the question

        B. Sentence that introduces second paragraph

        C. Sentence that introduces third paragraph

        D. Sentence that leads into the second paragraph. This is optional.

   II. The first point you have to make. It may be advantages, disadvantages, or just your first topic under discussion.

        A. Topic sentence

        B. Your first point (or advantages, etc.)

            1. Detail about the point

            2. Detail about the point

        C. Your second point

            1. Detail

            2. Detail

        D. Optional summary of the points made in the paragraph

  III. Your second point (which may be disadvantages, etc.)

        A. Topic sentence

        B. Your first point

            1. Detail

            2. Detail

        C. Your second point

            1. Detail

            2. Detail

        D. Optional conclusion

  IV. Conclusion to the essay

        A. Topic sentence—rephrases the question

        B. Sentence that summarizes the second paragraph

        C. Sentence that summarizes the third paragraph

        D. Overall conclusion that makes your point

A Second Way to Plan: The QAD Method

There are many other ways to plan your essay. One that many find helpful is called

Q	Question
A	Answer
D	Detail

and goes like this:

Question: Some believe that college is a waste of time and money, while others feel it is a valuable tool for happiness and success. Explain the advantages and disadvantages of going to college. Be specific.

Answer:	Advantages	Disadvantages
	become better educated	expensive
	meet people	lose time on career
	form new interests	a lot of what you learn not useful in career
	gain appreciation of culture	difficult to do

Details: There are two ways to do this:
You can ask yourself the following questions, when they apply:

What happens?	Where?
When?	Why?
How?	Who?

OR

List specific details you can use in the essay.

Advantages

I became better educated when I took Math 101 and chemistry. Even though I can't use either one of these courses in my job, I really feel it is important to understand how these fields work. I enjoyed learning about radical numbers and quadratic equations, and found the way molecules work fascinating. I think I'm more well-rounded for having studied these areas.

I met a lot of interesting people in college, people I would never have encountered in my home town. I remember especially someone from Hawaii and a few people from England and France, who told me all about their lives and culture. I still write to the Hawaiian and I stayed with my British friend last summer.

I became interested in gems and physical education in college, two fields I ignored in high school. The course in Jewelry Arts showed me all sorts of things I had never seen before—how to solder and hammer metal—and Physical Education got me involved in tennis and golf.

Disadvantages

My college charges $150.00 for one credit of study, and you need 125 credits to graduate. Counting room and board and fees, that's more than my parents paid for their first two homes combined!

I want to begin a career in landscaping and I can't afford to lose two or four years in a liberal arts college. I know there's a need for landscaping in my neighborhood and if I get started fast, I could have a thriving business.

I resent having to take math and science, which will be of no use to me in my planned career as a sales representative. Why should I spend all that time and money on something I'll never use?

WRITING YOUR ESSAY

Topic Sentences Are a Must

In a way, writing a good topic sentence is like aiming an arrow: If the topic sentence is aimed correctly, the whole paragraph will hit its mark and prove your point.

- *Every paragraph must have a topic sentence*. This includes the first, second, third, and last.

- The topic sentence expresses the main idea—the topic—of the paragraph.

- The topic sentence must join together all the ideas expressed in the paragraph.

- The topic sentence must be *limited* enough to be developed within a single paragraph but *broad* enough to have all the ideas that you need in that paragraph.

The more specific your topic sentence, the more detailed and descriptive your paragraph will be.

Limiting a Topic Sentence

Remember: A topic sentence has an idea that can be fully proven in one paragraph. For example, the sentence "You can learn a lot about human nature just by observing people" is so broad that it cannot be proven in one single paragraph. But if we write:

"You can learn a lot about human nature by watching people at a bus station"

OR

"You can learn a lot about human nature by watching people at the beach"

we have a topic that we can prove in one paragraph.

Expressing a Clear Controlling Idea

Another way to look at topic sentences is through the *controlling idea*. This is a *key word* or a *group of words* that expresses the basic idea of the sentence. When the controlling idea is clear, the entire sentence will be specific and clear.

Directions: Circle the controlling idea in the following sentences.

An encyclopedia is a handy book for students.

"Handy" is the controlling idea, and in the paragraph that follows, you will explain how the encyclopedia is handy.

1. Obtaining a driver's license is a difficult experience.

2. I have had several unusual experiences on dates.

3. Traveling by train has several advantages over traveling by car.

4. There are three steps in barbecuing hot dogs.

5. Good English is clear, appropriate, and vivid.

Answers:

1. difficult experience

2. unusual experiences

3. several advantages

4. three steps

5. clear, appropriate, vivid

Using Specific Words

To prove your point and make your writing interesting, you have to use specific words and phrases.

Directions: Select the most specific word from the list below in each example to make the most precise sentence.

His face was _____ with fright.
colorless   scarlet   chalky   pale

The answer is "chalky," for "colorless" and "pale" are too vague. "Scarlet" is also incorrect, for your face does not become scarlet (red) when you are afraid. "Chalky" is the best word, for in addition to color—a pale, dry white—it implies a *texture*—dry and lifeless. It is the most descriptive word and the one that will make this sentence most effective.

1 He wore a _____ shirt.
scarlet   colored   red   bright-colored

2 The playground was a sea of mud after the _____ .
cloudburst   precipitation   rain   moisture

3 The sun is high and hot; the air is sultry; it is _____ time.
siesta   sleep   nap   rest

Answers:

1 "Scarlet" is the most specific here, as it describes a bright red. Then would come:
red   bright-colored   colored

2 "Cloudburst" describes a specific kind of precipitation, a sudden, sharp downpour. In order of specific nature:
rain   precipitation (can also be snow, sleet, hail)   moisture

3 "Siesta" describes a nap that is taken when it is very warm during the middle of the day, and is thus the most precise. Then would come:
nap   (a short sleep)
sleep   (a type of rest)
rest   (any sitting down and relaxing)

Proofreading Can Raise Your Score

There is a great tendency to stand up the very minute you have finished writing and rush out of the room, relieved that it is all over. While we all have this feeling, *you must allow time for proofreading*. You can save yourself a great many unnecessary errors if you proofread your essay.

This is time very well spent. You must check over what you said, but *be sure to read what is there, not what you think is there*. Do not read too quickly, and go back over passages that seem unclear to you. Some find it helpful to put another piece of paper over the lines to help you focus on only one line at a time. In any event, make sure you check what you have said, even if all others are getting up around you. You'll improve your essay if you do.

Before You Go on to the Sample Topics, Review These Tips for Writing Better Essays

1 Sit in a quiet room all alone, without a television or radio. Make the room conditions as close to exam conditions as possible.

2 Allow yourself 45 minutes.

3 ORGANIZE before you write. We suggest the EGO method. This means you will

_____ Write down all the ideas you can think of about the question.

_____ Eliminate all doubles or vague ideas.

_____ Group the ideas into a form that will answer the question.

_____ Organize an outline and begin to write.

This whole process should only take a few moments.

4 After you finish writing, be sure to *proofread*. This is well worth the few moments it will take you. Check to make sure that you have provided specific examples, that you have proved what was asked of you, and that you have corrected all spelling, grammar, punctuation, and capitalization errors.

5 Try to turn in the best possible essay every time you write. Make each practice session count.

6 Try to get someone to read your essays and offer advice. They will be able to help you clear up any confusion in your thinking and make sure that you have proved your point.

PRACTICE WITH GED-TYPE ESSAY TOPICS

Directions: Each of the following essay topics is very much like what you will encounter on the GED. Write an essay for them as though you were actually taking the exam. Remember to include your own ideas and examples from your own experiences.

1 Recent antismoking laws have touched off a great deal of controversy, as anti-smokers feel their health is being endangered by smokers, and smokers feel they are being denied their rights by antismoking legislation. State your opinion concerning the antismoking laws and back it up with specific examples.

2 "When all guns are outlawed, only outlaws will have guns" a bumper sticker reads. Discuss the advantages and disadvantages of gun control.

3 Many states are passing laws so students cannot graduate without passing a series of competency exams. Is this good or bad? State your opinion and support with details.

4 The majority of mothers of young children now find it necessary to work outside of the home. How does this affect the American family? What might be the consequences to children and to society? Do you feel that this is a good thing or not? Support your views with specific examples.

5 There is current talk of putting weapons in our space stations in outer space. Could this create a possible danger? Is it necessary in terms of protecting our national security? Discuss, in detail, the advantages or dangers inherent in this idea.

6 Among the current ideas about changing Social Security is the question of putting a portion of its funds into the stock market. Another is to give the individual employee the opportunity to invest money for himself instead of letting the Social Security administration do it for him. What do you think of these ideas? Support your opinions with specific details.

7 "Buy American," orders a roadside billboard. Discuss the advantages and disadvantages of buying goods manufactured in the United States in preference to foreign products.

8 According to recent census figures, a large proportion of people living in our cities are foreign-born. What are the effects of this on our culture and on our country? What are the advantages and disadvantages? Support your opinions with specific details.

9 "Seat belts save lives" according to the television commercials. It has been shown that a greater number of Americans are surviving serious automobile accidents. Some people feel that passive restraint systems, such as air bags, could increase the survival rate even more, especially if they were required in every automobile sold in the United States. State your opinion concerning passive restraints and back it up with specific details.

10 While Americans love the automobile, people in many countries in Europe continue to rely on trains both for commuting and for leisure and holiday travel. What do you think about each of these modes of travel? What are the advantages and disadvantages, both personally and environmentally? Be sure to include specific examples in expressing your opinions.

SUMMING IT UP

What You Need to Know About the GED Language Arts, Writing Test, Essay

- The essay segment of the test consists of a single topic on which you are expected to write a well-organized, well-stated response in 45 minutes.

- The essay questions fall into two types: exposition and persuasion

After you finish writing, leave a few minutes to check over what you wrote. Make sure of the following:

- Did you answer the question?
- Did you provide good, *specific* detail to support your ideas?
- Did you organize your answer in the best possible way to make your point clearly?
- Did you check for errors in spelling, grammar, punctuation, words misused, and so forth?

PART IV

SOCIAL STUDIES REVIEW

All About the GED Social Studies Test

chapter 5

OVERVIEW
- Quick Tips!
- Taking the GED Social Studies test
- Summing it up

QUICK TIPS!

The best way to succeed in this area is to get used to reading the news section of a good newspaper every day, see the news on TV, listen to serious discussions on the radio, and think about current issues.

What are people saying about topics such as politics, abortion rights, economics, unemployment, education, crime, peace, world events, and other issues? Think about the interesting things that have happened in other times. Read about the experiences of people in other countries and of other eras. Weekly magazines, such as *Time* and *Newsweek*, are very useful and cover almost every topic. Go to your neighborhood library and glance through the atlases, maps, and magazines. If you have internet access, look up topics of interest to you.

You will become much better informed, have a good time, and do well on tests such as the GED Social Studies Test.

TAKING THE GED SOCIAL STUDIES TEST

The GED Social Studies Test Covers the Following Subject Areas:
- History (40%)
- Economics (20%)
- Civics and Government (25%)
- Geography (15%)

Many of the questions concern knowledge or skills taken from more than one subject area. For example, a single question may actually draw upon your knowledge of economic, geographic, political, and historical concepts in the process of asking you to make a decision or solve a problem. Some of the questions concern global issues such as how American history influences world affairs or how world affairs have altered the course of American history.

What Are the Questions Like on the Social Studies Test?

All questions on the GED Social Studies Test are multiple-choice questions, with five possible answers. You will be required to pick the best possible answer of the five. The test contains 50 questions. Many of these questions are based on written (printed) information. This information may be taken from any number of places: a speech, an editorial, a magazine article, a diary, a historic document, etc. The remaining questions are based on some sort of illustration: a table, a pie chart, an editorial cartoon, a map, a bar graph, etc.

Many questions are arranged in sets. A typical set might begin with an excerpt from a magazine article followed by five or six questions. Another set could begin with a table of business activity followed by four or five questions. The remaining questions in the test are single questions based on a very short reading or a single illustration.

GED Social Studies questions test your knowledge of important principles, concepts, events, and relationships. You will be asked to demonstrate a variety of reasoning skills in answering these questions:

① Understanding the meaning of both written and illustrated questions. (Comprehension)

- Can you restate information that was written or pictured in the original question?

- Can you summarize, that is, restate briefly, the important idea(s) of a reading passage, or picture?

- Can you determine the implications of a particular piece of information or event, that is, can you draw an inference?

② Taking the information or ideas in a question and applying it to a specific situation given in the question(s). (Application)

- Can you apply a principle to a new situation, not necessarily one you may have studied in a class?

③ Breaking down information into smaller parts/Looking at the relationships between the various parts of (larger) complete ideas. (Analysis)

- Can you tell the difference between a fact and an opinion or a hypothesis?

- Can you pick out the unstated assumptions in a question or a table or a reading passage?

- Can you separate a conclusion from the various supporting statements that help you reach that conclusion?

- Can you pick out cause-and-effect relationships?

④ Making judgments about the validity or accuracy of information or methods used to gather information or research data. (Evaluation)

- Can you look at information presented in a question and decide whether it really supports a hypothesis, conclusion, or generalization?

- Do you understand that certain values have often entered into the development of particular beliefs, policies, or instances of decision-making?

- Are you able to look critically at the accuracy of facts that are offered as "proof"?

- Can you find logical mistakes in arguments?

If you've decided at this point that the reasoning skills needed for the GED are rather overwhelming, remember this: You need to answer just about half of the questions correctly to pass the GED Social Studies Test.

What Topics Are Covered on the Social Studies Test?

This section of the GED will cover topics drawn from American and world history, economics, geography, civics, and government. Most of the questions will be based on a reading passage or some form of graphic presentation and will test your understanding and judgment about what is presented. Good reading and comprehension are vital skills that are necessary for success in this test.

Each test will contain a passage from one of the following: the Declaration of Independence, the United States Constitution, the Federalist Papers, or an important landmark Supreme Court case. There will also be a sample of a "practical document," such as a tax form, voters' guide, public notice, or advertisement.

If you find that you need more study in a particular area, you may also wish to consult a basic high school text such as:

American History

Holt American Nation, Success in History for Every Student, Holt, Rinehart and Winston (2003)

America: Pathways to the Present, Prentice Hall (2003)

World History

Holt World History: The Human Journey, From Ancient Cultures to the Modern World, Holt, Rinehart and Winston (2003)

World History, Connections to Today, Prentice Hall (2003)

Economics

Holt Economics, Down Wall Street and Your Street, Holt, Rinehart and Winston, (2003)

Economics: Principles in Action, Prentice Hall (2003)

Civics and Government

Holt American Civics, Holt, Rinehart and Winston (2003)

Holt American Government, Of the People, By the People...and For Your Students, Holt, Rinehart and Winston (2003)

Civics and Economics, Prentice Hall (2003)

Geography

Holt People, Places, and Change: An Introduction to World Studies, Around the World in One School Year, Holt, Rinehart and Winston (2003)

World Geography: Building a Global Perspective, Prentice Hall (2003)

EXERCISES: HISTORY

Directions: For each question, circle the number of the response that best answers the question or completes the statement. An Answer Key and Explanations are provided at the end of this section.

ITEM 1 IS BASED ON THE MAP BELOW.

Major Events in the Middle East, 1979–1990

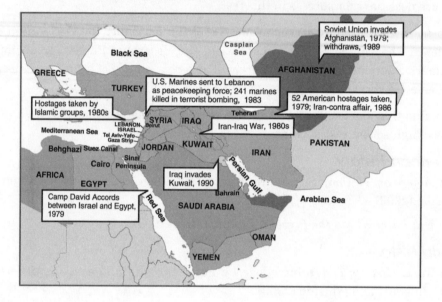

1. Based on the information in the map, which of the following statements is the most accurate?

   (1) During the 1980s, Iran was the Middle Eastern country most hostile toward the United States.

   (2) Afghanistan was the only Middle Eastern nation to be invaded by an aggressor during the 1980s.

   (3) The Middle East was a relatively peaceful region during the 1980s.

   (4) The U.S. and the Soviet Union managed to stay out of affairs in the Middle East during the 1980s.

   (5) There was no time during the 1980s when the entire Middle East region was without war or armed conflict.

2. George Washington was chosen president of the Constitutional Convention in 1787 and was then overwhelmingly elected to serve as the first president of the new republic in 1789 and 1792. Washington is associated with which of the following wars?

   (1) The French and Indian War

   (2) The Revolutionary War

   (3) The War of 1812

   (4) The Civil War

   (5) The Spanish American War

ITEMS 3 TO 7 REFER TO THE FOLLOWING INFORMATION.

Immigration Legislation in the United States

Legislation	Provisions
1. Literacy Test (1917)	People immigrating to the U.S. were required to pass a literacy test.
2. Immigration Act of 1921	Immigration limited to a total of 350,000 persons a year. Quota system limited numbers admitted of any nationality to 3% of total present in the U.S. in 1910.
3. National Origins System of 1929	Annual limit of 150,000 immigrants from outside Western Hemisphere, with quotas. No restrictions on Western Hemisphere immigration. Immigration from Asian countries prohibited.
4. Refugee and Displaced Persons Acts, 1940s	Limited immigration allowances for refugees from Nazi Germany and Eastern Europe.
5. McCarran-Walter Act of 1952	Total of 156,000 admitted with quota system for immigrants coming from outside the Western Hemisphere. 2,000 admitted from the Far East yearly. Careful screening for Communists.
6. Immigration Act of 1965	Quota system ended. 170,000 immigrants to be allowed from outside the Western Hemisphere, 120,000 from within. Those with "special talents" or resident relatives given preference.

3. According to this chart, which of the following is a fair assessment of the U.S. immigration policy in the twentieth century?

   (1) The United States has normally shown equal treatment to all prospective immigrants.

   (2) Most immigrants have come here from China and India.

   (3) There are still extensive waiting lists for entry from most countries.

   (4) European immigration policies are more open than those of the United States.

   (5) Most of the provisions seem to be restrictive or discriminatory.

4. Just two of the six legislative acts show a concern with the personal qualities of the prospective immigrant. They are numbers

   (1) 2 and 5.

   (2) 3 and 4.

   (3) 5 and 6.

   (4) 1 and 2.

   (5) 1 and 6.

5. Which of the laws concerns itself with the needs of people in crisis, rather than the needs or desires of the United States at the time the laws were enacted?

   (1) Act 2
   (2) Act 3
   (3) Act 1
   (4) Act 6
   (5) Act 4

6. Several laws show a long-term prejudice against people coming from Asia. These laws were finally changed in

   (1) 1929
   (2) 1917
   (3) 1999
   (4) 1965
   (5) None of the above

7. What might have been a reason for enacting the McCarran-Walter Act in 1952?

   (1) A fear of too many poor Mexican immigrants coming to this country.
   (2) The U.S. was in the midst of McCarthyism, which reflected fear of the spread of Communism to this country.
   (3) There was a great need for immigrant labor, so immigration was expanded.
   (4) McCarran and Walter wanted to limit immigration because they feared overpopulation.
   (5) All of the above

ITEMS 8 AND 9 REFER TO THE FOLLOWING PASSAGE.

The preamble to the Declaration of Independence states in part: "When in the course of human events it becomes necessary for one people to dissolve the political bands that have connected them with another . . . a decent respect to the opinions of mankind requires that they should declare the causes that impel them to separation."

8. Another word for *preamble* would be

   (1) conclusion.
   (2) introduction.
   (3) body.
   (4) appendix.
   (5) amendment.

9. What can you assume about the Declaration of Independence?

   (1) That it explains the laws of the land.
   (2) It gives the reasons for revolting against England.
   (3) It explains the Bill of Rights.
   (4) A new form of government for the colonies is explained.
   (5) It presents the reasons for the abolition of slavery.

ITEMS 10 AND 11 REFER TO THE FOLLOWING PASSAGE.

The invention of *food production*, or the growing of food crops, was a great advance in human civilization thousands of years ago. It involved the selection of one or more of the few wild plants that were edible in a particular region, and growing them so as to produce large amounts of food on a regular basis. Before humans learned to do this they were *hunter-gatherers*, or people who lived off the plants and animals that they happened to find as they traveled from place to place. The other advance was in the domestication of some wild animals and birds, such as chickens, cows, pigs, goats, sheep, horses, dogs, and cats.

10. Plant and animal domestication created many basic changes in the way people could live and organize their society. You can infer that among these was

    (1) the ability to stay put in a particular place.
    (2) the tendency to have more children.
    (3) an expansion of population.
    (4) a greater emphasis on government and social organization.
    (5) All of the above

11. The domestication of horses changed the character of warfare. How?

    (1) Potential fighters were turned into farmers.
    (2) Feed crops needed to be grown during warfare to feed the horses.
    (3) It probably gave the advantage to those warriors who were mounted on horses.
    (4) The eating of horse-meat became a staple of the fighters' diet.
    (5) The care of horses took a great deal of time.

ITEMS 12 AND 13 REFER TO THE INFORMATION BELOW.

"In the new code of law of which I suppose it will be necessary for you to make, I desire you would remember the ladies and be more generous and favorable to them than your ancestors. Do not put such unlimited power into the hands of husbands. Remember, all men would be tyrants if they could. If particular care and attention is not paid to the ladies, we are determined to foment a rebellion, and will not hold ourselves bound by any laws in which we have no voice or representation."

12. The writer of these lines might be described today as a

    (1) socialist.
    (2) revolutionary.
    (3) feminist.
    (4) patriot.
    (5) civil rights advocate.

13. The writer's argument and choice of words reflect the language and political vocabulary of a specific time period in United States history. This period is most likely

    (1) early colonial period.
    (2) Revolutionary War.
    (3) War of 1812.
    (4) annexation of Texas.
    (5) 1850s.

ITEMS 14 TO 16 REFER TO THE FOLLOWING CARTOON.

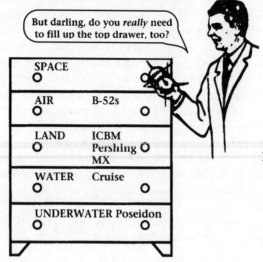

But darling, do you *really* need to fill up the top drawer, too?

SPACE

AIR　　B-52s

LAND　　ICBM
　　　　Pershing
　　　　MX

WATER　　Cruise

UNDERWATER Poseidon

14. The best title for this cartoon is

   (1) "Planning the Bedroom Furniture."

   (2) "Cooperative Planning."

   (3) "Arms Storage."

   (4) "Danger under the Sea."

   (5) "Science Fiction Thriller."

15. The cartoonist implies that

   (1) the submarine is the most important weapon.

   (2) we have enough weapons already.

   (3) countries with these weapons should negotiate.

   (4) we need more weapons below the earth.

   (5) the military budget is too low.

16. Nuclear weapons exist everywhere *but*

   (1) in space.

   (2) in the air.

   (3) on land.

   (4) on the water.

   (5) under the water.

ITEMS 17 TO 20 REFER TO THE FOLLOWING MAP.

Expansion of the Continental United States

17. According to the map, the last major expansion of the continental United States was made possible by the addition of

    (1) the Louisiana Purchase.

    (2) the Mexican Cession.

    (3) Oregon Country.

    (4) the Gadsden Purchase.

    (5) Florida

18. The Treaty of Guadeloupe Hidalgo ended the Mexican War of 1846-1848. Which large area of land was then added to the United States?

    (1) The Louisiana Purchase

    (2) The Mexican Cession

    (3) Oregon Country

    (4) The Gadsden Purchase

    (5) Florida

19. Based on the information on this map, which of the following is a reasonable conclusion to be drawn?

    (1) The United States grew quickly in the nineteenth century.

    (2) Most of the added land was gotten by aggression.

    (3) At one time, Spain and France owned the majority of North America.

    (4) Mexico once owned the whole western part of the United States.

    (5) Fillmore, Jefferson, Polk, or Pierce, who occupied the White House in the 1800s, were responsible for these acquisitions.

20. Which sentence is the best summary of the map's content?

    (1) Texas was annexed before the Gadsden Purchase was made.

    (2) The Louisiana Purchase extended from the Gulf of Mexico to the Canadian border.

    (3) At the time of the Constitutional Convention, the territory of the United States was all east of the Mississippi River.

    (4) The Oregon Country is north and west of the Louisiana Purchase.

    (5) The expansion of the continental United States was made up of adjoining pieces of land that were added during the nineteenth century.

ITEMS 21 TO 24 REFER TO THE INFORMATION BELOW.

The attitudes and values of a democratic society have been expressed in a variety of ways throughout history. The views of some members of a society often tend to express the underlying doubts, animosities, or culturally accepted reasons for pursuing war, even when this pursuit conflicts with the values of a democratic society. Each of the following quotations represents the time period of a particular conflict in which the United States was engaged. Choose the conflict each statement is most closely related to.

21. "*Sic semper tyrannis!* The South is avenged!"

    (1) Civil War
    (2) Spanish-American War
    (3) World War I
    (4) World War II
    (5) Vietnamese Conflict

22. "The tree of liberty must be refreshed from time to time with the blood of patriots and tyrants. It is its natural manure."

    (1) French and Indian War
    (2) American Revolution
    (3) War of 1812
    (4) Civil War
    (5) Spanish-American War

23. "A splendid little war"

    (1) Civil War
    (2) Spanish-American War
    (3) World War I
    (4) Korean Conflict
    (5) Vietnam Conflict

24. "Wrong and morally wrong in its conduct and consequences, it was nevertheless not evil, in intent or origin. What propelled us into this war was a corruption of the generous, idealistic, liberal impulse."

    (1) American Revolution
    (2) Spanish-American War
    (3) World War II
    (4) Korean Conflict
    (5) Vietnamese Conflict

ITEMS 25 AND 26 REFER TO THE FOLLOWING INFORMATION.

In the 1880s, large industrial monopolies controlled many industries. For example, the steel, oil, and meat-packing industries were each controlled by one major company. The result was that the consumer had to pay artificially high prices for these goods. Eventually laws were enacted to protect the consumers.

25. The writers who described the evils of the monopolies were called

    (1) communists.
    (2) libertarians.
    (3) progressives.
    (4) labor leaders.
    (5) muckrakers.

26. One of the laws that was enacted to curb monopolies was the

    (1) Stamp Act.
    (2) Sherman Anti-Trust Act.
    (3) National Recovery Act.
    (4) Great Society.
    (5) Marshall Plan.

27. For years, the United States took a hard-line stance against the communist Soviet Union. Now we are friendly and helpful toward Russia, the largest republic to result from the breakup of the Soviet Union. This change shows that U.S. foreign policy

    (1) is flexible enough to change when circumstances change.
    (2) reflects a wishy-washy attitude toward world events.
    (3) is staunchly against communism.
    (4) is subject to the whims of the president.
    (5) has not changed in at least fifty years.

28. "A man who lived in a certain country from 1865 to 1945 would have witnessed developments that in European history occupied several centuries: Absolute monarchy, constitutional monarchy, liberalism, imperialist expansion, military dictatorship, totalitarian fascism, foreign occupation." This description best fits

    (1) India.
    (2) China.
    (3) Japan.
    (4) Egypt.
    (5) Israel.

ITEMS 29 AND 30 REFER TO THE FOLLOWING INFORMATION.

The American Constitution provides for changes in society with a process for amendment, or change. Today, the Constitution includes twenty-six amendments. The first ten amendments, called the *Bill of Rights*, are outlined below:

BILL OF RIGHTS

First Amendment: Provides religious and political freedom

Second Amendment: Provides the right to bear arms

Third Amendment: Gives the right to refuse to house soldiers in peacetime

Fourth Amendment: Provides protection against unreasonable search and seizure

Fifth Amendment: Safeguards the right of accused persons to due process of the law

Sixth Amendment: Assures the right to a speedy and public trial

Seventh Amendment: Guarantees the right to a jury trial in civil cases

Eighth Amendment: Provides protection against cruel and unusual punishment

Ninth Amendment: Gives people the rights to powers that may not be spelled out in the Constitution

Tenth Amendment: Safeguards the rights of the people and the states to powers not otherwise given to the federal government, states, or people

29. Which two amendments provide for changes over time in the circumstances and realities of American life?

    (1) The First and Second Amendments
    (2) The Fifth and Sixth Amendments
    (3) The Thirds and Fourth Amendments
    (4) The Ninth and Tenth Amendments
    (5) The Seventh and Eighth Amendments

30. A family that was forced by the U.S. Army in 2005 to provide housing and food for a group of soldiers could appeal to the courts based on which amendment to the Constitution?

    (1) The Sixth Amendment
    (2) The Third Amendment
    (3) The Second Amendment
    (4) The Ninth Amendment
    (5) The Tenth Amendment

ANSWER KEY AND EXPLANATIONS

1. (5)	9. (2)	17. (4)	24. (5)
2. (2)	10. (5)	18. (2)	25. (5)
3. (5)	11. (3)	19. (1)	26. (2)
4. (5)	12. (3)	20. (5)	27. (1)
5. (5)	13. (2)	21. (1)	28. (3)
6. (4)	14. (3)	22. (2)	29. (4)
7. (2)	15. (2)	23. (2)	30. (2)
8. (2)	16. (1)		

1. **The correct answer is (5).** The Middle East was a hotbed of military conflict throughout the entire decade of the 1980s. There is no support for choice (1), and choices (2), (3), and (4) are contradicted by the passage. Therefore, they are incorrect.

2. **The correct answer is (2).** George Washington was a general and commander-in-chief of the colonial armies in the American Revolution. The dates of his presidency are clues you can use to arrive at the correct answer (the Revolution was fought between 1775-1783). The French and Indian War was earlier in the eighteenth century (1754-1763), while the remaining three wars were fought in the nineteenth century.

3. **The correct answer is (5).** The best answer is the last choice, since most of the legislation listed presents restrictions and quotas according to country of origin. No information is given in support of choices (2), (3), or (4), so they are incorrect, and choice (1) is the opposite.

4. **The correct answer is (5).** Laws number 1 and 6 concern themselves with literacy and the special talents, or training, that a prospective immigrant may have. The other laws do not.

5. **The correct answer is (5).** The title, *Refugee and Displaced Persons Act,* and the dates and information given in the right-hand column suggest that this law was enacted to help persons who were fleeing the Nazis during World War II and immediately after the war ended in 1945. These people were in crisis and needed to be helped by the United States, as well as other Allied countries. Unfortunately, the number limits placed on immigration doomed many persons, who were therefore unable to reach safety in the United States.

6. **The correct answer is (4).** Not until 1965 was the "quota" system, which restricted people from certain parts of the world, lifted. Provisions 3 and 5 specifically target those trying to immigrate to the United States from the Far East. This reflected the prejudices of the times against minority groups.

7. **The correct answer is (2).** Sometimes it is possible to guess at an answer by being alert and carefully reading the choices given. Of the first four choices, only choice (2) seems possible or likely. The United States was in a "cold war" with the powerful Soviet Union and feared the expansion of communism throughout the world and into the United States. That was the purpose of the last provision mentioned, the *careful screening for Communists.* You can use logic to see that the other choices do not make any sense and are therefore incorrect.

8. **The correct answer is (2).** The prefix "pre" indicates something that comes before, so *introduction* is the correct answer. The first choice is the opposite in meaning, and the other choices are unrelated.

9. **The correct answer is (2).** The passage indicates that the causes of separation, or reasons for revolting against England, will be discussed in the document to follow. This is the meaning of "declare the causes that impel them to separation."

10. **The correct answer is (5).** All of these things logically would happen after people learned to grow crops rather than being dependant on roaming around and being *hunter-gatherers*. Because of the local availability of food, they could stay put in a particular place. Not being nomadic to look for food would increase the tendency to have more children, who are a detriment to that type of living. The population would grow, since food would be more efficiently produced. And there would be a greater need for social organization and government as local groups of population increased in size and complexity.

11. **The correct answer is (3).** You can make the assumption that horses probably gave an advantage to the warriors who had them over those who did not. They could move much faster, overrun their enemies, and be less likely to be injured or killed than those fighting on foot. An example of this is the victory of invading Spaniards over the Incas and the Aztecs in South America in the fifteenth century. Even though these native populations vastly outnumbered the Spaniards, they were defeated partly because of their lack of domesticated horses.

12. **The correct answer is (3).** Feminists seek rights and power for women.

13. **The correct answer is (2).** Abigail Adams's style and word choice in this 1777 letter echo those of her husband and other leaders of the American colonies who deliberated and/or propagandized the cause of the Declaration of Independence.

14. **The correct answer is (3).** The cartoon depicts deployment of arms systems.

15. **The correct answer is (2).** The implication of the cartoon is that we have enough weapons already.

16. **The correct answer is (1).** The "Military Dresser" shows weapons everywhere except in space.

17. **The correct answer is (4).** This question tests your ability to read a map quickly and accurately. *The Gadsden Purchase* was added in 1853, making it the final acquisition to the continental, or mainland, United States.

18. **The correct answer is (2).** The *Mexican Cession* was added to the United States in 1848 as a result of the Mexican War, which ended that year.

19. **The correct answer is (1).** You can infer that the country grew quickly in the 1800s, or nineteenth century, because, according to the map, it almost doubled in size during this short period of time. The key phrase here is *based on this map*, meaning that you must disregard answer choices like (5), which are factually correct, but an incorrect answer to this question. There is no support for choices (2) or (3), which are therefore also incorrect. We are not told how all the lands were obtained.

20. **The correct answer is (5).** Only this answer summarizes the entire map, which is what the question requires. The other choices only describe limited parts of it.

21. **The correct answer is (1).** Spoken after Booth assassinated Lincoln at Ford's Theater on April 14, 1865, these words typified the lingering

animosity of the Reconstruction period to follow.

22. **The correct answer is (2).** Jefferson wrote these words during the Revolutionary War.

23. **The correct answer is (2).** These words were spoken by John Hay, Secretary of State, in 1898. The Spanish-American was the "littlest" of American wars, and highly manipulated by interests other than those of the territories directly involved.

24. **The correct answer is (5).** Alexander Bickel wrote these words in *The Morality of Consent*, after the conclusion of the Vietnamese Conflict.

25. **The correct answer is (5).** The "muckrakers" were authors who wrote about the abuses of the people by big business.

26. **The correct answer is (2).** The Sherman Anti-Trust Act of 1890 was the first federal act that sought to declare monopolies and attempts to restrain trade illegal.

27. **The correct answer is (1).** This is an example of foreign policy changing and adjusting with the times, which is a fairly common event. As the Soviet Union dissolved and Russia developed a nonaggressive leadership and became a more open and democratic society, it was no longer perceived as being a potential threat to the United States. Therefore, U.S. policy toward Russia changed positively.

28. **The correct answer is (3).** The series of events best describes the political changes within Japan during the time period given. It begins with the removal of the Tokigawa Shogun and the beginning of the Meiji Restoration in 1868. It ends with the American occupation of Japan at the end of World War II in 1945.

29. **The correct answer is (4).** The Ninth and Tenth Amendments give powers not otherwise described to the people and to the states. That means that if the federal government doesn't explicitly have a certain power, it can be assumed that the individual citizen, or individual state, can exercise that power.

30. **The correct answer is (2).** The Third Amendment protects citizens from having to house and feed troops during peacetime. This was a practice that was common during earlier periods of this country's history, and sometimes during wars that were closer to home, like the Civil War.

EXERCISES: ECONOMICS

Directions: For each question, circle the number of the response that best answers the question or completes the statement. An Answer Key and Explanations are provided at the end of this section.

YEAR	WHEAT PRODUCTION (thousands of bushels)	PRICE OF WHEAT (cents per bushel)
1875	2,450	51.9
1880	2,706	49.0
1885	3,058	42.2

1. The data in the chart above could best be used to illustrate which economic concept?

   (1) Recession

   (2) Inflation

   (3) Interdependence

   (4) Free enterprise

   (5) Supply and demand

2. "When prices of conventional fuels rise sufficiently to match the cost of solar energy, then solar energy will be able to supply more than 10 percent of our needs."

   In order to bring about greater use of solar energy, the author of this statement is relying primarily upon

   (1) the market system to cause consumers to switch to solar energy.

   (2) government policy to encourage solar energy at the expense of other fuels.

   (3) technological breakthroughs to reduce the cost of solar energy.

   (4) changes in the attitude of big business toward solar energy.

   (5) increase in availability of solar energy.

exercises

ITEMS 3 TO 6 REFER TO THE FOLLOWING CHART AND PASSAGE.

United Nations Millennium Project 2000

Rich countries should increase donations to 0.44 of their gross national income.	Rich countries should open their markets.	Wealthy countries should prepare for a quick response in case of an unexpected disaster.	Rich countries should target poor countries for rapid development.	More research needs to be done to address the causes of poverty in poor countries.	Poor countries need to improve efficiency, reduce corruption, and invest in their people wisely.

World leaders initiated the United Nations Millennium Project in order to alleviate hunger, disease, poverty, and misery in poor and developing countries. The goal is to halve world poverty by the year 2015. The above chart lists the main parts of this economic program. They include rich countries giving more financial aid to poor countries, targeting specific problems as they arise, increasing trade, and helping poor countries run their countries more efficiently so as to improve their ability to benefit from the aid given.

3. Which of the following actions of a poor country might be considered to be consistent with the goals of the Millennium Project?

  (1) Sending all young students to the movies.

  (2) Wiping out government waste and inefficiency.

  (3) Starting a boarding school for the sons of the rich and privileged.

  (4) Forbidding trade with other countries, especially the rich ones.

  (5) Increasing the number of national holidays.

4. It is suggested that rich countries

  (1) increase trade with poor countries.

  (2) increase tariffs.

  (3) improve the fairness of the World Court.

  (4) teach English in developing countries.

  (5) All of the above

5. Which of the following statements is TRUE according to the information given?

  (1) America is the most generous country in the developed world.

  (2) Only donor countries need to make changes to improve world prosperity.

  (3) Poverty is no longer a really serious problem.

  (4) The world's poorest nations are Haiti, Kenya, Indonesia, and Bangladesh.

  (5) Donor countries have been contributing less than .44 percent of their gross national income to developing countries.

6. Which of the following are possible reasons suggested by the information given as being at least partly responsible for the problem of poverty in developing countries?

   (1) Some areas of the earth have poor natural resources.

   (2) War and civil strife will often make a country poor.

   (3) Some countries may have corrupt or incompetent governments.

   (4) Colonialism has left many countries poorly equipped to rule itself wisely.

   (5) None of the above

   ITEMS 7 TO 10 REFER TO THE FOLLOWING PASSAGE.

President Lyndon B. Johnson was responsible for many programs in his *war on poverty*. The *Economic Opportunity Act of 1964* set up job-training programs, provided loans to college students and to small businesses that agreed to hire the unemployed, helped poverty-stricken Appalachia, and granted aid directly to needy elementary and secondary school students. The *Volunteers for America*, or *Vista*, was organized in 1965 in order to provide volunteers to work in rural poor areas with children, the elderly, Native Americans, agricultural migrant workers, and the mentally ill. *Operation Head Start, Job Corps*, and *Neighborhood Youth Corps* were also set up to help preschoolers and teenagers succeed. The *Community Action Program* was a way of encouraging self-help with financial aid for inner-city economic projects. Congress also approved a rent-supplement program under the Department of Housing and Urban Development, or HUD.

7. Which of the following statements is TRUE?

   (1) Very few of these programs really helped needy people.

   (2) The programs mentioned were part of Johnson's vision for a "great society."

   (3) Johnson was not concerned with the economic problems of the common man.

   (4) Congress failed to pass any of these programs.

   (5) None of these programs have survived in our day.

8. According to this passage, teenagers are directly helped by

   (1) Operation Head Start.

   (2) Community Action Program.

   (3) rent subsidies.

   (4) Job Corps and Neighborhood Youth Corps.

   (5) Volunteers for America.

9. Which program was designed to help increase employment?

   (1) Economic Opportunity Act

   (2) VISTA

   (3) Operation Head Start

   (4) Health Insurance Act

   (5) All of the above

10. Which of the following statements directly contradicts the philosophy behind President Johnson's *war on poverty* programs?

    (1) A dime saved is a dime earned.

    (2) Spare the rod and spoil the child.

    (3) Government should stay out of people's lives.

    (4) Everyone can use a helping hand from time to time.

    (5) Government is there to even the odds for economic success.

exercises

ITEMS 11 TO 16 REFER TO THE FOLLOWING PASSAGE.

Taxes are a fact of life in the United States. Income taxes in the United States did not exist prior to 1913, at which time reformers introduced legislation that became the Sixteenth Amendment. Soon, the federal income tax became the principal source of revenue for the federal government. The federal tax is an example of a *progressive* tax, meaning that people pay a higher proportion of their income in taxes as they make more money. This rule applies to state or local income taxes as well. However, Americans pay some *regressive* taxes also; these taxes are designed so that all people pay the same tax rate, no matter what their income. An example of a *regressive* tax would be an *excise* tax, which is a tax on some luxury items, like jewelry or furs.

Taxes are often collected before the money reaches your pockets. For example, your employer takes money out of your paycheck to pay your approximate federal, state, and local taxes. Also taken out of your paycheck are amounts for Social Security, which supports the elderly and handicapped, and Medicare, which pays for health care for the elderly. You pay other taxes as you purchase items in stores or pay for services.

11. In order to compute the income taxes you owe the federal government this year, your employer is required to give you a _____ that lists your earnings and withholding for the past year.

   (1) 1040A form
   (2) W2 form
   (3) Social Security form
   (4) Exemption statement
   (5) W4 form

12. Americans pay many different types of taxes to federal, state, and local governments. Choose the best example of a tax that we do NOT pay in the United States.

   (1) Payroll taxes
   (2) Excise taxes
   (3) Value-added taxes
   (4) Sales taxes
   (5) Income taxes

13. The major purpose of our tax system is to provide funds for the operation of the government. But taxes are also levied in order to

   (1) develop or protect certain industries.
   (2) redistribute income.
   (3) influence personal spending.
   (4) educate the young.
   (5) All of the above

14. A tax on perfume is an example of a(n)

   (1) income tax.
   (2) excise tax.
   (3) property tax.
   (4) estate tax.
   (5) stock transfer tax.

15. Susan Johnson earned $15,000 last year. Sam Milner earned $63,000 last year. Each person was required to pay a special tax of $350. Which of the following terms best describes this tax?

   (1) Proportional
   (2) Regressive
   (3) Inexpensive
   (4) Progressive
   (5) Unearned

16. Payments to a worker, his dependents, and/or survivors in the event of retirement, disability, or death are generally covered by the system of insurance known as

 (1) unemployment compensation.

 (2) Social Security.

 (3) worker's compensation.

 (4) pension fund.

 (5) profit sharing.

17. Most Americans seek to reduce the financial burdens that can occur in case of unusual illness, accident, fire, theft, or old age by purchasing insurance policies. Insurance serves as a means of guaranteeing individuals against losses of all kinds. Insurance policies are an example of

 (1) worker's compensation.

 (2) government taxes.

 (3) wasteful spending.

 (4) trusts.

 (5) good financial planning.

ITEMS 18 TO 20 REFER TO THE FOLLOWING GRAPH.

U.S. Balance of International Payments

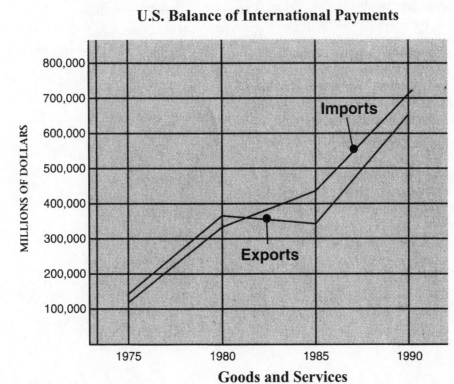

Goods and Services

18. According to the graph, the value of goods and services exported by the United States exceeded the value of goods and services imported during the years

 (1) 1975-1982

 (2) 1982-1985

 (3) 1980-1990

 (4) 1985-1990

 (5) The graph does not reveal this information.

19. The value of goods and services imported by the United States exceeded the value of goods and services exported during the years

 (1) 1975-1980

 (2) 1980-1985

 (3) 1980-1990

 (4) 1982-1990

 (5) The graph does not reveal this information.

20. By about how many millions of dollars did imports exceed exports in 1985? (Answer in millions of dollars.)

   (1) 4,000

   (2) 10,000

   (3) 40,000

   (4) 100,000

   (5) 1,000,000

ITEMS 21 AND 22 REFER TO THE FOLLOWING ARTICLE

Advertising of nonprescription medicine has become a frequent source of confusion and wasteful expense. Sometimes it can even damage health. Among heavily advertised patent medicines are those that claim to have rejuvenating powers and are sold to elderly people. One leading gerontologist has pointed out that most such medicines generally contain vitamins and alcohol, that the alcohol is cheaper at the liquor store, and most people do not need extra vitamins.

Television is especially convincing in the sale of drugs and medicine because it can show pseudoscientific demonstrations, featuring actors who look authentic and speak authoritatively—as if they were actually doctors, dentists, or scientists.

21. According to the selection above, the most frequent victims of patent medicines are

   (1) elderly people.

   (2) young children.

   (3) arthritis sufferers.

   (4) people with headaches.

   (5) people with dental problems.

22. Television as a sales medium is particularly effective because it

   (1) conveys the appearance of authenticity.

   (2) is usually in color.

   (3) is often watched by old people and children.

   (4) costs nothing.

   (5) can be repeated incessantly.

ITEM 23 REFERS TO THE FOLLOWING BAR GRAPH.

Federal Spending on Education, 1965 and 1971

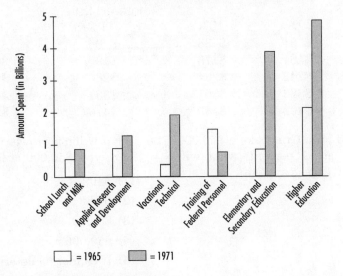

☐ = 1965   ▨ = 1971

23. Which of the following statements can be verified by information in the graph?

(1) In general, it was more expensive to fund elementary and secondary education than state universities during both those years.

(2) The cost of providing school lunches skyrocketed in 1971.

(3) The Federal government did not value research and development in the field of education very highly during 1965 and 1971.

(4) The importance of vocational education declined in 1971.

(5) In 1971, most Americans believed that federal funds for education were not being wisely spent.

ITEMS 24 TO 26 REFER TO THE TABLE BELOW.

30-Year Mortgage (Principal and Interest per Month)

Mortgage Amount			Interest Rate		
	9%	10%	11%	12%	13%
$10,000	$ 81	$ 88	$ 95	$103	$111
$20,000	$161	$176	$190	$206	$221
$30,000	$242	$264	$286	$309	$330
$40,000	$322	$351	$381	$411	$442
$50,000	$402	$439	$476	$515	$553

24. If Mr. and Mrs. Gray take a $40,000 mortgage at 11 percent, what will their mortgage payments be each month?

(1) $206

(2) $286

(3) $322

(4) $351

(5) $381

25. Which of the following statements is NOT supported by the information in the mortgage table?

(1) People will make higher mortgage payments as the interest rates increase.

(2) Mortgage payments will increase as the amount of money borrowed increases.

(3) It will cost more to borrow $10,000 at 13 percent than at 12 percent.

(4) It is more expensive to borrow $40,000 at 12 percent than $50,000 at 10 percent.

(5) It is cheaper to borrow $30,000 at 10 percent than at 12 percent.

26. What will a borrower pay in one year to borrow $50,000 at 9 percent?

(1) $402

(2) $4,824

(3) $5,530

(4) $50,000

(5) It cannot be determined.

ITEMS 27 AND 28 REFER TO THE FOLLOWING ILLUSTRATION.

Purchasing Power of the Dollar

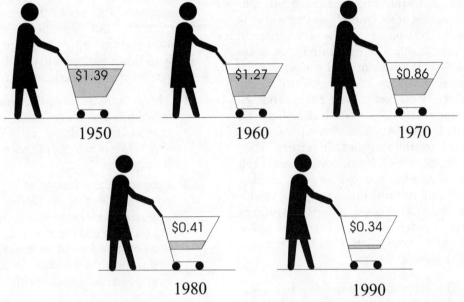

27. The illustration tells the story of the value of money in selected years. If you needed to assign a base year when a dollar would probably buy a dollar's worth of goods, which of the following is the most likely?

(1) 2006

(2) 1976

(3) 1967

(4) 1950

(5) 1955

28. With which of the following statements would the author of this illustration agree?

(1) The illustration probably shows the effects of inflation between 1950 and 1990.

(2) You should try to get the best interest rate on your savings to increase their value with time.

(3) To keep up with the cost of living, a worker who was employed during this time frame needed to get regular raises.

(4) A periodic increase in the minimum wage law is necessary.

(5) All of the above

ITEMS 29 AND 30 REFER TO THE FOLLOWING TEXT.

Currently, because of the growth of economic, cultural, and technological connections between countries, the world is actually getting smaller and smaller. In the year 2000, it is estimated that more than 50,000 multinational companies accounted for more than one fifth of the total world economy. That means that giant corporations like Shell and Microsoft are no longer "American" companies, but instead are international in nature. They hire employees, manufacture and sell their products, and get needed technological and natural materials on a worldwide basis. Therefore, potential workers in the United States need to compete more and more with workers from all over the world.

29. The economic phenomena being explained in this passage is called

   (1) globalization.

   (2) monopoly.

   (3) poor foreign policy.

   (4) stagnation.

   (5) recession.

30. The World Trade Organization was created in 1995 as the only international organization that deals with the rules governing trade among nations across the globe. Their meetings, with 143 member nations attending, have often been marked by sometimes violent anti-globalization street demonstrations. Why?

   (1) The demonstrators are holding multinational companies responsible for drugs, crime, and other problems of contemporary life.

   (2) Because of the feeling of powerlessness in the face of huge multinational conglomerates, which often put smaller local economies out of business and impose "American" or European culture on local people.

   (3) The demonstrators are out-of-control unemployed people.

   (4) The demonstrations show feelings of anti-Americanism.

   (5) The objections relate to the spread of English as the international language.

ANSWER KEY AND EXPLANATIONS

1. (5)	9. (1)	17. (5)	24. (5)
2. (1)	10. (3)	18. (1)	25. (4)
3. (2)	11. (2)	19. (4)	26. (2)
4. (1)	12. (3)	20. (4)	27. (3)
5. (5)	13. (5)	21. (1)	28. (5)
6. (3)	14. (2)	22. (1)	29. (1)
7. (2)	15. (2)	23. (3)	30. (2)
8. (4)	16. (2)		

1. **The correct answer is (5).** The data show that as the supply of wheat increased, the price decreased. This is an illustration of the concept of supply and demand.

2. **The correct answer is (1).** According to the author's point of view, solar energy will be used once its cost matches that of conventional fuels. If something is cheaper, and just as good or better, the consumer will buy it. This is an example of the market system at work.

3. **The correct answer is (2).** The Millennium Project requires poor countries to become more efficient and wise. Otherwise, foreign aid will not help them overcome poverty. The only choice given that meets this criterion is (2), *wiping out government waste and inefficiency,* meaning using money wisely and well. The other choices would not contribute toward the overall economic improvement of the country.

4. **The correct answer is (1).** The second column of the chart gives you the answer—"rich nations should open their markets," meaning that they should have greater business and trade with poor countries. The other choices given are irrelevant or nonsensical.

5. **The correct answer is (5).** The only statement supported by the information given is the last choice. The first column states a goal that countries increase their contribution to .44 percent, suggesting that they have been giving less than that amount. Nothing is stated indicating which country is the most generous or who the poorest nations are, so choices (1) and (4) are incorrect. The last column of the chart, which states that developing countries also must make changes in order to eliminate poverty in their countries, contradicts choice (2). Choice (3) is also contradicted by the entire passage.

6. **The correct answer is (3).** The last column in the chart, as well as the text below it, suggest that many poor countries are ruled poorly, with inefficient or corrupt governments, and an inability to use money wisely in such a way that the country will benefit. The topics of natural resources, wars, and colonialism are not mentioned or suggested in the passage.

7. **The correct answer is (2).** Johnson had a vision where the government was to help people achieve the best in terms of their education, economic well being, and quality of life, and this he called the "great society." These "war on poverty" programs were enacted to help achieve these aims. Choices (1) and (3) are clearly contradicted by the passage. Choice (4) is also incorrect, because if Congress had not passed legislation, none of these programs would have come to pass. Choice (5) is incorrect because the passage does not discuss

the present-day status of these programs.

8. **The correct answer is (4).** The programs that directly help teenagers and young adults are *Job Corps*, which is a program for school dropouts, and *Neighborhood Youth Corps,* which is for unemployed teenagers. *Head Start* is for preschoolers, rent subsidies are generally for low-income people, and *Volunteers for America* is a program of volunteerism to help needy people of all ages.

9. **The correct answer is (1).** By providing loans to small businesses that agreed to hire people who had been unemployed, the *Economic Opportunity Act* helped to lower unemployment among workers in the 1960s. The other choices are incorrect because they relate minimally or indirectly to efforts to improve work opportunities.

10. **The correct answer is (3).** President Johnson's philosophy seemed to be that there was a role for government in improving the quality of people's lives in economic and educational areas. Choice (3), government should stay out of people's lives, is the exact opposite, and therefore the correct answer. Choices (1) and (2), which deal with being frugal and with child-rearing, are irrelevant. Choices (4) and (5) seem to agree with Johnson's philosophy and are therefore also incorrect, since the question asks for a contradictory or opposite point of view.

11. **The correct answer is (2).** The W2 form specifies earnings and withholding.

12. **The correct answer is (3).** Value-added taxes are taxes based on the increase in price or value at each level of production of a product. They are not levied in the United States.

13. **The correct answer is (5).** Choices (1), (2), (3), and (4) are all reasons for tax levies.

14. **The correct answer is (2).** Excise taxes are taxes on luxury items.

15. **The correct answer is (2).** Regressive taxes are those levied without regard to the income of the taxpayer.

16. **The correct answer is (2).** Social Security covers all these.

17. **The correct answer is (5).** Making sure you don't go bankrupt as a result of some catastrophic event, like an accident or a fire, is an example of good financial planning. It shows that you are looking ahead and safeguarding your future. The other choices are irrelevant and incorrect.

18. **The correct answer is (1).** To find the years in which exports exceeded imports, find a section of the graph where the line that illustrates exports appears over the "imports" line. This happens in 1975, 1976, 1977, 1978, 1979, 1980, 1981, and 1982.

19. **The correct answer is (4).** Imports exceed exports when the "imports" line is over the "exports" line: from 1982 through the end of the graph.

20. **The correct answer is (4).** Imports in 1985 = around $460,000 million. Exports in 1985 = around $360,000 million. The difference is $100,000 million.

21. **The correct answer is (1).** The third sentence states that the most heavily advertised patent medicines are those that claim to have rejuvenating powers; they are sold to the elderly.

22. **The correct answer is (1).** Although all of the answers have some truth, the best answer is choice (1), since the major idea of authenticity is stressed in the passage.

23. **The correct answer is (3).** Since the Federal government spent only a small portion of its overall budget on *Applied Research and Development,* and since it didn't go up very much

between 1965 and 1971, you can assume that such work was not highly thought of at the time. Choice (1) is opposite to the information given on the graph. Choice (2) is an exaggeration, since costs only went up slightly. Choice (4) is incorrect, since spending for vocational education almost quadrupled in 1971. Choice (5) is not the topic of the bar graph and is therefore an incorrect answer.

24. **The correct answer is (5).** The table shows that $40,000 borrowed at 11 percent costs $381 per month.

25. **The correct answer is (4).** $40,000 borrowed at 12 percent costs $411 a month; $50,000 borrowed at 10 percent costs $439 a month. The $40,000 loan is cheaper, therefore choice (4) is false.

26. **The correct answer is (2).** A $50,000 loan at 9 percent costs $402 per month. $402 per month times 12 payments = $4,824 a year.

27. **The correct answer is (3).** You can see from the illustration that in 1960 you could buy $1.27 worth of goods for one dollar. In 1970, a dollar would only buy $0.86 or 86 cents worth of goods by comparison. So the answer lies some where in between 1960 and 1970, making choice (3), or 1967, the best estimated answer.

28. **The correct answer is (5).** Since the first four choices are in agreement with the illustration, the answer is choice (5), All of the above. What is being illustrated is the effect of *inflation,* which refers to the shrinking buying power of the dollar with time. Interest on your savings would make your balance go up, which is necessary to maintain the value. Wage increases and minimum wage laws that increase are also necessary to keep up with the rising cost of living.

29. **The correct answer is (1).** *Globalization* refers to the act of ignoring boundaries between countries in terms of economics. It means that the whole Earth, or *globe,* is potentially viewed as the source and location of business. For example, *Coca Cola* is enjoyed all over the world. Japanese cars are often assembled in the United States, just as American manufacturing plants are increasingly located in other countries, such as Mexico. The other answer choices are unrelated to the topic of the passage.

30. **The correct answer is (2).** There may be a thread of truth in all the answers, but the best answer is choice (2) because it summarizes the central complaint, which is the feeling of powerlessness. The demonstrators are often people from all over the world who feel angry because of the fast spread of these multinational companies that overtake competition, subvert local culture, and seem to take control away from locals. Sometimes there are feelings against the United States, because of its super-power strength, and sometimes the complaints involve feelings that age-old local language, customs, and traditions are being affected by American or western globalization.

answers exercises

EXERCISES: CIVICS AND GOVERNMENT

Directions: For each question, circle the number of the response that best answers the question or completes the statement. An Answer Key and Explanations are provided at the end of this section.

ITEMS 1 TO 5 REFER TO THE INFORMATION BELOW.

Politicians and big businesses are becoming increasingly adept at using propaganda techniques to influence the public. Many of the techniques used to create effective propaganda are known to us in everyday communications and conversation. Each of us has used or heard these techniques for separating the listener from thorough examination of the idea being conveyed. Listed below are five such techniques and brief descriptions of how each is used.

Plain folks	a speaker tries to convince an audience that we're all just plain folks who think alike and act alike
Glittering generality	a speaker associates his ideas with a "virtue"
Testimonial	a respected person is used to endorse an idea
Card stacking	a speaker uses untrue or illogical statements in order to make the best possible (or worst possible) case for an idea
Bandwagon	attempts to convince the audience that everyone in the group has accepted this idea

Based on the information above, look at the following quotations and situations to determine the propaganda technique being used.

1. At a scientific discussion on the worldwide extinction of the dinosaurs, a supporter leaves out the information that some dinosaurs were still living even after the "massive extinction" of "all" the dinosaurs.

   The propaganda technique in use is

   (1) plain folks.
   (2) glittering generality.
   (3) testimonial.
   (4) card stacking.
   (5) bandwagon.

2. As you flip on the television set, you see one of America's most famous actresses praising the quality and performance of a luxurious foreign sports car.

   The propaganda technique in use is

   (1) plain folks.
   (2) glittering generality.
   (3) testimonial.
   (4) card stacking.
   (5) bandwagon.

3. *Vogue, Glamour,* and *Harper's Bazaar* all decree that the fashionable skirt for spring ends just 3 inches above a woman's knee.

   The propaganda technique in use is

   (1) plain folks.

   (2) glittering generality.

   (3) testimonial.

   (4) card stacking.

   (5) bandwagon.

4. Taste testers for the cola companies descend upon unsuspecting shoppers in grocery stores and malls and record their results for television and cable audiences.

   The propaganda technique in use is

   (1) plain folks.

   (2) glittering generality.

   (3) testimonial.

   (4) card stacking.

   (5) bandwagon.

5. Campaigners of a particular party represent themselves and their ideas to the public as being the only ones on the side of values, goodness, and old-time morality.

   The propaganda technique in use is

   (1) plain folks.

   (2) glittering generality.

   (3) testimonial.

   (4) card stacking.

   (5) bandwagon.

exercises

ITEMS 6 TO 9 REFER TO THE FOLLOWING INFORMATION.

Americans are members of numerous special-interest groups, such as labor unions, professional organizations, and business organizations that exert pressure upon national, state, and local legislators. These special-interest groups often employ a specialist in placing pressure, otherwise called *a lobbyist*. Competent lobbyists push for favored treatment for their clients and use a number of techniques in the course of their work. Some of these techniques include:

Communications	letter-writing campaigns, personal visits, and telephone calls
Campaign contributions	lobbyists often find contributions for friendly legislators running for reelection
Social contacts	are used to build a network of friendships and obligations
Sanctions	can be applied against a legislator who does not recognize the causes advanced by the lobbyist
Formation of alliances	enables different groups to join together in support of or opposition to a proposed bill

Each of the following items describes the action of a lobby or special-interest group. Choose the term that most nearly identifies the technique being used.

6. A proposal to prohibit smoking in public places of assembly, restaurants, elevators, and schools has been brought before the state legislature. The state medical society, the "Right to Fresh Air" Committee, the state nurses association, and several county health departments have jointly endorsed the bill.

 The lobbying technique in use is

 (1) communications.
 (2) campaign contributions.
 (3) social contacts.
 (4) sanctions.
 (5) formation of alliances.

7. The Friends of Bergen County Public Library have endorsed a bill before the state legislature that will double the amount of state aid to every public library in the state. The bill is tied up in the Education Committee and it seems unlikely that the legislature will have the opportunity to take a vote. The president of the Friends group urges you to send a telegram to the chair of the Education Committee.

 The lobbying technique in use is

 (1) communications.
 (2) campaign contributions.
 (3) social contacts.
 (4) sanctions.
 (5) formation of alliances.

8. An industry group, the National Association of Television Station Owners, hosts a golf tournament each spring for senators and representatives and their staffs, by invitation only.

The lobbying technique in use is

(1) communications.
(2) campaign contributions.
(3) social contacts.
(4) sanctions.
(5) formation of alliances.

9. Congresswoman Greene took a strong stand against the "gun lobby" in the last two sessions of Congress. Illegal firearms have been the cause of a number of deaths in the suburban district she represents. In her next campaign for reelection she finds herself facing a challenge in the primaries. The candidate who opposes her is funded by several PACs (political action committees); among them is one funded by members of the National Rifle Association.

The lobbying technique in use is

(1) communications.
(2) campaign contributions.
(3) social contacts.
(4) sanctions.
(5) formation of alliances.

exercises

ITEM 10 REFERS TO THE PUBLIC OPINION SURVEY BELOW.

Question	PERCENT OF PUBLIC		
	Agree	Disagree	Not Sure
Campaigns for Congress should be supported by public funds only.	30	62	8
PACs (Political Action Committees) should be prohibited from contributing more than $5,000 to any congressional campaign.	35	53	12

10. The information in the chart above indicates that most of the people questioned

    (1) favored changes in campaign financing.

    (2) supported both statements.

    (3) were unclear about the issues.

    (4) were divided on the two questions.

    (5) favored the status quo.

11. Benjamin Franklin stated that "a free and independent press assures freedom from tyranny." As long as newspapers are free to express their political opinions, report the news as they see it, and advocate for the ideas that are important to them, the public will be protected. Currently, there is much consolidation of the public media. A couple of large companies are buying up many formerly independent newspapers throughout the country, as well as radio and television stations.

Why is this potentially dangerous?

    (1) Big companies would become a voice for big business.

    (2) Because it can lead to the public not getting a balanced picture by getting only one side of an argument or problem and of not being fully informed.

    (3) Large companies are often international, so that foreign political news will take precedence over pressing American concerns.

    (4) The author is wrong—this is not potentially dangerous, but will assure the more efficient gathering of information.

    (5) Large companies that overextend are more likely to go into bankruptcy, which would leave the nation without newspapers or other public media.

12. In a United States presidential election, the electoral vote was distributed as follows:

CANDIDATE	W	X	Y	Z
% of electoral vote	36%	36%	18%	10%

Based on this information, which of the following choices would be the most likely outcome of the election?

(1) Candidate W was declared the winner immediately after the election.

(2) Candidate W became president and candidate X became vice president.

(3) A new presidential election was held with only candidates W and X running for office.

(4) The president was chosen by the members of the House of Representatives.

(5) The president was chosen by a joint resolution of the Senate and the House.

ITEMS 13 TO 16 REFER TO THE INFORMATION BELOW.

In governing their various states, each governor receives administrative assistance from a variety of state officials, both elected and appointed. Most state governments typically include these officials:

Lieutenant governor   presides over the state senate; sits as acting governor when governor leaves the state

Attorney general   enforces state laws; represents the state in court as chief prosecutor or defense attorney; serves as legal advisor to the state government

Secretary of state   supervises the state's official business

State treasurer   collects taxes and pays bills

Superintendent of public instruction   supervises the administration of public schools and enforces the state education code

Each of the following items describes a situation in which a citizen or citizens would need to call upon the assistance of a state official. Choose the best official to deal with each problem.

13. A rapidly growing company decides to change its legal structure and become incorporated. Which official deals with this problem?

    (1) Lieutenant governor

    (2) Attorney general

    (3) Secretary of state

    (4) State treasurer

    (5) Superintendent of public instruction

14. In the Fort Deeges School District, handicapped children are entitled to attend classes along with nonhandicapped children as much as is physically possible. Mr. and Mrs. Jenkin's son, who is confined to a wheelchair, has been denied the right to attend chemistry or physics classes at his high school, despite appeals to the principal and the local school board. To which state official should the Jenkinses turn for help?

    (1) Lieutenant governor

    (2) Attorney general

    (3) Secretary of state

    (4) State treasurer

    (5) Superintendent of public instruction

15. The governor of the state resigns in the middle of his term to run for a seat in the U.S. Senate. Which official deals with this problem?

    (1) Lieutenant governor

    (2) Attorney general

    (3) Secretary of state

    (4) State treasurer

    (5) Superintendent of public instruction

16. A pyramid scheme, supposedly designed to make every participant rich in a short time, has collapsed. More than 100 people were victimized, and each one lost between $500 and $2,500. To whom should these victims turn for help?

    (1) Lieutenant governor

    (2) Attorney general

    (3) Secretary of state

    (4) State treasurer

    (5) Superintendent of public instruction

ITEM 17 IS BASED ON THE QUOTATIONS BELOW.

"Whenever . . . government becomes destructive to these ends it is the right of the people to alter or abolish it, and to institute new government. . . ."

—Thomas Jefferson

". . . there comes a time when people get tired. We are here this evening to say to those who have mistreated us so long that we are tired—tired of being segregated and humiliated, tired of being kicked about by the brutal feet of oppression. We have no alternative but to protest. . . ."

—Martin Luther King, Jr.

17. Which statement best summarizes the main idea of both quotations?

    (1) Violence is the only effective form of protest.
    (2) Government is harmful to freedom and human dignity.
    (3) Revolution is inevitable in a democratic society.
    (4) The people may ultimately have to force the government to meet their needs.
    (5) The people should ignore laws they do not agree with.

ITEMS 18 TO 19 REFER TO THE FOLLOWING QUOTATION FROM THE SUPREME COURT DECISION IN THE CASE OF *BROWN VS. BOARD OF EDUCATION OF TOPEKA, KANSAS.*

"We conclude that in the field of public education the doctrine of 'separate but equal' has no place. Separate educational facilities are inherently unequal. Therefore, we hold that the plaintiffs . . . are, by reason of the segregation complained of, deprived of the equal protection of the laws guaranteed by the Fourteenth Amendment."

18. This Supreme Court decision is based on the idea that segregation in education is likely to

    (1) deny individuals the opportunity to make upward social and economic progress.
    (2) create unnecessary administrative problems in the nation's schools.
    (3) place excessive burdens on school transportation systems.
    (4) result in unfair tax increases to support dual school systems.
    (5) result in higher educational standards.

19. This Supreme Court ruling can most accurately be said to have marked the beginning of the end of

    (1) racial violence.
    (2) public education.
    (3) legal racial discrimination.
    (4) the civil rights movement.
    (5) private education.

ITEMS 20 TO 22 REFER TO THE FOLLOWING PASSAGE.

Recent national elections have pinpointed some difficulties with the many voting machines in use throughout the country, with some voters questioning their consistency and reliability. With the passage of the Help America Vote Act (HAVA) and nearly $4 billion in funds from Washington to local districts to purchase new voting machines, software, and databases, it was hoped that the voting process would be modernized.

But as concerns over the security and reliability of the new direct-recording electronic voting machines (DRE's) have increased, so too has public concern over the political activity of some of the large companies that design, manufacture, and maintain them. These companies have been accused of having contributed to political campaigns and of having been engaged in lobbying activities.

20. Which of the following statements is supported by this passage?

(1) Many different types of voting methods were being employed throughout the country.

(2) Everyone in the mid-West was concerned about the machines being used in their states.

(3) All the voting machines being used were faulty.

(4) Only 54 percent of the adult population of the U.S. votes.

(5) DRE is the largest manufacturer of voting machines.

21. Why would it be undesirable for voting-machine manufacturers to be involved in political activity?

(1) They might amass too much money by becoming a monopoly.

(2) It might cast doubt on the reliability of the product they are creating, which might favor one party over another.

(3) No manufacturing company should be engaged in politics.

(4) It would not be undesirable, since we would then know their political leanings.

(5) They might spend more money on lobbying and not enough on perfecting voting machines.

22. A criticism of these new electronic voting machines is that they do not leave a "paper trail" in case a recount is needed. A "paper trail" refers to

(1) the messy paper that election organizers leave around after the election is over.

(2) the permanent paper ballots that are used in rural areas.

(3) newspaper articles about the elections.

(4) a record on paper of the voting activity on any particular machine.

(5) the banners that election organizers place in their headquarters.

ITEMS 23 AND 24 REFER TO THE FOLLOWING QUOTATION.

"An informed public depends on accurate and open reporting by the news media. No individual can obtain for himself the information needed for the intelligent discharge of his political responsibilities. . . . The press therefore acts as an agent of the public at large."

23. The quotation most clearly supports the idea that the news media have a responsibility to

(1) report news in an objective fashion.

(2) create national agreement on controversial issues.

(3) eliminate editorials on controversial news subjects.

(4) encourage public participation in news-gathering activities.

(5) report every story regardless of its source.

24. Which of the following does the speaker believe to be the major reason for keeping abreast of the news?

(1) To demonstrate intelligence

(2) To make sound political judgments

(3) To advance in your job

(4) To increase your store of information

(5) To know what to expect

25. The nine justices of the U.S. Supreme Court all receive lifetime appointments. In which of the following ways do you think that their legal decisions would probably be most affected by this fact?

(1) Because they have federal appointments, they probably favor the federal government over state governments when the two are on opposite sides of an issue.

(2) They work more slowly and carefully than they might if some oversight group could set the pace.

(3) They will tend to follow the beliefs of the president who nominated them.

(4) They probably tend to become fair and independent thinkers because they are not accountable to any politician or party.

(5) They rely more heavily on initial drafts of decisions that are written by their law clerks.

exercises

ITEMS 26 AND 27 REFER TO THE FOLLOWING QUOTATION.

"The accumulation of all powers, legislative, executive, and judiciary in the same hands . . . is the very definition of tyranny."

—From *Federalist 47* by James Madison

26. The fear expressed by James Madison is the fear of

    (1) concentration of power.
    (2) division of power.
    (3) executive authority.
    (4) an independent judiciary.
    (5) checks and balances.

27. The Constitution follows through on Madison's ideas by

    (1) dividing power between state and national governments.
    (2) separating power among the three branches of government.
    (3) adopting a Bill of Rights.
    (4) making ratification very difficult.
    (5) creating a complicated amending process.

28. U.S. Senators are elected for six-year terms. They are expected to represent the interests of their states and to take a long-range view of the needs of the entire country as well. Which qualities or experiences would be LEAST useful for a U.S. senator to have?

    (1) An ability to reach compromises on important issues.
    (2) A clear understanding of the meaning of the Constitution.
    (3) Strong financial and business skills.
    (4) Strong ties to a foreign government.
    (5) A good public speaking style.

29. George Washington set a precedent by not running for a third term as president of the United States. Later on, this practice became the law. Why is a two-term limit a good policy for the country?

    (1) Most people are too tired after two terms as president to be effective during a third term.
    (2) Many people want to be president, and it's not fair to them if one person has the job for too long.
    (3) One person should not have so much power for such a long period of time.
    (4) Members of Congress object to the predictable policies of a president who has held office for so long.
    (5) Most citizens get tired of listening to one leader after eight years and need to hear from someone else.

30. An American student in London becomes friendly with the "wrong crowd" and soon is involved in a bungled robbery. The robbers are apprehended and the American student calls the American Consulate for help. The Consul can offer advice and encouragement to the jailed student but he or she CANNOT

    (1) request the release of the student, as a U.S. citizen, for trial in the United States.
    (2) attend the trial as an observer.
    (3) communicate with the student's parents to reassure them that the student is being treated fairly.
    (4) visit the student in prison if the student is convicted.
    (5) bring the student small gifts from home

ANSWER KEY AND EXPLANATIONS

1. (4)	9. (4)	17. (4)	25. (4)
2. (3)	10. (5)	18. (1)	26. (1)
3. (5)	11. (2)	19. (3)	27. (2)
4. (1)	12. (4)	20. (1)	28. (4)
5. (2)	13. (3)	21. (2)	29. (3)
6. (5)	14. (5)	22. (4)	30. (1)
7. (1)	15. (1)	23. (1)	
8. (3)	16. (2)	24. (2)	

1. **The correct answer is (4).** By conveniently leaving out some facts, the speaker gives his side of the "argument" the strongest support.

2. **The correct answer is (3).** This is an example of a testimonial. The famous actress is associated with the car even though her testimonial may be paid by the car manufacturer.

3. **The correct answer is (5).** This is an example of the bandwagon technique: Everyone is doing it, that is, if your "everyone" includes the group that reads *Vogue, Glamour,* and *Harper's Bazaar.*

4. **The correct answer is (1).** These ordinary people shopping at the supermarket liked Coca Cola, and being just like them (us), so will you, is what the suggestion is that is being made to influence you.

5. **The correct answer is (2).** By associating themselves and their ideas with values, goodness, and morality, the implication is that the ideas are good and that the public, if they also want to be on the side of values and morality, should vote for the candidates of this party. The technique also serves the double purpose of painting the opposing party as probably *not* having those same values and ideals, which may in fact not be true.

6. **The correct answer is (5).** Each of these organizations represents distinct yet related interests. By forming an alliance or coalition they are able to overwhelm and convince legislators of the clout behind the advancement of the issue.

7. **The correct answer is (1).** Communication—letter writing, e-mails, faxes, telephone calls, and telegrams—is a valuable low-budget tool of lobbying groups as well as individual citizens who wish to express their viewpoints on any issue.

8. **The correct answer is (3).** This is an example of the use of social contacts. Large business and industrial groups frequently sponsor outings and social events for legislators and their staffs and families, especially legislators who sit on key committees that formulate laws restricting or supporting specific industries and types of businesses.

9. **The correct answer is (4).** Though the action involves political campaign contributions, sanctions are specifically being applied against the Congresswoman. The sanction consists of her opponent in the next re-election being supported by the "gun lobby."

10. **The correct answer is (5).** At the present time, campaigns for Congress are supported by private fortunes and donations from private citizens, special-interest groups, and business interests. A majority of the respondents disagreed quite clearly

answers exercises

with both questions (62 to 30 and 53 to 35), respectively, thereby eliminating choices (1), (2), and (4). We do not have any additional information about how or where or to whom these questions were administered; therefore, choice (3) is not an acceptable answer. Choice (5) is clearly supported by the statistics.

11. **The correct answer is (2).** The danger lies in the fact that having all the newspapers and other media controlled by just a couple of companies means that the programming on radio and television, as well as what is reported in the newspapers, could easily be slanted or limited to just one view. There would be no assurance of "freedom from tyranny" as Franklin warned, since people would not have alternative voices to listen to.

12. **The correct answer is (4).** If no candidate receives a majority of electoral votes, the election is decided by the House of Representatives.

13. **The correct answer is (3).** The secretary of state registers the state's official business, including the status of business corporations.

14. **The correct answer is (5).** Education is ultimately a state responsibility, and the state superintendent of public instruction (or his/her equivalent) is usually the final decision maker in conflicts concerning the application of state education regulations.

15. **The correct answer is (1).** Most states have a lieutenant governor who would fill the job of the governor should he/she retire, resign, die, or be impeached.

16. **The correct answer is (2).** The attorney general, often regarded as the second-most important job in state government, is highly visible and "political" as well as responsible for law enforcement within the state.

17. **The correct answer is (4).** Both Thomas Jefferson and Martin Luther King, Jr., supported the notion that a government is for the people and by the people. They believed that it was the people's right to rebel against an oppressive government (Jefferson) or protest against one that discriminated against one group, namely African Americans (King).

18. **The correct answer is (1).** The Supreme Court decision is based upon the idea that segregation in education is "unequal" and likely to deny African-American children the opportunity to make upward social and economic progress.

19. **The correct answer is (3).** By declaring segregated school systems to be unconstitutional, the Supreme Court ruling can most accurately be said to have marked the beginning of the end of legal racial discrimination.

20. **The correct answer is (1).** The first sentence of the passage confirms this answer—the many voting machines in use throughout the country. Choices (2) and (4) are not discussed. Choice (3) is an exaggeration—the passage states only that some voters saw a problem, not that all the machines were faulty. And DRE stands for direct-recording electronic machines, which are electronic voting machines, not the name of any company.

21. **The correct answer is (2).** It is felt that if a voting machine manufacturer is politically involved with one or the other side in an election, it might create a voting machine product that favors that side. Since these machines are computerized and very complicated, it would be difficult to detect a faulty machine. Therefore, it is very important for the manufacturer to be viewed by the public as being a highly credible and ethical

company with no political involvement.

22. **The correct answer is (4).** Because these new machines are electronic, they do not leave a record on paper, or a "paper trail," as the older machines do. The evidence is in the form of an electronic record only. Therefore, if a recount were needed, it would be impossible to do. The other answers are nonsensical and irrelevant.

23. **The correct answer is (1).** Accurate and objective news reports are for the purpose of informing the public so that individuals can make up their own minds about important issues.

24. **The correct answer is (2).** The speaker says that information is needed "for the intelligent discharge of . . . political responsibilities," in other words, to make sound political judgements. Choice (2) is the best answer even though there might be some truth to the other choices as well.

25. **The correct answer is (4).** This independence has led some justices, including some of the most famous, to follow their consciences, regardless of previous tilts toward liberal or conservative platforms and regardless of who the president was who initially nominated them for the Supreme Court position.

26. **The correct answer is (1).** Madison feared that the consequence of placing all governmental power in the hands of one person, or one branch of government, would be a *concentration of power* that could lead to a dictatorship or tyranny. Choices (2), (4), and (5) are the opposite in meaning here—division of power, independent courts, and maintaining checks and balances among the three branches of government assures that a tyranny is not created.

27. **The correct answer is (2).** The outline of government described in the Federalist Papers was carried out in the provisions of the Constitution, which created a separation of powers among the three branches of government—the administrative (or president), the legislative (Congress), and the judicial (the Supreme Court).

28. **The correct answer is (4).** You can infer that having strong ties to a foreign government might make it impossible for an elected American official to operate with the best interest of the United States in mind. The other qualities mentioned—an ability to compromise and a clear understanding of financial matters and Constitutional law, as well as a good persuasive speaking ability, are all important qualities that a senator must have to succeed in government.

29. **The correct answer is (3).** The two-term limit is part of the system of checks and balances, which prevents any one group or individual from gaining too much power in the nation. The longer a person remains in the office of the presidency, the more power he and his party are likely to accumulate.

30. **The correct answer is (1).** As a signatory of the Universal Declaration of Human Rights, the United States is bound to the precept that all American citizens accused of a crime in a foreign nation are subject to the laws of that nation. Given this fact, the Consul may not request the release of the student for trial in the United States as a U.S. citizen. He or she may, of course, observe the trial, visit the student, and communicate with the parents of the student.

answers exercises

EXERCISES: GEOGRAPHY

Directions: For each question, circle the number of the response that best answers the question or completes the statement. An Answer Key and Explanations are provided at the end of this section.

ITEMS 1 AND 2 REFER TO THE FOLLOWING ILLUSTRATION.

Latitude and Longitude

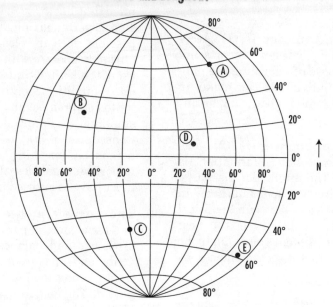

1. According to the illustration, which of the lettered points is found at 50 degrees south latitude and 20 degrees west longitude?

   (1) Point A

   (2) Point B

   (3) Point C

   (4) Point D

   (5) Point E

2. A traveler going from point D to point B would be traveling in which direction?

   (1) West, Northwest

   (2) East, Southeast

   (3) East, Northeast

   (4) West, Southwest

   (5) South

exercises

ITEM 3 REFERS TO THE FOLLOWING TABLE.

Center of Population: 1790 to 1900

"Center of population" is the point at which an imaginary flat, weightless, and rigid map of the United States would balance if weights of identical value were placed on it so that each weight represented the location of one person on the date of the census.

YEAR	NORTH LATITUDE ° ' "	WEST LATITUDE ° ' "	APPROXIMATE LOCATION
1790 (Aug. 2)	39 16 30	76 11 12	23 miles east of Baltimore, MD
1850 (June 1)	38 59 0	81 19 0	23 miles southeast of Parkersburg, WV
1900 (June 1)	39 9 36	85 48 54	6 miles southeast of Columbus, IN
1950 (Apr. 1)	38 50 21	88 9 33	8 miles north-northwest of Olney, Richland County, IL
1960 (Apr. 1)	38 35 58	89 12 85	In Clinton Co. about $6\frac{1}{2}$ miles northwest of Centralia, IL
1970 (Apr. 1)	38 27 47	89 42 22	5.3 miles east-southeast of the Mascoutah City Hall in St. Clair County, IL
1980 (Apr. 1)	38 8 13	90 34 26	$\frac{1}{4}$ mile west of De Soto in Jefferson County, MO
1990 (Apr. 1)	37 52 20	91 12 55	9.7 miles southeast of Steelville, MO

3. The information in the table is most likely a reflection of which of the following events in U.S. history?

   (1) Sectionalism
   (2) Reconstruction
   (3) The rise of industrialism
   (4) A decline in immigration
   (5) The growth of the west

ITEM 4 REFERS TO THE FOLLOWING TABLE.

RECENT POPULATION
FIGURES FOR COUNTRY X

Year	Birth Rate(1)	Death Rate(1)
1960	35.2	6.7
1970	24.8	6.7
1980	22.8	6.4
1882	21.2	6.6
1983	20.1	6.6

(1) per 1000 population

4. The information shown could be used to support which of the following statements?

    (1) The death rate is likely to decline through the 1990s.

    (2) The population has increased rapidly.

    (3) Population growth has been slowed.

    (4) The birth rate will increase slightly.

    (5) Population has decreased greatly.

ITEM 5 REFERS TO THE DIAGRAM BELOW.

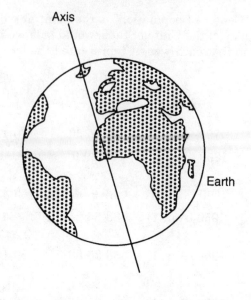

5. Based on the diagram and your knowledge of geography, the tilt of the earth's axis is a major cause of the occurrence of

    (1) tides.

    (2) rotation of the earth.

    (3) leap years in the calendar.

    (4) the change of seasons.

    (5) weather.

ITEM 6 REFERS TO THE INFORMATION BELOW.

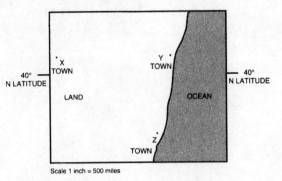

Scale 1 inch = 500 miles

The temperature of a place will be partly determined by its distance from the equator. The closer to the equator, the warmer it will be. Also, the ocean tends to moderate the chilling winds of winter. This map presents the geographic location of towns X, Y, and Z.

6. The information given could most accurately support which of the following statements about climate?

   (1) Z-town will have a tropical climate.

   (2) X-town will most likely have a warmer climate than Y-town.

   (3) All three towns will have similar climates.

   (4) X-town and Y-town will experience wetter summers than Z-town.

   (5) X-town is likely to have cooler winters than Y-town.

exercises

ITEMS 7 TO 9 REFER TO THE FOLLOWING MAP AND TEXT.

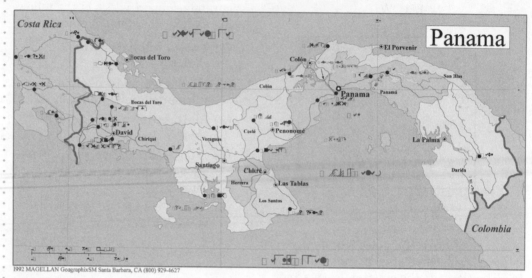

1992 MAGELLAN GeographixSM Santa Barbara, CA (800) 929-4627

The United States became interested in building a canal across the *isthmus* of Central America after it acquired Oregon and California. It signed a treaty with Colombia in 1846 that allowed the building of either a canal or railroad across Panama. In 1850, it was decided that the United States and Great Britain would have joint control over the canal that would be built, but the *Hay-Buuau-Varilla Treaty* in 1903 with Panama granted just the United States perpetual control of a canal zone 10 miles wide across the isthmus of Panama. The first ocean steamer sailed through the completed canal on August 15, 1914. The canal cost $275 million to build. Under President Carter in 1977, the 1903 treaty was renegotiated after many years of effort, with Panama gaining full control of the canal on December 31, 1999.

7. Why was the 1846 treaty allowing the building of the Panama Canal signed with Colombia?

(1) Colombia signed all South and Central American treaties.

(2) Panama was part of Colombia at that time.

(3) The United States was at war with Panama.

(4) Great Britain didn't trust the Panamanians to honor the treaty.

(5) All of the above

8. The most important reason for building the Panama Canal was that

(1) it provided employment for the Panamanians.

(2) the climate was better in the Caribbean than on the West Coast.

(3) it made it easier to sail from San Francisco to Japan.

(4) America needed better transportation to its new possessions in the Caribbean and Pacific.

(5) None of the above

9. What are the two countries that abut, or are neighbors of, Panama?

(1) Chile and Colombia

(2) United States and Colombia

(3) Costa Rica and Colombia

(4) Puerto Rico and Costa Rica

(5) Cuba and Costa Rica

ITEMS 10 TO 12 REFER TO THE FOLLOWING MAP AND TEXT.

Time Zones in the Continental United States

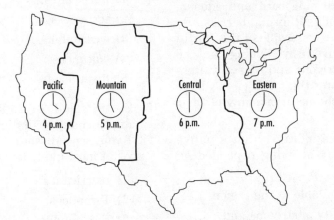

Travel and the great expansion of the United States territories during the 1800s made *standard time zones* necessary. After railroad systems in North America adopted the four time zones assigned to North America, the British helped gain support for time zone usage around the world. While most time zones remain standard, there are exceptions. China operates under a single time zone, and all of Russia falls within the same day's time.

10. Based on the information on the map, the sun would rise first in which of the following time zones?

   (1) Eastern

   (2) Pacific

   (3) Central

   (4) Mountain

   (5) The sun would rise at the same time everywhere.

11. A government worker in Washington, D.C., has to make a phone call to a Portland, Oregon, business that opens at 9 a.m. What is the earliest time in Washington, D.C., that the government worker can reach the Portland business?

   (1) 9 a.m.

   (2) 10 a.m.

   (3) 9 p.m.

   (4) 8 a.m.

   (5) Noon

12. If it is 7 a.m. in Beijing, China, what time is it in Hong Kong?

   (1) 7 p.m.

   (2) 7 a.m.

   (3) 10 a.m.

   (4) Eastern Standard Time

   (5) None of the above

13. The Eastern Woodland native people of North America lived in what is now the northeastern part of the United States. These groups lived by hunting, farming corn and squash, fishing, and gathering berries. By contrast, native people of the Northwest survived by fishing in the crowded streams and coastal waters and by using the trees of the huge forests of the area for many of their needs.

The passage indicates that a native people's way of living depended on the

- **(1)** fish available in the region.
- **(2)** proximity of streams and coastal waters.
- **(3)** crops and berries that grew in the region.
- **(4)** geography and resources of the region.
- **(5)** proximity of large forests.

ITEMS 14 TO 16 REFER TO THE FOLLOWING PASSAGE.

Although people sometimes think of the earth as unchanging and solid, this is not really true. In fact, the earth is changing constantly, both on and beneath the surface. Evidence of this activity can be seen in the United States today. Active volcanoes are found in both Oregon and Hawaii. Earthquakes are common in California, especially along the San Andreas Fault. The New Madrid Fault, a less active but well-known fault, runs from southern Illinois through Missouri, Tennessee, and Arkansas.

Weather has a positive and negative effect on the shape and form of the earth's surface. Tornadoes are common during some seasons in Iowa, Nebraska, Kansas, Illinois, and Wisconsin and other states in the Midwest. Heavy rains sometimes cause flash floods in Texas, Arizona, New Mexico, and California. Hurricanes are annual events and sometimes strike Florida, the Carolinas, and other states along the eastern seaboard.

14. Someone who lives near the San Andreas Fault probably worries most about the danger from

- **(1)** hurricanes.
- **(2)** tornadoes.
- **(3)** earthquakes.
- **(4)** volcanoes.
- **(5)** flash floods.

15. In 1811 and 1812, the Mississippi River changed its course through Tennessee, Missouri, and Arkansas. What most likely forced this change?

- **(1)** Hurricanes.
- **(2)** Tornadoes.
- **(3)** Earthquakes.
- **(4)** Volcanoes.
- **(5)** Flash floods.

16. Which of the following is NOT a true statement according to the passage?

- **(1)** Flash floods and hurricanes are common all along the eastern seaboard.
- **(2)** The flatness of much of Texas is probably related to its weather.
- **(3)** Tornadoes are common in Iowa.
- **(4)** There is a volcano in Hawaii.
- **(5)** All of the above.

exercises

ITEMS 17 TO 20 REFER TO THE FOLLOWING PASSAGE.

Article I, Section 2 of the U. S. Constitution calls for a *Census*, or enumeration of the people, every ten years, to be used for apportioning seats in the House of Representatives. The first Census was conducted in 1790 by Thomas Jefferson, who was then the Secretary of State. That Census, taken by U.S. marshals on horseback, counted 3.9 million inhabitants. Since that time, the Census has been conducted every decade, generally on April 1 in the years ending in a zero.

The Census Bureau since then has also provided the small-area population data needed to redraw state legislative and congressional districts. The data obtained is used for the distribution of funds for programs such as Medicaid and for determining the right locations for schools, roads, and other public facilities. Most Census data is available for many levels of government, including states, counties, cities, and towns. Because of its thoroughness, the 2000 census has turned out to be the most accurate in history, with the lowest undercount of minorities of any previous census.

Some of the many Census questions asked of every person include ethnic origin, race, income, work status, marital status, languages spoken in the home, occupation, citizenship, vehicle ownership, and characteristics of the home being lived in.

17. Why is it important to periodically do a national Census?

(1) So that radio stations will know their public.

(2) To find escaped criminals.

(3) To see if the average person is healthy.

(4) So that people can be represented fairly in government.

(5) To give people temporary employment as Census takers.

18. For which of the following would information from a Census be helpful?

(1) Making decisions about a school decoration project.

(2) Deciding on whether to give construction workers a raise.

(3) Determining the need for a regional office of the Motor Vehicle Department.

(4) Deciding whom to vote for in an election.

(5) Seeing which plants would thrive in your garden.

19. Which of the following is a FALSE statement?

(1) The population of the United States was 3.9 million in 1790.

(2) A Census is scheduled to take place in the year 2010 and then again in 2020.

(3) Many people are probably needed to conduct a Census.

(4) Some people may feel uncomfortable answering Census questions.

(5) Thomas Jefferson invented the Census.

20. A small town would want Census data before

(1) deciding on where to build a new elementary school.

(2) giving its mayor a raise.

(3) giving out dog permits.

(4) planning a community picnic.

(5) replacing books in the town library.

ITEM 21 REFERS TO THE CIRCLE GRAPH BELOW.

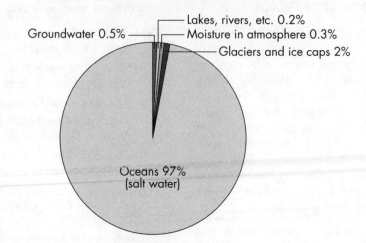

Groundwater 0.5% — Lakes, rivers, etc. 0.2%
— Moisture in atmosphere 0.3%
— Glaciers and ice caps 2%

Oceans 97%
(salt water)

Water Supply

21. The graph suggests that people could increase their fresh water supply significantly if they could find an inexpensive way to

   (1) melt the glaciers.

   (2) reach aquifers and other sources of groundwater.

   (3) turn salt water into fresh water.

   (4) channel water from places that have too much water to those that have too little.

   (5) clean up polluted rivers and lakes.

ITEM 22 REFERS TO THE FOLLOWING MAP AND TEXT.

The Arctic Ocean is the smallest of the world's five oceans (after the Pacific Ocean, Atlantic Ocean, Indian Ocean, and the recently delimited Southern Ocean). The Northwest Passage (U.S. and Canada) and Northern Sea Route (Norway and Russia) are two of its important seasonal waterways. A sparse network of air, ocean, river, and land routes circumscribes the Arctic Ocean.

22. Which of the following is an accurate statement based on the above information?

   (1) There are no passable waterways through the Arctic Ocean.

   (2) The Arctic polar ice cap is melting due to global warming.

   (3) The Arctic Ocean is the largest body of water and ice in the world.

   (4) The Arctic Ocean lies between Europe, Asia, and North America, and is mostly north of the Arctic Circle.

   (5) It is impossible to judge the depth of the ice in the Arctic.

ITEMS 23 AND 24 REFER TO THE FOLLOWING PARAGRAPH.

Today there are more than 200 reservations in the United States, established for various tribes of Native Americans through special treaties with the federal government. The largest is the Navajo reservation in Arizona, New Mexico, and Utah. Its 15 million acres make it about the size of New England. Many of the 1.4 million Native Americans have moved to cities where they have sought to maintain at least a semblance of tribal customs and organization in their new surroundings. Other groups, particularly in the Southwest, still maintain many elements of their ancient heritage.

23. According to this passage, which of the following is true about reservations?

    (1) Only the Navajos live on reservations.
    (2) All Native Americans live on reservations.
    (3) The Navajo reservation is in New England.
    (4) The largest reservation is in Arizona, New Mexico, and Utah.
    (5) There are 1.4 million Native Americans living on reservations.

24. The reservations were established

    (1) through treaties between the federal government and various tribes.
    (2) to keep all Native Americans in one place.
    (3) to make the Native Americans conform to the white man's ways.
    (4) through grants by the various state governments.
    (5) wherever Native Americans live.

ITEMS 25 AND 26 REFER TO THE FOLLOWING INFORMATION.

Some factors that may affect the climate of a region are:

- **Ocean currents** can warm or cool shorelines as they pass.

- **Oceans and large lakes,** which do not lose or gain heat as quickly as land does, may cause milder temperatures nearby.

- **Mountains**, which affect rainfall by forcing clouds to rise up and over them. As air rises, it cools. Since cold air cannot hold as much moisture as warm air, the clouds drop their moisture as they rise.

25. Inland areas, as opposed to places along an ocean, are likely to be

(1) similar in temperature and rainfall.

(2) warmer in winter.

(3) rainier all year long.

(4) drier.

(5) colder in winter.

26. Although Valdez, a port in Alaska, lies near the Arctic Circle, it is free of ice all year long. What is the most likely explanation?

(1) The winds that blow over the water are warmer than the winds that blow over the land.

(2) The mountains are blocking the cold winds.

(3) Valdez is warmed by an ocean current.

(4) The ocean does not gain or lose heat as quickly as land.

(5) Valdez is affected by prevailing wind patterns.

27. Having appropriate geographic information is often important. For which of the following activities would knowledge of relative *geographic location* be more helpful than just information about *longitude and latitude*?

(1) Piloting a long-distance plane.

(2) Driving a car.

(3) Sailing on the ocean.

(4) Surveying a state's borders.

(5) Laying out a new city.

ITEMS 28 TO 30 REFER TO THE FOLLOWING BAR GRAPH.

WORLD ENERGY PRODUCTION, CONSUMPTION, AND POPULATION, 2000

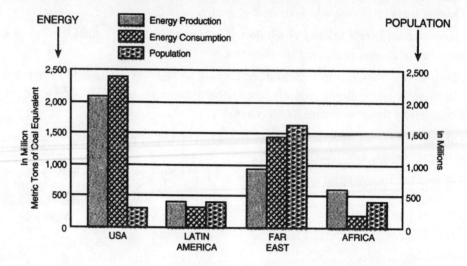

28. Which region used the most energy in 2000?

    (1) U.S.A.

    (2) Africa

    (3) Far East

    (4) Latin America

    (5) Impossible to determine from the information given.

29. According to the graph, which area's usage of energy most closely conformed to the size of its population in the year 2000?

    (1) U.S.A.

    (2) Africa

    (3) Far East

    (4) Latin America

    (5) Impossible to determine from the information given.

30. If all the people in the world were given the same amount of energy in order to survive, which region would need the most?

    (1) U.S.A.

    (2) Africa

    (3) Far East

    (4) Latin America

    (5) Impossible to determine from the information given.

ANSWER KEY AND EXPLANATIONS

1. (3)	9. (3)	17. (4)	25. (5)
2. (1)	10. (1)	18. (3)	26. (3)
3. (5)	11. (5)	19. (5)	27. (2)
4. (3)	12. (2)	20. (1)	28. (1)
5. (4)	13. (4)	21. (3)	29. (4)
6. (5)	14. (3)	22. (4)	30. (3)
7. (2)	15. (3)	23. (4)	
8. (4)	16. (1)	24. (1)	

1. **The correct answer is (3).** Just looking at the latitudes of the various options can tell you this answer. Only choices (3) and (5), points C and E, are in the south latitudes, so the other three choices can be eliminated immediately. Choice (5) is at 60 degrees south latitude, so choice (3), point C, can be determined to be the correct answer by the process of elimination.

2. **The correct answer is (1).** By locating points B and D on the globe, it should become apparent that point B is both west and north of point D, so choice (1) is correct.

3. **The correct answer is (5).** The center of population has shifted to the west because more "weight" has been applied to that portion of the country: the western portion has grown in both numbers and percentage of the population.

4. **The correct answer is (3).** The death rate has remained essentially the same and the birth rate has decreased; therefore, population growth has slowed.

5. **The correct answer is (4).** The northern hemisphere is tilted toward the sun part of the year and away from the sun for the remaining months. In winter, the rays strike the northern hemisphere indirectly; in spring, the hemisphere is warming; during summer, the rays of the sun strike directly; and in the fall, the hemisphere cools.

6. **The correct answer is (5).** Though X and Y are the same distance north of the equator, Y's climate will be moderated by the warming effects of the ocean while landlocked X will experience colder weather.

7. **The correct answer is (2).** The logical answer is choice (2), that Panama must have been part of Colombia at that time. Panama attained its independence after rising in revolt against Colombia in 1903. The other answer choices, (1), (3), and (4) are illogical and incorrect.

8. **The correct answer is (4).** The Panama Canal connects the Pacific Ocean from the west to the Caribbean Sea and the Atlantic Ocean beyond in the east. It saves having to go around Cape Horn, at the southern end of South America. The United States was in the midst of acquiring territories, such as the Philippines, Guam, Samoa, and Hawaii in the Pacific and Puerto Rico and the Virgin Islands in the Caribbean. It also wanted to be able to travel easily from coast to coast by water when necessary. The Panama Canal made that possible.

9. **The correct answer is (3).** As you can see on the map, the two countries that abut, or touch, Panama are Costa Rica and Colombia.

10. **The correct answer is (1).** The sun rises in the east and sets in the west. Therefore, the Eastern Time zone would see the sun first. According to the map, the sun would rise about 3 hours later in California than it does in New York.

11. **The correct answer is (5).** Because Washington, D.C., is in the Eastern time zone and Portland, Oregon, is in the Pacific time zone, the time difference is 3 hours. So when it is 9 a.m. is Portland, it is noon in Washington.

12. **The correct answer is (2).** According to the last sentence of the text, all of China operates under a single time zone, meaning that it is always the same time all over China. So if it is 7 a.m. in Beijing, it is also 7 a.m. in Hong Kong.

13. **The correct answer is (4).** The best answer of the choices given is choice (4). The passage shows that native people in both areas of the country relied on locally available game and plants (such as fish or berries) for food and on geographic characteristics, such as forests, for their other needs.

14. **The correct answer is (3).** Because the passage states that the San Andreas Fault is a major cause of earthquakes, people in the area would worry about this phenomenon as opposed to the other events.

15. **The correct answer is (3).** The passage described the New Madrid Fault as running through the area. Therefore, choice (3) is correct. The other choices occur in different parts of the country, so they are unlikely to have caused this effect on the Mississippi.

16. **The correct answer is (1).** This is an example of a statement that is only partly correct, and therefore, it is NOT a true statement and is the correct answer to this question. While hurricanes are listed as being "annual events" in some places along the east-

ern seaboard, flash floods are not. Choices (3) and (4) are also supported by the passage and are also therefore incorrect answers to the question.

17. **The correct answer is (4).** The first and second paragraphs tell us that the purpose of the Census is, first of all, to provide a basis for fairly apportioning seats in the House of Representatives and in Congress and also for drawing state legislative and congressional districts. These relate to fairness in government both on a federal and state level. People can then be represented according to population figures in a particular area, making it possible for everyone to have an equal voice in their government.

18. **The correct answer is (3).** The passage states that Census information tells the government about people living in an area, and their needs for government services, such as Motor Vehicle Departments. Also, the last paragraph mentions *vehicle ownership* directly, so knowing how many people in an area own a car would help the government decide whether a local Motor Vehicle Department was needed. The other choices given are incorrect because they do not concern the Census or the government in any direct way—decorating a school, voting choices, and wages are individual issues not necessarily related to government controls.

19. **The correct answer is (5).** All the statements are correct, except for the last choice. Thomas Jefferson *conducted*, or was in charge of, the first Census, as stated in the first paragraph. He did not invent it. Choice (1) is confirmed in the first paragraph. Since the Census is conducted every decade, or ten years, choice (2) is correct. Choice (3) can be *inferred;* since the United States is such a vast country, you can assume that

many people will be needed to conduct a Census. Choice (4) can be inferred as being correct also, since some people will feel uncomfortable answering the many personal questions required by the census.

20. **The correct answer is (1).** The second paragraph of the passage states that a Census presents useful information on local or town levels as well as for the country as a whole. So, knowing where and how many people with potentially school-aged children might be living would be vital information in deciding if a new school is needed and where it should be located for greatest access and convenience. For example, locating a school far from where it's needed would mean additional expenses for busing. The other answer choices do not represent decisions where Census data would necessarily be useful.

21. **The correct answer is (3).** Since the graph shows that most of the world's water supply is in the ocean, which is made up of salt water, it is reasonable to assume that finding an inexpensive way to convert it to fresh water would be very useful in increasing the supply.

22. **The correct answer is (4).** Even though the map is not fully labeled, you can see approximately where the Arctic Ocean lies—between Europe, Asia and North America—and also that it is mostly north of the Arctic Circle. Choice (1) is contradicted by the passage, which lists two seasonal waterways. Choices (2) and (5) are unrelated to the material presented. Choice (3) is the opposite; the Arctic is the smallest, not the largest, of the world's oceans.

23. **The correct answer is (4).** The second sentence gives this information. All of the other statements are contradicted by information in the article.

24. **The correct answer is (1).** The first sentence states that the reservations were established "through special treaties with the federal government."

25. **The correct answer is (5).** The passage refers to the effect of large bodies of water on temperature. It suggests that such bodies of water have a moderating effect on temperature. Therefore, places inland are likely to be colder in winter and warmer in summer than places near a coast.

26. **The correct answer is (3).** Even though you may be unfamiliar with the characteristics of ocean currents, you can derive the correct answer by eliminating the other choices, which are incorrect. As a port, Valdez lies along an ocean, so choice (2) is incorrect. Choices (1) and (4) are incorrect because they explain only why Valdez might have more moderate temperatures than places inland. They do not explain why those temperatures are above freezing. Choice (5) is incorrect because prevailing winds can bring warm or cold temperatures to a place. So that leaves choice (3) as the logical correct answer.

27. **The correct answer is (2).** Since drivers of cars have to rely on landmarks to find their way, latitude and longitude information would not be useful, so this is the correct answer. The other activities mentioned mainly require knowledge of *absolute location* geographically, or latitude or longitude.

28. **The correct answer is (1).** Looking at each of the "energy consumption" bars, the middle of each country's set of three, tells you that it is the United States that used the most energy.

answers exercises

29. **The correct answer is (4).** You are asked to compare each area's energy usage relative to its population. Choice (1) is incorrect, since the United States is seen to use *much more* energy by far than its population would justify. While Africa and the Far East use quite a bit less energy relative to population, it is seen that Latin America outdoes all other areas of the world in energy conservation.

30. **The correct answer is (3).** The question really is asking which area has the largest population, and since the graph tells you that that is the Far East, it follows that they would require the most energy. The larger the population, the greater the per capita consumption needed. So choice (3) is therefore correct.

SUMMING IT UP

What You Need to Know About the GED Social Studies Test

- The questions test your knowledge of important principles, concepts, events, and relationships

- The best way to succeed on this test is to get used to reading the news section of a good newspaper every day, watch the news on television, listen to serious discussions on the radio, and think about current issues. Go to your neighborhood library and glance through the atlases, maps, and magazines.

- Many of the questions concern knowledge or skills taken from more than one subject area.

- All questions will be multiple-choice questions, with 5 possible answers.

PART V

SCIENCE REVIEW

CHAPTER 6   All About the GED Science Test

All About the GED Science Test

OVERVIEW

- Quick Tips!
- Taking the GED Science test
- Summing it up

QUICK TIPS!

Much of what is included in science tests draws on knowledge that can be gained by being alert and involved in your daily surroundings.

See the many programs on television that deal with science, nature, health topics, environmental issues, medical research, space exploration, exercise, diet, and nutrition. Read the daily columns in newspapers about these same topics, as well as frequent articles in weekly magazines. Become a more knowledgeable consumer by reading the lists of ingredients on canned or prepared foods or on soaps and detergents. Be aware of vitamins and minerals in your diet. Think of environmental problems and the reasons for recycling garbage.

All of these and many other topics fall under the province of science in everyday life. If you become more aware of these, you will do much better on the GED science test.

TAKING THE GED SCIENCE TEST

The questions on the GED Science Test are based upon the basic concepts of science. The questions require the reading of passages and the comprehension of material presented in graphs, tables, and charts. The subject matter draws on the fields of life science (biology), physical science (physics and chemistry), and Earth and space science.

You will be asked to answer four different types of questions:

1. **Comprehension** questions, which require you to demonstrate an understanding of the meaning of the stimulus. Can you restate, summarize, or identify the implications of the information?

2. **Application** questions, which ask you to use the information in a context other than the one stated in the reading.

❸ Analysis questions, which call for breaking down the information. What are the facts and what are the hypotheses? Were there any assumptions? Can you distinguish between cause and effect?

❹ Evaluation questions, which require you to make a judgment based on the facts given. How accurate are the facts presented? Can you differentiate logic from beliefs and values?

Special emphasis is placed on the role science plays in our everyday lives with topics such as: how we are affected by pollution and disease; how our lives are changed with the improving effectiveness of medical technology; overpopulation issues and the adequacy of Earth's natural resources; changes in the ozone layer, and the "greenhouse effect;" or our increased understanding of the solar system. Topics often spoken of in the news are included.

The following outline of content areas from which science questions are likely to be drawn is based upon the National Science Education Standards of the National Academy of Sciences.

I. LIFE SCIENCE

  A. Characteristics of organisms

  B. Life cycle of organisms

  C. Organisms and environments

  D. Structure and function in living systems

  E. Reproduction and heredity

  F. Regulation and behavior

  G. Population and ecosystems

  H. Diversity and adaptation of organisms

  I. Interdependence of organisms

  J. Matter, energy, and organization in living systems

  K. Behavior of organisms

II. PHYSICAL SCIENCE

  A. Physics

    1. Properties of objects and materials

    2. Position and motion of objects

    3. Light, heat, electricity, and magnetism

    4. Interaction of energy and matter

    5. Motion and forces

    6. Transfer of energy

    7. Conservation of energy and increase in disorder

  B. Chemistry

    1. Structure of the atom

2. Properties and changes of properties in matter

3. Chemical reactions

III. EARTH and SPACE SCIENCE

  A. Earth's system

    1. Origin of Earth

    2. Earth's history

    3. Properties of Earth materials

    4. Structure of Earth's system

    5. Energy in Earth's system

  B. Objects in the sky

  C. Changes in earth and sky

  D. Earth in the solar system

  E. Geochemical systems

  F. Origin and evolution of the universe

For each of the three main sciences mentioned above, the GED also asks questions pertaining to how we learn about science through experimentation, research, and inquiry. Topics include:

✓ What is the history and nature of science?

  a. Science as a human endeavor

  b. Historical perspectives of science

✓ How do we learn about science?

  a. Abilities necessary to do scientific inquiry

  b. Evidence, models, and explanations

✓ Why is science important to our daily lives?

  a. Understanding about science and technology

  b. Innovations of technological design

Some Strategies for Answering Science Questions

❶ *Read* the passage or *study* the graphic material carefully. You may want to underline key words and phrases so that you can find them easily as you answer the questions following each reading.

Some people find it more effective to read the questions first so that they know just what to look for as they read the passage or study the graphs and tables. Try both methods on the practice questions that follow to see which one works better for you.

❷ *Reject* an argument or assertion if one exception is found to it. Look for the exception or contrary information and that may be your answer.

3 *Draw a quick sketch* where appropriate to help you understand a reading passage. Use very simple diagrams. An arrow or a small dot may help you change abstract written words to a concrete picture of what is happening.

For example, consider a problem that begins:

"If car 1 is traveling north at 50 miles/hour and car 2 is traveling east at 40 miles/hour, then . . ."

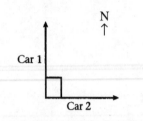

4 *Formula* problems can be solved by using simple "boxlike" fill-in inserts. For example, Rate × Time = Distance

$$R \times T = D$$
$$\square \times \square = \square$$

If you travel at 50 miles per hour, how long will it take to cover 200 miles?

$$\boxed{50} \times \square = \boxed{200}$$

5 *Use personal analogies* to reason through a problem. For example, imagine yourself as a bacteria placed in a petri dish. What would you do under the conditions presented in the problem?

6 *Use scrap paper* to jot down your thoughts, but don't let your notes get so jumbled and crowded that they confuse rather than help you.

HOW TO USE THIS SECTION EFFECTIVELY

After you have taken the Diagnostic Test and filled in the Error Analysis chart as directed, you will see at a glance which science areas need the most study. This section contains many questions based on what is taught in high school science courses. It will serve as a good review of these courses. In addition, it includes many science reading passages for practice in reading and interpreting scientific materials.

NOTE

This section is divided into three major subject areas: 1. Life Sciences; 2. Physical Science; 3. Earth and Space Science

You may wish to give equal study to all of these subjects or to spend more time concentrating on the weaknesses identified by your Diagnostic Test. If you find that you need more study in a particular area, you may also wish to consult a basic high school text, such as:

Life Science

Modern Biology, The Natural Selection, Holt, Rinehart and Winston (2002)

Biology: Exploring Life, Prentice Hall (2004)

Physical Science

Holt Physics, Build World Class Problem Solvers with Serway and Faughn, Holt, Rinehart and Winston (2002)

Holt Chemistry, Providing the Core Elements of Chemistry for Every Student, Holt, Rinehart and Winston *(2004)*

Physical Science: Concepts in Action, Prentice Hall (2004)

Earth and Space Science

Modern Earth Science, Holt, Rinehart and Winston (2002)

Glencoe Science: An Introduction to the Life, Earth, and Physical Sciences, Glencoe/McGraw-Hill (2003)

EXERCISES: LIFE SCIENCE

> **Directions:** For each question, circle the number of the response that best answers the question or completes the statement. An Answer Key and Explanations are provided at the end of the section.

ITEMS 1 TO 3 REFER TO THE FOLLOWING INFORMATION.

What is life? Biologists define life as the ability to carry out all of the basic life functions. Some of the life functions are described below.

Regulation	controlling all of the other life processes
Ingestion	taking food in
Digestion	breaking down food
Circulation	moving food to all parts of an organism
Respiration	burning food to make energy
Assimilation	changing food into useful substances
Excretion	removing waste products
Reproduction	making more of the same kind

1. Fire is almost alive, except it cannot carry out which of the following life functions?

   (1) Regulation
   (2) Digestion
   (3) Respiration
   (4) Excretion
   (5) Reproduction

2. Which of the following life processes is necessary to ensure the survival of the species?

   (1) Regulation
   (2) Circulation
   (3) Respiration
   (4) Excretion
   (5) Reproduction

3. Which of the following describes an organism that carries out all its life functions?

   (1) A plant
   (2) An animal
   (3) Incapable of intelligent thought
   (4) Alive
   (5) In danger of extinction

ITEM 4 REFERS TO THE FOLLOWING DIAGRAM.

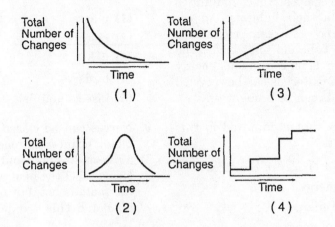

4. Niles Eldridge and Stephen Jay Gould are neo-Darwinists. While they believe that Darwin was essentially correct in his theory of natural selection and evolution, they feel there are points that should be refined as scientists learn more. Specifically, they feel that large and sudden changes in the environment will cause changes in the rate of speciation. Which of the graphs above best illustrates their position?

(1) 1
(2) 2
(3) 3
(4) 4
(5) 1 and 3

ITEM 5 REFERS TO THE FOLLOWING DIAGRAM.

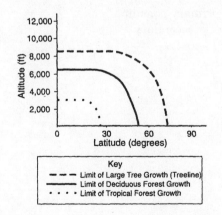

5. The diagram shows that trees cannot live above

(1) 3,000 feet.
(2) 6,200 feet.
(3) 8,200 feet.
(4) 28 degrees latitude.
(5) 52 degrees latitude.

ITEMS 6 TO 8 REFER TO THE FOLLOWING INFORMATION.

Ecosystems are composed of communities of organisms in their habitats. An example would be a stream containing plants, insects, fish, and some birds. The ecosystem depends on continuous energy input, although materials can be recycled or new materials can be brought in.

6. The energy that is inputted in this ecosystem is

    (1) the heat energy of the stream.
    (2) solar energy.
    (3) kinetic energy.
    (4) chemical energy.
    (5) built up downstream in a lake.

7. Assume that the insects are herbivorous and the fish eat the insects. Which statement is then correct?

    (1) The insects are producers and the fish primary consumers.
    (2) The insects are producers and the fish secondary consumers.
    (3) The insects are primary consumers and the fish secondary consumers.
    (4) The insects are secondary consumers and the fish tertiary consumers.
    (5) The plants are primary consumers and the insects secondary consumers.

8. If there were a spill of DDT into the stream, the most DDT per kilogram would be found in

    (1) plants.
    (2) insects.
    (3) fish.
    (4) birds.
    (5) insects and fish.

9. Nerves can be classified as sensory, motor, or interneurons. Suppose that a person has his hand on a hot plate. He can feel the heat and knows that the plate is hot, but he cannot move his hand. This is indication of

    (1) sensory neuron damage.
    (2) motor neuron damage.
    (3) interneuron damage.
    (4) brain damage.
    (5) reflex reaction.

ITEMS 10 AND 11 REFER TO THE FOLLOWING INFORMATION.

A student wanted to do an experiment to find the best conditions for growing brine shrimp. She set up 6 beakers with the following conditions and placed a half-teaspoon of eggs in each one:

Beaker Number	Salt Content	Temperature
1	0%	10° C
2	3%	10° C
3	5%	10° C
4	0%	20° C
5	3%	20° C
6	5%	20° C

She sampled them each day for five days, and she found that the greatest number of shrimp grew at 3% salt at either temperature.

10. In this experiment the dependent variable(s) is (are)

   (1) percentage of salt.
   (2) temperature.
   (3) number of shrimp.
   (4) number of days.
   (5) percentage of salt and temperature.

11. The student was not satisfied with her results. She wanted results that could help her better distinguish the preferred growth conditions. To improve her experiment, she should

   (1) use finer divisions for the percentage of salt.
   (2) use finer divisions for the temperature.
   (3) let the experiment run longer.
   (4) be more careful about the volume of water the eggs were growing in.
   (5) be more careful about adding a specific number of shrimp eggs.

ITEMS 12 AND 13 REFER TO THE FOLLOWING INFORMATION.

The four major blood groups in humans are A, B, AB, and O. People who are Type A have a certain protein on their red blood cells (RBCs) that is referred to as "A." People with Type B blood lack the "A" protein and have "B" instead. People with Type AB have both proteins, while those with Type O have neither protein on their RBCs. People with type O blood are called universal donors because they can give blood to individuals of any other blood group, since the recipients will not form antibodies to the O blood, which carries neither protein. Every person receives half of his or her blood group type from the mother and half from the father, so that everyone has two alleles, or gene types, for the ABO blood groups.

12. Which of the following statements is incorrect, according to the information above and your knowledge of biology?

    (1) People with blood Type AB cannot receive blood from a Type B donor.

    (2) People with blood Type O cannot receive blood from a person with Type AB.

    (3) People with blood Type A, whose mother is Type B, can donate blood to Type A individuals.

    (4) Some people with blood Type AB had a parent whose Type was A.

    (5) Antibodies are proteins formed by the recipient that attack the proteins on the donor's RBCs.

13. A man with Type B blood married a woman with Type O blood. Which of the following blood groups could their children inherit?

    (1) Type AB
    (2) Type B
    (3) Type O
    (4) Types AB and O
    (5) Types B and O

ITEMS 14 AND 15 REFER TO THE FOLLOWING PASSAGE AND DIAGRAM.

A student read reports of lead being removed from gasoline because it was harmful to humans. She hypothesized that it was harmful to other living things as well and developed a test for lead in water systems using small onions. She cut the end off the onions where the roots grew and placed each onion in a test tube containing lead nitrate solutions. The concentrations of lead are shown on the diagram. Here is a diagram of her experiment:

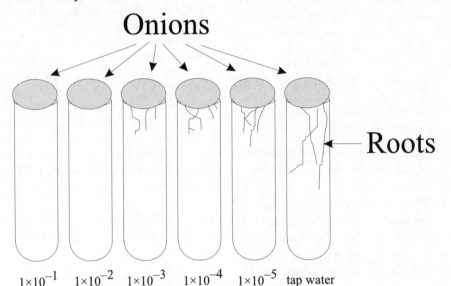

1×10^{-1} 1×10^{-2} 1×10^{-3} 1×10^{-4} 1×10^{-5} tap water

14. Which of the following statements is false?

    (1) The more lead in the solution, the less water.

    (2) Lead caused the onion roots to grow more slowly.

    (3) People should not eat onions that have been growing in lead.

    (4) From left to right, the concentration of lead increases.

    (5) Even small amounts of lead keep roots from growing.

15. Which of the following statements is true?

    (1) There is half as much lead in the first tube than the second tube (reading left to right).

    (2) The first tube has 100 times more lead than the third tube.

    (3) The amount of lead increases as you move left to right.

    (4) There is twice the amount of lead in the first tube than the second tube.

    (5) The fifth tube has five times the amount of lead as the first.

16. In 1998, the FDC ruled that the vitamin folic acid had to be added to flour. The purpose of this action was to reduce the number of neural tube birth defects (such as spina bifida). Before the policy was put into effect, the number of neural tube defects per 100,000 births was 37.8. In 2000, the number per 100,000 births was 30.5. In the same year, a study showed that women age 15–44 averaged more than double the amount of folic acid in their blood than did women studied before the mandatory fortification. Which of the following statements is correct?

(1) There was a 19 percent decrease in the number of neural tube defects between 1998 and 2000.

(2) There was a 7.3 percent decrease in the number of neural defects between 1998 and 2000.

(3) If women would double their intake of folic acid, they could reduce the number of birth defects by half.

(4) This study was faulty, because some women take vitamin supplements.

(5) The number of neural tube birth defects per million women in 2000 was 378.

ITEMS 17 TO 19 REFER TO THE FOLLOWING PASSAGE.

A virus is a small particle consisting of nucleic acid surrounded by a protein coat. Viruses are active only if they are in living cells because they reproduce more viruses by commandeering the host cell's machinery. If the nucleic acid is RNA, the virus is said to be a retrovirus. It is called a retrovirus because it must change its RNA to DNA before it can take over the host cell. When a retrovirus makes DNA from RNA, it uses an enzyme-reverse transcriptase. Viruses that contain DNA as their nucleic acid do not require this additional step and behave more like their hosts in that they follow the central dogma of modern biology: DNA makes RNA, which makes proteins.

17. In order for any virus to become pathogenic in a cell, it must

(1) be alive.

(2) contain RNA.

(3) be a retrovirus.

(4) have DNA.

(5) have a protein coat.

18. Retroviruses are viruses that contain

(1) only RNA and a protein coat.

(2) RNA, DNA, and protein.

(3) some of the host's machinery.

(4) proteins that will convert RNA to DNA.

(5) None of the above

19. In order to harm a host, retroviruses must

(1) be in the host's nucleus.

(2) use the host's cellular machinery to make new virus particles.

(3) use an enzyme that will convert their RNA to DNA.

(4) commandeer the host's cell machinery.

(5) All of the above

ITEMS 20 AND 21 REFER TO THE FOLLOWING DIAGRAM OF A FLOWER.

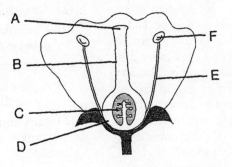

20. Pollen is produced in the structure labeled

    (1) A
    (2) C
    (3) D
    (4) E
    (5) F

21. The stamen is (are) part(s)

    (1) A
    (2) A and B
    (3) F
    (4) E
    (5) F and E

22. A scientist hypothesized that certain kinds of foods would help travelers avoid jet lag. She fed Group A a high-protein diet and Group B a high-carbohydrate diet before a flight from New Jersey to Europe. She tested both groups 24 hours later for signs of jet lag.

    What is the most important element *missing* from this experimental design?

    (1) The scientist's observations are not included.
    (2) The scientist did not consider the age of the subjects.
    (3) The scientist did not include a control group.
    (4) There was no mention of the number of time zones involved.
    (5) The scientist did not include a high-fat diet.

(vertical right margin) exercises

ITEM 23 REFERS TO THE FOLLOWING PARAGRAPH.

Evolution is defined as changes in gene frequencies in a population over time. Evolution is a basic concept in biology. It is important to understand that individuals do not evolve; species evolve. The basic principal underlying evolution is *survival of the fittest*: some individuals in a species have the right combination of genes to survive better than competitors and to reproduce readily in their environment. Their genes are, therefore, passed on to future generations, and those genes determine the future genetic composition of the species.

23. Which of the following conditions is necessary for evolution to occur?

   (1) A stable environment
   (2) A population with a stable genetic composition
   (3) A lack of genetic mutations
   (4) A population with genetic variability
   (5) An unlimited amount of resources

ITEM 24 REFERS TO THE FOLLOWING ILLUSTRATION.

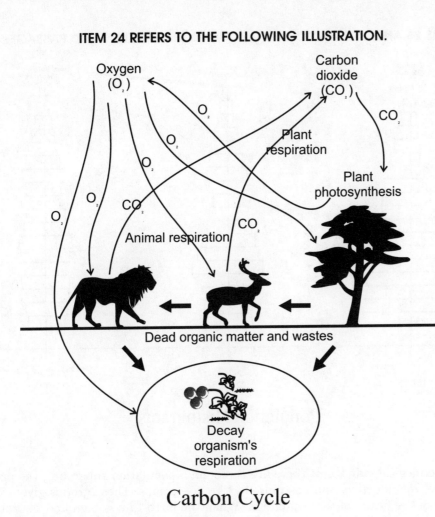

Carbon Cycle

24. Which of the following is a FALSE statement according to this illustration?

    (1) Carbon dioxide is not a vital part of life, just a waste byproduct.

    (2) Animals take in oxygen and breathe out carbon dioxide.

    (3) Both plants and animals must "breathe" to survive.

    (4) Oxygen is vital both for plant and animal life.

    (5) Even dead material has a place in the *carbon cycle* of life.

ITEMS 25 AND 26 REFER TO THE FOLLOWING ILLUSTRATION AND PASSAGE.

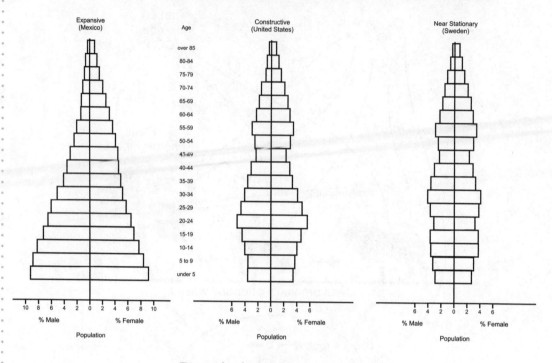

Population Histograms

From an ecological standpoint there are three main population subgroups: the prere-productive, reproductive, and postreproductive age groups. These groups give a very good idea of the future of the population. When the birth rate is high and the rate of population growth is exponential, then a population histogram is in the shape of a pyramid (shown on the left). A histogram with a tapering base shows a lower future growth due to the smaller prereproductive segment of the population (middle). A histogram that shows no constriction or expansion of the base shows a stationary population (right). These histograms are important to politicians, business leaders, and educators who have to plan for the future.

25. A population histogram plots

   (1) wealthy countries against less-developed countries.

   (2) the percent of the population in each age group by sex.

   (3) population growth as well as limiting factors.

   (4) the biotic potential against the environmental resistance.

   (5) the rate of population growth for a given country.

26. One of the least intrusive ways to reduce the birthrate in a country is to

   (1) limit the number of children a family may have.

   (2) use machinery in agriculture in place of children.

   (3) educate and employ the women.

   (4) ensure that women have many domestic duties.

   (5) have male babies remain in the family but have female babies put up for adoption.

ITEMS 27 TO 29 REFER TO THE FOLLOWING ILLUSTRATION AND INFORMATION.

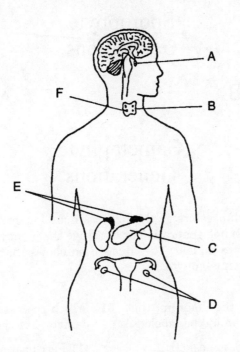

The endocrine glands pictured above secrete hormones into the bloodstream that act on certain tissues, known as target tissues, that have hormone receptors. These tissues respond to the hormones while others do not.

27. Which of the glands produce hormones that act on other glands?

　(1) A
　(2) A and B
　(3) C
　(4) D
　(5) A and D

28. Which gland produces hormones that can increase your blood pressure and make your heart rate go up?

　(1) A
　(2) B
　(3) C
　(4) D
　(5) E

29. Insulin and glucagon are produced by which gland?

　(1) A
　(2) B
　(3) C
　(4) D
　(5) E

ITEMS 30 AND 31 REFER TO THE FOLLOWING ILLUSTRATION AND INFORMATION.

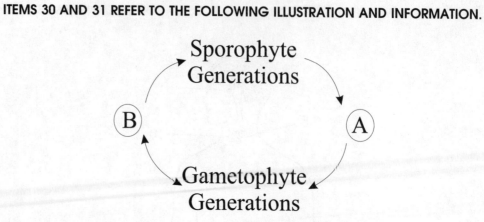

Green plants and their ancestors go through a unique life cycle known as the alternation of generations. In one generation or life stage the plant structures are haploid, and in the other they are diploid. The illustration shows that these two stages are called sporophyte and gametophyte.

30. To correctly fill in the diagram, the (A) and (B) spaces would be labeled

    (1) fertilization (A), meiosis (B).

    (2) meiosis (A), fertilization (B).

    (3) spores (A), meiosis (B).

    (4) meiosis (A), gametes (B).

    (5) spores (A), gametes (B).

31. Which process must occur before the gametophyte generation?

    (1) Fertilization

    (2) Mitosis

    (3) Germination

    (4) Meiosis

    (5) Evolution

ITEMS 32 AND 33 REFER TO THE FOLLOWING ILLUSTRATION AND INFORMATION.

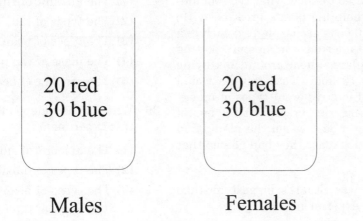

20 red
30 blue

20 red
30 blue

Males   Females

Each beaker represents the frequency of certain alleles of a gene pair in a sexually reproducing population. Assume that the beaker on the left represents males and the one on the right represents females.

32. If the act of sexual reproduction is the union of one allele from each container, what is the probability that the first union will be one red and one blue?

(1) 0.24

(2) 0.36

(3) 0.48

(4) 0.50

(5) 0.60

33. If these ratios represented the allele frequency of a genetic disease that would affect a person with two blue alleles, what percentage of the population is affected?

(1) 24%

(2) 36%

(3) 48%

(4) 50%

(5) 60%

exercises

**ITEMS 34 TO 36 REFER TO THE
FOLLOWING INFORMATION.**

Stuart wanted to know what types of music would help his plants grow best. He obtained 10 bean seeds, planted each in a quart container of commercial potting mix, and placed them around his living room. For 10 hours each day he would play one of four different types of music: classical, jazz, rap, or pop. At the end of each day he would weigh the plants and see how much mass they had gained that day.

34. What was Stuart's biggest mistake in his experimental design?

   (1) He didn't use enough beans.
   (2) He placed the beans in different areas of his living room.
   (3) He switched music too often.
   (4) His balance scale wasn't tested when he began.
   (5) He can't tell how much a plant grows by weighing it.

35. What is the dependent variable in this experiment?

   (1) The amount of sunlight
   (2) The types of music
   (3) The types of beans
   (4) The mass of the plants
   (5) The number of bean seeds

36. What is the independent variable in this experiment?

   (1) The amount of sunlight
   (2) The types of music
   (3) The types of beans
   (4) The mass of the plants
   (5) The number of bean seeds

ITEMS 37 AND 38 REFER TO THE FOLLOWING ILLUSTRATION.

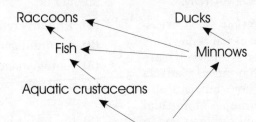

37. The diagram above shows that

   (1) algae and floating plants are the primary consumers.

   (2) aquatic crustaceans and minnows are the primary consumers.

   (3) fish and ducks are the primary consumers.

   (4) raccoons are the quaternary consumers.

   (5) fish eat raccoons.

38. If water contained 0.001 ppm of a nonbiodegradable substance, such as DDT, which of the following statements is the least likely to be correct?

   (1) The amount of DDT is more in 1 gram of duck than in 1 gram of minnow.

   (2) The amount of DDT could be as high as 10 ppm in raccoons.

   (3) The amount of DDT is higher in fish than in raccoons.

   (4) The amount of DDT is higher in crustaceans than in plants.

   (5) The amount of DDT could be as high as 1 ppm in fish.

exercises

ITEMS 39 AND 40 REFER TO THE FOLLOWING INFORMATION.

In the human population in America there is a genetic condition known as sickle-cell anemia. It is a relatively rare hereditary disorder that mostly affects people of African ancestry, but can also occur in other ethnic groups. More than 80,000 African Americans or about one in 400 have some form of sickle cell anemia. This genetic disease is the result of an individual inheriting two recessive alleles, causing his or her red blood cells to become sickle-shaped, instead of flexible and round, under some conditions. Individuals who have one normal allele and one sickle trait are said to have the sickle-cell trait, which does not cause them bouts of pain in the chest, stomach, arms, legs, or other parts of the body. Another two million African Americans, or eight percent of the African American population, carry the sickle cell trait, a genetic predisposition toward sickle cell anemia that can be passed down to their children. A child who has inherited the sickle cell gene from only one parent will not develop the disease, but will have sickle cell trait. There is a 50 percent chance that a child born to parents who both carry a sickle cell gene will have the trait. There is a 25 percent chance that the child will have sickle cell disease. There also is a 25 percent chance that the child will have neither the trait nor the disease.

39. What percentage of African Americans carries the sickle-cell trait?

(1) 8 percent
(2) 12 percent
(3) 25 percent
(4) 50 percent
(5) 80 percent

40. The passage implies that sickle cell anemia is

(1) a relatively new disorder
(2) a painful genetic disease
(3) contagious and life-threatening
(4) most common in Asian populations
(5) the result of two dominant alleles

ITEMS 41 TO 43 REFER TO THE FOLLOWING ARTICLE.

Vitamins are organic compounds necessary in small amounts in the diet for the normal growth and maintenance of life of animals, including man.

They do not provide energy nor do they construct or build any part of the body. They are needed for transforming foods into energy and body maintenance. There are thirteen or more of them, and if any is missing a deficiency disease becomes apparent.

Vitamins are similar because they are made of the same elements—carbon, hydrogen, oxygen, and sometimes nitrogen. (Vitamin B_{12} also contains cobalt.) They are different in that their elements are arranged differently, and each vitamin performs one or more specific functions in the body.

Getting enough vitamins is essential to life, although the body has no nutritional use for excess vitamins, and some vitamins can be stored only for relatively short periods. Many people, nevertheless, believe in being on the "safe side" and thus take extra vitamins. However, a well-balanced diet will usually meet all the body's vitamin needs.

So-called average or normal eaters probably never need supplemental vitamins, although many think they do. Vitamin deficiency diseases are rarely seen in the U.S. population. People known to have deficient diets require supplemental vitamins, as do those recovering from certain illnesses or vitamin deficiencies.

People who are interested in nutrition and good health should become familiar with the initials U.S. RDI. "United States Recommended Daily Intake" was adopted by the FDA for use in nutrition labeling and special dietary foods. They are the highest amounts of vitamins, minerals, and proteins that are needed by most people each day.

41. Which of the following statements about vitamins is NOT true?

    (1) Vitamins contain carbon, hydrogen, and oxygen atoms.
    (2) Vitamins provide energy for growth.
    (3) Vitamins help prevent diseases.
    (4) Only a small amount of a vitamin is needed for it to work.
    (5) Each vitamin performs a different function in the body.

42. According to this article, supplemental vitamins are required for

    (1) everyone interested in nutrition and good health.
    (2) people who eat a balanced diet.
    (3) people known to have deficient diets.
    (4) average or normal eaters.
    (5) people who exercise vigorously.

43. Recommended Daily Intake was adopted by the FDA to indicate the

    (1) minimum amount of food a person needs to stay alive.
    (2) optimum amount of food needed each day to maintain normal weight.
    (3) minimum amount of vitamins necessary to prevent deficiency diseases.
    (4) highest amount of vitamins, minerals, and proteins needed by most people each day.
    (5) amount of food taken in by average or normal eaters each day.

exercises

ITEMS 44 TO 47 REFER TO THE FOLLOWING INFORMATION.

Plant survival depends on the plant's ability to disperse its seeds to different areas. If the seeds are too close together, they will compete for the limited land and water and very few will survive. Therefore nature has given plants many allies in spreading their seeds. They are as follows:

1. Wind	Many seeds are able to catch the wind and be carried by it.
2. Water	Some seeds have the ability to float on water. They will germinate when they are able to anchor into the soil.
3. Animals	Some seeds attach to the fur of passing animals; other seeds are eaten by animals and scattered when the animal leaves its waste.
4. Insects	Pollen attaches to the insect and is carried from one plant to another.
5. Man	Farmers and scientists are able to spread seeds that they feel will be most advantageous for growth and crop yield.

Each of the following items describes a situation in which a seed is spread by one of the methods of seed dispersal listed above. For each item, choose the one method that best describes the situation. Each of the methods may be used more than once in the following set of items.

44. An explorer on a South Pacific Island found only one coconut tree. The nearest coconut trees were found almost 300 miles away. He reasoned that the coconut seed had been carried by

   (1) wind.
   (2) water.
   (3) animals.
   (4) insects.
   (5) man.

45. My lawn has hundreds of dandelions each spring. I see these little seeds with a white puff of silky hairs attached to them. My neighbors sometimes get angry at this because they do not want dandelions on their lawns. Dandelion seeds are spread by

   (1) wind.
   (2) water.
   (3) animals.
   (4) insects.
   (5) man.

46. In a field about 10 miles from an apple orchard may be found a lone apple tree. People seldom travel or camp there, but deer and bears are known to travel through the area. How did the apple seeds travel there?

   (1) Wind
   (2) Water
   (3) Animals
   (4) Insects
   (5) Man

47. A cocklebur is an interesting plant. It produces a seed that has stickers or little barbs on the end. In an area untouched by civilization, how would these seeds be dispersed?

   (1) Wind
   (2) Water
   (3) Animals
   (4) Insects
   (5) Man

ITEMS 48 TO 50 REFER TO THE GRAPH BELOW.

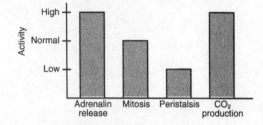

The graph above shows the rate of performance of four activities as they occurred in a man immediately after he had been frightened.

48. From the graph, what can be inferred about the movement of the diaphragm immediately after one has been frightened?

    (1) It becomes more rapid.

    (2) It slows down.

    (3) It ceases for a brief period.

    (4) It is unaffected.

    (5) It becomes more rapid, then suddenly slows down.

49. From the graph, one can assume that there was a decrease in activity in which of the following organs?

    (1) Thyroid

    (2) Kidney

    (3) Stomach

    (4) Lungs

    (5) Brain

50. An analysis of the graph would lead one to assume that which of the following temporarily increased?

    (1) Amount of DNA in the nuclei

    (2) Synthesis of protein

    (3) Storage of glucose in the liver

    (4) Production of red blood cells

    (5) Concentration of glucose in the blood

exercises

ANSWER KEY AND EXPLANATIONS

1. (1)	11. (1)	21. (5)	31. (4)	41. (2)
2. (5)	12. (1)	22. (3)	32. (3)	42. (3)
3. (4)	13. (5)	23. (4)	33. (2)	43. (4)
4. (4)	14. (4)	24. (1)	34. (2)	44. (2)
5. (3)	15. (2)	25. (2)	35. (4)	45. (1)
6. (2)	16. (1)	26. (3)	36. (2)	46. (3)
7. (3)	17. (4)	27. (5)	37. (2)	47. (3)
8. (4)	18. (4)	28. (5)	38. (3)	48. (1)
9. (2)	19. (5)	29. (3)	39. (1)	49. (3)
10. (3)	20. (5)	30. (5)	40. (2)	50. (5)

1. **The correct answer is (1).** Fire is incapable of controlling itself. It does perform the other functions mentioned, however—it digests (or burns up), it breathes (it uses air), it excretes (creates wastes, or ashes), and it reproduces (it spreads).

2. **The correct answer is (5).** Without the ability to reproduce, an organism will die out, or cease to exist.

3. **The correct answer is (4).** If an organism carries out all its basic life functions, it is alive.

4. **The correct answer is (4).** The horizontal line parallel to the *x*-axis shows no change over time. The vertical lines parallel to the *y*-axis connote periods of numerous changes over very short time spans.

5. **The correct answer is (3).** The graph shows the limits of growth. For the tree line it is about 8,200 feet and 72 degrees latitude.

6. **The correct answer is (2).** Streams, like most other systems, depend on the sun for energy. The sun's radiant energy is transformed by producers of energy to chemical energy that other organisms can use.

7. **The correct answer is (3).** The food chain moves from: plants to insects to fish to birds, meaning that the insects eat the plants, the fish eat the insects, and the birds eat the fish. Plants are *producers*, in that they produce chemical energy from radiant energy from the sun. The organisms that eat plants are *herbivores* or primary consumers. The organisms that feed on primary consumers are *secondary consumers*.

8. **The correct answer is (4).** *Biological magnification* is the term used to describe this event. It means that nonbiodegradable substances taken in by organisms build up in the food chain. This happens because many plants are eaten by the insects during the insect's lifetime before the insects are eaten by the fish. Of course, the fish eat many insects. Unfortunately, this is a true story, and even penguins in the South Pole region have DDT from pesticides in their tissues although no spraying ever occurred there.

9. **The correct answer is (2).** Sensory neurons receive stimuli and pass the message to the *interneurons* in the central nervous system. The motor neurons take this information from the central nervous system to an *effector*, which may be another nerve or a gland or muscle. In this case the information was processed as far as the central nervous system but somewhere in the motor neurons there was a fault.

10. **The correct answer is (3).** The *in-dependent* variable is the *cause* and the *dependent* variable is the *effect*. The independent variable is placed on the *x*-axis and the dependent on the *y*-axis when graphing results.

11. **The correct answer is (1).** We know that temperature is not the variable to change since she tested at two different temperatures with the same result. The volume of water and the amount of eggs she put into each container are, or should be, controls. Controls are experimental conditions that should be the same, so that the independent variable is the only thing that changes.

12. **The correct answer is (1).** Type AB is considered the universal recipient. Because people with AB have both proteins on their own RBC's, they won't produce antibodies to either A or B proteins on donated RBC's.

13. **The correct answer is (5).** A person with type B could have the alleles BB or BO.

14. **The correct answer is (4).** As one moves from left to right, the concentration of lead goes down. 1 times 10 to the minus 1 is the same as 0.1 M, while 1 times 10 to the minus 5 is 0.00001 M solution.

15. **The correct answer is (2).** See number 14.

16. **The correct answer is (1).** To figure out the decrease, subtract the difference and divide by the current number: $(37.8 - 30.5) \div 37.8$.

17. **The correct answer is (4).** A virus cannot commandeer the cell's machinery without using its own DNA.

18. **The correct answer is (4).** A retrovirus must contain reverse transcriptase, the enzyme (protein) that converts its RNA to DNA.

19. **The correct answer is (5).** DNA is found only in the nucleus. The rest of the answers are descriptive of a virus's interaction with its host.

20. **The correct answer is (5).** Most flowers have both male and female structures. The male structure is the stamen, which is made of the filament (E) and anther (F). The pollen is produced in the anther, while the eggs are produced in the ovary (D).

21. **The correct answer is (5).** See number 20.

22. **The correct answer is (3).** A control group is always necessary in any experiment. The groups must be tested against a control, in this case a group of passengers who did not receive any special diet. Choice (1) is incorrect because the scientist's observations would have preceded the hypothesis. Choice (2) is incorrect because the age of the subjects in the experiment was not being tested (but the scientist should have considered age as a potential confounding variable). Choice (4) is incorrect because time zones are not important as long as they remain constant between the groups. However, this would be important information to report, so that future work could investigate any interaction between diet and number of time zones. Choice (5) is incorrect because including a high-fat diet was not necessary to the experiment, and not doing so does not bias her results.

23. **The correct answer is (4).** Gene frequencies cannot change if there is no genetic variability, i.e., if every one of the species shared the same genetic pool. Choices (1) and (2) are incorrect because evolution is more likely to occur in an unstable environment and requires genetic variability. Choice (3) is incorrect because mutations can *enhance* evolution. Choice (5) is incorrect because, as population increases, resources become limited. At this point, natural selection, or *survival*

of the fittest, can lead to evolutionary change.

24. **The correct answer is (1).** The question asks you to find the *incorrect* statement, which is choice (1). The illustration shows that carbon dioxide is indeed important; it is created by "animal respiration" and taken in by plants as part of the process of *photosynthesis.* The other choices are supported by the illustration: animals do take in oxygen and breathe out carbon dioxide. Both animals and plants "breathe." As part of the cycle, oxygen is important. The last choice is true also; dead organic matter is created by both animal and plant life, and it is then decayed by bacteria to put nutrients back into the soil.

25. **The correct answer is (2).** A histogram shows the percent of the population, by sex, in each age group. It does not show limiting factors, carry capacity, or break down results by country. It also does not show rate of population growth; a line graph would be needed to do that.

26. **The correct answer is (3).** Education and employment of women reduce the birthrate and are less invasive than the other measures listed. Choices (1), (2), and (5) are very invasive, whereas choice (4) would not reduce the birth rate.

27. **The correct answer is (5).** The pituitary gland is the master gland that can control other glands, although it is under the guidance of the hypothalamus. The ovaries also produce hormones that provide feedback to the pituitary and to the hypothalamus.

28. **The correct answer is (5).** Epinephrine is produced in the adrenal glands, which are anterior to (on top of) the kidneys.

29. **The correct answer is (3).** The pancreas produces these important hormones, which regulate blood glucose levels.

30. **The correct answer is (5).** Sporophytes produce spores and gametophytes produce gametes.

31. **The correct answer is (4).** Meiosis produces haploid spores, which germinate into haploid gametophytes, which produce haploid reproductive structures that become diploid with fertilization.

32. **The correct answer is (3).** The proportion of red is 20/50 or 0.4, and that of blue is 30/50 or 0.6. The chance of drawing a red from the male is 0.4, and the chance of drawing a blue from the female is 0.6. The probability of two simultaneous events is the product of their individual probabilities, or 0.24. However, one could also draw a blue from the male and a red from the female (another 0.24 probability), so that there are 2 times 0.24, or a 0.48 chance.

33. **The correct answer is (2).** The frequency of the blue allele is 0.6. Those that have *two* copies of the allele would be 0.6 times 0.6, or 36% of each population.

34. **The correct answer is (2).** All variables, including light, need to be controlled as tightly as possible so that one can best determine the effect of the experimental variable, which is sound.

35. **The correct answer is (4).** The *dependent* variable is what is measured as a result of the *independent* variable. Stuart was using the mass as a measure of plant growth.

36. **The correct answer is (2).** Stuart was changing the types of music to see if they had an effect on plant growth, or mass.

37. **The correct answer is (2).** Primary consumers are *herbivores,* which eat the green plants, or producers.

38. **The correct answer is (3).** As one moves up the food chain, each level will accumulate nonbiodegradable poisons in the tissues. This buildup is termed *biological magnification.*

39. **The correct answer is (1).** The passage states that two million African Americans, or eight percent, carry the sickle cell trait.

40. **The correct answer is (2).** The passage mentions that those who carry the sickle cell trait and not the sickle cell disease would not have painful symptoms. The passage does imply that the pain in the chest, stomach, arms, legs, or other parts of the body is consistent with symptoms associated with sickle cell disease.

41. **The correct answer is (2).** Paragraph two states that vitamins "do not provide energy nor do they construct or build any part of the body."

42. **The correct answer is (3).** The fifth paragraph of the passage indicates that supplemental vitamins are required for people known to have deficient diets and those recovering from certain illnesses.

43. **The correct answer is (4).** The last sentence of the article defines *Recommended Daily Intake* as the highest amount of vitamins, minerals, and proteins needed by most people each day.

44. **The correct answer is (2).** Coconut seeds float on water and have been known to travel thousands of miles.

45. **The correct answer is (1).** Dandelion seeds catch the wind and travel in the air.

46. **The correct answer is (3).** Animals eat the apples and drop the seeds in their waste as they pass through an area.

47. **The correct answer is (3).** Cockleburs attach to the fur of passing animals and fall off as the animals walk. The passage also specifically says that man is not present in the area.

48. **The correct answer is (1).** The graph shows a high rate of carbon dioxide production. When the supply of carbon dioxide in the blood increases, the breathing rate is increased. The brain is stimulated by increased amounts of carbon dioxide in the blood and sends impulses to the diaphragm and chest muscles, which then move more rapidly. As a result, the rate of breathing is speeded up.

49. **The correct answer is (3).** *Peristalsis* is the term applied to the rhythmic contractions of the smooth muscles in the wall of the alimentary canal. The stomach is one of its organs. The graph shows that there is a low rate of peristalsis, which means there is little digestion going on in the stomach.

50. **The correct answer is (5).** The graph shows a high rate of adrenaline release. One of the effects of adrenaline is to cause a conversion of glycogen, which is stored in the liver, into glucose, which becomes dissolved in the blood. The high concentration of glucose supplies the extra energy that results when large amounts of adrenaline are released.

answers exercises

EXERCISES: PHYSICAL SCIENCE

Directions: For each question, circle the number of the response that best answers the question or completes the statement. An Answer Key and Explanations are provided at the end of this section.

1. The flow of electrons through a wire is similar to the flow of water through a pipe: The greater the diameter and the shorter the length of pipe, the easier it is for the water to flow and the less is the resistance. The diagram below represents a portion of an electrical wire with a length of (l) and thickness of (t).

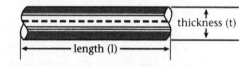

The resistance of the wire

(1) increases with length; increases with thickness.

(2) increases with length; decreases with thickness.

(3) decreases with length; decreases with thickness.

(4) decreases with length; increases with thickness.

(5) is unchanged by changes in length or thickness.

ITEM 2 REFERS TO THE ILLUSTRATION BELOW.

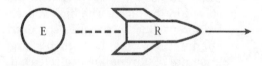

2. In the diagram above, a rocket (R) has just left Earth (E). The attractive force between R and E is

(1) magnetic.

(2) electrical.

(3) centripetal.

(4) gravitational.

(5) nuclear.

3. Work measures the product of the force (W) exerted on an object and the resulting displacement (d) of that object. The formula for work is: $work = W \times d$.

In the diagram below, a Weight (W) is pulled a distance (d). If W is doubled, the work required is

(1) halved.

(2) quadrupled.

(3) doubled.

(4) quartered.

(5) unchanged.

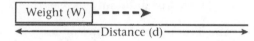

4. The diagram below represents a tall mountain. The atmospheric pressure at the bottom is 14.7 pounds per square inch.

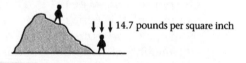

At the top of the mountain, the atmospheric pressure is

(1) less because of a smaller amount of atmosphere pushing down.

(2) less because of the greater amount of atmosphere pushing down.

(3) greater since the ambient temperature is lower.

(4) greater since there is a greater proximity to the clouds.

(5) the same.

ITEMS 5 TO 7 REFER TO THE FOLLOWING GRAPH.

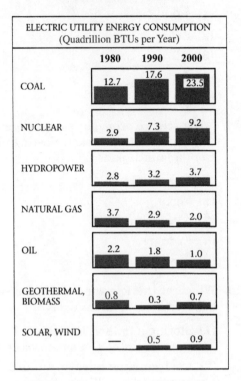

ELECTRIC UTILITY ENERGY CONSUMPTION
(Quadrillion BTUs per Year)

	1980	1990	2000
COAL	12.7	17.6	23.5
NUCLEAR	2.9	7.3	9.2
HYDROPOWER	2.8	3.2	3.7
NATURAL GAS	3.7	2.9	2.0
OIL	2.2	1.8	1.0
GEOTHERMAL, BIOMASS	0.8	0.3	0.7
SOLAR, WIND	—	0.5	0.9

5. The fuel that supplies the greatest amount of energy is

   (1) nuclear.
   (2) natural gas.
   (3) coal.
   (4) hydropower.
   (5) solar and wind.

6. All of the following fuels are expected to increase in consumption EXCEPT

   (1) coal.
   (2) nuclear.
   (3) hydropower.
   (4) natural gas.
   (5) geothermal, biomass.

7. Besides coal, the greatest increase in fuel consumption in BTUs is projected for

   (1) nuclear.
   (2) hydropower.
   (3) natural gas.
   (4) oil.
   (5) solar, wind.

ITEMS 8 TO 11 REFER TO THE FOLLOWING GRAPH.

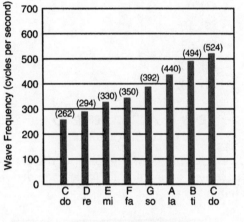

Notes on a Musical Scale

In the above graph, the notes C-D-E-F-G-A-B-C constitute a major scale. The sound frequencies produced by each note are indicated.

8. If a major scale is played, the frequencies

   (1) go up by even steps.
   (2) go up but not evenly.
   (3) decrease evenly.
   (4) decrease but not evenly.
   (5) stay the same.

9. Compared to the frequency of the first C, the second C is

   (1) twice as much.
   (2) half as much.
   (3) four times as much.
   (4) the same.
   (5) one quarter as much.

10. The lowest pitch indicated in the graph is

   (1) A

   (2) B

   (3) C

   (4) D

   (5) E

11. "The Star-Spangled Banner" begins with the notes G and E. What is the change in frequency between these two notes?

   (1) 0

   (2) 10

   (3) 62

   (4) 330

   (5) 392

ITEMS 12 AND 13 REFER TO THE FOLLOWING GRAPH.

The following graph represents the disintegration of a sample of a radioactive element.

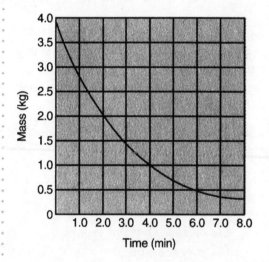

12. What mass of the material remains at 4.0 minutes?

   (1) 1 kg

   (2) 2 kg

   (3) 3 kg

   (4) 4 kg

   (5) 5 kg

13. What is the half-life of the isotope (in minutes)?

   (1) 1.0

   (2) 2.0

   (3) 3.0

   (4) 4.0

   (5) 5.0

14. What science principle is most closely associated with a rocket blasting off from a launch pad?

   (1) Momentum

   (2) Force

   (3) Action-reaction

   (4) Entropy

   (5) Synergy

15. Which of the following tasks can be handled by computers today?

   (1) Storing a million DNA sequences in the Genome project

   (2) Analyzing the census results of hundreds of millions of people

   (3) Designing new complex technology using 3-dimensional imaging

   (4) Analyzing information about the galaxies in the universe

   (5) All of the above

16. Ellen, a champion cyclist, wanted to see the effect of tire pressure on the speed of her bike. She set up an experiment. If she planned to make five experimental tests runs, what variable would she most likely have had to change in each run?

   (1) Length of the test course

   (2) Weight she carried

   (3) Wind velocity

   (4) Tire pressure

   (5) Type of bike

ITEMS 17 AND 18 REFER TO THE FOLLOWING CHART.

PROJECTED U.S. CARBON DIOXIDE EMISSIONS BY SECTOR AND FUEL, 1990–2020 (MILLION METRIC TONS CARBON EQUIVALENT)

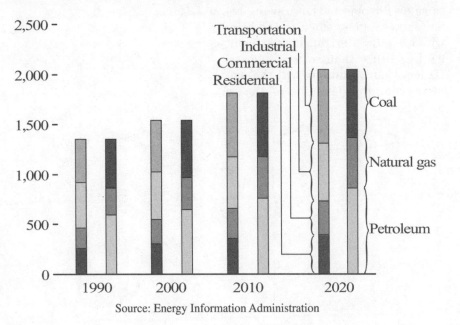

Source: Energy Information Administration

17. What fuel produces the largest amount of CO_2 emissions in the United States?

(1) Coal

(2) Natural gas

(3) Nuclear

(4) Petroleum

(5) Wood burning

18. An alternative fuel that does not produce carbon dioxide is

(1) coal.

(2) natural gas.

(3) nuclear.

(4) petroleum.

(5) wood burning.

19. The *Principle of Archimedes* states that buoyant force is equal to the weight of water displaced. This means that a floating object pushes up an amount of water weighing the same as the object. The drawing below shows a glass filled to the brim with ice and water. Since ice is about 9% less dense than water, it floats. Under what conditions will the water overflow the glass after all the ice melts?

(1) The water will never overflow the glass.

(2) The water will overflow as soon as any ice melts.

(3) The water will overflow if there is more than 9% ice.

(4) The water will overflow if there is more than 18% ice.

(5) The water will overflow if there is more than 91% ice.

ITEMS 20 TO 22 REFER TO THE FOLLOWING INFORMATION AND ILLUSTRATION.

The graph below shows the absorption of optical fiber used to carry data and voice in telecommunications networks. Fibers with less absorption are desired because they can carry signals farther before they need to be amplified. The distance between amplifiers is inversely proportional to the absorption coefficient, which means that if the absorption is doubled, the distance is halved. While lower-absorption fiber is generally more expensive, the higher cost of the fiber is more than compensated for by the lower total cost of amplifiers.

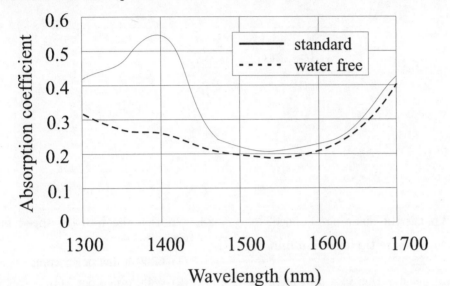

20. Why is the absorption important in optical communication?

    (1) Data is lost when light is absorbed in the fiber.

    (2) More data can be sent down a fiber with less absorption.

    (3) Data can be sent over longer distances with less absorption.

    (4) Absorption determines the spacing of optical amplifiers.

    (5) Low-absorption fiber is more expensive.

21. For a communications system operating at 1400 nm with 20 amplifiers using standard fiber, how many amplifiers can be saved by converting to water-free fiber?

    (1) None

    (2) 5

    (3) 10

    (4) 15

    (5) 20

22. The owner of an optical link that uses standard fiber at 1310 nm is considering upgrading the link. Which change would result in the greatest savings in the number of amplifiers?

    (1) Change the wavelength to 1550 nm.

    (2) Install water-free fiber.

    (3) Install water-free fiber and change the wavelength to 1400 nm.

    (4) Install water-free fiber and change the wavelength to 1550 nm.

    (5) None of the above

ITEMS 23 TO 25 REFER TO THE FOLLOWING GRAPHS.

WORLD SPEED RECORDS:
(DISTANCE TRAVELED BY EACH IN ONE HOUR)

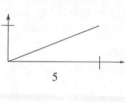

Fastest Horse

Fastest Swimmer

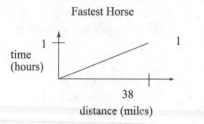

38

5

distance (miles)

Fastest Car

Fastest Plane

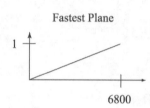

763

6800

23. What is the meaning of speed?

   (1) distance traveled in a unit of time
   (2) acceleration in a unit of time
   (3) momentum magnitude in one direction
   (4) motion of an object
   (5) pressure change

24. What is the speed, in miles per hour, of the fastest vehicle at 3,400 miles from start?

   (1) 1,000
   (2) 1,700
   (3) 3,400
   (4) 6,800
   (5) Not enough information is given.

25. What is the limit of speed for *any* object?

   (1) 6800 miles per second
   (2) 6800 miles per hour
   (3) 186,000 miles per second
   (4) 186,000 miles per hour
   (5) There is no limit.

ITEMS 26 AND 27 REFER TO THE FOLLOWING GRAPHICS AND PASSAGE.

Periodic Table of Elements (Number 1–18)

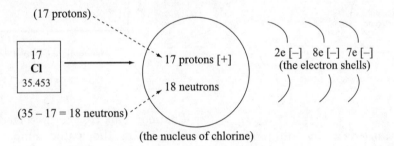

	Atomic Number	→ 1
	Symbol	→ **H**
	Atomic Mass	→ 1.01

Period:	1A	2A	3A	4A	5A	6A	7A	8A
Row: 1	1 **H** 1.01							2 **He** 4.00
2	3 **Li** 6.94	4 **Be** 9.01	5 **B** 10.81	6 **C** 12.01	7 **N** 14.01	8 **O** 16.00	9 **F** 19.00	10 **Ne** 20.18
3	11 **Na** 22.99	12 **Mg** 24.31	13 **Al** 29.98	14 **Si** 28.09	15 **P** 30.97	16 **S** 32.06	17 **Cl** 35.45	18 **Ar** 39.95

Drawing a Chlorine Atom Using the Periodic Table of Elements

(17 protons)

17	
Cl	→ 17 protons [+]
35.453	18 neutrons

2e [–] 8e [–] 7e [–]
(the electron shells)

(35 – 17 = 18 neutrons)

(the nucleus of chlorine)

The Periodic Table of Elements is an important tool used by physicists and engineers to understand the chemical properties of elements. Developed by Dmitri Mendeleev (1869), it contains the symbols of all known elements listed in order of their masses. On the left side of the table (see the darkened step beginning between Be and B) are the metals; on the right are the nonmetals.

26. Why do scientists and engineers often refer to the Periodic Table of Elements?

   (1) It organizes the 92 elements in patterns.

   (2) It predicts chemical properties.

   (3) It predicts physical properties.

   (4) It helps to develop new materials.

   (5) All of the above

27. How many [neutrons], [protons] and [electrons] are in a boron (B) atom?

   (1) 6 [neutrons], 5 [protons], 5 [electrons]

   (2) 5,5,6

   (3) 6,5,6

   (4) 5,6,5

   (5) 6,6,5

28. The smallest particle of gold that still retains its characteristics is a(n)

   (1) molecule of gold.

   (2) proton.

   (3) electron.

   (4) gold granule.

   (5) atom of gold.

29. The diagram below represents the formation of an

   (1) atom.

   (2) isotope.

   (3) isobar.

   (4) electron.

   (5) ion.

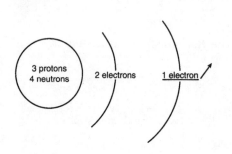

30. Substances can be altered macroscopically or at an atomic level. A piece of paper is torn. This is an example of a

   (1) chemical change.

   (2) combustion process.

   (3) nuclear change.

   (4) physical change.

   (5) Carnot process.

31. Water is electrolyzed to produce oxygen and hydrogen. This is an example of a

   (1) chemical change.

   (2) combustion process.

   (3) nuclear change.

   (4) physical change.

   (5) Carnot process.

32. Which of the following processes is responsible for clothes drying on the line on a warm summer day?

   (1) Freezing

   (2) Condensation

   (3) Sublimation

   (4) Evaporation

   (5) Melting

ITEMS 33 TO 36 REFER TO THE GRAPH AND INFORMATION BELOW.

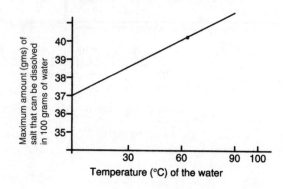

Common salt can be dissolved in water. The hotter the water temperature, the more salt can be dissolved. In the graph above, the line shows the maximum amount (grams) of salt that can be dissolved in 100 grams of water at various temperatures.

33. What is the maximum number of grams of salt that can be dissolved in 100 grams of water at 30°C?

   (1) 34

   (2) 36

   (3) 38

   (4) 40

   (5) 0

34. At what temperature will the water dissolve a maximum of 40 grams of salt?

    (1) 0°C
    (2) 30°C
    (3) 60°C
    (4) 90°C
    (5) 100°C

35. At 60°C, 100 grams of water can dissolve any of the following amounts of salt EXCEPT

    (1) 30 grams.
    (2) 38 grams.
    (3) 39 grams.
    (4) 40 grams.
    (5) 41 grams.

36. By raising the temperature of the water from 0°C to 100°C, how many more grams of salt can be dissolved?

    (1) 0 grams
    (2) 1 gram
    (3) 2 grams
    (4) 3 grams
    (5) 4 grams

37. Seawater consists mostly of salt dissolved in water. In order to effectively make seawater pure enough to drink, that water must first be

    (1) chlorinated.
    (2) distilled.
    (3) filtered.
    (4) oxidized.
    (5) aerated.

ITEM 38 REFERS TO THE FOLLOWING PASSAGE.

According to the *Big Bang* theory, about ten to twenty billion years ago the universe began in a gigantic explosion. The explosion caused clouds of matter to form that cooled and condensed into atoms. Condensation continued, causing atoms to become stars, stars to form star clusters, clusters to become galaxies, and galaxies to form clusters of galaxies. Scientists are using physics, the science that deals with matter and energy and their interactions, to try to understand how this happened.

What will happen to the universe in the future depends upon the total matter residing in the universe and on the forces of gravity pulling them together. If there is too little mass, the universe will keep expanding. This is known as the "expanding universe" model. Too much gravity and it will begin to contract, making it shrink. Eventually it will collapse in the same way as it formed. This is known as the "big crunch" model.

38. What does the "big crunch" model predict will happen in the future? The universe will

    (1) expand due to gravity.
    (2) expand due to pressure.
    (3) contract due to gravity.
    (4) contract due to thermal fusion.
    (5) stay the same.

ITEMS 39 AND 40 REFER TO THE FOLLOWING PASSAGE.

In his book, *The Sun, The Genome and The Internet* (1999), the world-famous physicist Freeman Dyson discusses the question of whether modern technology could be used to narrow the gap between rich and poor. Solar power, he says, could be used as an inexpensive way to connect people all over the world with the Internet and end the cultural isolation of poor countries. Decoding the *genome*, or genetic engineering, would encourage breakthroughs in genetics, which could promote better health in children as well as better crops in poorer countries to help them compete in the global economy. These potential developments in the fields of genetic engineering and worldwide communication would create a more equal distribution of wealth to people throughout the world.

39. Which of the following is an incorrect inference according to this passage?

   (1) Scientists work only on issues relating to pure science

   (2) Freeman Dyson is focused on applying the uses of science to problems of poverty throughout the world.

   (3) The fields of physics, biology, and economics are sometimes interrelated.

   (4) The Internet is a modern worldwide means of communication.

   (5) Freeman Dyson is a physicist and author.

40. How does Dyson propose to utilize the sun's energy?

   (1) As a nation-wide substitute for coal

   (2) To heat houses

   (3) To power the Internet

   (4) To produce artificial food

   (5) All of the above

ANSWER KEY AND EXPLANATIONS

1. (2)	9. (1)	17. (4)	25. (3)	33. (3)
2. (4)	10. (3)	18. (3)	26. (5)	34. (3)
3. (3)	11. (3)	19. (1)	27. (1)	35. (5)
4. (1)	12. (1)	20. (4)	28. (5)	36. (4)
5. (3)	13. (2)	21. (3)	29. (5)	37. (2)
6. (4)	14. (3)	22. (4)	30. (4)	38. (3)
7. (1)	15. (5)	23. (1)	31. (1)	39. (1)
8. (2)	16. (4)	24. (4)	32. (4)	40. (3)

1. **The correct answer is (2).** The longer and thinner the wire, the harder it is for electrons to travel through it. It is easier to think about how water flows through a pipe. If the diameter is very small, it's naturally harder for the water to get through it. In addition, it is more difficult for water to flow through a 1,000-foot length of pipe than it is to travel through a 10-foot pipe. Choices (1), (3), and (4) do not fulfill *both* of these conditions for length and diameter.

2. **The correct answer is (4).** Gravity is the attraction between any two objects. The other choices are incorrect: Magnetic forces depend on the direction of electron flow; electrical forces depend on the charges of particles; centripetal forces concern rotating bodies; and nuclear forces act only in the nucleus of an atom.

3. **The correct answer is (3).** Using the formula, work = weight (W) × distance (d), then twice as much work is needed to move twice the weight over the same distance. The other choices are incorrect since they don't make sense when applied to the work formula.

4. **The correct answer is (1).** The farther up the mountain you climb, the less atmosphere is above you, and therefore the less pressure pushing down on you. Remember that outer space has no atmosphere. All the other choices contradict this fact.

5. **The correct answer is (3).** Coal is the highest bar for each year. In the year 2000, coal is 23.5 quadrillion BTUs per year; choice (1), nuclear, is 9.2; choice (2), natural gas, is 2.0; choice (4), hydropower, is 3.7; and choice (5), solar and wind power, is 0.9.

6. **The correct answer is (4).** The best way of predicting the future is to look at the trends of the past. Of the choices given, only natural gas shows a decrease from year to year. For example, choice (1), coal, increases from 12.7 (1980) to 17.6 (1990) and to 23.5 (2000).

7. **The correct answer is (1).** Nuclear energy consumption increases the most: 9.2 - 2.9 = 6.3 quadrillion BTUs in 20 years. Choice (3), natural gas, and choice (4), oil, are incorrect because they both decrease. The other two choices have smaller increases than does nuclear energy consumption.

8. **The correct answer is (2).** The bar length for each successive note increases. But each successive increment is not an even amount. For example, the step size between C and D is 294 − 262, or *32 cycles per second*, and between D and E it is 330 − 294, or *36 cycles per second*. Since these are *not even*, choice (1) is incorrect. Since the frequency *increases with each note*, choices (3), (4), and (5) are all incorrect. *Note: To understand a graph, it is important*

to try to make sense of the graphics: here, if you know that a musical scale gets higher and higher as you go up from "do", then the bars should get longer too.

9. **The correct answer is (1).** The wave frequency for the second C note is exactly twice as much as the frequency of the first C note: 2 × 262 = 524.

10. **The correct answer is (3).** Pitch is measured by frequency. Therefore, the lowest pitch on the graph corresponds to the lowest frequency, which is C (at 262 cycles per second).

11. **The correct answer is (3).** The difference in frequencies is: 392(G) − 330(E) = 62 cycles per second.

12. **The correct answer is (1).** Locate 4.0 minutes on the time axis. Then proceed vertically up, until the curve is reached. Next, move horizontally toward the *mass* axis. The value on the mass axis is 1.0 kg (kilogram), the quantity of radioactive element remaining after 4.0 minutes.

13. **The correct answer is (2).** By definition, the half-life is the time for one-half of the original sample to disintegrate or change to another element. The nucleus of the original element changes while it emits radiation, making it radioactive. The graph indicates that at 2.0 minutes, 2.0 kg of a 4.0 kg sample remains. 2.0 kg/ 4.0 kg = 1/2.

14. **The correct answer is (3).** The gases pushing downward (action) lift the rocket upward (reaction). Choices (1), (2) and (4) each take part in the rocket motion, but none describes the *opposing* forces. Choice (5), synergy, is not applicable since it means the interaction of two or more forces so that their combined effect is greater than the sum of their individual effects.

15. **The correct answer is (5).** Because of their fast speed and large memo-

ries, computers of today are capable of handling each of the four listed choices.

16. **The correct answer is (4).** Ellen would need to see how her speed *depended on* the change of tire pressure. Therefore, the independent variable of the experiment is the *tire pressure*; the dependent variable is her speed. She would have had to vary the tire pressure between each test trial, keeping all the other variables constant. All other choices would measure another independent variable instead. For example, choice (3) would have measured the effect of wind velocity on her speed.

17. **The correct answer is (4).** According to the chart, the length of all line segments (see the right-hand bar for each year) for petroleum, from 1990 to 2020, is greater than that of either coal (choice 1) or natural gas (choice 2). This means that petroleum produces more carbon dioxide than does either natural gas or coal. Choice (3), *nuclear*, and choice (5), *wood burning*, are not major sources of energy in the United States.

18. **The correct answer is (3).** Nuclear energy does not depend on burning a carbon-containing substance and therefore does not produce carbon dioxide when used. Since carbon dioxide is a major contributor to the problem of global warming, this is an advantage that nuclear power has over power generated by fossil fuels such as coal or gas. All the other choices are hydrocarbons and *do* produce carbon dioxide.

19. **The correct answer is (1).** The ice has more volume than the water it displaces, but its volume will be reduced when it melts, since it is less dense than water. The *Principle of Archimedes* guarantees that the volume of water added from melting ice is equal to the volume of water displaced since their weights are the same.

20. **The correct answer is (4).** As the passage explains, lower absorption allows the amplifier to be more sparsely spaced. The absorption neither affects the data capacity of the fiber, choices (1) and (2), nor the total range of fiber transmission, choice (3). While low-absorption fiber is more expensive, it is not the reason that absorption is important. Applying physical science understandings to the development of important technology, such as telecommunication, is important to our modern life style.

21. **The correct answer is (3).** At a wavelength of 1400 nm, the absorption is reduced from about 0.55 (on the solid line), to 0.27 (on the dashed line): a factor of two. Since the amplifier span is inversely proportional to the absorption, the distance between amplifiers can be doubled, reducing the number of amplifiers by half, from 20 to 10. It is always important to try to to make sense of the graphics. Here, *It makes sense* that the higher the absorption, the more information is lost, and therefore the more amplifiers are needed to send the signal through the fibers. All other choices are incorrect since they don't represent the *greatest savings in the number of amplifiers* corresponding to the greatest reduction in the absorption coefficient.

22. **The correct answer is (4).** The lowest absorption is for water-free fiber at 1550 nm, so the greatest savings of amplifiers is achieved by changing to that fiber type and wavelength. This maximum change can be determined by noting the change of the absorption coefficient, from the initial point in the problem, at 1300 nm, of 0.4, to the final point, at 1550 nm, of 0.2.

23. **The correct answer is (1).** Speed is the distance covered in a unit of time. Here each speed is measured in miles per hour. Speed differs from velocity, which is a measure of the speed in a *particular direction*. The other choices are incorrect.

24. **The correct answer is (4).** The plane, which is the fastest vehicle, is shown traveling at 6,800 miles in 1 hour, or 6,800 miles per hour. Since the graph is a straight line, the speed is constant. It would travel 3,400 miles in *1/2 hour,* which is the same as 6,800 miles per *hour.* Choice (3), 3,400 miles per hour is incorrect because the ordinate of the graph at 3,400 miles is *not 1* but *1/2.* Similarly, choices (1) and (2) are incorrect. There *is* enough information, so choice (5) is incorrect.

25. **The correct answer is (3).** According to Einstein's theory of relativity, the fastest any object can travel is 186,000 miles per second. The reason it can't travel any faster is that its mass actually gets measurably larger as it gets closer to this speed, which will slow it down. Only photons with zero mass travel that fast. For this reason, there *is* a limit and choice (5) is incorrect.

26. **The correct answer is (5).** The table helps to make sense of the 92 different elements, arranging them in order of size (choice 1); to identify metals and nonmetals (choice 2); to predict some physical properties such as atomic radii, electronegativity, and ionization energy (choice 3); and to help scientists to predict behavior of chemicals in order to develop new materials (choice 4). All choices are correct.

27. **The correct answer is (1).** The boron box in the Periodic Table looks like:

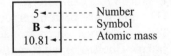

The atomic number, 5, gives the number of protons and electrons in an atom. The atomic mass is equivalent (approximately) to the number of protons and neutrons; round it to

11. Therefore, the number of (neutrons) = (atomic mass) − (protons) = 6. Therefore there are **6**[neutrons], **5**[protons], and **5**[electrons], **choice (1)**. *Note: in drawing the atom, the number of valence electrons (electrons in the outer shell) can be determined by the column in which the atom appears.* Here, since boron is in column 3A, it will have 3 valence electrons. The maximum number of electrons for the atoms in the first 3 rows shown are 2 (in the first), 8 (in the second), and 8 (in the third).

28. **The correct answer is (5).** An atom is the smallest part of an element retaining its properties. If gold is broken down into smaller and smaller pieces, even the tinniest granules are made of *gold atoms* (choice 4). If it were possible to end up with a single atom of gold, then any smaller subdivision would consist of the individual parts of the atom, namely neutrons, protons (choice 2); and electrons (choice 3).

29. **The correct answer is (5).** An ion is formed when an atom gains or loses electrons, usually leaving a complete outer electron shell. Here, an atom of lithium, atomic number 3, loses an electron to become a lithium ion. Choice (1) is incorrect because an atom with 3 protons must have 3 electrons. Choice (2) is incorrect since an isotope of the element contains a different number of *neutrons* in the nucleus. Choice (3), *isobars* have the same atomic mass but different numbers of protons. From the picture choice (4) is meaningless.

30. **The correct answer is (4).** The paper is only being changed physically. Neither its chemical nor nuclear make-up has been altered, so choices (1) and (3) are both incorrect. Choice (2) is incorrect since it hasn't been burnt. Choice (5) isn't applicable.

31. **The correct answer is (1).** Electrolysis breaks up water, chemically, into hydrogen and oxygen. These two products do not resemble the proper-ties of the original water molecule so choice (4) is incorrect. Choice (2) is incorrect since water is not combining with an oxidant; it is just being decomposed. A chemical change only deals with changes in the electron shells, not the nucleus, choice (3).

32. **The correct answer is (4).** *Evaporation* is described by the following: *water (liquid) → water (gas)*. Here, the water in the clothes is heated by the sun's energy. The molecules of water move faster and eventually turn into gas, which escape into the air. The opposite is *condensation* (choice 2), when humid air cools down and releases water. In freezing, the surroundings *cool* the water, turning it into a solid (choice 1); its opposite is *melting* (choice 5). *Sublimation* (choice 3) changes a solid directly into a gas, like dry ice to carbon dioxide.

33. **The correct answer is (3).** Find 30°C on the abscissa (the bottom scale). Move up to the line, then move straight across and read the figure from the ordinate (the scale on the left), 38 grams. *Try to understand the meaning of all graphics. Here, at a given temperature, if more salt is added than the maximum amount as seen on the line, then it falls to the bottom of the container; less than that amount, and it is totally dissolved in the water.*

34. **The correct answer is (3).** From 40 grams on the ordinate, move to the right until the line is met; then read the value below on the abscissa, 60°C.

35. **The correct answer is (5).** At 60°C, the maximum amount that can be dissolved is 40 grams; 41 grams is too much. Choices (1) through (4) can all dissolve because each lies below the line at 60°C.

36. **The correct answer is (4).** Follow the graph from the initial to the final temperature. At 0°C, 37 grams can be dissolved; at 60°C, 40 grams can

be dissolved. Therefore 3 more grams of salt can be dissolved by raising the temperature of the water from 0°C to 100°C.

37. **The correct answer is (2).** During the distillation process, the impurities are removed by vaporizing the water, leaving behind the salt. Choices (1), (4), and (5) just add chlorine, oxygen, and air to the water but don't remove the salt. The salt can not be filtered (choice 3) since it is dissolved in the water.

38. **The correct answer is (3).** Gravity is the force of attraction between two bodies such as between you and the center of the earth holding you down to its surface. If the sum of all the matter in the universe were large enough, the matter would attract other matter and contract due to gravity. You can think of it as the reverse of the Big Bang theory, pulling all matter to a common center. Thermal fusion, the energy given off by stars, doesn't contract matter (choice 4). The concept of *crunching* something makes it contract, *not expand*, nor stay the same, so choices (1), (2), and (5) are incorrect.

39. **The correct answer is (1).** The question asks you to identify the *incorrect* inference, so this is the correct answer. The first sentence tells you that this world-renowned physicist is interested not only in studying pure science but also in applying it to societal problems such as in *narrowing the gap between rich and poor*. Choice (2) is corroborated by the last sentence. Choice (3) is suggested by the idea of using these various disciplines to increase crop production. Choices (4) and (5) are stated in the passage.

40. **The correct answer is (3).** Dyson is a socially responsible scientist who wants to narrow the large economic gap existing between richer and poorer countries. Small solar power generators, he says, could be developed in order to connect people in poorer countries to the Internet, giving them access to improved knowledge and communication. Choices (1), (2), and (4) are not mentioned in the passage. However, it is true that solar power can be used in houses as well as in greenhouses; and as for coal, it produces 80 percent of our electric power, while solar power is presently limited to smaller applications.

answers exercises

EXERCISES: EARTH AND SPACE SCIENCE

Directions: For each question, circle the number of the response that best answers the question or completes the statement. An Answer Key and Explanations are provided at the end of this section.

ITEMS 1 TO 4 REFER TO THE FOLLOWING PASSAGE.

On December 18, 1999, the National Aeronautics and Space Administration (NASA) launched *Terra*, its Earth Observing System (EOS) flagship satellite. In February 2000, *Terra* opened its Earth-viewing doors to begin one of humanity's largest and most ambitious science missions ever undertaken—to give Earth its first physical check-up.

In particular, the mission is designed to improve understanding of the movements of carbon and energy throughout Earth's climate system. Forest fires, for example those caused by lightning strikes, have long been part of many ecosystems. However, fires are having greater and greater impacts on the land and the atmosphere as the scale of the burning increases with human activity. Yearly burning of forest and grassland is used in many regions, such as in Southeast Asia and in South America, for the purpose of land clearing.

Among other pollutants and particles, burning releases high amounts of carbon monoxide (CO) into the atmosphere. High atmospheric CO levels have been measured since March 2000 by the remote-sensing instruments onboard NASA's *Terra* satellite.

1. *Terra* is

   (1) the name of NASA's earth-observing satellite.
   (2) one of the causes of pollutants and particles in the air.
   (3) on a mission to watch ocean currents.
   (4) a spaceship on the way to Mars.
   (5) a method of cleaning up toxic waste.

2. Which of the following is a TRUE statement?

   (1) Land clearing on Earth has declined since 1999.
   (2) Lightning and accidents cause most fires on Earth.
   (3) EOS stands for Earth and Ocean Standards.
   (4) Much land clearing takes place in North and South America.
   (5) Burning forests and grasslands causes the release of environmental pollutants, like carbon monoxide.

3. What do you think is probably the most important reason that forests and grasslands are being burned in some areas of the Earth?

   (1) New varieties of experimental vegetation are being created.
   (2) Manmade lakes are being planned in these areas.
   (3) The lands are needed by farmers and are being prepared for raising crops.
   (4) The local population in these areas is declining.
   (5) Local streams and rivers are being rerouted.

4. Which of the following is the most important reason for the existence of a satellite like *Terra?*

(1) Several countries can see it at the same time.

(2) It is able to observe and study the Earth on a total worldwide basis.

(3) The satellite is able to locate things that can't be seen on the ground.

(4) It is able to follow the movements of wildlife.

(5) All of the above

ITEM 5 REFERS TO THE FOLLOWING DIAGRAM.

The Greenhouse Effect

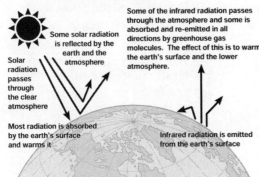

Source: Environmental Protection Agency

5. Why is this phenomena called "the greenhouse effect"?

(1) The sun helps make chlorophyll, which gives green color to plants.

(2) Radiation from the green spectrum of sunlight predominates.

(3) A greenhouse has high humidity.

(4) A greenhouse holds in heat.

(5) A greenhouse depletes the ozone.

ITEM 6 REFERS TO THE FOLLOWING GRAPH.

The amount of ozone existing over the Antarctic between 1979 and 1997.

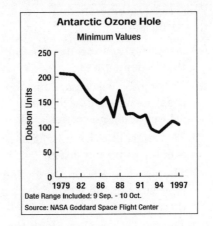

Source: Environmental Protection Agency

6. Why is the shape of this graph so alarming?

(1) Ozone is increasing.

(2) Ozone is decreasing.

(3) The rate of increase of ozone is very high.

(4) The rate of decrease of ozone is very high.

(5) It is not alarming since it's happening in Antarctica only.

7. During the winter season, cities located along the eastern seaboard of the United States consistently record higher temperatures than inland cities in the same states. Which of the following statements might explain this situation?

   (1) Eastern cities receive more sun than inland cities.

   (2) The winter weather along the coast is milder due to the influence of the ocean.

   (3) The angle of the sunlight is greater in inland cities.

   (4) The average amount of daylight is greater in the winter than in the summer.

   (5) The winter weather along the coast is milder due to the location of the Appalachian Mountains.

   ITEMS 8 TO 10 REFER TO THE FOLLOWING INFORMATION.

   Tsunamis are powerful ocean waves caused by sudden undersea disturbances such as earthquakes. They can reach great heights and travel at speeds averaging 450 miles per hour. Tsunamis can be devastating, causing death and destruction in their path.

   On December 26, 2004, a giant earthquake, the fourth most powerful in 100 years, hit the Indian Ocean, creating an enormous tsunami. Indonesia, East Africa, India, and Sri Lanka were hit. There were no early warning systems to alert people, so large numbers living along the water were unable to reach the safety of higher altitudes or inland areas. There were more than 200,000 deaths, and 1 million homes were lost.

   Interestingly enough, NASA scientists have calculated that this earthquake slightly changed our planet's shape, shaved almost 3 microseconds from the length of the day, and shifted the North Pole by several centimeters. The scientists calculated that Earth's *oblateness* (flattening on the top and bulging at the equator) decreased by a small amount. This continues the trend of earthquakes making Earth less oblate, or rounder. They also found that the earthquake decreased the length of the day by 2.68 microseconds. In other words, our Earth now spins a little faster than it did before. This change in spin is related to the change in oblateness.

8. A *tsunami* is a powerful ocean wave that can

   (1) cause much damage to property.

   (2) wipe out crops and rip up trees.

   (3) kill or harm many people and animals.

   (4) happen unexpectedly.

   (5) All of the above

9. Which of the following is a TRUE statement, according to the passage?

   (1) Powerful earthquakes are capable of changing the shape of the earth.

   (2) The causes of tsunamis are totally unknown to scientists.

   (3) Much aid has been sent to the victims of the December 2004 tsunami.

   (4) Much better earthquake and tsunami detection devices are being worked on at NASA.

   (5) Tsunamis occur only in the Indian Ocean.

10. How is the length of the day on Earth affected by its changed *oblateness* after the December 2004 earthquake?

  (1) As the Earth becomes less *oblate,* the length of the day remains the same.

  (2) The length of the day is affected by the position of the North Pole, not the change in its *oblateness.*

  (3) Because the Earth is less *oblate,* or rounder, there is a slight shortening in the length of a day.

  (4) The earthquake caused an increase, not decrease, in the earth's *oblateness.*

  (5) The earthquake did not affect the length of the day on Earth.

ITEM 11 REFERS TO THE FOLLOWING PASSAGE.

In June 1991, Mount Pinatubo in the Philippines began one of the most violent volcanic eruptions of the twentieth century. More than 200,000 acres were covered with a thick coat of volcanic ash, pumice, and debris. In some places the coating became 15 feet thick. More than 600 people died. Some were killed by the ash, others from inhaling the deadly gases Mount Pinatubo gave off. Experts believe that the gases and ash thrown into the upper atmosphere were the cause of below-average worldwide temperatures the following year.

11. What was the major worldwide effect of Mount Pinatubo's explosion in 1991?

  (1) Debris

  (2) A thick coat of ash

  (3) Pumice

  (4) Cooling temperatures

  (5) Deadly gases

ITEM 12 REFERS TO THE FOLLOWING PARAGRAPH.

Early proponents of the theory of continental drift, which was the forerunner of the concept of *plate tectonics,* did not have an easy time defending their ideas against a scientific community that adamantly believed in the theory of fixed continents. In the sixteenth century, maps began to show that the Western Hemisphere on the one hand, and Europe and Asia on the other, appeared to have been pulled apart since, in interlocking fashion, they seemed to fit together nicely into one another. This evidence suggested that a sudden, cataclysmic split had occurred between the eastern and western hemispheres, and that the earth's crust, like a glacier, was moving infinitesimally slowly in one direction or another.

12. The term *plate tectonics* refers to the theory that

  (1) magma can be found deep within the earth's crust.

  (2) the continents of the earth are drifting closer together over geological time.

  (3) the crust of the earth is made of great moving plates driven by powerful forces within the earth.

  (4) glaciers form crevasses as they move over uneven ground.

  (5) the earth's center is a very dense core.

exercises

13. On August 10, 1972, a great fireball streaked northward across the bright afternoon skies of the western United States. It was visible to amazed observers for over a minute and a half as it traced a 900-mile path from Utah to Alberta, Canada, leaving behind it a smoky trail that lingered in the air for 20 minutes. In Montana, people heard a sonic boom at the time it passed by. Over Canada, it disappeared.

This paragraph most likely describes the appearance of

(1) an F-14 fighter.

(2) the space shuttle.

(3) a disintegrating artificial satellite.

(4) a UFO.

(5) a meteor.

ITEMS 14 AND 15 REFER TO THE FOLLOWING ARTICLE.

The principle of balloon flight is simple. The propane is ignited in a burner that is placed directly beneath the opening in the bottom of the balloon. The balloon rises because the air inside the bag is warmer, therefore lighter, than the outside air. If the balloon begins to descend too soon, the crew reignites the burner, sending another blast of lift-producing heat into the bag.

A balloon consists of only three major parts: bag, basket, and burner. The bags (or envelopes, as they are technically called) are made of nylon or polyester. They range in capacity from 33,000 to 100,000 cubic feet, and some reach as high as a seven-story building. The crew basket, constructed from wicker or aluminum, is suspended from the bag by strong tapes. The burner is fixed to a metal platform above the basket.

14. The crew basket on a balloon is usually constructed of wicker or aluminum. What might you predict as an outcome if the crew basket were exchanged for one made of iron or steel?

(1) The balloon would be harder to control.

(2) The balloon would rise more easily from the ground.

(3) The balloon would be unlikely to rise from the ground at all.

(4) The balloon would be struck by lightning.

(5) No change would be likely.

15. In the article, the balloon rises because the air inside the bag is warmer. This occurs because

(1) When air is heated, its density changes.

(2) the balloon is constructed of light materials.

(3) molecules move more violently in cool air.

(4) cool air always moves toward warm air.

(5) air absorbs heat more rapidly than water.

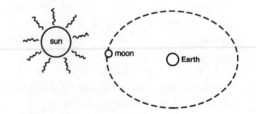

16. The illustration above is an example of

(1) the phases of the moon.

(2) the seasons of the year.

(3) a lunar eclipse.

(4) a solar eclipse.

(5) radiation.

ITEMS 17 AND 18 REFER TO THE INFORMATION AND MAP BELOW.

Few areas in the United States are free from thunderstorms and their attendant hazards, but some areas have more storms than others. The map below shows the incidence of thunderstorm days—days on which thunderstorms are observed—for the United States.

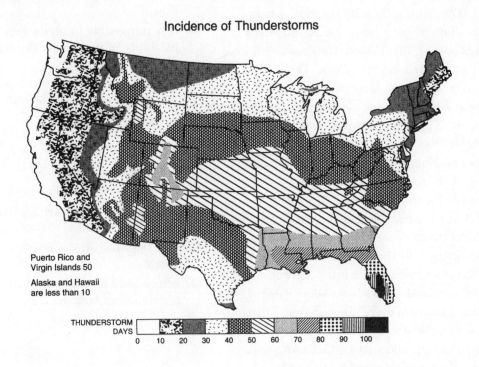

Incidence of Thunderstorms

Puerto Rico and Virgin Islands 50

Alaska and Hawaii are less than 10

THUNDERSTORM DAYS

0   10   20   30   40   50   60   70   80   90   100

17. Mary and Phil are looking forward to a carefree camping vacation. They would like to avoid the frequent thunderstorms that spoiled their last camping trip. Based on the information in the map, which region of the country would they be LEAST likely to choose for their next vacation?

(1) California, Oregon, Washington

(2) Florida, Georgia, Alabama

(3) Kentucky, Virginia, West Virginia

(4) Missouri, Iowa, Illinois

(5) Texas, Louisiana, Oklahoma

18. If Mary and Phil should experience a thunderstorm despite their careful planning, they should do any of the following EXCEPT

(1) stay inside a solid building.

(2) remain in an all-metal automobile.

(3) stand under a tall tree.

(4) go to a low place such as a ravine or valley.

(5) get off and away from bicycles, motorcycles, and golf carts.

ITEMS 19 TO 21 REFER TO THE FOLLOWING TEXT.

It has been more than 75 years since Clyde W. Tombaugh discovered the planet Pluto. He was a young man from a Kansas farm with only a high school education when he got a job as an astronomer's assistant at the Lowell Observatory in Flagstaff, Arizona, in 1929. There had been a suspicion since the turn of the century that a huge planet, nicknamed Planet X, with a mass seven times greater than Earth, existed beyond Uranus and Neptune. The gravitational pull of such a planet, it was believed, would account for observed irregularities in the orbit of Uranus. Using a series of photographs taken of an area of the constellation Gemini, Tombaugh made an unusual observation, which was later determined to be a planet in our own solar system. Other astronomers calculated that Pluto is a mean distance of 3.67 billion miles from the Sun and takes 248 Earth years to make a complete orbit of the Sun. In 1976, it was finally determined that Pluto was small in both diameter and mass, smaller in fact than Earth's moon. It might be as small as 1,750 miles in diameter. Astronomers now believe that no Planet X exists anywhere in our solar system.

19. Based on the information given above, one can conclude that

(1) Planet X does exist but has not yet been found.

(2) the calculations that predicted Planet X were incorrect.

(3) Pluto is a huge planet that affects the orbit of Uranus.

(4) Pluto is in the constellation Gemini.

(5) the planet Pluto must be Planet X.

20. It is known from the information given that

(1) Pluto is closer to the sun than the Earth.

(2) Mars is farther from the sun than Pluto.

(3) it is impossible to predict the existence of previously unseen planets.

(4) since its discovery, Pluto has not yet made an orbit of the sun.

(5) None of the above

21. The diameter of Pluto is

(1) equal to that of Planet X.

(2) as large as that of the Earth.

(3) accounts for irregularities in the orbit of Uranus.

(4) less than the size of Earth's moon.

(5) somewhere in the area of the constellation Gemini.

exercises

ITEMS 22 TO 25 REFER TO THE FOLLOWING ARTICLE.

The Orbiter has only one washroom and toilet. Crew members take turns like a traveling family sharing a motel room. Sanitation facilities are much the same as on the Earth. Airflow substitutes for gravity in carrying away the wastes. Plastic sleeves around the hand-wash basin keep spray droplets from floating away into the cabin.

Toilet waste is pushed by airstreams into a container. Some waste may be intentionally saved. Its analysis tells doctors which minerals crew members may lose excessively in weightlessness.

Crew members may use conventional shaving cream and safety razors and disposable towels. For those preferring electric shavers, there is a wind-up shaver operating like an electric model but requiring no plug or battery. It has a built-in vacuum device that sucks up whiskers as the shaving proceeds. For a sponge-bath, the only kind available, there is a watergun adjustable for temperatures from 18 to 35° C (65 to 95° F).

22. How are droplets of water prevented from leaving the sink and entering the cabin?

(1) The water is frozen.

(2) Droplets are centrifuged down the drain.

(3) Droplets are convected by fans.

(4) Plastic sleeves contain the droplets.

(5) Water is not used.

23. Why are air streams used to collect toilet waste?

(1) The wastes are poisonous.

(2) The wastes are heavy in space.

(3) The wastes are weightless.

(4) Astronauts reuse the wastes.

(5) Wastes must be tested in labs.

24. According to the passage, what floating material could foul up the cabin and harm the crew?

(1) Boots, fuel, wastes

(2) Boots, beds, wastes

(3) Whiskers, bolts, wastes

(4) Landing pods, insulation tiles

(5) Whiskers, water, wastes

25. How much would you weigh while in space?

(1) Twice the earth weight

(2) Earth weight

(3) 50 percent of the earth weight

(4) 25 percent of the earth weight

(5) No weight

ITEMS 26 AND 27 REFER TO THE GRAPH BELOW.

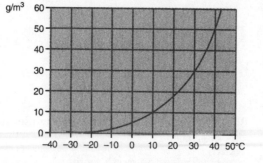

26. Air temperature affects relative humidity, that is, the amount of water vapor in the air compared to the amount of water vapor the air could hold at that temperature. Based on the graph shown above, how much water is needed to saturate each cubic meter of air at 30°C?

(1) 17 g

(2) 20 g

(3) 30 g

(4) 35 g

(5) 50 g

27. The cooling of this air will cause it to become saturated with water vapor. The temperature at which the air becomes saturated is called

(1) break point.

(2) condensation.

(3) dew point.

(4) discomfort index.

(5) relative humidity.

28. In 1969, Neil Armstrong and Edwin Aldrin successfully landed a lunar lander on the surface of the moon and then blasted off again. The property of the Earth that would have prevented the same lunar lander from blasting off from the Kennedy Space Center is its

(1) mass.

(2) revolution.

(3) rotation.

(4) surface temperature.

(5) atmosphere.

ITEM 29 REFERS TO THE FOLLOWING INFORMATION.

The following research has been recently conducted in space:

- Growing insulin crystals to cure diabetes

- Helping plants to extract nitrogen from the air

- Developing new varieties of plants

- Developing new fragrances from flowers

29. These research projects are all related to what type of technology?

(1) Agricultural

(2) Biological

(3) Chemical

(4) Industrial

(5) Pharmaceutical

ITEM 30 REFERS TO THE FOLLOWING DIAGRAM.

Ozone Depletion Process

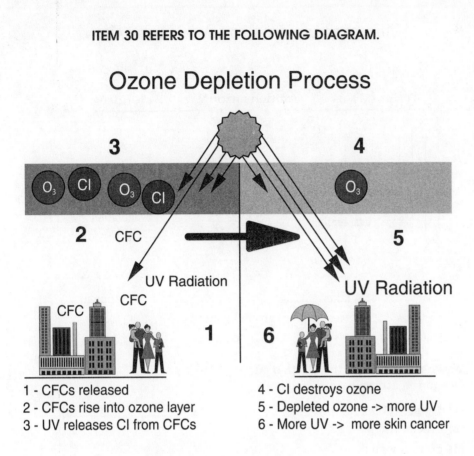

1 - CFCs released
2 - CFCs rise into ozone layer
3 - UV releases Cl from CFCs
4 - Cl destroys ozone
5 - Depleted ozone -> more UV
6 - More UV -> more skin cancer

Source: Environmental Protection Agency

30. Why is the ozone layer important to people?

   (1) It destroys harmful CFCs.

   (2) It filters out pollution.

   (3) It helps us to get suntanned.

   (4) It cuts down on harmful UV radiation.

   (5) It reduces rainfall.

exercises

ITEM 31 REFERS TO THE FOLLOWING ILLUSTRATION.

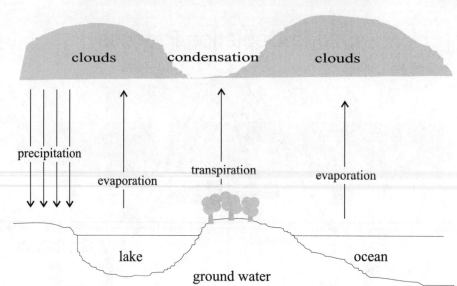

31. Water returns from the Earth's surface to the atmosphere through

(1) transpiration
(2) precipitation
(3) ground water
(4) ocean currents
(5) All of the above

ITEM 32 REFERS TO THE FOLLOWING ILLUSTRATION.

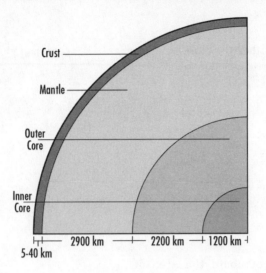

32. Which of the following observations supports the conclusion that the temperature of the Earth's crust rises as you get deeper?

(1) It is cool at the top of coal mines.

(2) Earthquakes generate much heat.

(3) Hot air balloons rise as the air is heated.

(4) The Earth absorbs the sun's hot rays.

(5) Oil pumped from deep wells is often very hot.

ITEM 33 REFERS TO THE FOLLOWING DIAGRAM.

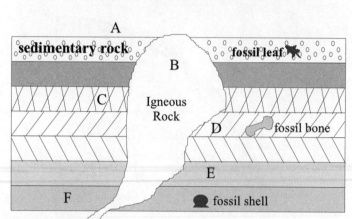

33. Which statement about the area of the Earth represented by the diagram is incorrect?

(1) Many different types of fossils may be found there.

(2) The sedimentary layers are older than the igneous rock.

(3) The sedimentary layers have been tilted at an angle from their original position.

(4) Layer F was underwater at one time.

(5) Weathering is most likely taking place at the point indicated by letter A.

ITEMS 34 AND 35 REFER TO THE FOLLOWING PASSAGE.

NASA's twin robot geologists, the Mars Exploration Rovers named *Spirit* and *Opportunity*, landed on Mars in January 2004 after being launched the previous summer. At that time, the idea that the Red Planet had once been covered with rivers, lakes, and seas was just a theory. But soon these two quad-bike-sized roving laboratories collected abundant evidence on the ground that turned that idea into an established fact. Stratified sediments and minerals that normally form in the presence of water were seen everywhere on this currently cold and frost-locked planet.

Landing sites were carefully selected to be those that might have flowed with water in warmer periods of the planet's history. *Spirit* arrived at the Gusev Crater, the possible site of a prehistoric lake just south of the Martian equator. Its twin *Opportunity* landed on the other side of Mars at the Meridiani Planum, a possible site of ancient water action. The landings were flawless, and the Rovers, which are 6-wheeled 400-pound contraptions, have performed beyond expectation in exploring the planet. They have found such evidence as hematite, a mineral that usually forms in the presence of water, as well as clay and gypsum deposits that are formed by water in the soil.

34. What is the most important significance of finding signs of water on Mars?

(1) Since water is needed for many chemical reactions, this means that many different rocks, minerals, and soil types are similar to those on Earth.

(2) Since water is vital to life here on Earth, this suggests that there may have been Earth-like life there as well.

(3) It may mean that Mars was once a warmer place than the Earth.

(4) It means that many of the weather patterns will be the same on Mars and the Earth.

(5) It suggests that it may have been completely covered with water at one time.

35. Scientists recently found evidence of bacteria while drilling deep in 30,000-year-old ice in Fox, Alaska. Much to their surprise, this newly discovered life form that had been frozen so many years ago started swimming as soon as the ice thawed. How does this possibly relate to the "frost-locked planet" of Mars?

(1) It suggests that bacteria can only survive in ice, not water.

(2) It means that bacteria are the same on Earth and Mars.

(3) The bacteria no doubt were once present in Mars, since the cold conditions of the planet would be similar to the climate in Alaska.

(4) It suggests that if bacteria could remain alive in ice here, it might have done the same on Mars.

(5) It suggests that the diseases on Mars were similar to those on Earth.

ANSWER KEY AND EXPLANATIONS

1. (1)	10. (3)	19. (2)	28. (1)
2. (5)	11. (4)	20. (4)	29. (2)
3. (3)	12. (3)	21. (4)	30. (4)
4. (2)	13. (5)	22. (4)	31. (1)
5. (4)	14. (3)	23. (3)	32. (5)
6. (4)	15. (1)	24. (5)	33. (3)
7. (2)	16. (4)	25. (5)	34. (2)
8. (5)	17. (2)	26. (3)	35. (4)
9. (1)	18. (3)	27. (3)	

1. **The correct answer is (1).** The correct answer is given in the first sentence of the passage. It is an EOS, or *earth observing satellite,* under the control of NASA. Choice (2) is incorrect because nothing is stated about *Terra* itself as a cause of pollution. According to the passage, *Terra* is there to observe the condition of the Earth's climate systems. Choices (3), (4), and (5) are topics not discussed in the passage, so they are also incorrect.

2. **The correct answer is (5).** The second paragraph tells you that this is a correct statement—extensive burning causes the release of carbon monoxide, which is a pollutant. Choice (1) is the opposite; land clearing by burning has *increased,* not declined, according to the second paragraph, which refers to *the scale of burning increasing with human activity.* Choice (2) is only partly correct, since the role of accidental fires is not mentioned. Choice (3) is incorrect; EOS stands for *Earth Observing System.* Because the land clearing issue concerns Asia and South America, not North America, choice (4) is incorrect.

3. **The correct answer is (3).** The most logical explanation for extensive and purposeful burning of forests and grasslands is the need for more farmland in those areas. Choice (1) doesn't really make sense and is also not discussed in the passage. Choice (2) is a possibility, but not as likely as choice (3), so it is incorrect. Choice (4) is probably opposite; you can assume that the local population in these areas is *increasing,* not decreasing, if people are clearing these lands for use. Choice (5) is not likely, since rerouting rivers would probably not necessitate the mass burning of vegetation.

4. **The correct answer is (2).** Because of its distant vantagepoint as it circles our planet, the satellite *Terra* is able to observe the Earth on a total worldwide basis and study problems that cross international boundaries. Issues like different kinds of environmental pollution, global warming, ozone depletion, and extreme weather patterns are worldwide problems that go across borders and must be studied on a global level.

5. **The correct answer is (4).** Energy from the sun heats up the earth's surface. Then the earth radiates energy back into space. Greenhouse gases, such as carbon dioxide and water vapor, trap some of this energy, keeping the heat on a high level. This is also the way glass roofs and windows retain heat inside a greenhouse, which is where the name *greenhouse effect* comes from.

6. **The correct answer is (4).** In less than twenty years, between 1979 and 1997, the amount of ozone has rapidly decreased by more than 50 percent from about 200 to below 100 units. Reductions of ozone levels are occurring all around the earth's atmosphere and are leading to higher levels of ultraviolet radiation reaching the earth's surface. This is putting people at greater risk for developing health problems, including skin cancer and cataracts.

7. **The correct answer is (2).** Bodies of water exert a *moderating influence* on temperature along the coast by giving up heat *more slowly* in the winter and by absorbing it *more slowly* in the summer. So, cities located along the Eastern seaboard, along the Atlantic Ocean, will remain at a more even temperature, being cooler in the summer and warmer in the winter. The other answer choices are incorrect because they discuss issues that are irrelevant to this question, such as the amount of light, angle of sunlight, or presence of mountain ranges.

8. **The correct answer is (5).** From the descriptions in the first and second paragraphs of the passage, you can infer that a tsunami can damage property, kill and hurt people and animals, and happen unexpectedly. So, choice (5) is the best answer to this question.

9. **The correct answer is (1).** The first sentence of the third paragraph confirms that the Earth's shape, as well as other factors, can be changed by a powerful earthquake. There is no indication that scientists are unaware of the causes of tsunamis, so choice (2) is incorrect. Choice (3) is not supported by the passage, although it might be a true statement. NASA is reported in the passage to be working on the effects of this earthquake, not on detection devices, so choice (4) is incorrect. Nothing is stated about the locations of tsunamis in general, so choice (5) is unsupported and incorrect.

10. **The correct answer is (3).** The passage tells you that the lessened *oblateness*, or greater roundness of the earth as a result of the earthquake, causes the earth to spin a little more quickly. If the earth spins more quickly, that means that the length of the day is shorter as a result. A comparison might be gotten in watching a spinning skater. As the skater draws her arms closer to the body, she is able to spin faster. So also as the earth becomes rounder (or less *oblate)*, it also spins faster, thereby shortening the length of the day.

11. **The correct answer is (4).** All of the choices describe the effects of the Mount Pinatubo eruption, but only choice (4) describes an effect that touched the whole world, which is what the question asks.

12. **The correct answer is (3).** This can be deduced from the paragraph as a whole, especially the reference to a "cataclysmic split" and the comparison of the movement of the earth's crust to that of a glacier.

13. **The correct answer is (5).** The sky show was produced by a *meteor*, a solid piece of material from outer space that was rushing through the atmosphere, but was too large to be completely changed into a gas. Pieces that reach the earth before burning up completely are called *meteorites*.

14. **The correct answer is (3).** The weight of the basket would be considerably heavier due to the density of the iron or steel. It would therefore not be easy to lift it off the ground.

15. **The correct answer is (1).** When air is heated, molecules are more active, and the density of the air decreases.

answers exercises

16. **The correct answer is (4).** During a solar eclipse the moon travels between the sun and the earth, blocking out the view of the sun totally or partially on at least some part of the Earth.

17. **The correct answer is (2).** Based on the map, Florida shows the highest incidence of thunderstorm activity, up to 100 thunderstorm days per year.

18. **The correct answer is (3).** Standing under a tall tree, or telephone pole, or on the top of a hill creates a natural lightning rod, and that would make it easier to be hit by lightening. In a forest, seek shelter under a thick growth of small trees. In open areas, go to a low place, such as a ravine or valley.

19. **The correct answer is (2).** It would appear that someone was calculating very badly. Look at the last sentence.

20. **The correct answer is (4).** Since it takes 248 Earth years for Pluto to orbit our Sun, according to the information given, and since it was discovered only 75 years ago, that distant planet has a long way to go.

21. **The correct answer is (4).** Pluto, being only about 1,750 miles in diameter, is smaller in diameter than the earth's moon, which is 2,160 miles in diameter.

22. **The correct answer is (4).** The last sentence in the first paragraph says that "plastic sleeves around the hand-wash basin keep spray droplets from floating away into the cabin."

23. **The correct answer is (3).** From your knowledge of space travel, you know that everything in space is weightless; therefore, an external force is necessary to move the wastes.

24. **The correct answer is (5).** Floating material described here includes whiskers and water and wastes.

25. **The correct answer is (5).** A person in space is too far from Earth's gravitational pull and therefore is weightless.

26. **The correct answer is (3).** The graph shows that it takes 30 grams of water per cubic meter to saturate air at 30 degrees centigrade.

27. **The correct answer is (3).** The dew point is defined as the temperature at which the air becomes saturated with water. Condensation refers to the process of a gas changing to a liquid.

28. **The correct answer is (1).** Since the mass of the earth is so much larger than that of the moon, its gravity is also much larger—six times larger. Since weight is proportional to gravity, the weight of the lunar lander would have been far too great for its smaller engines to be able to lift it off the Earth.

29. **The correct answer is (2).** Each of the research projects mentioned refers to a topic in biology, which is the study of life and living organisms.

30. **The correct answer is (4).** The ozone layer protects us from some of the dangerous ultraviolet (UV) radiation that comes from the sun. As more of the layer is depleted due to the release of certain man-made industrial chemicals into the atmosphere, less UV radiation is filtered out, putting people at greater risk of developing skin cancer, cataracts, and weakened immune systems.

31. **The correct answer is (1).** Transpiration is one of the two processes shown that returns water from the earth's surface to the atmosphere, the other being evaporation. Transpiration refers to water that reaches the atmosphere when green plants produce water vapor during photosynthesis. Choice (2), *precipitation,* is the opposite process, and occurs when the air becomes saturated with water, which then condenses

into water droplets or freezes into ice crystals. The droplets become too heavy to stay suspended in the atmosphere and fall toward the surface of the earth in the form of rain or snow. This is part of the *hydrologic cycle,* which refers to the movement of water on and within the Earth.

32. **The correct answer is (5).** Only this answer relates to the increasing warmth of the Earth's crust. The other choices are either irrelevant or incorrect. This outer crust is increasingly hot the deeper you get because the *mantle,* which is immediately beneath it, consists of a layer of very hot rock that flows like plastic and extends halfway to the center of the Earth.

33. **The correct answer is (3).** This question, which asks for the *incorrect* statement, brings together much information on Earth history and fossils. Therefore choice (3) is the right answer because the sedimentary layers are seen in the illustration to be *horizontal,* as they were when they were laid down. Choice (1) is a correct statement because the diagram shows at least three different types of fossils. Choice (2) is correct also because we know that intrusions are younger than the surrounding sedimentary layers. Choice (4) is correct because the fossil shell suggests that the area was once underwater. Choice (5) is correct because weathering has revealed the top of the igneous intrusion at the surface.

34. **The correct answer is (2).** The main motive for going to Mars, and for looking for water, is to search for signs of life there, especially Earthlike life. Water is essential to life on our planet, so finding signs of past or present evidence of water raises the likelihood that life existed on Mars as well. Water would be a necessary ingredient of an environment conducive to life. No evidence is offered for choices (1) and (5). Choice (3) is a possibility, but not confirmed by the passage and not the best answer. Choice (4) is not discussed.

35. **The correct answer is (4).** You are told in the first paragraph about Mars being a *currently cold and frost-locked planet.* The ice-bound bacteria that were found in Alaska remained alive for 30,000 years and came to life after being thawed. So the idea is that perhaps forms of life exist in the ice on Mars just as they do here. Choices (1) and (2) are not supported by the passage. Choice (3) is an overstatement; it is going too far to say that the same bacteria were present in Mars. Not all bacteria cause disease, and we're not told anything about what kind of bacteria this was, or that this bacteria even exists on Mars, so choice (5) is incorrect also.

answers exercises

SUMMING IT UP

What You Need to Know About the GED Science Test

- The questions are based upon the basic concepts of science.

- The questions will require the reading of passages and the comprehension of material presented in graphs, tables, and charts.

- The subject matter will draw on the fields of Life Science, Physical Science, and Earth and Space Science.

- Special emphasis will be placed on the role science plays in our everyday lives.

PART VI

LANGUAGE ARTS, READING REVIEW

CHAPTER 7   All About the GED Language Arts, Reading Test

All About the GED Language Arts, Reading Test

OVERVIEW

- Quick Tips!
- Taking the GED language arts, reading test
- Critical reading
- Reading in the content areas
- Reading charts, graphs, maps, and illustrations
- Business reading
- Summing it up

QUICK TIPS!

In order to become a fluent, skillful reader, get used to doing some reading every day—at least for a half hour. Whatever catches your eye is fine—like a good newspaper, magazine, or book. If you like to play word games, like Scrabble, or do puzzles, these are excellent ways of improving your vocabulary and having a good time.

Notice the spellings and meanings of words, the way sentences are put together, and the usage of familiar and unfamiliar words. If possible, use a dictionary to look up words you don't know. You can also infer the meanings of a lot of unfamiliar words by guessing from the context.

If you can, visit your local bookstore or library. Ask the sales people or the librarians to help you find books on topics in which you might be interested. Walk around and browse. Take your time. Don't overlook the Young People's sections, and the sections that feature practical writings for daily use.

Have fun, and improve your reading skills at the same time!

TAKING THE GED LANGUAGE ARTS, READING TEST

The GED Language Arts, Reading Test consists of selections drawn from fiction and nonfiction passages. You will have to read the passages and then answer 5 or 6 questions about what you have read. There will be approximately 7 passages with 40 multiple-choice questions on each Language Arts, Reading Test. You will have 65 minutes to complete all the test items.

The passages used on the GED Language Arts, Reading Test will come from books, short stories, magazine or newspaper articles, or business or practical documents. They will include readings from poetry, drama, fiction, and nonfiction prose. You will see a wide range of different types of writing, some of it recent and familiar in style and some that will be more difficult.

The distribution of selections for each test will be the following:

- Literary (75%)
- Nonfiction (25%)

The questions you will be asked on the GED Language Arts, Reading Test will fall into one of the following four categories:

NOTE

Approximately one third of the questions will be Comprehension or Application questions. One third will be Analysis questions. The rest will be Synthesis questions.

❶ *Comprehension:* These questions ask you to demonstrate a literal understanding of what you have read, such as the specific facts. Questions about meaning and the intentions of the writer are in this category. For example, what color was the house? Who won the ball game? Who surrendered at Saratoga?

❷ *Application questions:* These questions ask you to apply what you have read to a different situation. For example, if you read that cork is a light wood that floats and fishermen use it to support their nets in water, you might be asked how you could use cork if you were in a shipwreck.

❸ *Analysis questions:* These questions ask you to break down and really analyze the information you are given. You will have to see relationships between ideas, recognize comparisons and contrasts, and understand cause-and-effect. These questions will test your reasoning ability.

❹ *Synthesis questions:* These are the more difficult kinds of questions to answer. They will require you to make inferences, to come to conclusions, and to draw your own theories about what you are reading. For example, what is a possible outcome of what the author wrote? What idea can be related to what you have read?

CRITICAL READING

Your success on all of the tests in the GED test battery depends to a large extent on your reading comprehension skills. Whether the test is in the area of science, social studies, literature and the arts, or even mathematics, it will test your ability to use **critical reading skills** to **comprehend, apply, analyze, synthesize,** and **evaluate** what you read. Each of these categories is represented by a number of different types of test questions. Some of the types you are most likely to find on the GED are illustrated below.

Comprehension Skills

These are the skills you might think of as "remembering" skills. They do not ask you to go beyond what you have read; they simply ask you to recall facts and details. Read this example and then try your hand at the types of questions below.

> The social standing of a wife in colonial days was determined by the standing of her husband as well as by her own ability and resourcefulness. She married not only a husband but also a career. Her position in the community was established in part by the quality of the bread she baked, by the food she preserved for the winter's use, by the whiteness of her washing on the line, by the way her children were clothed, and by her skill in nursing. Doctors were scarce. In case of the illness or death of a neighbor, a woman would put aside her own work to help, and she was honored for what she could do.

Paraphrasing

This kind of question asks you to repeat what the author said, usually in slightly different words.

> **Q**   According to the author, which of these was true of colonial wives?
>
>   **(1)** They married their husbands young.
>   **(2)** Their husbands often had careers.
>   **(3)** They married careers as well as husbands.
>   **(4)** Their husbands married often.
>   **(5)** Their careers ended with their marriages.
>
> **A**   Choice (3) is an accurate restatement of the author's second sentence.

Identifying Main Idea

Main idea questions often present several titles and ask you to choose the one that expresses the main idea or thought of the passage.

Q   The title that best expresses the main idea of this selection is

    (1) "Care of Children in Colonial Times."
    (2) "Community Spirit."
    (3) "Medical Care in Pre-Revolutionary Times."
    (4) "The Colonial Housewife."
    (5) "Clothing and Food in Early America."

A   **The correct answer is (4).** This selection describes the various homemaking duties a colonial woman was expected to perform.

Recalling Details

Details are the facts and ideas in a selection that explain and support the main idea.

Q   When might a colonial woman put aside her own work?

    (1) When a neighbor was ill
    (2) When she reached middle age
    (3) At her marriage
    (4) When her children were born
    (5) Only at her death

A   **The correct answer is (1).** The last sentence of the selection includes the detail that women might put aside their work "in case of the illness or death of a neighbor."

Summarizing

Some comprehension questions require you to restate the central premise of a passage in a sentence or two.

Q   Which of these sentences best summarizes the selection?

    (1) Colonial women needed help from doctors.
    (2) Colonial women's social standings were influenced by their work.
    (3) Most of us would not have succeeded in colonial times.
    (4) Very few colonists were women.
    (5) Unless a woman married well, her life was one of toil.

A   The only choice that takes the whole selection and condenses it accurately into a single idea is (2).

Defining Vocabulary Words

This kind of question, sometimes called "words in context," asks you to choose a synonym for one of the words in the passage.

> **Q** In the selection, what does the word "standing" mean?
>
> **(1)** Unmoving
> **(2)** Idle
> **(3)** Permanent
> **(4)** Operative
> **(5)** Status
>
> **A** **The correct answer is (5).** Try it in the selection in place of the word "standing." Although each of the choices is a possible synonym for "standing," only "status" makes sense and keeps the meaning of the sentence intact.

Application Skills

When you take what you have read and apply it to a new context, you are using application skills. Nearly any word problem you solve in mathematics is an example of application skills in action. You take a formula you know—for example, the area of a triangle—and apply it to a problem you have not seen before. As you follow the written directions that tell you how to take a test, you are using application skills. Application skills may also involve organizing information in new ways. Read this example and try the questions that follow.

> There are many signs by which people predict the weather. Some of these have a true basis, but many do not. There is, for example, no evidence that it is more likely to storm during one phase of the moon than during another. If it happens to rain on Easter, there is no reason to think that it will rain for the next seven Sundays. The groundhog may or may not see his shadow on Groundhog Day, but it probably won't affect the weather anyway.

Classifying

When you classify, you organize information in groups that are somehow related.

> **Q** Which of these might the author also include in the list of false weather predictors?
>
> **(1)** Heat lightning
> **(2)** Local weather reports
> **(3)** Weather maps
> **(4)** Tornado warnings
> **(5)** Unusual caterpillar markings
>
> **A** **The correct answer is (5).** Only choice (5) fits with the author's other suggested false weather predictors: phases of the moon, rain on a holiday, and a groundhog's prediction.

NOTE

HELP YOURSELF by looking for similar ideas or concepts.

Generalizing

This kind of question asks you to take new information and compare or contrast it with information in the selection. Once you have made the comparison, you often must draw a conclusion.

> **Q** In 1994 it rained in Tampa on Easter Sunday. Which of the following would be a logical assumption, according to the author?
>
>   **(1)** It rained for the next seven Sundays.
>   **(2)** It rained on Easter Sunday in 1995.
>   **(3)** It did not rain the next Sunday.
>   **(4)** It may or may not have rained the next Sunday.
>   **(5)** It rained on Easter Monday as well.
>
> **A** **The correct answer is (4).** Since the author states that rain on Easter Sunday is not a good predictor of future rain, only choice (4) is a possible answer.

Analysis Skills

NOTE

HELP YOURSELF by looking for connections among ideas.

Analysis skills enable you to examine relationships among facts and ideas. When you read critically, you constantly ask yourself questions such as these: What caused X to happen? What was the result of Y? Is X true? What does Y mean? What conclusion can I draw from X and Y? Read this selection and test yourself on the questions that follow.

> The facts, as we see them, on drug use and the dangerous behaviors caused by drugs are that some people do get into trouble while using drugs, and some of those drug users are dangerous to others. Sometimes a drug is a necessary element in order for a person to commit a crime, although it might not be the cause of his or her criminality. On the other hand, the use of a drug sometimes seems to be the only convenient excuse by means of which the observer can account for the undesirable behavior. We spend millions of dollars a year incarcerating drug abusers. Clearly, drugs do more harm than good, but there were criminals before there were drugs. Tunnel vision on this issue will keep us spending irrationally without ever seeing the results we desire.

Determining Cause and Effect

A cause leads to an effect. For example, striking a bell can be the cause of an effect—a ringing noise. Often, to understand a passage, you must look at the connections among causes and effects.

> **Q** According to the author, taking drugs might lead to which of these things?
>
>   **(1)** Dangerous behavior
>   **(2)** Criminality
>   **(3)** Addiction
>   **(4)** Making excuses
>   **(5)** None of the above

A **The correct answer is (1).** Only choice (1) is directly stated as an effect of taking drugs. The author states that choice (2) might *not* be caused by drugs and never mentions choice (3).

Distinguishing Fact from Opinion

An important critical reading skill is the ability to tell when an author is giving you a verifiable fact and when he or she is simply stating a personal belief.

Q Which of these statements is the author's opinion and NOT a fact?

(1) Some people do get into trouble while using drugs.
(2) Drugs do more harm than good.
(3) Some drug users are dangerous to others.
(4) Drug users might commit crimes.
(5) We spend millions of dollars a year incarcerating drug abusers.

A **The correct answer is (2).** Only one of these statements is not easily verifiable—choice (2). Had the author said "All people who use drugs get into trouble" instead of choice (1) or "Drug users are always dangerous" instead of choice (3), either of these might have been considered an opinion as well.

Interpreting Figurative Language

This is a particular kind of vocabulary skill that is most often found in literature selections. Authors may use words in a colorful, imaginative way that defies literal interpretation. You must use the surrounding context and make connections among ideas to determine what their words really mean.

Q What does the author mean by "tunnel vision"?

(1) Concentration on the future
(2) Desire to run underground at a sign of trouble
(3) Bad eyesight
(4) Failure to see more than one point of view
(5) Heedless belief in what we see on TV

A **The correct answer is (4).** Even if you have never seen the phrase before, you can tell from context that the author is concerned with people's easy connection of drugs to crime, which he sees as too often being an excuse and not a solution. This failure to see more than one point of view, an insistence on looking in only one direction, choice (4), he calls "tunnel vision."

Drawing Conclusions

Many questions on the GED require you to draw a conclusion from something that is implied but not directly stated in the text. You must analyze the whole passage in order to draw conclusions accurately.

Q Which conclusion can you draw from this selection?

(1) The use of drugs always results in crime.

(2) Drugs and crime are only sometimes related.

(3) Drug use does not cause crime.

(4) Drugs are usually an element in accidents.

(5) Most criminals use drugs of one sort or another.

A **The correct answer is (2).** The author states that drugs are sometimes a necessary element in a crime, but at other times are just an excuse for criminal behavior.

Synthesis Skills

Synthesis skills involve letting your mind and your imagination take over where the writer has left off. It means that you arrive at a logical idea or *theory* of your own based on the ideas given in the text.

It involves using the above-mentioned comprehension and analysis skills and going further with them.

For example, you can ask yourself:

- If I asked the author what he thought about this idea, what would he say?

- What hypothesis, or theory, can I derive from an event described in a text?

- What would have happened if this thing had not taken place?

In other words, what ideas can you think of based on what you have read?

Expanded Synthesis Questions

You may be asked a type of question called an "expanded synthesis" question. These questions are not harder than others, but they will give you a piece of information in the text of the question itself. Then, you will be asked to combine this information with information from the reading. In other words, this requires you to incorporate information from two sources: the reading selection and the question itself. Then, you will be asked to draw some sort of a conclusion based on this information.

Rosa felt awkward in school. Her skirt was too long. Her hair was still in old-fashioned braids, like in the old country. While she could easily understand and speak English, she felt that her accent differentiated her from the others. The school was large and unfamiliar, and she worried that she'd get lost in the long halls, which all looked alike to her. She spent most of her time on the sidelines and alone.

Now, answer the following question.

Q Rosa's teacher, Miss Lewis, noticed Rosa's obvious discomfort in the large school where she was the only child from a foreign country. If Miss Lewis wants to help Rosa feel more at ease, which of the following might be the most effective means?

  (1) She might help her dress better and encourage her to cut her hair.
  (2) She could make friends with her.
  (3) She could hook up Rosa with a friendly group of girls.
  (4) Rosa should just be left alone, and things will improve on their own.
  (5) The teacher could call in Rosa's mother for a conference.

A In order to answer this question, you will need to read the selection and also use the information given in the question itself.

  The correct answer is (3). In giving this answer, you have come to a conclusion that is not explicitly stated in the above reading, but which your own logic tells you is correct. You have arrived at a theory that hopefully being helped to become "one of the gang" will be better for Rosa than any of the other actions the teacher might take.

  This is an example of a synthesis type of question you will sometimes encounter.

Evaluation Skills

Evaluation skills involve assessing the quality of ideas. As you read, you ask yourself: Is X reasonable? Is Y logical? What is the author's point of view? Why did he or she say X and Y? Evaluation skills are the most advanced reading skills because they require you to take what you read with a grain of salt. You really *can't* believe everything you read; you have to make up your own mind based on everything you know about the topic and the author. Read this selection and try the questions that follow.

NOTE

HELP YOURSELF by considering the author's relationship to the text.

The question has to be: Why would anyone *not* exercise his or her right to vote? Our founding fathers (and mothers) fought a war of independence to give us the right to choose our own government. Emerging countries the world over are judged by their commitment to democracy and to free elections. Yet in our own town, fewer than 35 percent of registered voters turn out to the polls in an average year. That does not even count those thousands of adults 18 and over who have not bothered to register. Last year, our town justice won by only 42 votes! When I sit at a booth downtown and try to sign up new voters, I hear all kinds of excuses. "One vote doesn't matter," people say. "I don't really know much about the issues," say others. I have a million responses, but they seem not to sway the nonvoters.

Determining Author's Point of View

Every author writes from a particular point of view. Writers have individual sets of beliefs and standards that influence their writing. Thinking about who the author is and where he or she stands on the issue will help you better understand a selection.

How does the author feel about voting?

(1) It is a privilege, not a right.
(2) Voting is more important in emerging countries than it is here.
(3) Voting was once vitally important.
(4) One vote really can't make a difference.
(5) There is no excuse not to vote.

A **The correct answer is (5).** The author's description of the excuses offered for not voting and her response to them makes it clear that she believes that there is no excuse not to vote.

Judging Author's Intent

Sometimes understanding *why* an author wrote a selection helps you understand the writing itself. Most writing is done for one of these purposes or a combination thereof: to inform, to persuade, to entertain, to reflect, or to describe.

 What does the author's purpose seem to be in writing this passage?

(1) To inform
(2) To persuade
(3) To entertain
(4) To reflect
(5) To describe

A **The correct answer is (2).** Although it is not directly stated, the author, who spends time registering voters, seems to want to persuade her readers of the importance of voting.

Verifying Facts

Any piece of writing must be read with certain questions in mind: Was I given enough information? Is the information verifiable? Did the author leave something out accidentally or on purpose? Did the author have all the facts?

Q Which statement might the author use to counter the excuse "One vote doesn't matter"?

(1) Thousands of adults have not bothered to register.
(2) Fewer than 35 percent of registered voters turn out to the polls.
(3) Emerging countries are judged by their commitment to democracy.
(4) Our town justice won by only 42 votes.
(5) I have a million responses.

A **The correct answer is (4).** Choice (4) counters the argument by describing a situation in which very small numbers of votes counted a great deal.

READING IN THE CONTENT AREAS

You do not use the same strategies when you read science material as you do when you read a novel. Your strategies change when you read math problems, and they change again when you read a paragraph from a history text. The reasons for this are complex. Usually expository material in the content areas includes a lot of **technical vocabulary.** The density of ideas in content-rich material from social studies or science requires you to change your **reading rate.** Some expository writing contains **graphic aids** that alert you to key concepts and may help you define unfamiliar words. Reading expository writing can be difficult, but by using **active reading strategies**, you can improve your understanding of selections in the content areas.

Technical Vocabulary

Readers are often put off and frustrated when their reading contains large numbers of words they don't recognize. You don't have to understand every word; often you can distill the meaning from a sentence without knowing a key word. There are active reading strategies that can help you.

Using Context Clues

Everything that surrounds an unfamiliar word may contain a clue to that word's meaning. Try to decipher the meanings of the nonsense words in these three sentences.

1 Doctors rely on *wrpfls* to help them remove cysts without surgery.

2 After years of *vcxyz*, Uruguay finally saw a decade of peace.

3 To find the area of a circle, you must know the *qmjkb* of its radius.

Here are the clues from sentence 1.

> **Doctors** rely on *wrpfls* to help them **remove cysts without surgery.** You know that doctors use this mysterious thing, and you know what they use it for. Even if you don't know the word *cysts,* you can tell that *wrpfls* must be a kind of nonsurgical tool for removing something in a medical process. You probably know enough to continue reading about the topic.

Here are the clues from sentence 2.

> **After years** of *vcxyz*, Uruguay finally saw **a decade of peace.** You don't need to know where Uruguay is or even what it is. This sentence sets up a contrast between "a decade of peace" and "years of *vcxyz*." This unfamiliar word must contrast with *peace*—it is probably a synonym for *war.*

Here are the clues from sentence 3.

> To find the **area of a circle,** you must know the *qmjkb* of **its radius.** You know that you are trying to find a measurement, so it makes sense that you need a number in order to find it. Even if you never heard of a *radius,* you should be able to tell that a *qmjkb* is some kind of measurement. Obviously, the more you know about finding the area of a circle, the closer you will come to the precise meaning of *qmjkb,* but an active reader can come close enough to get the gist of the sentence even without knowing much geometry.

Using Structural Clues

Besides the meaning of surrounding words, sentences give you additional clues to the meaning of unfamiliar words. What can you figure out about the meaning of these nonsense words?

1 I bought *oiues* at the grocery.

2 He is never very *uaoie* in crowds.

3 In winter, deer often *aeiou* in fields.

In sentence 1, the position of the unfamiliar word marks it as a noun. In addition, the *s* at the end tells you the word is plural. In sentence 2, the word is obviously an adjective, and in sentence 3, it is a verb. These clues alone are not enough for you to define the words accurately, but an active reader will file the information away in case the words turn up in a clearer context later on.

Looking for Familiar Roots

By the time you take the GED, you have spent years enlarging your vocabulary. You often have information about unfamiliar words stored in your brain from encounters with similar words. The key is to access this information and apply it to the new word. Try these made-up words. What do you know that might help you determine their meanings?

1 The snowshoe hare *rebrowned* when spring arrived.

2 The accident occurred when the driver *misbraked* on the turn.

3 People *grieffully* filled the streets for the funeral procession.

These words don't really exist—but you can use what you know about roots, prefixes, and suffixes to guess their meanings.

Take sentence 1. The root is *brown,* and it is being used as a verb. That's unusual, but not unheard of—think of "browning meat in the pan." The prefix *re-* means "again," and the *-ed* ending puts the verb into the past tense. Thus, the sentence means: "The snowshoe hare became brown again when spring arrived."

Try sentence 2. Again, the word is a verb in past tense. The root is a familiar one: *brake.* The prefix *mis-* often means "wrong." The sentence, then, means, "The accident occurred when the driver braked incorrectly on the turn."

Turn to sentence 3. Here, the recognizable root is *grief.* The dual suffix *-fully* means "in a way that was full of _____." The people filling the streets, then, did so "in a way that was full of grief."

Reading Rate

You must read more slowly when you read content-dense material. However, when you are taking a timed test, reading slowly can be a handicap. For speed and accuracy in reading and answering comprehension questions, practice and use these skimming and scanning techniques.

Answering Main Idea and Inference Questions

1 Use your index finger as a guide and a pacer, and read the selection through quickly.

2 As you move your finger across each line, concentrate on looking at three- or four-word phrases, not one word at a time. Try not to "say" the words in your mind as you go.

3 Follow your finger only with your eyes, not with your whole head.

4 Your purpose is to locate the topic sentence, the main idea, and the major supporting details. This information should enable you to answer most main idea and inference questions.

Answering Vocabulary and Detail Questions

1 Take a key word from the question you want to answer, and "lock" it into your mind.

2 Using your index finger as a guide, scan the lines for that word.

3 DO NOT READ when you scan! You are simply looking for the key word.

4 When you find the word, STOP! The answer to your question will usually be in the same sentence.

5 Read the entire sentence carefully before choosing an answer.

The two most important ingredients in a successful test performance are accuracy and speed. Keep track of your time as you complete the sample tests in this book. Use the active reading strategies above to improve your rate.

Graphic Aids

Often, expository writing includes aids to assist you in discovering key concepts and defining key vocabulary. When you see these aids, be sure to use them.

Italicized or Boldfaced Words

These alert you to vocabulary the author considers important.

1 The geese *migrate* annually, following the same path each year.

2 To assess **rate,** consider **velocity** and **time.**

Parenthetical Definitions and Pronunciation Keys

These can help you define unfamiliar words and recognize words you have heard but never seen.

1 The kulaks (wealthy peasant farmers) controlled the local economy.

2 Below the columns ran a frieze ('frēz) depicting historical scenes.

Headings and Marginalia

These alert you to key concepts and help you find the main idea of a passage.

Local Government

Geographical Subdivisions   Our district is divided into counties, which are then subdivided into towns. Each town has a village as its center.

Governmental Subdivisions   The counties are run by a county board, chaired by the county commissioner. The towns each have a town board and a town supervisor, and the villages are run by a mayor and a village council.

READING CHARTS, GRAPHS, MAPS, AND ILLUSTRATIONS

Many of the questions on the GED feature graphics. Your ability to retrieve information quickly and accurately from charts, graphs, maps, and illustrations can make a huge difference in your overall score. Below are descriptions of some of the most common graphics found on the GED.

Charts

A chart or table is a simple way of presenting a great deal of data clearly and concisely. Charts highlight information by placing it in columns and rows.

United States School Enrollment, 1996–2000			
Year	Elementary	Secondary	College
1996	28,226,000	16,939,000	12,504,000
1997	28,536,000	16,950,000	12,766,000
1998	28,451,000	16,980,000	13,055,000
1999	28,782,000	17,099,000	13,458,000
2000	29,680,000	16,541,000	13,711,000

Once the information is presented, you may be asked to use the chart to answer any of several types of questions.

Locating Data

You may be asked simply to locate and report information directly from the chart or table.

Q   What was the secondary school enrollment in the year 1997?

    (1) 16,980,000

    (2) 28,536,000

    (3) 16,950,000

    (4) 16,939,000

    (5) None of the above

A   **The correct answer is (3).** First locate the row labeled "1997" under the heading "Year." Then locate the column labeled "Secondary." Travel across the row and down the column until the two intersect.

Comparing Data

More often, you will need to do something with the information on the chart or table. A typical question might have you compare two or more figures.

 In which year was college enrollment highest?

(1) 1996
(2) 1997
(3) 1998
(4) 1999
(5) 2000

A **The correct answer is (5).** Find the column labeled "College." Then read the column, comparing the numbers. When you find the highest number, read across the row to find the year.

Manipulating Data

You may be asked to do more than simply compare two figures. Some questions may require more advanced number operations.

Q Between which two years did elementary enrollment increase most?

(1) 1996 and 1997
(2) 1997 and 1998
(3) 1998 and 1999
(4) 1999 and 2000
(5) Not enough information is given.

A **The correct answer is (4).** Look first for the column labeled "Elementary." Then compare the figures for each pair of years mentioned. You can easily eliminate choice (2)—between those two years, enrollment actually declined. Because the numbers are clearly aligned on the chart, it is easy to compare digits and estimate the answer. The biggest jump seems to be between 1999 and 2000, choice (4), and a quick subtraction check will prove this to be so.

Drawing Conclusions

This is the most complex of the types of questions you may be asked. Here you must take the data given and use it to make projections, infer unstated information, or make generalizations.

 Based on the information on this chart, which of these is a logical conclusion?

(1) Elementary schools are larger than secondary schools.
(2) School enrollment does not always increase over time.
(3) College enrollment will double by the year 2010.
(4) The high school drop-out rate is increasing.
(5) Elementary school enrollment is declining steadily.

A **The correct answer is (2).** The only one of these conclusions that is upheld by the chart is choice (2). You cannot tell the size of schools, choice (1), from the chart; nor can you tell anything about the high school drop-out rate, choice (4). Choice (5) is untrue, and the trend shown gives little evidence to support the projection in choice (3).

Graphs

Graphs provide a clear way to view and compare data. The kinds of graphs you are most likely to find on the GED are those shown below.

Pictographs

In a pictograph, a symbol is used to represent a number. A key tells you how many items each symbol represents.

Commercial Planes Landing at Airport X

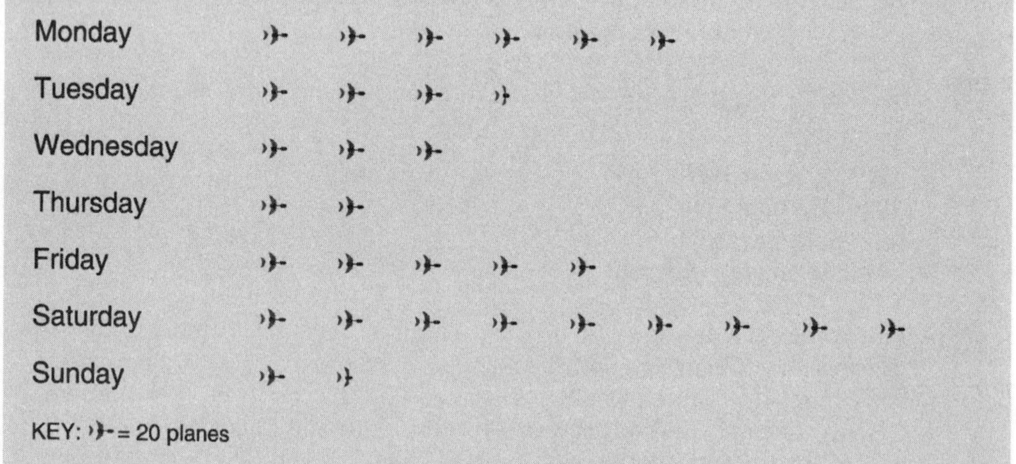
Monday
Tuesday
Wednesday
Thursday
Friday
Saturday
Sunday
KEY: = 20 planes

Just as for charts and tables, the types of questions you are asked will involve *locating data, comparing data, manipulating data,* and *drawing conclusions*. Try these typical questions.

Q How many planes landed at Airport X on Tuesday?

(1) 20
(2) 50
(3) 60
(4) 70
(5) 80

A **The correct answer is (4).** If the symbol equals 20 planes, half of the symbol equals 10. There are three whole symbols and one half in the row labeled "Tuesday"—3(20) + 10 = 70.

Q On which day did the fewest planes land?

(1) Monday

(2) Tuesday

(3) Wednesday

(4) Thursday

(5) Sunday

A **The correct answer is (5).** Counting symbols shows that only 30 planes landed on Sunday, compared with 40 on Thursday.

Q This week, how many more planes landed on the busiest day than landed on Monday?

(1) 3 more

(2) 30 more

(3) 60 more

(4) 100 more

(5) Not enough information is given.

A **The correct answer is (3).** Count by twenties to answer this question. The busiest day was Saturday, when 180 planes landed. Only 120 landed on Monday, so Saturday had 60 more.

Q Based on the information on this graph, which of these is a logical conclusion?

(1) More planes take off from Airport X than land there.

(2) Business travelers tend to arrive at Airport X early in the week.

(3) This week was not a typical week for Airport X.

(4) Airport X is in a small resort community.

(5) Airport X is in an industrial city.

A **The correct answer is (2).** The graph shows that Airport X has two peak arrival days—Monday and Saturday. Weekend arrivals would tend to mean vacationers, but there are too many arrivals for choice (4) to be true. There is no evidence to support choices (1), (3), or (5). Business travelers would tend to arrive on a weekday, and the high numbers for Monday make choice (2) a likely choice.

Bar Graphs

Where a pictograph uses pictures, a bar graph uses bars, which makes comparing data very easy. The bars may be vertical or horizontal.

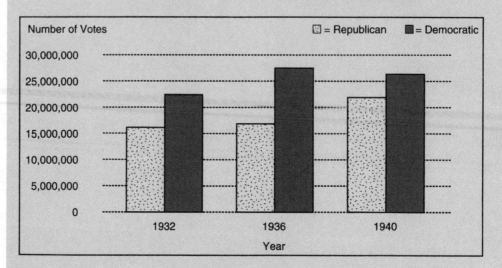

Popular Votes Cast for President, 1932–1940

Here, the number of votes are shown along the vertical axis. The year is shown along the horizontal axis. A key tells you that the dotted bar represents Republican votes, and the black bar represents Democratic votes. By reading up from the bottom and then across from the top of each bar, you can tell how many votes were cast.

Here are some questions you might be asked about this bar graph. The first asks you to *locate data,* and the second asks you to *draw conclusions.*

Q In 1932, about how many popular votes were earned by the Republican candidate?

(1) 10,000,000
(2) 15,000,000
(3) 20,000,000
(4) 25,000,000
(5) 30,000,000

A **The correct answer is (2).** Find the year 1932 on the horizontal axis. Then find the bar for "Republican," which, according to the key, is the dotted bar. Read across from the top of the bar to the numbers on the vertical axis.

Q Based on the information on this graph, which of these is a logical conclusion?

> **(1)** The closest election of the three was in 1940.
> **(2)** The same people ran for office in all three election years.
> **(3)** Fewer people voted in 1940 than in 1936.
> **(4)** The Republicans won the election in 1944.
> **(5)** A third-party vote skewed the results in 1940.

A **The correct answer is (1).** Comparing the bars will show you quickly that choice (1) is true. There is no evidence to support choices (2), (4), or (5); choice (3) is simply wrong.

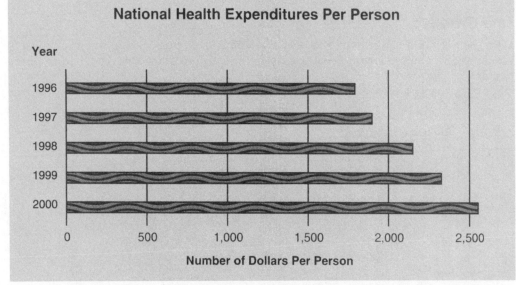

National Health Expenditures Per Person

Here, the bars are horizontal. Dollars spent per person appear on the horizontal axis, and years are on the vertical axis. Read across and then down from the end of each bar to find how much was spent in each year.

Here are some questions you might be asked about this bar graph. The first asks you to *compare data* and the second asks you to *manipulate data*.

Q Between which two years did the smallest increase in health expenditures per person occur?

> **(1)** 1996 and 1997
> **(2)** 1997 and 1998
> **(3)** 1998 and 1999
> **(4)** 1999 and 2000
> **(5)** Not enough information is given.

A **The correct answer is (1).** You do not really need to count, subtract, or even look at numbers here. Simply comparing lengths of bars should show you that the least difference was between 1996 and 1997.

Q In all, about how much money per person was spent on national health from 1996 to 2000?

   (1) $2,000

   (2) $4,000

   (3) $11,000

   (4) $18,000

   (5) $25,000

A **The correct answer is (3).** The words *in all* alert you that this problem requires you to add. The word *about* means that this is an approximation. Read down from the end of each bar and add up the figures in your head. Your answer should be around $11,000, choice (3).

Line Graphs

Line graphs are a convenient way to show trends over time. Some line graphs use a single line to show a trend; some use more than one to allow the reader to compare trends.

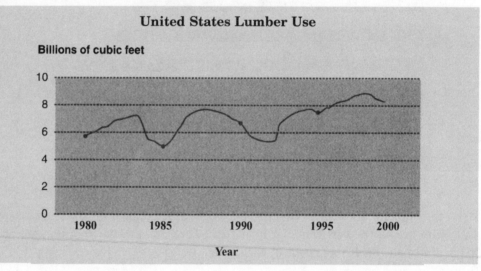

On this graph, the year is shown across the horizontal axis. Rather than simply showing data for individual years, however, the line graph shows fluid change over time. Notice that the years are shown in intervals of five. Suppose you need to find information for the year 1991. Move a bit to the right of 1990. Then move straight up until you intersect with the line. That point shows you the billions of cubic feet of lumber consumed in the United States in 1991.

Try these questions. The first asks you to *locate data;* the second asks you to *draw conclusions.*

Q About how many cubic feet of lumber were consumed in the United States in 1994?

    (1) 6 billion
    (2) 6.5 billion
    (3) 7.5 billion
    (4) 8 billion
    (5) 8.5 billion

A **The correct answer is (3).** Find 1995 and trace to the left a bit. Then move up to intersect with the line. Read across from that point, and you will land between 6 and 8 billion, at a point that is close to 7.5, as in choice (3).

Q Based on the information on this graph, which of these is a logical conclusion?

    (1) Lumber is no longer a popular building material.
    (2) Lumber consumption declined in the late 1980s.
    (3) Fewer houses were built before 1980 than after 1980.
    (4) Lumber use has steadily increased since 1980.
    (5) In the years since 1998, lumber consumption has risen.

A **The correct answer is (2).** No evidence exists to support choices (3) or (5), and choices (1) and (4) are actually contradicted by the graph. The only generalization that is accurate is choice (2).

Some line graphs compare trends over time.

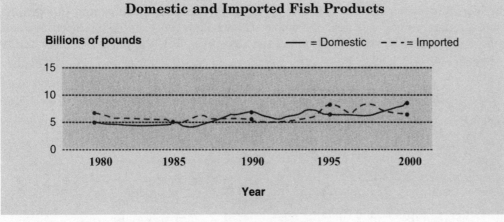

This graph tells you the numbers of fish that were domestically caught versus the numbers that were imported. By comparing the levels of the lines and watching for places where the lines cross, you can determine a lot about consumption of fish products.

These questions test your ability to *compare data* and to *manipulate data*.

 In which year was the domestic catch less than the imported catch?

   (1) 1990
   (2) 1992
   (3) 1995
   (4) 1999
   (5) 2000

The correct answer is (3). The key tells you that domestic catch is represented by a solid line, and imported catch is represented by a dashed line. You need to find a point at which the solid line falls below the dashed line. The only one that names a year in which that happened is choice (3).

About how many more pounds of fish were caught domestically in 2000 than were imported?

   (1) 3 million
   (2) 3 billion
   (3) 5 million
   (4) 5 billion
   (5) Not enough information is given.

The correct answer is (2). The words *how many more* imply a subtraction problem. The point showing domestic catch in 2000 is at about 10, meaning 10 billion pounds. The point for imported catch is at about 7.

10 billion − 7 billion = 3 billion

Circle Graphs

Circle graphs are decidedly different from pictographs, bar graphs, and line graphs. They compare numbers as part of a whole. The whole is represented by the circle itself, and its parts are shown as fractions of the circle. Usually, the parts are indicated as percents, with the whole circle equal to 100%.

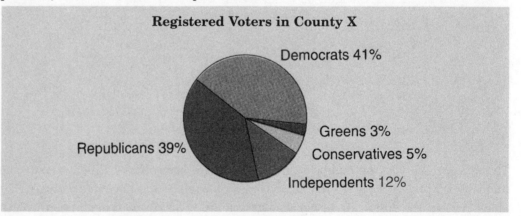

Comparing the relative sizes of the circle's slices gives you instant information about the relative numbers of registered voters in each party.

These questions ask you to *locate data, compare data, manipulate data,* and *draw conclusions* from the circle graph on the previous page.

Q What percentage of registered voters are not affiliated with a specific party?

    (1) 39%

    (2) 41%

    (3) 3%

    (4) 5%

    (5) 12%

A **The correct answer is (5).** Independent voters, voters who are not registered with any particular party, make up 12% of the circle graph.

Q Which list orders registered voters from greatest number to least number?

    (1) Democrats, Republicans, Independents, Greens, Conservatives

    (2) Republicans, Independents, Conservatives, Greens, Democrats

    (3) Greens, Conservatives, Independents, Republicans, Democrats

    (4) Democrats, Republicans, Independents, Conservatives, Greens

    (5) Democrats, Republicans, Conservatives, Greens, Independents

A **The correct answer is (4).** The relative sizes of circle parts and the percentages given show you that the order from greatest to least is Democrats (41%), Republicans (39%), Independents (12%), Conservatives (5%), and Greens (3%).

Q If the total population of registered voters in County X is 1,000, how many of those are Greens?

    (1) 3

    (2) 13

    (3) 30

    (4) 300

    (5) Not enough information is given.

A **The correct answer is (3).** Remember that any circle graph represents 100%. If 100% = 1,000, then 3% = 30.

Based on the information on this circle graph, which of these is a logical conclusion?

(1) Major party election results in County X are often very close.

(2) The number of Green voters has declined over time.

(3) Republicans can never be elected in County X.

(4) One hundred percent of County X's voters vote annually.

(5) County X has a large student population.

A **The correct answer is (1).** There is no indication from the graph alone that choices (2), (4), or (5) are true. Since voters need not vote their party line, choice (3) is certainly not true. However, since the numbers for Democrats and Republicans are so close, choice (1) is probably true and is a logical conclusion.

Maps

Maps give a reader information about a particular place. They can show political divisions between countries or states, geographic features such as mountains and rivers, man-made features such as highways and campgrounds, weather patterns, crops and exports, or any combination of these.

U.S. Congressional Representation in 1990 and Changes Since 1980

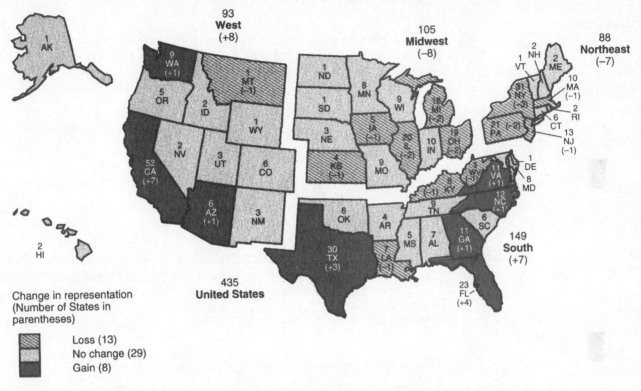

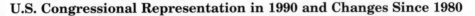

This map has a title that lets you know its focus. It has a key that helps you interpret the information shown. Each state contains a number, followed by the state abbreviation. The number is the number of representatives in Congress from that state in the year 1990. Some states also show a second number, preceded by a plus or minus sign. That number indicates whether the state gained or lost representatives between 1980 and 1990. In addition, the states are shaded according to whether they won seats in Congress, lost seats in Congress, or had no change in representation over the ten-year period.

Q How many representatives did Florida have in Congress in 1990?

   (1) 4

   (2) 23

   (3) 27

   (4) 149

   (5) Not enough information is given.

A **The correct answer is (2).** First, locate Florida (FL). The number above the state abbreviation is 23. The "+4" below means that Florida gained 4 seats between 1980 and 1990.

Q Which state lost the most seats in Congress over this ten-year period?

   (1) California

   (2) Texas

   (3) New York

   (4) Ohio

   (5) West Virginia

A **The correct answer is (3).** The key alerts you to look only at those states shaded gray, since those are the states that lost representatives. Of the three choices that are gray states—New York, Ohio, and West Virginia—New York lost 3, Ohio 2, and West Virginia 1.

Q How many representatives did Texas have in Congress in 1980?

   (1) 8

   (2) 27

   (3) 30

   (4) 33

   (5) Not enough information is given.

A **The correct answer is (2).** Find Texas (TX). The numbers show you that Texas had 30 representatives in 1990, which was a gain of 3 from 1980. That means that in 1980, Texas had 27 representatives.

Q Congressional representation is based on population. Knowing that and using the information on the map, which of these is a logical conclusion?

   (1) California and Florida had population booms between 1980 and 1990.

   (2) Many people moved from Louisiana to Texas between 1980 and 1990.

   (3) Manufacturing jobs are leaving the Northeast.

   (4) The total population of the United States grew between 1980 and 1990.

   (5) The Midwest and West saw a migration from the East in the 1980s.

The correct answer is (1). You cannot tell who moved where—choices (2) and (5)—from this map; nor can you tell why they moved, choice (3). Choice (4) may be true, but the map tends to contradict rather than support it. Since California and Florida increased their representation most dramatically of any states, it is fair to assume that their populations grew dramatically during this ten-year period.

Illustrations

The drawings you see on the GED will most likely appear in the mathematics, science, and social studies sections. These are the kinds of illustrations you are likely to see.

Geometric Figures

Many questions on the mathematics section of the GED refer you to illustrations of geometric figures.

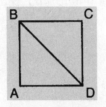

Recognizing the figure is important, but so is reading the figure correctly. Make sure you understand the points to which letters refer; this will help you answer questions about the figure.

Q   Which segment would form a right angle with $\overline{BD}$?

 (1) $\overline{AB}$
 (2) $\overline{BC}$
 (3) $\overline{CD}$
 (4) $\overline{DB}$
 (5) $\overline{BD}$

A   **The correct answer is (5).** A close reading of the illustration shows you that $\overline{BD}$ is a diagonal of the square. It would form right angles with the other diagonal, $\overline{AC}$.

Diagrams

In the science section of the GED, you may be asked to read and interpret diagrams.

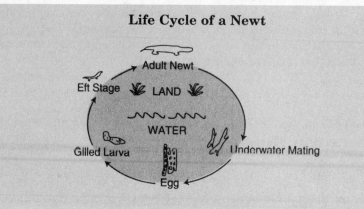

Life Cycle of a Newt

Titles, labels, and/or captions can help you read and answer questions about a diagram.

Q   Based on this illustration, which of these is a logical conclusion?

    (1) Newts are entirely aquatic.

    (2) Newts have an aquatic stage early in their development.

    (3) Adult newts have gills.

    (4) The female newt stays with the eggs until they hatch.

    (5) All of the above

A   **The correct answer is (2).** Choice (1) is certainly not true, according to the upper half of the diagram. For that reason, too, choice (3) is unlikely. There is no evidence for choice (4). Since the diagram clearly shows that newts start out their lives underwater, choice (2) is supported by the evidence and is a logical conclusion.

Cartoons

In the social studies section of the GED, you may be asked to read and interpret political cartoons.

In any cartoon, the title, caption, dialogue balloons, and/or drawings themselves tell you what the artist wants to say. Most questions about cartoons of this sort will involve *analysis* or *evaluation skills*.

Q   According to the artist, what will happen if income taxes disappear?

  (1) The taxpayer will be jailed.
  (2) Property taxes will disappear as well.
  (3) They will reappear as property taxes.
  (4) People will be better off.
  (5) More housing will be built.

A   **The correct answer is (3).** The cartoon shows the taxpayer burden, represented by a labeled coin, shifting from income tax (the handkerchief) to property tax (the bucket). The best interpretation of the artist's meaning is given in choice (3).

Q Which word best describes the artist's attitude toward the gubernatorial candidate?

    (1) Fond
    (2) Irate
    (3) Repelled
    (4) Approving
    (5) Cynical

A **The correct answer is (5).** The candidate has been portrayed as a magician, someone whose job it is to fool a gullible public. There is no sense of anger, choice (2), or disgust, choice (3), in the art, but there is certainly a cynical leaning to the cartoon.

BUSINESS READING

By "Business Reading" we mean the reading you must often do to get through daily life—at work and at home and even at school. This may include work-related documents, practical "how to" pieces, loan and lease agreements, financial writings, legal settlements, credit card applications, and similar readings. It is very important to be at ease reading these kinds of documents. They appear on the GED—and everywhere!

Read on for some general reading tips, as well as practice reading and answering questions to test your ability in understanding some typical business selections. Remember, you will now have to read these in various parts of the GED Test.

Reading Tips

1 Remember, you may be reading important material that is giving you some *information*, *explanation*, or *advice*. It is important to pay close and serious attention. Reading business-type material gets easier with practice, so don't be discouraged.

2 First, skim the entire document. Usually, it's not going to be that long. This should give you a general idea of its contents and its purpose.

3 Then, carefully read the piece in its entirety. Read it several times, if necessary, until you are totally certain you understand all the details.

4 If you are given an application to deal with, remember that the form of the reading is different, nothing else. Approach it as you would any other type of written communication.

5 Don't confuse what the document is saying with your own ideas about the subject. Be sure you know what the author of the piece is saying. Don't assume anything unless it is clearly stated or implied in the document.

EXERCISES: BUSINESS READING

Directions: Read each of the following selections carefully. Take your time. Then circle the number of the response that best answers the question or completes the statement. An Answer Key and Explanations are provided at the end of this section.

The first selection below is typical of the many informative articles about the practical and financial aspects of higher education. Read it carefully, then answer the questions that follow.

How do I find out about getting financial aid for college?

Education or training after high school costs more than ever. But postsecondary education is more important than ever, so you need to learn about as many sources of aid as you can. The major sources you can use to find out about federal and other student aid are described below:

* The financial aid administrator at each school in which you're interested can tell you what aid programs are available there and how much the total cost of attendance will be.

* Two federal income tax credits—dollar-for-dollar reductions in tax liability—are available for higher education expenses. The Hope Credit, a tax credit worth up to $1500 per student, is available to first- and second-year students enrolled at least half time. The Lifetime Learning Credit is a tax credit equal to 20 percent of a family's tuition expenses, up to $5000 for virtually any postsecondary education and training, including subsequent undergraduate years, graduate and professional schools, and even less-than-half-time study.

For more information on the Hope Credit, the Lifetime Learning Credit, and other tax benefits for postsecondary students, see the Internal Revenue Service's Publication 970. You can get a copy by calling 1-800-829-3676, or download the publication from the Internet at: www.irs.ustreas.gov/prod/forms_pubs/

* The state higher education agency in your home state can give you information about state aid—including aid from the Leveraging Educational Assistance Partnership (LEAP) Program, which is funded jointly by individual states and the U.S. Department of Education.

* The AmeriCorps program provides full-time educational awards in return for work in community service. You can work before, during, or after your postsecondary education, and you can use the funds either to pay current educational expenses or to repay federal student loans. For information, call toll-free 1-800-942-2677, or look it up on the Internet at: www.americorps.org.

* The federal government's Access America for Students Web site provides access to a multitude of government resources to assist students in planning and paying for their education. Access America for Students is a federal initiative designed to make interacting with the government easier for students. In addition to providing financial aid information, students can use the Web site to file their taxes, search for a job, and take advantage of a host of other government services. The Internet address is: www.students.gov.

From *Financial Aid, The Student Guide,*

2000–2001 edition, U.S. Dept. of Education

Used by permission.

1. After reading this article, what do you think is meant by postsecondary education?

   (1) A program for GED test preparation

   (2) Any formal education after high school

   (3) Federally funded education

   (4) Any kind of adult education program

   (5) The last year of high school

2. Rose wants specifics about her college loan, information on filing her taxes, and possible leads for finding a job after she graduates. Where is the best place for her to start?

   (1) Her state Office for Loans and Unemployment

   (2) Her own family accountant

   (3) The manager for her college loan

   (4) By calling 1-800-942-2677

   (5) The Internet site for Access America for Students

3. According to this selection, which of the following can you reasonably infer?

   (1) Getting funds for education will probably require a lot of effort.

   (2) If you apply, the federal government will pay most of the cost of your tuition expenses.

   (3) If you work it out with your accountant, you will get most of your school costs back in the form of income tax credits.

   (4) Any school you attend will only be concerned with your education, not with how your expenses will be covered.

   (5) The cost of a college education has finally stabilized.

4. All of the following are sources of information about financial aid for education EXCEPT

   (1) the AmeriCorps program.

   (2) the higher education agency of each state.

   (3) I.R.S. publication 970.

   (4) Access America for Students.

   (5) the U.S. Department of Education.

5. Which of the following is the only program described in this reading that allows a student to pay for his or her education with something other than money?

   (1) The LEAP Program

   (2) Access America for Students

   (3) The Hope Credit

   (4) The AmeriCorps Program

   (5) There is no such program.

exercises

Directions: The following is a practical selection about saving and investing for your future. (Note: It is NOT meant to be taken literally by the reader—it is just here to provide practice reading these kinds of selections.) Read it and then answer the questions that follow.

How do you invest for your future?

It is very important to save some money for your old age. Why? First, there may not be other sources of income that will keep you comfortable. Most people don't have pensions when they retire. Social Security gives people minimal income that cannot be depended upon to do the entire job. Your children may help, or they may be unable to. In any case, it is best to do the job right and be as independent as you can, even when your working days are over.

So, when should you start saving? The best thing to do is start early—the earlier the better. If you start in your twenties, rather than when you are older, the money will have plenty of time to grow.

How do you do this? Start by putting a certain amount aside each pay period. Take money that you can do without, perhaps $50.00 a week, and put it away in a separate savings account. Don't think of it as part of your salary; pretend that you're making $50.00 less per week. You will be surprised at how quickly this money will add up. When you have accumulated a few thousand dollars, you are ready to do some serious investing. Look at newspaper ads for a company that sells mutual funds. Or, if you have access to a computer, you can easily do some research to find the names of mutual fund companies. Mutual stock funds are groups of stocks that are picked and managed by a fund adviser. They are less risky than just buying single stocks. Put your money in a mutual fund.

How do you know which fund to pick? If you go to a reputable company, they will advise you about a good, all-purpose fund. Then, as time goes by, you will become more knowledgeable about the different kinds of funds— large company funds, small company funds, international funds, growth funds, value funds, and so on. You may want to add money to your original fund, or branch out into some of the other types mentioned above. Again, if you have a computer, you can track your funds on a daily basis and compare your funds to others.

If you can do this, then you will develop good habits of money management, as well as having a prosperous old age.

6. What is the main idea of this reading selection?

    (1) The dangers of the stock market

    (2) How to pick stocks

    (3) How a person should save for the future with mutual funds

    (4) Why mutual funds are better than bank savings accounts

    (5) Poverty and old age

7. In the first paragraph, what does the writer mean by "do the job right"?

    (1) He is referring to the job of saving.

    (2) He is referring to the task of working and saving.

    (3) He means you won't be getting even minimal Social Security.

    (4) He means the entire job of supporting you in old age.

    (5) All of the above

8. Which of the following can you infer from this article?

    (1) Put money regularly in mutual funds, and you'll be more comfortable in old age.

    (2) Don't save, and you might be poor some day.

    (3) You will learn more about investing as you do it.

    (4) There are many kinds of mutual funds.

    (5) All of the above

9. A mutual stock fund is

    (1) a collection of sure-fire stocks.

    (2) a selected group of different stocks.

    (3) a banking company.

    (4) a kind of savings account.

    (5) more risky than buying a single stock.

10. Why does the article advise people to start saving while still in their twenties?

    (1) The investment will have a longer time to grow.

    (2) Later on, they won't have the extra money to save.

    (3) Mutual funds may be unavailable in the future.

    (4) Social Security will cease to exist.

    (5) Most people don't have pensions.

Directions: The following is an excerpt from a divorce settlement. It is similar to many documents of this kind. It requires careful reading. Note what *is* stated and what is *not* stated. While it may or may not appear on the GED, you will find documents of a similar nature to read.

Child Support Agreement

(A) The Father shall pay to the Mother the sum of $400.00 per month for child support, said payments to be made to the Mother at her address on the first day of the month following the execution of this agreement.

(B) In addition, the parties agree to share other extraordinary expenses, including child care (after school, summer camp), school-related costs, and unreimbursed medical expenses. These shared expenses will continue until the Child becomes emancipated.

(C) For the purposes of this agreement, the Child will be considered emancipated upon the earliest happening of any of the following:

1. Reaching the age of twenty-one years, or finishing four years of college, but in no case beyond the date on which the Child reaches the age of twenty-two years. However, the Child shall be unemancipated beyond the age of twenty-one only as long as he attends college on a full-time basis, but not beyond the age of twenty-two years.

2. Marriage of the Child.

3. Permanent residence by the Child away from the mother.

4. Death of the Father or of the Child.

5. Entry by the Child into the armed forces. If the Child is discharged from the Armed Forces before reaching the age of majority, the Child shall be deemed not to have been fully emancipated.

6. Working on a full-time basis after reaching the age of eighteen years, except that engaging by the Child in partial, part-time or sporadic employment shall not be considered emancipation. Full-time employment during vacation and summer periods shall also not be considered emancipation.

(D) The payments by the Father to the Mother shall be adjusted on a regular basis. The monthly payments will increase by 5 percent after every three years from the signing of this agreement, on a $400.00 per month basis, compounded. For example, in 2005, the Father will pay $400.00, plus 5 percent, or $420.00 for the next three years, and in 2008 the Father will pay an additional 5 percent, or $441 for the next three years, and so on, until the Father is no longer obligated to support the Child.

—March 31, 2005

11. What is the purpose of this legal document?

   (1) It states how much money the mother needs for her child.

   (2) It states when the child can be visited by the father.

   (3) It spells out the financial support responsibilities of the father toward the child.

   (4) It summarizes how much it costs to raise a child.

   (5) It makes sure the child goes to college.

12. According to this child support agreement, the father needs to support his child until age 21, instead of 18, unless the child

   (1) is already working full-time.

   (2) gets married.

   (3) joins the armed services.

   (4) All of the above

   (5) None of the above

13. What can you infer about the meaning of the word "emancipated" from the way it is used in this document?

   (1) It means the child is financially independent of his parents.

   (2) It refers to the child getting out of the armed services.

   (3) It suggests that the child has dropped out of college temporarily.

   (4) It means that the child only needs his mother's support, not his father's.

   (5) It refers to the child no longer having to listen to his parents.

14. The father loses his job in the year 2007. How much monthly child support will he legally be responsible for paying at that time?

   (1) None, since he isn't working

   (2) $420.00

   (3) $400.00

   (4) $441.00

   (5) $463.00

15. The child turns 18 and is working full-time as a shoe salesman. While on the way to his Tuesday night college course, he falls and sprains his ankle. Who is legally responsible for his medical bills?

   (1) His father is responsible since he is under 21 years of age and still taking classes.

   (2) According to part B, his parents share his unreimbursed medical expenses.

   (3) His mother is responsible since he's living with her.

   (4) Both the parents share the costs equally with the child.

   (5) Neither parent is legally responsible any longer.

exercises

Directions: The following selection talks about the things a person needs to know before signing up for a credit card. Read the article carefully, then answer the questions that follow.

How Do You Go About Choosing a Credit Card?

Before you choose a credit card, consider and compare all terms, including the following:

Annual Percentage Rate (APR)

The cost of credit as a yearly rate.

Free or Grace Period

This allows you to avoid any finance charge by paying your balance in full before the due date. If there is no free period, you will pay a finance charge from the date of the transaction, even if you pay your entire balance when you receive your bill.

Fees and Charges

Most issuers charge an annual fee; some also might charge a fee for a cash advance or if you fail to make a payment on time or go over your credit limit.

Credit Card Insurance

Is unnecessary because it duplicates protections you already have under law in case your credit card is lost or stolen. Of course, the loss of the card must be reported promptly.

If you pay bills in full each month, the size of the annual fee or other fees will be more important. If you carry a balance, the APR and the method used to figure your balance are key.

Get all terms and fees in writing,

including whether a deposit is required.

Apply directly to the card issuer.

Don't give money to a company that offers to get you a credit card for a fee. You may not get a card or your money back.

Beware of "credit cards" that only allow you to buy from their own catalogs.

Avoid companies that promise instant credit.

Or guarantee you a credit card "even if you have bad credit history." No one can guarantee you credit in advance.

Be cautious of offers for secured credit cards.

These cards usually require you to set aside money in a separate bank account in an amount equal to the line of credit on the card to guarantee that you will pay the credit card debt. Some of these offers advertise that secured cards can be used to repair a bad credit record, but no matter how well you handle this account, your payment history on your past debts still will be taken into consideration when you apply for credit, employment, or housing.

Excerpt from *The Consumer Action Handbook*, 2004 Edition.

16. Why is it preferable to get a credit card with a free or grace period?

    (1) You will be able to avoid all fees.

    (2) You can avoid finance charges by paying the balance on time.

    (3) You can charge larger amounts.

    (4) It makes no difference either way.

    (5) None of the above

17. The assistant branch manager of your bank explains the benefits of getting a MasterCard from his bank. His explanations are clear and convincing, and you want a credit card. What should you do?

    (1) Do nothing until you see the offer in writing.

    (2) Take the offer, since he is an official employee of the bank.

    (3) Think about it, then take it.

    (4) Ask someone who knows, then go and sign up for the card.

    (5) All of the above

18. According to this article, you can infer the following:

    (1) All credit cards are pretty much the same.

    (2) You should be able to charge as much as you want if you get credit card insurance.

    (3) Avoid all credit cards, since they will cost you money in fees even if you don't charge anything.

    (4) It may pay to search around before getting a credit card.

    (5) You should insist on getting a card that guarantees you unlimited credit.

19. What happens if you lose your credit card?

    (1) You will be liable for all charges incurred, regardless.

    (2) You will not be liable, but only if you are insured.

    (3) You will be legally protected if the loss is reported.

    (4) You will be unable to get a new card for six months.

    (5) You can ignore all charges if they weren't yours.

20. Which kind of credit card requires you to make a prior bank deposit?

    (1) MasterCard

    (2) APRs

    (3) Most cards

    (4) Insured credit cards

    (5) Secured credit cards

exercises

Directions: The next selection gives an overall picture of how to write a resume. Read the following, then test yourself with the questions that follow.

How Do You Write a Resume?

What is the general purpose of a resume? It is to give a brief summary of details about you that would be important to a potential employer. While everyone's resume is going to be different, there are four basic sections that should be included in each and every resume.

First, a section called "Educational Background" is expected. Starting with your last school first, give the dates for each type of schooling, the name of the school attended, the type of program, and the degree you obtained, if any. If you did an apprenticeship, attended a training program, or even learned a skill on your own, this should be listed and briefly explained here.

Next, under the heading of "Experience," list the jobs you have held, again starting with the last or present employment first, and working your way backward. This should be a complete list. The names of the companies, dates of employment, and your job title(s) should be given here. You could present a brief phrase or two explaining what you did, whom you worked for in the firm, and what your responsibilities were. In this section you can also include volunteer experience or unpaid work you have done; this is particularly important if your experience with paying jobs is very limited. If you were a student for most of your life, don't forget to include summer jobs, temporary experience, and seasonal holiday work.

In the third section, give a list of three to five references, with addresses and telephone numbers. These should include former employers as well as teachers or reputable people in your community who know and like you.

The fourth section is one that can be loosely labeled "Skills." Here you have the chance to tell potential employers about your special abilities and qualities. For example, you may know much about doing certain tasks on the computer, or you may be very good at taking care of children. Or, more generally, perhaps you are excellent at doing work that requires care and patience or that requires strength and energy. Are you at ease dealing with lots of people, good on the telephone, capable of writing easily, quick to learn new skills? These are all skills and characteristics about which an employer would want to know.

Of course, all of this must be preceded with a heading that includes your name, address, and telephone number. Keep your resume up to date, organize it neatly, and check the spelling. Don't be modest in describing yourself. And, good luck!

21. Which of the following statements is most clearly inferred by this article?

    (1) Everyone needs a resume.

    (2) Not all work experience should be mentioned on a resume.

    (3) A resume should reveal all there is to know about you.

    (4) A resume is not necessary unless you're going to apply for a major job.

    (5) Your resume should reflect relevant accomplishments and abilities.

22. Josh spent his last two summers using his photography skills in filming weddings. In what part of the resume could this be mentioned?

    (1) Under "Experience"

    (2) In the fourth section, under "Skills"

    (3) The "References" section

    (4) Choices (1), (2), and (3)

    (5) Only in the "Education Background" section

23. Marie has not yet finished high school and has had very little work experience. However, she helped in the family store for much of her life and has many skills. According to this article, how should she compose a resume?

    (1) Marie needs to list her skills, consider the family business as experience, and list the owners as references.

    (2) She should put off writing a resume until she has some real experience working.

    (3) Since she hasn't finished high school, Marie doesn't need to complete the educational background section, but she can mention her work in the store under "Experience."

    (4) Family members can't be good references, so she really can't mention any. However, she has good work experience to list.

    (5) Marie needs to finish high school first, then work on her resume.

24. Ruth has made the following list for the "Experience" section of her resume. According to this article, which one should she emphasize?

    (1) Babysitting the neighbor's kids during the last three years

    (2) Helping out with her parents' yardwork

    (3) Eight months of volunteer work on an emergency ambulance team

    (4) Washing cars during the summer

    (5) Helping out at her church charity bazaar

25. All of the following could appropriately be listed in the "Skills" section of your resume, EXCEPT your

    (1) boss's name.

    (2) 70 w.p.m. typing ability.

    (3) knowledge of Spanish.

    (4) ability to work long hours, if necessary.

    (5) capacity for keeping cool under pressure.

ANSWER KEY AND EXPLANATIONS

1. (2)	6. (3)	11. (3)	16. (2)	21. (5)
2. (5)	7. (4)	12. (4)	17. (1)	22. (4)
3. (1)	8. (5)	13. (1)	18. (4)	23. (1)
4. (5)	9. (2)	14. (2)	19. (3)	24. (3)
5. (4)	10. (1)	15. (5)	20. (5)	25. (1)

1. **The correct answer is (2).** The term "secondary school" usually refers to high school, while "postsecondary" refers to what comes beyond that. The first sentence suggests that this article deals with education after high school.

2. **The correct answer is (5).** Access America for Students is described as a source of information about financial aid (which includes loans), job searching, and even filing taxes. This would be the best place for Rose to get the information she needs.

3. **The correct answer is (1).** Reading this piece suggests that getting information about financing education is no simple matter. Since there seem to be so many places to look, it appears that it will take some work and effort to get your education paid for.

4. **The correct answer is (5).** The U.S. Department of Education is not mentioned as a source of financial aid information. It is only stated that the Department partly funds one of the programs.

5. **The correct answer is (4).** The second-to-last paragraph states that it is possible to do community service through the AmeriCorps program, and thereby pay for postsecondary educational expenses.

6. **The correct answer is (3).** The article says you should plan financially for the future by investing regularly. It talks of mutual funds but doesn't discuss the dangers, nor does it discuss other possibilities for investing money.

7. **The correct answer is (4).** He is talking about the sources of income in old age, and whether they will be adequate in supporting you at that time.

8. **The correct answer is (5).** All of these points are made directly or implied by the article.

9. **The correct answer is (2).** The article states that a mutual stock fund is a group of stocks selected and managed by an adviser.

10. **The correct answer is (1).** Presumably, you won't need the money until you are retired. That means that your investment will then have many years to grow.

11. **The correct answer is (3).** The title of this article tells us it involves child support. The first line tells us that it's the father's responsibility that is spelled out here.

12. **The correct answer is (4).** Section C, numbers 2, 5, and 6 give the criteria of defining a child who is already independent and not in need of parental support. Therefore, according to this legal agreement, only a child who is still in college full-time would be required to be supported by the father past the age of 18.

13. **The correct answer is (1).** You can infer that it means a child who can take care of himself or who has moved away from home and is therefore independent of his parents' financial support.

14. **The correct answer is (2).** There is nothing stated in the agreement

about the event of the father losing his job. Therefore, he is still legally responsible for support of his child even though he isn't working.

15. The correct answer is (5). Since he is already 18 years old and working full-time he is considered "emancipated" according to Section C, part 6 of the Agreement. Therefore, he is responsible for his own medical expenses.

16. The correct answer is (2). A card that doesn't have a grace period will impose finance charges from the day you use it for a transaction, according to the information in this article. Cards that give you a grace period will not impose any finance charges if you pay your total balance on time. Of course, there may be other charges you will have to pay.

17. The correct answer is (1). The article states that you should see the written contract. Even the assistant branch manager may not know all the facts about the cards his bank offers, and he may give you some misinformation.

18. The correct answer is (4). The point of the whole article is that there are many differences between existing cards. It infers that you should look around for the best deal.

19. The correct answer is (3). The selection states that you are legally protected and that credit card insurance is not necessary. It also states that you must report the loss to the company issuing the card.

20. The correct answer is (5). According to the last paragraph, secured credit cards are the ones that require a prior bank deposit to guarantee charges made on your card.

21. The correct answer is (5). The article states that a resume should summarize your background in school, on the job, and in terms of abilities and skills you have developed. It doesn't state who needs one or that it should necessarily reveal everything about you.

22. The correct answer is (4). This summer work will allow Josh to list his talents and abilities under "Skills," as well as the job itself under "Experience." The names of his employers can be added to his list of references as well. Therefore, choice (4) is correct.

23. The correct answer is (1). Marie's skills and work in connection with her family's store are legitimate and important work experience that she can proudly detail in her resume. She should make the most of it. Under the circumstances, she should also list the owners as references, even if they are her parents.

24. The correct answer is (3). Even though some other choices here reflect paid as opposed to voluntary employment, the ambulance work is the most impressive and unusual of Ruth's experiences and requires the most ability and knowledge. It should therefore be stressed in her resume.

25. The correct answer is (1). The boss's name belongs in the resume, but not in the "Skills" section. All the other choices do.

EXERCISES: READING SELECTIONS

> **Directions:** In this section, you will have the opportunity to work on a large number of practice readings that are very similar to the ones you will see on the actual GED test. Among the various pieces are poems, drama excerpts, fiction, and nonfiction passages.
>
> Working on these will improve your skills in reading these kinds of passages. Take your time with each selection. Scan it first to get the general idea, then read it again carefully. If it isn't clear to you, read it again.
>
> Then, for each question circle the number of the response that best answers the question or completes the statement. Correct and explanatory answers are provided at the end of the section.

ITEMS 1 TO 5 REFER TO THE FOLLOWING EXCERPT FROM AN AUTOBIOGRAPHY.

How Did Frederick Douglass Get an Education?

Line From this time I was most narrowly watched. If I was in a separate room any considerable length of time, I was sure to be suspected of having a book, and was at once called to give an account of myself. All this, however, was too late. The first step had been taken. Mistress, in teaching me the alphabet, had given me the inch,
(5) and no precaution could prevent me from taking the ell.

The plan which I adopted, and the one by which I was most successful, was that of making friends of all the little white boys whom I met in the street. As many of these as I could, I converted into teachers. With their kindly aid, obtained at different times and in different places, I finally succeeded in learning to read. When
(10) I was sent on errands, I always took my book with me, and by doing one part of my errand quickly, I found time to get a lesson before my return. I used also to carry bread with me, enough of which was always in the house, and to which I was always welcome; for I was much better off in this regard than many of the poor white children in our neighborhood. This bread I used to bestow upon the hungry little
(15) urchins, who, in return, would give me the more valuable bread of knowledge.

I am strongly tempted to give the names of two or three of those little boys, as a testimonial of the gratitude and affection I bear them; but prudence forbids;—not that it would injure me, but it might embarrass them; for it is almost an unpardonable offense to teach slaves to read in this Christian country. It is enough to say of
(20) the dear little fellows that they lived on Philpot Street, very near Durgin and Bailey's ship-yard. I used to talk this matter of slavery over with them. I would sometimes say to them, I wished I could be as free as they would be when they got to be men. "You will be free as soon as you are twenty-one, but I am a slave for life! Have not I as good a right to be free as you have?" These words seemed to trouble
(25) them; they would express for me the liveliest sympathy, and console with the hope that something would occur by which I might be free.

—*from* Narrative of the Life of Frederick Douglass

1. Based on information in this selection, when was Frederick Douglass's *Narrative* written?

   (1) During the Middle Ages
   (2) During the Renaissance
   (3) Before the Civil War
   (4) Between 1880 and 1900
   (5) After 1900

2. According to the information in the passage, how did Douglass learn to read?

   (1) By his own efforts
   (2) From his mistress
   (3) With the help of young white boys
   (4) By using his time in a clever way
   (5) By going to school

3. Which of the following would be the most suitable title for this selection?

   (1) "The Yearning for Freedom"
   (2) "The Burning for Success"
   (3) "As the World Turns"
   (4) "How I Learned to Read"
   (5) "A Lover is Spurned"

4. Why does Douglass withhold the names of his young white friends?

   (1) They asked him not to give their names.
   (2) They might be embarrassed.
   (3) He never learned their names.
   (4) He had forgotten their names.
   (5) He feared injury to himself.

5. Douglass states that ". . . in teaching me the alphabet (she) had given me an inch, and no precaution could prevent me from taking the ell." This can be interpreted as which of the following?

   (1) The use of knowledge is a criminal conspiracy.
   (2) Once started, learning is self-generating.
   (3) A slave could not be stopped from reading.
   (4) The alphabet is a powerful tool.
   (5) Douglass's need to know was a powerful motivator.

**ITEMS 6 TO 9 REFER TO THE
FOLLOWING POEM.**

**How Does This Poet Feel
about His Love?**

Line She walks in beauty, like the night
    Of cloudless climes and starry skies;
And all that's best of dark and bright
    Meet in her aspect and her eyes:
(5) Thus mellow'd to that tender light
    Which heaven to gaudy day denies.

One shade the more, one ray the less,
    Had half impair'd the nameless grace
Which waves in every raven tress,
(10)   Or softly lightens o'er her face;
Where thoughts serenely sweet express
    How pure, how dear their dwelling-place.
And on that cheek, and o'er that brow,
    So soft, so calm, yet eloquent,
(15) The smiles that win, the tints that glow,
    But tell of days in goodness spent,
A mind at peace with all below,
A heart whose love is innocent!

    —Lord George Gordon Byron,
        "She Walks in Beauty"

6. Personification is a technique used by writers to ascribe human characteristics to a nonliving object. In the first stanza, what is being personified?

(1) Eyes

(2) Aspect

(3) Night

(4) Beauty

(5) Walking

7. According to this poem and by using the poet's actual words, what "tell of days in goodness spent"? (line 16)

(1) "the night/of cloudless climes" (lines 1–2)

(2) "a heart whose love is innocent" (line 18)

(3) "A mind at peace with all below" (line 17)

(4) "How pure, how dear their dwelling-place" (line 12)

(5) "the smiles that win, the tints that glow" (line 15)

8. The technique used in the poet's comparison of his love to the night is called

(1) metaphor.

(2) simile.

(3) hyperbole.

(4) personification.

(5) oxymoron.

9. The tone of the poet's writing is

(1) worshipful.

(2) cynical.

(3) scornful.

(4) mocking.

(5) arrogant.

**ITEMS 10 TO 15 REFER TO THE
FOLLOWING EXCERPT.**

Why Is This Fight Going to Take Place?

Line "Johnson," Wolf Larsen said, with an air of dismissing all that had gone before as introductory to the main business in hand, "I understand you're not quite satisfied with those oilskins?"

"No, I am not. They are no good, sir."

(5) "And you've been shooting off your mouth about them."

"I say what I think, sir," the sailor answered courageously, not failing at the same time in ship courtesy, which demanded that "sir" be appended to each speech he made.

It was at this moment that I chanced to glance at Johansen. His big fists were

(10) clenching and unclenching, and his face was positively fiendish, so malignantly did he look at Johnson. I noticed a black discoloration, still faintly visible, under Johansen's eye, a mark of the thrashing he had received a few nights before from the sailor. For the first time I began to divine that something terrible was about to be enacted—what, I could not imagine.

(15) "Do you know what happens to men who say what you've said about my slop-chest and me?" Wolf Larsen was demanding.

"I know, sir," was the answer.

"What?" Wolf Larsen demanded, sharply and imperatively.

"What you and the mate there are going to do to me, sir."

(20) "Look at him, Hump," Wolf Larsen said to me, "look at this bit of animated dust, this aggregation of matter that moves and breathes and defies me and thoroughly believes itself to be compounded of something good; that is impressed with certain human fictions such as righteousness and honesty, and that will live up to them in spite of all personal discomforts and menaces. What do you think of him, Hump?

(25) What do you think of him?"

"I think that he is a better man than you are," I answered, impelled, somehow, with a desire to draw upon myself a portion of the wrath I felt was about to break upon his head. "His human fictions, as you choose to call them, make for nobility and manhood. You have no fictions, no dreams, no ideals. You are a pauper."

(30) He nodded his head with a savage pleasantness. "Quite true, Hump, quite true. I have no fictions that make for nobility and manhood. A living dog is better than a dead lion, say I with the preacher. My only doctrine is the doctrine of expediency, and it makes for surviving. This bit of the ferment, only dust and ashes, will have no more nobility than any dust and ashes, while I shall still be alive and roaring."

(35) "Do you know what I am going to do?" he questioned. I shook my head.

"Well, I am going to exercise my prerogative of roaring and show you how fares nobility. Watch me."

I cannot give the further particulars of the horrible scene that followed. It was too revolting. It turns me sick even now when I think of it. Johnson fought bravely

(40) enough, but he was no match for Wolf Larsen, much less for Wolf Larsen and the mate.

—*Jack London,* The Sea Wolf

10. Where does this scene probably take place?

    (1) In a court of law
    (2) In the street
    (3) In a boxing ring
    (4) On a ship
    (5) On a freight train

11. Wolf Larsen appears to be

    (1) a sailor with the same status as Johnson.
    (2) a man who is in authority.
    (3) the first mate of the ship.
    (4) a policeman.
    (5) a mutineer.

12. Judging from the selection, what can we infer about Hump?

    (1) He is a person who has no strong feelings.
    (2) He is a strong man who is able to defeat Larsen.
    (3) He can argue with Larsen.
    (4) He is an out-and-out coward.
    (5) He is a champion of all "underdogs."

13. What does Hump mean when he says, "You are a pauper"?

    (1) Larsen has no money.
    (2) Larsen is too much of an idealist and pays no attention to the realities of life.
    (3) Larsen is poor because he has none of the thoughts that make life worth living.
    (4) Larsen's oilskins in his slop-chest are worthless.
    (5) Larsen once read the book *The Prince and the Pauper.*

14. Larsen's idea of the doctrine of expediency is

    (1) not to worry about right or wrong but to survive by any means.
    (2) to cheat everyone when possible.
    (3) never to admit he was wrong in any situation.
    (4) to follow the ideals of nobility only when it suits him to do so.
    (5) to sell poor-quality merchandise.

15. How can Larsen best be described?

    (1) As brutal and stupid
    (2) As cynical and cruel
    (3) As intellectual and lenient
    (4) As gentle but stern
    (5) As arrogant but with a heart of gold

exercises

ITEMS 16 TO 20 REFER TO THE FOLLOWING POEM.

Who Is Being Welcomed?
The New Colossus

Line   Not like the brazen giant of Greek fame
With conquering limbs astride from land to land
Here at our sea-washed, sunset gates shall stand
A mighty woman with a torch, whose flame
(5)   Is the imprisoned lightning, and her name
Mother of Exiles. From her beacon hand
Glows world-wide welcome; her mild eyes command
The air-bridged harbor that twin cities frame.
"Keep, ancient lands, your storied pomp!" cries she
(10)   with silent lips. "Give me your tired, your poor,
Your huddled masses yearning to breathe free,
The wretched refuse of your teeming shore,
Send these, the homeless, tempest-tost, to me.
I lift my lamp beside the golden door!"

             —*Emma Lazarus*

16. Which of the following statements best describes the purpose of this poem?

   (1) To memorialize the poet's mother

   (2) To insult European governments

   (3) To glorify the Greek myths

   (4) To justify calls for restrictions on immigration

   (5) To proclaim that America is a safe haven

17. What does the subtitle of the poem seem to imply?

   (1) The United States is a giant new country.

   (2) There was a similar statue in ancient times.

   (3) Italian refugees are particularly welcome.

   (4) New York City is a great modern place.

   (5) The old Colossus of Rhodes has been replaced.

18. What is the form of this poem?

   (1) A sonnet

   (2) Blank verse

   (3) Free verse

   (4) A ballad

   (5) A rondel

19. What does the phrase "the wretched refuse of your teeming shore" (line 12) suggest?

   (1) America is for rich people only.

   (2) Only poor people want to come here.

   (3) All immigrants are political refugees.

   (4) Americans look up to Europeans.

   (5) America is wide open and empty.

20. What is the tone of this poem?

   (1) Sorrowful

   (2) Scornful

   (3) Delightful

   (4) Bewildered

   (5) Exalted

ITEMS 21 TO 25 REFER TO THE FOLLOWING PASSAGE.

What Were the Soldiers' Feelings after the Battle?

Line The First Brigade, after pushing its way through the throng at the river with the point of the bayonet, was already forming on the crest of the hill. Now and then we heard the pattering sounds of bullets, stragglers from the leaden storm above, falling upon the roofs of the boats. Our horses were quickly disembarked, and with
(5) the First Brigade in columns closed in mass, leaving orders for the rest of the Division to follow as soon as landed, we moved toward the point indicated by the firing. Directly we saw evidence of close and terrible fighting. Artillery horses dead, cannon dismounted, accouterments torn and bloody appeared everywhere. The first dead soldier we saw had fallen in the road; our artillery had crushed and mangled
(10) his limbs, and ground him into the mire. He lay a bloody, loathsome mass, the scraps of his blue uniform furnishing the only distinguishable evidence that a hero there had died. At this sight, I saw a manly fellow gulp down his heart, which swelled too closely into his throat. Near him lay a slender rebel boy—his face in the mud, his brown hair floating in a bloody pool. Soon a dead Major, then a Colonel,
(15) then the lamented Wallace, yet alive, were passed in quick and sickening succession. The gray gleaming of the misty morning gave a ghostly pallor to the faces of the dead. The disordered hair, dripping from the night's rain, the distorted and passion-marked faces, the stony, glaring eyes, the blue lips, the glistening teeth, the shriveled and contracted hands, the wild agony of pain and passion in the attitudes
(20) of the dead—all the horrid circumstances with which death surrounds the brave when torn from life in the whirlwind of battle—were seen as we marched over the field, the beseeching cries of the wounded from their bloody and miry beds meanwhile saluting our ears and cutting to our hearts.

—*Daniel McCook,* The Second
Division at Shiloh

21. At the beginning of this selection, the First Brigade

  (1) has just come ashore from landing craft.

  (2) is retreating.

  (3) has spent the night in battle.

  (4) has been wiped out.

  (5) has killed some Union soldiers.

22. What is the author's attitude toward the dead soldiers he sees?

  (1) It reflects pity and sorrow.

  (2) It shows disgust and hatred.

  (3) It indicates scorn and revulsion.

  (4) It is full of humor and delight.

  (5) None of the above

23. It is apparent that the

  (1) battle is over.

  (2) battle has just begun.

  (3) First Brigade has been fighting for hours.

  (4) battle has been going on for some time.

  (5) First Brigade is retreating.

24. What can the reader infer from the author's choice of language?

    (1) He glories in combat.

    (2) War disgusts and horrifies him.

    (3) He regards battle as a comic adventure.

    (4) He wants to desert.

    (5) He feels the Union must be preserved.

25. Which word best describes the general mood of this piece?

    (1) Distinguished

    (2) Excited

    (3) Sorrowful

    (4) Patriotic

    (5) Humorous

ITEMS 26 TO 30 REFER TO THE REVIEW BELOW.

What Is It Like at the Metropolitan Opera?

Line Earlier this month, Adrienne Dugger, a native of Atlanta, Georgia, stood in front of the curtain of the Metropolitan Opera with a huge grin on her face. It was not the compulsive smile of a diva who needs to wring a few more seconds of applause from her fans. Instead, it was the unbelieving smile of a woman who has come through

(5) danger intact. Dugger had stepped in on short notice to sing the lead in Puccini's "Turandot," one of the most taxing roles in the soprano repertory. At first, her voice sounded unsteady, especially in those cruelly exposed lines of "In questa reggia" with which she had to make her entrance. But she did not lack power, and her high C's cut thrillingly through the choral and orchestral climaxes of Act II. More than

(10) that, she acted the role with intelligence and passion, sharply telegraphing the rage of this proud princess who must surrender herself to a nameless foreigner. At one point, she shot the tenor Richard Margison a glance that might have given even Pavarotti the chills. She did all this while wearing cumbersome headgear that seemed to have upside-down bowling pins attached to it—part of the imperishable

(15) bric-a-brac of Franco Zeffirelli's 1987 production. A star is born? Hard to say. But the soprano gave flesh and blood to a character who is often little more than an onslaught of high notes.

    Dugger's last-minute triumph was one of several unexpected pleasures in the first few weeks of the Met season. Trips to the big house are more fun than they were six

(20) or eight years ago, when Disneyland scenery rumbled on and off the stage and recording stars went through the motions. Productions are more thoughtful, and the repertory has broadened bit by bit. Best of all, the new stars are taking care to act their roles, as well as sing them. On opening night, Bryn Terfel painted Don Giovanni as a rapacious thug who edged into insanity during the ordinarily chipper

(25) Champagne Aria. Renée Fleming kept pace with him, ruffling her customary poise and emitting, on the third syllable of the word "Abbastanza," the loveliest note of the year. Karita Mattila, heading a new production of "Fidelio," gave a performance that will be talked about for years. Singers of the post-Pavarotti generation are dispensing with operatic cliches and trying to build character gesture by gesture.

(30) They may not have the purely vocal charisma of Corelli or Tebaldi, but their energy is giving the art new strength.

—An excerpt from *"Semper Fidelio,"* by Alex Ross, *The New Yorker,*
October 30, 2000. Used by permission.

26. What is this article about?

    (1) An opera singer's efforts to bring more life into her roles

    (2) Adrienne Dugger's debut

    (3) Adrienne Dugger's performance, and the quality of this season's performances at the Metropolitan Opera

    (4) Puccini's "Turandot"

    (5) The costumes and sets of current opera productions

27. What was Adrienne Dugger's main accomplishment?

    (1) She hit a lot of high C's throughout the evening.

    (2) She successfully took over a difficult operatic role on short notice.

    (3) She came through danger intact inspite of cumbersome headgear.

    (4) She took her bows and smiled graciously.

    (5) She was an excellent costume designer.

28. The productions of the Metropolitan Opera, according to the writer, are better now than in previous years because

    (1) the singers are better able to act as well as sing.

    (2) productions are more thoughtfully presented.

    (3) there is a wider selection of operas given.

    (4) Choices (1), (2), and (3)

    (5) the singing is better.

29. The reviewer mentions Don Giovanni and Fidelio. What (or who) are they?

    (1) Operas produced at the Metropolitan this season

    (2) Singers who are in the production of "Turandot"

    (3) Names of opera houses

    (4) Famous producers of opera

    (5) Great sopranos from the past

30. In lines 29–30, the reviewer states, "Singers of the post-Pavarotti generation are dispensing with operatic cliches and trying to build character gesture by gesture." What does he mean?

    (1) Younger singers are better than they used to be.

    (2) Singers are using many gestures on stage.

    (3) Singers now are trying to imitate Pavarotti gesture by gesture.

    (4) They are trying to be funnier on stage by turning their roles into comical characters.

    (5) Singers are no longer copying their predecessors but are establishing their own more realistic interpretations of their roles.

ITEMS 31 TO 36 REFER TO THE FOLLOWING POEM.

Is There Any Advantage to Dying Young?

Line The time you won your town the race
We chaired you through the market-place;
Ma and boy stood cheering by,
And home we brought you shoulder-high.

(5) Today, the road all runners come,
Shoulder-high we bring you home,
And set you at your threshold down,
Townsman of a stiller town.

Smart lad, to slip betimes away
(10) From fields where glory does not stay,
And early though the laurel grows
It withers quicker than the rose.

Eyes the shady night has shut
Cannot see the record cut,
(15) And silence sounds no worse than cheers
After earth has stopped the ears.

Now you will not swell the rout
Of lads that wore their honors out
Runners whom renown outran
(20) And the name died before the man.

So set, before its echoes fade,
The fleet foot on the sill of shade,
And hold to the low lintel up
The still-defended challenge-cup.

(25) And round that early-laurelled head
Will flock to gaze the strength less dead,
And find unwithered on its curls
The garland briefer than a girl's.

—A. E. Housman,
"To an Athlete Dying Young"

31. What did the athlete in this poem do?

(1) He was a runner.

(2) He played football.

(3) He was a basketball star.

(4) He excelled in many sports.

(5) He was a tennis champion.

32. In line 7, the word "threshold" is a metaphor for which of the following words?

(1) The grave

(2) Sports

(3) Home

(4) Life

(5) Glory

33. "Stiller town" in line 8 is a metaphor for

    (1) a country village.
    (2) old age.
    (3) death.
    (4) love.
    (5) home.

34. Why does the poet praise the athlete?

    (1) For winning the race
    (2) For wearing the laurel of victory
    (3) For breaking a record
    (4) For returning to his hometown
    (5) For dying young

35. What advantage does the poet see to the athlete's death at this time?

    (1) He was beginning to slow down.
    (2) He had been forgotten by his fans.
    (3) He had been ill and suffered greatly.
    (4) He died while he still had fame.
    (5) He has lost all his money.

36. What is the general mood of this poem?

    (1) Victorious
    (2) Somber
    (3) Cheerful
    (4) Hopeless
    (5) Matter-of-fact

exercises

ITEMS 37 TO 41 REFER TO THE BUSINESS READING BELOW.

What Are the Rules of This Lease?

LEASE AGREEMENT FOR PARKING

(excerpt)

(1). The make, model, and year of the motor vehicle to be parked is:

Make _____ Model _____ Year _____

(2). Until further notice as hereafter provided, the annual fee for the Lease herein granted shall be $1,200, payable in advance in equal monthly installments of $100 on the first day of each and every calendar month of this Agreement.

(3). The aforesaid motor vehicle must be maintained in operating condition as confirmed by a current inspection sticker, current registration, current insurance, and current driver's license. Failing to maintain the vehicle in operating condition shall be cause for immediate termination of this Agreement.

(4). The aforesaid parking space shall be used by the Renter for parking a private passenger car or station wagon and for no other purpose whatsoever. No other vehicle of any kind shall be permitted to park on the property. The parking of vans, trucks, recreational vehicles, and motorcycles and/or other power driven scooters is strictly prohibited.

(5). The Garage shall have the right, from time to time, to increase the aforesaid fee.

(6). The Renter's automobile shall be stored at his/her own risk and the Garage and/or employees shall not be liable for any loss or damage to said vehicle. The Garage shall likewise not be liable for any damage to the stored vehicle or its contents or injury to said Renter resulting from any cause whatsoever.

(7). This Lease cannot be assigned, sublet, loaned, or otherwise transferred by Renter nor may Renter permit the parking space herein to be used by anyone other than the Renter without the prior consent of the Garage in each instance. This Lease may not be changed orally.

(8). If the Renter acquires another vehicle to replace the one parked during the term of the Lease, the new current inspection sticker, current registration, and current insurance must be presented to the Garage.

(9). Any motor vehicle parked pursuant to the provisions of this Agreement shall be subject to towing in the event it does not display a current registration sticker, license plates, or inspection sticker.

37. What is the purpose of this lease?

    (1) To charge a fee for the rental of a parking space

    (2) To guarantee the safety of the stored vehicle

    (3) To get cars off the streets

    (4) To park vans and trucks for a fee for a given period of time

    (5) To establish a legal basis for the storage of a car or station wagon

38. Jeff has a small truck that he uses for business purposes, in addition to a car that he stores in this garage. Regarding the truck, which of the following statements is true?

    (1) He can keep the truck in the garage if he's got his car out.

    (2) He may not park his truck in the garage at all.

    (3) Jeff can occasionally put his truck into his spot if the garage is not too full.

    (4) He may rent a larger space in the garage, and keep his truck there.

    (5) None of the above

39. While storing his car in the garage, Michael's brand new tape deck is stolen. According to the lease, who is going to be responsible for its replacement?

    (1) The garage insurance will cover the cost.

    (2) The attendants who worked the day the tape deck disappeared.

    (3) Michael will be solely responsible for the loss.

    (4) The cost will be split between the owners of the garage and Michael's insurance.

    (5) Any of these is a possibility. It depends on the circumstances.

40. Regarding the cost of the Lease, which of the following statements is true?

    (1) The cost is $1,200 per year, but it may go up.

    (2) The cost is $100, due at the end of each month.

    (3) The cost has not been determined.

    (4) It will cost $1,200 per year for the next three years, then be raised.

    (5) The cost is $1,200 per year, in addition to monthly payments of $100.

41. Derrick's station wagon, for which he has one more year on his Lease Agreement for Parking, is smashed up in an accident. According to the Agreement, Derrick can

    (1) give his parking spot to his sister, who needs one.

    (2) get his money back for the year left on the Lease.

    (3) store his motorcycle in the spot.

    (4) use the space for his current rental car.

    (5) All of the above

exercises

ITEMS 42 TO 47 REFER TO THE FOLLOWING POEM.

What Was the "Shot Heard Round the World"?

Concord Hymn

Line   By the rude bridge that arched the flood,
       Their flag to April's breeze unfurled,
       Here once the embattled farmers stood
       And fired the shot heard round the world.

(5)   The foe long since in silence slept;
       Alike the conqueror silent sleeps;
       And Time the ruined bridge has swept
       Down the dark stream which seaward creeps.

       On this green bank, by this soft stream,
(10)   We set this day a votive stone;
       That memory may their deed redeem,
       When, like our sires, our sons are gone.

       Spirit, that made those heroes dare
       To die, and leave their children free,
(15)   Bid Time and Nature gently spare
       The shaft we raise to them and thee.
                    —*Ralph Waldo Emerson*

42. The poet uses the words "slept" and "sleeps" (lines 5–6) to mean what about the protagonists?

   (1) They do not know each other.
   (2) They remain watchful.
   (3) They have finished fighting.
   (4) They are resting before battle.
   (5) They are long dead.

43. Which might be the best word to replace "sires"? (line 12)

   (1) Rulers
   (2) Kings
   (3) Forefathers
   (4) Producers
   (5) Breeders

44. How would you describe the main purpose of this poem?

   (1) Commemorative
   (2) Persuasive
   (3) Informational
   (4) Critical
   (5) Descriptive

45. The allusions to Time and Nature (line 15) are examples of which literary term?

   (1) Personification
   (2) Rhyme
   (3) Metaphor
   (4) Simile
   (5) Onomatopoeia

46. What event is being described in the third stanza?

   (1) Poetry is being recited in honor of the dead.
   (2) People are reflecting on the passage of time.
   (3) Stones are being put onto the banks of the stream.
   (4) A commemorative monument of some kind is being laid down.
   (5) The broken bridge is being rebuilt.

47. What is implied by the phrase "the shot heard round the world" (line 4)?

   (1) That it was an extremely loud sound.

   (2) That it was a shot that started a battle with great consequences.

   (3) That it started an avalanche.

   (4) This is a phrase used for dramatic effect.

   (5) None of the above

ITEMS 48 TO 52 REFER TO THE FOLLOWING EXCERPT FROM A PLAY.

How Does Undershaft Feel About the Salvation Army?

Line *Undershaft:* One moment, Mr. Lomax. I am rather interested in the Salvation Army. Its motto might be my own: Blood and Fire.

Lomax (shocked): But not your sort of blood and fire, you know.

Undershaft: My sort of blood cleanses: my sort of fire purifies.

(5) *Barbara:* So do ours. Come down tomorrow to my shelter—the West Ham Shelter—and see what we are doing. We're going to march to a great meeting in the Assembly at Mile End. Come and see the shelter and then march with us: It will do you a lot of good. Can you play anything?

Undershaft: In my youth I earned pennies, and even shillings occasionally, in the
(10) streets and in public house parlors by my natural talent for stepdancing. Later on, I became a member of the Undershaft Orchestra Society, and performed passably on the tenor trombone.

Lomax (scandalized—putting down the concertina): Oh I say!

Barbara: Many a sinner has played himself into heaven on the trombone, thanks
(15) to the Army.

Lomax (to Barbara, still rather shocked): Yes; but what about the cannon business, don't you know? *(to Undershaft)* Getting into heaven is not exactly in your line, is it?

Lady Britomart: Charles!!!

(20) *Lomax:* Well; but it stands to reason, don't it? The cannon business may be necessary and all that; we can't get along without cannons; but it isn't right, you know. On the other hand, there may be a certain amount of tosh about the Salvation Army—I belong to the Established Church myself—but still you can't deny that it's religion; and you can't go against religion, can you? At least unless
(25) you're downright immoral, don't you know.

—from *Major Barbara,* by George Bernard Shaw, by permission of the Society of Authors on behalf of the George Bernard Shaw Estate.

48. Which of the following can be inferred from this selection?

   (1) Undershaft is a professional trombone player.

   (2) Lomax is forthright and determined.

   (3) Lady Britomart is the wife of Lomax.

   (4) Undershaft is a munitions manufacturer.

   (5) Lomax does not believe in organized religion.

49. Which of the following words best describes the tone of Lomax's statement, "We can't get along without cannons; but it isn't right, you know"? (lines 21–22)

   (1) Cynical

   (2) Idealistic

   (3) Sarcastic

   (4) Hypocritical

   (5) Bitter

50. What does Undershaft's description of himself lead the reader to believe?

   (1) He is sorry for his mistakes.

   (2) He should give more to charity.

   (3) He hates the Salvation Army.

   (4) He was poor as a young man.

   (5) He comes from a wealthy family.

51. What does Lomax mean when he describes the Salvation Army as "tosh"? (line 22)

   (1) It is not good to join the Salvation Army.

   (2) A lot of nonsense is associated with the Salvation Army.

   (3) The Salvation Army gives away tosh, a kind of English candy.

   (4) The Salvation Army consists of many wealthy people.

   (5) The Salvation Army does a lot for the average person.

52. From the description of Barbara in the selection, which of the following is she most likely seeking?

   (1) To enjoy life

   (2) To punish her father

   (3) To do good for people

   (4) To make even more money

   (5) To marry Lomax

ITEMS 53 TO 57 REFER TO THE POEM BELOW.

What Is Weir Like?

Line The skies they were ashen and sober;
      The leaves they were crisped and sere—
      The leaves they were withering and sere:
      It was night in the lonesome October
(5) Of my most immemorial year;
      It was hard by the dim lake of Auber,
      In the misty mid region of Weir—
      It was down by the dank tarn of Auber
      In the ghoul-haunted woodland of Weir

—from "Ulalume" by
Edgar Allen Poe

53. From the context, what is "Weir"?

   (1) The name of the main character
   (2) The narrator
   (3) The setting of the poem
   (4) A ghoul, or ghost
   (5) None of the above

54. Which of the following best describes these lines of poetry?

   (1) They seem to be meaningless.
   (2) They suggest boredom and the author's lack of interest in Weir.
   (3) They are the concluding lines of a narrative poem.
   (4) They present a picture of the poet's nightmares.
   (5) They effectively set up a feeling of suspense.

55. Which of the following pairs of words best describes the atmosphere of this poem?

   (1) Mysterious and horrifying
   (2) Quiet and tranquil
   (3) Silent and lonely
   (4) Frivolous and high spirited
   (5) Quiet and contemplative

56. What does the author mean when he says "my most immemorial year"? (line 5)

   (1) The year he remembers most easily
   (2) His most important year
   (3) The year he cannot remember
   (4) The most horrifying year of his life
   (5) The year he traveled to Weir

57. Why does the author use the words "ashen" (line 1), "sere" (line 3), and "dank" (line 8)?

   (1) To show his hatred of Ulalume
   (2) To underscore his love of Auber
   (3) To exhibit his distrust of October
   (4) To establish the mood of the country
   (5) To reassure the reader

exercises

ITEMS 58 TO 63 REFER TO THE FOLLOWING SELECTION.

Did Lewy Clement Have a Nice Life?

Line   Lewy Clement's life was not terrifically tossed. Saltless, rather. Or like an un-
mixed batter. Lumpy.

   Little Clement's mother had grown listless after the desertion. She looked as
though she had been scrubbed, up and down, on the washing board, doused from
(5)   time to time in gray and noisome water. But little Clement looked alert, he looked
happy, he was always spirited. He was in second grade. He did his work, and had
always been promoted. At home he sang. He recited little poems. He told his mother
little stories wound out of the air by himself. His mother glanced at him once in a
while. She would have been proud of him if she had had the time.

(10)   She started toward her housemaid's work each morning at seven. She left a glass
of milk and a bowl of dry cereal and a dish of prunes on the table, and set the alarm
clock for eight. At eight little Clement punched off the alarm, stretched, got up,
washed, dressed, combed, brushed, ate his breakfast. It was quiet in the apartment.
He hurried off to school. At noon he returned from school, opened the door with his
(15)   key. It was quiet in the apartment. He poured himself a second glass of milk, got
more prunes, and ate a slice—"just one slice," his mother had cautioned—of bread
and butter. He went back to school. At three o'clock he returned from school, opened
the door with his key. It was quiet in the apartment. He got a couple of graham
crackers out of the cookie can. He drew himself a glass of water. He changed his
(20)   clothes. Then he went out to play, leaving behind him the two rooms. Leaving
behind him the brass beds, the lamp with the faded silk tassel and frayed cord, the
hooked oven door, the cracks in the walls and the quiet. As he played, he kept a
lookout for his mother, who usually arrived at seven or near that hour. When he saw
her rounding the corner, his little face underwent a transformation. His eyes lashed
(25)   into brightness, his lips opened suddenly and became a smile, and his eyebrows
climbed toward his hairline in relief and joy.

   He would run to his mother and almost throw his little body at her. "Here I am,
mother! Here I am! Here I am!"

—from "Neighbors" by Gwendolyn Brooks

58. Why is the author's introductory paragraph effective in capturing the reader's interest?

   (1) It relies on the author's personal experience.

   (2) It refers to ideas about maturity that are familiar to most readers.

   (3) It explains the advantages and disadvantages of Lewy's upbringing.

   (4) It has a variety of sentence lengths and descriptive words.

   (5) It explains why Lewy behaves the way he does.

59. Which of the following choices is especially effective in describing Lewy's home life?

   (1) "glass of milk," "bowl of dry cereal"

   (2) "faded silk tassel," "cracks in the wall"

   (3) "hurried off to school," "returned from school"

   (4) "glass of water," "changed his clothes"

   (5) "punched the alarm," "rounding the corner"

60. How does Lewy feel about his mother?

(1) He resents her for working such long hours.

(2) He blames her for his father's desertion.

(3) He is indifferent to her.

(4) He adores her.

(5) He wishes she was proud of him.

61. Which of the following words best describes the author's attitude toward Mrs. Clement?

(1) Admiring

(2) Bitter

(3) Indignant

(4) Neutral

(5) Worshipful

62. Of the statements below, which one is supported by the story?

(1) Lewy was a lonely little boy who lived in a fantasy world.

(2) Mrs. Clement was a thoughtless parent.

(3) Lewy suffered acutely because of his father's desertion of the family.

(4) There was little excuse for the mother's frequent absences from home.

(5) Lewy was well looked-after by his mother.

63. Small children who are left to themselves at home are sometimes referred to as "latchkey" kids. How does this relate to the events in this story?

(1) Lewy was a very imaginative little boy who did well in school, and therefore could not be called a "latchkey" child.

(2) He was a very mature child for his age, like most "latchkey" children.

(3) Lewy's mother worked and had to leave him alone during the day.

(4) Children don't need as much supervision as people think.

(5) Lewy was a neglected child.

ITEMS 64 TO 69 REFER TO THE STORY BELOW.

How Do the Three Friends Feel?

Line Abandoning his bicycle, which fell before a servant could catch it, the young man sprang up on to the verandah. He was all animation. "Hamidullah, Hamidullah! Am I late?" he cried.

"Do not apologize," said his host. "You are always late."

(5) "Kindly answer my question. Am I late? Has Mahmoud Ali eaten all the food? If so I go elsewhere. Mr. Mahmoud Ali, how are you?"

"Thank you, Dr. Aziz, I am dying."

"Dying before your dinner? Oh, poor Mahmoud Ali!"

"Hamidullah here is actually dead. He passed away just as you rode up on your (10) bike."

"Yes, that is so," said the other. "Imagine us both as addressing you from another and a happier world."

"Does there happen to be such a thing as a hookah in that happier world of yours?"

"Aziz, don't chatter. We are having a very sad talk."

(15) The hookah had been packed too tight, as was usual in his friend's house, and bubbled sulkily. He coaxed it. Yielding at last, the tobacco jetted up into his lungs and nostrils, driving out the smoke of burning cow dung that had filled them as he rode through the bazaar. It was delicious. He lay in a trance, sensuous but healthy, through which the talk of the two others did not seem particularly sad—they were (20) discussing as to whether or not it was possible to be friends with an Englishman. Mahmoud Ali argued that it was not, Hamidullah disagreed, but with so many reservations that there was no friction between them. Delicious indeed to lie on the broad verandah with the moon rising in front and the servants preparing dinner behind, and no trouble happening.

(25) "Well, look at my own experience this morning."

"I only contend that it is possible in England," replied Hamidullah, who had been to that country long ago, before the big rush, and had received a cordial welcome at Cambridge.

"It is impossible here. Aziz! The red-nosed boy has again insulted me in Court. I do (30) not blame him. He was told that he ought to insult me. Until lately he was quite a nice boy, but the others have got hold of him."

"Yes, they have no chance here, that is my point. They come out intending to be gentlemen, and are told it will not do. Look at Lesley, look at Blakiston, now it is your red-nosed boy, and Fielding will go next. Why, I remember when Turton came (35) out first. It was in another part of the Province. You fellows will not believe me, but I have driven with Turton in his carriage—Turton! Oh yes, we were once quite intimate. He has shown me his stamp collection."

"He would expect you to steal it now. Turton! But red-nosed boy will be far worse than Turton!"

—from *A Passage to India,*
by E. M. Forster. Used by permission.

64. Which of the following choices best describes the general tone of this selection?

(1) Humorous and sarcastic
(2) Worried and whining
(3) Hopelessly depresssed
(4) Guardedly hopeful
(5) Sad but optimistic

65. From the context, what does a "hookah" seem to be?

(1) A bicycle
(2) A long sofa to lie on
(3) A pair of binoculars
(4) A porch near a gurgling brook
(5) A device for smoking tobacco

66. The name of the man who came to dinner by bicycle in this selection is

(1) Hamidullah.
(2) Dr. Aziz.
(3) Mahmoud Ali.
(4) Fielding.
(5) Blakiston.

67. What can be assumed about the hosts in this story?

(1) They are Englishmen.
(2) They are students in England.
(3) They are prosperous.
(4) They are servants of the English.
(5) They all ride bicycles.

68. What did Hamidullah mean by "I only contend that it is possible in England"? (line 27)

(1) You can only get a hookah there.
(2) That was the only place to go to school.
(3) That dinner will be served there.
(4) It is only possible to be treated well by the English there.
(5) None of the above

69. In this conversation, the speakers portray Englishmen as

(1) cruel and violent.
(2) socially inferior.
(3) soldiers.
(4) stamp collectors.
(5) being undependable friends.

ITEMS 70 TO 74 REFER TO THE FOLLOWING REVIEW OF A FILM DOCUMENTARY.

What Does This Film Say About Italian Trains?

Line   In September 2002, there was a preview of a wonderful documentary film. It was called "Italy—from top to toe!" It was produced by Ursula Lewis Films, and ran 106 minutes. It showed wonderful camera work, and the commentary was lively and informative.

(5)   According to the film, trains are the way to go in Italy, and perhaps in Europe as a whole. Trains are cheap, convenient, and go everywhere. They also offer the opportunity to meet the Italians, who are almost always friendly, helpful, and informative.

Italian scenery is breathtaking and varied—from small hills to great Alpine peaks, *(10)* rolling farmlands, great old cities, huge beautiful lakes, a continuous coastline, and never-ending beautiful views of one kind or another—all of it to be seen from the comforts and luxury of an Italian train. All in all, it is an extremely colorful country in all possible ways.

The film showed some beautiful train rides. For example, the train ride from
(15) Locarno to Desenzano, in northern Italy, passes high over magnificent canyons, mountains, and river scenery. Also seen was the Cuneo to Breil ride, starting from Turin, which goes over countless viaducts and bridges. Also in the north, the documentary showed the many medieval castles and wild Alpine mountain scenery on the route between Bolzano and Brennero. Further south, the train ride from
(20) Naples to Siracusa, in Sicily, follows along the shores of the wonderful Mediterranean Sea, with the train going right onto a ferryboat and continuing on its way once on the other side.

Also shown were some magnificent train rides in Sicily. For example, along the coast from Messina to Taormina, with magnificent Mt. Etna in the background. Or,
(25) from Palermo going west to Trapani, the train passed alternately rugged rocky countryside and gently rolling hills, interspersed with the ancient Greek cities of Segesta and Erice. Then, it continued south to the well-known old city of Agrigento, with its many revered Greek temples.

We really recommend this documentary if you can catch it. Next to actually being
(30) on those trains, this is a great vicarious experience. See it! It will give you the wanderlust!

70. What is the main theme of this film review?

(1) The beauty of Italy's coastline
(2) European friendliness to tourists
(3) The wonderful experience of seeing Italy from a train
(4) Photographing Italy's colorful towns and scenery
(5) The people of Italy

71. Which of the following statements about Italian trains is true?

(1) Italy is completely covered with hills and mountains.
(2) Train travel is a good way to meet the friendly Italians.
(3) Italian trains are comfortable but expensive.
(4) There are very few really beautiful train rides in Italy.
(5) Some train rides are probably dangerous.

72. According to this piece, trains are the best means of transport for getting around Italy because they

(1) are very speedy and run frequently.
(2) serve delicious Italian food in the dining car.
(3) go to the most scenic areas.
(4) can easily cross all inaccessible and rustic mountains.
(5) go everywhere and are economical.

73. How does the train go into Sicily?

(1) It can't—Sicily is an island.
(2) It must go across the Sicily Bridge.
(3) It goes along the Adriatic coast.
(4) It gets driven onto a ferryboat.
(5) It goes from Naples to Brindisi.

74. What are "Locarno to Desenzano," "Bolzano to Brennero," and "Messina to Taormina"?

(1) Some of Italy's beautiful train routes
(2) Coastal cities in Italy
(3) Huge mountain ranges
(4) Northern Alpine peaks
(5) Sicilian regions

ANSWER KEY AND EXPLANATIONS

1. (3)	17. (1)	33. (3)	49. (4)	65. (5)
2. (3)	18. (1)	34. (5)	50. (4)	66. (2)
3. (4)	19. (2)	35. (4)	51. (2)	67. (3)
4. (2)	20. (5)	36. (2)	52. (3)	68. (4)
5. (5)	21. (1)	37. (5)	53. (3)	69. (5)
6. (3)	22. (1)	38. (2)	54. (5)	70. (3)
7. (5)	23. (4)	39. (3)	55. (1)	71. (2)
8. (2)	24. (2)	40. (1)	56. (2)	72. (5)
9. (1)	25. (3)	41. (4)	57. (4)	73. (4)
10. (4)	26. (3)	42. (5)	58. (4)	74. (1)
11. (2)	27. (2)	43. (3)	59. (2)	
12. (3)	28. (4)	44. (1)	60. (4)	
13. (3)	29. (1)	45. (1)	61. (1)	
14. (1)	30. (5)	46. (4)	62. (5)	
15. (2)	31. (1)	47. (2)	63. (3)	
16. (5)	32. (1)	48. (4)	64. (1)	

1. **The correct answer is (3).** Douglass uses the present tense and indicates that slavery still exists. Slavery was abolished in the United States just after the Civil War.

2. **The correct answer is (3).** He made the boys into teachers, and they taught him to read.

3. **The correct answer is (4).** These paragraphs are about learning to read.

4. **The correct answer is (2).** Douglass states the reason in the first sentence of the third paragraph.

5. **The correct answer is (5).** The final clause refers to Douglass's own will.

6. **The correct answer is (3).** The poet said that "she walks in beauty, like the night." The night is being personified because it is given the ability to walk like a living person.

7. **The correct answer is (5).** "The smiles that win, the tints that glow" tell of "days in goodness spent."

8. **The correct answer is (2).** A simile uses the words "like" or "as" to make a comparison: "She walks . . . like the night."

9. **The correct answer is (1).** The poet is certainly worshipful.

10. **The correct answer is (4).** There are several hints that this scene takes place on a ship, such as the use of "sir" toward Larsen, the reference to ship courtesy, and Johansen being described as "mate."

11. **The correct answer is (2).** Larsen is the leader and has authority over Johnson, as Johnson admits. We do not know exactly what rank Larsen has, though, but we can guess he is the captain. He does not act or talk like a policeman on duty.

12. **The correct answer is (3).** We know that Hump has strong feelings because he has argued bitterly against Larsen. He is not a coward because it is apparently dangerous to argue with Larsen. Yet we can infer Hump is not a strong man since he

does not go to Johnson's defense in the fight.

13. **The correct answer is (3).** Hump says that Larsen is a pauper because he has "no dreams, no ideals." Therefore, Larsen cannot be an idealist. We don't know if Larsen has money or not, or if his oilskins are worthless.

14. **The correct answer is (1).** Choice (2) is nearly correct, but is only part of Larsen's system of life. He might admit he was wrong if such a confession didn't threaten him. He certainly has no use for the ideals for nobility. Therefore, it is choice (1) that sums up what he believes in.

15. **The correct answer is (2).** The other three answers are partly right, but only choice (2) is completely true. Larsen is brutal, but he is not stupid. He is intellectual, but he is not lenient. He is stern, but not gentle. He has a low opinion of men so he is cynical. That he is cruel is obvious.

16. **The correct answer is (5).** The phrases "Mother of Exiles," "worldwide welcome," and "send these, the homeless . . . to me" are positive and proud and indicate that the poet is eager to tell the world about "this land of opportunity." The poem could easily be twisted and be used by advocates of restrictive immigration, but that is clearly not the intent of the poet.

17. **The correct answer is (1).** America is a *new* colossus, symbolized by "a mighty woman with a torch," the Statue of Liberty.

18. **The correct answer is (1).** This is a sonnet, a 14-line poem with a specific rhyming scheme.

19. **The correct answer is (2).** The phrase suggests that only poor people seek refuge. The idea that immigrants to America are wretched or unwanted in their own countries is certainly not always true.

20. **The correct answer is (5).** The tone is exalted, uplifting, ringing.

21. **The correct answer is (1).** The key word in the third sentence is "disembarked."

22. **The correct answer is (1).** The feeling is that of pity and sorrow for the fallen soldiers of both sides.

23. **The correct answer is (4).** The number of dead and the continuing pattern of firing indicates that the battle has been going on for some time.

24. **The correct answer is (2).** The war horrifies and disgusts the writer.

25. **The correct answer is (3).** The whole piece is an expression of sorrow about the terrible effects of war on the young soldiers involved, as well as those who follow them.

26. **The correct answer is (3).** The first paragraph reviews Adrienne Dugger's performance in "Turandot" and discusses her strengths. The second paragraph speaks of the current quality of the Metropolitan Opera performances.

27. **The correct answer is (2).** She was apparently the understudy who had to cover for an ailing singer. The reviewer praises her wonderful singing and her excellent portrayal of the lead character.

28. **The correct answer is (4).** The writer praises the Metropolitan Opera for all three reasons: the good acting (Bryn Terfel's "rapacious thug" characterization of Don Giovanni), the "thoughtful" productions, and the "broadened" repertory.

29. **The correct answer is (1).** These are the names of operas, as mentioned in the second paragraph. "Don Giovanni" was the opening night production. "Fidelio" is mentioned in the middle of the second paragraph as starring Karita Mattila.

30. **The correct answer is (5).** The writer makes the point that post-Pavarotti, or current younger singers, are really acting well and figuring out their roles for themselves instead of acting in more traditional ways. The word "cliches" as used here refers to the customary ways of doing things on stage.

31. **The correct answer is (1).** The poet states the athlete "won your town the race" and several times refers to running.

32. **The correct answer is (1).** You know by the title of the poem that the athlete has died. The whole implication of the second stanza is that he is being carried on his funeral day.

33. **The correct answer is (3).** If this is the athlete's funeral day, it becomes obvious that "stiller town" stands for death.

34. **The correct answer is (5).** The poet states that the athlete won the big race in the first stanza, that he broke the record in the fourth stanza, and since he is the champion, the laurel of victory is his. But he does not necessarily praise him for these things. However, he calls him a "smart lad, to slip betimes away" to die.

35. **The correct answer is (4).** Choices (1) and (2) are obviously false. We don't know if choice (3) is true or not. But the poet states that "Now you will not swell the rout of lads that wore their honors out" and says the athlete is smart to leave "fields where glory does not stay."

36. **The correct answer is (2).** The image presented of a young athlete who dies while at the height of his capabilities creates a somber tone to this poem.

37. **The correct answer is (5).** The purpose is to make clear what the rules, or legalities, are when you park your car in this garage. Since non-running cars, trucks, and vans can't be kept there, choices (3) and (4) are clearly wrong. Since the lease states it's not responsible for damage to the cars, choice (2) is incorrect. While the lease does establish the fee, choice (1) is also not correct since it's an incomplete description of what the lease accomplishes.

38. **The correct answer is (2).** Section 4 states that trucks may not be stored in this garage. There are no exceptions mentioned; therefore, choice (2) is the only correct answer.

39. **The correct answer is (3).** Paragraph (6) indicates that the garage is not "liable for any damage to the stored vehicle or its contents." So, Michael will have to be solely responsible for his loss.

40. **The correct answer is (1).** The second statement says that the cost is $1,200 per year, paid at the rate of $100 at the beginning of each month. Choice (5) states that rates may be increased. Therefore, choice (1) is the correct answer.

41. **The correct answer is (4).** According to the agreement, Derrick can only park his own car there. Since there is nothing that says he can't park a rental car, he should be able to do that if he can prove to the garage owner that it is truly his own rental and not someone else's. The other choices are clearly against the rules given.

42. **The correct answer is (5).** Stanza 2 is all about the passage of time.

43. **The correct answer is (3).** Only "forefathers" has the correct connotation here.

44. **The correct answer is (1).** The purpose is clearly to commemorate the embattled farmers of Concord and their quest "to leave their children free."

answers exercises

45. The correct answer is (1). Time and Nature are given human traits; that means that this is an example of personification.

46. The correct answer is (4). A "votive stone" implies a memorial stone of some kind. A dedication of this monument was taking place, so that future generations would remember the event.

47. The correct answer is (2). The implication is that this shot led to other major events and so was a decisive shot with great and universal importance.

48. The correct answer is (4). Undershaft is a maker of cannon. Lady Britomart's address of "Charles!!!" might well come from an embarrassed wife, but without more information, she might also be his mother or a stern aunt.

49. The correct answer is (4). It is hypocritical, because he degrades it while acknowledging its necessity.

50. The correct answer is (4). Undershaft tells how he danced in the streets for pennies, indicating a childhood of poverty.

51. The correct answer is (2). We can infer that "tosh" means "nonsense" by the phrase "on the other hand," which indicates that "tosh" must be a contrast to the description that comes after it. Although there may be a certain amount of *tosh* in the Salvation Army, it is still religion.

52. The correct answer is (3). As a member of the Salvation Army, Barbara is in charge of a "shelter" for indigents or derelicts. She is obviously interested in doing good.

53. The correct answer is (3). Weir appears to be a region, perhaps in England, with a lake and a "ghoul-haunted woodland." It is the setting of events about to be described by the poet.

54. The correct answer is (5). Words like "night" and "ghoul-haunted" suggest a feeling of suspense and mystery. The lines appear to be the beginning of a narrative poem, which is a poem that tells a story. The lines are not meaningless, and do not suggest a feeling of boredom.

55. The correct answer is (1). Poe uses words like "withering," "lonesome," "misty," and "ghoul-haunted" to establish an atmosphere of mystery and horror.

56. The correct answer is (2). "Immemorial" means "beyond memory." But this is poetry, and Poe has used poetic license to use "immemorial" to mean "most memorable." It is obvious from the poem that the poet remembers the year well.

57. The correct answer is (4). These words establish the haunted mood of the setting.

58. The correct answer is (4). The author uses short sentences, long sentences, and descriptive words such as "saltless" and "lumpy" to get the reader's attention. Choice (1) is incorrect because we have no way of knowing whether or not this story is based on the author's own experience. Choice (2) is wrong because most readers may not have had a childhood like Lewy's. The opening does not explain the advantages or disadvantages of Lewy's life, choice (3), or explain Lewy's behavior, choice (5).

59. The correct answer is (2). This choice describes Lewy's life most effectively. The "faded silk tassel" indicates how his mother tried to bring some beauty into the home, but it has faded with the father's departure. "Cracks in the wall" describes their present poverty.

60. The correct answer is (4). The final paragraph indicates Lewy's love for his mother.

61. The correct answer is (1). The author admires Mrs. Clement for doing such a fine job raising her son despite her own sorrow at the breakup of her marriage (see paragraph 2). Even though she works long hours, she has managed to keep her son well-fed, clean, and happy.

62. The correct answer is (5). Although his mother left him to go to work, she took care of his needs as best she could before she left. Little Lewy apparently understood the need for her to be away from him. The story presents him as a happy, well looked-after child.

63. The correct answer is (3). Lewy is certainly a "latchkey" child, according to the facts presented in this story. His mother left for work early, and he used his "latchkey" to get in and out of his house by himself.

64. The correct answer is (1). The first half of this selection is full of humor, such as "Dying before your dinner? Oh, poor Mahmoud Ali!" Then, the passage becomes more sarcastic and bitter as the guests speak of more serious matters.

65. The correct answer is (5). The sentence "Yielding at last, the tobacco jetted up into his lungs" tells us that a "hookah" is used for smoking tobacco.

66. The correct answer is (2). The other guest, Mahmoud Ali, is the first to address the newcomer by his name, which is Dr. Aziz.

67. The correct answer is (3). The mention of servants preparing their dinner while they converse leisurely on the veranda, or porch, suggests that this is a prosperous home.

68. The correct answer is (4). The discussion indicates that, back home in England, the English treat their guests with due respect, while here in another country, they gradually seem unable to do so.

69. The correct answer is (5). The men discuss how the English treat them in a friendly, trusting manner one day, then become rude the next. This suggests that they are not dependable as friends.

70. The correct answer is (3). The film review is about seeing Italy by train, which is described as a comfortable and practical means of transportation.

71. The correct answer is (2). The writer indicates in the second paragraph that the trains in Italy provide a good chance to meet the local people.

72. The correct answer is (5). The second paragraph of this review states that trains are "cheap, convenient, and go everywhere." There is no suggestion of their being speedy, running frequently, serving food, or that they are the best way to get into scenic or rustic areas.

73. The correct answer is (4). In the fourth paragraph, in describing the Naples to Siracusa trip, we are told that the train goes "right onto a ferryboat" on the way to Sicily. There is no mention of a bridge.

74. The correct answer is (1). These are among the examples given of the beautiful train routes that a tourist can enjoy in Italy, as shown in the film and as described by the reviewer. They are mentioned in the fourth and fifth paragraphs of this review.

ERROR ANALYSIS FOR PRACTICE READING QUESTIONS

Circle the number of each question you answered incorrectly. Count the number of circles in each content area and write the total number missed in the column headed "No. Incorrect." A large number of incorrect responses in a particular area indicates the need for further study in that area.

BY CONTENT	QUESTIONS	NO. INCORRECT
Drama and Poetry	6, 7, 8, 9, 16, 17, 18, 19, 20, 31, 32, 33, 34, 35, 36, 42, 43, 44, 45, 46, 47, 48, 49, 50, 51, 52, 53, 54, 55, 56, 57	
Fiction	10, 11, 12, 13, 14, 15, 21, 22, 23, 24, 25, 58, 59, 60, 61, 62, 63, 64, 65, 66, 67, 68, 69	
Nonfiction	1, 2, 3, 4, 5, 26, 27, 28, 29, 30, 70, 71, 72, 73, 74	
Business Documents	37, 38, 39, 40, 41	

SUMMING IT UP

What You Need to Know about the GED Language Arts, Reading Test

- The test consists of selections drawn from fiction and nonfiction passages.

- There are approximately 7 passages with 40 multiple-choice questions.

- The passages come from books, short stories, magazine of newspaper articles, or business or practical documents. The passages include readings from poetry, drama, fiction, and nonfiction prose.

- The questions fall into one of the following categories: comprehension, application, analysis, or synthesis.

PART VII

MATHEMATICS REVIEW

CHAPTER 8   All About the GED
            Mathematics Test

All About the GED Mathematics Test

OVERVIEW

- Quick Tips!
- Taking the GED mathematics test
- Introduction to using the calculator
- How to mark your answer sheet
- Fractions
- Decimals
- Percents
- Shortcuts in multiplication and division
- Powers and roots
- Table of measures
- Denominate numbers (measurement)
- Statistics and probability
- Graphs
- Payroll
- Sequences
- Operations with algebraic expressions: vocabulary
- Equations, inequalities, and problems in algebra
- Geometry and trigonometry
- Coordinate geometry
- Summing it up

QUICK TIPS!

In order to improve your math, it is very easy to practice daily in an informal way.

For example, when you are shopping for a few items in a grocery or clothing store, you could add up the cost mentally before coming to the cash register to see how close you can get to the actual amount.

Or, when you are going a long distance by car, ask yourself how much the trip is costing you (in gas, tolls, etc.), and also, how long the trip will take relative to the speed you're going.

In making a dress or in knitting a sweater, figure out how much material or yarn you will need.

On all of these and many other occasions, think in terms of using numbers, and you will become very good at doing mental arithmetic. This will put you at ease and make it much easier to study for tests such as the mathematics test on the GED.

TAKING THE GED MATHEMATICS TEST

The questions in the GED Mathematics Test are based on short readings or on graphs, charts, tables, or diagrams.

They will stress higher-level thinking (applications, analysis, and evaluation) as well as problem-solving ability. Special emphasis will be placed on realistic situations such as those found in home, consumer, civics, and workplace contexts. Many solutions will require multiple-step solutions.

Sometimes, a problem will not give enough information to solve it. In that case, the answer will be "not enough information is given." At other times, unneeded information will be given, so be sure to read the problem carefully.

The math test will be divided into two parts. The first part will allow the use of a scientific calculator provided to you at the time of the test. It will be a Casio FX-260 Solar model. You will be given an instruction sheet explaining how to use the calculator and a short time in which to familiarize yourself with the calculator.

Each of the major skills necessary to successfully answer the GED Mathematics questions is presented in this section along with helpful exercises.

INTRODUCTION TO USING THE CALCULATOR

Since half the math questions on the GED will allow you to use a calculator, it is important to become familiar with its use. Typical problems in which calculators may help you to more quickly reach an answer may include:

- Addition of decimals: $12.34 + 5.67 + 890.12 + 3.45 =$

- Addition of fractions: $12\frac{3}{4} + 5\frac{6}{7} =$

- Finding square roots: $\sqrt{8}$

The following section will introduce you to the calculator by explaining:

- how to get started using your calculator;
- what are the most *important keys* you will need to know for the test.

Important:

Your calculator will be an aid to you in taking Part 1 of the GED Math Test. However, using it may be tricky and require your full understanding of its operation. Practice using the calculator on the Application and Practice Problems given below, as well as in the actual test problems in this book. It is important to familiarize yourself with its individual features and to learn how you can effectively use it to solve problems. The more you practice, the more successful you will become in mastering the math portion of the GED.

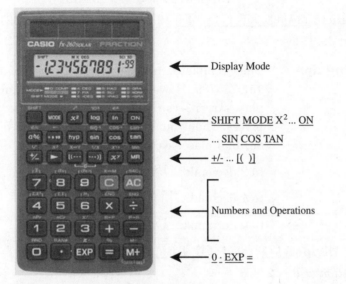

Display Mode

SHIFT MODE X^2... ON

... SIN COS TAN

+/- ... [( )]

Numbers and Operations

0 · EXP =

Getting Started Using Your Calculator

A Typical Scientific Calculator: The Casio FX-260 Solar Model

Knowing how to use the following keys will help you get started using your calculator.

❶ The *ON key* (top right): If the display screen is blank, say when you first open the calculator, by hitting the ON key, a "0." appears in the display and you are ready to begin.

❷ The *Number keys:* 0, 1, 2, 3, 4, 5, 6, 7, 8, 9

❸ The *Decimal point:* Use to write decimal numbers like, $26.95 or 3.141592654

❹ The *red "C"* or correction key: If you make an error, inadvertently hitting a wrong number, then hitting the C key will clear the last number from the screen. You may then continue your calculation.

❺ The *red "AC"* correction key: This is the "All Clear" button. When you have completed a calculation, pushing the AC button will erase the numbers on the display, leaving a "0." displayed. You are now ready to begin the next calculation.

Getting to Know the Important Calculator Keys

You are now ready to begin doing basic calculations with your calculator.

The calculator has many keys with which you can do all sorts of problems. The following will be the most helpful to you in mastering the GED.

Note: Throughout this part, when you see the word ⒸⒶⓁⒸⓊⓁⒶⓉⓄⓇ written at the beginning of a line, please refer to your calculator buttons.

Add, Subtract ⒸⒶⓁⒸⓊⓁⒶⓉⓄⓇ   **Keys → + −**

Illustration a: 3 + 4 − 5

Application: ⒸⒶⓁⒸⓊⓁⒶⓉⓄⓇ 3 + 4 − 5 =

Answer: 2

Illustration b: (Rounding off an answer)

$$12.3456789 + 8.76 - 5.4321$$

Application: ⒸⒶⓁⒸⓊⓁⒶⓉⓄⓇ 12.3456789 ₁ 8.76 − 5.4321 =

Answer: 15.6735 . . .

Test-taking tip: The complete number appearing in the display is 15.6735789. However, when writing the answer in the display screen, you need only include the first 4 decimal places. Then round off as required based on the number of decimal places called for in the answer:

to 2 decimals: 15.67~~35~~   15.67

to 1 decimal: 15.6~~735~~   15.7

to 0 decimals: 15~~.6735~~   16

Multiply, Divide ⒸⒶⓁⒸⓊⓁⒶⓉⓄⓇ   **Keys → × ÷**

Illustration a: 8 ÷ 2 × 3

Application: ⒸⒶⓁⒸⓊⓁⒶⓉⓄⓇ 8 ÷ 2 × 3 =

Answer: 12

Illustration b: (Order of Operation)

$$3 \times 4 + 5 - 8 \div 2$$

Application: ⒸⒶⓁⒸⓊⓁⒶⓉⓄⓇ 3 × 4 + 5 − 8 ÷ 2 =

Answer: 13

ⒸⒶⓁⒸⓊⓁⒶⓉⓄⓇ *Note: The Casio FX-260 Solar calculator will automatically perform multiplication and division *before* it does addition and subtraction.

Signed numbers ⒸⒶⓁⒸⓊⓁⒶⓉⓄⓇ   **Key → N +/-**

Illustration: 3.87 + (−2.64)

Application: ⒸⒶⓁⒸⓊⓁⒶⓉⓄⓇ 3.87 + 2.64 +/- =

Answer: 1.23

*Note: N stands for number.

ⒸⒶⓁⒸⓊⓁⒶⓉⓄⓇ *Note: 1.23 is actually obtained by pressing the individual numbers, and decimal points, and function keys one-at-a-time like: 3.87 + 2.64 +/− =

Pi C A L C U L A T O R   **Key → SHIFT EXP**

Illustration: $\pi \times 4.32$

Application: C A L C U L A T O R SHIFT EXP $\times$ 4.32 =

Answer: 13.5716 . . .

Parenthesis C A L C U L A T O R **[(N * N)]**

Illustration a: $(2 + 4)(2 + 5)$

Application: C A L C U L A T O R $(2 + 4) \times (2 + 5)$ =

Answer: 42

*Note: Don't forget to include a "multiplication" sign, between the two parentheses.

Illustration b: $27 - (60 \div 6 + 5)$

Application: C A L C U L A T O R $27 - (60 \div 6 + 5)$ =

Answer: 12

Illustration c: $4 + (6 \times 3)$

Application: C A L C U L A T O R $4 + (6 \times 3)$ =

Answer: 22

        or alternatively,

Illustration: C A L C U L A T O R $4 + 6 \times 3$ =

Answer: 22

*Note: Parentheses *are not always necessary*. Here, the Casio FX-260 calculator automatically follows the Order of Operations rule: multiplication is done before addition.

Squaring N C A L C U L A T O R   **Key → N X^2**

Illustration: 3×5^2

Application: C A L C U L A T O R $3 \times 5\, X^2$ =

Answer: 75

Square Root of N C A L C U L A T O R   **Key → N shift X^2**

Illustration: $\sqrt{(4 + 5)}$

Application: C A L C U L A T O R $(4 + 5)$ shift X^2 =

Answer: 3

Trigonometric Ratios

sin A CALCULATOR   **Key → A sin**

   Illustration: sin 30°

   Application: CALCULATOR 30 sin

   Answer: 0.5

cos B CALCULATOR   **Key → B cos**

   Illustration: cos 30°

   Application: CALCULATOR 30 cos

   Answer: 0.8660 . . .

tan C CALCULATOR   **Key → C tan**

   Illustration: tan 30°

   Application: CALCULATOR 30 tan

   Answer: 0.5773 . . .

FORMULAS

Description	Formula
AREA (A) of a:	
square	$A = s^2$; where s = side
rectangle	$A = lw$; where l = length, w = width
parallelogram	$A = bh$; where b = base, h = height
triangle	$A = \frac{1}{2} bh$; where b = base, h = height
circle	$A = \pi r^2$; where π = 3.14, r = radius
PERIMETER (P) of a:	
square	$P = 4s$; where s = side
rectangle	$P = 2l + 2w$; where l = length, w = width
triangle	$P = a + b + c$; where a, b, and c are the sides
Circumference (C) of a circle	$C = \pi d$; where π = 3.14, d = diameter
VOLUME (V) of a:	
cube	$V = s^3$; where s = side
rectangular container	$V = lwh$; where l = length, w = width, h = height
cylinder	$V = \pi r^2 h$; where π = 3.14, r = radius, h = height
square pyramid	Volume $= \frac{1}{3} \times (\text{base edge})^2 \times \text{height}$
cone	Volume $= \frac{1}{3} \times \pi \times \text{radius}^2 \times \text{height}$; π is approximately equal to 3.14.
Pythagorean theorem	$c^2 = a^2 + b^2$; where c = hypotenuse, a and b are legs of a right triangle
distance (d) between two points in a plane	$d = \sqrt{(x_2 - x_1)^2 + (y_2 - y_1)^2}$; where (x_1, y_1) and (x_2, y_2) are two points in a plane
slope of a line (m)	$m = \dfrac{y_2 - y_1}{x_2 - x_1}$ where (x_1, y_1) and (x_2, y_2) are two points in a plane
trigonometric ratios	given an acute angle with measure x of a right triangle, $\sin x = \dfrac{\text{opposite}}{\text{hypotenuse}}$, $\cos x = \dfrac{\text{adjacent}}{\text{hypotenuse}}$, $\tan x = \dfrac{\text{opposite}}{\text{adjacent}}$
mean	mean $= \dfrac{x_1 + x_2 + \cdots + x_n}{n}$; where the x's are the values for which a mean is desired, and n = number of values in the series
median	median = the point in an ordered set of numbers at which half of the numbers are above and half of the numbers are below this value
simple interest (i)	$i = prt$; where p = principal, r = rate, t = time
distance (d) as function of rate and time	$d = rt$; where r = rate, t = time
total cost (c)	$c = nr$; where n = number of units, r = cost per unit

EXERCISES: USING THE CALCULATOR

With the help of the Formula page and your calculator, answer the following questions. Check your answers with the Answer Explanations following this practice exercise.

Test-taking tip: Try to mentally estimate your answers to check whether the results you got with the calculator seem reasonable and that you didn't inadvertently press the wrong key.

1. Shopping: Joan went shopping and spent $2.15 for bread, $12.93 for meat, $8.36 for vegetables and potatoes, and $9.86 for dessert. How much did she spend in total?

   (1) $21.66
   (2) $31.23
   (3) $33.30
   (4) $41.30
   (5) $52.65

2. Change: Jessie gave the cashier $50 for a $28.92 meal with $2.39 tax. How much change should he receive?

   (1) $18.69
   (2) $23.47
   (3) $28.69
   (4) $76.53
   (5) $81.31

3. Balancing a checkbook: Jane began the month with $567.89. During the month she deposited a total of $520, and wrote a total of $98.76 in checks. What was her balance at the end of the month?

   (1) $50.87
   (2) $146.65
   (3) $989.13
   (4) $1,000.00
   (5) $1,186.65

4. Circumference: The circumference of the clock was 42 inches. Find the diameter in inches.

   (1) 7.5
   (2) 13.4
   (3) 38.9
   (4) 45.14
   (5) 131.9

5. Distance between points on a graph: Find the distance between the following coordinate points: (7,5) and (2, −3).

   (1) 3.6
   (2) 5.4
   (3) 7.9
   (4) 9.4
   (5) 10.6

ITEM 6 REFERS TO THE DIAGRAM BELOW.

6. Right triangles:

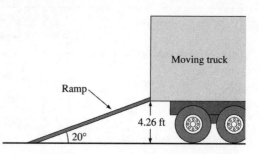

A ramp is placed on the back of a moving truck, 4.26 feet above the ground (see diagram above). If the angle it makes with the ground is 20°, then what is the length of the ramp?

   (1) 1.5
   (2) 4.5
   (3) 10.2
   (4) 11.7
   (5) 12.5

ANSWER KEY AND EXPLANATIONS

1. (3)	3. (3)	5. (4)
2. (1)	4. (2)	6. (5)

1. **The correct answer is (3).** Add the four items.

   `CALCULATOR` 2.15 + 12.93 + 8.36 + 9.86 =

   [Answer: she spent **$33.30**]

   As a quick "mental check," estimate the items by rounding to the nearest dollar as follows:

   2 + 13 + 8 + 10 = 33 (The estimate *is close to the answer*. Okay.)

2. **The correct answer is (1).** Subtract the sum of the meal and the tax from the $50.00.

   `CALCULATOR` 50.00 − (28.92 + 2.39) =

   [Answer: the change is **$18.69**]

   As a check, estimate the answer by rounding off each item to the nearest dollar.

   50 − (29 + 2) = 19 (The estimate *is close to the answer*. Okay.)

3. **The correct answer is (3).** From the initial balance ($567.89) add the deposits and subtract the checks.

   `CALCULATOR` 567.89 + 520 − 98.76 =

   [Answer: her balance was $ **989.13**]

4. **The correct answer is (2).** From the Formula page, the Circumference of a circle, $C = \pi \times diameter$

   $C = \pi \times d$; Dividing both sides by π: $d = \dfrac{C}{\pi}$

   `CALCULATOR` 42 ÷ SHIFT EXP =

   [Answer: the diameter is 13.3690; rounded to **13.4** inches]

5. **The correct answer is (4).**

The distance between two points $\sqrt{(x_2 - x_1)^2 + (y_2 - y_1)^2}$

The two points* are: Point 1 $(x_1, y_1) = (7,5)$

Point 2 $(x_2, y_2) = (2, -3)$

[*Note: It doesn't matter which of the two points is Point 1 or Point 2.]

By substituting, $\sqrt{(2 - 7)^2 + (-3 - 5)^2}$

$\boxed{\text{CALCULATOR}}$ [(2 − 7) X^2 + (3 +/− 5) X^2)] SHIFT X^2 =

[Answer is 9.4339, rounded to **9.4** inches]

6. **The correct answer is (5).** The ratio that relates to the angle 20°, the side opposite it (4.26), and the hypotenuse (length of the ramp, R) is $\sin 20° = \dfrac{4.26}{R}$; Multiplying both sides by R: $R \times \sin 20° = 4.26$

Dividing both sides by $\sin 20°$,

$\boxed{\text{CALCULATOR}}$ 4.26 ÷ 20 sin =

[Answer: the ramp is 12.4554 . . .; rounded to **12.5** feet]

HOW TO MARK YOUR ANSWER SHEET

The answer sheet is divided into two separate parts: in Part 1, you are permitted to use a calculator; in Part 2, you are not. All answers require you to shade in appropriate circles that represent the correct answer. There are three different types of answers:

Answer type 1—multiple choice: These are regular format questions requiring multiple-choice answers. They require you to fill in the circle that represents *the correct choice*: 1, 2, 3, 4, or 5.

Answer type 2—standard grid: These are alternate format questions requiring you to fill in the circles representing the *correct number, including decimal or divisor signs where appropriate* (for example, 3.14, 22/7, etc.).

Answer type 3—coordinate plane grid: These are alternate format questions requiring you to fill in the circles representing the *coordinates of the solution to a graph item* [for example, (3,5), (−2,6), etc.].

Now let us try to do an example of *each type of answer* mentioned above and practice writing the answer in the answer sheet provided.

Sample problems using the answer sheets on pages 465 and 466

PART 1 (CALCULATOR IS PERMITTED)

Sample problem A. This is a regular format, multiple-choice type question.

1. Find the average of the following numbers: 12.34, 23.45, 32.10

   (1) 26.23
   (2) 22.63
   (3) 36.22
   (4) 63.22
   (5) 36.23

   The correct answer is (2).

Sample problem B. This is an alternate format, standard grid-type question.

4. The area of a circular swimming pool is 700.0 ft^2. Find its radius. Give your answer to one decimal place.
   Mark your answer in the circles in the grid on your answer sheet.

   The correct answer is 14.9 feet.

Sample problem C. This is an alternate format, coordinate plane grid-type question.

17.   Item 17 refers to the following graph showing triangle ABC.

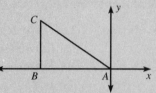

If the coordinates of B are $(-5,0)$, and angle BAC is $38.6°$, find the coordinates of point C. [Round off the coordinates to the nearest whole numbers.]

DO NOT MARK THE POINT ON THE GRAPH ABOVE.

Mark your answer on the coordinate plane grid on your answer sheet.

The correct answer is $(-5, 4)$.

Part 2 (no calculator permitted)

Sample problem D. This is a regular format, multiple-choice type question.

26.   How much change in dollars should John get if he paid the salesperson $100.00 for a $59.95 printer?

   (1) $39.95
   (2) $40.05
   (3) $41.10
   (4) $49.95
   (5) $51.15

The correct answer is (2).

Sample problem E. This is an alternate format standard grid-type question.

31.   Maria made a 24-hour pie chart describing her weekday time schedule. What is the total fraction of her day budgeted if she has already budgeted $\frac{3}{8}$, $\frac{1}{5}$, and $\frac{1}{4}$ of her pie chart?
   Mark your answer in the circles in the grid on your answer sheet.

The correct answer is $\frac{33}{40}$.

Sample problem F. This is an alternate format coordinate plane grid-type question.

---

37. A system of two linear equations is given below.

$$x + 3y = 0$$
$$x + y = 4$$

What point represents the common solution for this system of equations?

DO NOT WRITE IN THIS TEST BOOKLET.

Mark your answer on the coordinate plane grid on your answer sheet.

The correct answer is (6, −2).

Answer sheet marked for selected sample problems

TEST 5: MATHEMATICS - PART 1

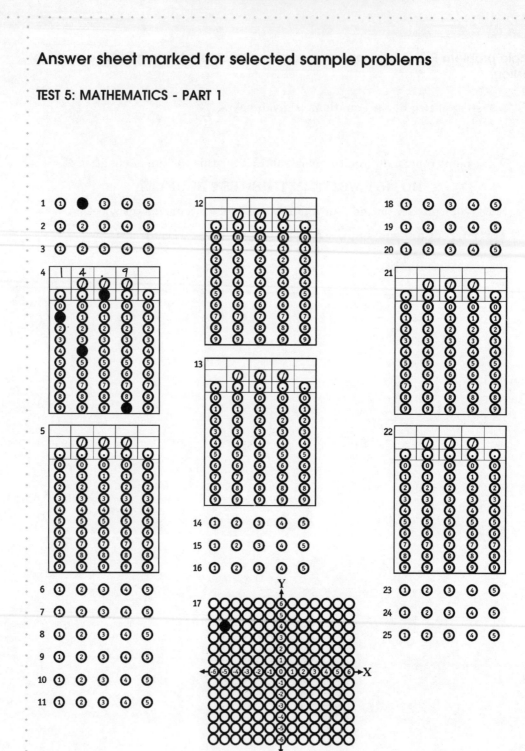

Please return your calculator.

TEST 5: MATHEMATICS - PART 2

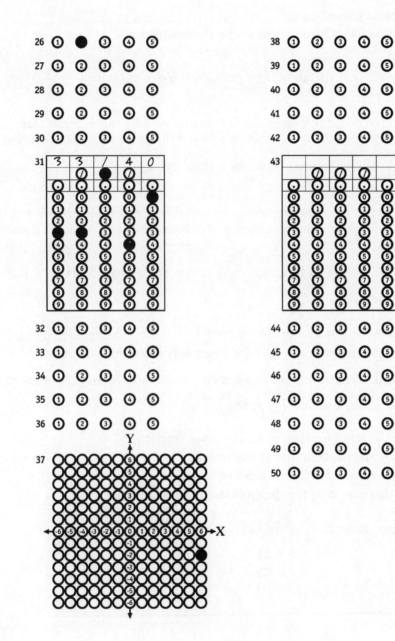

FRACTIONS

Fractions and Mixed Numbers

1. A **fraction** is part of a unit.
   a. A fraction has a **numerator** and a **denominator**.

In the fraction $\frac{3}{4}$, 3 is the numerator and 4 is the denominator.

    b. In any fraction, the numerator is being divided by the denominator.

The fraction $\frac{2}{7}$ indicates that 2 is being divided by 7.

    c. In a fraction problem, the whole quantity is 1, which may be expressed by a fraction in which the numerator and denominator are the same number.

If the problem involves $\frac{1}{8}$ of a quantity, then the whole quantity is $\frac{8}{8}$, or 1.

2. A **mixed number** is an integer together with a fraction, such as $2\frac{3}{5}$, $7\frac{3}{8}$, etc. The integer is the integral part, and the fraction is the fractional part.

3. An **improper fraction** is one in which the numerator is equal to or greater than the denominator, such as $\frac{19}{6}$, $\frac{25}{4}$, or $\frac{10}{10}$.

4. To rewrite a mixed number as an improper fraction:
   a. Multiply the denominator of the fraction by the integer.
   b. Add the numerator to this product.
   c. Place this sum over the denominator of the fraction.

Illustration: Rewrite $3\frac{4}{7}$ as an improper fraction.

Solution:
$$7 \times 3 = 21$$
$$21 + 4 = 25$$

$$3\frac{4}{7} = \frac{25}{7}$$

Answer: $\frac{25}{7}$

5. To rewrite an improper fraction as a mixed number:

    a. Divide the numerator by the denominator. The quotient, disregarding the remainder, is the whole number (integral) part of the mixed number.

    b. Place the remainder, if any, over the denominator. This is the fractional part of the mixed number.

    Illustration: Rewrite $\dfrac{36}{13}$ as a mixed number.

    Solution:

    $$\begin{array}{r} 2 \\ 13\overline{)36} \\ \underline{26} \\ 10 \end{array} \text{ remainder}$$

    $$\frac{36}{13} = 2\frac{10}{13}$$

    Answer: $2\dfrac{10}{13}$

6. The numerator and denominator of a fraction may be changed by multiplying both by the same number, without affecting the value of the fraction.

    The value of the fraction $\dfrac{2}{5}$ will not be altered if the numerator and the denominator are multiplied by 2, to result in $\dfrac{4}{10}$.

7. The numerator and the denominator of a fraction may be changed by dividing both by the same number, without affecting the value of the fraction. This process is called **simplifying the fraction**. A fraction that has been simplified as much as possible is said to be in **simplest form**.

    The value of the fraction $\dfrac{3}{12}$ will not be altered if the numerator and denominator are divided by 3, to result in $\dfrac{1}{4}$.

    If $\dfrac{6}{30}$ is simplified to simplest form (by dividing both numerator and denominator by 6), the result is $\dfrac{1}{5}$.

8. As a final answer to a problem:
   a. Improper fractions should be rewritten as mixed numbers.
   b. Fractions should be simplified to simplest form.

Addition of Fractions

9. Fractions cannot be added unless the denominators are all the same.
   a. If the denominators are the same, add all the numerators and place this sum over the common denominator. In the case of mixed numbers, follow the above rule for the fractions and then add the integers.

The sum of $2\dfrac{3}{8} + 3\dfrac{1}{8} + \dfrac{3}{8} = 5\dfrac{7}{8}$.

   b. If the denominators are not the same, the fractions, in order to be added, must be rewritten as ones having the same denominator. To do this, it is first necessary to find the least common denominator.

10. The **least common denominator** (henceforth called the LCD) is the least number that can be divided evenly by all the given denominators. If no two of the given denominators can be divided by the same number, then the LCD is the product of all the denominators.

The LCD of $\dfrac{1}{2}, \dfrac{1}{3}$, and $\dfrac{1}{5}$ is $2 \times 3 \times 5 = 30$.

11. To find the LCD when two or more of the given denominators can be divided by the same number:
    a. Write down the denominators, leaving plenty of space between the numbers.
    b. Select the least number (other than 1) by which one or more of the denominators can be divided evenly.
    c. Divide the denominators by this number, copying down those that cannot be divided evenly. Place this number to one side.
    d. Repeat this process, placing each divisor to one side until there are no longer any denominators that can be divided evenly by any selected number.
    e. Multiply all the divisors to find the LCD.

Illustration: Find the LCD of $\dfrac{1}{5}, \dfrac{1}{7}, \dfrac{1}{10}$, and $\dfrac{1}{14}$.
Solution:

$$
\begin{array}{ccccc}
 & 5 & 7 & \underline{10} & \underline{14} \\
(2) & 5 & 7 & \underline{5} & 7 \\
(5) & 1 & 7 & 1 & \underline{7} \\
(7) & 1 & 1 & 1 & 1 \\
\end{array}
$$
$$7 \times 5 \times 2 = 70$$

Answer: The LCD is 70.

12. To add fractions having different denominators:
    a. Find the LCD of the denominators.
    b. Rewrite each fraction as an equivalent fraction having the LCD as its denominator.
    c. When all of the fractions have the same denominator, they may be added, as in the example following item 9a.

    Illustration: Add $\frac{1}{4}$, $\frac{3}{10}$, and $\frac{2}{5}$.

    Solution: Find the LCD:

    $$
    \begin{array}{cccc}
    2) & 4 & 10 & 5 \\
    2) & \underline{2} & 5 & 5 \\
    5) & 1 & \underline{5} & 5 \\
       & 1 & 1 & 1
    \end{array}
    $$

    $$\text{LCD} = 2 \times 2 \times 5 = 20$$

    $$
    \begin{aligned}
    \frac{1}{4} &= \frac{5}{20} \\
    \frac{3}{10} &= \frac{6}{20} \\
    +\frac{2}{5} &= +\frac{8}{20} \\
    \hline
    &\quad\ \frac{19}{20}
    \end{aligned}
    $$

    Answer: $\frac{19}{20}$

13. To add mixed numbers in which the fractions have different denominators, add the fractions by following the rules in item 12 above, then add the integers.

    Illustration: Add $2\frac{5}{7}$, $5\frac{1}{2}$, and 8.

    Solution: LCD = 14

    $$
    \begin{aligned}
    2\frac{5}{7} &= 2\frac{10}{14} \\
    5\frac{1}{2} &= 5\frac{7}{14} \\
    +8 &= +8 \\
    \hline
    &\ 15\frac{17}{14} = 16\frac{3}{14}
    \end{aligned}
    $$

    Answer: $16\frac{3}{14}$

Subtraction of Fractions

14. a. Unlike addition, which may involve adding more than two numbers at the same time, subtraction involves only two numbers.

    b. In subtraction, as in addition, the denominators must be the same.

15. To subtract fractions:

    a. Find the LCD.

    b. Rewrite both fractions so that each has the LCD as the denominator.

    c. Subtract the numerator of the second fraction from the numerator of the first, and place this difference over the LCD.

    d. Simplify, if possible.

    Illustration: Find the difference of $\frac{5}{8}$ and $\frac{1}{4}$.

    Solution: LCD = 8

    $$\begin{array}{rcl} \frac{5}{8} &=& \frac{5}{8} \\ -\frac{1}{4} &=& -\frac{2}{8} \\ \hline && \frac{3}{8} \end{array}$$

    Answer: $\frac{3}{8}$

16. To subtract mixed numbers:

    a. It may be necessary to "borrow" so that the fractional part of the first term is greater than the fractional part of the second term.

    b. Subtract the fractional parts of the mixed numbers and simplify.

    c. Subtract the integers.

    Illustration: Subtract $16\frac{4}{5}$ from $29\frac{1}{3}$.

    Solution: LCD = 15

    $$\begin{array}{rcl} 29\frac{1}{3} &=& 29\frac{5}{15} \\ -16\frac{4}{5} &=& -16\frac{12}{15} \\ \hline \end{array}$$

    Note that $\frac{5}{15}$ is less than $\frac{12}{15}$. "Borrow" 1 from 29, and rewrite as $\frac{15}{15}$.

    $$\begin{array}{rcl} 29\frac{5}{15} &=& 28\frac{20}{15} \\ -16\frac{4}{5} &=& -16\frac{12}{15} \\ \hline && 12\frac{8}{15} \end{array}$$

    Answer: $12\frac{8}{15}$

Multiplication of Fractions

17. a. To be multiplied, fractions need not have the same denominators.
    b. A whole number has the denominator 1 understood.

18. To multiply fractions:
    a. Rewrite the mixed numbers, if any, as improper fractions.
    b. Multiply all the numerators, and place this product over the product of the denominators.
    c. Simplify, if possible.

    Illustration: Multiply $\frac{2}{3} \times 2\frac{4}{7} \times \frac{5}{9}$

    Solution:

    $$2\frac{4}{7} = \frac{18}{7}$$

    $$\frac{2}{3} \times \frac{18}{7} \times \frac{5}{9} = \frac{180}{189}$$

    $$= \frac{20}{21}$$

    Answer: $\frac{20}{21}$

19. a. **Dividing common factors** is a device to facilitate multiplication. This means to divide a numerator and a denominator by the same number in a multiplication problem.

    In the problem $\frac{4}{7} \times \frac{5}{6}$, the numerator 4 and the denominator 6 may be divided by 2.

    $$\frac{\overset{2}{\cancel{4}}}{7} \times \frac{5}{\underset{3}{\cancel{6}}} = \frac{10}{21}$$

    b. The word "of" is often used to mean "multiply."

    $$\frac{1}{2} \text{ of } \frac{1}{2} = \frac{1}{2} \times \frac{1}{2} = \frac{1}{4}$$

20. To multiply a whole number by a mixed number:
    a. Multiply the whole number by the fractional part of the mixed number.
    b. Multiply the whole number by the integral part of the mixed number.
    c. Add both products.

    Illustration: Multiply $23\frac{3}{4}$ by 95.

    Solution:

    $$\frac{95}{1} \times \frac{3}{4} = \frac{285}{4}$$

    $$= 71\frac{1}{4}$$

    $$95 \times 23 = 2185$$

    $$2185 + 71\frac{1}{4} = 2256\frac{1}{4}$$

    Answer: $2256\frac{1}{4}$

Division of Fractions

21. The **reciprocal** of a fraction is a fraction that when multiplied by the original fraction results in 1.

    a. In simplest terms, the reciprocal of a fraction is when the numerator becomes the denominator and the denominator becomes the numerator.

    The reciprocal of $\frac{3}{8}$ is $\frac{8}{3}$.

    The reciprocal of $\frac{1}{3}$ is $\frac{3}{1}$, or simply 3.

    b. Since every whole number has the denominator 1 understood, the reciprocal of a whole number is a fraction having 1 as the numerator and the number itself as the denominator.

    The reciprocal of 5 (expressed fractionally as $\frac{5}{1}$) is $\frac{1}{5}$.

22. To divide fractions:
    a. Rename all the mixed numbers, if any, as improper fractions.
    b. Multiply by the reciprocal of the second fraction.
    c. Simplify, if possible.

    Illustration: Divide $\frac{2}{3}$ by $2\frac{1}{4}$.

    Solution:

    $$2\frac{1}{4} = \frac{9}{4}$$

    $$\frac{2}{3} \div \frac{9}{4} = \frac{2}{3} \times \frac{4}{9}$$

    $$= \frac{8}{27}$$

    Answer: $\frac{8}{27}$

23. A **complex fraction** is one that has a fraction as the numerator, or as the denominator, or as both.

    $\dfrac{\frac{2}{3}}{\frac{5}{}}$ is a complex fraction.

24. To simplify a complex fraction:
    a. Divide the numerator by the denominator.
    b. Simplify, if possible.

    Illustration: Simplify $\dfrac{\frac{3}{7}}{\frac{5}{14}}$

    Solution:

    $$\frac{3}{7} \div \frac{5}{14} = \frac{3}{7} \times \frac{14}{5} = \frac{42}{35}$$

    $$= \frac{6}{5}$$

    $$= 1\frac{1}{5}$$

    Answer: $1\frac{1}{5}$

Comparing Fractions

25. If two fractions have the same denominator, the one having the greater numerator is the greater fraction.

$\frac{3}{7}$ is greater than $\frac{2}{7}$.

26. If two fractions have the same numerator, the one having the greater denominator is the least fraction.

$\frac{5}{12}$ is less than $\frac{5}{11}$.

27. To compare two fractions having different numerators and different denominators:

    a. Rewrite the fractions as equivalent fractions having their LCD as their new denominator.

    b. Compare, as in the example following item 25.

    Illustration: Compare $\frac{4}{7}$ and $\frac{5}{8}$.

    Solution: LCD = $7 \times 8 = 56$

    $$\frac{4}{7} = \frac{32}{56}$$
    $$\frac{5}{8} = \frac{35}{56}$$

    Answer: Since $\frac{35}{56}$ is greater than $\frac{32}{56}$, $\frac{5}{8}$ is greater than $\frac{4}{7}$.

Fraction Problems

28. Most fraction problems can be arranged in the form: "What fraction of a number is another number?" This form contains three important parts:

    • The fractional part
    • The number following "of"
    • The number following "is"

    a. If the fraction and the "of" number are given, multiply them to find the "is" number.

    Illustration: What is $\frac{3}{4}$ of 20?

    Solution: Write the question as "$\frac{3}{4}$ of 20 is what number?" Then multiply the fraction $\frac{3}{4}$ by the "of" number, 20:

    $$\frac{3}{\cancel{4}} \times \cancel{20}^{5} = 15$$

    Answer: 15

b. If the fractional part and the "is" number are given, divide the "is" number by the fraction to find the "of" number.

Illustration: $\frac{4}{5}$ of what number is 40?

Solution: To find the "of" number, divide 40 by $\frac{4}{5}$:

$$40 \div \frac{4}{5} = \frac{\overset{10}{\cancel{40}}}{1} \times \frac{5}{\underset{1}{\cancel{4}}}$$

$$= 50$$

Answer: 50

c. To find the fractional part when the other two numbers are known, divide the "is" number by the "of" number.

Illustration: What part of 12 is 9?

Solution:

$$9 \div 12 = \frac{9}{12}$$

$$= \frac{3}{4}$$

Answer: $\frac{3}{4}$

EXERCISES: FRACTIONS

1. Simplify to simplest form: $\frac{60}{108}$.

   (1) $\frac{1}{48}$

   (2) $\frac{1}{3}$

   (3) $\frac{20}{39}$

   (4) $\frac{10}{18}$

   (5) $\frac{5}{9}$

2. Rewrite $\frac{27}{7}$ as a mixed number.

   (1) $2\frac{1}{7}$

   (2) $3\frac{6}{7}$

   (3) $6\frac{1}{3}$

   (4) $7\frac{1}{2}$

   (5) 8

3. Rewrite $4\frac{2}{3}$ as an improper fraction.

   (1) $\frac{10}{3}$

   (2) $\frac{11}{3}$

   (3) $\frac{14}{3}$

   (4) $\frac{42}{3}$

   (5) $\frac{49}{3}$

4. Find the LCD of $\frac{1}{6}$, $\frac{1}{10}$, $\frac{1}{18}$, and $\frac{1}{21}$.

   (1) 160

   (2) 330

   (3) 630

   (4) 1260

   (5) 1420

5. Add $16\frac{3}{8}$, $4\frac{4}{5}$, $12\frac{3}{4}$, and $23\frac{5}{6}$.

   (1) $57\frac{91}{120}$

   (2) $57\frac{1}{4}$

   (3) 58

   (4) 59

   (5) 60

6. Subtract $27\frac{5}{14}$ from $43\frac{1}{6}$.

   (1) $15\frac{1}{48}$

   (2) $15\frac{7}{21}$

   (3) $15\frac{9}{21}$

   (4) $15\frac{17}{21}$

   (5) 17

7. Multiply $17\frac{5}{8}$ by 128.

   (1) 2200

   (2) 2205

   (3) 2240

   (4) 2256

   (5) 2400

8. Divide $1\frac{2}{3}$ by $1\frac{1}{9}$.

   (1) $\frac{2}{3}$

   (2) $1\frac{1}{2}$

   (3) $1\frac{23}{27}$

   (4) 6

   (5) $7\frac{23}{27}$

9. What is the value of $12\frac{1}{6} - 2\frac{3}{8} - 7\frac{2}{3} + 19\frac{3}{4}$?

   (1) 21

   (2) $21\frac{7}{8}$

   (3) $21\frac{8}{9}$

   (4) 22

   (5) 23

10. Simplify the complex fraction $\dfrac{\frac{4}{9}}{\frac{2}{5}}$.

   (1) $\frac{1}{2}$

   (2) $\frac{9}{10}$

   (3) $\frac{2}{5}$

   (4) $1\frac{8}{9}$

   (5) $1\frac{1}{9}$

11. Which fraction is greatest?

   (1) $\frac{9}{16}$

   (2) $\frac{7}{10}$

   (3) $\frac{5}{8}$

   (4) $\frac{4}{5}$

   (5) $\frac{3}{4}$

12. One brass rod measures $3\frac{5}{16}$ inches long and another brass rod measures $2\frac{3}{4}$ inches long. Together their length is

   (1) $\frac{9}{16}$

   (2) $5\frac{1}{8}$

   (3) $6\frac{1}{16}$

   (4) $7\frac{1}{16}$

   (5) $7\frac{1}{8}$

13. The number of half-pound packages of tea that can be weighed out of a box that holds $10\frac{1}{2}$ lbs. of tea is

   (1) 5

   (2) $10\frac{1}{2}$

   (3) $20\frac{1}{2}$

   (4) 21

   (5) $21\frac{1}{2}$

14. If each bag of tokens weighs $5\frac{3}{4}$ pounds, how many pounds do 3 bags weigh?

   (1) $7\frac{1}{4}$

   (2) $15\frac{3}{4}$

   (3) $16\frac{1}{2}$

   (4) $17\frac{1}{4}$

   (5) $17\frac{1}{2}$

exercises

15. During one week, a man traveled $3\frac{1}{2}$, $1\frac{1}{4}$, $1\frac{1}{6}$, and $2\frac{3}{8}$ miles. The next week he traveled $\frac{1}{4}$, $\frac{3}{8}$, $\frac{9}{16}$, $3\frac{1}{16}$, $2\frac{5}{8}$, and $3\frac{3}{16}$ miles. How many more miles did he travel the second week than the first week?

(1) $1\frac{37}{48}$

(2) $2\frac{1}{2}$

(3) $2\frac{3}{4}$

(4) 3

(5) $3\frac{5}{8}$

16. A certain type of board is sold only in lengths of multiples of 2 feet. The shortest board sold is 6 feet and the longest is 24 feet.

A builder needs a large quantity of this type of board in $5\frac{1}{2}$-foot lengths. For minimum waste, the lengths to be ordered should be

(1) 6 ft
(2) 12 ft
(3) 22 ft
(4) 24 ft
(5) 26 ft

17. A man spent $\frac{15}{16}$ of his entire fortune in buying a car for $7500. How much money did he possess?

(1) $6000
(2) $6500
(3) $7000
(4) $7500
(5) $8000

18. The population of a town was 54,000 in the last census. It has increased $\frac{2}{3}$ since then. Its present population is

(1) 18,000
(2) 36,000
(3) 72,000
(4) 80,000
(5) 90,000

19. If one third of the liquid contents of a can evaporates on the first day and three fourths of the remainder evaporates on the second day, the fractional part of the original contents remaining at the close of the second day is

(1) $\frac{5}{12}$

(2) $\frac{7}{12}$

(3) $\frac{1}{6}$

(4) $\frac{1}{2}$

(5) $\frac{3}{4}$

20. A car is run until the gas tank is $\frac{1}{8}$ full. The tank is then filled to capacity by putting in 14 gallons. The capacity of the gas tank of the car is

(1) 14
(2) 15
(3) 16
(4) 17
(5) 18

ANSWER KEY AND EXPLANATIONS

1. (5)	6. (4)	11. (4)	16. (3)
2. (2)	7. (4)	12. (3)	17. (5)
3. (3)	8. (2)	13. (4)	18. (5)
4. (3)	9. (2)	14. (4)	19. (3)
5. (1)	10. (5)	15. (1)	20. (3)

1. The correct answer is (5).

Divide the numerator and denominator by 12:

$$\frac{60 \div 12}{108 \div 12} = \frac{5}{9}$$

One alternate method (there are several) is to divide the numerator and denominator by 6 and then by 2:

$$\frac{60 \div 6}{108 \div 6} = \frac{10}{18}$$

$$\frac{10 \div 2}{18 \div 2} = \frac{5}{9}$$

2. The correct answer is (2).

Divide the numerator (27) by the denominator (7):

$$7)\overline{27} \quad \begin{array}{c} 3 \\ \end{array}$$
$$\underline{21}$$
$$6 \text{ remainder}$$

$$\frac{27}{7} = 3\frac{6}{7}$$

3. The correct answer is (3).

$$4 \times 3 = 12$$
$$12 + 2 = 14$$
$$4\frac{2}{3} = \frac{14}{3}$$

4. The correct answer is (3).

2)	6	10	18	21	(2 is a divisor of 6, 10, and 18)
3)	3	5	9	21	(3 is a divisor of 3, 9, and 21)
3)	1	5	3	7	(3 is a divisor of 3)
5)	1	5	1	7	(5 is a divisor of 5)
7)	1	1	1	7	(7 is a divisor of 7)
	1	1	1	1	

$$\text{LCD} = 2 \times 3 \times 3 \times 5 \times 7 = 630$$

5. The correct answer is (1).

$$\text{LCD} = 120$$

$$16\frac{3}{8} = 16\frac{45}{120}$$
$$4\frac{4}{5} = 4\frac{96}{120}$$
$$12\frac{3}{4} = 12\frac{90}{120}$$
$$+23\frac{5}{6} = 23\frac{100}{120}$$
$$\overline{\phantom{+23\frac{5}{6}} \quad 55\frac{331}{120} = 57\frac{91}{120}}$$

answers exercises

6. The correct answer is (4).

LCD = 42

$$43\frac{1}{6} = 43\frac{7}{42} = 42\frac{49}{42}$$
$$-27\frac{5}{14} = -27\frac{15}{42} = -27\frac{15}{42}$$
$$15\frac{34}{42} = 15\frac{17}{21}$$

7. The correct answer is (4).

$$17\frac{5}{8} = \frac{141}{8}$$

$$\frac{141}{\cancel{8}} \times \frac{\cancel{128}^{16}}{1} = 2256$$

8. The correct answer is (2).

$$1\frac{2}{3} \div 1\frac{1}{9} = \frac{5}{3} \div \frac{10}{9}$$
$$= \frac{\cancel{5}^{1}}{\cancel{3}_{1}} \times \frac{\cancel{9}^{3}}{\cancel{10}_{2}}$$
$$= \frac{3}{2}$$
$$= 1\frac{1}{2}$$

9. The correct answer is (2).

LCD = 24

$$12\frac{1}{6} = 12\frac{4}{24} = 11\frac{28}{24}$$
$$-2\frac{3}{8} = -2\frac{9}{24} = -2\frac{9}{24}$$
$$9\frac{19}{24} = 9\frac{19}{24}$$

$$-7\frac{2}{3} = -7\frac{16}{24}$$
$$2\frac{3}{24} = 2\frac{3}{24}$$
$$+19\frac{3}{4} = +19\frac{18}{24}$$
$$21\frac{21}{24}$$
$$21\frac{21}{24} = 21\frac{7}{8}$$

10. The correct answer is (5).

To simplify a complex fraction, divide the numerator by the denominator.

$$\frac{4}{9} \div \frac{2}{5} = \frac{\cancel{4}^{2}}{9} \times \frac{5}{\cancel{2}_{1}}$$
$$= \frac{10}{9}$$
$$= 1\frac{1}{9}$$

11. The correct answer is (4).

Write all of the fractions with the same denominator. LCD = 80

$$\frac{9}{16} = \frac{45}{80}$$
$$\frac{7}{10} = \frac{56}{80}$$
$$\frac{5}{8} = \frac{50}{80}$$
$$\frac{4}{5} = \frac{64}{80}$$
$$\frac{3}{4} = \frac{60}{80}$$

12. The correct answer is (3).

$$3\frac{5}{16} = 3\frac{5}{16}$$
$$+2\frac{3}{4} = +2\frac{12}{16}$$
$$= 5\frac{17}{16}$$
$$= 6\frac{1}{16}$$

13. The correct answer is (4).

$$10\frac{1}{2} \div \frac{1}{2} = \frac{21}{2} \div \frac{1}{2}$$
$$= \frac{21}{\overset{1}{\cancel{2}}} \times \frac{\overset{1}{\cancel{2}}}{1}$$
$$= 21$$

14. The correct answer is (4).

$$5\frac{3}{4} \times 3 = \frac{23}{4} \times \frac{3}{1}$$
$$= \frac{69}{4}$$
$$= 17\frac{1}{4}$$

15. The correct answer is (1).

First week: LCD = 24

$$3\frac{1}{2} = 3\frac{12}{24} \text{ miles}$$
$$1\frac{1}{4} = 1\frac{6}{24}$$
$$1\frac{1}{6} = 1\frac{4}{24}$$
$$+2\frac{3}{8} = +2\frac{9}{24}$$
$$7\frac{31}{24} = 8\frac{7}{24} \text{ miles}$$

Second week:

LCD = 16

$$\frac{1}{4} = \frac{4}{16} \text{ miles}$$
$$\frac{3}{8} = \frac{6}{16}$$
$$\frac{9}{16} = \frac{9}{16}$$
$$3\frac{1}{16} = 3\frac{1}{16}$$
$$2\frac{5}{8} = 2\frac{10}{16}$$
$$+3\frac{3}{16} = +3\frac{3}{16}$$
$$8\frac{33}{16} = 10\frac{1}{16} \text{ miles}$$

LCD = 48

$$10\frac{1}{16} = 9\frac{51}{48} \quad \text{miles second week}$$
$$-8\frac{7}{24} = -8\frac{14}{48} \quad \text{miles first week}$$
$$1\frac{37}{48} \quad \begin{array}{l}\text{miles more}\\\text{traveled}\end{array}$$

answers exercises

16. The correct answer is (3).

Consider each choice:

Each 6-ft board yields one $5\frac{1}{2}$- board with $\frac{1}{2}$-ft waste.

Each 12-ft board yields two $5\frac{1}{2}$-ft boards with 1-ft waste. $2 \times 5\frac{1}{2} = 11$; $12 - 11 = 1$ ft waste)

Each 24-ft board yields four $5\frac{1}{2}$-boards with 2-ft waste. ($4 \times 5\frac{1}{2} = 22$; $24 - 22 = 2$-ft waste)

Each 22-ft board may be divided into four $5\frac{1}{2}$-ft boards with no waste. ($4 \times 5\frac{1}{2} = 22$ exactly)

17. The correct answer is (5).

$\frac{15}{16}$ of fortune is $7500.

Therefore, his fortune $7500 \div \frac{15}{16}$

$= \frac{\overset{500}{\cancel{7500}}}{1} \times \frac{16}{\underset{1}{\cancel{15}}}$

$= 8000$

18. The correct answer is (5).

$\frac{2}{3}$ of 54,000 = increase

Increase $= \frac{2}{\underset{1}{\cancel{3}}} \times \overset{18,000}{\cancel{54,000}}$

$= 36,000$

Present
Population $= 54,000 + 36,000$
$ = 90,000$

19. The correct answer is (3).

First day: $\frac{1}{3}$ evaporates $\frac{2}{3}$ remains

Second day: $\frac{3}{4}$ of $\frac{2}{3}$ evaporates

$\frac{1}{4}$ of $\frac{2}{3}$ remains

The amount remaining is

$\frac{1}{\underset{2}{\cancel{4}}} \times \frac{\overset{1}{\cancel{2}}}{3} = \frac{1}{6}$

of original contents

20. The correct answer is (3).

$\frac{7}{8}$ of capacity = 14 gal

Therefore, capacity $= 14 \div \frac{7}{8}$

$= \frac{\overset{2}{\cancel{14}}}{1} \times \frac{8}{\underset{1}{\cancel{7}}}$

$= 16 \, \text{gal}$

DECIMALS

1. A **decimal,** which is a number with a decimal point (.), is actually a fraction, the denominator of which is understood to be 10 or some power of 10.

   a. The number of digits, or places, after a decimal point determines which power of 10 the denominator is. If there is one digit, the denominator is understood to be 10; if there are two digits, the denominator is understood to be 100, etc.

   $$.3 = \frac{3}{10}, \ .57 = \frac{57}{100}, \ .643 = \frac{643}{1000}$$

   b. The addition of zeros after a decimal point does not change the value of the decimal. The zeros may be removed without changing the value of the decimal.

   $$.7 = .70 = .700 \text{ and vice versa, } .700 = .70 = .7$$

   c. Since a decimal point is understood to exist after any whole number, the addition of any number of zeros after such a decimal point does not change the value of the number.

   $$2 = 2.0 = 2.00 = 2.000$$

Addition of Decimals

2. Decimals are added in the same way that whole numbers are added, with the provision that the decimal points must be kept in a vertical line, one under the other. This determines the place of the decimal point in the answer.

Illustration: Add 2.31, .037, 4, and 5.0017

Solution: 2.3100
                  .0370
               4.0000
             + 5.0017
              11.3487

Answer: 11.3487

Subtraction of Decimals

3. Decimals are subtracted in the same way that whole numbers are subtracted, with the provision that, as in addition, the decimal points must be kept in a vertical line, one under the other. This determines the place of the decimal point in the answer.

Illustration: Subtract 4.0037 from 15.3

Solution: 15.3000
            − 4.0037
             11.2963

Answer: 11.2963

Multiplication of Decimals

4. Decimals are multiplied in the same way that whole numbers are multiplied.
   a. The number of decimal places in the product equals the sum of the decimal places in the multiplicand and in the multiplier.
   b. If there are fewer places in the product than this sum, then a sufficient number of zeros must be added in front of the product to equal the number of places required, and a decimal point is written in front of the zeros.

Illustration: Multiply 2.372 by .012

Solution:

  2.372 (3 decimal places)
×   .012 (3 decimal places)
  4744
  2372
.028464 (6 decimal places)

Answer: .028464

5. A decimal can be multiplied by a power of 10 by moving the decimal point to the *right* as many places as indicated by the power. If multiplied by 10, the decimal point is moved one place to the right; if multiplied by 100, the decimal point is moved two places to the right, etc.

$$.235 \times 10 = 2.35$$
$$.235 \times 100 = 23.5$$
$$.235 \times 1000 = 235$$

Division of Decimals

6. There are four types of division involving decimals:

   ❶ When the dividend only is a decimal.
   ❷ When the divisor only is a decimal.
   ❸ When both are decimals.
   ❹ When neither dividend nor divisor is a decimal.

   a. When the dividend only is a decimal, the division is the same as that of whole numbers, except that a decimal point must be placed in the quotient exactly above that in the dividend.

Illustration: Divide 12.864 by 32

Solution:

$$
\begin{array}{r}
.402 \\
32 \overline{)\ 12.864} \\
\underline{12\ 8} \\
064 \\
\underline{64}
\end{array}
$$

Answer: .402

   b. When the divisor only is a decimal, the decimal point in the divisor is omitted and as many zeros are placed to the right of the dividend as there were decimal places in the divisor.

Illustration: Divide 211327 by 6.817

Solution:

$$
6.817 \overline{)211327} = 6817 \overline{)211327000}
$$

(3 decimal places) $\underline{20451}$ (3 zeros added)

$\quad\quad\quad\quad 31000$

$\quad\quad\quad\quad 6817$

$\quad\quad\quad\quad \underline{6817}$

Answer: 31000

c. When both divisor and dividend are decimals, the decimal point in the divisor is omitted and the decimal point in the dividend must be moved to the right as many decimal places as there were in the divisor. If there are not enough places in the dividend, zeros must be added to make up the difference.

Illustration: Divide 2.62 by .131

Solution:

$$.131\overline{)2.62} = 131\overline{)2620} \quad \frac{20}{}$$

$$262$$

Answer: 20

d. In instances when neither the divisor nor the dividend is a decimal, a problem may still involve decimals. This occurs in two cases: when the dividend is less than the divisor and when it is required to work out a division to a certain number of decimal places. In either case, write in a decimal point after the dividend, add as many zeros as necessary, and place a decimal point in the quotient above that in the dividend.

Illustration: Divide 7 by 50.

Solution:

$$50\overline{)7.00} \quad \frac{.14}{}$$

$$\underline{5\,0}$$
$$2\,00$$
$$\underline{2\,00}$$

Answer: .14

Illustration: What is 155 divided by 40, carried out to 3 decimal places?

Solution:

$$40\overline{)155.000} \quad \frac{3.875}{}$$

$$\underline{120}$$
$$35\,0$$
$$\underline{32\,0}$$
$$3\,00$$
$$\underline{2\,80}$$
$$200$$
$$200$$

Answer: 3.875

7. A decimal can be divided by a power of 10 by moving the decimal to the *left* as many places as indicated by the power. If divided by 10, the decimal point is moved one place to the left: if divided by 100, the decimal point is moved two places to the left, etc. If there are not enough places, add zeros in front of the number to make up the difference, and add a decimal point.

.4 divided by 10 = .04
.4 divided by 100 = .004

Rounding Decimals

8. To round a number to a given decimal place:
   a. Locate the given place.
   b. If the digit to the right is less than 5, omit all digits following the given place.
   c. If the digit to the right is 5 or greater, increase the given place by 1 and omit all digits following the given place.

4.27 = 4.3 to the nearest tenth
.71345 = .713 to the nearest thousandth

9. In problems involving money, answers are usually rounded to the nearest cent.

Rewriting Fractions as Decimals

10. A fraction can be rewritten as a decimal by dividing the numerator by the denominator and working out the division to as many decimal places as required.

Illustration: Rewrite $\frac{5}{11}$ as a decimal of 2 places.

Solution:

$$\frac{5}{11} = 11{\overline{\smash{)}5.00}}$$

$$\begin{array}{r} .454 \\ 11{\overline{\smash{)}5.00}} \\ \underline{44} \\ 60 \\ \underline{55} \\ 5 \end{array}$$

Answer: .45

11. To simplify fractions containing a decimal in either the numerator or the denominator, or in both, divide the numerator by the denominator.

    Illustration: What is the value of $\dfrac{2.34}{.6}$?

    Solution:

    $$\frac{2.34}{.6} = .6\overline{)2.34} = 6\overline{)23.4}$$

    $$\begin{array}{r} 3.9 \\ 6\overline{)23.4} \\ \underline{18} \\ 5\ 4 \\ \underline{5\ 4} \end{array}$$

    Answer: 3.9

Rewriting Decimals as Fractions

12. Since a decimal point indicates a number having a denominator that is a power of 10, a decimal can be expressed as a fraction, the numerator of which is the number itself and the denominator of which is the power indicated by the number of decimal places in the decimal.

    $$.3 = \frac{3}{10}, .47 = \frac{47}{100}$$

13. When the decimal is a mixed number, divide by the power of 10 indicated by its number of decimal places. The fraction does not count as a decimal place.

    Illustration: Rewrite $.25\dfrac{1}{3}$ as a fraction.

    Solution:

    $$.25\frac{1}{3} = 25\frac{1}{3} \div 100$$

    $$= \frac{76}{3} \times \frac{1}{100}$$

    $$= \frac{76}{300} = \frac{19}{75}$$

    Answer: $\dfrac{19}{75}$

14. When to rewrite decimals as fractions:

    a. When dealing with whole numbers, do not rewrite the decimal.

    In the problem 12 × .14, it is better to keep the decimal:
    12 × .14 = 1.68

b. When dealing with fractions, rewrite the decimal as a fraction.

In the problem $\frac{3}{5} \times .17$, it is best to rewrite the decimal as a fraction:

$$\frac{3}{5} \times .17 = \frac{3}{5} \times \frac{17}{100} = \frac{51}{500}$$

15. Because decimal equivalents of fractions are often used, it is helpful to be familiar with the most common ones.

    Note that the left column contains exact values. The values in the right column have been rounded to the nearest ten-thousandth.

    $\frac{1}{2} = .5$ $\frac{1}{3} \approx .3333$

    $\frac{1}{4} = .25$ $\frac{2}{3} \approx .6667$

    $\frac{3}{4} = .75$ $\frac{1}{6} \approx .1667$

    $\frac{1}{5} = .2$ $\frac{1}{7} \approx .1429$

    $\frac{1}{8} = .125$ $\frac{1}{9} \approx .1111$

    $\frac{1}{16} = .0625$ $\frac{1}{12} \approx .0833$

EXERCISES: DECIMALS

1. Add 37.03, 11.5627, 3.4005, 3423, and 1.141.
   - (1) 3476.1342
   - (2) 3500
   - (3) 3524.4322
   - (4) 3424.1342
   - (5) 3452.4852

2. Subtract 4.64324 from 7.
   - (1) 3.35676
   - (2) 2.35676
   - (3) 2.45676
   - (4) 2.36676
   - (5) 2.36576

3. Multiply 27.34 by 16.943.
   - (1) 463.22162
   - (2) 453.52162
   - (3) 462.52162
   - (4) 462.53162
   - (5) 463.52162

4. What is 19.6 divided by 3.2, carried out to 3 decimal places?
   - (1) 6.125
   - (2) 6.124
   - (3) 6.123
   - (4) 5.123
   - (5) 5.013

5. What is $\frac{5}{11}$ in decimal form (to the nearest hundredth)?
   - (1) .44
   - (2) .55
   - (3) .40
   - (4) .42
   - (5) .45

6. What is $.64\frac{2}{3}$ in fraction form?
   - (1) $\frac{97}{120}$
   - (2) $\frac{97}{150}$
   - (3) $\frac{97}{130}$
   - (4) $\frac{98}{130}$
   - (5) $\frac{99}{140}$

7. What is the difference between $\frac{9}{8}$ and $\frac{3}{5}$ expressed decimally?
   - (1) .550
   - (2) .425
   - (3) .520
   - (4) .500
   - (5) .525

8. A boy saved up $4.56 the first month, $3.82 the second month, and $5.06 the third month. How much did he save altogether?
   - (1) $12.56
   - (2) $13.28
   - (3) $13.44
   - (4) $14.02
   - (5) $14.44

9. The diameter of a certain rod is required to be $1.51 \pm .015$ inches. The rod would not be acceptable if the diameter measured
   - (1) 1.490 inches
   - (2) 1.500 inches
   - (3) 1.510 inches
   - (4) 1.525 inches
   - (5) 1.511 inches

10. After an employer figures out an employee's salary of $190.57, he deducts $3.05 for Social Security and $5.68 for pension. What is the amount of the check after these deductions?

    (1) $181.84
    (2) $181.92
    (3) $181.93
    (4) $181.99
    (5) $182.00

11. If the outer diameter of a metal pipe is 2.84 inches and the inner diameter is 1.94 inches, the thickness of the metal is

    (1) .45 inches
    (2) .90 inches
    (3) 1.94 inches
    (4) 2.39 inches
    (5) 2.50 inches

12. A boy earns $20.56 on Monday, $32.90 on Tuesday, and $20.78 on Wednesday. He spends half of all that he earned during the three days. How much has he left?

    (1) $29.19
    (2) $31.23
    (3) $34.27
    (4) $37.12
    (5) $38.00

13. The total cost of $3\frac{1}{2}$ pounds of meat at $1.69 a pound and 20 lemons at $.60 a dozen will be

    (1) $6.00
    (2) $6.40
    (3) $6.52
    (4) $6.82
    (5) $6.92

14. A reel of cable weighs 1279 lb. If the empty reel weighs 285 lb. and the cable weighs 7.1 lb. per foot, the number of feet of cable on the reel is

    (1) 220
    (2) 180
    (3) 140
    (4) 100
    (5) 80

15. 345 fasteners at $4.15 per hundred will cost

    (1) $ .1432
    (2) $1.4320
    (3) $14.32
    (4) $143.20
    (5) $149.20

ANSWER KEY AND EXPLANATIONS

1. (1)	6. (2)	11. (1)
2. (2)	7. (5)	12. (4)
3. (1)	8. (3)	13. (5)
4. (1)	9. (1)	14. (3)
5. (5)	10. (1)	15. (3)

1. The correct answer is (1).

Line up all the decimal points one under the other. Then add:

```
  37.03
  11.5627
   3.4005
3423.0000
+  1.141
─────────
3476.1342
```

2. The correct answer is (2).

Add a decimal point and five zeros to the 7. Then subtract:

```
 7.00000
-4.64324
────────
 2.35676
```

3. The correct answer is (1).

Since there are two decimal places in the multiplicand and three decimal places in the multiplier, there will be 2 + 3 = 5 decimal places in the product.

```
    27.34
  ×16.943
  ───────
     8202
   1 0936
  24 606
 164 04
 273 4
 ─────────
 463.22162
```

4. The correct answer is (1).

Omit the decimal point in the divisor by moving it one place to the right. Move the decimal point in the dividend one place to the right and add three zeros in order to carry your answer out to three decimal places, as instructed in the problem.

```
          6.125
3.2.)19.6.000
      19.2
      ────
       4 0
       3 2
       ───
         80
         64
         ──
        160
        160
```

5. The correct answer is (5).

To rewrite a fraction as a decimal, divide the numerator by the denominator:

```
       .454
   11) 5.000
       4 4
       ───
        60
        55
        ──
        50
        44
        ──
         6
```

6. **The correct answer is (2).**

   To rewrite a decimal as a fraction, divide by the power of 10 indicated by the number of decimal places. (The fraction does not count as a decimal place.)

   $$64\frac{2}{3} \div 100 = \frac{194}{3} \div \frac{100}{1}$$
   $$= \frac{194}{3} \times \frac{1}{100}$$
   $$= \frac{194}{300}$$
   $$= \frac{97}{150}$$

7. **The correct answer is (5).**

   Rewrite each fraction as a decimal and subtract to find the difference:

   $$\frac{9}{8} = 1.125 \qquad \frac{3}{5} = .60$$

   ```
     1.125
    -.60
     .525
   ```

8. **The correct answer is (3).**

   Add the savings for each month:

   ```
    $4.56
     3.82
    +5.06
   $13.44
   ```

9. **The correct answer is (1).**

   ```
    1.51        1.510
   +.015       -.015
    1.525       1.495
   ```

   The rod may have a diameter from 1.495 inches to 1.525 inches inclusive.

10. **The correct answer is (1).**

    Add to find total deductions:

    ```
     $3.05
    + 5.68
     $8.73
    ```

    Subtract total deductions from salary to find amount of check:

    ```
    $190.57
      -8.73
    $181.84
    ```

11. **The correct answer is (1).**

    The difference of the two diameters equals the total thickness of the metal on both ends of the inner diameter.

    ```
     2.84     .90 ÷ 2 = .45 = thickness of metal
    -1.94
     .90
    ```

12. **The correct answer is (4).**

    Add daily earnings to find total earnings:

    ```
    $20.56
     32.90
    + 20.78
    $74.24
    ```

    Divide total earnings by 2 to find out what he has left:

    ```
        $37.12
    2)$74.24
    ```

13. The correct answer is (5).

Find cost of $3\frac{1}{2}$ pounds of meat:

$$
\begin{array}{r}
\$1.69 \\
\times\ 3.5 \\
\hline
845 \\
5\ 07 \\
\hline
\end{array}
$$

$\$5.915 = \$5.92$ to the nearest cent

Find cost of 20 lemons:

$\$.60 \div 12 = \$.05$ (for 1 lemon)

$\$.05 \times 20 = \$1.00$ (for 20 lemons)

Add cost of meat and cost of lemons:

$$
\begin{array}{r}
\$5.92 \\
+\ 1.00 \\
\hline
\$6.92
\end{array}
$$

14. The correct answer is (3).

Subtract weight of empty reel from total weight to find weight of cable:

$$
\begin{array}{r}
1279\ \text{lb} \\
-\ 285\ \text{lb} \\
\hline
994\ \text{lb}
\end{array}
$$

Each foot of cable weighs 7.1 lb. Therefore, to find the number of feet of cable on the reel, divide 994 by 7.1

$$
\begin{array}{r}
14\ 0. \\
7.1\overline{)994.0.} \\
\underline{71} \\
284 \\
\underline{284} \\
0\ 0
\end{array}
$$

15. The correct answer is (3).

Each fastener costs:

$\$4.15 \div 100 = \$.0415$

345 fasteners cost:

$$
\begin{array}{r}
345 \\
\times\ .0415 \\
\hline
1725 \\
345 \\
13\ 80 \\
\hline
14.3175
\end{array}
$$

PERCENTS

1. The **percent symbol** (%) means "parts of a hundred." Some problems involve expressing a fraction or a decimal as a percent. In other problems, it is necessary to express a percent as a fraction or a decimal in order to perform the calculations.

2. To rewrite a whole number or a decimal as a percent:
   a. Multiply the number by 100.
   b. Affix a % sign.

   Illustration: Rewrite 3 as a percent.

   Solution: $3 \times 100 = 300$
   $$3 = 300\%$$

   Answer: 300%

   Illustration: Rewrite .67 as a percent.

   Solution: $.67 \times 100 = 67$
   $$.67 = 67\%$$

   Answer: 67%

3. To rewrite a fraction or a mixed number as a percent:
   a. Multiply the fraction or mixed number by 100.
   b. Simplify, if possible.
   c. Affix a % sign.

   Illustration: Rewrite $\frac{1}{7}$ as a percent.

   Solution:

   $$\frac{1}{7} \times 100 = \frac{100}{7}$$
   $$= 14\frac{2}{7}$$
   $$\frac{1}{7} = 14\frac{2}{7}\%$$

   Answer: $14\frac{2}{7}\%$

Illustration: Rewrite $4\frac{2}{3}$ as a percent.

Solution:

$$4\frac{2}{3} \times 100 = \frac{14}{3} \times 100 = \frac{1400}{3}$$

$$= 466\frac{2}{3}$$

$$4\frac{2}{3} = 466\frac{2}{3}\%$$

Answer: $466\frac{2}{3}\%$

4. To rewrite a decimal percent as a decimal, divide the decimal by 100. If necessary, the resulting decimal may then be rewritten as a fraction.

   Illustration: Rewrite .5% as a decimal and as a fraction.

   Solution:

   $$.5\% = .5 \div 100 = .005$$

   $$.005 = \frac{5}{1000} = \frac{1}{200}$$

   Answer: .5% = .005

   $$.5\% = \frac{1}{200}$$

5. To rewrite a fractional percent, divide the fraction or mixed number by 100 and simplify, if possible. If necessary, the resulting fraction may then be rewritten as a decimal.

   Illustration: Rewrite $\frac{3}{4}\%$ as a fraction and as a decimal.

   Solution:

   $$\frac{3}{4}\% = \frac{3}{4} \div 100 = \frac{3}{4} \times \frac{1}{100} = \frac{3}{400}$$

   $$\frac{3}{400} = 400\overline{)3.0000}^{\,.0075}$$

   Answer: $\frac{3}{4}\% = \frac{3}{400}$

   $$\frac{3}{4}\% = .0075$$

6. To rewrite a decimal percent that includes a fraction, divide the decimal by 100. If necessary, the resulting number may then be rewritten as a fraction.

Illustration: Rewrite $.05\frac{1}{3}$ as a fraction.

Solution: $5\frac{1}{3}\% = .05\frac{1}{3}$

$$= \frac{5\frac{1}{3}}{100}$$

$$= 5\frac{1}{3} \div 100$$

$$= \frac{16}{3} \times \frac{1}{100}$$

$$= \frac{16}{300}$$

$$= \frac{4}{75}$$

Answer: $5\frac{1}{3}\% = \frac{4}{75}$

7. Some fraction-percent equivalents are used so frequently that it is helpful to be familiar with them.

$\frac{1}{25} = 4\%$	$\frac{1}{5} = 20\%$
$\frac{1}{20} = 5\%$	$\frac{1}{4} = 25\%$
$\frac{1}{12} = 8\frac{1}{3}\%$	$\frac{1}{3} = 33\frac{1}{3}\%$
$\frac{1}{10} = 10\%$	$\frac{1}{2} = 50\%$
$\frac{1}{8} = 12\frac{1}{2}\%$	$\frac{2}{3} = 66\frac{2}{3}\%$
$\frac{1}{6} = 16\frac{2}{3}\%$	$\frac{3}{4} = 75\%$

Solving Percent Problems

8. Most percent problems involve three quantities:
   - The rate, R, which is followed by a % sign.
   - The base, B, which follows the word "of."
   - The amount or percentage, P, which usually follows the word "is."

   a. If the rate (R) and the base (B) are known, then the percentage (P) = $R \times B$.

Illustration: Find 15% of 50.

Solution:

Rate = 15%

Base = 50

$$P = R \times B$$
$$P = 15\% \times 50$$
$$= .15 \times 50$$
$$= 7.5$$

Answer: 7.5

   b. If the rate (R) and the percentage (P) are known, then the base (B) = $\dfrac{P}{R}$.

Illustration: 7% of what number is 35?

Solution:

Rate = 7%

Percentage = 35

$$B = \frac{P}{R}$$
$$B = \frac{35}{7\%}$$
$$= 35 \div .07$$
$$= 500$$

Answer: 500

c. If the percentage (P) and the base (B) are known, the rate (R) = $\dfrac{P}{B}$.

Illustration: There are 96 men in a group of 150 people. What percent of the group are men?

Solution:

$$\text{Base} = 150$$
$$\text{Percentage (amount)} = 96$$
$$\text{Rate} = \frac{96}{150}$$
$$= .64$$
$$= 64\%$$

Answer: 64%

Illustration: In a tank holding 20 gallons of solution, 1 gallon is alcohol. What is the strength of the solution in percent?

Solution:

$$\text{Percentage (amount)} = 1 \text{ gallon}$$
$$\text{Base} = 20 \text{ gallons}$$
$$\text{Rate} = \frac{1}{20}$$
$$= .05$$
$$= 5\%$$

Answer: 5%

9. In a percent problem, the whole is 100%.

If a problem involves 10% of a quantity, the rest of the quantity is 90%.

If a quantity has been increased by 5%, the new amount is 105% of the original quantity.

If a quantity has been decreased by 15%, the new amount is 85% of the original quantity.

EXERCISES: PERCENTS

1. 10% written as a decimal is

   (1) 1.0
   (2) 0.01
   (3) 0.001
   (4) 0.1
   (5) .101

2. What is 5.37% in fraction form?

   (1) $\dfrac{537}{10,000}$

   (2) $5\dfrac{37}{10,000}$

   (3) $\dfrac{537}{1000}$

   (4) $5\dfrac{37}{100}$

   (5) $\dfrac{537}{100}$

3. What percent of $\dfrac{5}{6}$ is $\dfrac{3}{4}$?

   (1) 75%
   (2) 60%
   (3) 80%
   (4) 85%
   (5) 90%

4. What percent is 14 of 24?

   (1) $62\dfrac{1}{4}\%$

   (2) $58\dfrac{1}{3}\%$

   (3) $41\dfrac{2}{3}\%$

   (4) $33\dfrac{3}{5}\%$

   (5) $73\dfrac{1}{8}\%$

5. 200% of 800 equals

   (1) 2500
   (2) 16
   (3) 1600
   (4) 4
   (5) 2

6. If John must have a mark of 80% to pass a test of 35 items, the number of items he may miss and still pass the test is

   (1) 7
   (2) 8
   (3) 11
   (4) 28
   (5) 30

7. The regular price of a TV set that sold for $118.80 at a 20% reduction sale is

   (1) $148.50
   (2) $142.60
   (3) $138.84
   (4) $ 95.04
   (5) $ 90.04

8. A circle graph of a budget shows the expenditure of 26.2% for housing, 28.4% for food, 12% for clothing, 12.7% for taxes, and the balance for miscellaneous items. The percent for miscellaneous items is

   (1) 31.5%
   (2) 79.3%
   (3) 20.7%
   (4) 68.5%
   (5) 80.5%

9. Two dozen shuttlecocks and four badminton rackets are to be purchased for a playground. The shuttlecocks are priced at $.35 each and the rackets at $2.75 each. The playground receives a discount of 30% from these prices. The total cost of this equipment is

    (1) $7.29
    (2) $11.43
    (3) $13.58
    (4) $18.60
    (5) $20.60

10. A piece of wood weighing 10 ounces is found to have a weight of 8 ounces after drying. The moisture content was

    (1) 25%
    (2) $33\frac{1}{3}\%$
    (3) 20%
    (4) 40%
    (5) 60%

11. A bag contains 800 coins. Of these, 10 percent are dimes, 30 percent are nickels, and the rest are quarters. The amount of money in the bag is

    (1) less than $150.
    (2) between $150 and $300.
    (3) between $301 and $450.
    (4) between $451 and $499.
    (5) more than $500.

12. Six quarts of a 20% solution of alcohol in water are mixed with 4 quarts of a 60% solution of alcohol in water. The alcoholic strength of the mixture is

    (1) 80%
    (2) 40%
    (3) 36%
    (4) 72%
    (5) 75%

13. A man insures 80% of his property and pays a $2\frac{1}{2}\%$ premium amounting to $348. What is the total value of his property?

    (1) $17,000
    (2) $18,000
    (3) $18,400
    (4) $17,400
    (5) $19,000

14. A clerk divided his 35-hour work week as follows: $\frac{1}{5}$ of his time was spent in sorting mail, $\frac{1}{2}$ of his time in filing letters, and $\frac{1}{7}$ of his time in reception work. The rest of his time was devoted to messenger work. The percent of time spent on messenger work by the clerk during the week was most nearly

    (1) 6%
    (2) 10%
    (3) 14%
    (4) 15%
    (5) 16%

15. In a school in which 40% of the enrolled students are boys, 80% of the boys are present on a certain day. If 1,152 boys are present, the total school enrollment is

    (1) 1,440
    (2) 2,880
    (3) 3,600
    (4) 5,400
    (5) 5,600

exercises

ANSWER KEY AND EXPLANATIONS

1. (4)	6. (1)	11. (1)
2. (1)	7. (1)	12. (3)
3. (5)	8. (3)	13. (4)
4. (2)	9. (3)	14. (5)
5. (3)	10. (3)	15. (3)

1. The correct answer is (4).

$$10\% = .10 = .1$$

2. The correct answer is (1).

$$5.37\% = .0537 = \frac{537}{10,000}$$

3. The correct answer is (5).

Base (number following "of") = $\frac{5}{6}$

Percentage (number following "is") = $\frac{3}{4}$

$$Rate = \frac{Percentage}{Base}$$
$$= Percentage \div Base$$

$$Rate = \frac{3}{4} \div \frac{5}{6}$$

$$= \frac{3}{\underset{2}{\cancel{4}}} \times \frac{\overset{3}{\cancel{6}}}{5}$$

$$= \frac{9}{10}$$

$$\frac{9}{10} = .9 = 90\%$$

4. The correct answer is (2).

Base (number following "of") = 24

Percentage (number following "is") = 14

Rate = Percentage ÷ Base

Rate = $14 \div 24$

$$= .58\frac{1}{3}$$

$$= 58\frac{1}{3}\%$$

5. The correct answer is (3).

$$200\% \text{ of } 800 = 2.00 \times 800$$
$$= 1600$$

6. The correct answer is (1).

He must answer 80% of 35 correctly. Therefore, he may miss 20% of 35.

$$20\% \text{ of } 35 = .20 \times 35$$
$$= 7$$

7. The correct answer is (1).

Since $118.80 represents a 20% reduction, $118.80 = 80% of the regular price.

$$Regular\ price = \frac{\$118.80}{80\%}$$

$$= \$118.80 \div .80$$

$$= \$148.50$$

8. The correct answer is (3).

All the items in a circle graph total 100%. Add the figures given for housing, food, clothing, and taxes:

$$\begin{array}{r} 26.2\% \\ 28.4\% \\ 12\ \% \\ +12.7\% \\ \hline 79.3\% \end{array}$$

Subtract this total from 100% to find the percent for miscellaneous items:

$$\begin{array}{r} 100.0\% \\ -\ 79.3\% \\ \hline 20.7\% \end{array}$$

9. The correct answer is (3).

Price of shuttlecocks =
$24 \times \$ .35 = \$8.40$

Price of rackets =
$4 \times \$2.75 = \$11.00$

Total price = $19.40

Discount is 30%, and
$100\% - 30\% = 70\%$

$$\begin{aligned} \text{Actual cost} &= 70\% \text{ of } 19.40 \\ &= .70 \times 19.40 \\ &= 13.58 \end{aligned}$$

10. The correct answer is (3).

Subtract weight of wood after drying from original weight of wood to find amount of moisture in wood:

$$\begin{array}{r} 10 \\ -8 \\ \hline 2 \text{ ounces of moisture in wood} \end{array}$$

Moisture content =

$$\frac{2 \text{ ounces}}{10 \text{ ounces}} = .2 = 20\%$$

11. The correct answer is (1).

Find the number of each kind of coin:

10% of 800 = .10 × 800 = 80 dimes

30% of 800 = .30 × 800 = 240 nickels

60% of 800 = .60 × 800 = 480 quarters

Find the value of the coins:

80 dimes = 80 × .10 = $ 8.00

240 nickels = 240 × .05 = 12.00

480 quarters = 480 × .25 = 120.00

Total $140.00

12. The correct answer is (3).

First solution contains 20% of 6 quarts of alcohol.

$$\begin{aligned} \text{Alcohol content} &= .20 \times 6 \\ &= 1.2 \text{ quarts} \end{aligned}$$

Second solution contains 60% of 4 quarts of alcohol.

$$\begin{aligned} \text{Alcohol content} &= .60 \times 4 \\ &= 2.4 \text{ quarts} \end{aligned}$$

Mixture contains:

$1.2 + 2.4 = 3.6$ quarts alcohol

$6 + 4 = 10$ quarts liquid

Alcoholic strength of mixture $= \dfrac{3.6}{10} = 36\%$

answers exercises

13. The correct answer is (4).

$2\frac{1}{2}\%$ of insured value = $348

$$\text{Insured value} = \frac{348}{2\frac{1}{2}\%}$$

$$= 348 \div .025$$

$$= \$13,920$$

$13,920 is 80% of total value

$$\text{Total value} = \frac{\$13,920}{80\%}$$

$$= \$13,920 \div .80$$

$$= \$17,400$$

14. The correct answer is (5).

$\dfrac{1}{5} \times 35 = 7$ hr sorting mail

$\dfrac{1}{2} \times 35 = 17\dfrac{1}{2}$ hr filing

$\dfrac{1}{7} \times 35 = \underline{ 5}$ hr reception

$ 29\dfrac{1}{2}$ hr accounted for

$35 - 29\dfrac{1}{2} = 5\dfrac{1}{2}$ hr left for messenger work

% spent on messenger work:

$$= \frac{5\frac{1}{2}}{35}$$

$$= 5\frac{1}{2} \div 35$$

$$= \frac{11}{2} \times \frac{1}{35}$$

$$= \frac{11}{70}$$

$$= .15\frac{5}{7}$$

$.15\dfrac{5}{7}$ is most nearly 16%.

15. The correct answer is (3).

80% of the boys = 1152

$\text{Number of boys} = \dfrac{1152}{80\%}$

$$= 1152 \div .80$$

$$= 1440$$

40% of students = 1440

Total number of students:

$$= \frac{1440}{40\%}$$

$$= 1440 \div .40$$

$$= 3600$$

SHORTCUTS IN MULTIPLICATION AND DIVISION

There are several shortcuts for simplifying multiplication and division. Following the description of each shortcut, practice problems are provided.

Dropping Final Zeros

1. a. A zero in a whole number is considered a "final zero" if it appears in the units column or if all columns to its right are filled with zeros. A final zero may be omitted in certain kinds of problems.

   b. In decimal numbers a zero appearing in the extreme right column may be dropped with no effect on the solution of a problem.

2. In multiplying whole numbers, the final zero(s) may be dropped during computation and simply transferred to the answer.

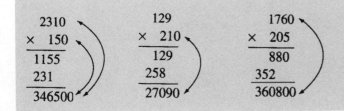

$$
\begin{array}{r}
2310 \\
\times\ 150 \\
\hline
1155 \\
231\ \ \ \\
\hline
346500
\end{array}
\qquad
\begin{array}{r}
129 \\
\times\ 210 \\
\hline
129 \\
258\ \ \ \\
\hline
27090
\end{array}
\qquad
\begin{array}{r}
1760 \\
\times\ 205 \\
\hline
880 \\
352\ \ \ \\
\hline
360800
\end{array}
$$

Practice Problems

Solve the following multiplication problems, dropping the final zeros during computation.

1. $\begin{array}{r} 230 \\ \times\ \ 12 \\ \hline \end{array}$

2. $\begin{array}{r} 175 \\ \times\ 130 \\ \hline \end{array}$

3. $\begin{array}{r} 203 \\ \times\ \ 14 \\ \hline \end{array}$

4. $\begin{array}{r} 621 \\ \times\ 140 \\ \hline \end{array}$

5. $\begin{array}{r} 430 \\ \times\ 360 \\ \hline \end{array}$

6. $\begin{array}{r} 132 \\ \times\ 310 \\ \hline \end{array}$

7. $\begin{array}{r} 350 \\ \times\ \ 24 \\ \hline \end{array}$

8. $\begin{array}{r} 520 \\ \times\ 410 \\ \hline \end{array}$

9. $\begin{array}{r} 634 \\ \times\ 120 \\ \hline \end{array}$

10. $\begin{array}{r} 431 \\ \times\ 230 \\ \hline \end{array}$

Answers

1.
$$
\begin{array}{r}
230 \\
\times\ 12 \\
\hline
46 \\
23 \\
\hline
2760
\end{array}
$$

2.
$$
\begin{array}{r}
175 \\
\times\ 130 \\
\hline
525 \\
175 \\
\hline
22750
\end{array}
$$

3.
$$
\begin{array}{r}
203 \\
\times\ 14 \\
\hline
812 \\
203 \\
\hline
2842
\end{array}
$$

(no final zeros)

4.
$$
\begin{array}{r}
621 \\
\times\ 140 \\
\hline
2484 \\
621 \\
\hline
86940
\end{array}
$$

5.
$$
\begin{array}{r}
430 \\
\times\ 360 \\
\hline
258 \\
129 \\
\hline
154800
\end{array}
$$

6.
$$
\begin{array}{r}
132 \\
\times\ 310 \\
\hline
132 \\
396 \\
\hline
40920
\end{array}
$$

7.
$$
\begin{array}{r}
350 \\
\times\ 24 \\
\hline
140 \\
70 \\
\hline
8400
\end{array}
$$

8.
$$
\begin{array}{r}
520 \\
\times\ 410 \\
\hline
52 \\
208 \\
\hline
213200
\end{array}
$$

9.
$$
\begin{array}{r}
634 \\
\times\ 120 \\
\hline
1268 \\
634 \\
\hline
76080
\end{array}
$$

10.
$$
\begin{array}{r}
431 \\
\times\ 230 \\
\hline
1293 \\
862 \\
\hline
99130
\end{array}
$$

Multiplying Whole Numbers by Decimals

3. In multiplying a whole number by a decimal number, if there are one or more final zeros in the multiplicand, move the decimal point in the multiplier to the right the same number of places as there are final zeros in the multiplicand. Then cross out the final zero(s) in the multiplicand.

$$
\begin{array}{r} 27500 \\ \times\ .15 \\ \hline \end{array}
=
\begin{array}{r} 275 \\ \times\ 15 \\ \hline \end{array}
$$

$$
\begin{array}{r} 1250 \\ \times\ .345 \\ \hline \end{array}
=
\begin{array}{r} 125 \\ \times\ 3.45 \\ \hline \end{array}
$$

Practice Problems

Rewrite the following problems, dropping the final zeros and moving decimal points the appropriate number of spaces. Then compute the answers.

1. $\begin{array}{r} 2400 \\ \times\ \ .02 \\ \hline \end{array}$

2. $\begin{array}{r} 620 \\ \times\ \ .04 \\ \hline \end{array}$

3. $\begin{array}{r} 800 \\ \times\ \ .005 \\ \hline \end{array}$

4. $\begin{array}{r} 600 \\ \times\ \ .002 \\ \hline \end{array}$

5. $\begin{array}{r} 340 \\ \times\ \ .08 \\ \hline \end{array}$

6. $\begin{array}{r} 480 \\ \times\ \ .4 \\ \hline \end{array}$

7. $\begin{array}{r} 400 \\ \times\ \ .04 \\ \hline \end{array}$

8. $\begin{array}{r} 5300 \\ \times\ \ .5 \\ \hline \end{array}$

9. $\begin{array}{r} 930 \\ \times\ \ .3 \\ \hline \end{array}$

10. $\begin{array}{r} 9000 \\ \times\ \ .001 \\ \hline \end{array}$

Answers

The rewritten problems are shown, along with the answers.

1.	$\begin{array}{r} 24 \\ \times\ 2 \\ \hline 48 \end{array}$		**6.**	$\begin{array}{r} 48 \\ \times\ 4 \\ \hline 192 \end{array}$
2.	$\begin{array}{r} 62 \\ \times\ .4 \\ \hline 24.8 \end{array}$		**7.**	$\begin{array}{r} 4 \\ \times\ 4 \\ \hline 16 \end{array}$
3.	$\begin{array}{r} 8 \\ \times\ .5 \\ \hline 4.0 \end{array}$		**8.**	$\begin{array}{r} 53 \\ \times\ 50 \\ \hline 2650 \end{array}$
4.	$\begin{array}{r} 6 \\ \times\ .2 \\ \hline 1.2 \end{array}$		**9.**	$\begin{array}{r} 93 \\ \times\ 3 \\ \hline 279 \end{array}$
5.	$\begin{array}{r} 34 \\ \times\ .8 \\ \hline 27.2 \end{array}$		**10.**	$\begin{array}{r} 9 \\ \times\ 1 \\ \hline 9 \end{array}$

Dividing by Whole Numbers

4. a. When there are final zeros in the divisor but no final zeros in the dividend, move the decimal point in the dividend to the left as many places as there are final zeros in the divisor, then omit the final zeros.

$$2700.\overline{)37523.} = 27.\overline{)375.23}$$

b. When there are fewer final zeros in the divisor than there are in the dividend, drop the same number of final zeros from the dividend as there are final zeros in the divisor.

$$250.\overline{)45300.} = 25.\overline{)4530}$$

c. When there are more final zeros in the divisor than there are in the dividend, move the decimal point in the dividend to the left as many places as there are final zeros in the divisor, then omit the final zeros.

$$2300.\overline{)690.} = 23.\overline{)6.9}$$

d. When there are no final zeros in the divisor, no zeros can be dropped in the dividend.

$$23.\overline{)690.} = 23.\overline{)690.}$$

Practice Problems

Rewrite the following problems, dropping the final zeros and moving the decimal points the appropriate number of places. Then compute the quotients.

1. $600.\overline{)72.}$

2. $310.\overline{)6200.}$

3. $7600.\overline{)1520.}$

4. $46.\overline{)920.}$

5. $11.0\overline{)220.}$

6. $700.\overline{)84.}$

7. $90.\overline{)8100.}$

8. $8100.\overline{)1620.}$

9. $25.\overline{)5250.}$

10. $41.0\overline{)820.}$

11. $800.\overline{)96.}$

12. $650.\overline{)1300.}$

13. $5500.\overline{)110.}$

14. $36.\overline{)720.}$

15. $87.0\overline{)1740.}$

Rewritten Practice Problems

1. $6.\overline{).72}$

2. $31.\overline{)620.}$

3. $76.\overline{)15.2}$

4. $46.\overline{)920.}$

5. $11.\overline{)220.}$

6. $7.\overline{).84}$

7. $9.\overline{)810.}$

8. $81.\overline{)16.2}$

9. $25.\overline{)5250.}$

10. $41.\overline{)820.}$

11. $8.\overline{).96}$

12. $65.\overline{)130.}$

13. $55.\overline{)1.1}$

14. $36.\overline{)720.}$

15. $87.\overline{)1740.}$

Answers

1. $6. \overline{\smash{)}.72}$ quotient $.12$

2. $31. \overline{\smash{)}620.}$ quotient 20
    $\underline{62}$
    00

3. $76. \overline{\smash{)}15.2}$ quotient $.2$
    $\underline{15\ 2}$
    00

4. $46. \overline{\smash{)}920.}$ quotient 20
    $\underline{92}$
    00

5. $11. \overline{\smash{)}220.}$ quotient 20
    $\underline{22}$
    00

6. $7. \overline{\smash{)}.84}$ quotient $.12$

7. $9. \overline{\smash{)}810.}$ quotient 90

8. $81. \overline{\smash{)}16.2}$ quotient $.2$
    $\underline{16\ 2}$
    $0\ 0$

9. $25. \overline{\smash{)}5250.}$ quotient 210
    $\underline{50}$
    25
    $\underline{25}$
    00

10. $41. \overline{\smash{)}820.}$ quotient 20
    $\underline{82}$
    00

11. $8. \overline{\smash{)}.96}$ quotient $.12$

12. $65. \overline{\smash{)}130.}$ quotient 2
    $\underline{130}$
    00

13. $55. \overline{\smash{)}1.10}$ quotient $.02$
    $\underline{1\ 10}$
    00

14. $36. \overline{\smash{)}720.}$ quotient 20
    $\underline{72}$
    00

15. $87. \overline{\smash{)}1740}$ quotient 20
    $\underline{174}$
    00

Division by Multiplication

5. Instead of dividing by a particular number, the same answer is obtained by multiplying by the equivalent multiplier.

6. To find the equivalent multiplier of a given divisor, divide 1 by the divisor.

The equivalent multiplier of $12\frac{1}{2}$ is $1 \div 12\frac{1}{2}$ or .08. The division problem $100 \div 12\frac{1}{2}$ may be more easily solved as the multiplication problem $100 \times .08$. The answer will be the same.

7. Common divisors and their equivalent multipliers are shown below:

Divisor	Equivalent Multiplier
$11\frac{1}{9}$	.09
$12\frac{1}{2}$	.08
$14\frac{2}{7}$	.07
$16\frac{2}{3}$	.06
20	.05
25	.04
$33\frac{1}{3}$	.03
50	.02

8. A divisor may be multiplied or divided by any power of 10, and the only change in its equivalent multiplier will be in the placement of the decimal point, as may be seen in the following table:

Divisor	Equivalent Multiplier
.025	40.
.25	4.
2.5	.4
25.	.04
250.	.004
2500.	.0004

Practice Problems

Rewrite and solve each of the following problems by using equivalent multipliers. Drop the final zeros where appropriate.

1. $100 \div 16\frac{2}{3} =$

2. $200 \div 25 =$

3. $300 \div 33\frac{1}{3} =$

4. $250 \div 50 =$

5. $80 \div 12\frac{1}{2} =$

6. $800 \div 14\frac{2}{7} =$

7. $620 \div 20 =$

8. $500 \div 11\frac{1}{9} =$

9. $420 \div 16\frac{2}{3} =$

10. $1200 \div 33\frac{1}{3} =$

11. $955 \div 50 =$

12. $450 \div 25 =$

13. $275 \div 12\frac{1}{2} =$

14. $625 \div 25 =$

15. $244 \div 20 =$

16. $350 \div 16\frac{2}{3} =$

17. $400 \div 33\frac{1}{3} =$

18. $375 \div 25 =$

19. $460 \div 20 =$

20. $250 \div 12\frac{1}{2} =$

Answers

The rewritten problems and their solutions appear below:

1. $100 \times .06 = 1 \times 6 = 6$

2. $200 \times .04 = 2 \times 4 = 8$

3. $300 \times .03 = 3 \times 3 = 9$

4. $250 \times .02 = 25 \times .2 = 5$

5. $80 \times .08 = 8 \times .8 = 6.4$

6. $800 \times .07 = 8 \times 7 = 56$

7. $620 \times .05 = 62 \times .5 = 31$

8. $500 \times .09 = 5 \times 9 = 45$

9. $420 \times .06 = 42 \times .6 = 25.2$

10. $1200 \times .03 = 12 \times 3 = 36$

11. $955 \times .02 = 19.1$

12. $450 \times .25 = 112.5$

13. $275 \times .08 = 22$

14. $625 \times .04 = 25$

15. $244 \times .05 = 12.2$

16. $350 \times .06 = 35 \times .6 = 21$

17. $400 \times .03 = 4 \times 3 = 12$

18. $375 \times .04 = 15$

19. $460 \times .05 = 46 \times .5 = 23$

20. $250 \times .08 = 25 \times .8 = 20$

Multiplication by Division

9. Just as some division problems are made easier by rewriting them as equivalent multiplication problems, certain multiplication problems are made easier by rewriting them as equivalent division problems.

10. Instead of arriving at an answer by multiplying by a particular number, the same answer is obtained by dividing by the equivalent divisor.

11. To find the equivalent divisor of a given multiplier, divide 1 by the multiplier.

12. Common multipliers and their equivalent divisors are shown below:

Divisor	*Equivalent Multiplier*
$11\dfrac{1}{9}$	.09
$12\dfrac{1}{2}$	.08
$14\dfrac{2}{7}$	.07
$16\dfrac{2}{3}$	.06
20	.05
25	.04
$33\dfrac{1}{3}$	.03
50	.02

Notice that the multiplier-equivalent divisor pairs are the same as the divisor-equivalent multiplier pairs given earlier.

Practice Problems

Rewrite and solve each of the following problems by using division. Drop the final zeros where appropriate.

1. $77 \times 14\frac{2}{7} =$

2. $81 \times 11\frac{1}{9} =$

3. $475 \times 20 =$

4. $42 \times 50 =$

5. $36 \times 33\frac{1}{3} =$

6. $96 \times 12\frac{1}{2} =$

7. $126 \times 16\frac{2}{3} =$

8. $48 \times 25 =$

9. $33 \times 33\frac{1}{3} =$

10. $84 \times 14\frac{2}{7} =$

11. $99 \times 11\frac{1}{9} =$

12. $126 \times 33\frac{1}{3} =$

13. $168 \times 12\frac{1}{2} =$

14. $654 \times 16\frac{2}{3} =$

15. $154 \times 14\frac{2}{7} =$

16. $5250 \times 50 =$

17. $324 \times 25 =$

18. $625 \times 20 =$

19. $198 \times 11\frac{1}{9} =$

20. $224 \times 14\frac{2}{7} =$

Answers

The rewritten problems and their solutions appear below:

1. $.07\overline{)77.} = 7\overline{)7700.}^{1100.}$

2. $.09\overline{)81.} = 9\overline{)8100.}^{900.}$

3. $.05\overline{)475.} = 5\overline{)47500.}^{9500.}$

4. $.02\overline{)42.} = 2\overline{)4200.}^{2100.}$

5. $.03\overline{)36.} = 3\overline{)3600.}^{1200.}$

6. $.08\overline{)96.} = 8\overline{)9600.}^{1200.}$

7. $.06\overline{)126.} = 6\overline{)12600.}^{2100.}$

8. $.04\overline{)48.} = 4\overline{)4800.}^{1200.}$

9. $.03\overline{)33.}$ = $3\overline{)3300.}^{1100.}$

10. $.07\overline{)84.}$ = $7\overline{)8400.}^{1200.}$

11. $.09\overline{)99.}$ = $9\overline{)9900.}^{1100.}$

12. $.03\overline{)126.}$ = $3\overline{)12600.}^{4200.}$

13. $.08\overline{)168.}$ = $8\overline{)16800.}^{2100.}$

14. $.06\overline{)654.}$ = $6\overline{)65400.}^{10900.}$

15. $.07\overline{)154.}$ = $7\overline{)15400.}^{2200.}$

16. $.02\overline{)5250.}$ = $2\overline{)525000.}^{262500.}$

17. $.04\overline{)324.}$ = $4\overline{)32400.}^{8100.}$

18. $.05\overline{)625.}$ = $5\overline{)62500.}^{12500.}$

19. $.09\overline{)198.}$ = $9\overline{)19800.}^{2200.}$

20. $.07\overline{)224.}$ = $7\overline{)22400.}^{3200.}$

POWERS AND ROOTS

1. The numbers that are multiplied to give a product are called the **factors** of the product.

In $2 \times 3 = 6$, 2 and 3 are factors.

2. If the factors are the same, an **exponent** may be used to indicate the number of times the factor appears.

In $3 \times 3 = 3^2$, the number 3 appears as a factor twice, as is indicated by the exponent 2.

3. When a product is written in exponential form, the number the exponent refers to is called the **base**. The product itself is called the **power**.

In 2^5, the number 2 is the base and 5 is the exponent.
$2^5 = 2 \times 2 \times 2 \times 2 \times 2 = 32$, so 32 is the power.

4. a. If the exponent used is 2, we say that the base has been **squared**, or raised to the second power.

6^2 is read "six squared" or "six to the second power."

b. If the exponent used is 3, we say that the base has been **cubed**, or raised to the third power.

5^3 is read "five cubed" or "five to the third power."

c. If the exponent is 4, we say that the base has been raised to the fourth power. If the exponent is 5, we say the base has been raised to the fifth power, etc.

2^8 is read "two to the eighth power."

5. A number that is the product of a number squared is called a **perfect square**.

25 is a perfect square because $25 = 5^2$.

6. a. If a number has exactly two equal factors, each factor is called the **square root of the number.**

$9 = 3 \times 3$; therefore, 3 is the square root of 9.

b. The symbol $\sqrt{}$ is used to indicate square root.

$\sqrt{9} = 3$ means that the square root of 9 is 3, or $3 \times 3 = 9$.

7. The square root of the most common perfect squares can be found by using the following table, or by trial and error; that is, by finding the number that, when squared, yields the given perfect square.

Number	Perfect Square	Number	Perfect Square
1	1	10	100
2	4	11	121
3	9	12	144
4	16	13	169
5	25	14	196
6	36	15	225
7	49	20	400
8	64	25	625
9	81	30	900

To find $\sqrt{81}$, note that 81 is the perfect square of 9, or $9^2 = 81$. Therefore, $\sqrt{81} = 9$.

8. To find the square root of a number that is not a perfect square, use the following method:
   a. Locate the decimal point.
   b. Mark off the digits in groups of two in both directions beginning at the decimal point.
   c. Mark the decimal point for the answer just above the decimal point of the number whose square root is to be taken.
   d. Find the greatest perfect square contained in the left-hand group of two.
   e. Place its square root in the answer. Subtract the perfect square from the first digit or pair of digits.
   f. Bring down the next pair.
   g. Double the partial answer.
   h. Place a trial digit to the right of the doubled partial answer. Multiply this new number by the trial digit. If the product is the greatest possible without being more than the number from (f), this is the next digit in the answer.
   i. Subtract the product.
   j. Repeat steps (f–i) as often as necessary.

You will notice that you get one digit in the answer for every group of two you marked off in the original number.

Illustration: Find the square root of 138,384.

Solution:

$$
\begin{array}{r}
3\ \underline{7}\ \underline{\underline{2}} \\
\sqrt{13'83'84'.} \\
3^2 = -9 \\
\hline
4\ 83 \\
\underline{7} \times 6\underline{7} = -4\ 69 \\
\hline
14\ 84 \\
\underline{\underline{2}} \times 74\underline{\underline{2}} = -14\ 84 \\
\hline
\end{array}
$$

The number must first be marked off in groups of two figures each, beginning at the decimal point, which, in the case of a whole number, is at the right. The number of figures in the root will be the same as the number of groups so obtained.

The greatest square less than 13 is 9. $\sqrt{9} = 3$

Place its square root in the answer. Subtract the perfect square from the first digit or pair of digits. Bring down the next pair. To form our trial divisor, double the partial answer ($3 \times 2 = 6$) and place a trial digit next to it (enter 8 first).

Multiplying the trial divisor 68 by 8, we obtain 544, which is too great. We then use 7 and try multiplying 67 by 7. This is correct. Place the new digit in the answer. Subtract the product and bring down the final group. Double the partial answer (37) and place a trial digit (372). Multiply 2×372 and get 1484 so the final answer is 372.

Illustration: Find the square root of 3 to the nearest hundredth.

Solution:

$$
\begin{array}{r}
1.\ 7\ \ 3\ \ 2 \\
\sqrt{3.00'00'00} \\
1^2 = \quad 1 \\
\hline
2\ 00 \\
\underline{7} \times 2\underline{7} = \quad 1\ 89 \\
\hline
11\ 00 \\
\underline{3} \times 34\underline{3} = \quad 10\ 29 \\
\hline
71\ 00 \\
\underline{\underline{2}} \times 346\underline{\underline{2}} = \quad 69\ 24 \\
\hline
\end{array}
$$

We can stop here because we only need it to the nearest hundredth.

Answer: 1.73

9. To find the square root of a fraction, find the square root of its numerator and of its denominator.

$$\sqrt{\frac{4}{9}} = \frac{\sqrt{4}}{\sqrt{9}} = \frac{2}{3}$$

10. a. If a number has exactly three equal factors, each factor is called the **cube root** of the number.

    b. The symbol $\sqrt[3]{}$ is used to indicate the cube root.

$$8 = 2 \times 2 \times 2; \text{ therefore, } \sqrt[3]{8} = 2$$

EXERCISES: POWERS AND ROOTS

1. The square of 10 is

(1) 1

(2) 2

(3) 5

(4) 100

(5) 105

2. The cube of 9 is

(1) 3

(2) 27

(3) 81

(4) 99

(5) 729

3. The fourth power of 2 is

(1) 2

(2) 4

(3) 8

(4) 16

(5) 32

4. The product $7 \times 7 \times 7 \times 7 \times 7$ may be written in exponential form as

(1) 5^7

(2) 7^5

(3) 2^7

(4) 7^2

(5) 2^5

5. The value of 3^5 is

(1) 243

(2) 125

(3) 35

(4) 25

(5) 15

6. The square root of 1175, to the nearest whole number, is

(1) 32

(2) 33

(3) 34

(4) 35

(5) 36

7. Find $\sqrt{503}$ to the nearest tenth.

(1) 22.4

(2) 22.5

(3) 22.6

(4) 22.7

(5) 22.8

8. Find $\sqrt{\dfrac{1}{4}}$.

(1) 2

(2) $\dfrac{1}{2}$

(3) $\dfrac{1}{8}$

(4) $\dfrac{1}{16}$

(5) $\dfrac{1}{16}$

9. Find $\sqrt[3]{64}$.

(1) 3

(2) 4

(3) 8

(4) 32

(5) 40

10. The sum of 2^2 and 2^3 is

(1) 9

(2) 10

(3) 12

(4) 32

(5) 44

ANSWER KEY AND EXPLANATIONS

1. (4)	5. (1)	8. (2)
2. (5)	6. (3)	9. (2)
3. (4)	7. (1)	10. (3)
4. (2)		

1. The correct answer is (4).

$$10^2 = 10 \times 10 = 100$$

2. The correct answer is (5).

$$9^3 = 9 \times 9 \times 9$$
$$= 81 \times 9$$
$$= 729$$

3. The correct answer is (4).

$$2^4 = 2 \times 2 \times 2 \times 2$$
$$= 4 \times 2 \times 2$$
$$= 8 \times 2$$
$$= 16$$

4. The correct answer is (2).

$$7 \times 7 \times 7 \times 7 \times 7 = 7^5$$

5. The correct answer is (1).

$$3^5 = 3 \times 3 \times 3 \times 3 \times 3$$
$$= 243$$

6. The correct answer is (3).

$$
\begin{array}{r}
3\ \ 4.\ \ 2 = 34 \text{ to the nearest} \\
\sqrt{11'75.00} \quad \text{whole number} \\
\end{array}
$$

$$
\begin{array}{rr}
3^2 = & 9 \\
\hline
& 2\,75 \\
4 \times 6\underline{4} = & 2\,56 \\
\hline
& 19\,00 \\
2 \times 68\underline{2} = & 13\,64 \\
\hline
& 5\,36 \\
\end{array}
$$

7. The correct answer is (1).

$$
\begin{array}{r}
2\ \ 2.\ 4\ \ 2 \\
\sqrt{5'03.00'00}
\end{array}
= 22.4 \text{ to the nearest tenth}
$$

$$
\begin{array}{rr}
2^2 = & 4 \\
\hline
& 1\ 03 \\
2 \times 4\underline{2} = & 84 \\
\hline
& 19\ 00 \\
4 \times 44\underline{4} = & 17\ 76 \\
\hline
& 1\ 24\ 00 \\
2 \times 448\underline{2} = & 89\ 64 \\
\hline
& 34\ 36 \\
\end{array}
$$

8. The correct answer is (2).

$$\sqrt{\frac{1}{4}} = \frac{\sqrt{1}}{\sqrt{4}} = \frac{1}{2}$$

9. The correct answer is (2).

Since $4 \times 4 \times 4 = 64$, $\sqrt[3]{64} = 4$

10. The correct answer is (3).

$$2^2 + 2^3 = 4 + 8 = 12$$

TABLE OF MEASURES

English Measures

Length

1 foot (ft or ') = 12 inches (in or ")

1 yard (yd) = 36 inches

1 yard = 3 feet

1 rod (rd) = $6\frac{1}{2}$ feet

1 mile (mi) = 5,280 feet

1 mile = 1760 yards

1 mile = 320 rods

Weight

1 pound (lb) = 16 ounces (oz)

1 hundredweight (cwt) = 100 pounds

1 ton (T) = 2,000 pounds

Area

1 square foot (ft^2) = 144 square inches (in^2)

1 square yard (yd^2) = 9 square feet

General Measures

Time

1 minute (min) = 60 seconds (sec)

1 hour (hr) = 60 minutes

1 day = 24 hours

1 week = 7 days

1 year = 52 weeks

1 calendar year = 365 days

Liquid Measure

1 cup (c) = 8 fluid ounces (fl oz)

1 pint (pt) = 2 cups

1 pint = 4 gills (gi)

1 quart (qt) = 2 pints

1 gallon (gal) = 4 quarts

1 barrel (bl) = $31\frac{1}{2}$ gallons

Dry Measure

1 quart (qt) = 2 pints (pt)

1 peck (pk) = 8 quarts

1 bushel (bu) = 4 pecks

Volume

1 cubic foot (ft^3 or cu ft) = 1728 cubic inches

1 cubic yard (yd^3 or cu yd) = 27 cubic feet

1 gallon = 231 cubic inches

Angles and Arcs

1 minute (') = 60 second (sec)

1 degree (°) = 60 minutes

1 circle = 360 degrees

Counting

1 dozen (doz) = 12 units

1 gross (gr) = 12 dozen

1 gross = 144 units

English–Metric Conversions (Approximate)

English to Metric	Metric to English
1 inch = 2.54 centimeters	1 centimeter = .39 inches
1 yard = .9 meters	1 meter = 1.1 yards
1 mile = 1.6 kilometers	1 kilometer = .6 miles
1 ounce = 28 grams	1 kilogram = 2.2 pounds
1 pound = 454 grams	1 liter = 1.06 liquid quart
1 fluid ounce = 30 milliliters	
1 liquid quart = .95 liters	

Table of Metric Conversions

1 liter = 1,000 cubic centimeters (cm³)

1 milliliter = 1 cubic centimeter

1 liter of water weighs 1 kilogram*

1 milliliter of water weighs 1 gram*

The Metric System

Length

Unit	Abbreviation	Number of Meters
myriameter	mym	10,000
kilometer	km	1,000
hectometer	hm	100
dekameter	dam	10
meter	m	1
decimeter	dm	0.1
centimeter	cm	0.01
millimeter	mm	0.001

Area

Unit	Abbreviation	Number of Square Meters
square kilometer	sq km *or* km²	1,000,000
hectare	ha	10,000
are	a	100
centare	ca	1
square centimeter	sq cm *or* cm²	0.0001

*These conversions are exact only under specific conditions. If the conditions are not met, the conversions are approximate.

Volume

Unit	Abbreviation	Number of Cubic Meters
dekastere	das	10
stere	s	1
decistere	ds	0.10
cubic centimeter	cu cm *or* cm³ *or* cc	0.000001

Capacity

Unit	Abbreviation	Number of Liters
kiloliter	kl	1,000
hectoliter	hl	100
dekaliter	dal	10
liter	*l*	1
deciliter	dl	0.10
centiliter	cl	0.01
milliliter	ml	0.001

Mass and Weight

Unit	Abbreviation	Number of Grams
metric ton	MT *or* t	1,000,000
quintal	q	100,000
kilogram	kg	1,000
hectogram	hg	100
dekagram	dag	10
gram	g *or* gm	1
decigram	dg	0.10
centigram	cg	0.01
milligram	mg	0.001

DENOMINATE NUMBERS (MEASUREMENT)

1. A **denominate number** is a number that specifies a given measurement. The unit of measure is called the **denomination.**

   7 miles, 3 quarts, and 5 grams are denominate numbers.

2. a. The English system of measurement uses such denominations as pints, ounces, pounds, and feet.

   b. The metric system of measurement uses such denominations as grams, liters, and meters.

English System of Measurement

3. To convert from one unit of measure to another, find in the Table of Measures how many units of the smaller denomination equal one unit of the larger denomination. This number is called the **conversion number.**

4. To convert from one unit of measure to a smaller unit, multiply the given number of units by the conversion number.

   Illustration: Convert 7 yards to inches.

   Solution: 1 yard = 36 inches (conversion number)

   $$7 \text{ yards} = 7 \times 36 \text{ inches}$$
   $$= 252 \text{ inches}$$

   Answer: 252 inches

   Illustration: Convert 2 hours 12 minutes to minutes.

   Solution: 1 hour = 60 minutes (conversion number)

   $$2 \text{ hr } 12 \text{ min} = 2 \text{ hr} + 12 \text{ min}$$
   $$2 \text{ hr} = 2 \times 60 \text{ min} = 120 \text{ min}$$
   $$2 \text{ hr } 12 \text{ min} = 120 \text{ min} + 12 \text{ min}$$
   $$= 132 \text{ min}$$

   Answer: 132 min

5. To convert from one unit of measure to a larger unit:
   a. Divide the given number of units by the conversion number.

   Illustration: Convert 48 inches to feet.

   Solution: 1 foot = 12 inches (conversion number)

   $$48 \text{ in} \div 12 = 4 \text{ ft}$$

   Answer: 4 ft

b. If there is a remainder, it is expressed in terms of the smaller unit of measure.

Illustration: Convert 35 ounces to pounds and ounces.

Solution: 1 pound = 16 ounces (conversion number)

$$35 \text{ oz} \div 16 = 16\overline{)\begin{array}{l} 2 \text{ lb} \\ 35 \text{ oz} \end{array}}$$

$$\underline{32}$$

$$3 \text{ oz}$$

$$= 2 \text{ lb } 3 \text{ oz}$$

Answer: 2 lb 3 oz

6. To add denominate numbers, arrange them in columns by common unit, then add each column. If necessary, simplify the answer, starting with the smallest unit.

Illustration: Add 1 yd 2 ft 8 in, 2 yd 2 ft 10 in, and 3 yd 1 ft 9 in.

Solution: 1 yd 2 ft   8 in

                2 yd 2 ft 10 in

         + 3 yd 1 ft   9 in

                6 yd 5 ft 27 in

= 6 yd 7 ft 3 in (since 27 in = 2 ft 3 in)

= 8 yd 1 ft 3 in (since 7 ft = 2 yd 1 ft)

Answer: 8 yd 1 ft 3 in

7. To subtract denominate numbers, arrange them in columns by common unit, then subtract each column starting with the smallest unit. If necessary, rename to increase the number of a particular unit.

Illustration: Subtract 2 gal 3 qt from 7 gal 1 qt.

Solution: 7 gal 1 qt = 6 gal 5 qt

         − 2 gal 3 qt = −2 gal 3 qt

                    4 gal 2 qt

Note that 1 gal was renamed as 4 qt.

Therefore, 7 gal 1 qt = 6 gal 5 qt

Answer: 4 gal 2 qt

8. To multiply a denominate number by a given number:
   a. If the denominate number contains only one unit, multiply the numbers and write the unit.

3 oz × 4 = 12 oz

   b. If the denominate number contains more than one unit of measurement, multiply the number of each unit by the given number and simplify the answer, if necessary.

Illustration: Multiply 4 yd 2 ft 8 in by 2.

Solution: 4 yd 2 ft   8 in

          × 2

          8 yd 4 ft 16 in

   = 8 yd 5 ft 4 in (since 16 in = 1 ft 4 in)

   = 9 yd 2 ft 4 in (since 5 ft = 1 yd 2 ft)

Answer: 9 yd 2 ft 4 in

9. To divide a denominate number by a given number, convert all units to the smallest unit, then divide. Simplify the answer, if necessary.

Illustration: Divide 5 lb 12 oz by 4.

Solution: 1 lb = 16 oz, therefore
          5 lb 12 oz = 92 oz
          92 oz ÷ 4 = 23 oz
                   = 1 lb 7 oz

Answer: 1 lb 7 oz

10. Alternate method of division:
    a. Divide the number of the largest unit by the given number.
    b. Convert any remainder to the next largest unit.
    c. Divide the total number of that unit by the given number.
    d. Again, convert any remainder to the next unit and divide.
    e. Repeat until no units remain.

Illustration: Divide 9 hr 21 min 40 sec by 4.

Solution:

$$
\begin{array}{r}
\text{2 hr} \quad \text{20 min} \quad \text{25 sec} \\
\overline{4)\ \text{9 hr} \quad \text{21 min} \quad \text{40 sec}} \\
\underline{\text{8 hr}} \quad\quad\quad\quad\quad\quad \\
\text{1 hr} = \underline{\text{60 min}} \quad\quad\quad \\
\text{81 min} \quad\quad \\
\underline{\text{80 min}} \quad\quad \\
\text{1 min} = \underline{\text{60 sec}} \\
\text{100 sec} \\
\underline{\text{100 sec}} \\
\text{0 sec}
\end{array}
$$

Answer: 2 hr 20 min 25 sec

Metric Measurement

11. The basic units of the metric system are the meter (m), which is used for length; the gram (g), which is used for weight; and the liter (1), which is used for capacity, or volume.

12. The prefixes that are used with the basic units, and their meanings, are:

Prefix	Abbreviation	Meaning
micro-	m	one millionth of (.000001)
milli-	ml	one thousandth of (.001)
centi-	c	one hundredth of (.01)
deci-	d	one tenth of (.1)
deka-	da *or* dk	ten times (10)
hecto-	h	one hundred times (100)
kilo-	k	one thousand times (1000)
mega-	M	one million times (1,000,000)

13. To convert *to* a basic metric unit from a prefixed metric unit, multiply by the number indicated in the prefix.

> Convert 72 millimeters to meters.
> 72 millimeters = 72 × .001 meters
>   = .072 meters
>
> Convert 4 kiloliters to liters.
> 4 kiloliters = 4 × 1000 liters
>   = 4000 liters

14. To convert *from* a basic unit to a prefixed unit, divide by the number indicated in the prefix.

> Convert 300 liters to hectoliters.
> 300 liters = 300 ÷ 100 hectoliters
>   = 3 hectoliters
>
> Convert 4.5 meters to decimeters.
> 4.5 meters = 4.5 ÷ .1 decimeters
> = 45 decimeters

15. To convert from any prefixed metric unit to another prefixed unit, first convert to a basic unit, then convert the basic unit to the desired unit.

    Illustration: Convert 420 decigrams to kilograms.

    Solution: 420 dg = 420 × .1 g = 42 g
            42 g = 42 ÷ 1000 kg = .042 kg

    Answer: .042 kg

16. To add, subtract, multiply, or divide using metric measurement, first convert all units to the same unit, then perform the desired operation.

    Illustration: Subtract 1200 g from 2.5 kg.

    Solution:

    $$\begin{array}{r} 2.5\,\text{kg} = 2500\,\text{g} \\ -1200\,\text{g} = -1200\,\text{g} \\ \hline 1300\,\text{g} \end{array}$$

    Answer: 1300 g or 1.3 kg

17. To convert from a metric measure to an English measure, or the reverse:
    a. In the Table of English-Metric Conversions, find how many units of the desired measure are equal to one unit of the given measure.
    b. Multiply the given number by the number found in the table.

Illustration: Find the number of pounds in 4 kilograms.

Solution:

From the table, 1 kg = 2.2 lb

$$4 \text{ kg} = 4 \times 2.2 \text{ lb}$$
$$= 8.8 \text{ lb}$$

Answer: 8.8 lb

Illustration: Find the number of meters in 5 yards.

Solution: 1 yd = .9 m

$$5 \text{ yd} = 5 \times .9 \text{ m}$$
$$= 4.5 \text{ m}$$

Answer: 4.5 m

Temperature Measurement

18. The temperature measurement currently used in the United States is the degree Fahrenheit (°F). The metric measurement for temperature is the degree Celsius (°C), also called degree Centigrade.
19.

Degrees Celsius can be converted to degrees Fahrenheit by the formula:

$$°F = \frac{9}{5}°C + 32°$$

Illustration: Water boils at 100°C. Convert this to °F.

Solution:

$$°F = \frac{9}{\cancel{5}} \times \cancel{100}^{20} + 32°$$

$$°F = 180° + 32°$$
$$= 212°$$

Answer: 100°C = 212°F

20. Degrees Fahrenheit can be converted to degrees Celsius by the formula:

$$°C = \frac{5}{9}(°F - 32°)$$

In using this formula, perform the subtraction in the parentheses first, then multiply by $\frac{5}{9}$.

Illustration: If normal body temperature is 98.6°F, what is it on the Celsius scale?

Solution:

$$°C = \frac{5}{9}(98.6° - 32°)$$

$$= \frac{5}{9} \times 66.6°$$

$$= \frac{333°}{9}$$

$$= 37°$$

Answer: 37°C

EXERCISES: MEASUREMENT

1. A carpenter needs boards for 4 shelves, each 2'9" long. How many feet of board should he buy?

    (1) 11

    (2) $11\frac{1}{6}$

    (3) 13

    (4) $15\frac{1}{2}$

    (5) 16

2. The number of half-pints in 19 gallons of milk is

    (1) 76

    (2) 152

    (3) 304

    (4) 608

    (5) 904

3. The product of 8 ft 7 in multiplied by 8 is

    (1) 69 feet 6 inches

    (2) 68.8 feet

    (3) $68\frac{2}{3}$ feet

    (4) 68 feet 2 inches

    (5) 68 feet 6 inches

4. $\frac{1}{3}$ of 7 yards is

    (1) 2 yards

    (2) 4 feet

    (3) $3\frac{1}{2}$ yards

    (4) 5 yards

    (5) 7 feet

5. Six gross of special drawing pencils were purchased for use in an office. If the pencils were used at the rate of 24 a week, the maximum number of weeks that the six gross of pencils would last is

    (1) 6 weeks

    (2) 12 weeks

    (3) 24 weeks

    (4) 36 weeks

    (5) 42 weeks

6. If 7 ft 9 in is cut from a piece of wood that is 9 ft 6 in, the piece left is

    (1) 1 foot 9 inches

    (2) 1 foot 10 inches

    (3) 2 feet 2 inches

    (4) 2 feet 5 inches

    (5) 2 feet 9 inches

7. Subtract 3 hours 49 minutes from 5 hours 13 minutes.

    (1) 1 hour 5 minutes

    (2) 1 hour 10 minutes

    (3) 1 hour 18 minutes

    (4) 1 hour 20 minutes

    (5) 1 hour 24 minutes

8. A piece of wood 35 feet 6 inches long was used to make 4 shelves of equal lengths. The length of each shelf was

    (1) 8.9 inches

    (2) 8 feet 9 inches

    (3) 8 feet $9\frac{1}{2}$ inches

    (4) 8 feet $10\frac{1}{2}$ inches

    (5) 8 feet 11 inches

9. The number of yards equal to 126 inches is

   (1) 3.5
   (2) 10.5
   (3) 1,260
   (4) 1,512
   (5) 1,560

10. If there are 231 cubic inches in one gallon, the number of cubic inches in 3 pints is closest to which one of the following?

    (1) 24
    (2) 29
    (3) 57
    (4) 87
    (5) 89

11. The sum of 5 feet $2\frac{3}{4}$ inches, 8 feet $\frac{1}{2}$ inch, and $12\frac{1}{2}$ inches is

    (1) 14 feet $3\frac{3}{4}$ inches

    (2) 14 feet $5\frac{3}{4}$ inches

    (3) 14 feet $9\frac{1}{4}$ inches

    (4) 15 feet $\frac{1}{2}$ inches

    (5) 16 feet $\frac{1}{2}$ inches

12. Add 5 hr 13 min, 3 hr 49 min, and 14 min. The sum is

    (1) 8 hours 16 minutes
    (2) 9 hours 16 minutes
    (3) 9 hours 76 minutes
    (4) 8 hours 6 minutes
    (5) 9 hours 26 minutes

13. Assuming that 2.54 centimeters = 1 inch, a metal rod that measures $1\frac{1}{2}$ feet would most nearly equal which one of the following?

    (1) 380 centimeters
    (2) 46 centimeters
    (3) 30 centimeters
    (4) 18 centimeters
    (5) 10 centimeters

14. A micromillimeter is defined as one millionth of a millimeter. A length of 17 micromillimeters may be represented as

    (1) .00017 mm
    (2) .0000017 mm
    (3) .000017 mm
    (4) .00000017 mm
    (5) 0.17 mm

15. How many liters are equal to 4,200 ml?

    (1) .42
    (2) 42
    (3) 420
    (4) 420,000
    (5) 4.2

16. Add 26 dg, .4 kg, 5 g, and 184 cg.

    (1) 215.40 grams
    (2) 319.34 grams
    (3) 409.44 grams
    (4) 849.00 grams
    (5) 869.00 grams

17. Four full bottles of equal size contain a total of 1.28 liters of cleaning solution. How many milliliters are in each bottle?

    (1) 3.20
    (2) 5.12
    (3) 320
    (4) 512
    (5) 620

18. How many liters of water can be held in a 5-gallon jug? (See Conversion Table.)

   (1) 19

   (2) 38

   (3) 40

   (4) 50

   (5) 60

19. To the nearest degree, what is a temperature of 12°C equal to on the Fahrenheit scale?

   (1) 19°

   (2) 54°

   (3) 57°

   (4) 60°

   (5) 79°

20. A company requires that the temperature in its offices be kept at 68°F. What is this in °C?

   (1) 10°

   (2) 15°

   (3) 20°

   (4) 25°

   (5) 30°

ANSWER KEY AND EXPLANATIONS

1. (1)	6. (1)	11. (1)	16. (3)
2. (3)	7. (5)	12. (2)	17. (3)
3. (3)	8. (4)	13. (2)	18. (1)
4. (5)	9. (1)	14. (3)	19. (2)
5. (4)	10. (4)	15. (5)	20. (3)

1. The correct answer is (1).

$$\begin{array}{r} 2 \text{ ft } 9 \text{ in} \\ \times \quad\quad 4 \\ \hline 8 \text{ ft } 36 \text{ in} = 11 \text{ ft} \end{array}$$

2. The correct answer is (3).

Find the number of half-pints in 1 gallon:

1 gal = 4 qts
4 qts = 4×2 pts = 8 pts
8 pts = 8×2 = 16 half-pints

Multiply to find the number of half-pints in 19 gallons:
19 gal = 19×16 half-pints

$\qquad$ = 304 half-pints

3. The correct answer is (3).

$$\begin{array}{r} 8 \text{ ft } 7 \text{ in} \\ \times \quad\quad 8 \\ \hline 64 \text{ ft } 56 \text{ in} \quad = 68 \text{ ft } 8 \text{ in} \end{array}$$
(since 56 in = 4 ft 8 in)

$$8 \text{ in} = \frac{8}{12} \text{ ft} = \frac{2}{3} \text{ ft}$$

$$68 \text{ ft } 8 \text{ in} = 68\frac{2}{3} \text{ ft}$$

4. The correct answer is (5).

$$\begin{aligned} \frac{1}{3} \times 7 \text{ yd} &= 2\frac{1}{3} \text{ yd} \\ &= 2 \text{ yd } 1 \text{ ft} \\ &= 2 \times 3 \text{ ft} + 1 \text{ ft} \\ &= 7 \text{ ft} \end{aligned}$$

5. The correct answer is (4).

Find the number of units in 6 gross:

1 gross = 144 units
6 gross = 6×144 units
$\qquad$ = 864 units

Divide units by rate of use:

$864 \div 24 = 36$

6. The correct answer is (1).

$$\begin{array}{r} 9 \text{ ft } 6 \text{ in} = \quad 8 \text{ ft } 18 \text{ in} \\ -7 \text{ ft } 9 \text{ in} = \quad -7 \text{ ft } \;\; 9 \text{ in} \\ \hline 1 \text{ ft } \;\; 9 \text{ in} \end{array}$$

7. The correct answer is (5).

$$\begin{array}{rcl}
5 \text{ hours } 13 \text{ minutes} & = & 4 \text{ hours } 73 \text{ minutes} \\
\underline{-3 \text{ hours } 49 \text{ minutes}} & = & \underline{- \; 3 \text{ hours } 49 \text{ minutes}} \\
 & & 1 \text{ hour } \;\; 24 \text{ minutes}
\end{array}$$

8. The correct answer is (4).

$$8 \text{ feet } \;\; 10 \text{ inches} + \frac{2}{4} \text{ inches} = 8 \text{ ft } 10\frac{1}{2} \text{ in}$$

$$\begin{array}{r}
4\overline{)35 \text{ feet } 6 \text{ inches}} \\
\underline{32 \text{ feet}} \\
\underline{3 \text{ feet} = 36 \text{ inches}} \\
42 \text{ inches} \\
\underline{40 \text{ inches}} \\
2 \text{ inches}
\end{array}$$

9. The correct answer is (1).

$$1 \text{ yd} = 36 \text{ in}$$
$$126 \div 36 = 3.5$$

10. The correct answer is (4).

$$1 \text{ gal} = 4 \text{ qt} = 8 \text{ pt}$$
$$\begin{aligned}
\text{Therefore, } 1 \text{ pt} &= 231 \text{ cubic inches} \div 8 \\
&= 28.875 \text{ cubic inches} \\
3 \text{ pts} &= 3 \times 28.875 \text{ cubic inches} \\
&= 86.625 \text{ cubic inches}
\end{aligned}$$

11. The correct answer is (1).

$$\begin{array}{rl}
5 \text{ feet} & 2\frac{3}{4} \text{ inches} \\
8 \text{ feet} & \frac{1}{2} \text{ inches} \\
+ & 12\frac{1}{2} \text{ inches} \\
\hline
13 \text{ feet} & 15\frac{3}{4} \text{ inches} \\
= 14 \text{ feet} & 3\frac{3}{4} \text{ inches}
\end{array}$$

12. The correct answer is (2).

$$\begin{array}{rl}
& 5 \text{ hr } 13 \text{ min.} \\
& 3 \text{ hr } 49 \text{ min.} \\
\underline{+} & \underline{14 \text{ min.}} \\
& 8 \text{ hr } 76 \text{ min} \\
= & 9 \text{ hr } 16 \text{ min}
\end{array}$$

13. The correct answer is (2).

$$1 \text{ foot} = 12 \text{ inches}$$
$$1\frac{1}{2} \text{ feet} = 1\frac{1}{2} \times 12 \text{ inches} =$$
$$18 \text{ inches}$$
$$1 \text{ inch} = 2.54 \text{ cm}$$

Therefore,
$$\begin{aligned}
18 \text{ inches} &= 18 \times 2.54 \text{ cm} \\
&= 45.72 \text{ cm}
\end{aligned}$$

14. The correct answer is (3).

$$\begin{aligned}
1 \text{ micromillimeter} &= .000001 \text{ mm} \\
17 \text{ micromilliters} &= 17 \times .000001 \text{ mm} \\
&= .000017 \text{ mm}
\end{aligned}$$

15. The correct answer is (5).

$$\begin{aligned}
4200 \text{ ml} &= 4200 \times .001 \, l \\
&= 4.200 \, l
\end{aligned}$$

16. The correct answer is (3).

Convert all of the units to grams:

$$\begin{array}{llll}
26 \text{ dg} & = 26 \times .1 & = & 2.6 \text{ g} \\
.4 \text{ kg} & = .4 \times 1000 \text{g} & = 400 & \text{g} \\
5 \text{g} & = & & 5 \;\; \text{g} \\
184 \text{ cg} & = 184 \times .01 \text{ g} & = & \underline{1.84 \text{g}} \\
& & & 409.44 \text{ g}
\end{array}$$

17. The correct answer is (3).

$$1.28 \text{ liters} \div 4 = .32 \text{ liters}$$
$$32 \text{ liters} = .32 \div .001 \text{ ml}$$
$$= 320 \text{ ml}$$

18. The correct answer is (1).

Find the number of liters in 1 gallon:

$$1 \text{ qt} = .95 \, l$$
$$1 \text{ gal} = 4 \text{ qts}$$
$$1 \text{ gal} = 4 \times .95 \, l = 3.8 \, l$$

Multiply to find the number of liters in 5 gallons:

$$5 \text{ gal} = 5 \times 3.8 \, l = 19 \, l$$

19. The correct answer is (2).

$$°F = \frac{9}{5} \times 12° + 32°$$
$$= \frac{108°}{5} + 32°$$
$$= 21.6° + 32°$$
$$= 53.6°$$

20. The correct answer is (3).

$$°C = \frac{5}{9}\left(68° - 32°\right)$$
$$= \frac{5}{\cancel{9}} \times \cancel{36°}^{4}$$
$$= 20°$$

answers

exercises

STATISTICS AND PROBABILITY

Statistics

1. The averages used in statistics include the **arithmetic mean**, the **median**, and the **mode**.

2. a. The most commonly used average of a group of numbers is the **arithmetic mean**. It is found by adding the numbers given and then dividing this sum by the number of items being averaged.

   Illustration: Find the arithmetic mean of 2, 8, 5, 9, 6, and 12.

   Solution: There are 6 numbers.

   $$\text{Arithmetic mean} = \frac{2+8+5+9+6+12}{6}$$
   $$= \frac{42}{6}$$
   $$= 7$$

   Answer: The arithmetic mean is 7.

   b. If a problem calls for simply the "average" or the "mean," it is referring to the arithmetic mean.

3. If a group of numbers is arranged in order, the middle number is called the **median**. If there is no single middle number (this occurs when there is an even number of items), the median is found by computing the arithmetic mean of the two middle numbers.

   The median of 6, 8, 10, 12, and 14 is 10.

   The median of 6, 8, 10, 12, 14, and 16 is the arithmetic mean of 10 and 12.
   $$\frac{10 + 12}{2} = \frac{22}{2} = 11$$

4. The **mode** of a group of numbers is the number that appears most often.

   The mode of 10, 5, 7, 9, 12, 5, 10, 5, and 9 is 5.

5. To obtain the average of quantities that are weighted:

   a. Set up a table listing the quantities, their respective weights, and their respective values.

   b. Multiply the value of each quantity by its respective weight.

   c. Add up these products.

   d. Add up the weights.

   e. Divide the sum of the products by the sum of the weights.

   Illustration: Assume that the weights for the following subjects are: English 3, History 2, Mathematics 2, Foreign Languages 2, and Art 1. What would be the average of a student whose marks are: English 80, History 85, Algebra 84, Spanish 82, and Art 90?

   Solution:

Subject	Weight	Mark
English	3	80
History	2	85
Algebra	2	84
Spanish	2	82
Art	1	90

English	$3 \times 80 = 240$
History	$2 \times 85 = 170$
Algebra	$2 \times 84 = 168$
Spanish	$2 \times 82 = 164$
Art	$1 \times 90 = \underline{90}$
	832

   Sum of the weights: $3 + 2 + 2 + 2 + 1 = 10$

   $832 \div 10 = 83.2$

   Answer: Average = 83.2

Probability

6. The study of probability deals with predicting the outcome of chance events; that is, events in which one has no control over the results.

Tossing a coin, rolling dice, and drawing concealed objects from a bag are chance events.

7. The probability of a particular outcome is equal to the number of ways that outcome can occur, divided by the total number of possible outcomes.

In tossing a coin, there are 2 possible outcomes: heads or tails. The probability that the coin will turn up heads is $1 \div 2$ or $\frac{1}{2}$.

If a bag contains 5 balls of which 3 are red, the probability of drawing a red ball is $\frac{3}{5}$. The probability of drawing a non-red ball is $\frac{2}{5}$.

8. a. If an event is certain, its probability is 1.

If a bag contains only red balls, the probability of drawing a red ball is 1.

   b. If an event is impossible, its probability is 0.

If a bag contains only red balls, the probability of drawing a green ball is 0.

9. Probability may be expressed in fractional, decimal, or percent form.

An event having a probability of $\frac{1}{2}$ is said to be 50% probable.

10. A probability determined by random sampling of a group of items is assumed to apply to other items in that group and in other similar groups.

Illustration: A random sampling of 100 items produced in a factory shows that 7 are defective. How many items of the total production of 50,000 can be expected to be defective?

Solution: The probability of an item being defective is $\frac{7}{100}$, or 7%. Of the total production, 7% can be expected to be defective.

$7\% \times 50,000 = .07 \times 50,000 = 3500$

Answer: 3500 items

EXERCISES: STATISTICS AND PROBABILITY

1. The arithmetic mean of 73.8, 92.2, 64.7, 43.8, 56.5, and 46.4 is

   (1) 60.6
   (2) 61.00
   (3) 61.28
   (4) 61.48
   (5) 62.9

2. The median of the numbers 8, 5, 7, 5, 9, 9, 1, 8, 10, 5, and 10 is

   (1) 5
   (2) 7
   (3) 8
   (4) 9
   (5) 10

3. The mode of the numbers 16, 15, 17, 12, 15, 15, 18, 19, and 18 is

   (1) 15
   (2) 16
   (3) 17
   (4) 18
   (5) 19

4. A clerk filed 73 forms on Monday, 85 forms on Tuesday, 54 on Wednesday, 92 on Thursday, and 66 on Friday. What was the average number of forms filed per day?

   (1) 60
   (2) 72
   (3) 74
   (4) 92
   (5) 94

5. The grades received on a test by twenty students were: 100, 55, 75, 80, 65, 65, 85, 90, 80, 45, 40, 50, 85, 85, 85, 80, 80, 70, 65, and 60. The average of these grades is

   (1) 70
   (2) 72
   (3) 77
   (4) 80
   (5) 87

6. A buyer purchased 75 six-inch rulers costing 15¢ each, 100 one-foot rulers costing 30¢ each, and 50 one-yard rulers costing 72¢ each. What was the average price per ruler?

   (1) $26\frac{1}{8}$¢
   (2) $34\frac{1}{3}$¢
   (3) 39¢
   (4) 42¢
   (5) 49¢

7. What is the average of a student who received 90 in English, 84 in algebra, 75 in French, and 76 in music, if the subjects have the following weights: English 4, algebra 3, French 3, and music 1?

   (1) 81
   (2) $81\frac{1}{2}$
   (3) 82
   (4) 83
   (5) 84

ITEMS 8 TO 11 REFER TO THE FOLLOWING INFORMATION.

A census shows that on a certain block the number of children in each family is 3, 4, 4, 0, 1, 2, 0, 2, and 2, respectively.

8. Find the average number of children per family.

   (1) 2
   (2) $2\frac{1}{2}$
   (3) 3
   (4) $3\frac{1}{2}$
   (5) 4

9. Find the median number of children.

   (1) 6
   (2) 5
   (3) 4
   (4) 3
   (5) 2

10. Find the mode of the number of children.

   (1) 0
   (2) 1
   (3) 2
   (4) 4
   (5) 5

11. What is the probability that a family chosen at random on this block will have 4 children?

   (1) $\frac{4}{9}$

   (2) $\frac{2}{9}$

   (3) $\frac{4}{7}$

   (4) $\frac{2}{1}$

   (5) $\frac{4}{7}$

12. What is the probability that an even number will come up when a single standard die is thrown?

   (1) $\frac{1}{6}$

   (2) $\frac{1}{5}$

   (3) $\frac{1}{4}$

   (4) $\frac{1}{3}$

   (5) $\frac{1}{2}$

13. A bag contains 3 black balls, 2 yellow balls, and 4 red balls. What is the probability of drawing a black ball?

   (1) $\frac{1}{2}$

   (2) $\frac{1}{3}$

   (3) $\frac{2}{3}$

   (4) $\frac{4}{9}$

   (5) $\frac{4}{5}$

14. In a group of 1,000 adults, 682 are women. What is the probability that a person chosen at random from this group will be a man?

   (1) .318
   (2) .682
   (3) .5
   (4) 1
   (5) 1.5

15. In a balloon factory, a random sampling of 100 balloons showed that 3 had pinholes in them. In a sampling of 2,500 balloons, how many may be expected to have pinholes?

   (1) 30
   (2) 75
   (3) 100
   (4) 750
   (5) 800

ANSWER KEY AND EXPLANATIONS

1. (5)	6. (2)	11. (2)
2. (3)	7. (4)	12. (5)
3. (1)	8. (1)	13. (2)
4. (3)	9. (5)	14. (1)
5. (2)	10. (3)	15. (2)

1. The correct answer is (5).

Find the sum of the values:

73.8 + 92.2 + 64.7 + 43.8 + 56.5 + 46.4 = 377.4

There are 6 values.

Arithmetic mean = $\dfrac{377.4}{6}$ = 62.9

2. The correct answer is (3).

Arrange the numbers in order:

1, 5, 5, 5, 7, 8, 8, 9, 9, 10, 10

The middle number, or median, is 8.

3. The correct answer is (1).

The mode is the number that appears most frequently. The number 15 appears three times.

4. The correct answer is (3).

Average = $\dfrac{73 + 85 + 54 + 92 + 66}{5}$

$= \dfrac{370}{5}$

$= 74$

5. The correct answer is (2).

Sum of the grades = 1440
$\dfrac{1440}{20}$ = 72

6. The correct answer is (2).

$$
\begin{array}{r}
75 \times 15¢ = 1125¢ \\
100 \times 30¢ = 3000¢ \\
\underline{50 \times 72¢ = 3600¢} \\
225 \qquad\quad 7725¢
\end{array}
$$

$\dfrac{7725¢}{225} = 34\dfrac{1}{3}¢$

7. The correct answer is (4).

Subject	Grade	Weight
English	90	4
Algebra	84	3
French	75	3
Music	76	1

$(90 \times 4) + (84 \times 3) + (75 \times 3) + (76 \times 1)$

360 + 252 + 225 + 76 = 913

Weight = 4 + 3 + 3 + 1 = 11

913 ÷ 11 = 83 average

8. The correct answer is (1).

Average = $\dfrac{3+4+4+0+1+2+0+2+2}{9}$

$= \dfrac{18}{9}$

$= 2$

9. The correct answer is (5).

Arrange the numbers in order:

0, 0, 1, 2, 2, 2, 3, 4, 4

Of the 9 numbers, the fifth (middle) number is 2.

10. The correct answer is (3).

The number appearing most often is 2.

11. The correct answer is (2).

There are 9 families, 2 of which have 4 children. The probability is $\frac{2}{9}$.

12. The correct answer is (5).

Of the six possible numbers, three are even (2, 4, and 6). The probability is $\frac{3}{6}$ or $\frac{1}{2}$.

13. The correct answer is (2).

There are 9 balls in all. The probability of drawing a black ball is $\frac{3}{9}$ or $\frac{1}{3}$.

14. The correct answer is (1).

If 682 people of the 1000 are women, $1000 - 682 = 318$ are men. The probability of choosing a man is $\frac{318}{1000} = .318$.

15. The correct answer is (2).

There is a probability of $\frac{3}{100} = 3\%$ that a balloon may have a pinhole.

$3\% \times 2500 = 75.00$

GRAPHS

1. **Graphs** illustrate comparisons and trends in statistical information. The most commonly used graphs are **bar graphs**, **line graphs**, **circle graphs**, and **pictographs**.

Bar Graphs

2. **Bar graphs** are used to compare various quantities. Each bar may represent a single quantity or may be divided to represent several quantities.

3. Bar graphs may have horizontal or vertical bars.

Illustration:

Municipal Expenditure Per Capita

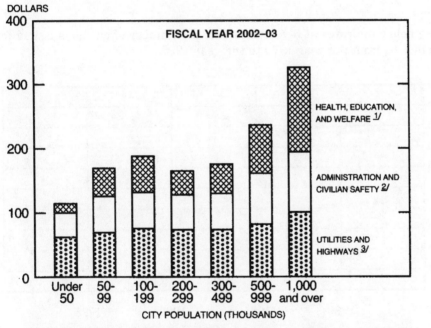

1/ PUBLIC WELFARE, EDUCATION, HOSPITALS, HEALTH, LIBRARIES, AND HOUSING AND URBAN RENEWAL.
2/ POLICE AND FIRE PROTECTION, FINANCIAL ADMINISTRATION, GENERAL CONTROL, GENERAL PUBLIC BUILDINGS, INTEREST ON GENERAL DEBT, AND OTHER.
3/ HIGHWAYS, SEWERAGE, SANITATION, PARKS AND RECREATION, AND UTILITIES.
SOURCE: DEPARTMENT OF COMMERCE.

Question 1: What was the approximate municipal expenditure per capita in cities having populations of 200,000 to 299,000?

Answer: The middle of the seven bars shown represents cities having populations from 200,000 to 299,000. This bar reaches about halfway between 100 and 200. Therefore, the per capita expenditure was approximately $150.

Question 2: Which cities spent the most per capita on health, education, and welfare?

Answer: The bar for cities having populations of 1,000,000 and over has a larger cross-hatched section than the other bars. Therefore, those cities spent the most.

Question 3: Of the three categories of expenditures, which was least dependent on city size?

Answer: The expenditures for utilities and highways, the dotted part of each bar, varied least as city size increased.

Line Graphs

4. **Line graphs** are used to show trends, often over a period of time.

5. A line graph may include more than one line, with each line representing a different item.

Illustration:

The graph below indicates at 5-year intervals the number of citations issued for various offenses from the year 1975 to the year 1995.

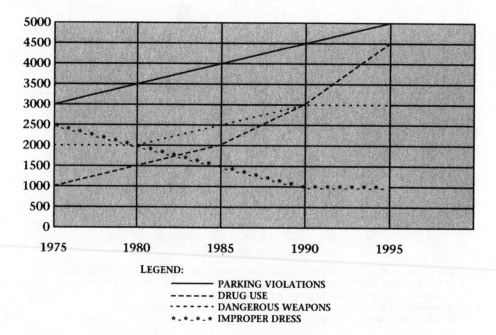

LEGEND:
——————— PARKING VIOLATIONS
- - - - - - DRUG USE
· · · · · · DANGEROUS WEAPONS
-·--·-* IMPROPER DRESS

Question 4: Over the 20-year period, which offense shows an average rate of increase of more than 150 citations per year?

Answer: Drug-use citations increased from 1000 in 1975 to 4500 in 1995. The average increase over the 20-year period is $\frac{3500}{20} = 175$.

Question 5: Over the 20-year period, which offense shows a constant rate of increase or decrease?

Answer: A straight line indicates a constant rate of increase or decrease. Of the four lines, the one representing parking violations is the only straight one.

Question 6: Which offense shows a total increase or decrease of 50% for the full 20-year period?

Answer: Dangerous weapons citations increased from 2000 in 1975 to 3000 in 1995, which is an increase of 50%.

Circle Graphs

6. **Circle graphs** are used to show the relationship of various parts of a quantity to each other and to the whole quantity.

7. Percents are often used in circle graphs. The 360 degrees of the circle represent 100%.

8. Each part of the circle graph is called a sector.

Illustration:

The following circle graph shows how the federal budget of $300.4 billion was spent.

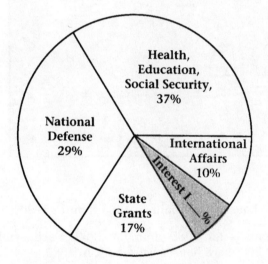

Question 7: What is the value of I?

Answer: There must be a total of 100% in a circle graph. The sum of the other sectors is:

17% + 29% + 37% + 10% = 93%

Therefore, I = 100% − 93% = 7%.

Question 8: How much money was actually spent on national defense?

Answer: 29% × $300.4 billion = $87.116 billion

= $87,116,000,000

Question 9: How much more money was spent on state grants than on interest?

Answer: 17% − 7% = 10%

10% × $300.4 billion = $30.04 billion

= $30,040,000,000

Pictographs

9. **Pictographs** allow comparisons of quantities by using symbols. Each symbol represents a given number of a particular item.

Illustration:

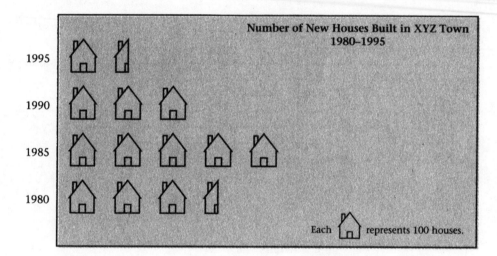

Question 10: How many more new houses were built in 1985 than in 1990?

Answer: There are two more symbols for 1985 than for 1990. Each symbol represents 100 houses. Therefore, 200 more houses were built in 1985.

Question 11: How many new houses were built in 1980?

Answer: There are $3\frac{1}{2}$ symbols shown for 1980; $3\frac{1}{2} \times 100 = 350$ houses.

Question 12: In which year were half as many houses built as in 1990?

Answer: In 1990, 3 × 100 = 300 houses were built. Half of 300, or 150, houses were built in 1995.

EXERCISES: GRAPHS

ITEMS 1 TO 4 REFER TO THE FOLLOWING GRAPH.

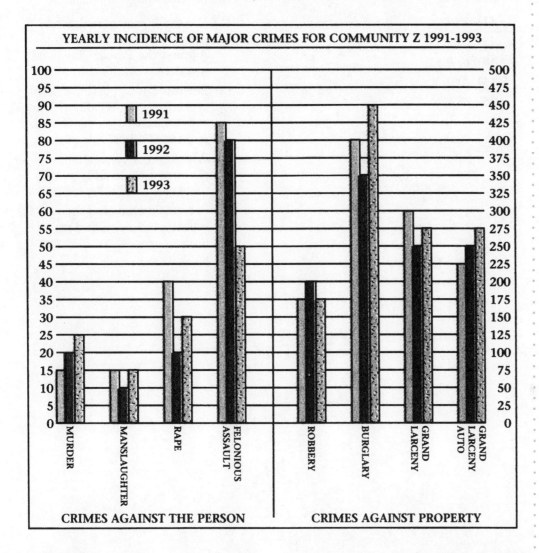

YEARLY INCIDENCE OF MAJOR CRIMES FOR COMMUNITY Z 1991-1993

CRIMES AGAINST THE PERSON   CRIMES AGAINST PROPERTY

1. In 1993 the incidence of which of the following crimes was greater than in the previous two years?

   (1) Grand larceny

   (2) Murder

   (3) Rape

   (4) Robbery

   (5) None of the above

2. If the incidence of burglary in 1994 were to have increased over 1993 by the same number as it had increased in 1993 over 1992, then the average for this crime for the four-year period from 1991 through 1993 would be most nearly

   (1) 100

   (2) 400

   (3) 425

   (4) 440

   (5) 450

3. The graph on the previous page indicates that the *percentage* increase in grand larceny auto from 1992 to 1993 was

   (1) 5%

   (2) 10%

   (3) 15%

   (4) 20%

   (5) 25%

4. Which of the following cannot be determined because there is not enough information in the graph on the previous page to do so?

   (1) For the 3-year period, what percentage of all "Crimes Against the Person" involved murders committed in 1992?

   (2) For the 3-year period, what percentage of all "Major Crimes" was committed in the first six months of 1992?

   (3) Which major crimes followed a pattern of continuing yearly increases for the 3-year period?

   (4) For 1993, what was the ratio of robbery, burglary, and grand larceny crimes?

   (5) None of the above

ITEMS 5 TO 7 REFER TO THE FOLLOWING GRAPH.

In the graph below, the lines labeled "A" and "B" represent the cumulative progress in the work of two file clerks, each of whom was given 500 consecutively numbered applications to file in the proper cabinets over a five-day work week.

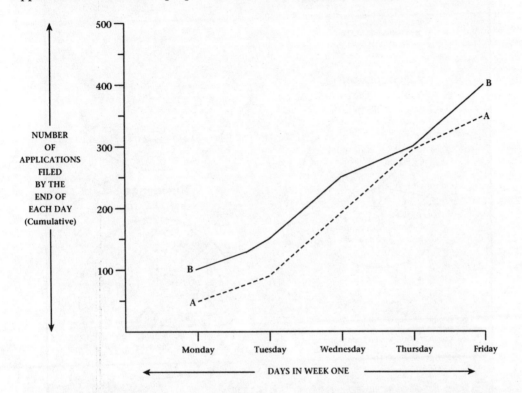

NUMBER OF APPLICATIONS FILED BY THE END OF EACH DAY (Cumulative)

DAYS IN WEEK ONE

5. The day during which the greatest number of applications was filed by both clerks was

   (1) Monday.

   (2) Tuesday.

   (3) Wednesday.

   (4) Thursday.

   (5) Friday.

6. At the end of the second day, the approximate percentage of applications still to be filed was

   (1) 25%

   (2) 37%

   (3) 50%

   (4) 66%

   (5) 75%

7. Assuming that the production pattern is the same the following week as the week shown in the chart, the day on which Clerk B will finish this assignment will be

   (1) Monday.

   (2) Tuesday.

   (3) Wednesday.

   (4) Thursday.

   (5) Friday.

ITEMS 8 TO 11 REFER TO THE FOLLOWING GRAPH.

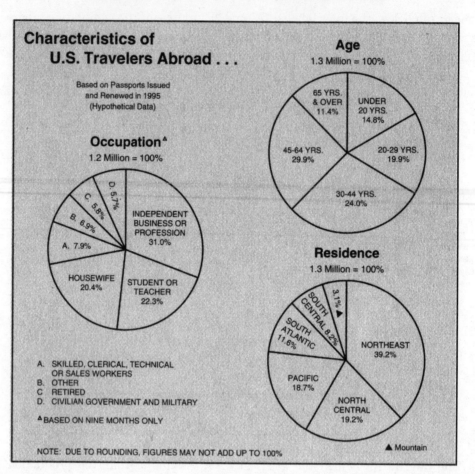

Characteristics of U.S. Travelers Abroad . . .

Based on Passports Issued and Renewed in 1995 (Hypothetical Data)

Occupation▲
1.2 Million = 100%

D. 5.7%
C. 5.8%
B. 6.9%
A. 7.9%
INDEPENDENT BUSINESS OR PROFESSION 31.0%
HOUSEWIFE 20.4%
STUDENT OR TEACHER 22.3%

A. SKILLED, CLERICAL, TECHNICAL OR SALES WORKERS
B. OTHER
C. RETIRED
D. CIVILIAN GOVERNMENT AND MILITARY

▲ BASED ON NINE MONTHS ONLY

Age
1.3 Million = 100%

65 YRS. & OVER 11.4%
UNDER 20 YRS. 14.8%
45-64 YRS. 29.9%
20-29 YRS. 19.9%
30-44 YRS. 24.0%

Residence
1.3 Million = 100%

SOUTH CENTRAL 8.2%
3.1% ▲
SOUTH ATLANTIC 11.6%
NORTHEAST 39.2%
PACIFIC 18.7%
NORTH CENTRAL 19.2%

▲ Mountain

NOTE: DUE TO ROUNDING, FIGURES MAY NOT ADD UP TO 100%

8. Approximately how many persons aged 29 or younger traveled abroad in 1995?

(1) 175,000
(2) 245,000
(3) 385,000
(4) 400,000
(5) 450,000

9. Of the people who did not live in the Northeast, what percent came from the North Central states?

(1) 19.2%
(2) 19.9%
(3) 26.5%
(4) 30.00%
(5) 31.6%

10. The fraction of travelers from the four smallest occupation groups is most nearly equal to the fraction of travelers

(1) under age 20 and 65 and over, combined.
(2) from the North Central and Mountain states.
(3) between 45 and 64 years of age.
(4) from the Housewife and Other categories.
(5) from the Pacific states.

11. If the South Central, Mountain, and Pacific sections were considered as a single classification, how many degrees would its sector include?

(1) 30°   (4) 120°
(2) 67°   (5) 130°
(3) 108°

ITEMS 12 TO 15 REFER TO THE FOLLOWING GRAPH.

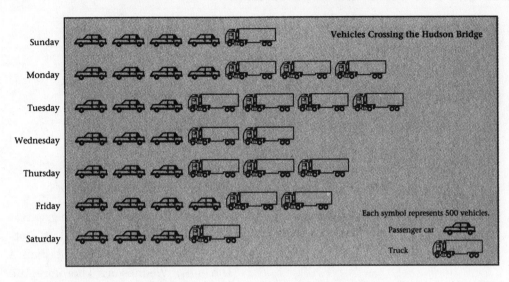

Vehicles Crossing the Hudson Bridge

Each symbol represents 500 vehicles.

Passenger car

Truck

12. What percent of the total number of vehicles on Wednesday were cars?

(1) 20%
(2) 30%
(3) 50%
(4) 60%
(5) 75%

13. What was the total number of vehicles crossing the bridge on Tuesday?

(1) 7
(2) 700
(3) 1,100
(4) 3,500
(5) 3,700

14. How many more trucks crossed on Monday than on Saturday?

(1) 200
(2) 1,000
(3) 1,500
(4) 2,000
(5) 2,500

15. If trucks paid a toll of $1.00 and cars paid a toll of $.50, how much money was collected in tolls on Friday?

(1) $400
(2) $600
(3) $1,000
(4) $1,500
(5) $2,000

ANSWER KEY AND EXPLANATIONS

1. (2)	6. (5)	11. (3)
2. (4)	7. (1)	12. (4)
3. (2)	8. (5)	13. (4)
4. (2)	9. (5)	14. (2)
5. (3)	10. (1)	15. (5)

1. The correct answer is (2).

The incidence of murder increased from 15 in 1991 to 20 in 1992 to 25 in 1993.

2. The correct answer is (4).

The incidence of burglary in 1991 was 400; in 1992 it was 350; and in 1993 it was 450. The increase from 1992 to 1993 was 100. An increase of 100 from 1993 gives 550 in 1994.

The average of 400, 350, 450, and 550 is

$$\frac{400+350+450+550}{4} = \frac{1750}{4}$$
$$= 437.5$$

3. The correct answer is (2).

The incidence of grand larceny auto went from 250 in 1992 to 275 in 1993, an increase of 25. The percent increase is

$$\frac{25}{250} = .10 = 10\%$$

4. The correct answer is (2).

This graph gives information by year, not month. It is impossible to determine from the graph the percentage of crimes committed during the first six months of any year.

5. The correct answer is (3).

For both Clerks A and B, the greatest increase in the cumulative totals occurred from the end of Tuesday until the end of Wednesday. Therefore, the greatest number of applications was filed on Wednesday.

6. The correct answer is (5).

By the end of Tuesday, Clerk A had filed approximately 100 applications and Clerk B had filed approximately 150, for a total of 250. This left 750 of the original 1,000 applications.
$$\frac{750}{1000} = .75 = 75\%$$

7. The correct answer is (1).

During Week One, Clerk B files 100 applications on Monday, 50 on Tuesday, 100 on Wednesday, 50 on Thursday, and 100 on Friday, a total of 400. On Monday of Week Two, he will file numbers 401 to 500.

8. The correct answer is (5).

20−29 yr.:	19.9%
Under 20 yr.:	+ 14.8%
	34.7%

$34.7\% \times 1.3$ million $= .4511$ million
$$= 451,100$$

9. The correct answer is (5).

100% − 39.2% = 60.8% did not live in Northeast

19.2% lived in North Central

$\dfrac{19.2}{60.8}$ = .316 approximately

10. The correct answer is (1).

Four smallest groups of occupation:

7.9 + 6.9 + 5.8 + 5.7 = 26.3

Age groups under 20 and over 65:

14.8 + 11.4 = 26.2

11. The correct answer is (3).

South Central:	8.2%
Mountain:	3.1%
Pacific:	<u>18.7%</u>
	30.0%

30% × 360° = 108°

12. The correct answer is (4).

There are 5 vehicle symbols, of which 3 are cars. $\dfrac{3}{5}$ = 60%

13. The correct answer is (4).

On Tuesday, there were 3 × 500 = 1500 cars and 4 × 500 = 2000 trucks. The total number of vehicles was 3500.

14. The correct answer is (2).

The graph shows 2 more truck symbols on Monday than on Saturday. Each symbol represents 500 trucks, so there were 2 × 500 = 1000 more trucks on Monday.

15. The correct answer is (5).

On Friday there were

4 × 500 = 2000 cars

2 × 500 = 1000 trucks

Car tolls:	2000 × $ .50 = $1000
Truck tolls:	1000 × $1.00 = <u>+ $1000</u>
Total tolls:	$2000

answers exercises

PAYROLL

1. **Salaries** are computed over various time periods: hourly, daily, weekly, biweekly (every 2 weeks), semimonthly (twice each month), monthly, and yearly.

2. **Overtime** is usually computed as "time and a half"; that is, each hour in excess of the number of hours in the standard workday or workweek is paid at $1\frac{1}{2}$ times the regular hourly rate. Some companies pay "double time," twice the regular hourly rate, for work on Sundays and holidays.

Illustration: An employee is paid weekly, based on a 40-hour workweek, with time and a half for overtime. If the employee's regular hourly rate is $4.50, how much will he earn for working 47 hours in one week?

Solution: Overtime hours = 47 − 40 = 7 hours

Overtime pay = $1\frac{1}{2} \times \$4.50 = \$6.75$ per hour

Overtime pay for 7 hours:

$$7 \times \$6.75 = \$47.25$$

Regular pay for 40 hours:

$$40 \times \$4.50 = \$180.00$$

Total pay = $47.25 + $180 = $227.25

Answer: $227.25

3. a. In occupations such as retail sales, real estate, and insurance, earnings may be based on **commission,** which is a percent of the sales or a percent of the value of the transactions that are completed.

   b. Earnings may be from straight commission only, from salary plus commission, or from a commission that is graduated according to transaction volume.

Illustration: A salesman earns a salary of $200 weekly, plus a commission based on sales volume for the week. The commission is 7% for the first $1,500 of sales and 10% for all sales in excess of $1,500. How much did he earn in a week in which his sales totaled $3,200?

Solution: $3200 − $1500 = 1700 excess sales

.07 × $1500 = $105 commission on first $1500

.10 × $1700 = $170 commission on excess sales

$\underline{+\$200}$ weekly salary

$475 total earnings

Answer: $475

4. **Gross pay** refers to the amount of money earned, whether from salary, commission, or both, before any deductions are made.

5. There are several deductions that are usually made from gross pay:
   a. **Withholding tax** is the amount of money withheld for income tax. It is based on wages, marital status, and number of exemptions (also called allowances) claimed by the employee. The withholding tax is found by referring to tables supplied by the federal, state, or city governments.

MARRIED PERSONS—WEEKLY PAYROLL PERIOD

Wages		Number of witholding allowances claimed				
At	But less	0	1	2	3	4
least	than	Amount of income tax to be withheld				
400	410	73.00	67.60	62.30	57.70	53.10
410	420	75.80	70.40	65.00	60.10	55.50
420	430	78.60	73.20	67.80	62.50	57.90
430	440	81.40	76.00	70.60	65.20	60.30
440	450	84.20	78.80	73.40	68.00	62.70
450	460	87.00	81.60	76.20	70.80	65.40
460	470	90.20	84.40	79.00	73.60	68.20
470	480	93.40	87.30	81.80	76.40	71.00
480	490	96.60	90.50	84.60	79.20	73.80
490	500	99.80	93.70	87.50	82.00	76.60

Based on the above table, an employee who is married, claims three exemptions, and is paid a weekly wage of $434.50 will have $65.20 withheld for income tax. If the same employee earned $440 weekly, it would be necessary to look on the next line for "at least $440 but less than $450" to find that $68.00 would be withheld.

   b. The FICA (Federal Insurance Contribution Act) tax is also called the Social Security tax. In 1982, the FICA tax was 6.7% of the first $32,400 of annual wages; the wages in excess of $32,400 were not subject to the tax.

The FICA tax may be found by multiplying the wages up to and including $32,400 by .067, or by using tables such as the one below.

SOCIAL SECURITY EMPLOYEE TAX TABLE
6.7 percent employee tax deductions

| Wages | | | Wages | | |
At least	But less than	Tax	At least	But less than	Tax
$78.14	$78.28	$5.24	$84.26	$84.40	$5.65
78.29	78.43	5.25	84.41	84.55	5.66
78.44	78.58	5.26	84.56	84.70	5.67
78.59	78.73	5.27	84.71	84.85	5.68
78.74	78.88	5.28	84.86	84.99	5.69
78.89	79.03	5.29	85.00	85.14	5.70
79.04	79.18	5.30	85.15	85.29	5.71
79.19	79.33	5.31	85.30	85.44	5.72
79.34	79.48	5.32	85.45	85.59	5.73
79.49	79.63	5.33	85.60	85.74	5.74
79.64	79.78	5.34	85.75	85.89	5.75
79.79	79.93	5.35			

According to the table above, the Social Security tax, or FICA tax, on wages of $84.80 is $5.68. The FICA tax on $84.92 is $5.69.

Illustration: Based on 1982 tax figures, what is the total FICA tax on an annual salary of $30,000?

Solution: .067 × $30,000 = $2010.00

Answer: $2,010.00

c. Other deductions that may be made from gross pay are deductions for pension plans, loan payments, payroll savings plans, and union dues.

6. The **net pay,** or **take-home pay**, is equal to gross pay less the total deductions.

Illustration: Mr. Jay earns $550 salary per week, with the following deductions: federal withholding tax, $106.70; FICA tax, $36.85; state tax, $22.83; pension payment, $6.42; union dues, $5.84. How much take-home pay does he receive?

Solution: Deductions : $106.70
                                36.85
                                22.83
                                 6.42
                                 5.84
                              _____
                              $178.64

Gross pay = $550.00
Deductions = −178.64
              _____
Net pay = $371.36

Answer: His take-home pay is $371.36

EXERCISES: PAYROLL

1. Jane Rose's semimonthly salary is $750. Her yearly salary is

   (1) $9,000

   (2) $12,500

   (3) $18,000

   (4) $19,500

   (5) $21,000

2. John Doe earns $300 for a 40-hour week. If he receives time and a half for overtime, what is his hourly overtime wage?

   (1) $7.50

   (2) $9.25

   (3) $10.50

   (4) $11.25

   (5) $15.00

3. Which salary is greater?

   (1) $50 daily per 5-day work week

   (2) $350 weekly

   (3) $1378 monthly

   (4) $17,000 annually

   (5) $646 biweekly

4. A factory worker is paid on the basis of an 8-hour day, with an hourly rate of $3.50 and time and a half for overtime. Find his gross pay for a week in which he worked the following hours:

Monday, 8; Tuesday, 9; Wednesday, $9\frac{1}{2}$; Thursday, $8\frac{1}{2}$; Friday, 9.

   (1) $140

   (2) $154

   (3) $161

   (4) $174

   (5) $231

ITEMS 5 AND 6 REFER TO THE FOLLOWING TABLE.

SINGLE PERSONS—WEEKLY PAYROLL PERIOD

Wages		Number of withholding allowances claimed				
At least	But less than	0	1	2	3	4
		Amount of income tax to be withheld				
$370	$380	$ 83.60	$ 77.10	$ 70.50	$64.50	$58.90
380	390	87.00	80.50	73.90	67.50	61.90
390	400	90.40	83.90	77.30	70.80	64.80
400	410	93.80	87.30	80.70	74.20	67.80
410	420	97.20	90.70	84.10	77.60	71.10
420	430	100.60	94.10	87.50	81.00	74.50
430	440	104.10	97.50	90.90	84.40	77.90
440	450	108.00	100.90	94.30	87.80	81.30
450	460	111.90	104.40	97.70	91.20	84.70
460	470	115.80	108.30	101.10	94.60	88.10

5. According to the table above, if an employee is single and has one exemption, the income tax withheld from his weekly salary of $389.90 is

   (1) $90.40
   (2) $87.00
   (3) $83.90
   (4) $83.60
   (5) $80.50

6. According to the table above, if a single person with two exemptions has $90.90 withheld for income tax, her weekly salary could not be

   (1) $430.00
   (2) $435.25
   (3) $437.80
   (4) $439.50
   (5) $440.00

7. Sam Richards earns $1,200 monthly. The following deductions are made from his gross pay monthly: federal withholding tax, $188.40; FICA tax, $80.40; state tax, $36.78; city tax, $9.24; savings bond, $37.50; pension plan, $5.32; repayment of pension loan, $42.30. His monthly net pay is

   (1) $800.06
   (2) $807.90
   (3) $808.90
   (4) $809.90
   (5) $810.06

8. A salesman is paid a straight commission that is 23% of his sales. What is his commission on $1,260 of sales?

   (1) $232.40
   (2) $246.80
   (3) $259.60
   (4) $289.80
   (5) $298.60

9. Ann Johnson earns a salary of $150 weekly plus a commission of 9% of sales in excess of $500 for the week. For a week in which her sales were $1,496, her earnings were

(1) $223.64
(2) $239.64
(3) $253.64
(4) $284.64
(5) $293.64

10. A salesperson is paid a 6% commission on the first $2,500 of sales for the week, and $7\frac{1}{2}$% on that portion of sales in excess of $2,500. What is the commission earned in a week in which sales were $3,280?

(1) $150.00
(2) $196.80
(3) $208.50
(4) $224.30
(5) $246.00

ANSWER KEY AND EXPLANATIONS

1. (3)	6. (5)
2. (4)	7. (1)
3. (2)	8. (4)
4. (3)	9. (2)
5. (5)	10. (3)

1. The correct answer is (3).

A semimonthly salary is paid twice a month. She receives $750 × 2 = $1500 each month, which is $1500 × 12 = $18,000 per year.

2. The correct answer is (4).

The regular hourly rate is

$300 ÷ 40 = $7.50

The overtime rate is

$7.50 × $\frac{1}{2}$ = $7.50 × 1.5

= $11.25

3. The correct answer is (2).

Write each salary as its yearly equivalent:

$$\begin{aligned}
\$50\,daily &= 50 \times 5\,days \\
&= \$250\,weekly \\
&= \$250 \times 52\,weeks \\
&= \$13,000\,yearly \\
\$350\,weekly &= \$350 \times 52\,weeks \\
&= \$18,200\,yearly \\
\$1378\,monthly &= \$1378 \times 12\,months \\
&= \$16,536\,yearly \\
\$17,000\,annually &= \$17,000\,yearly \\
\$646\,biweekly &= \$646 \div 2\,weeks \\
&= \$323\,weekly \\
&= \$323 \times 52\,weeks \\
&= \$16,796\,yearly
\end{aligned}$$

4. The correct answer is (3).

His overtime hours were:

Monday	0
Tuesday	1
Wednesday	$1\frac{1}{2}$
Thursday	$\frac{1}{2}$
Friday	1
Total	4 hours overtime

$$\begin{aligned}
\text{Overtime rate per hour} &= 1\frac{1}{2} \times \$3.50 \\
&= 1.5 \times \$3.50 \\
&= \$5.25 \\
\text{Overtime pay} &= 4 \times \$5.25 \\
&= \$21
\end{aligned}$$

Regular pay for 8 hours per day for 5 days or 40 hours

Regular pay = 40 × $3.50 = $140

Total wages = $140 + $21 = $161

5. The correct answer is (5).

The correct amount is found on the line for wages of at least $380 but less than $390, and in the column under "1" withholding allowance. The amount withheld is $80.50.

6. The correct answer is (5).

In the column for 2 exemptions, or withholding allowances, $90.90 is found on the line for wages of at least $430, but less than $440. Choice (5) does not fall within that range.

7. The correct answer is (1).

Deductions:	$188.40
	80.40
	36.78
	9.24
	37.50
	5.32
	+ 42.30
Total	$399.94
Gross Pay	= $1200.00
Total Deductions	= − 399.94
	$ 800.06

8. The correct answer is (4).

23% of $1,260 = .23 × $1,260

= $289.80

9. The correct answer is (2).

$1,496 − 500 = $996 excess sales

9% of $996 = .09 × $996

$89.64 commission

$150.00 salary
+ 89.64 commission
$239.64 total earnings

10. The correct answer is (3).

$3,280 − $2,500 = $780 excess sales

Commission on $2,500:

.06 × $2500 = $150.00

Commission on $780:

.075 × $780 = + 58.50

Total = $208.50

SEQUENCES

1. A **sequence** is a list of numbers based on a certain pattern. There are three main types of sequences:
   a. If each term in a sequence is being increased or diminished by the same number to form the next term, then it is an **arithmetic sequence.** The number being added or subtracted is called the **common difference.**

   > 2, 4, 6, 8, 10 . . . is an arithmetic sequence in which the common difference is 2.
   >
   > 14, 11, 8, 5, 2 . . . is an arithmetic sequence in which the common difference is 3.

   b. If each term of a sequence is being multiplied by the same number to form the next term, then it is a **geometric sequence**. The number multiplying each term is called the **common ratio.**

   > 2, 6, 18, 54 . . . is a geometric sequence in which the common ratio is 3.
   >
   > 64, 16, 4, 1 . . . is a geometric sequence in which the common ratio is $\frac{1}{4}$.

   c. If the sequence is neither arithmetic nor geometric, it is a **miscellaneous sequence.** Such a sequence may have each term a square or a cube, or the difference may be squares or cubes; or there may be a varied pattern in the sequence that must be determined.

2. A sequence may be ascending, that is, the numbers increase; or descending, that is, the numbers decrease, or neither.

3. To determine whether the sequence is arithmetic:
   a. If the sequence is ascending, subtract the first term from the second, and the second term from the third. If the difference is the same in both cases, the sequence is arithmetic.
   b. If the sequence is descending, subtract the second term from the first, and the third term from the second. If the difference is the same in both cases, the sequence is arithmetic.

4. To determine whether the sequence is geometric, divide the second term by the first, and the third term by the second. If the ratio is the same in both cases, the sequence is geometric.

5. To find a missing term in an arithmetic sequence that is ascending:
   a. Subtract any term from the one following it to find the common difference.
   b. Add the common difference to the term preceding the missing term.
   c. If the missing term is the first term, it may be found by subtracting the common difference from the second term.

Illustration: What number follows $16\frac{1}{3}$ in this sequence: 3, $6\frac{1}{3}$, $9\frac{2}{3}$, 13, $16\frac{1}{3}$ ...

Solution: $6\frac{1}{3} - 3 = 3\frac{1}{3}$, $9\frac{2}{3} - 6\frac{1}{3} = 3\frac{1}{3}$

The sequence is arithmetic; the common difference is $3\frac{1}{3}$.

$16\frac{1}{3} + 3\frac{1}{3} = 19\frac{2}{3}$

Answer: The missing term, which is the term following $16\frac{1}{3}$, is $19\frac{2}{3}$.

6. To find a missing term in an arithmetic sequence that is descending:
   a. Subtract any term from the one preceding it to find the common difference.
   b. Subtract the common difference from the term preceding the missing term.
   c. If the missing term is the first term, it may be found by adding the common difference to the second term.

Illustration: Find the first term in the sequence:

___, 16, $13\frac{1}{2}$, 11, $8\frac{1}{2}$, 6 ...

Solution: $16 - 13\frac{1}{2} = 2\frac{1}{2}$, $13\frac{1}{2} - 11 = 2\frac{1}{2}$

The sequence is arithmetic; the common difference is $2\frac{1}{2}$. $16 + 2\frac{1}{2} = 18\frac{1}{2}$

Answer: The term preceding 16 is $18\frac{1}{2}$.

7. To find a missing term in a geometric sequence:
   a. Divide any term by the one preceding it to find the common ratio.
   b. Multiply the term preceding the missing term by the common ratio.
   c. If the missing term is the first term, it may be found by dividing the second term by the common ratio.

Illustration: Find the missing term in the sequence:

2, 6, 18, 54,

Solution: $6 \div 2 = 3$, $18 \div 6 = 3$

The sequence is geometric; the common ratio is 3.

$54 \times 3 = 162$

Answer: The missing term is 162.

Illustration: Find the missing term in the sequence:

___, 32, 16, 8, 4, 2

Solution: $16 \div 32 = \dfrac{1}{2}$ (common ratio)

$$32 \div \frac{1}{2} = 32 \times \frac{2}{1}$$
$$= 64$$

Answer: The first term is 64.

8. If, after trial, a sequence is neither arithmetic nor geometric, it must be one of a miscellaneous type. Test to see whether it is a sequence of squares or cubes or whether the difference is the squarc or the cube of the same number, or the same number may be first squared, then cubed, etc.

EXERCISES: SEQUENCES

Find the missing term in each of the following sequences:

1. ___, 7, 10, 13

2. 5, 10, 20, ___, 80

3. 49, 45, 41, ___, 33, 29

4. 1.002, 1.004, 1.006,___

5. 1, 4, 9, 16,___

6. $10, 7\dfrac{7}{8}, 5\dfrac{3}{4}, 3\dfrac{5}{8},$___

7. ___, $3, 4\dfrac{1}{2}, 6\dfrac{3}{4}$

8. 55, 40, 28, 19, 13,___

9. $9, 3, 1, \dfrac{1}{3}, \dfrac{1}{9},$___

10. 1, 3, 7, 15, 31,___

ANSWER KEY AND EXPLANATIONS

1. 4	6. $1\frac{1}{2}$
2. 40	7. 2
3. 37	8. 10
4. 1.008	9. $\frac{1}{27}$
5. 25	10. 63

1. This is an ascending arithmetic sequence in which the common difference is $10 - 7$, or 3. The first term is $7 - 3 = 4$.

2. This is a geometric sequence in which the common ratio is $10 \div 5$, or 2. The missing term is $20 \times 2 = 40$.

3. This is a descending arithmetic sequence in which the common difference is $49 - 45$, or 4. The missing term is $41 - 4 = 37$.

4. This is an ascending arithmetic sequence in which the common difference is $1.004 - 1.002$, or .002. The missing term is $1.006 + .002 = 1.008$.

5. This sequence is neither arithmetic nor geometric. However, if the numbers are rewritten as 1^2, 2^2, 3^2, and 4^2, it is clear that the next number must be 5^2, or 25.

6. This is a descending arithmetic sequence in which the common difference is $10 - 7\frac{7}{8} = 2\frac{1}{8}$. The missing term is $3\frac{5}{8} - 2\frac{1}{8} = 1\frac{4}{8}$, or $1\frac{1}{2}$.

7. This is a geometric sequence in which the common ratio is:

$$4\frac{1}{2} \div 3 = \frac{9}{2} \times \frac{1}{3}$$
$$= \frac{3}{2}$$

The first term is $\quad 3 \div \frac{3}{2} = 3 \times \frac{2}{3}$
$$= 2$$

Therefore, the missing term is 2.

8. There is no common difference and no common ratio in this sequence. However, note the differences between terms:

55	40	28	19	13
	15	12	9	6
	5×3	4×3	3×3	2×3

The differences are multiples of 3. Following the same pattern, the difference between 13 and the next term must be 1×3, or 3. The missing term is then $13 - 3 = 10$.

9. This is a geometric sequence in which the common ratio is $3 \div 9 = \frac{1}{3}$. The missing term is $\frac{1}{9} \times \frac{1}{3} = \frac{1}{27}$.

10. This sequence is neither arithmetic nor geometric. However, note the difference between terms:

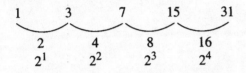

The difference between 31 and the next term must be 2^5, or 32. The missing term is thus $31 + 32 = 63$.

OPERATIONS WITH ALGEBRAIC EXPRESSIONS: VOCABULARY

1. **a.** In addition, the numbers that are being added are called the **addends.** The solution to an addition problem is the **sum** or **total**.

   b. There are several ways to express an addition problem such as $10 + 2$:

the sum of 10 and 2	2 more than 10
the total of 10 and 2	2 greater than 10
2 added to 10	10 increased by 2

2. **a.** In subtraction, the number from which something is subtracted is the **minuend,** the number being subtracted is the **subtrahend,** and the answer is the **difference.**

   In $25 - 22 = 3$, the minuend is 25, the subtrahend is 22, and the difference is 3.

   b. A subtraction problem such as $25 - 22$ may be expressed as:

25 minus 22	from 25 take 22
25 less 22	25 decreased by 22
the difference of 25 and 22	22 less than 25
subtract 22 from 25	

3. **a.** In multiplication, the answer is called the **product** and the numbers being multiplied are the **factors** of the product.

   b. In the multiplication $3 \times 5 = 15$ [which may also be written as $3(5) = 15$ or $(3)(5) = 15$] all of the following expressions apply:

15 is the product of 3 and 5	15 is a multiple of 3
3 is a factor of 15	15 is a multiple of 5
5 is a factor of 15	

4. **a.** In division, the number being divided is the **dividend,** the number the dividend is divided by is the **divisor,** and the answer is the **quotient.** Any number left over in the division is the **remainder.**

   In $12 \div 2 = 6$, the dividend is 12, the divisor is 2, and the quotient is 6.

$$\text{In } 3\overline{)22}$$
$$\underline{21}$$
$$1$$
$$7$$

22 is the dividend
3 is the divisor
1 is the remainder
7 is the quotient

  b. The division problem $12 \div 2$ may be expressed as:

  12 divided by 2   2 divides 12
  the quotient of 12 and 2

Because $12 \div 2 = 6$ with no remainder, 2 is called **a divisor** of 12, and 12 is said to be **divisible** by 2.

Properties

5. Addition is a **commutative** operation; this means that two numbers may be added in either order without changing their sum:

$$2 + 3 = 3 + 2$$
$$a + b = b + a$$

6. Multiplication is also commutative:

$$4 \cdot 5 = 5 \cdot 4$$
$$ab = ba$$

7. Subtraction and division problems are *not* commutative; changing the order within a subtraction or division problem may affect the answer:

$$10 - 6 \neq 6 - 10$$
$$8 \div 4 \neq 4 \div 8$$

8. Addition and multiplication are **associative;** that is, if a problem involves only addition or only multiplication, the parentheses may be changed without affecting the answer. Parentheses are grouping symbols that indicate work to be done first.

$$(5 + 6) + 7 = 5 + (6 + 7)$$
$$(2 \times 3) \times 4 = 2 \times (3 \times 4)$$
$$(a + b) + c = a + (b + c)$$
$$(ab)c = a(bc)$$

9. Subtraction and division are not associative. Work within parentheses must be performed first.

$$(8 - 5) - 2 \neq 8 - (5 - 2)$$
$$(80 \div 4) \div 2 \neq 80 \div (4 \div 2)$$

10. a. Multiplication is **distributive** over addition. If a sum is to be multiplied by a number, instead of adding first and then multiplying, each addend may be multiplied by the number and the products added.

$$5(6 + 3) = 5 \times 6 + 5 \times 3$$

$$a(b + c) = ab + ac$$

   b. Multiplication is also distributive over subtraction.

$$8(10 - 6) = 8 \times 10 - 8 \times 6$$

$$a(b - c) = ab - ac$$

   c. The distributive property may be used in both directions.

$$5a + 3a = (5 + 3)\, a = 8a$$

$$847 \times 94 + 847 \times 6 = 847\,(94 + 6) = 847\,(100) = 84,700$$

Signed Numbers

11. a. A **signed number** is a number with a positive (+) or negative (−) sign in front of it. Signed numbers may be represented on a number line as follows:

   b. If a number (except zero) is written without a sign, it is assumed to be **positive.**

   c. Zero is considered a signed number even though it is neither positive nor negative.

   d. The magnitude, or **absolute value,** of a signed number is the number without its sign. The symbol used for absolute value is | |.

The absolute value of −3 is 3.
   $|-3| = 3$
The absolute value of +6 is 6.
   $|6| = 6$

12. a. To add two signed numbers that have the same sign, add their absolute values and give the answer the common sign.

$(+3) + (+4) = +7$
$(-6) + (-2) = -8$

   b. To add two signed numbers that have different signs, subtract their absolute values. Give the answer the sign of the number with the greater absolute value.

$(-4) + (+1) = -3$
$(+5) + (-9) = -4$
$(-6) + (+7) = +1$

13. To subtract two signed numbers, change the sign of the subtrahend. Then use the rules for addition of signed numbers.

$$(-3)-(-5)=(-3)+(+5)=+2$$
$$(+10)-(-6)=(+10)+(+6)=+16$$
$$(+8)-(+9)=(+8)+(-9)=-1$$
$$(-7)-(+3)=(-7)+(-3)=-10$$

14. To multiply two signed numbers, multiply their absolute values. If the signed numbers have the same sign, the answer is positive. If the signed numbers have different signs, the answer is negative.

$$(+3)(+4)=+12$$
$$(-5)(-2)=+10$$
$$(-6)(+3)=-18$$
$$(+8)(-1)=-8$$

15. To divide two signed numbers, divide their absolute values. If the signed numbers have the same sign, the answer is positive. If the signed numbers have different signs, the answer is negative.

$$(+20)\div(+4)=+5$$
$$(-18)\div(-9)=+2$$
$$(-14)\div(+2)=-7$$
$$(+15)\div(-5)=-3$$

16. To evaluate algebraic equations and formulas:
    a. Substitute the given values for the letters in the expression.
    b. Perform the arithmetic in the following order:
       First, perform the operations within parentheses (if any);
       Second, compute all powers and roots;
       Third, perform all multiplications and divisions in order from left to right;
       Fourth, perform all additions and subtractions in order from left to right.
       There is a mnemonic (saying) that can help you remember the order of these math operations: **P**lease **e**xcuse **m**y **d**ear **A**unt **S**ally (parenthesis, exponents, multiplication, division, addition, subtraction).

Illustration: If $P = 2(L + W)$, find P when $L = 10$ and $W = 5$.

Solution: Substitute 10 for L and 5 for W:

$P = 2(10 + 5)$ First, add number in parentheses.

$= 2(15)$ Then multiply 2 by 15.

$= 30$

Answer: 30

Illustration: Evaluate $5a^2 - 2b$ if $a = 3$ and $b = 10$.

Solution: Substitute 3 for a and 10 for b:

$5 \times 3^2 - 2 \times 10$ First, find 3^2.

$5 \times 9 - 2 \times 10$ Next, multiply 5×9 and 2×10.

$45 - 20$ Then subtract 20 from 45.

25

Answer: 25

17. a. Algebraic expressions may contain numbers (constants) or letters (variables) or both.

   b. In an algebraic expression, if several quantities are being added or subtracted, each of these quantities is called a term.

In $4x^2 + 5y + 6$, the terms are: $4x^2$, $5y$, 6.

   c. The number factor of each term is called the **coefficient.** The letter part is called the **literal factor.**

In $3x^2$, 3 is the coefficient and x^2 is the literal factor. Note that 2 is the exponent and is part of the literal factor.

   d. Any variable appearing without a coefficient is assumed to have a coefficient of 1: $b = 1b$

   e. Any variable appearing without an exponent is assumed to have an exponent of 1: $b = b^1$

18. a. If two or more terms have identical literal factors, they are called **like terms.**

$3a$, $6a$, and a are like terms.

$2x^4$ and $5x^2$ are *not* like terms.

   b. Terms may be added (or subtracted) only if they are like terms. Add (or subtract) the coefficients and repeat the literal factor. This is called **combining like terms.**

$$3d + 2d = 5d$$
$$6xy + (-4)xy = 2 \times y$$
$$10z^3 + 5z^3 - 8z^3 = 7z^3$$

c. In most algebraic expressions it is easier to consider the operation that separates terms to be addition only, and the + or − sign immediately preceding each term to be the sign of the coefficient of that term.

Polynomials

19. An expression containing a single term is called a **monomial.** An expression containing more than one term is called a **polynomial.** Special polynomials are **binomials** (two terms) and **trinomials** (three terms).

20. To add (or subtract) two polynomials, add (or subtract) the coefficients of the like terms and repeat the literal factors. The unlike terms may not be combined.

Add $4x^2 - 3x + 2$

$\underline{2x^2 - 7x - 5}$

$6x^2 - 10x - 3$

Subtract $7a - 2b + 4c$ (Recall that in subtraction the sign of the subtrahend

$\underline{9a + 6b - 2c}$ is changed and the rules of addition are used.)

$-2a - 8b + 6c$

21. To multiply two monomials, multiply their coefficients and add the exponents of like variables.

$$2x^5 \cdot 3x^4 = 6x^9$$
$$y^4 \cdot y^{10} = y^{14}$$
$$9b^3 \cdot 2b = 18b^4 \qquad \text{(Note that } 2b = 2b^1\text{)}$$
$$(-4a^2b^3)(-3a^{11}b^8) = +12a^{13}b^{11}$$

22. To multiply a polynomial by a monomial, use the distributive property and multiply each term of the polynomial by the monomial.

$$3(2x + 4y) = 6x + 12y$$
$$y^2(5y - 3y^5) = 5y^3 - 3y^7$$

23. To multiply a polynomial by a polynomial, multiply each term of the first polynomial by each term of the second polynomial; then add any like terms in the answer.

$$(x+3)(x+4) = x^2 + 4x + 3x + 12$$
$$= x^2 + 7x + 12$$
$$(a-1)(b+5) = ab + 5a - 1b - 5$$
$$(y+4)(y^2 + 2y - 3) = y^3 + 2y^2 - 3y + 4y^2 + 8y - 12$$
$$= y^3 + 6y^2 + 5y - 12$$

24. To divide two monomials, divide their coefficients and subtract the exponents of like variables.

$$\frac{12a^5}{3a^2} = 4a^3$$

$$\frac{ac^7}{ac^5} = c^2 \ (Note \ that \ \frac{a}{a} = 1)$$

$$\frac{-6b^{10}c^7}{2bc^2} = -3b^9c^5$$

25. To divide a polynomial by a monomial, divide each term of the polynomial by the monomial.

$$\frac{15a^2 - 12a}{3} = 5a^2 - 4a$$

$$(12x^3 - 8x^2 + 20x) \div 4x = 3x^2 - 2x + 5$$

Simplifying Algebraic Expressions

26. Algebraic expressions containing parentheses can be simplified by using the following rules:
    a. If a positive (+) sign is immediately before the parentheses, the parentheses may simply be omitted.

$$3x + (2y + z) = 3x + 2y + z$$

    b. If a negative (−) sign immediately precedes the parentheses, the sign of each term within the parentheses must be changed. The parentheses may then be omitted.

$$4 - (2x - y + z) = 4 - 2x + y - z$$

c. If a number or letter is indicated as a multiplier immediately before the parentheses, the distributive property is used to multiply each term inside the parentheses by the multiplier.

$$a - 3(b + c) = a - 3b - 3c$$

d. After removing the parentheses, combine like terms.

$$5z + 2(3z - 4) = 5z + 6z - 8$$
$$= 11z - 8$$

Factoring

27. To **factor** an expression means to find those quantities whose product is the original expression.

28. **Common factors:**

    If all of the terms of a polynomial have a common factor, the distributive property may be used.

$$ax + ay = a(x + y)$$
$$12d - 8f = 4(3d - 2f)$$
$$x^3 + 2x^2 - 4x = x(x^2 + 2x - 4)$$

29. **Difference of two squares:**

    A binomial that is the difference of two squares has as its factors two binomials, one the sum of the square roots, the other the difference of the square roots.

$$x^2 - 9 = (x + 3)(x - 3)$$
$$25 - y^2 = (5 + y)(5 - y)$$

30. **Trinomials:**

    a. Quadratic trinomials are of the form: $ax^2 + bx + c$, where a, b, and c are constants and $a \neq 0$. Some—but not all—quadratic trinomials can be factored into two binomials, each the sum of an x term and a numerical term.

    b. When $a = 1$, the trinomial is written $x^2 + bx + c$. Each binomial factor will be the sum of x and a number. The product of the numbers is c; their sum is b.

    Illustration: Factor $x^2 + 7x + 12$

    Solution: The product of the numerical parts of the factors must be 12. Pairs of numbers whose product is 12 are:

1 and 12	−1 and −12
2 and 6	−2 and −6
3 and 4	−3 and −4

Of these pairs, the only one whose sum is 7 is 3 and 4. Therefore, the factors are $(x + 3)$ and $(x + 4)$.

Answer: $x^2 + 7x + 12 = (x + 3)(x + 4)$

Illustration: Factor $y^2 + 5y - 6$

Solution: Pairs of numbers whose product is -6 are:
   -1 and $+6$
   $+1$ and -6
   $+2$ and -3
   -2 and $+3$

The pair whose sum is $+5$ is -1 and $+6$. Therefore, the factors are $(y - 1)$ and $(y + 6)$.

Answer: $y^2 + 5y - 6 = (y - 1)(y + 6)$

Illustration: Factor $z^2 - 11z + 10$

Solution: The numbers whose product is positive are either both positive or both negative. In this case the sum of the numbers is negative, so consider only the negative pairs. The pairs of negative numbers whose product is $+10$ are:
   -1 and -10
   -2 and -5

The pair with -11 as its sum is -1 and -10. Therefore, the factors are $(z - 1)$ and $(z - 10)$.

Answer: $z^2 - 11z + 10 = (z - 1)(z - 10)$

c. When $a \neq 1$ in the trinomial $ax^2 + bx + c$, the product of the x terms in the binomial factors must be ax^2, the product of the number terms must be c, and when the binomials are multiplied their product must be $ax^2 + bx + c$.

While there will be more than one possible pair of factors in which the product of the number terms is c, the correct pair is the only one whose product is the original trinomial.

Illustration: Factor $3x^2 + 10x + 8$

Solution: The possible pairs of factors to be considered are:
   $(3x + 1)(x + 8)$
   $(3x + 8)(x + 1)$
   $(3x + 2)(x + 4)$
   $(3x + 4)(x + 2)$

In each case the product of the x terms is $3x^2$ and the product of the number terms is 8. Since the middle term is positive, any negative possibilities are ignored. Multiplying each pair of factors shows:

Answer: $3x^2 + 10x + 8$ may be factored as $(3x + 4)(x + 2)$.

31. An expression may require more than one type of factoring before it is factored completely. To factor *completely*:
   a. Use the distributive property to remove the greatest common factor from each term.
   b. If possible, factor the resulting polynomial as the difference of two squares or as a quadratic trinomial.

$$3x^2 - 48 = 3\left(x^2 - 16\right)$$
$$= 3(x+4)(x-4)$$

$$2ay^2 + 12ay - 14a = 2a\left(y^2 + 6y - 7\right)$$
$$= 2a(y+7)(y-1)$$

Radicals

32. The symbol $\sqrt{x}$ means the positive square root of x. The $\sqrt{}$ is called the **radical sign,** and x is called the **radicand.** The symbol $-\sqrt{x}$ means the negative square root of x.

33. Many radicals may be simplified by using the principle $\sqrt{ab} = \sqrt{a} \cdot \sqrt{b}$.

$$\sqrt{100} = \sqrt{25}\sqrt{4} = 5 \cdot 2 = 10$$
$$\sqrt{18} = \sqrt{9}\sqrt{2} = 3\sqrt{2}$$
$$\sqrt{75} = \sqrt{25}\sqrt{3} = 5\sqrt{3}$$

Note that the factors chosen must include at least one perfect square.

34. a. Radicals with the same radicands may be added or subtracted as like terms.

$$3\sqrt{5} + 4\sqrt{5} = 7\sqrt{5}$$
$$10\sqrt{2} - 6\sqrt{2} = 4\sqrt{2}$$

    b. Radicals with different radicands may be combined only if they can be simplified to have like radicands.

$$\sqrt{50} + \sqrt{32} - 2\sqrt{2} + \sqrt{3} = \sqrt{25}\sqrt{2} + \sqrt{16}\sqrt{2} - 2\sqrt{2} + \sqrt{3}$$
$$= 5\sqrt{2} + 4\sqrt{2} - 2\sqrt{2} + \sqrt{3}$$
$$= 7\sqrt{2} + \sqrt{3}$$

35. To multiply radicals, first multiply the coefficients. Then multiply the radicands.

$$2\sqrt{3} \cdot 4\sqrt{5} = 8\sqrt{15}$$

36. To divide radicals, first divide the coefficients. Then divide the radicands.

$$\frac{14\sqrt{20}}{2\sqrt{2}} = 7\sqrt{10}$$

Summary of Kinds of Numbers

37. The numbers that have been used in this section are called **real numbers** and may be grouped into special categories.

   a. The **natural** numbers, or counting numbers, are:
      1, 2, 3, 4, 5, 6, 7, 8, 9, 10, 11, 12, . . .

   b. A natural number (other than 1) is a **prime** number if it has exactly two factors (itself and 1). If a natural number has other factors, it is a **composite** number. The numbers 2, 3, 5, 7, and 11 are prime numbers, while 4, 6, 8, 9 and 12 are composites. The number 1 is neither prime nor composite.

   c. The **whole** numbers consist of 0 and the natural numbers:
      0, 1, 2, 3, . . .

   d. The **integers** consist of the natural numbers, the negatives of the natural numbers, and zero:
      . . . −3, −2, −1, 0, 1, 2, 3, 4, . . .
      Even integers are exactly divisible by 2:
      . . . −6, −4, −2, 0, 2, 4, 6, 8, . . .
      Odd integers are not divisible by 2:
      . . . −5, −3, −1, 1, 3, 5, 7, 9, . . .

   e. The **rational** numbers are numbers that can be expressed as the quotient of two integers (excluding division by 0). Rational numbers include integers, fractions, terminating decimals (such as 1.5 or .293) and repeating decimals (such as .333 . . . or .74867676767 . . .).

   f. The **irrational** numbers cannot be expressed as the quotient of two integers, but can be written as nonterminating, nonrepeating decimals. The numbers $\sqrt{2}$ and π are irrational.

EXERCISES: OPERATIONS WITH ALGEBRAIC EXPRESSIONS

1. The value of $2(-3) - |-4|$ is

    (1) -10

    (2) -2

    (3) 2

    (4) 10

    (5) 12

2. The value of $3a^2 + 2a - 1$ when $a = -1$ is

    (1) -3

    (2) 0

    (3) 3

    (4) 6

    (5) 9

3. If $2x^4$ is multiplied by $7x^3$ the product is

    (1) $9x^7$

    (2) $9x^{12}$

    (3) $9x^{14}$

    (4) $14x^{12}$

    (5) $14x^7$

4. The expression $3(x - 4) - (3x - 5) + 2(x + 6)$ is equivalent to

    (1) $2x - 15$

    (2) $2x + 23$

    (3) $2x + 5$

    (4) $-2x - 15$

    (5) $-2x + 20$

5. The product of $(x + 5)$ and $(x + 5)$ is

    (1) $2x + 10$

    (2) $x^2 + 25$

    (3) $x^2 + 10x + 25$

    (4) $x^2 + 10$

    (5) $x^2 + 20$

6. The quotient of $(4x^3 - 2x^2) \div (x^2)$ is

    (1) $4x^3 - 1$

    (2) $4x - 2x^2$

    (3) $4x^5 - 2x^4$

    (4) $4x - 2$

    (5) $4x + 2$

7. The expression $(+3x^4)^2$ is equal to

    (1) $6x^8$

    (2) $6x^6$

    (3) $9x^8$

    (4) $9x^6$

    (5) $9x^4$

8. If $3x - 1$ is multiplied by $2x$, the product is

    (1) $4x$

    (2) $5x^2$

    (3) $6x^2 - 1$

    (4) $6x^2 - x$

    (5) $6x^2 - 2x$

9. One factor of the trinomial $x^2 - 3x - 18$ is

    (1) $x - 9$

    (2) $x - 6$

    (3) $x - 3$

    (4) $x + 9$

    (5) $x + 6$

10. The sum of $\sqrt{18}$ and $\sqrt{72}$ is

    (1) $18\sqrt{2}$

    (2) $9\sqrt{2}$

    (3) $3\sqrt{10}$

    (4) 40

    (5) 49

ANSWER KEY AND EXPLANATIONS

1. (1)	5. (3)	8. (5)
2. (2)	6. (4)	9. (2)
3. (5)	7. (3)	10. (2)
4. (3)		

1. The correct answer is (1).

$$2(-3) - |-4| = -6 - 4$$
$$= -10$$

Recall that $|-4|$ means the *absolute value* of -4, which is 4.

2. The correct answer is (2).

If $a = -1$

$$3a^2 + 2a - 1 = 3(-1)^2 + 2(-1) - 1$$
$$= 3(+1) + 2(-1) - 1$$
$$= 3 - 2 - 1$$
$$= 0$$

3. The correct answer is (5).

$$(2x^4)(7x^3) = 14x^7$$

To multiply monomials, multiply coefficients and add exponents of like variables.

4. The correct answer is (3).

$$3(x-4) - (3x-5) + 2(x+6)$$
$$= 3x - 12 - 3x + 5 + 2x + 12$$
$$= 2x + 5$$

5. The correct answer is (3).

$$(x+5)(x+5) = x^2 + 5x + 5x + 25$$
$$= x^2 + 10x + 25$$

6. The correct answer is (4).

$$(4x^3 - 2x^2) \div x^2 = 4x^3 \div x^2 - 2x^2 \div x^2$$
$$= 4x - 2$$

7. The correct answer is (3).

$$(+3x^4)^2 = (+3x^4) + 3x^4$$
$$= 9x^8$$

8. The correct answer is (5).

$$2x(3x-1) = 2x \cdot 3x - 2x \cdot 1$$
$$= 6x^2 - 2x$$

9. The correct answer is (2).

Factor $x^2 - 3x - 18$ by finding two numbers whose product is -18 and whose sum is -3. Pairs of numbers whose product is -18 are:

-1 and $+18$
$+1$ and -18
-9 and $+2$
$+9$ and -2
-6 and $+3$
$+6$ and -3

Of these pairs, the one whose sum is -3 is -6 and $+3$. Therefore, the factors of $x^2 - 3x - 18$ are $(x - 6)$ and $(x + 3)$.

10. The correct answer is (2).

$$\sqrt{18} + \sqrt{72} = \sqrt{9}\sqrt{2} + \sqrt{36}\sqrt{2}$$
$$= 3\sqrt{2} + 6\sqrt{2}$$
$$= 9\sqrt{2}$$

EQUATIONS, INEQUALITIES, AND PROBLEMS IN ALGEBRA

Equations

1. a. An **equation** states that two quantities are equal.

   b. The solution to an equation is a number that can be substituted for the letter, or **variable**, to give a true statement.

> In the equation $x + 7 = 10$, if 5 is substituted for x, the equation becomes $5 + 7 = 10$, which is false. If 3 is substituted for x, the equation becomes $3 + 7 = 10$, which is true. Therefore, $x = 3$ is a solution for the equation $x + 7 = 10$.

   c. To **solve an equation** means to find all solutions for the variables.

2. a. An equation has been solved when it is transformed or rearranged so that a variable is isolated on one side of the equal sign and a number is on the other side.

   b. There are two basic principles that are used to transform equations:
   I) The same quantity may be added to, or subtracted from, both sides of an equation.

> To solve the equation $x - 3 = 2$, add 3 to both sides:
>
> $$\begin{aligned} x - 3 &= 2 \\ +3 &= +3 \\ \hline x &= 5 \end{aligned}$$

Adding 3 isolates x on one side and leaves a number on the other side. The solution to the equation is $x = 5$.

> To solve the equation $y + 4 = 10$, subtract 4 from both sides (adding -4 to both sides will have the same effect):
>
> $$\begin{aligned} y + 4 &= 10 \\ -4 &= -4 \\ \hline y &= 6 \end{aligned}$$

The variable has been isolated on one side of the equation. The solution is $y = 6$.

   II) Both sides of an equation may be multiplied by, or divided by, the same quantity.

> To solve $2a = 12$, divide both sides by 2:
>
> $$\frac{2a}{2} = \frac{12}{2}$$
> $$a = 6$$

To solve $\dfrac{b}{5} = 10$, multiply both sides by 5:

$$5 \cdot \dfrac{b}{5} = 10 \cdot 5$$
$$b = 50$$

3. To solve equations containing more than one operation:
   a. First eliminate any number that is being added to or subtracted from the variable.
   b. Then eliminate any number that is multiplying or dividing the variable.

Illustration: Solve $3x - 6 = 9$

$$\underline{+6 \quad +6} \quad \text{Adding 6 eliminates } -6.$$
$$3x = 15$$
$$\dfrac{3x}{3} = \dfrac{15}{3} \quad \text{Dividing 3 eliminates the 3, which is multiplying the } x.$$
$$x = 5$$

4. A variable term may be added to, or subtracted from, both sides of an equation. This is necessary when the variable appears on both sides of the original equation.

Illustration: Solve $6y + 9 = 2y + 1$

$$
\begin{array}{rcl}
6y + 9 & = & 2y + 1 \\
\underline{-2y} & & \underline{-2y} \\
4y + 9 & = & +1 \\
\underline{-9} & & \underline{-9} \\
4y & = & -8 \\
\dfrac{4y}{4} & = & \dfrac{-8}{4} \\
y & & -2
\end{array}
$$

Eliminate the y term from the right side by subtracting $2y$ from both sides.
Eliminate 9 from the left side by subtracting 9 from both sides.
Divide both sides by 4 to eliminate the multiplication by 4 and isolate the y.

5. It may be necessary to first simplify the expression on each side of an equation by removing parentheses or combining like terms.

Illustration: Solve

$$5z - 3(z - 2) = 8$$
$$5z - 3z + 6 = 8 \quad \text{Remove parentheses first.}$$
$$2z + 6 = 8 \quad \text{Combine like terms.}$$
$$\underline{-6 \quad -6} \quad \text{Subtract 6 from both sides.}$$
$$\dfrac{2z}{2} = \dfrac{2}{2} \quad \text{Divide by 2 to isolate the } z.$$
$$z = 1$$

6. To check the solution to any equation, replace the variable with the solution in the original equation, perform the indicated operations, and determine whether a true statement results.

Earlier it was found that $x = 5$ is the solution for the equation $3x - 6 = 9$. To check, substitute 5 for x in the equation:

$3 \cdot 5 - 6 = 9$ Perform the operations on the left side.

$15 - 6 = 9$

$9 = 9$ A true statement results; therefore the solution is correct.

Solving Problems

7. Many types of problems can be solved by using algebra. To solve a problem:
   a. Read it carefully. Determine what information is given and what information is unknown and must be found.
   b. Represent the *unknown* quantity with a letter.
   c. Write an equation that expresses the relationship given in the problem.
   d. Solve the equation.

If 7 is added to twice a number, the result is 23. Find the number.

Solution: Let $x =$ the unknown number. Then write the equation:

$7 + 2x = 23$

$\underline{-7 \qquad -7}$

$\dfrac{2x}{2} = \dfrac{16}{2}$

$x = 8$

Answer: 8

There are 6 more women than men in a group of 26 people. How many women are there?

Solution: Let $m =$ the number of men. Then, $m + 6 =$ the number of women.

$(m + 6) + m = 26$

$m + 6 + m = 26$ Remove parentheses.

$2m + 6 = 26$ Combine like terms.

$\underline{\qquad -6 \qquad -6}$

$\dfrac{2m}{2} = \dfrac{20}{2}$

$m = 10$

$m + 6 = 16$

Answer: There are 16 women.

John is 3 years older than Mary. If the sum of their ages is 39, how old is Mary?

Solution: Let m = Mary's age. Then, $m + 3$ = John's age. The sum of their ages is

$$m + (m + 3) = 39$$
$$m + m + 3 = 39$$
$$2m + 3 = 39$$
$$\underline{-3 \quad -3}$$
$$\frac{2m}{2} = \frac{36}{2}$$
$$m = 18$$

Answer: Mary is 18 years old.

Consecutive Integer Problems

8. a. **Consecutive integers** are integers that follow one another.

7, 8, 9, and 10 are consecutive integers.
$-5, -4, -3, -2,$ and -1 are consecutive integers.

   b. Consecutive integers may be represented in algebra as:

$x, x + 1, x + 2, x + 3, \ldots$

Find three consecutive integers whose sum is 39.

Solution: Let x = first consecutive integer. Then, $x + 1$ = second consecutive integer, and $x + 2$ = third consecutive integer.

$$x + (x + 1) + (x + 2) = 39$$
$$x + x + 1 + x + 2 = 39$$
$$3x + 3 = 39$$
$$\underline{-3 \quad = -3}$$
$$\frac{3x}{3} = \frac{36}{3}$$
$$x = 12$$

Answer: The integers are 12, 13, and 14.

9. Consecutive even and consecutive odd integers are both represented as $x, x + 2, x + 4, x + 6, \ldots$

If x is even, then $x + 2, x + 4, x + 6, \ldots$ will all be even.

If x is odd, then $x + 2, x + 4, x + 6, \ldots$ will all be odd.

Find four consecutive odd integers such that the sum of the greatest and twice the least is 21.

Solution: Let x, $x + 2$, $x + 4$, and $x + 6$ be the four consecutive odd integers. Here, x is the least and $x + 6$ is the greatest. The greatest integer plus twice the least is 21.

$$x + 6 + 2x = 21$$
$$3x + 6 = 21$$
$$\underline{ -6 = -6}$$
$$\frac{3x}{3} = \frac{15}{3}$$
$$x = 5$$

Answer: The integers are 5, 7, 9, and 11.

Motion Problems

10. **Motion problems** are based on the following relationship:

Rate · Time = Distance
Rate is usually given in miles per hour. Time is usually given in hours and distance is given in miles.

A man traveled 225 miles in 5 hours. How fast was he traveling (what was his rate)?

Solution: Let r = rate

$$\text{rate} \cdot \text{time} = \text{distance}$$
$$r \cdot 5 = 225$$
$$\frac{5r}{5} = \frac{225}{5}$$
$$r = 45 \text{ miles per hour}$$

Answer: He was traveling 45 miles per hour.

John and Henry start at the same time from cities 180 miles apart and travel toward each other. John travels at 40 miles per hour and Henry travels at 50 miles per hour. In how many hours will they meet?

Solution: Let h = number of hours. Then, $40h$ = distance traveled by John, and $50h$ = distance traveled by Henry. The total distance is 180 miles.

$$40h + 50h = 180$$
$$\frac{90h}{90} = \frac{180}{90}$$
$$h = 2 \text{ hours}$$

Answer: They will meet in 2 hours.

Perimeter Problems

11. To solve a perimeter problem, express each side of the figure algebraically. The **perimeter** of the figure is equal to the sum of the lengths of all of the sides.

A rectangle has four sides. One side is the length and the side next to it is the width. The opposite sides of a rectangle are equal. In a particular rectangle, the length is one less than twice the width. If the perimeter is 16, find the length and the width.

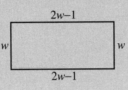

Solution:

$$\text{Let } w = \text{width}$$
$$\text{Then } 2w-1 = \text{length}$$

The sum of the four sides is 16.

$$w+(2w-1)+w+(2w-1)=16$$
$$w+2w-1+w+2w-1=16$$
$$6w-2=16$$
$$\underline{+2 \quad +2}$$
$$\frac{6w}{6}=\frac{18}{6}$$
$$w=3$$
$$2w-1=2(3)-1=5$$

Answer: The width is 3 and the length is 5.

Ratio and Proportion Problems

12. a. A ratio is the quotient of two numbers. The ratio of 2 to 5 may be expressed $2 \div 5$, $\frac{2}{5}$, 2 is to 5, 2:5, or algebraically as $2x{:}5x$.

    The numbers in a ratio are called the terms of the ratio.

Two numbers are in the ratio 3:4. Their sum is 35. Find the numbers.

Solution:

Let $3x =$ the first number

$ 4x =$ the second number

Note that $\dfrac{3x}{4x} = \dfrac{3}{4} = 3:4$

The sum of the numbers is 35.

$$3x + 4x = 35$$

$$\frac{7x}{7} = \frac{35}{7}$$

$$x = 5$$

$$3x = 15$$

$$4x = 20$$

Answer: The numbers are 15 and 20.

b. A ratio involving more than two numbers may also be expressed algebraically. The ratio 2:3:7 is equal to $2x:3x:7x$. The individual quantities in the ratio are $2x$, $3x$, and $7x$.

13. a. A **proportion** states that two ratios are equal.

   b. In the proportion a:b = c:d (which may also be written $\dfrac{a}{b} = \dfrac{c}{d}$), the inner terms, b and c, are called the **means**; the outer terms, a and d, are called the **extremes.**

> In 3:6 = 5:10, the means are 6 and 5; the extremes are 3 and 10.

   c. In any proportion, the product of the means equals the product of the extremes. In $a:b = c:d$, $bc = ad$.

> In 3:6 = 5:10, or $\dfrac{3}{6} = \dfrac{5}{10}$, $6 \cdot 5 = 3 \cdot 10$.

   d. In many problems, the quantities involved are in proportion. If three quantities are given in a problem and the fourth quantity is unknown, determine whether the quantities should form a proportion. The proportion will be the equation for the problem.

> A tree that is 20 feet tall casts a shadow 12 feet long. At the same time, a pole casts a shadow 3 feet long. How tall is the pole?

Solution: Let p = height of pole. The heights of objects and their shadows are in proportion.

$$\frac{\text{tree}}{\text{tree's shadow}} = \frac{\text{pole}}{\text{pole's shadow}}$$

$$\frac{20}{12} = \frac{p}{3}$$

$12p = 60$ The product of the means equals the product of the extremes.

$$\frac{12p}{12} = \frac{60}{12}$$

$$p = 5$$

Answer: The pole is 5 feet tall.

> The scale on a map is 3 cm = 500 km. If two cities appear 15 cm apart on the map, how far apart are they actually?

Solution: Let d = actual distance. The quantities on maps and scale drawings are in proportion with the quantities they represent.

$$\frac{\text{first map distance}}{\text{first actual distance}} = \frac{\text{second map distance}}{\text{second actual distance}}$$

$$\frac{3\,\text{cm}}{500\,\text{km}} = \frac{15\,\text{cm}}{d\,\text{km}}$$

$3d = 7500$ The product of the means equals the product of the extremes.

$$\frac{3d}{3} = \frac{7500}{3}$$

$$d = 2500$$

Answer: The cities are 2,500 km apart.

Percent Problems

14. **Percent** problems may be solved algebraically by translating the relationship in the problem into an equation. The word *of* means multiplication, and *is* means equal to.

> 45% of what number is 27?

Solution: Let n = the unknown number. 45% of n is 27.

$.45n = 27$ Change the % to a decimal $(45\% = .45)$

$45n = 2700$ Multiplying both sides by 100 eliminates the decimal.

$$\frac{45n}{45} = \frac{2700}{45}$$

$$n = 60$$

> Mr. Jones receives a salary raise from $15,000 to $16,200. Find the percent of increase.

Solution: Let p = percent. The increase is $16{,}200 - 15{,}000 = 1{,}200$. What percent of 15,000 is 1,200?

$$p \cdot 15{,}000 = 1{,}200$$

$$\frac{p \cdot 15{,}000}{15{,}000} \qquad p = \frac{1{,}200}{15{,}000}$$

$$p = .08 = 8\%$$

15. **Interest** is the price paid for the use of money in loans, savings, and investments. Interest problems are solved using the formula $I = \mathbf{prt}$, where:

I = interest

p = principal (amount of money bearing interest)

r = rate of interest, in %

t = time, in years

> How long must $2,000 be invested at 6% to earn $240 in interest?

Solution:

Let t = time

$\quad I = \$240$

$\quad p = \$2000$

$\quad r = 6\%$ or .06

$$240 = 2000(.06)t$$

$$\frac{240}{120} = \frac{120t}{120}$$

$$2 = t$$

Answer: The $2,000 must be invested for 2 years.

16. a. A **discount** is a percent that is deducted from a marked price. The marked price is considered to be 100% of itself.

> If an item is discounted 20%, its selling price is $100\% - 20\%$, or 80%, of its marked price.

> A radio is tagged with a sale price of $42.50, which is 15% off the regular price. What is the regular price?

Solution: Let r = regular price. The sale price is 100% − 15%, or 85%, of the regular price. 85% of r = $42.50

$.85r = \$42.50$

$$\frac{85r}{85} = \frac{4250}{85}$$ Multiply by 100 to eliminate the decimals.

$$r = 50$$

Answer: The regular price was $50.

b. If two discounts are given in a problem, an intermediate price is computed by taking the first discount on the marked price. The second discount is then computed on the intermediate price.

An appliance company gives a 15% discount for purchases made during a sale, and an additional 5% discount if payment is made in cash. What will the price of an $800 refrigerator be if both discounts are taken?

Solution: First discount: 100% − 15% = 85%

After the first discount, the refrigerator will cost:

85% of $800 = .85($800)

$\qquad = \$680$

The intermediate price is $680.

Second discount: 100% − 5% = 95%.

After the second discount, the refrigerator will cost:

95% of $680 = .95 ($680) = $646.

Answer: The final price will be $646.

17. a. **Profit** is the amount of money added to the dealer's cost of an item to find the selling price. The cost price is considered 100% of itself.

If the profit is 20% of the cost, the selling price must be 100% + 20%, or 120% of the cost.

A furniture dealer sells a sofa at $870, which represents a 45% profit over the cost. What was the cost to the dealer?

Solution: Let c = cost price. 100% + 45% = 145%. The selling price is 145% of the cost.

145% of c = $870

$\qquad 1.45c = 870$

$$\frac{145c}{145} = \frac{87000}{145}$$

$$c = 600$$

Answer: The sofa cost the dealer $600.

b. If an article is sold at **a loss**, the amount of the loss is deducted from the cost price to find the selling price.

An article that is sold at a 25% loss has a selling price of 100% − 25%, or 75%, of the cost price.

Mr. Charles bought a car for $8,000. After a while he sold it to Mr. David at a 30% loss. What did Mr. David pay for the car?

Solution: The car was sold for 100% − 30%, or 70%, of its cost price.

70% of $8000 = .70 ($8000)

$$= \$5600$$

Answer: Mr. David paid $5,600 for the car.

18. Tax is computed by finding a percent of a base amount.

A homeowner pays $2,500 in school taxes. What is the assessed value of his property if school taxes are 3.2% of the assessed value?

Solution: Let v = assessed value.

$$3.2\% \text{ of } v = 2500$$

$$.032v = 2500$$

$$\frac{32v}{32} = \frac{2500000}{32} \qquad \text{(Multiply by 1000 to eliminate decimals)}$$

$$v = 78125$$

Answer: The value of the property is $78,125.

Inequalities

19. a. The = symbol indicates the relationship between two equal quantities. The symbols used to indicate other relationships between two quantities are:
≠ not equal to
> greater than
< less than
≥ greater than or equal to
≤ less than or equal to

b. A number is **greater** than any number appearing to its left on the number line. A number is **less** than any number appearing to its right on the number line.

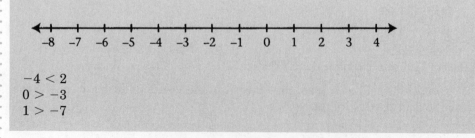

$$-4 < 2$$
$$0 > -3$$
$$1 > -7$$

20. a.

An **inequality** states that one quantity is greater than, or less than, another quantity.

b. Inequalities are solved in the same way as equations, except that in multiplying or dividing both sides of an inequality by a negative quantity, the inequality symbol is reversed.

Solve for x:

$$3x - 4 > 11$$
$$\underline{+4 \quad +4} \qquad \text{Add 4 to both sides.}$$
$$\frac{3x}{3} > \frac{15}{3} \qquad \text{Divide both sides by 3. Since 3 is positive,}$$
$$\text{the inequality symbol remains the same.}$$
$$x > 5$$

The solution $x > 5$ means that all numbers greater than 5 are solutions to the inequality.

Solve for y:

$$2y + 3 > 7y - 2$$
$$\underline{-7y \qquad -7y} \qquad \text{Subtract } 7y \text{ from both sides.}$$
$$-5y + 3 > \quad -2$$
$$\underline{-3 \qquad -3} \qquad \text{Subtract 3 from both sides.}$$
$$-5y > \quad -5 \qquad \text{Divide both sides by } -5. \text{ When dividing both sides by a}$$
$$y < \quad 1 \qquad \text{negative number, reverse the inequality symbol.}$$

Quadratic Equations

21. a. A **quadratic equation** is an equation in which the variable has 2 as its greatest exponent. Quadratic equations may be put into the form $ax^2 + bx + c = 0$, where a, b, and c are constants and $a \neq 0$.

b. The solution of quadratic equations is based on the principle that if the product of two quantities is zero, at least one of those quantities must be zero.

If one side of a quadratic equation is zero and the other side can be written as the product of two factors, each of those factors may be set equal to zero and the resulting equations solved.

Solve $x^2 - 7x + 10 = 0$

$$x^2 - 7x + 10 = 0$$

The factors of the trinomial are	$(x-2)(x-5) = 0$
Set each factor equal to zero:	$x - 2 = 0; \quad x - 5 = 0$
Solve each equation:	$x = 2; \qquad x = 5$

The solutions of $x^2 - 7x + 10 = 0$ are 2 and 5.

Solve $x^2 - 5 = 4$

$$\begin{array}{ll} x^2 - 5 = 4 \\ \underline{ -4 -4} & \text{Add } -4 \text{ to both sides to obtain 0 on the right side.} \end{array}$$

$$x^2 - 9 = 0$$

$$(x + 3)(x - 3) = 0 \qquad \text{Factor } x^2 - 9.$$

$$\begin{array}{ll} x + 3 = 0 \qquad\quad x - 3 = 0 & \text{Set each factor equal to zero.} \\ \underline{-3 -3} \qquad \underline{+3 +3} & \text{Solve each equation.} \\ x = -3 \qquad\quad x = 3 \end{array}$$

The solutions of $x^2 - 5 = 4$ are 3 and -3.

Solve $3z^2 - 12z = 0$ Factor $3z^2 - 12z$

$$\begin{array}{ll} 3z(z - 4) = 0 & z - 4 = 0 \quad \text{Set each factor equal to zero.} \\ \dfrac{3z}{3} = \dfrac{0}{3} & \underline{+4 +4} \\ z = 0 & z = 4 \quad \text{Solve each equation.} \end{array}$$

The solutions of $3z^2 - 12z = 0$ are 0 and 4.

EXERCISES: EQUATIONS, INEQUALITIES, AND PROBLEMS

1. If $6x - (2x + 6) = x + 3$, then $x =$

   (1) -3
   (2) -1
   (3) 1
   (4) 2
   (5) 3

2. If $y^2 - 5y - 6 = 0$, then $y =$

   (1) 6 or -1
   (2) -6 or 1
   (3) -2 or 3
   (4) 2 or -3
   (5) 2 or 3

3. Solve for z: $8z + 5 - 10z > -3$

   (1) $z > 4$
   (2) $z > -4$
   (3) $z < 4$
   (4) $z < -4$
   (5) $z < 16$

4. If $2x^3 + 5x = 4x^3 - 2x^3 + 10$, then $x =$

   (1) -2
   (2) -1
   (3) 1
   (4) 2
   (5) 3

5. One number is three times another number. If their difference is 30, the lesser number is

   (1) 5
   (2) 10
   (3) 15
   (4) 20
   (5) 25

6. The perimeter of the figure below is 41. The length of the longest side is

   (1) 10
   (2) 11
   (3) 12
   (4) 13
   (5) 14

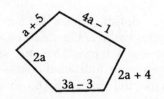

7. The sum of four consecutive even integers is 12. The least of the integers is

   (1) 4
   (2) 3
   (3) 2
   (4) 1
   (5) 0

8. An estate was divided among three heirs, A, B, and C, in the ratio 2:3:4. If the total estate was $22,500, what was the least inheritance?

   (1) $1,000
   (2) $1,250
   (3) $2,500
   (4) $5,000
   (5) $7,500

9. A dealer buys a TV set for $550 and wishes to sell it at a 20% profit. What should his selling price be?

   (1) $570
   (2) $600
   (3) $660
   (4) $672
   (5) $680

10. Michael earns $50 for 8 hours of work. At the same rate of pay, how much will he earn for 28 hours of work?

   (1) $150

   (2) $175

   (3) $186

   (4) $232

   (5) $286

11. Mrs. Smith wishes to purchase a freezer with a list price of $500. If she waits for a "15% off" sale and receives an additional discount of 2% for paying cash, how much will she save?

   (1) $75.50

   (2) $83.50

   (3) $85.00

   (4) $150.00

   (5) $185.00

12. A photograph is 8" wide and 10" long. If it is enlarged so that the new length is 25", the new width will be

   (1) $18\frac{1}{2}$"

   (2) 20"

   (3) 24"

   (4) $31\frac{1}{4}$"

   (5) 34"

13. Jean sells cosmetics, earning a 12% commission on all sales. How much will she need in sales to earn $300 in commission?

   (1) $1,800

   (2) $1,900

   (3) $2,100

   (4) $2,300

   (5) $2,500

14. Mr. Taylor leaves home at 8 a.m., traveling at 45 miles per hour. Mrs. Taylor follows him, leaving home at 10 a.m. and traveling at 55 miles per hour. How long will it take Mrs. Taylor to catch up with Mr. Taylor?

   (1) 7 hours

   (2) 8 hours

   (3) 9 hours

   (4) 10 hours

   (5) 11 hours

15. Sam buys a jacket marked $85. He pays $90.95 including sales tax. What percent sales tax does he pay?

   (1) 4%

   (2) 5%

   (3) 6%

   (4) 7%

   (5) 8%

ANSWER KEY AND EXPLANATIONS

1. (5)	6. (2)	11. (2)
2. (1)	7. (5)	12. (2)
3. (3)	8. (4)	13. (5)
4. (4)	9. (3)	14. (3)
5. (3)	10. (2)	15. (4)

1. The correct answer is (5).

$$6x - (2x + 6) = x + 3$$

$6x - 2x - 6 = x + 3$ Remove parentheses first.

$4x - 6 = x + 3$ Combine the like terms on the left side.

$\dfrac{-x \quad -x}{}$ Eliminate the x term from the right side.

$3x - 6 = \quad 3$

$\dfrac{+6 \quad +6}{}$ Eliminate the number term from the left side.

$\dfrac{3x}{3} = \dfrac{9}{3}$ Divide both sides by 3 to isolate x.

$x = 3$

2. The correct answer is (1).

$$y^2 - 5y - 6 = 0$$

$(y - 6)(y + 1) = 0$ Factor the trinomial side of the quadratic equation.

$y - 6 = 0 \quad y + 1 = 0$ Set each factor equal to zero.

$\dfrac{+6 \quad\quad +6}{} \quad \dfrac{-1 \quad\quad -1}{}$

$y = 6 \quad\quad y = -1$ Solve each equation.

3. The correct answer is (3).

$$8z + 5 - 10z > -3$$

$-2z + 5 > -3$ Combine the like terms on the left side.

$\dfrac{-5 \quad -5}{}$ Eliminate the number term from the left side.

$-2z > -8$ Divide both sides by -2 and reverse the inequality symbol.

$z < 4$

4. The correct answer is (4).

$$2x^3 + 5x = 4x^3 - 2x^3 + 10$$
$$2x^3 + 5x = 2x^3 + 10 \quad \text{Combine the like terms on the right side.}$$
$$\underline{-2x^3 \qquad -2x^3} \quad \text{Subtracting } 2x^3 \text{ from both sides leaves a simple equation.}$$
$$\frac{5x}{5} = \frac{10}{5}$$
$$x = 2$$

5. The correct answer is (3).

Let n = the lesser number. Then $3n$ = the greater number. The difference of the numbers is 30.

$$3n - n = 30$$
$$\frac{2n}{2} = \frac{30}{2}$$
$$n = 15$$

6. The correct answer is (2).

The perimeter is equal to the sum of the sides.

$$a + 5 + 4a - 1 + 2a + 4 + 3a - 3 + 2a = 41$$

$$12a + 5 = 41 \quad \text{Combine like terms.}$$
$$\underline{-5 \qquad -5}$$
$$\frac{12a}{12} = \frac{36}{12}$$
$$a = 3$$

The sides are:

$$a + 5 = 3 + 5 = 8$$
$$4a - 1 = 4 \cdot 3 - 1 = 11$$
$$2a + 4 = 2 \cdot 3 + 4 = 10$$
$$3a - 3 = 3 \cdot 3 - 3 = 6$$
$$2a = 2 \cdot 3 = 6$$

The longest side is 11.

7. The correct answer is (5).

Let x, $x + 2$, $x + 4$, and $x + 6$ represent the four consecutive even integers. The sum of the integers is 12.

$$x + x + 2 + x + 4 + x + 6 = 12$$
$$4x + 12 = 12$$
$$\underline{-12 \quad -12}$$
$$\frac{4x}{4} = \frac{0}{4}$$
$$x = 0$$
$$x + 2 = 2,\ x + 4 = 4,\ x + 6 = 6$$

The least integer is 0.

8. The correct answer is (4).

Let $2x$, $3x$, and $4x$ represent the shares of the inheritance. The total estate was $22,500.

$$2x + 3x + 4x = 22500$$
$$\frac{9x}{9} = \frac{22500}{9}$$
$$x = 2500$$
$$2x = 2 \cdot 2500 = 5000$$
$$3x = 3 \cdot 2500 = 7500$$
$$4x = 4 \cdot 2500 = 10,000$$

The least inheritance was $2x$, or $5,000.

9. The correct answer is (3).

His selling price will be $(100\% + 20\%)$ of his cost price.

$$120\% \text{ of } \$550 = 1.20(\$550)$$
$$= \$660$$

10. The correct answer is (2).

The amount earned is proportional to the number of hours worked.

Let m = unknown pay

$$\frac{m}{28} = \frac{50}{8}$$
$$8m = 28 \cdot 50 \qquad \text{The product of the means is equal to the product of the extremes.}$$
$$\frac{8m}{8} = \frac{1400}{8}$$
$$m = 175$$

11. The correct answer is (2).

The selling price after the 15% discount is 85% of list.
selling price = .85(500)
$$= 425$$
The selling price after the additional 2% discount is 98% of 425.
new selling price = .98(425)
$$= 416.50$$
The original price was $500. Mrs. Smith buys at $416.50. She saves $500 − $416.50 = $83.50

12. The correct answer is (2).

The old dimensions and the new dimensions are in proportion. Let w = new width.

$$\frac{\text{new width}}{\text{old width}} = \frac{\text{new length}}{\text{old length}}$$

$$\frac{w}{8} = \frac{25}{10}$$

$$10w = 200$$

$$w = 20$$

13. The correct answer is (5).

Let s = needed sales. 12% of sales will be $300.

$$\frac{12s}{.12} = \frac{300}{.12}$$ Divide by .12, or first multiply by 100 to

$$s = 2500$$ clear the decimal, then divide by 12.

14. The correct answer is (3).

Let h = the number of hours needed by Mrs. Taylor. Mr. Taylor started two hours earlier; therefore, he travels $h + 2$ hours. Mrs. Taylor's distance is $55h$. Mr. Taylor's distance is $45(h + 2)$. When Mrs. Taylor catches up with Mr. Taylor, they will have traveled equal distances.

$$55h = 45(h + 2)$$

$$55h = 45h + 90$$

$$\frac{-45h}{10h} = \frac{-45h}{90}$$

$$h = 9$$

15. The correct answer is (4).

The amount of tax is $90.95 − $85 = $5.95. Find the percent $5.95 is of $85. Let p = percent.

$$\frac{p \cdot 85}{85} = \frac{5.95}{85}$$

$$p = .07 = 7\%$$

GEOMETRY AND TRIGONOMETRY

Angles

1. a. An **angle** is the figure formed by two rays meeting at a point.

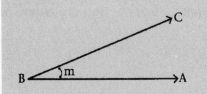

   b. The point B is the **vertex** of the angle and the rays $\overline{BA}$ and $\overline{BC}$ are the **sides** of the angle.

2. There are three common ways of naming an angle:
   a. By a small letter or figure written within the angle, as ∢ m.
   b. By the capital letter at its vertex, as ∢ B.
   c. By three capital letters, the middle letter being the vertex letter, as ∢ ABC.

3. a. When two straight lines intersect (cut each other), four angles are formed. If these four angles are congruent, each angle is a **right angle** and measures 90°. The symbol ⌐ is used to indicate a right angle.

   b. An angle less than a right angle is an **acute angle**.

   c. If the two sides of an angle extend in opposite directions forming a straight line, the angle is a **straight angle** and measures 180°.

   d. An angle greater than a right angle (90°) and less than a straight angle (180°) is an **obtuse angle**.

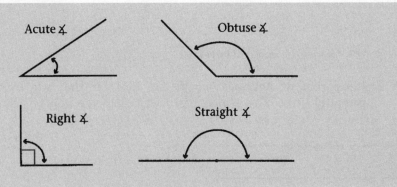

4. a. Two angles are **complementary** if the sum of their measures is 90°. To find the complement of an angle, subtract the measure of the angle from 90°.

The complement of 60° is 90° − 60° = 30°.

b. Two angles are **supplementary** if the sum of their measures is 180°. To find the supplement of an angle, subtract the measure of the angle from 180°.

The supplement of 60° is 180° − 60° = 120°.

5. When two straight lines intersect, any pair of opposite angles are called **vertical angles** and are congruent.

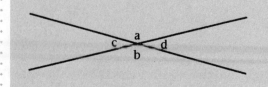

∢ a and ∢ b are vertical angles

m ∢ a = m ∢ b

∢ c and ∢ d are vertical angles

m ∢ c = m ∢ d

6. Two lines are **perpendicular** to each other if they meet to form a right angle. The symbol ⊥ is used to indicate that the lines are perpendicular.

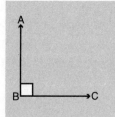

∢ ABC is a right angle. Therefore, $\overrightarrow{AB} \perp \overrightarrow{BC}$.

7. a. Lines that do not meet no matter how far they are extended are called **parallel lines**. The symbol ∥ is used to indicate that two lines are parallel.

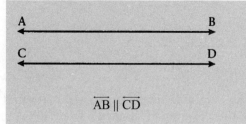

$\overrightarrow{AB} \parallel \overrightarrow{CD}$

b. A line that intersects parallel lines is called a **transversal**. The pairs of angles formed have special names and relationships.

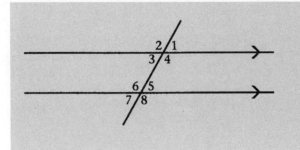

alternate interior angles:
m ∢ 3 = m ∢5
m ∢ 4 = m ∢ 6
corresponding angles:
m ∢ 1 = m ∢ 5
m ∢ 2 = m ∢ 6
m ∢ 3 = m ∢ 7
m ∢ 4 = m ∢ 8

Several pairs of angles, such as ∢ 1 and ∢ 2, are supplementary. Several pairs, such as ∢ 6 and ∢ 8, are vertical angles and are therefore congruent.

Triangles

8. A triangle is a closed, three-sided figure. The following figures are triangles.

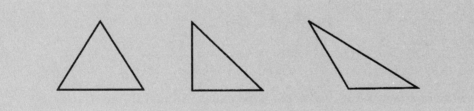

9. a. The sum of the measures of the three angles of a triangle is 180°.

b. To find the measures of the an angle of a triangle given the measures of the other two angles, add the given measures and subtract their sum from 180°.

Illustration: The measures of two angles of a triangle are 60° and 40°. Find the measure of the third angle.

Solution: 60° + 40° = 100°
         180° − 100° = 80°

Answer: The measure of the third angle is 80°.

10. a. A triangle with two congruent sides is called an **isosceles triangle**.

    b. In an isosceles triangle, the angles opposite the congruent sides are also congruent.

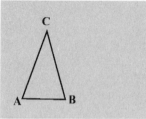

If AC = BC, then m $\sphericalangle$ A = m $\sphericalangle$ B

11. a. A triangle with all three sides congruent is called an **equilateral triangle**.

    b. The measure of each angle of an equilateral triangle is 60°.

12. a. A triangle with a right angle is called a **right triangle**.

    b. In a right triangle, the two acute angles are complementary.

    c. In a right triangle, the side opposite the right angle is called the **hypotenuse** and is the longest side. The other two sides are called legs.

In right triangle ABC, $\overline{AC}$ is the hypotenuse. $\overline{AB}$ and $\overline{BC}$ are the legs.

13. The **Pythagorean theorem** states that in a right triangle, the square of the hypotenuse equals the sum of the squares of the legs.

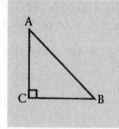

$(AC)^2 + (BC)^2 = (AB)^2$

Illustration: Find the hypotenuse (h) in a right triangle that has legs 6 and 8.

Solution:

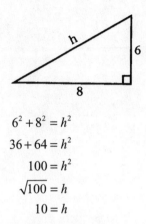

$$6^2 + 8^2 = h^2$$
$$36 + 64 = h^2$$
$$100 = h^2$$
$$\sqrt{100} = h$$
$$10 = h$$

Illustration: One leg of a right triangle is 5. The hypotenuse is 13. Find the other leg.

Solution: Let the unknown leg be represented by x.

$$5^2 + x^2 = 13^2$$
$$25 + x^2 = 169$$
$$\underline{-25 \qquad = -25}$$
$$x^2 = 144$$
$$x = \sqrt{144}$$
$$x = 12$$

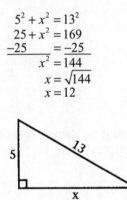

Answer: The other leg is 12.

14. a. In a right triangle with congruent legs (an isosceles right triangle), each acute
       angle measures 45°. There are special relationships between the legs and the
       hypotenuse:

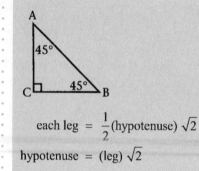

$$\text{each leg} = \frac{1}{2}(\text{hypotenuse})\sqrt{2}$$

$$\text{hypotenuse} = (\text{leg})\sqrt{2}$$

$$AC = BC = \frac{1}{2}(AB)\sqrt{2}$$

$$AB = (AC)\sqrt{2} = (BC)\sqrt{2}$$

In isosceles right triangle RST:

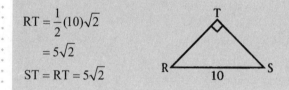

$$RT = \frac{1}{2}(10)\sqrt{2}$$

$$= 5\sqrt{2}$$

$$ST = RT = 5\sqrt{2}$$

   b. In a right triangle with acute angles measuring 30° and 60°, the leg opposite
      the 30° angle is one-half the hypotenuse. The leg opposite the 60° angle is
      one-half the hypotenuse multiplied by $\sqrt{3}$.

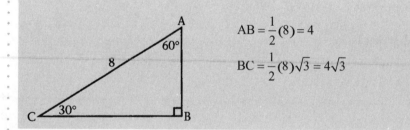

$$AB = \frac{1}{2}(8) = 4$$

$$BC = \frac{1}{2}(8)\sqrt{3} = 4\sqrt{3}$$

Quadrilaterals

15. a. A quadrilateral is a closed, four-sided figure in two dimensions. Common
       quadrilaterals are the **parallelogram**, **rectangle**, and **square**.

   b. The sum of the measures of the four angles of a quadrilateral is 360°.

16. a. A **parallelogram** is a quadrilateral in which both pairs of opposite sides are parallel.

   b. Opposite sides of a parallelogram are congruent.

   c. Opposite angles of a parallelogram are congruent.

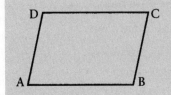

In parallelogram ABCD,

$\overline{AB} \parallel \overline{CD}$, AB = CD, m ∢ A = m ∢ C

$\overline{AD} \parallel \overline{BC}$, AD = BC, m ∢ B = m ∢ D

17. a. A **rhombus** is a parallelogram that has all sides congruent.

   b. A **rectangle** is a parallelogram that has all right angles.

   c. A **square** is a rectangle that has all sides congruent. A square is also a rhombus.

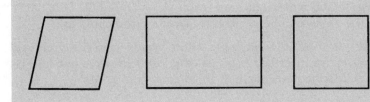

18. A **trapezoid** is a quadrilateral with one and only one pair of opposite sides parallel.

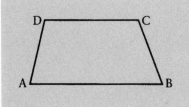

In trapezoid ABCD, $\overline{AB} \parallel \overline{CD}$

Circles

19. A **circle** is a closed plane curve, all points of which are equidistant from a point within called the center.

20. a. A **complete circle** contains 360°.

   b. A **semi-circle** contains 180°.

21. a. A **chord** is a line segment connecting any two points on the circle.

 b. A **radius** of a circle is a line segment connecting the center with any point on the circle.

 c. A **diameter** is a chord passing through the center of the circle.

 d. A **secant** is a chord extended in either one or both directions.

 e. A **tangent** is a line touching a circle at one point and only one.

 f. The **circumference** is the curved line bounding the circle.

 g. An **arc** of a circle is any part of the circumference.

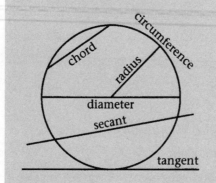

22. a. **A central angle**, as ∢ AOB in the figure below, is an angle whose vertex is the center of the circle and whose sides are radii. A central angle is equal in degrees to (or has the same number of degrees as) its intercepted arc.

 b. An **inscribed angle**, as ∢ MNP, is an angle whose vertex is on the circle and whose sides are chords. An inscribed angle is equal in degrees to one-half its intercepted arc. m ∢ MNP equals one-half the degrees in arc MP.

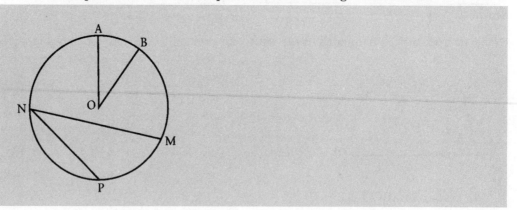

Perimeter

23. The **perimeter** of a two-dimensional figure is the distance around the figure.

The perimeter of the figure below is 9 + 8 + 4 + 5 + 3 = 29.

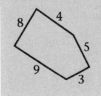

24. a. The perimeter of a triangle is found by adding all of its sides.

If the sides of a triangle are 4, 5, and 7, its perimeter is 4 + 5 + 7 = 16.

   b. If the perimeter and two sides of a triangle are given, the third side is found
      by adding the two given sides and subtracting this sum from the perimeter.

   Illustration: Two sides of a triangle are 12 and 15. The perimeter is 37. Find the
   other side.

   Solution: 12 + 15 = 27

   37 − 27 = 10

   Answer: The third side is 10.

25. The perimeter of a rectangle equals twice the sum of the length and the width. The
    length is any side; the width is the side adjacent to the length. The formula is:
    P = 2(l + w).

The perimeter of a rectangle whose length is 7 feet and width is 3 feet equals 2
(7 + 3) = 2 × 10 = 20 ft.

26. The perimeter of a square equals one side multiplied by 4. The formula is: P = 4s.

The perimeter of a square one side of which is 5 feet equals 4 × 5 feet = 20
feet.

27. a. The **circumference** of a circle is equal to the product of the diameter multi-
      plied by π . The formula is C = πd.
   b. The number π (pi) is approximately equal to $\frac{22}{7}$, or 3.14 (3.1416 for greater
      accuracy). The problem will state which value to use; otherwise, express the
      answer in terms of pi, π.

The circumference of a circle whose diameter is 4 inches = 4π inches; or, if it is stated
that $\pi = \frac{22}{7}$, then the circumference = $4 \times \frac{22}{7} = \frac{88}{7} = 12\frac{4}{7}$ inches.

   c. Since the diameter is twice the radius, the circumference equals twice the
      radius multiplied by π. The formula is C = 2πr.

If the radius of a circle is 3 inches, then the circumference = 6π inches.

   d. The diameter of a circle equals the circumference divided by π.

If the circumference of a circle is 11 inches, then, assuming $\pi = \dfrac{22}{7}$,

$$\text{diameter} = 11 \div \dfrac{22}{7} \text{ inches}$$

$$= \overset{1}{\cancel{11}} \times \dfrac{7}{\underset{2}{\cancel{22}}}$$

$$= \dfrac{7}{2} \text{ inches, or } 3\dfrac{1}{2} \text{ inches}$$

Area

28. a. In a figure of two dimensions, the total space within the figure is called the **area**.

   b. Area is expressed in square units, such as **square inches, square centimeters, and square miles.**

   c. In computing area, all dimensions must be in the same units.

29. The area of a square is equal to the square of the length of any side. The formula is $A = s^2$.

The area of a square one side of which is 6 inches is $6 \times 6 = 36$ square inches.

30. a. The area of a rectangle equals the product of the length multiplied by the width. The formula is $A = l \times w$.

If the length of a rectangle is 6 feet and its width is 4 feet, then the area is $6 \times 4 = 24$ square feet.

   b. If given the area of a rectangle and one dimension, you can find the other dimension by dividing the area by the given dimension.

If the area of a rectangle is 48 square feet and one dimension is 4 feet, then the other dimension is $48 \div 4 = 12$ feet.

31. a. The altitude, or height, of a parallelogram is a line drawn from a vertex perpendicular to the opposite side, or base.

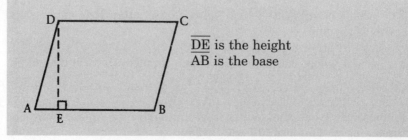

$\overline{DE}$ is the height
$\overline{AB}$ is the base

b. The area of a parallelogram is equal to the product of its base and its height. The formula is $A = b \times h$.

If the base of a parallelogram is 10 centimeters and its height is 5 centimeters, its area is $10 \times 5 = 50$ square centimeters.

c. To find the base or the height of a parallelogram given one of these dimensions and given the area, divide the area by the given dimension.

If the area of a parallelogram is 40 square inches and its height is 8 inches, its base is $40 \div 8 = 5$ inches.

32. a. The **altitude**, or height, of a triangle is a line drawn from a vertex perpendicular to the opposite side, called the **base**.

b. The area of a triangle is equal to one-half the product of the base and the height. The formula is $A = \frac{1}{2}b \times h$.

The area of a triangle that has a height of 5 inches and a base of 4 inches is $\frac{1}{2} \times 5 \times 4 = \frac{1}{2} \times 20 = 10$ square inches.

c. In a right triangle, one leg may be considered the height and the other leg the base. Therefore, the area of a right triangle is equal to one-half the product of the legs.

The legs of a right triangle are 3 and 4. Its area is $\frac{1}{2} \times 3 \times 4 = 6$ square units.

33. The area of a rhombus is equal to one-half the product of its diagonals. The formula is:

$$A = \frac{1}{2} \cdot d_1 \cdot d_2$$

If the diagonals of a rhombus are 4 and 6,

$$Area = \frac{1}{2} \cdot 4 \cdot 6$$
$$= 12$$

34. The area of a trapezoid is equal to one-half the product of the height and the sum of the bases.

$$\text{Area} = \frac{1}{2} h \,(\text{base}_1 + \text{base}_2)$$

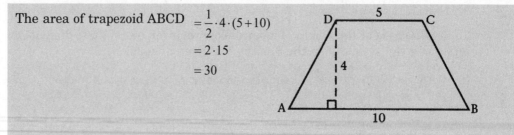

The area of trapezoid ABCD
$$= \frac{1}{2} \cdot 4 \cdot (5 + 10)$$
$$= 2 \cdot 15$$
$$= 30$$

35. a. The area of a circle is equal to the radius squared multiplied by π. The formula is $A = \pi r^2$.

If the radius of a circle is 6 inches, then the area = 36p square inches.

  b. To find the radius of a circle given the area, divide the area by π and find the square root of the quotient.

To find the radius of a circle of area 100π:

$$\frac{100\pi}{\pi} = 100$$
$$\sqrt{100} = 10 = \text{radius}$$

36. Some figures are composed of several geometric shapes. To find the area of such figures, it is necessary to find the area of each of their parts.

Illustration: Find the area of the figure below:

Solution: The figure is composed of three parts: a square of side 4, a semi-circle of diameter 4 (the lower side of the square), and a right triangle with legs 3 and 4 (the right side of the square).

$$\text{Area of square} = 4^2 = 16$$

$$\text{Area of triangle} = \frac{1}{2} \times 3 \times 4 = 6$$

$$\text{Area of semicircle is } \frac{1}{2} \text{ area of circle} = \frac{1}{2}\pi r^2$$

$$\text{Radius} = \frac{1}{2} \times 4 = 2$$

$$\text{Area} = \frac{1}{2} = \pi r^2$$

$$= \frac{1}{2}\pi 2^2 = 2\pi$$

$$\text{Total area} = 16 + 6 + 2\pi = 22 + 2\pi$$

Three-Dimensional Figures

37. a. In a three-dimensional figure, the total space contained within the figure is called the **volume** and is expressed in cubic units.

   b. The total outside surface is called the **surface area** and it is expressed in square units.

   c. In computing volume and surface area, all dimensions must be expressed in the same units.

38. a. A rectangular solid is a figure of three dimensions having six rectangular faces meeting each other at right angles. The three dimensions are **length, width,** and **height.** The figure below is a rectangular solid: "l" is the length, "w" is the width, and "h" is the height.

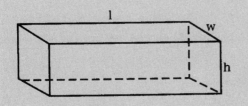

   b. The volume of a rectangular solid is the product of the length, width, and height: $V = l \times w \times h$.

The volume of a rectangular solid whose length is 6 ft, width 3 ft, and height 4 ft is $6 \times 3 \times 4 = 72$ cubic ft.

39. a. A **cube** is a rectangular solid whose edges are congruent. The figure below is a cube: the length, width, and height are all equal to "e."

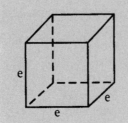

b. The volume of a cube is equal to the edge cubed: $V = e^3$.

The volume of a cube whose height is 6 inches equals $6^3 = 6 \times 6 \times 6 = 216$ cubic inches.

c. The surface area of a cube is equal to the area of any side multiplied by 6.

The surface area of a cube whose length is 5 inches $= 5^2 \times 6 = 25 \times 6 = 150$ square inches.

40. The volume of a cylinder is equal to the product of π, the radius squared, and the height.

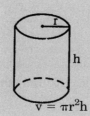

$v = \pi r^2 h$

Trigonometry

Trigonometry has been developed to help solve problems concerning the *sides* and *angles* of right triangles.

For example, suppose triangle ABC looks like this:

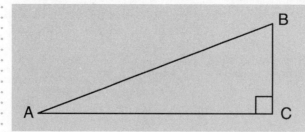

Then, angle C, in the right-triangle ABC, is a right angle (90°), and $\overline{AB}$ is the hypotenuse.

Angle A is *opposite* side $\overline{BC}$, and *adjacent* to side $\overline{AC}$.

If you are standing at a point A, then the ratio of the length of the side opposite you (BC) to the hypotenuse (AB) is equal to the sine of angle A, or *sin A*. Thus,

$$\sin A = \frac{BC}{AB}$$

The value of sin A can be found using the calculator. Suppose m $\angle$ A = 30°. By using the calculator, you can find that sin 30° = 0.5.

CALCULATOR   30 sin [the result is **0.5**]

Consider right triangle, ABC above. If Joe is standing at point A, which is 30°, and point A is 400 feet from point B (AB = 400), then find the distance from B to C (BC).

In right triangle ABC, angle A and length AB are known. The trigonometric function that relate both of these measurements to the unknown, BC, is

$$\sin A = \frac{BC}{AB}$$ (1) Substituting the known values,

$$\sin 30° = \frac{BC}{400}$$ (2) Solve for BC by first multiplying both sides by 400,

$$BC = 400 \times \sin 30°$$

CALCULATOR   400 × 30 sin [the result is **200 feet**]

The Trigonometric Functions

$$\sin = \frac{\text{opposite side}}{\text{hypotenuse}}$$ $$\sin A = \frac{BC}{AB}$$

$$\cos = \frac{\text{adjacent side}}{\text{hypotenuse}}$$ $$\cos A = \frac{AC}{AB}$$

$$\tan = \frac{\text{opposite side}}{\text{adjacent side}}$$ $$\tan A = \frac{BC}{AC}$$

Note: It is not necessary to memorize these functions since they will be given to you in a Formula page at the time of the test.

Evaluate the values of sin, cos, and tan for 30°, 45°, and 60°.

Selected examples, using the calculator, are as follows:

CALCULATOR   60 sin [the result is: **sin 60° = 0.8660. . .**]

CALCULATOR   60 cos [the result is: **cos 60° = 0.5**]

CALCULATOR   60 tan [the result is: **tan 60° = 1.7320 . . .**]

Set up a table to organize the results. Where necessary, truncate the results to 4 decimal places.

	sin	cos	tan
30	0.5	0.8660	0.5773
45	0.7071	0.7071	1.
60	0.8660	0.5	1.7320

A water slide will be constructed at Aqua-Land Amusement Park. It will form a right triangle, PBT, and will empty into a pool of water at point P, making a 20° angle with the ground, as shown below. Find the length of ground (BP) needed to construct the slide. [Give your answer to the nearest tenth of a foot.]

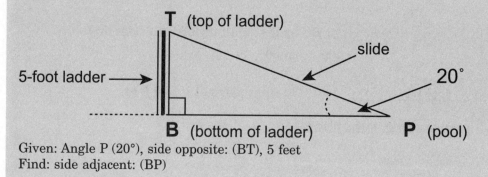

Given: Angle P (20°), side opposite: (BT), 5 feet
Find: side adjacent: (BP)

The trigonometric function that relates these measurements to the unknown, BP, is:

$$\tan P = \frac{\text{opposite}}{\text{adjacent}} = \frac{BT}{BP}; \quad \tan 20° = \frac{5}{BP} \quad \text{(equation 1)}$$

Multiplying both sides of (1) by BP and dividing by tan 20°,

$$BP = \frac{5}{\tan 20°} \quad \text{(equation 2)}$$

CALCULATOR   5 ÷ 20 tan = [Answer: 13.7373. . ., rounded to **13.7** feet]

Summary of Geometry and Trigonometry Formulas

Perimeter

Any 2-dimensional figure:	P = sum of all the sides
Rectangle:	P = 2(l + w)
Square:	P = 4s
Circle:	Circumference = $2\pi r = \pi d$

Area

Square:	$A = s^2$
Rectangle:	$A = l \cdot w$
Parallelogram:	$A = b \cdot h$
Triangle:	$A = \dfrac{1}{2} \cdot b \cdot h$
Right triangle:	$A = \dfrac{1}{2} \cdot \text{leg}_1 \cdot \text{leg}_2$
Rhombus:	$A = \dfrac{1}{2} \cdot d_1 \cdot d_2$
Trapezoid:	$A = \dfrac{1}{2} \cdot h(b_1 + b_2)$
Circle:	$A = \pi r^2$

Volume

Rectangular solid:	$V = l \cdot w \cdot h$
Cube:	$V = e^3$
Cylinder:	$V = \pi r^2 h$
Sphere:	$V = \dfrac{3}{4}\pi r^3$
Cone:	$V = \dfrac{1}{3}\pi r^2 h$
Pyramid:	$V = \dfrac{1}{3} \cdot B \cdot h$ (B = area of base)

Trigonometry

Given an acute angle with measure x of a right triangle.

sine:	$\sin x = \dfrac{\text{opposite side}}{\text{hypotenuse}}$
cosine:	$\cos x = \dfrac{\text{adjacent side}}{\text{hypotenuse}}$
tangent:	$\tan x = \dfrac{\text{opposite side}}{\text{adjacent side}}$

EXERCISES: GEOMETRY AND TRIGONOMETRY

1. If the perimeter of a rectangle is 68 yards and the width is 48 feet, the length is

   (1) 10 yards.
   (2) 18 yards.
   (3) 20 feet.
   (4) 56 feet.
   (5) 60 feet.

2. The total length of fencing needed to enclose a rectangular area 46 feet by 34 feet is

   (1) 26 yards 1 foot.
   (2) $26\frac{2}{3}$ yards.
   (3) 52 yards 2 feet.
   (4) $53\frac{1}{3}$ yards.
   (5) 54 yards.

3. The area of a square is $49x^2$. What is the length of a diagonal of the square?

   (1) $7x$
   (2) $7x\sqrt{2}$
   (3) $14x$
   (4) $7x^2$
   (5) $\dfrac{7x}{\sqrt{2}}$

4. A road runs 1,200 ft from A to B, and then makes a right angle going to C, a distance of 500 ft. A new road is being built directly from A to C. How much shorter will the new road be?

   (1) 400 feet
   (2) 609 feet
   (3) 850 feet
   (4) 1,300 feet
   (5) 1,350 feet

5. A certain triangle has sides that are, respectively, 6 inches, 8 inches, and 10 inches long. A rectangle equal in area to that of the triangle has a width of 3 inches. The perimeter of the rectangle, expressed in inches, is

   (1) 11
   (2) 16
   (3) 18
   (4) 20
   (5) 22

6. If $\overline{AB} \parallel \overline{DE}$, $\measuredangle C = 50°$ and $\measuredangle 1 = 60°$ in the figure below, then $\measuredangle A =$

   (1) 30°
   (2) 60°
   (3) 70°
   (4) 50°
   (5) 80°

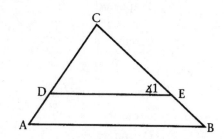

7. A rectangular bin 4 feet long, 3 feet wide, and 2 feet high is solidly packed with bricks whose dimensions are 8 inches, 4 inches, and 2 inches. The number of bricks in the bin is

   (1) 54
   (2) 648
   (3) 1,296
   (4) 1,300
   (5) None of the above

8. If the cost of digging a trench is $2.12 a cubic yard, what would be the cost of digging a trench 2 yards by 5 yards by 4 yards?

   (1) $21.20
   (2) $40.00
   (3) $64.00
   (4) $84.80
   (5) $90.00

9. A piece of wire is shaped to enclose a square whose area is 121 square inches. It is then reshaped to enclose a rectangle whose length is 13 inches. The area of the rectangle, in square inches, is

   (1) 64
   (2) 96
   (3) 117
   (4) 144
   (5) 169

10. The area of a 2-foot-wide walk around a garden that is 30 feet long and 20 feet wide is

   (1) 104 square feet.
   (2) 120 square feet.
   (3) 180 square feet.
   (4) 200 square feet.
   (5) 216 square feet.

11. The area of a circle is 49π. Find its circumference, in terms of π.

   (1) 14π
   (2) 28π
   (3) 49π
   (4) 98π
   (5) 100π

12. In two hours, the minute hand of a clock rotates through an angle of

   (1) 90°
   (2) 180°
   (3) 360°
   (4) 720°
   (5) 900°

13. Anne's kite, on a 500-foot string, is flying directly over Max's head. If the angle the string makes with the ground is 83°, approximately how far is Max standing from Anne?

   (1) 50 feet
   (2) 60 feet
   (3) 61 feet
   (4) 100 feet
   (5) 496 feet

14. The width of a rectangular playing field is 100 feet. A line is painted across the diagonal, forming a 40° angle with the length. Find the approximate length of the field.

   (1) 64
   (2) 84
   (3) 100
   (4) 115
   (5) 119

15. The roof of Nick's house is 25 feet on each side and forms a right angle at the top. If the sides form a triangle with the floor of the attic, what is the sine of the angle that the side makes with the floor?

   (1) 0.57
   (2) 0.71
   (3) 0.86
   (4) 1.00
   (5) 1.40

ANSWER KEY AND EXPLANATIONS

1. (2)	6. (3)	11. (1)
2. (4)	7. (2)	12. (4)
3. (2)	8. (4)	13. (3)
4. (1)	9. (3)	14. (5)
5. (5)	10. (5)	15. (2)

1. The correct answer is (2).

Perimeter $= 2(l + w)$. Let the length be x yards.

$$\text{Each width} = 48 \text{ ft} \div 3$$
$$= 16 \text{ yd}$$
$$2(x + 16) = 68$$
$$2x + 32 = 68$$
$$\underline{-32 \quad -32}$$
$$\frac{2x}{2} = \frac{36}{2}$$
$$x = 18$$

2. The correct answer is (4).

Perimeter

$$= 2(l + w)$$
$$= 2(46 + 34) \text{ feet}$$
$$= 2 \times 80 \text{ feet}$$
$$= 160 \text{ feet}$$

$$160 \text{ feet} = 160 \div 3 \text{ yards} = 53\frac{1}{3} \text{ yards}$$

3. The correct answer is (2).

If the area is $49x^2$, the side of the square is $7x$. Therefore, the diagonal of the square must be the hypotenuse of a right isosceles triangle of leg $7x$. Hence, diagonal $= 7x\sqrt{2}$.

4. The correct answer is (1).

The new road is the hypotenuse of a right triangle whose legs are the old road.

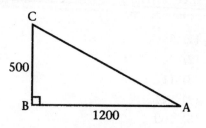

$$(AC)^2 = 500^2 + 1200^2$$
$$= 250000 + 1440000$$
$$= 1690000$$
$$AC = \sqrt{1690000}$$
$$= \sqrt{169} \cdot \sqrt{10000}$$
$$= 13 \cdot 100$$
$$= 1300$$

Old road $= 500 \text{ ft} + 1200 \text{ ft}$
$$= 1700 \text{ ft}$$

New road $= 1300 \text{ ft}$

Difference $= 400 \text{ ft}$

5. The correct answer is (5).

Since $6^2 + 8^2 = 10^2$, or $36 + 64 = 100$, the triangle is a right triangle. Its area is $\frac{1}{2} \times 6 \times 8 = 24$ sq in (area of a triangle $= \frac{1}{2} \cdot b \cdot h$). Therefore, the area of the rectangle is also 24 square inches. If the width of the rectangle is 3 inches, the length is $24 \div 3 = 8$ inches. Then, the perimeter of the rectangle is $2(3 + 8) = 2 \times 11 = 22$ inches.

6. The correct answer is (3).

∢ B and ∢ 1 are corresponding angles formed by the parallel lines AB and DE and the transversal BC. Therefore, m ∢ 1 = m ∢ B = 60°.

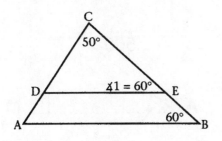

The sum of the measures of the angles of a triangle is 180°.

$$\angle A + \angle B + \angle C = 180°$$
$$\angle A + 60° + 50° = 180°$$
$$\angle A + 110° = 180°$$
$$\underline{-110°} = \underline{110°}$$
$$\angle A \quad = 70°$$

7. The correct answer is (2).

Convert the dimensions of the bin to inches:
  4 feet = 48 inches
  3 feet = 36 inches
  2 feet = 24 inches

Volume of bin = 48 × 36 × 24 cubic in
        = 41,472 cubic in

Volume of each brick = 8 × 4 × 2 cubic in
        = 64 cubic in

41,472 ÷ 64 = 648 bricks

8. The correct answer is (4).

The trench contains:
2 yd × 5 yd × 4 yd = 40 cubic yards

40 × $2.12 = $84.80

9. The correct answer is (3).

If the area of the square is 121 square inches, each side is $\sqrt{121} = 11$ inches and the perimeter is $4 \times 11 = 44$ inches. The perimeter of the rectangle is then 44 inches. If the two lengths are each 13 inches, their total is 26 inches. $44 - 26 = 18$ inches remain for the two widths. Therefore, each width is equal to $18 \div 2 = 9$ inches.

The area of a rectangle with length 13 inches and width 9 inches is $13 \times 9 = 117$ square inches.

10. The correct answer is (5).

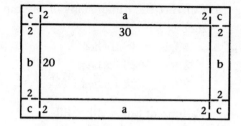

The walk consists of:

a) 2 rectangles of length 30 ft and width 2 ft
Area of each = 2 × 30 = 60 sq ft
Area of both = 120 sq ft

b) 2 rectangles of length 20 ft and width 2 ft
Area of each = 2 × 20 = 40 sq ft
Area of both = 80 sq ft

c) 4 squares, each having a side of 2 ft
Area of each square = 2^2 = 4 sq ft
Area of 4 squares = 16 sq ft
Total area of walk = 120 + 80 + 16 = 216 sq ft

Alternatively, you may solve this problem by finding the area of the garden and the area of the garden plus the walk, then subtracting to find the area of the walk alone:

Area of garden = 20 × 30 = 600 sq ft

Area of garden + walk:

(20 + 2 + 2) × (30 + 2 + 2) = 24 × 34

= 816 sq ft

Area of walk alone:

816 − 600 = 216 sq ft

11. The correct answer is (1).

Area of a circle = πr^2. If the area is 49π, the radius is $\sqrt{49}$ = 7.
Circumference = $2\pi r$

$$= 2 \times \pi \times 7$$
$$= 14\pi$$

12. The correct answer is (4).

In one hour, the minute hand rotates through 360°. In two hours, it rotates through 2 × 360° = 720°.

13. The correct answer is (3).

Make a labeled sketch of the problem:

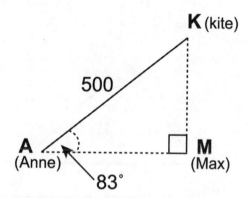

Given: hypotenuse AK and angle A.

Find: the adjacent side AM

$$\cos A = \frac{\text{adjacent}}{\text{hypotenuse}} = \frac{AM}{AK}$$

Substituting the values, $\cos 83° = \dfrac{AM}{500}$

Solve for AM by multiplying both sides by 500: 500 × cos 83° = AM

⌨ CALCULATOR   500 × 83 cos

[Answer: 60.9346. . ., rounded to **61 feet**]

14. The correct answer is (5).

Make a sketch of the problem.

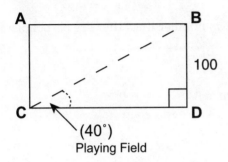

(40°)
Playing Field

Given: Rectangle ABCD,

Angle BCD (40°),

side opposite, BD

(width = 100 feet)

Find: side adjacent, CD

$$\tan BCD = \frac{\text{opposite}}{\text{adjacent}} = \frac{BD}{DC}$$

$\tan 40° = \dfrac{100}{CD}$; multiplying both sides

by CD and then dividing by tan 40°,

$$CD = \frac{100}{\tan 40°}$$

CALCULATOR 100 ÷ 40 tan =
[Answer: 119.1753. . ., rounded to **119 feet**]

15. The correct answer is (2).

Make a sketch of the problem:

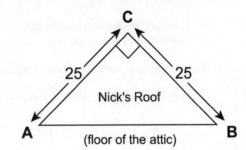

Nick's Roof

(floor of the attic)

Plan: Use Pythagorean theorem to

find AB

$$AB = \sqrt{25^2 + 25^2}$$

CALCULATOR $(25\ X^2 + 25\ X^2)$
SHIFT X^2 =

[Answer: 35.3553. . ., rounded to **35**]

$$\sin A = \frac{\text{opposite}}{\text{hypotenuse}} = \frac{25}{AB}$$

sin A = 25 / 35 = 0.7148. . ., rounded
to **0.71**

answers exercises

COORDINATE GEOMETRY

1. a. **Coordinate geometry** is used to locate and to graph points and lines on a plane.

   b. The coordinate system is made up of two number lines that are perpendicular and that intersect at 0.

   The horizontal number line is called the **x-axis**.

   The vertical number line is called the **y-axis**.

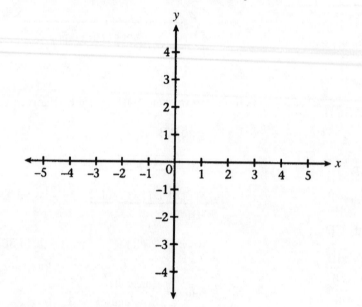

Graphing Points

2. a. Any point on the plane has two numbers (**coordinates**), that indicate its location. The **x-coordinate (abscissa)** is found by drawing a vertical line from the point to the x-axis. The number on the x-axis where the vertical line meets it is the x-coordinate of the point.

   The **y-coordinate (ordinate)** is found by drawing a horizontal line from the point to the y-axis. The number on the y-axis where the horizontal line meets it is the y-coordinate of the point. The two coordinates are always given in the order (x,y).

The *x*-coordinate of point A is 3.
The *y*-coordinate of point A is 2.
The coordinates of point A are given by the ordered pair (3,2).
Point B has coordinates (−1,4).
Point C has coordinates (−4,−3).
Point D has coordinates (2,−3).

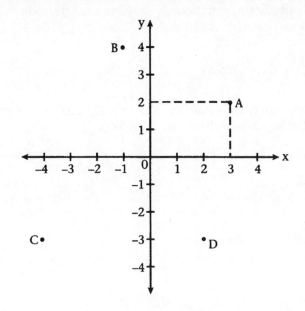

b. The point at which the *x*-axis and the *y*-axis meet has coordinates (0,0) and is called the **origin**.

c. Any point on the *y*-axis has 0 as its *x*-coordinate. Any point on the *x*-axis has 0 as its *y*-coordinate.

3. To graph a point whose coordinates are given, first locate the *x*-coordinate on the *x*-axis. From that position, move vertically the number of spaces indicated by the *y*-coordinate.

To graph (4,−2), locate 4 on the *x*-axis. Then move −2 spaces vertically (2 spaces down) to find the given point.

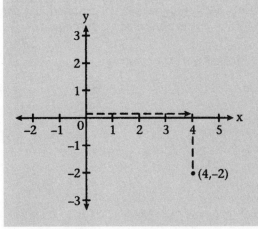

Graphing Equations

4. a. For any equation in x or y or both, ordered pairs (x,y) may be found that are solutions for (or that "satisfy") the equation.

> $(3,4)$, $(1,6)$, and $(7,0)$ are solutions to the equation $x + y = 7$, since $3 + 4 = 7$, $1 + 6 = 7$, and $7 + 0 = 7$.

> $(2,0)$, $(2,1)$, $(2,3)$, and $(2,10)$ all satisfy the equation $x = 2$. Note that the value of y is irrelevant in this equation.

> $(-3,1)$, $(4,1)$, and $(12,1)$ all satisfy the equation $y = 1$.

   b. To find ordered pairs that satisfy an equation, it is usually easiest to substitute any value for x and solve the resulting equation for y.

> For the equation $y = 2x - 1$: if $x = 3$, $\begin{aligned} y &= 2(3) - 1 \\ &= 6 - 1 \\ &= 5 \end{aligned}$

Therefore, $(3,5)$ is a solution to the equation.

if $x = -2$, $y = 2(-2) - 1$

$$= -4 - 1$$

$$= -5$$

Therefore, $(-2,-5)$ is a solution to the equation.

if $x = 0$, $y = 2(0) - 1$

$$= 0 - 1$$

$$= -1$$

Therefore, $(0,-1)$ is a solution to the equation.

   c. If two or more ordered pairs that satisfy a given equation are graphed and the points are connected, the resulting line is the graph of the given equation.

To draw the graph of $y = 2x - 1$, graph the points $(3,5)$, $(-2,-5)$, and $(0,-1)$. Then draw the line passing through all of them.

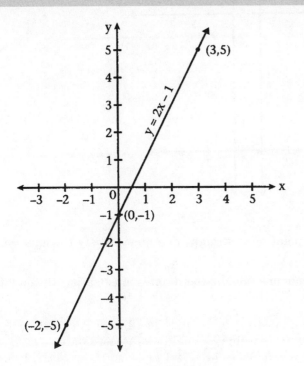

5. Any equation that can be written in the form $y = mx + b$, where m and b remain constant, is called a **linear equation** and has a straight line as its graph.

$y = x$ may be written $y = 1x + 0$ and has a straight-line graph.

The equation $y - 3 = 2x$ may be rewritten:

$$y - 3 = 2x$$
$$\underline{+3 = \quad +3}$$
$$y \quad = 2x + 3$$

Therefore, the graph of $y - 3 = 2x$ is a straight line.

6. a. Any line parallel to the x-axis has the equation $y = a$, where a is constant.

   b. Any line parallel to the y-axis has the equation $x = b$, where b is constant.

The graph of $y = 5$ is parallel to the x-axis and passes through the y-axis at 5.

The graph of $x = -1$ is parallel to the y-axis and passes through the x-axis at -1.

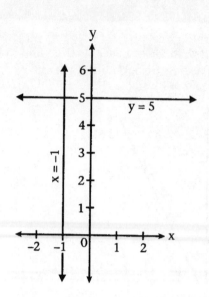

7. a. The coordinates of any point on a straight line must satisfy the equation of that line.

   b. If a point lies on more than one line, its coordinates must satisfy the equation of each of the lines.

Any point on the graph of $y = 2$ must have 2 as its y-coordinate. Any point on the graph of $y = x$ must have its x-coordinate equal to its y-coordinate.

The point where the two lines meet must have coordinates that satisfy both equations. Its coordinates are (2,2).

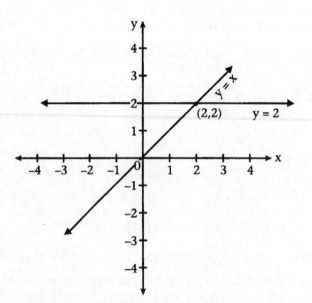

Solving Pairs of Equations

8. To find the ordered pair that is a solution to a pair of equations, graph both equations and find the point at which their corresponding lines meet.

Solve the pair of equations:
$x + y = 5$
   $y = x + 1$

Graph both equations:

The pairs (0,5), (1,4), and (5,0) are solutions for $x + y = 5$.

The pairs (0,1), (1,2), and (3,4) are solutions for $y = x + 1$.

The lines meet at the point (2,3). The pair (2,3) is a solution to both equations.

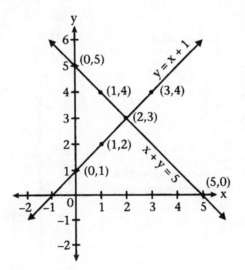

Distance Between Two Points

9. The distance d between any two points (x_1, y_1) and (x_2, y_2) is given by the formula:

$$d = \sqrt{(x_1 - x_2)^2 + (y_1 - y_2)^2}$$

The distance between the points (13,5) and (1,0) is:

$$d = \sqrt{(13 - 1)^2 + (5 - 0)^2}$$

$$= \sqrt{(12)^2 + (5)^2}$$

$$= \sqrt{144 + 25}$$

$$= \sqrt{169}$$

$$= 13$$

EXERCISES: COORDINATE GEOMETRY

1. In the graph below, the coordinates of point A are

  (1) $(-1,3)$

  (2) $(-3,1)$

  (3) $(1,-3)$

  (4) $(3,-1)$

  (5) $(1,3)$

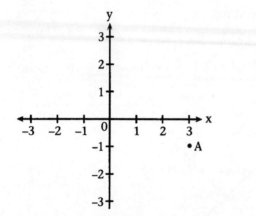

2. A circle has its center at $(0,0)$ and diameter $\overline{AB}$. If the coordinates of A are $(-4,0)$, then the coordinates of B are

  (1) $(4,0)$

  (2) $(0,4)$

  (3) $(0,-4)$

  (4) $(4,-4)$

  (5) $(4,4)$

3. Point R lies on the graph of $y = 3x - 4$. If the abscissa of R is 1, the ordinate of R is

  (1) 3

  (2) 2

  (3) 1

  (4) 0

  (5) -1

4. The lines $y = 4$ and $x = 7$ intersect at the point

  (1) $(4,7)$

  (2) $(7,4)$

  (3) $(3,0)$

  (4) $(0,3)$

  (5) $(3,3)$

5. The distance from point A to point B in the graph below is

  (1) 3

  (2) 4

  (3) 5

  (4) 6

  (5) 7

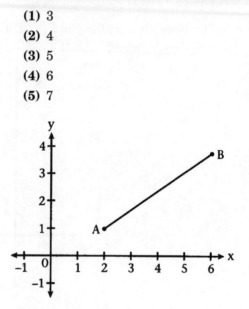

6. The line shown in the graph below has which of the following equations?

  (1) $x = 2$

  (2) $y = -2$

  (3) $y = x + 2$

  (4) $x = y + 2$

  (5) $y = x$

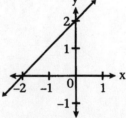

7. The graph of $x + 2y = 6$ intersects the y-axis at the point

(1) $(0,3)$

(2) $(0,-3)$

(3) $(3,0)$

(4) $(-3,0)$

(5) $(3,3)$

8. The graphs of $y = 2x$ and $y = x + 1$ intersect at the point

(1) $(1,2)$

(2) $(0,1)$

(3) $(2,1)$

(4) $(1,0)$

(5) $(0,2)$

9. The distance from $(-1,0)$ to $(5,-2)$ is

(1) $4\frac{1}{2}$

(2) $5\frac{1}{2}$

(3) $\sqrt{10}$

(4) $2\sqrt{10}$

(5) $3\sqrt{10}$

10. A triangle has vertices A(1,2), B(11,2), and C(4,5). How many square units are in the area of triangle ABC?

(1) 40

(2) 30

(3) 25

(4) 20

(5) 15

exercises

ANSWER KEY AND EXPLANATIONS

1. (4)	3. (5)	5. (3)	7. (1)	9. (4)
2. (1)	4. (2)	6. (3)	8. (1)	10. (5)

1. The correct answer is (4).

A vertical line through A meets the x-axis at 3; therefore, the x-coordinate is 3.

A horizontal line through A meets the y-axis at -1; therefore, the y-coordinate is -1.

The coordinates of point A are $(3, -1)$.

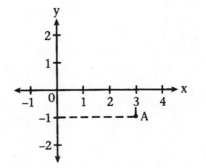

2. The correct answer is (1).

The diameter of a circle is a straight line passing through the center of the circle. The endpoints of the diameter are the same distance from the center.

The center of the given circle is on the x-axis, at the origin. Point A is also on the x-axis, 4 units from the center. Point B must be on the x-axis, 4 units from the center.

The coordinates of B are $(4,0)$.

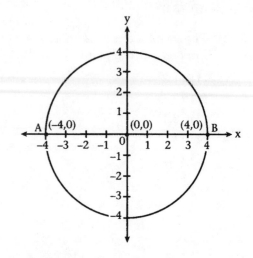

3. The correct answer is (5).

Substitute 1 for x in the equation:

$y = 3 \cdot 1 - 4$

$= 3 - 4$

$= -1$

4. The correct answer is (2).

The coordinates of the point of intersection must satisfy both equations. Choice (2) has x-coordinate $= 7$ and y-coordinate $= 4$.

5. The correct answer is (3).

Point A has coordinates (2,1) and point B has coordinates (6,4). Using the distance formula,

$$d = \sqrt{(6-2)^2 + (4-1)^2}$$

$$= \sqrt{(4)^2 + (3)^2}$$

$$= \sqrt{16+9}$$

$$= \sqrt{25}$$

$$= 5$$

An alternate solution is to consider the right triangle formed by $\overline{AB}$ and the lines of the graph paper, with the right angle vertex at (6,1). Find the lengths of the legs by counting the spaces on the graph. The horizontal leg is 4 and the vertical leg is 3.

Using the Pythagorean theorem,

$$(AB)^2 = 3^2 + 4^2$$

$$= 9 + 16$$

$$= 25$$

$$AB = \sqrt{25} = 5$$

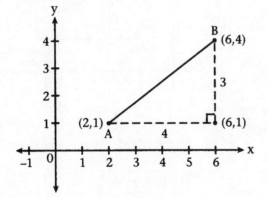

6. The correct answer is (3).

The line passes through the points $(-2,0)$ and $(0,2)$. Choice (3) is the only equation that is satisfied by both ordered pairs.

$$(-2,0): y = x + 2$$

$$0 = -2 + 2$$

$$(0,2): y = x + 2$$

$$2 = 0 + 2$$

7. The correct answer is (1).

Any point on the y-axis has its x-coordinate equal to 0. Substituting 0 for x in the equation,

$$x + 2y = 6$$

$$0 + 2y = 6$$

$$2y = 6$$

$$y = 3$$

8. The correct answer is (1).

Graph both lines on the same set of axes. To find points on the graph of each line, choose any value for x and find the corresponding y.

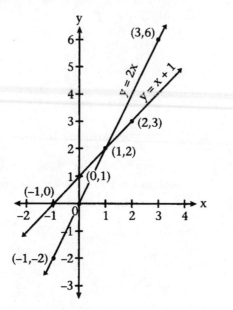

For $y = 2x$:
  if $x = 0$, $y = 2 \cdot 0 = 0$ $(0,0)$
  if $x = 3$, $y = 2 \cdot 3 = 6$ $(3,6)$
  if $x = -1$, $y = 2(-1) = -2$ $(-1,-2)$

For $y = x + 1$:
  if $x = -1$, $y = -1 + 1 = 0$ $(-1,0)$
  if $x = 2$, $y = 2 + 1 = 3$ $(2,3)$
  if $x = 0$, $y = 0 + 1 = 1$ $(0,1)$

The point of intersection of the two lines is $(1,2)$.

An alternate solution is to determine which of the given choices satisfies both equations.

9. The correct answer is (4).

Using the distance formula,

$$d = \sqrt{\left(x_1 - x_2\right)^2 + \left(y_1 - y_2\right)^2}$$

$$d = \sqrt{\left[(-1) - 5\right]^2 + \left[0 - (-2)\right]^2}$$

$$= \sqrt{(-6)^2 + (+2)^2}$$

$$= \sqrt{36 + 4}$$

$$= \sqrt{40}$$

$$= \sqrt{4}\sqrt{10}$$

$$= 2\sqrt{10}$$

10. The correct answer is (5).

Base AB = 10

Height = 3

$$\text{Area} = \frac{1}{2} \, (\text{base})(\text{height})$$

$$= \frac{1}{2} \cdot 10 \cdot 3$$

$$= 15$$

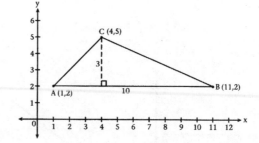

EXERCISES: MATHEMATICS

Directions: Study each of the following problems and work out your answers in the margins or on a piece of scratch paper. After each problem, you will find five suggested answers, numbered from 1 to 5. Circle the number of the answer you have figured out to be correct. Solutions for each problem appear at the end of the examination.

1. The difference between 304,802 and 212,810 is

    (1) 91,992
    (2) 96,592
    (3) 182,328
    (4) 209,328
    (5) 210,972

2. Joan earns $4.00 per hour. On a day that she works from 9:30 a.m. to 3:00 p.m., how much will she earn?

    (1) $14.00
    (2) $18.00
    (3) $22.00
    (4) $26.00
    (5) $30.00

3. The product of .010 and .001 is

    (1) .00001
    (2) .01000
    (3) .01010
    (4) .01100
    (5) .10100

4. If $2x + y = 7$, what is the value of y when $x = 3$?

    (1) 1
    (2) 3
    (3) 5
    (4) 7
    (5) 9

5. Paul received a bonus of $750, which was 5% of his annual salary. His annual salary was

    (1) $37,500
    (2) $25,000
    (3) $22,500
    (4) $15,000
    (5) $7,500

6. The value of $(-6) + (-2)(-3)$ is

    (1) -24
    (2) -12
    (3) 0
    (4) 12
    (5) 24

7. Round 825.6347 to the nearest hundredth.

    (1) 800
    (2) 825.63
    (3) 825.64
    (4) 825.635
    (5) 825.645

exercises

8. The coordinates of point P on the graph are

(1) $(2,-3)$

(2) $(-3,2)$

(3) $(-2,3)$

(4) $(3,-2)$

(5) $(-2,-3)$

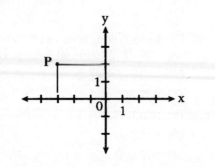

9. A boy buys oranges at 3 for 30¢ and sells them at 5 for 60¢. How many oranges must he sell in order to make a profit of 50¢?

(1) 12

(2) 25

(3) 50

(4) 75

(5) 100

10. The formula for the volume of a right circular cone is $V = \frac{1}{3}\pi r^2 h$, where r is the radius and h is the height. Find the approximate volume of a right circular cone that has radius 3 inches and height 14 inches (π is approximately $\frac{22}{7}$).

(1) 33 cubic inches

(2) 132 cubic inches

(3) 396 cubic inches

(4) 686 cubic inches

(5) 1,188 cubic inches

11. Of the following, the number that is nearest in value to 5 is

(1) 4.985

(2) 5.005

(3) 5.01

(4) 5.1

(5) 5.105

12. If a rope four yards long is cut into three equal pieces, how long will each piece be?

(1) 4 feet

(2) $3\frac{1}{2}$ feet

(3) $3\frac{1}{3}$ feet

(4) 3 feet

(5) $2\frac{1}{4}$ feet

ITEM 13 REFERS TO THE TRIANGLE BELOW.

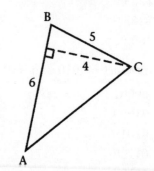

13. The number of square units in the area of triangle ABC above is

(1) 35

(2) 28

(3) 24

(4) 14

(5) 12

14. The cost of 30 sandwich rolls at $1.50 per dozen is

    (1) $3.00
    (2) $3.45
    (3) $3.75
    (4) $4.50
    (5) $4.80

15. If P = 2(a + b), find P when $a = 3$ and $b = 4$.

    (1) 9
    (2) 10
    (3) 14
    (4) 24
    (5) 28

16. Two angles of a triangle measure 30° and 50°. The measure of the third angle in degrees is

    (1) 10
    (2) 40
    (3) 50
    (4) 90
    (5) 100

17. A map is drawn to the scale $1\frac{1}{2}$ inches = 50 miles. What is the actual distance between two towns that are $4\frac{1}{2}$ inches apart on the map?

    (1) 45 miles
    (2) 90 miles
    (3) 120 miles
    (4) 150 miles
    (5) 300 miles

18. The numbers in the sequence 1, 4, 9, 16, 25, . . . follow a particular pattern. If the pattern is continued, what number should appear after 25?

    (1) 28
    (2) 30
    (3) 34
    (4) 36
    (5) 40

19. If shipping charges to a certain point are $1.24 for the first five ounces and 16 cents for each additional ounce, the weight of a package for which the charges are $3.32 is

    (1) 13 ounces
    (2) 15 ounces
    (3) $1\frac{1}{8}$ pounds
    (4) $1\frac{1}{4}$ pounds
    (5) $1\frac{1}{2}$ pounds

20. If a recipe for a cake calls for $2\frac{1}{2}$ cups of flour, and Mary wishes to make three such cakes, the number of cups of flour she must use is

    (1) 6
    (2) $6\frac{1}{2}$
    (3) $7\frac{1}{2}$
    (4) 9
    (5) $9\frac{1}{2}$

21. The equation of the line passing through the points $(-2,2)$ and $(3,-3)$ is

    (1) $x + y = 5$
    (2) $x - y = 5$
    (3) $y - x = 5$
    (4) $y = x$
    (5) $y = -x$

22. What will it cost to carpet a room 12 feet wide and 15 feet long if carpeting costs $20.80 per square yard?

    (1) $334.60
    (2) $374.40
    (3) $416.00
    (4) $504.60
    (5) $560.00

exercises

23. If a five-pound mixture of nuts contains two pounds of cashews and the rest peanuts, what percent of the mixture is peanuts?

   (1) 20

   (2) 30

   (3) 40

   (4) 50

   (5) 60

ITEMS 24 TO 26 REFER TO THE GRAPH BELOW.

Rainfall in Damp City January–July 2002

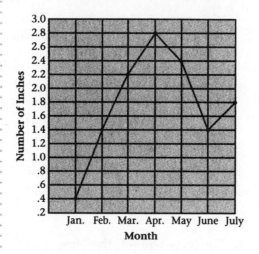

24. The total rainfall for the months January, February, and March was, in inches,

   (1) 2.2

   (2) 3.4

   (3) 4.0

   (4) 4.8

   (5) 7.6

25. The average monthly rainfall, in inches, for April, May, and June was

   (1) 2.0

   (2) 2.1

   (3) 2.2

   (4) 2.3

   (5) 2.4

26. Which statement about the information given in the graph is false?

   (1) The rainfall in April was twice the rainfall in February.

   (2) June had greater rainfall than February.

   (3) The month with the least rainfall was January.

   (4) March had .4 inch greater rainfall than July.

   (5) May had more rain than March.

27. How long will the shadow of a five-foot-tall person be at the same time that an eight-foot-high pole casts a shadow 24 feet long?

   (1) 1 foot

   (2) 8 feet

   (3) 15 feet

   (4) $32\frac{1}{2}$ feet

   (5) 72 feet

28. George has a five-dollar bill and a ten- dollar bill. If he buys one item costing \$7.32 and another item costing \$1.68, how much money will he have left?

   (1) \$1.10

   (2) \$5.64

   (3) \$6.00

   (4) \$9.00

   (5) \$9.90

29. If one card is picked at random from a deck of cards, the probability that it is a club is

   (1) 1

   (2) $\frac{1}{52}$

   (3) $\frac{1}{13}$

   (4) $\frac{1}{10}$

   (5) $\frac{1}{4}$

30. Jack can ride his bicycle 6 miles in 48 minutes. At the same rate, how long will it take him to ride 15 miles?

    (1) 1 hour 20 minutes

    (2) 2 hours

    (3) 2 hours 12 minutes

    (4) 3 hours

    (5) 3 hours 12 minutes

31. If $2x - 7 = 3$, then $3x + 1 =$

    (1) 4

    (2) 5

    (3) 7

    (4) 12

    (5) 16

32. Over a four-year period, the sales of the Acme Company increased from $13,382,675 to $17,394,683. The average yearly increase was

    (1) $4,012,008

    (2) $3,146,014

    (3) $2,869,054

    (4) $1,060,252

    (5) $1,003,002

33. The perimeter of figure ABCDE is

    (1) 18

    (2) 25

    (3) 38

    (4) 44

    (5) 45

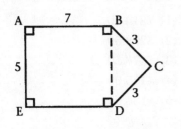

34. Of the following, the unit that would most likely be used to measure the distance from New York to Albany is the

    (1) liter.

    (2) kilometer.

    (3) centigram.

    (4) millimeter.

    (5) degree Celsius.

35. The simple interest on $200 at 12% for 2 years is

    (1) $6

    (2) $12

    (3) $24

    (4) $48

    (5) $120

exercises

ITEMS 36 TO 38 REFER TO THE PICTURE GRAPH BELOW.

This picture graph represents how many men ☿, women ☿, boys ◯, and girls △ visited a museum one particular week. Each figure represents 100.

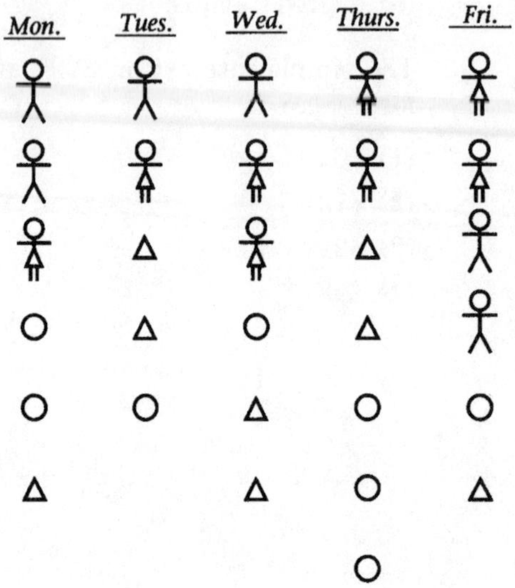

Mon.	Tues.	Wed.	Thurs.	Fri.

36. Over the five-day period, the ratio of men visitors to women visitors was

(1) 3:4

(2) 4:3

(3) 3:7

(4) 4:7

(5) 7:3

37. If the admission price was 50¢ per child and $1.50 per adult, the combined revenue on Monday and Thursday was

(1) $11.50

(2) $260

(3) $1,150

(4) $2,600

(5) $11,500

38. The total number of visitors to the museum during the week was

(1) 3,000

(2) 2,200

(3) 1,400

(4) 300

(5) 30

39. A man spent exactly one dollar in the purchase of 3-cent stamps and 5-cent stamps. The number of 5-cent stamps that he could not have purchased under the circumstances is

(1) 5

(2) 8

(3) 9

(4) 11

(5) 14

40. The number of grams in one kilogram is

(1) .001

(2) .01

(3) .1

(4) 10

(5) 1,000

41. An appliance store gives a 15% discount off the list price of all of its merchandise. An additional 30% reduction of the store price is made for the purchase of a floor model. A television set that has a list price of $300 and is a floor model sells for

(1) $210.00

(2) $228.50

(3) $178.50

(4) $165.00

(5) $135.00

42. Mrs. Jones wishes to buy exactly 72 ounces of canned beans for the least possible cost. Which of the following should she buy?

(1) Six 12-ounce cans at 39¢ per can

(2) Seven 10-ounce cans at 34¢ per can

(3) Three 24-ounce cans at 79¢ per can

(4) Two 25-ounce cans at 62¢ per can

(5) Five 13-ounce cans at 37¢ per can

43. In the graph below, the distance from point A to point B is

(1) 3

(2) 5

(3) 6

(4) $\sqrt{5}$

(5) $\sqrt{7}$

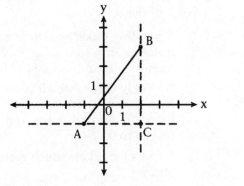

44. If $x^2 - x - 6 = 0$, then x is equal to

(1) 3 only

(2) −2 only

(3) −3 or 2

(4) 3 or −2

(5) −3 or −2

45. Which quantity is NOT equal to $75(32 + 88)$?

(1) $75 \cdot 32 + 75 \cdot 88$

(2) $(75 \cdot 32) + 88$

(3) $75(88 + 32)$

(4) $(88 + 32) \cdot 75$

(5) $88 \cdot 75 + 32 \cdot 75$

46. In a certain boys' camp, 30% of the boys are from New York State and 20% of these are from New York City. What percent of the boys in the camp are from New York City?

(1) 60

(2) 50

(3) 20

(4) 10

(5) 6

47. If 1 ounce is approximately equal to 28 grams, then 1 pound is approximately equal to

(1) 250 grams.

(2) 350 grams.

(3) 450 grams.

(4) 550 grams.

(5) 650 grams.

48. Which fraction is equal to .25%?

(1) $\dfrac{1}{400}$

(2) $\dfrac{1}{40}$

(3) $\dfrac{1}{4}$

(4) $\dfrac{5}{2}$

(5) $\dfrac{50}{2}$

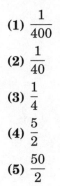

ITEMS 49 AND 50 REFER TO THE TABLE BELOW.

VALUE OF PROPERTY STOLEN—2001 AND 2002
LARCENY

	2001		2002	
Category	**# of Offenses**	**Value of Stolen Property**	**# of Offenses**	**Value of Stolen Property**
Pocket-picking	20	$ 1,950	10	$ 950
Purse-snatching	175	5,750	120	12,050
Shoplifting	155	7,950	225	17,350
Automobile thefts	1040	127,050	860	108,000
Thefts of automobile accessories	1135	34,950	970	24,400
Bicycle thefts	355	8,250	240	6,350
All other thefts	1375	187,150	1300	153,150

49. Of the total number of larcenies reported in 2001, automobile thefts accounted for, most nearly,

   (1) 5%
   (2) 15%
   (3) 25%
   (4) 50%
   (5) 65%

50. Of the following, the category that had the greatest reduction in value of stolen property from 2001 to 2002 was

   (1) pocket-picking.
   (2) automobile thefts.
   (3) shoplifting.
   (4) bicycle thefts.
   (5) purse-snatching.

ITEMS 51 TO 54 REFER TO THE FOLLOWING INFORMATION.

Mike is starting a new job on April 15. His working hours are 8:30 to 4:30 from Monday through Friday and his starting pay is $18,500 per year. To get to this job, Mike will have to take a train each day. The railroad offers only the following types of tickets:

1. A monthly ticket, which is good from the first to the last day of each month and costs $129.00

2. A weekly ticket, which is good from Saturday morning to Friday night each week and costs $40.00

3. A one-way ticket, which costs $6.25

The calendar for the month in which Mike starts to work is shown below.

APRIL						
S	M	T	W	T	F	S
	1	2	3	4	5	6
7	8	9	10	11	12	13
14	15	16	17	18	19	20
21	22	23	24	25	26	27
28	29	30				

51. Based on the fare schedule and the calendar shown, which is the least costly method for Mike to get to work from April 15 through April 30?

  (1) Buying one-way tickets for first week, a weekly ticket for the next week, and then one-way tickets for the last 2 days

  (2) Buying 1 monthly ticket

  (3) Buying 2 weekly tickets and one-way tickets for 2 days

  (4) Buying 3 weekly tickets

  (5) Buying one-way tickets for each trip

52. What is the total difference in cost between buying one-way tickets for each trip every day from April 15—April 30 and buying 3 weekly tickets?

  (1) $5

  (2) $10

  (3) $20

  (4) $25

  (5) $30

53. Mike wants to take an apartment closer to his new job so that he can decrease his transportation expense. He has determined that he cannot afford to pay more than 30% of his salary for rent. What is the greatest monthly rental Mike can afford if he is to stay within his own budget guidelines?

  (1) $555

  (2) $462

  (3) $384

  (4) $355

  (5) Not enough information is given.

54. If Mike eliminates his train fare by moving closer to his job, what effect will this have on his available cash?

  (1) He will have $129 more cash each month.

  (2) He will have $40 more cash each week.

  (3) He will have $1,584 more cash each year.

  (4) He will have 10% more available cash.

  (5) Not enough information is given.

55. A 32-foot pole holds up the sail to Captain Ahab's boat, as shown in the diagram below. How many feet from the bottom of the sail should he attach the end of the sail, if the angle it must make with the boat is 75°?

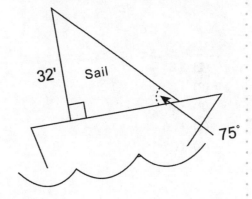

  (1) 36.2

  (2) 30.9

  (3) 15.0

  (4) 8.6

  (5) 8.3

56. Raj, an artist, needs to construct a rod to support his new 12 foot × 1 foot × 1 foot, glass, cube-shaped sculpture in the museum. The rod is attached to the side of the cube and to the floor, 4 feet from the corner of the base, making a 70° angle with the floor, as shown below. How long should he make the rod, in feet?

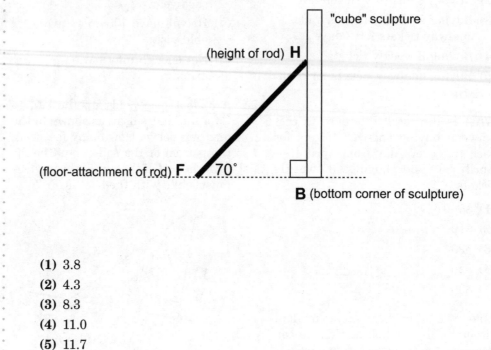

(1) 3.8
(2) 4.3
(3) 8.3
(4) 11.0
(5) 11.7

ANSWER KEY AND EXPLANATIONS

1. (1)	13. (5)	24. (3)	35. (4)	46. (5)
2. (3)	14. (3)	25. (3)	36. (1)	47. (3)
3. (1)	15. (3)	26. (2)	37. (3)	48. (1)
4. (1)	16. (5)	27. (3)	38. (1)	49. (3)
5. (4)	17. (4)	28. (3)	39. (3)	50. (2)
6. (3)	18. (4)	29. (5)	40. (5)	51. (3)
7. (2)	19. (3)	30. (2)	41. (3)	52. (5)
8. (2)	20. (3)	31. (5)	42. (1)	53. (2)
9. (2)	21. (5)	32. (5)	43. (2)	54. (5)
10. (2)	22. (3)	33. (2)	44. (4)	55. (4)
11. (2)	23. (5)	34. (2)	45. (2)	56. (5)
12. (1)				

1. The correct answer is (1).

$$\begin{array}{r} 304{,}802 \\ -212{,}810 \\ \hline 91{,}992 \end{array}$$

2. The correct answer is (3).

From 9:30 a.m. to 3 p.m. is $5\frac{1}{2}$ hours.

$$\$4 \cdot 5\frac{1}{2} = \$22$$

3. The correct answer is (1).

$$\begin{array}{ll} .010 & \text{(3 decimal places)} \\ \times .001 & \text{(3 decimal places)} \\ \hline .000010 & \text{(6 decimal places)} \end{array}$$

The final zero may be dropped:

$.000010 = .00001$

4. The correct answer is (1).

When $x = 3$, $2x + y = 7$ becomes

Solve for y:
$$\begin{array}{r} 2 \cdot 3 + y = 7 \\ 6 + y = 7 \\ \underline{-6 \qquad -6} \\ y = 1 \end{array}$$

5. The correct answer is (4).

Let s = Paul's annual salary

$$\begin{array}{l} 5\% \text{ of } s = \$750 \\ .05s = \$750 \\ \dfrac{.05s}{.05} = \dfrac{\$750}{.05} \\ s = \$15{,}000 \end{array}$$

6. The correct answer is (3).

$$(-6) + (-2)(-3) = (-6) + (+6)$$

First multiply, then add.

7. The correct answer is (2).

To round 825.6347 to the nearest hundredth, consider 4, the digit in the thousandths place. Since it is less than 5, drop all digits to the right of the hundredths place.

$825.6347 = 825.63$ to the nearest hundredth

8. The correct answer is (2).

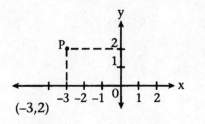

(−3,2)

Point P has coordinates $x = -3$ and $y = 2$.

9. The correct answer is (2).

The boy buys oranges for 10¢ each (30¢ ÷ 3). He sells them for 12¢ each (60¢ ÷ 5). Therefore his profit is 2¢ per orange. He must sell 50¢ ÷ 2¢ = 25 oranges for a 50¢ profit.

10. The correct answer is (2).

$$V = \frac{1}{3}\pi r^2 h, \ r = 3'', h = 14''$$

$$V = \frac{1}{\cancel{3}} \times \frac{22}{\cancel{7}} \times \cancel{3} \times 3 \times \cancel{14}^{2}$$

$$V = \frac{22 \times 3 \times 2}{1}$$

$$V = 132$$

11. The correct answer is (2).

Find the difference between each choice and 5:

5.000	5.005	5.01	5.1	5.105
−4.985	−5.000	−5.00	−5.0	−5.000
.015	.005	.01	.1	.105

The least difference is .005; therefore, 5.005 is closer than the other choices to 5.

12. The correct answer is (1).

4 yards = 4 · 3 feet = 12 feet
12 feet ÷ 3 = 4 feet per piece

13. The correct answer is (5).

Area of a triangle $= \frac{1}{2} \cdot$ base $\cdot$ height

The height, which is 4, is drawn to base $\overline{AB}$, which is 6.

$$\text{Area} = \frac{1}{2} \cdot 6 \cdot 4$$
$$= 3 \cdot 4$$
$$= 12$$

14. The correct answer is (3).

If 1 dozen rolls costs $1.50, each roll costs

$1.50 ÷ 12 = $.125

Then 30 rolls will cost

30($.125) = $3.75

15. The correct answer is (3).

$$P = 2(a + b)$$
If $a = 3$ and $b = 4$,
$$P = 2(3 + 4)$$
$$= 2(7)$$
$$= 14$$

16. The correct answer is (5).

The sum of the measures of the angles of a triangle is 180°.

The two given angles total 80°.

180° − 80° = 100°

The third angle is 100°.

17. The correct answer is (4).

Let x represent the actual distance between towns, then write a proportion:

$$\frac{x}{50} = \frac{4\frac{1}{2}}{1\frac{1}{2}}$$

$$\frac{x}{50} = 3 \ (Since \ 4\frac{1}{2} \div 1\frac{1}{2} = 3)$$

$$x = 150$$

18. The correct answer is (4).

Each of the numbers in the sequence is a perfect square:

1, 4, 9, 16, 25, . . .

$1^2, 2^2, 3^2, 4^2, 5^2, . . .$

The next number is 6^2, or 36.

19. The correct answer is (3).

$ 3.32 total charge

$-$ 1.24 charge for first five ounces

$ 2.08 charge for additional weight at $.16 per ounce

$$2.08 \div .16 = 13$$
$$5 \text{ ounces} + 13 \text{ ounces} = 18 \text{ ounces}$$
$$= 1 \text{ pound } 2 \text{ ounces}$$
$$= 1\frac{1}{8} \text{ pound}$$

20. The correct answer is (3).

$$2\frac{1}{2} \times 3 = \frac{5}{2} \times 3$$
$$= \frac{15}{2}$$
$$= 7\frac{1}{2}$$

21. The correct answer is (5).

Substitute the coordinates of each point in each equation. Only $y = -x$ is satisfied by the coordinates of the points:

$$(-2,2): \quad 2 = -(-2)$$
$$(3,-3): \quad -3 = -(3)$$

22. The correct answer is (3).

12 feet = 4 yards

15 feet = 5 yards

4 yards $\cdot$ 5 yards = 20 square yards

$20.80   per square yard

$\times$ 20   square yards

$416.00

23. The correct answer is (5).

There are three pounds of peanuts.

$$\frac{3}{5} = .60 = 60\%$$

24. The correct answer is (3).

January:	.4
February:	1.4
March:	2.2
Total:	4.0

25. The correct answer is (3).

April:	2.8
May:	2.4
June:	1.4
Total:	6.6

Average: 6.6 ÷ 3 = 2.2

26. The correct answer is (2).

The rainfall in June was 1.4 inches, the same as the rainfall in February.

27. The correct answer is (3).

Let x represent the person's height, and write a proportion:

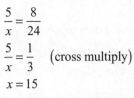

$$\frac{5}{x} = \frac{8}{24}$$
$$\frac{5}{x} = \frac{1}{3} \quad \text{(cross multiply)}$$
$$x = 15$$

28. The correct answer is (3).

George has $15.00. His total purchase is:

$7.32

+ 1.68

$9.00

He will have $15.00 $-$ $9.00 = $6.00 left.

29. The correct answer is (5).

There are 52 cards in a deck, of which 13 are clubs. The probability of picking a club is $\frac{13}{52} = \frac{1}{4}$.

30. The correct answer is (2).

It takes Jack 48 minutes ÷ 6 miles = 8 minutes for each mile. At that rate it will take him 15 · 8 = 120 minutes for 15 miles.

120 minutes = 2 hours

31. The correct answer is (5).

$$\begin{array}{rcl} 2x - 7 &=& 3 \\ +7 && +7 \\ \hline 2x &=& 10 \\ x &=& 5 \end{array}$$

If $x = 5$, $3x + 1 = 3 \cdot 5 + 1 = 16$

32. The correct answer is (5).

The increase in sales was

$$\begin{array}{r} \$17,394,683 \\ -13,382,675 \\ \hline \$4,012,008 \end{array}$$

The average yearly increase over 4 years was

$4,012,008 ÷ 4 = 1,003,002$

33. The correct answer is (2).

The perimeter is the sum of all the lengths of the sides of the figure. ABDE is a rectangle, so side ED = 7.

Perimeter = 7 + 5 + 7 + 3 + 3 = 25

34. The correct answer is (2).

Kilometers are used to measure long distances.

35. The correct answer is (4).

$I = p \cdot r \cdot t$, where I = interest, p = principal, r = rate, t = time in years. If p = \$200, r = 12%, and t = 2 years,

$$\begin{array}{rcl} I &=& (\$200)(12\%)(2) \\ &=& (\$200)(.12)(2) \\ &=& \$48.00 \end{array}$$

36. The correct answer is (1).

There are 6 symbols representing men and 8 symbols representing women. The ratio is 6:8, or 3:4.

37. The correct answer is (3).

Monday:	300 children	300 adults
Thursday:	500 children	200 adults
Total:	800 children	500 adults

$$\begin{array}{rcl} \text{Total revenue} &=& 800(\$.50) + 500(\$1.50) \\ &=& \$400 + \$750 \\ &=& \$1,150 \end{array}$$

38. The correct answer is (1).

There are 30 symbols in all. Each symbol represents 100 people.

$30 \times 100 = 3,000$

39. The correct answer is (3).

Try each choice:

(1) 5 5¢ stamps = 25¢

    100¢ − 25¢ = 75¢

           = exactly 25 3¢ stamps

(2) 8 5¢ stamps = 40¢

    100¢ − 40¢ = 60¢

           = exactly 20 3¢ stamps

(3) 9 5¢ stamps = 45¢

    100¢ − 45¢ = 55¢

           = 18 3¢ stamps and 1¢ change

(4) 11 5¢ stamps = 55¢

    100¢ − 55¢ = 45¢

           = exactly 15 3¢ stamps

(5) 14 5¢ stamps = 70¢

    100¢ − 70¢ = 30¢

           = exactly 10 3¢ stamps

In choice (3), exactly $1.00 cannot be spent.

40. The correct answer is (5).

1 kilogram = 1,000 grams

41. The correct answer is (3).

The price after the 15% discount is 85% of $300 = .85($300)

            = $255

The price after the 30% discount is 70% of $255 = .70($255)

            = $178.50

42. The correct answer is (1).

Only choices (1) and (3) represent 72 ounces.

Choice (1): 6($.39) = $2.34

Choice (3): 3($.79) = $2.37

43. The correct answer is (2).

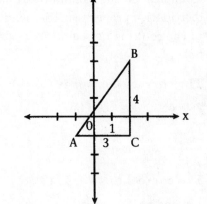

ABC is a right triangle.

  AC = 3

  BC = 4

Using the Pythagorean theorem,

$$(AB)^2 = 3^2 + 4^2$$
$$= 9 + 16$$
$$= 25$$
$$AB = \sqrt{25} = 5$$

Note that ABC is a 3-4-5 right triangle.

44. The correct answer is (4).

$$x^2 - x - 6 = 0$$
$$(x - 3)(x + 2) = 0$$
$$x - 3 = 0 \quad x + 2 = 0$$
$$x = 3 \quad\quad x = -2$$

An alternate method is to substitute each given answer into the equation to determine which are solutions. For example, in choice (3), $x = -3$.

$$(-3)^2 - (-3) - 6 = 9 + 3 - 6 = 6 \neq 0$$

Therefore, $x = -3$ is not a solution of $x^2 - x - 6 = 0$.

answers exercises

45. The correct answer is (2).

Choices (1), (3), (4), and (5) are all examples of the commutative and distributive properties. The quantity in choice (2) is not equal to $75(32 + 88)$.

46. The correct answer is (5).

$$20\% \text{ of } 30\% = (.20)(.30)$$
$$= .06$$
$$= 6\%$$

47. The correct answer is (3).

$$1 \text{ pound} = 16 \text{ ounces}$$
$$(16)(28) = 448$$

48. The correct answer is (1).

$$.25\% = .0025$$
$$= \frac{\times\ 25}{10000}$$
$$= \frac{1}{400}$$

49. The correct answer is (3).

Total larcenies in 2001:

$$\begin{array}{r} 20 \\ 175 \\ 155 \\ 1040 \\ 1135 \\ 355 \\ +1375 \\ \hline 4255 \end{array}$$

$$\frac{\text{Auto thefts}}{\text{Total}} = \frac{1040}{4255}$$
$$= .24 \text{ (approximately)}$$
$$= 24\%$$

50. The correct answer is (2).

Pocket-picking:

$$\begin{array}{r} 1950 \\ -\ 950 \\ \hline 1000\ \ \text{reduction} \end{array}$$

Auto thefts:

$$\begin{array}{r} 127{,}050 \\ -108{,}000 \\ \hline 19{,}050\ \ \text{reduction} \end{array}$$

Shoplifting: increased

Bicycle thefts:

$$\begin{array}{r} 8250 \\ -6350 \\ \hline 1900\ \ \text{reduction} \end{array}$$

Purse-snatching: increased

51. The correct answer is (3).

Calculate the cost of each combination of tickets.

1. One-way tickets for the first 5 days = $\$6.25 \times 2 \times 5 = \$62.50$
   1 weekly ticket = $\$40.00$
   One-way tickets for 2 days = $\$6.25 \times 2 \times 2 = \$25.00$
   Total cost = $\$62.50 + \$40 + \$25 = \$127.50$

2. 1 monthly ticket = $\$129$

3. 2 weekly tickets = $\$40 \times 2 = \$80$
   4 one-way tickets = $6.25 \times 4 = \$25$ (2 directions, 2 days)
   Total cost = $\$80 + 25 = \$105$

4. 3 weekly tickets = $\$40 \times 3 = \$120$

5. One-way tickets for each trip = $\$6.25 \times 2 \times 12 = \$150$
   Comparing the total costs, you can see that option 3 is the least expensive.

52. The correct answer is (5).

Using the calculations you have just made in question 51, you know that the cost of one-way tickets for each trip = $150. The cost of 3 weekly tickets = $40 × 3 = $120. The difference between these costs is $150 − $120 = $30.

53. The correct answer is (2).

First find out how much money Mike makes each month.

$18,500 ÷ 12 = $1,541.67 per month

To find 30% of his monthly income, multiply $1,541.67 by .30

$1,541.67 × .30 = $462.50

54. The correct answer is (5).

Although you know that Mike will no longer have to pay train fare, you do not know whether or not he will have to pay bus or subway fare or parking fees. Nor do you know what other expenses he will have in connection with the apartment.

55. The correct answer is (4).

Make a *simplified, labeled** sketch:

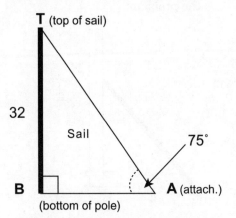

Given: angle A, side opposite (BT)

Find: side adjacent (BA)

$$\tan A = \frac{BT}{BA}$$

Substituting the values,

$$\tan 75° = \frac{32}{BA}$$

Solve for BA by multiplying both sides by BA and then dividing by tan 75°:

$$BA = \frac{32}{\tan 75°}$$

␣C␣A␣L␣C␣U␣L␣A␣T␣O␣R␣ 32 ÷ 75 tan =

[Answer: 8.5743. . .; rounded to **8.6 feet**]

*Hint: Sometimes, it may be helpful to use *convenient* letter-labels on your sketches to represent corresponding parts of the problem. For example, in this problem, you might use "T" to represent the top of the sail; "B" to stand for bottom; and "A" to represent the point where the sail will be attached to the side of the boat. Of course, these letters are arbitrary.

answers exercises

56. The correct answer is (5).

Make a *simplified**, *labeled* sketch of the problem:

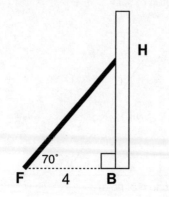

Given: angle F, side adjacent (BF)

Find: hypotenuse (HF)

$$\cos F = \frac{BF}{HF}$$

Substituting the values,

$$\cos 70° = 4HF$$

Solve for HF by multiplying both sides by HF and then dividing by cos 70°:

$$HF = \frac{4}{\cos 70°}$$

⌨ CALCULATOR   4 ÷ 70 cos =

[Answer: 11.6952. . .; rounded to **11.7 feet**]

*Hint: To save time during a *timed* test, draw a very simple working sketch. For example, compare the sketch illustrated in the problem statement (it's elaborate) with the one presented in the solution above (it's more basic and simple).

SUMMING IT UP

What You Need to Know About the GED Mathematics Test

- The questions are based on short readings or on graphs, charts, tables, or diagrams.

- They will stress higher-level thinking as well as problem-solving ability.

- Special emphasis will be place on realistic situations, such as those found in home, consumer, civics, and workplace contexts.

- The test is divided into two parts: Part 1 will allow the use of a scientific calculator that will be provided to you. Make sure you practice with the calculator before the test. Part 2 does not allow the use of the calculator.

PART VIII

TWO PRACTICE TESTS

Practice Test 2

DIRECTIONS FOR TAKING THE PRACTICE TEST

Directions: The GED Practice Test has five separate tests: Language Arts, Writing; Social Studies; Science; Language Arts, Reading; and Mathematics.

1 Read and follow the directions given at the start of each test.

2 Stick to the time limits.

3 Enter your answers on the tear-out Answer Sheets provided on pages 649–653.

4 When you have completed the entire test, compare your answers with the correct answers given in the Answer Key and Explanations at the end of this practice test.

5 Use the Error Analysis Chart following each practice test to see where you are weak and where you are strong.

6 Don't forget to consult the "Assessing Your Readiness" section to gauge how close you are to mastering the GED tests.

practice test 2

ANSWER SHEET PRACTICE TEST 2

Correct answers for this test begin on page 726.

Test 1. Language Arts, Writing—Part 1

1. ①②③④⑤   11. ①②③④⑤   21. ①②③④⑤   31. ①②③④⑤   41. ①②③④⑤
2. ①②③④⑤   12. ①②③④⑤   22. ①②③④⑤   32. ①②③④⑤   42. ①②③④⑤
3. ①②③④⑤   13. ①②③④⑤   23. ①②③④⑤   33. ①②③④⑤   43. ①②③④⑤
4. ①②③④⑤   14. ①②③④⑤   24. ①②③④⑤   34. ①②③④⑤   44. ①②③④⑤
5. ①②③④⑤   15. ①②③④⑤   25. ①②③④⑤   35. ①②③④⑤   45. ①②③④⑤
6. ①②③④⑤   16. ①②③④⑤   26. ①②③④⑤   36. ①②③④⑤   46. ①②③④⑤
7. ①②③④⑤   17. ①②③④⑤   27. ①②③④⑤   37. ①②③④⑤   47. ①②③④⑤
8. ①②③④⑤   18. ①②③④⑤   28. ①②③④⑤   38. ①②③④⑤   48. ①②③④⑤
9. ①②③④⑤   19. ①②③④⑤   29. ①②③④⑤   39. ①②③④⑤   49. ①②③④⑤
10. ①②③④⑤   20. ①②③④⑤   30. ①②③④⑤   40. ①②③④⑤   50. ①②③④⑤

Test 2. Social Studies

1. ①②③④⑤   11. ①②③④⑤   21. ①②③④⑤   31. ①②③④⑤   41. ①②③④⑤
2. ①②③④⑤   12. ①②③④⑤   22. ①②③④⑤   32. ①②③④⑤   42. ①②③④⑤
3. ①②③④⑤   13. ①②③④⑤   23. ①②③④⑤   33. ①②③④⑤   43. ①②③④⑤
4. ①②③④⑤   14. ①②③④⑤   24. ①②③④⑤   34. ①②③④⑤   44. ①②③④⑤
5. ①②③④⑤   15. ①②③④⑤   25. ①②③④⑤   35. ①②③④⑤   45. ①②③④⑤
6. ①②③④⑤   16. ①②③④⑤   26. ①②③④⑤   36. ①②③④⑤   46. ①②③④⑤
7. ①②③④⑤   17. ①②③④⑤   27. ①②③④⑤   37. ①②③④⑤   47. ①②③④⑤
8. ①②③④⑤   18. ①②③④⑤   28. ①②③④⑤   38. ①②③④⑤   48. ①②③④⑤
9. ①②③④⑤   19. ①②③④⑤   29. ①②③④⑤   39. ①②③④⑤   49. ①②③④⑤
10. ①②③④⑤   20. ①②③④⑤   30. ①②③④⑤   40. ①②③④⑤   50. ①②③④⑤

Test 3. Science

1. ①②③④⑤   11. ①②③④⑤   21. ①②③④⑤   31. ①②③④⑤   41. ①②③④⑤
2. ①②③④⑤   12. ①②③④⑤   22. ①②③④⑤   32. ①②③④⑤   42. ①②③④⑤
3. ①②③④⑤   13. ①②③④⑤   23. ①②③④⑤   33. ①②③④⑤   43. ①②③④⑤
4. ①②③④⑤   14. ①②③④⑤   24. ①②③④⑤   34. ①②③④⑤   44. ①②③④⑤
5. ①②③④⑤   15. ①②③④⑤   25. ①②③④⑤   35. ①②③④⑤   45. ①②③④⑤
6. ①②③④⑤   16. ①②③④⑤   26. ①②③④⑤   36. ①②③④⑤   46. ①②③④⑤
7. ①②③④⑤   17. ①②③④⑤   27. ①②③④⑤   37. ①②③④⑤   47. ①②③④⑤
8. ①②③④⑤   18. ①②③④⑤   28. ①②③④⑤   38. ①②③④⑤   48. ①②③④⑤
9. ①②③④⑤   19. ①②③④⑤   29. ①②③④⑤   39. ①②③④⑤   49. ①②③④⑤
10. ①②③④⑤   20. ①②③④⑤   30. ①②③④⑤   40. ①②③④⑤   50. ①②③④⑤

answer sheet

Test 4. Language Arts, Reading

1. ①②③④⑤   11. ①②③④⑤   21. ①②③④⑤   31. ①②③④⑤
2. ①②③④⑤   12. ①②③④⑤   22. ①②③④⑤   32. ①②③④⑤
3. ①②③④⑤   13. ①②③④⑤   23. ①②③④⑤   33. ①②③④⑤
4. ①②③④⑤   14. ①②③④⑤   24. ①②③④⑤   34. ①②③④⑤
5. ①②③④⑤   15. ①②③④⑤   25. ①②③④⑤   35. ①②③④⑤
6. ①②③④⑤   16. ①②③④⑤   26. ①②③④⑤   36. ①②③④⑤
7. ①②③④⑤   17. ①②③④⑤   27. ①②③④⑤   37. ①②③④⑤
8. ①②③④⑤   18. ①②③④⑤   28. ①②③④⑤   38. ①②③④⑤
9. ①②③④⑤   19. ①②③④⑤   29. ①②③④⑤   39. ①②③④⑤
10. ①②③④⑤   20. ①②③④⑤   30. ①②③④⑤   40. ①②③④⑤

Test 5. Mathematics—Part 1

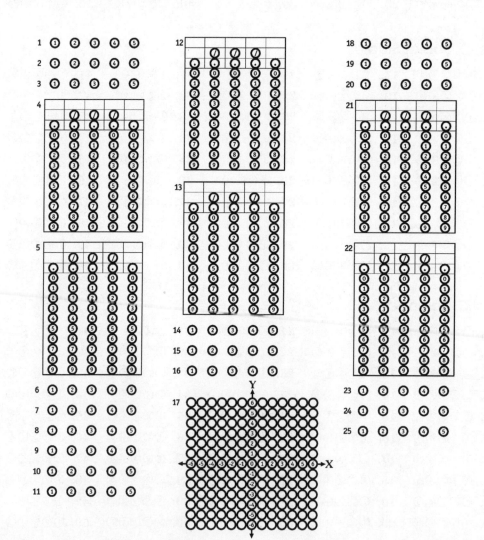

Test 5. Mathematics—Part 2

26 ① ② ③ ④ ⑤   38 ① ② ③ ④ ⑤
27 ① ② ③ ④ ⑤   39 ① ② ③ ④ ⑤
28 ① ② ③ ④ ⑤   40 ① ② ③ ④ ⑤
29 ① ② ③ ④ ⑤   41 ① ② ③ ④ ⑤
30 ① ② ③ ④ ⑤   42 ① ② ③ ④ ⑤

31 [grid-in answer field]   43 [grid-in answer field]

32 ① ② ③ ④ ⑤   44 ① ② ③ ④ ⑤
33 ① ② ③ ④ ⑤   45 ① ② ③ ④ ⑤
34 ① ② ③ ④ ⑤   46 ① ② ③ ④ ⑤
35 ① ② ③ ④ ⑤   47 ① ② ③ ④ ⑤
36 ① ② ③ ④ ⑤   48 ① ② ③ ④ ⑤
                 49 ① ② ③ ④ ⑤
37 [coordinate grid answer field]   50 ① ② ③ ④ ⑤

answer sheet

ANSWER SHEET PRACTICE TEST 2

Language Arts, Writing—Part 2 Essay Test

_____

_____

_____

_____

_____

_____

_____

_____

_____

_____

_____

_____

_____

_____

_____

_____

_____

Language Arts, Writing—Part 2 Essay Test (continued)

_____

_____

_____

_____

_____

_____

_____

_____

_____

_____

_____

_____

_____

_____

_____

_____

_____

answer sheet

TEST 1: LANGUAGE ARTS, WRITING

This test has two parts. Part 1 measures your ability to recognize errors in written material. Part 2 tests your ability to write a short essay.

Part 1. Recognizing and Correcting Errors

75 Minutes • 50 Questions

Directions: The Language Arts, Writing Test consists of several written passages with numbered sentences and lettered paragraphs. Some of the sentences contain errors in sentence structure, usage, or mechanics. There are also a few errors of organization that require moving a sentence or paragraph, or deleting or replacing a sentence. Read each passage carefully first, then answer the questions that follow. For each question, choose the answer that will correct an error and result in the most effective writing. The best answer must be consistent with the meaning and tone of the passage. Record your answers in the Language Arts, Writing Section of the answer sheet.

Q Often their are two equally effective ways to solve a problem.
What correction should be made to this sentence?

(1) replace their with there
(2) change are to is
(3) change two to too
(4) insert a comma after equally
(5) no change is necessary

● ② ③ ④ ⑤

A In this example, the word *their*, which means "belonging to them," is incorrectly substituted for the word *there*. To indicate this correction, mark answer space (1) on your answer sheet.

practice test

ITEMS 1 TO 7 REFER TO THE FOLLOWING ARTICLE.

How Do You Prepare for a Job Interview?

A

(1) A job interview is one of the more intimidating experiences of a person's work life. (2) It is something that everyone dreads. (3) If you are prepared, however, you will do better on the interview and increase the likelihood that you will get that job. (4) What will the interview be like?

B

(5) The employer has a position to fill and he wants knowing if you can do the job. (6) He will tell you briefly what kind of job it is, what the duties are, and what the company is expecting of its employees. (7) While he is talking, think of how you can contribute if you are hired. (8) Can you see yourself in the job he describes? (9) Do you have special skills, experiences, or ideas that would fit in? (10) If the position seems to be one you would like, let the interviewer know that you are interested letting him know that you understand what he needs and that you are the right person for the job. (11) Tell the interviewer of similar jobs and experiences you have had with success. (12) Smile, and be positive and enthusiastic in your manner.

C

(13) It is important to look good for interviews. (14) You will be treated better the nicer you look. (15) If you aren't sure what to wear, remember that it is better to be over-dressed than too casual in appearance. (16) Dress conservatively with shined shoes a pressed dress shirt and even a jacket. (17) Make sure you go to sleep early the night before the interview, give yourself plenty of time too get ready, and arrive for the interview promptly. (18) Then, relax and look forward to making a very good impression.

1. Sentence (4): **What will the interview be like?**

Which revision should be made to sentence (4) to improve the organization of this text?

(1) move sentence (4) to the beginning of paragraph C

(2) move sentence (4) to the beginning of paragraph B

(3) move sentence (4) to follow sentence (11)

(4) delete sentence (4)

(5) no revision is necessary

2. Sentence (5): **The employer has a position to fill and he wants knowing if you can do the job.**

What correction should be made to this sentence?

(1) capitalize <u>employer</u>

(2) change <u>has</u> to <u>had</u>

(3) change <u>to fill</u> to <u>unfilled</u>

(4) change <u>knowing</u> to <u>to know</u>

(5) no correction is necessary

3. Sentence (6): **He will tell you briefly what kind of job it is, what the duties are, and <u>what the company is expecting</u> of its employees.**

Which of the following is the best way to write the underlined portion of the sentence? If you think the original is the best way to write the sentence, choose option (1).

(1) what the company is expecting

(2) how the company's expecting

(3) which the company is expecting

(4) what the company's expected

(5) what the company expects

4. Sentence (10): **If the position seems to be one you would like, let the interviewer know that you are <u>interested letting him</u> know that you understand what he needs and that you are the right person for the job.**

Which of the following is the best way to write the underlined portion of the sentence? If you think the original is the best way to write the sentence, choose option (1).

  (1) interested letting him

  (2) interested. Letting him

  (3) interesting to let him

  (4) interested: let him

  (5) interested. Let him

5. Sentence (14): **You will be treated better the nicer you look.**

If you rewrote sentence (14) beginning with the words <u>The nicer you look</u>, the next words would be

  (1) you will

  (2) how you

  (3) the better

  (4) better treatment

  (5) your treatment

6. Sentence (16): **Dress conservatively with shined shoes a pressed dress shirt and even a jacket.**

What correction should be made to this sentence?

  (1) insert a comma after <u>Dress conservatively</u>

  (2) change <u>Dress</u> to <u>Dressing</u>

  (3) insert a comma after <u>Dress conservatively</u> and after <u>shined shoes</u>

  (4) change <u>dress shirt</u> to <u>dressed shirt</u>

  (5) change <u>conservatively</u> to <u>conservative</u>

7. Sentence (17): **Make sure you go to sleep early the night before the interview, give yourself plenty of <u>time too get ready,</u> and arrive for the interview promptly.**

Which of the following is the best way to write the underlined portion of the sentence? If you think the original is the best way to write the sentence, choose option (1).

  (1) time too get ready,

  (2) time to get ready,

  (3) time too getting ready,

  (4) time, too get ready,

  (5) time too getting ready,

ITEMS 8 TO 14 REFER TO THE FOLLOWING PIECE.

Social Support Systems

A

  (1) Mutual help was been practiced since families first existed. (2) As social beings, all of us need to be accepted, cared for, and emotionally supported. (3) We also find it satisfying to care for and support those around us. (4) Within the most natural mutual help networks with families and friends, we establish the one-to-one contact so important to our happiness and well-being. (5) This informal support is such a basic part of our social character that we are apt to take them for granted, but it clearly influences our ability to handle distressing aspects of our lives.

B

  (6) Many of our daily conversations are actually mutual counseling sessions, wherein we exchange the reassurance and advice that help us deal with routine stresses. (7) In fact, research scientists have found that there is a strong link between the strength of our social support system and our health. (8) Many studies show that such support helps prevent ill health and promotes recovery when an illness or accident does occur. (9) What is the meaning of "mutual help"?

C

(10) The personal support we receive from family and friends, however, is only one part of the support network that helps sustain us through life. (11) As we develop Socially and Intellectually, we tend to associate with others who have similar interests and beliefs. (12) In groups such as religious congregations, civic and fraternal organizations, and social clubs, members benefit from a shared identity and a sense of common purpose. (13) Some informal groups are aimed primarily at social enjoyment. (14) Other groups come together to bring about social change: through combined effort, the group can often achieve what the individual can not accomplish alone.

8. Sentence (1): **Mutual help was been practiced since families first existed.**

Which of the following is the best way to write the underlined portion of this sentence? If you think the original is the best way to write the sentence, choose option (1).

(1) help was been practiced

(2) help is been practiced

(3) help is being practiced

(4) help is practicing

(5) help has been practiced

9. Sentence (5): **This informal support is such a basic part of our social character that we are apt to take them for granted, but it clearly influences our ability to handle distressing aspects of our lives.**

What correction should be made to this sentence?

(1) change is to was

(2) change This informal support to This informal supporting

(3) change we are apt to they are apt

(4) change to take them to to take it

(5) change our social character to your social character

10. Sentence (8): **Many studies show that such support helps prevent ill health and promotes recovery when an illness or accident does occur.**

If you rewrote sentence (8) beginning with When an illness or accident does occur, the next words should be

(1) many studies

(2) such support

(3) that such

(4) and promotes

(5) helps prevent

11. Sentence (9): **What is the meaning of "mutual help"?**

What revision can be made to sentence (9) to improve the organization of this text?

(1) move sentence (9) to the beginning of paragraph C

(2) place sentence (9) before sentence (8)

(3) delete sentence (9)

(4) move sentence (9) after sentence (4)

(5) no revision is necessary

12. Sentence (11): **As we develop Socially and Intellectually, we tend to associate with others who have similar interests and beliefs.**

    Which of the following is the best way to write the underlined portion of this sentence? If you think the original is the best way to write the sentence, choose option (1).

    (1) develop Socially and Intellectually,
    (2) develop socially and intellectually,
    (3) developing Socially and Intellectually,
    (4) developed Socially and Intellectually,
    (5) have developed Social and Intellectual,

13. Sentence (12): **In groups such as religious congregations, civic and fraternal organizations, and social clubs, members benefit from a shared identity and a sense of common purpose.**

    If you rewrote sentence (12) beginning with The benefits of a shared identity and a sense of common purpose, the next words would be

    (1) are often obtained
    (2) in groups
    (3) in social clubs and civic groups
    (4) group members
    (5) in religious congregations

14. Sentence (14): **Other groups come together to bring about social change: through combined effort, the group can often achieve what the individual can not accomplish alone.**

    Which of the following is the best way to write the underlined portion of this sentence? If you think the original is the best way to write the sentence, choose option (1).

    (1) social change: through
    (2) social change through
    (3) social change, through
    (4) social change. Through
    (5) social change; Through

ITEMS 15 TO 21 REFER TO THE FOLLOWING ARTICLE.

The Tricks of Microwave Cooking

A

(1) More and more people have microwave ovens in their homes and find themselves facing a thoroughly different method of cooking. (2) Let's look at how microwave ovens work, and how that effects their use with perishable goods, particularly meat and poultry. (3) Microwaves are extra-short radio waves produced in the oven. (4) A movement of molecules (friction) is caused inside the food by these waves they actually do the cooking. (5) The air in the oven usually doesn't heat up very much. (6) The waves bounce around inside the oven, penetrating the food repeatedly. (7) This causes cooking to begin just below the food's surface. (8) Full cooking is achieved as the heat starts to spread threw the rest of the food.

B

(9) While microwaving is quick, it does not always cook food evenly. (10) Before novice microwave oven owners master their appliances, they often find that some spots in a food will over-cook, while others remain uncooked. (11) To completing cooking of the whole food without over-cooking these high-heat spots, many microwave recipes call for a 10- to 15-minute standing time following cooking. (12) That allows cooking to continue after you take the food out of the oven as the heat spreads evenly throughout the food.

15. Sentence (2): **Let's look at how microwave ovens work, and how that effects their use with perishable goods, particularly meat and poultry.**

What correction should be made to this sentence?

(1) change <u>work</u> to <u>works</u>
(2) change <u>effects</u> to <u>affects</u>
(3) change <u>use</u> to <u>used</u>
(4) remove the comma after <u>goods</u>
(5) insert a comma after <u>meat</u>

16. Sentence (4): **A movement of molecules (friction) is caused inside the food by these <u>waves they</u> actually do the cooking.**

Which of the following is the best way to write the underlined portion of this sentence? If you think the original is the best way to write the sentence, choose option (1).

(1) waves they
(2) waves, they
(3) waves who
(4) waves. They
(5) waves' they

17. Sentence (5): **The air in the oven usually doesn't heat up very much.**

What correction should be made to this sentence?

(1) insert a comma after <u>air</u>
(2) insert a semicolon after <u>oven</u>
(3) remove the word <u>up</u>
(4) change <u>doesn't</u> to <u>don't</u>
(5) no correction is necessary

18. Sentence (6): **The waves bounce around inside the oven, penetrating the food repeatedly.**

If you rewrote sentence (6) beginning with <u>Inside the oven</u>, the next word(s) should be

(1) food repeatedly

(2) around inside

(3) the food

(4) the waves

(5) bounce around

19. Sentence (8): **Full cooking is achieved as the heat starts to spread threw the rest of the food.**

What correction should be made to this sentence?

(1) change <u>heat</u> to <u>heating</u>

(2) change <u>threw</u> to <u>through</u>

(3) put a comma after <u>achieved</u>

(4) change <u>starts</u> to <u>starting</u>

(5) change <u>spread</u> to <u>spreads</u>

20. Sentence (11): <u>**To completing cooking of**</u> **the whole food without overcooking these high-heat spots, many microwave recipes call for a 10- to 15-minute standing time following power cooking.**

Which of the following is the best way to write the underlined portion of this sentence? If you think the original is the best way to write the sentence, choose option (1).

(1) To completing cooking of

(2) To completing cook of

(3) To complete cooking of

(4) To complete the cook of

(5) To cook completely for

21. Which revision would improve the organization and clarity of "The Tricks of Microwave Cooking"?

Start a new paragraph

(1) with sentence (3).

(2) with sentence (5).

(3) with sentence (7).

(4) with sentence (8).

(5) with sentence (11).

ITEMS 22 TO 29 REFER TO THE FOLLOWING BUSINESS COMMUNICATION.

Memo: To all members of the Trumansberg Citizens' Consumer Association (CCA)

Re: Meeting with representative of National Organization of CCA on 6/6/04, at 8:30 p.m.

A

(1) For members who was unable to attend this very informative meeting, the following is a summary of the helpful recommendations made to us.

B

(2) Before starting a home improvement project it is important to do some preliminary planning. (3) Here are some tips.

(4) **Plan ahead,** Know what you want or need to have done before contacting a contractor.

(5) **Ask family and friends** for recommendations for contractors.

(6) **Get at least three written estimates** from contractors who have come to your home to evaluate what needs to be done. (7) **Contact your local "consumer agency" and Better Business Bureau** for information on the contractors' licensing or registration requirements and complaint records.

(8) **Get references** and talk to people for whom the contractor has done similar work.

(9) **Be sure your contractor has the required personally liability and workers' compensation insurance** for his/her workers.

C

(10) **Insist on a complete written contract** and exactly what work will be done, the quality of materials that will be used, what warranties apply, and the total price of the job.

(11) **Try to limit your down payment.**

(12) **Don't make final payments until you are sure** that the work has been completed to your satisfaction.

(13) **Pay by credit card** when you can, because you could then refuse to pay the credit card company until possible problems with the job are corrected.

(14) **Be especially cautious if the contractor,**
- Comes door-to-door;
- Quotes a price that's out of line with other estimates;
- Pressures you for an immediate decision;
- Drives an unmarked van or has out-of-state plates on his/her vehicle.

6/25/05

22. Sentence (1): **For members who was unable to attend this very informative meeting, the following is a summary of the helpful recommendations made to us.**

What correction should be made to this sentence?

(1) change <u>attend</u> to <u>attending</u>

(2) change the comma to a period

(3) change <u>was unable</u> to <u>were unable</u>

(4) change <u>summary</u> to <u>summarizing</u>

(5) no correction is necessary

23. Sentence (4): **Plan ahead, Know what you want or need to have done before contacting a contractor.**

Which of the following choices is the best way to write the underlined portion of this sentence? If the original way is best, choose option (1).

(1) Plan ahead, Know what

(2) Plan ahead, and Know

(3) Planning ahead, knowing

(4) Plans ahead, know what

(5) Plan ahead. Know what

24. Sentence (7): **Contact your local "consumer agency" and Better Business Bureau for information on the contractors' licensing or registration requirements and complaint records.**

What correction should be made to sentence (7)?

(1) change <u>contractors'</u> to <u>contractors</u>

(2) change <u>"consumer agency"</u> to <u>consumer agency</u>

(3) change <u>registration requirements</u> to <u>registration requirements'</u>

(4) change <u>Better Business Bureau</u> to <u>better business bureau</u>

(5) put a comma after <u>licensing</u>

25. Sentence (9): **Be sure your contractor has <u>the required personally liability</u> and workers' compensation insurance for his/her workers.**

Which of the following choices is the best way to write the underlined portion of this sentence? If you think that the original is best, then choose option (1).

(1) the required personally liability

(2) the requiring personally liability

(3) the required personality liability

(4) the required personal liability

(5) the required personally liable

26. What revision could be made to the text of this selection to improve its organization?

(1) create a new paragraph with sentence (14)

(2) move paragraph B in front of paragraph A

(3) move sentence (1) to the end of the memo

(4) eliminate the creation of paragraphs A, B, and C

(5) move sentence (11) before sentence (5)

27. Sentence (10): **Insist on a complete written contract and exactly what work will be done, the quality of materials that will be used, what warranties apply, and the total price of the job.**

What correction should be made to the above sentence?

(1) change the period after <u>job</u> to a question mark

(2) change <u>warranties</u> to <u>warranty</u>

(3) change <u>and exactly</u> to <u>and know exactly</u>

(4) change <u>complete written contract</u> to <u>completely written contract</u>

(5) no correction is necessary

28. Sentence (13): **Pay by credit card when you can, because you could then refuse to pay the credit card company until possible problems with the job are corrected.**

If you rewrote this sentence beginning with <u>Because you could then refuse to pay the credit card company</u>, the next words should be

(1) until possible

(2) by credit

(3) when you

(4) possible problems

(5) you can

29. Sentence (14): **Be especially <u>cautious if the contractor,</u>**
— Comes door-to-door;
— Quotes a price that's out of line with other estimates;
— Pressures you for an immediate decision;
— Drives an unmarked van or has out-of-state plates on his/her vehicle.

Which of the following is the best way to write the underlined portion of this sentence? If you think that the original is best, choose option (1).

(1) cautious if the contractor,

(2) cautious if the contractor:

(3) cautious because the contractor,

(4) cautious if the contractor.

(5) cautious, in case the contractor,

ITEMS 30 TO 36 REFER TO THE FOLLOWING SELECTION.

Parents and Teens

A

(1) For parents, it is a challenge to recognize and keep a balanced perspective on they're teenager's emotional roller coaster ride. (2) As their children bounce back and forth between childishness and mature behavior, alternating irresponsibility with responsibility, blatantly testing parental authority one moment and depending on it the next, parents often do not know what to expect. (3) They must maintain needed discipline, yet understand the teenager's growing need for independent action, even for rebellion.

B

(4) It is easy to understand, why many parents and adolescents find this such a difficult period to survive. (5) But once it is over, even the most rebellious child often becomes appreciative, affectionate, and devoted. (6) With maturity comes the realization that much of their parents' behavior, once so irritated, was motivated by feelings of love. (7) Also, having children of their own brings an understanding of the pressures all parents face. (8) Parents should also be aware of their own imperfections.

C

(9) At times, lack of knowledge, poor advice, community pressures, or their own stresses can cause them to overreact to teenage behaviors. (10) To avoid making the same mistakes as their own parents, or to make up for what they missed in their childhood, parents sometimes poor judgment. (11) Adolescence was a trying period, but it is also an exciting one. (12) If parents and teenagers keep tuned in to each other and are able to maintain a sense of humor, this period may seem less trying and more fun for everyone.

30. Sentence (1): **For parents, it is a challenge to recognize and keep a balanced perspective on they're teenager's emotional roller coaster ride.**

What correction should be made to this sentence?

(1) change <u>parents,</u> to <u>parent's,</u>

(2) change <u>and keep</u> to <u>to keep</u>

(3) change <u>they're</u> to <u>their</u>

(4) change <u>teenager's</u> to <u>teenagers</u>

(5) no correction is necessary

31. Sentence (4): **It is easy to under-stand, why many parents and adolescents find this such a diffi-cult period to survive**.

    Which of the following is the best way to write the underlined portion of this sentence? If you think the original is the best way to write the sentence, choose option (1).

    (1) It is easy to understand,
    (2) It is easy to understand
    (3) Easy to understand,
    (4) Easiest to understand,
    (5) To try to understand,

32. Sentence (5): **But once it is over, even the most rebellious child of-ten becomes appreciative, affec-tionate, and devoted.**

    If you rewrote sentence (5) beginning with Even the most rebellious child the next words should be

    (1) often becomes
    (2) it is over
    (3) and devoted
    (4) but once
    (5) once it

33. Sentence (6): **With maturity comes the realization that much of their parents' behavior, once so irritated, was motivated by feel-ings of love for them**.

    What correction should be made to this sentence?

    (1) change comes to come
    (2) change realization to realizing
    (3) change parents' to parents
    (4) change irritated to irritating
    (5) no correction is necessary

34. Sentence (10): **To avoid making the same mistakes as their own parents, or to make up for what they missed in their childhood, parents sometimes poor judg-ment.**

    What correction should be made in sentence (10)?

    (1) remove the comma after parents
    (2) change or to make to and to make
    (3) add the word show after parents sometimes
    (4) insert making after sometimes
    (5) change To avoid to Avoiding

35. Sentence (11): **Adolescence was a trying period, but it is also an exciting one.**

    Which of the following is the best way to write the underlined portion of this sentence? If you think the original is the best way to write the sentence, choose option (1).

    (1) Adolescence was
    (2) Adolescence is
    (3) Adolescence to be
    (4) Adolescence were
    (5) Adolescence had been

36. Which revision would improve the organization of the text, "*Parents and Teens*"?

    (1) move sentence (3) to the beginning of paragraph B
    (2) move sentence (4) to the beginning of paragraph A
    (3) move paragraph A to follow paragraph C
    (4) move sentence (8) to the beginning of paragraph C
    (5) no revision is necessary

ITEMS 37 TO 43 REFER TO THE FOLLOWING ARTICLE.

The Beginning of "Quality Measurement"

A

(1) By "quality measurement" is meant the accurate, clear, and consistant ability to measure something in terms of its quality. (2) Quality measurement is a comparatively modern development. (3) Although man having been measuring sizes and distances—more or less accurately—since the dawn of recorded history. (4) In ancient egypt, the length of the pharaoh's foot was an official measurement. (5) Quality measurement, however, did not appear until a few hundred years ago.

B

(6) Probably it was the consumers in thirteenth-century England who got the benefit of the first real quality standards when the king decreed "assizes" for bread. (7) These assizes were enforced by local officials to make sure that bakers gave full quality and wait in their loaves. (8) This assured that people got a consistently good quality product when they bought bread. (9) Since bread constituted the major part of a person's diet at that time, this was a very important development.

C

(10) Under the method of measurement using the assize, "simnel loaves" had to be made from the finest white bread flour. (11) There was also a "wastrel loaf," far inferior to the first two kinds. (12) "Horse bread" was made from beans, and seems to sell primarily to unwary travelers at the local inns. (13) The price of the loaves was fixed, and the required size of each kind varied according to the price of the type of grain used. (14) "Treet bread" was brown bread, fairly close to simnel loaf in quality. (15) The standards weren't too exact, and local officials are serving as "graders" when there was a dispute.

37. Sentence (3): **Although man having been measuring sizes and distances—more or less accurately—since the dawn of recorded history.**

What correction should be made to this sentence?

- **(1)** change the dashes to commas
- **(2)** change Although man having to Man has
- **(3)** change having to have
- **(4)** change sizes and distances to size and distance
- **(5)** change recorded history to history recording

38. Sentence (4): **In ancient egypt, the length of the pharaoh's foot was an official measurement.**

What correction should be made to this sentence?

- **(1)** change egypt to Egypt
- **(2)** change pharaoh to Pharaoh
- **(3)** change foot to feet
- **(4)** change measurement to measuring
- **(5)** no correction is necessary

39. Sentence (7): **These assizes were enforced by local officials to make sure that bakers gave full quality and wait in their loaves.**

What correction should be made to this sentence?

- **(1)** change enforced to unforced
- **(2)** change make to makes
- **(3)** change bakers to bakers'
- **(4)** change wait to weight
- **(5)** change local officials to local official

40. Sentence (9): **Since bread constituted the major part of a per-
son's diet at that time, this was a
very important development.**

If you rewrote sentence (9) beginning
with the words <u>This was a very important development</u>, the next words
would be

- **(1)** bread constituted
- **(2)** of a person's
- **(3)** since bread
- **(4)** constituting the
- **(5)** that time

41. Sentence (12): **"Horse bread" was
made from beans, and <u>seems to
sell</u> primarily to unwary travelers at the local inns.**

Which of the following is the best
way to write the underlined portion
of this sentence? If you think the
original is the best way to write the
sentence, choose option (1).

- **(1)** seems to sell
- **(2)** seems to be selling
- **(3)** was selling
- **(4)** was sold
- **(5)** seems selling

42. Which one of the following revisions
should be made to sentence (14) in
order to improve the clarity and organization of this reading selection?

- **(1)** move sentence (14) to the end of
paragraph A
- **(2)** move sentence (14) to the end of
paragraph B
- **(3)** move sentence (14) to follow
sentence (10)
- **(4)** remove sentence (14)
- **(5)** no revision is necessary

43. Sentence (15): **The standards
weren't too exact, and <u>local officials are serving</u> as "graders"
when there was a dispute.**

Which choice is the best way to write
the underlined portion of the sentence? If you think the original is the
best, choose option (1).

- **(1)** local officials are serving
- **(2)** locally officials serving
- **(3)** local officials will serve
- **(4)** local official's served
- **(5)** local officials served

ITEMS 44 TO 50 REFER TO THE NEXT ARTICLE.

Justice in Old Athens

A

(1) As in the United States today, Athens had Courts where a wrong might be righted. (2) Since any citizen could accuse another of a crime, the Athenian courts of law were very busy. (3) In fact, unless a citizen was unusually peaceful or very unimportant, they would be sure to appear in the courts at least once every few years.

B

(4) Judging a trial, the jury was chosen from the members of the assembly who had reached 30 years of age. (5) The Athenian juries were very large, often consisting of 201, 401, 501, 1,001 or more men, depending upon the importance of the case being tried. (6) Each juryman swore by the gods to listen carefully to both sides, of the question and to give his honest opinion of the case. (7) He gave his decision by depositing a white or black stone in a box. (8) To keep citizens from being too careless in accusing each other, there was a very important rule. (9) If the person accused did not receive a certain number of negative votes, the accuser was condemned instead!

C

(10) At a trial, both the accuser and the person accused were allowed a certain amount of time to speak. (11) The length of time marked by a water clock. (12) Free men testified under oath as they do today, but the oath of a slave was counted as worthless.

44. Sentence (1): **As in the United States today, Athens had Courts where a wrong might be righted.**

Which of the following is the best way to write the underlined portion of this sentence? If you think the original is the best way to write the sentence, choose option (1).

(1) Athens had Courts where
(2) Athens had Courts. Where
(3) Athens had courts where
(4) Athens where Courts had
(5) Athens: had Courts where

45. Sentence (3): **In fact, unless a citizen was unusually peaceful or very unimportant, they would be sure to appear in the courts at least once every few years.**

What correction should be made to this sentence?

(1) delete the comma after fact
(2) change was to were
(3) begin a new sentence with They
(4) change they to he
(5) insert a comma after courts

46. Sentence (4): **Judging a trial, the jury was chosen from the members of the assembly who had reached 30 years of age.**

What correction should be made to this sentence?

(1) change Judging to To judge
(2) change was to were
(3) change from to among
(4) change who to whom
(5) change had reached to reaching

47. Sentence (5): **The Athenian juries were very large, often consisting of 201, 401, 501, 1,001 or more men, depending upon the importance of the case being tried.**

If you rewrote sentence (5) beginning with Depending upon the importance of the case being tried, the next words should be

(1) often consisting
(2) 201, 401, 501, 1,001
(3) very large
(4) juries were
(5) the Athenian

48. Sentence (6): **Each juryman swore by the gods to listen carefully to both sides, of the question and to give his honest opinion of the case.**

What correction should be made to sentence (6)?

(1) change the gods to the Gods
(2) change both sides, of to both sides. Of
(3) remove the comma
(4) change juryman to jurymen
(5) no correction is needed

49. Sentence (11): **The length of time marked by a water clock.**

Which of the following is the best way to write the underlined portion of this sentence? If you think the original is the best way to write the sentence, choose option (1).

(1) marked by
(2) marking by
(3) is marked by
(4) was marked by
(5) to be marked by

50. Which revision would improve the text, "Justice in Old Athens"?

(1) move paragraph A to follow paragraph B
(2) move sentence (3) to follow sentence (12)
(3) move sentence (8) to follow sentence (12)
(4) move paragraph B to follow paragraph C
(5) move sentence (12) to follow sentence (8)

Part 2. Essay Test

45 Minutes • 1 Essay

Directions: This part of the GED is designed to find out how well you write. You will be given one question that asks you to either explain something or present an opinion on an issue. In constructing your answer for this part of the exam, you should think of your own observations and experiences, and take the following steps:

1. Before you begin to write your answer, read the directions and the question carefully.

2. Think of what you wish to say and plan your essay in detail before you begin to write.

3. Use the blank pages in the test booklet (or scrap paper provided for you) to make notes for planning your essay.

4. Write your essay neatly on the separate answer sheet.

5. Carefully read over what you have written and make any changes that will improve your work.

6. Check your paragraphing, sentence structure, spelling, punctuation, capitalization, and language usage, and correct any errors.

You will have 45 minutes to write a response to the question you are given. Write clearly with a ballpoint pen so the evaluators can read what you have written. Any notes you make on the blank pages or scratch paper will not be included in your evaluation.

Your essay will be scored by at least two trained readers who will evaluate the paper according to its overall impact. They will be concerned with how clearly you made your main points, how thoroughly your ideas are supported, and how effective and correct your writing is throughout the entire composition. You will receive no credit for writing on a topic other than the one assigned.

Sample Topic

More than 85 percent of households in America clip and redeem supermarket coupons and refund offers.

Write a composition of about 250 words in which you explain why you think people take the time to do this. Be specific, and use examples from your own experience to support your view.

TEST 2: SOCIAL STUDIES

70 Minutes • 50 Questions

Directions: The Social Studies Test consists of multiple-choice questions intended to measure your knowledge of general concepts in history, economics, geography, and civics and government. The questions are based on reading passages, maps, graphs, charts, and cartoons. For each question, first study the information given and then answer the questions about it. You may refer to the readings or graphs as often as necessary in order to answer the questions. Record your answers in the Social Studies Section of your answer sheet.

Q Which medium most regularly presents opinions and interpretations of the news?

    (1) National television news programs

    (2) Local television news programs

    (3) Newspaper editorial pages

    (4) Teletype news agency reports

    (5) Radio news broadcasts

                                           ① ② ● ④ ⑤

A The correct answer is "newspaper editorial pages." Therefore, you should mark answer space (3) on your answer sheet.

ITEMS 1 TO 5 REFER TO THE FOLLOWING SELECTION.

Labor conditions in the South differed markedly from those in the North. For one thing, until well after the beginning of the twentieth century, the South failed to attract immigrant labor or even the children of immigrants. Whites from the poorer lands of the Piedmont and from the mountains supplied the bulk of the labor for the textile mills and such others as required skilled operatives, while a preponderance of blacks did the harder work in the mines, the blast furnaces, and the lumber industry. Only in rare instances were the two races employed side by side at the same tasks; industries that used both blacks and whites took care to maintain a division of labor be-tween the races, regularly assigning the inferior position to the blacks.

In the textile mills, the employment of women and children was practically universal, although the extent to which young children were exploited has probably been exaggerated. Nevertheless, the opportunity for the whole family to be gainfully employed was one of the chief attractions of the mills to the rural whites. Wages were low, at first far lower than wages paid in the Northern mills. With the mother and children and the father all at work, however, the total income was much larger than that from a run-down farm, and the temptation to leave that farm for the factory was almost irresistible.

1. Based on the information in this article, which phrase most clearly describes the economic condition of Southern farmers at the beginning of the twentieth century?

   (1) Poor but encouraging

   (2) Comparatively worse than the condition of mill workers

   (3) Unaffected by racial tensions

   (4) Determined by prices paid in Northern cities

   (5) Attractive to immigrant labor

2. Early in this century, who was most likely to have received training for skilled jobs in Southern factories?

   (1) Blacks and whites alike

   (2) White children only

   (3) Educated whites

   (4) Immigrant labor

   (5) White men

3. From this selection, what can be inferred about early twentieth-century rural life in the South?

   (1) Higher education did not play a major role.

   (2) There were few racial barriers.

   (3) It was far better than life in the North.

   (4) It was marked by rapid technological change.

   (5) It depended on immigrant labor.

4. Why did whites gradually move toward work in factories and mills?

   (1) Cotton was king in the South.

   (2) Land was not economically productive.

   (3) More money could be made there by the whole family.

   (4) Blacks were taking over the farms.

   (5) Northern competition was intense.

5. Based on the information in this article, which of the following reasons best explains why industries did not exploit child labor to a greater extent?

   (1) There were not enough children available.

   (2) The children were in school half the day.

   (3) It was not economically practical.

   (4) Parents refused to allow their young children to work.

   (5) The children rebelled against the work.

ITEMS 6 TO 8 REFER TO THE FOLLOWING MAP.

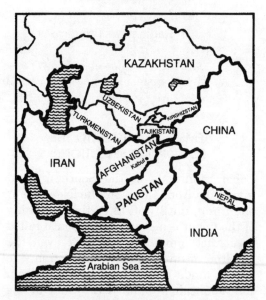

6. Which of the following statements most likely explains why Afghanistan has had difficulty getting its exports to foreign markets?

   (1) It does not produce enough.

   (2) It is a primitive country.

   (3) It is hated by its neighbors.

   (4) It has a low literacy rate among its inhabitants.

   (5) It has no access to the sea.

7. The people of Afghanistan are divided into various ethnic groups, including Pushtuns, Tajiks, Uzbeks, and Hazaras. About 50 percent of its 19,500,000 people speak Pushtu, another 35 percent speak Persian, and 11 percent speak Turkic languages, while the remaining people speak a variety of different languages. The country is about one-fifth the physical size of the United States. Only about 10 percent of the people are literate in any language. Based on this information, which conclusion is most likely?

   (1) Afghanistan is a rich, well-run nation.

   (2) Afghanistan has heavy industry and technologically advanced corporations.

   (3) Afghanistan is essentially an agricultural economy.

   (4) The capital of Afghanistan is a major Asian city.

   (5) Afghanistan cannot support its own army.

8. Which of the following statements is best supported by the map?

   (1) Fish makes up the main part of the Afghan diet.

   (2) The climate of Afghanistan is similar to that of Tajikistan.

   (3) Kabul is a strategic middle European port.

   (4) Afghanistan was once a part of Pakistan.

   (5) Afghanistan is bordered by mountains.

ITEMS 9 TO 13 REFER TO THE FOLLOWING SELECTION.

Certain kinds of deceptive advertising appeals and claims appear over and over again despite continued efforts to halt them. Advertisers who make such claims generally have found them so successful that they can make a great deal of profit before any action can be taken to force them to stop. Listed here are five types of deceptive advertising practices:

1. Meaningless claims	Ads that appear to supply useful facts but, upon closer examination, the information is meaningless.
2. **Misrepresentation**	Ads that exaggerate or make false claims about a product.
3. **"Bait and switch"**	An insincere offer to sell a product or service that the advertiser does not really wish or intend to sell. When the shopper shows interest in the product, the advertiser offers another, of higher price.

4. **Referral sales schemes** Ads that offer purchasers bonuses for providing the seller with names of other prospective buyers.

5. **Fictitious pricing** Overstatement of the "list price" in order to convince shoppers that advertised prices offer special pricing.

Each of the following statements illustrates a type of deceptive advertising. Choose the deceptive practice being used in each situation. The categories may be used more than once in the set of items but no one question has more than one best answer.

9. "You may never need to buy another pair of socks again—unless the laundry loses them! We guarantee it!"

(1) Meaningless claim

(2) Misrepresentation

(3) "Bait and switch"

(4) Referral sales scheme

(5) Fictitious pricing

10. "Scientific studies prove that Cleer detergent is absolutely guaranteed to last 40% longer or your money will be cheerfully refunded."

(1) Meaningless claim

(2) Misrepresentation

(3) "Bait and switch"

(4) Referral sales scheme

(5) Fictitious pricing

11. The Simmons family arrives at Giant Furniture in response to the following ad: "Three rooms of furniture—only $200!" At Giant, the Simmonses are shown a bed, a sofa, and a dining room table, all scratched and in poor condition. The salesman diverts them to more expensive items in better condition.

(1) Meaningless claim

(2) Misrepresentation

(3) "Bait and switch"

(4) Referral sales scheme

(5) Fictitious pricing

12. Television City claims that the manufacturer's suggested price on the 19-inch color television is $500, and the $400 Television City special sale price therefore represents a $100 savings over list. In actuality, the manufacturer's suggested price is $398.99.

(1) Meaningless claim

(2) Misrepresentation

(3) "Bait and switch"

(4) Referral sales scheme

(5) Fictitious pricing

13. "It's official! CHATTERING TEDDY BEARS sold by competitive companies are now outselling virtually every other toy in America! Demand is so great that even models introduced one year ago still sell for much more in the stores! But we are able to offer these adorable toys at far, far less, through this special introductory mail offer."

(1) Meaningless claim

(2) Misrepresentation

(3) "Bait and switch"

(4) Referral sales scheme

(5) Fictitious pricing

**ITEMS 14 TO 17 REFER TO THE
FOLLOWING MAPS.**

North America in 1689

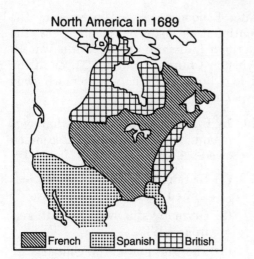

North America in 1763

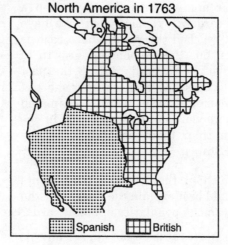

14. Which of the following choices best explains the changes between the two maps?

    (1) The French defeated the British in the French and Indian Wars, 1754–1763.

    (2) The Spanish diverted their forces to do battle in Mexico.

    (3) The British made the colonies bear their part in the cost of maintaining the British Empire.

    (4) The Treaty of Paris eliminated France as a colonial power in North America.

    (5) The American colonists gained valuable military experience.

15. According to the map, which power controlled British Columbia in 1689?

    (1) France

    (2) Spain

    (3) England

    (4) England and France

    (5) None of the above

16. According to the map, which power controlled Louisiana in 1689?

    (1) France

    (2) England and France

    (3) Spain

    (4) England

    (5) France and Spain

17. Based on the map, which power controlled the Mississippi River in 1763?

    (1) Spain

    (2) England

    (3) Spain and England

    (4) Spain and France

    (5) France

ITEM 18 REFERS TO THE FOLLOWING INFORMATION.

How far are we from the day when a plastic card will replace cash? We have not yet reached the point where cash is obsolete, but the tremendous growth in the use of credit cards during the past three decades has been nothing short of phenomenal. A recent survey estimated that there were more credit cards in circulation than there are people in the United States.

18. Which of the following statements would best explain the reason for the enormous popularity of credit cards?

    (1) Most cards do not charge any interest payments, making it much smarter to use cards than cash.

    (2) Most credit cards have an unlimited ceiling.

    (3) Merchants encourage people to obtain cards to spur sales.

    (4) Cards are sent free to people, even when they did not request them.

    (5) Credit cards are convenient and relatively safe.

19. In a map of the world, $1\frac{1}{2}$ inches represents 1,000 miles. How many inches should be used to indicate the distance from New York to San Francisco?

    (1) $1\frac{1}{2}$

    (2) 3

    (3) $4\frac{1}{2}$

    (4) 5

    (5) 6

ITEM 20 REFERS TO THE FOLLOWING STATEMENT.

After London succeeded in resisting the continual devastating bombing by the German Luftwaffe during World War II, Winston Churchill stated, "Never in the field of human conflict was so much owed by so many to so few."

20. In the statement above, what was meant by the phrase ". . . so much owed . . ."?

    (1) Britain owed so much to the United States for Lend Lease.

    (2) Germany still owed reparations from WWI.

    (3) The world owed the United States thanks for the D-Day invasion

    (4) The allies owed Britain gratitude for withstanding the bombing.

    (5) Germany owed a debt to the countries it invaded.

21. Beginning in 1957, the United States and Russia were in a "space-race." In 1957 the Soviets launched Sputnik. What event in 1969 marked a turning point for the U.S. in this race?

    (1) The first satellite orbited the earth

    (2) The construction of a space station

    (3) The first space walk

    (4) The first manned landing on the moon

    (5) The first multistage rocket launching

ITEM 22 REFERS TO THE FOLLOWING ANNOUNCEMENT.

TOWN SELECTMEN MEETING

Shepherd Hall

Lenox, North Dakota

June 15, 2004

Meeting will start at 7 p.m. sharp!

TOPIC: SEWERS

Please attend this very important meeting. The Sewer Committee will discuss the possibility of extending the sewer system to Goodrich Street, Mason Shores, Mason Terrace, and houses on Bean Hill Road.

Issues to be discussed include individual costs, the engineering report, state and county grant and loan options, and possible costs to homeowners.

DO NOT MISS THIS MEETING!

---

22. The announcement on the left is an example of which one of the following?

   (1) Participatory government
   (2) Absentee ballots
   (3) Republicanism
   (4) Environmental activism
   (5) None of the above

23. The eighteenth-century idea that it is not the business of governments to interfere with the economy is called

   (1) liberalism.
   (2) optimism.
   (3) uniformity.
   (4) laissez-faire.
   (5) Darwinism.

ITEMS 24 TO 28 REFER TO THE FOLLOWING CARTOON.

24. The cartoon above illustrates the problem of

    (1) toxic waste pollution.
    (2) solid waste disposal.
    (3) global warming.
    (4) poor international relations.
    (5) acid rain.

25. An acronym that might apply to the situation depicted is

    (1) ACWA.
    (2) IATA.
    (3) COCOM.
    (4) NIMBY.
    (5) DoD.

26. The most viable long-term solution to the problem is likely to lie in

    (1) compacting.
    (2) legislation.
    (3) recycling.
    (4) sanctions.
    (5) burning.

27. This problem is not limited to the United States, but it is a greater problem in the United States than it is elsewhere because the United States

    (1) has a "throw-away" ethic.
    (2) is the largest nation.
    (3) has the greatest population.
    (4) has a high water table.
    (5) has an obstructionist Congress.

28. This cartoon would be most likely to have appeared in a

    (1) children's picture book.
    (2) fashion magazine.
    (3) PTA newsletter.
    (4) food processor user manual.
    (5) daily newspaper.

ITEMS 29 TO 32 REFER TO THE FOLLOWING MAP AND TEXT.

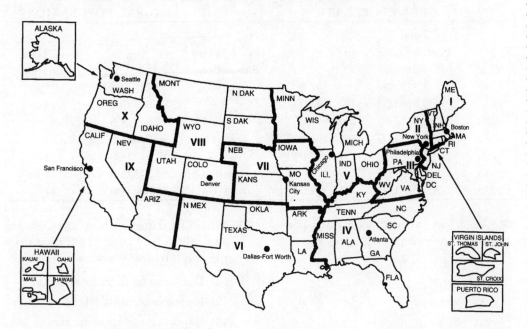

In order to make the federal government more accessible to the people who need its services, the executive branch is divided into ten geographical regions as shown on the map above. The dots in each region locate the regional headquarters city.

29. If you are a resident of Salt Lake City, where is the regional headquarters for your area?

(1) Seattle

(2) Chicago

(3) Atlanta

(4) Denver

(5) Kansas City

30. If you are a resident of Puerto Rico, where is the regional headquarters for your area?

(1) Atlanta

(2) Miami

(3) Philadelphia

(4) New York City

(5) Boston

31. What states does Region VII include?

(1) South Dakota, Iowa, Kansas, Missouri

(2) Arkansas, Illinois, Missouri, Iowa

(3) Iowa, Missouri, Kansas, Nebraska

(4) Iowa, Colorado, Missouri, Kansas

(5) Arkansas, Oklahoma, Kansas, Nebraska

32. From the information presented on the map, which of the following best explains why Region II is so small?

(1) It is close to Washington, D.C.

(2) It is densely populated.

(3) It receives a great deal of federal assistance.

(4) It has powerful congressmen and senators.

(5) It lacks a headquarter city.

ITEMS 33 TO 35 REFER TO THE FOLLOWING CHART.

	URBAN POPULATION			RURAL POPULATION	
Year	Total United States Population		% of Total Population		% of Total Population
1790	3,929,000	202,000	5%	3,728,000	95%
1820	9,618,000	693,000	7	8,945,000	93
1850	23,261,000	3,544,000	15	19,648,000	85
1880	50,262,000	14,130,000	28	36,026,000	72
1910	92,407,000	41,999,000	45	49,973,000	55
1940	132,122,000	74,424,000	56	57,245,000	44
1970	203,810,000	149,325,000	73	54,054,000	27

33. A net loss in rural population is evident in which period?

(1) 1790–1820

(2) 1820–1850

(3) 1880–1910

(4) 1910–1940

(5) 1940–1970

34. Which statement is best supported by the data in the chart?

(1) The number of people living in rural areas in 1970 was lower than the number living in rural areas in 1880.

(2) The percentage of the total population living in rural areas increased during the 1900s.

(3) The number of people living in urban areas declined during the nineteenth century.

(4) A majority of the people were living in urban areas by 1940.

(5) The number of people living in rural areas decreased steadily from 1880 to 1970.

35. Which explanation best accounts for the change in urban population during the late 1800s and early 1900s?

(1) Decrease in farm production

(2) Increase in industrial jobs

(3) Expansion of immigration quotas

(4) Improvements in transportation

(5) Decrease in birth rate

ITEMS 36 TO 40 REFER TO THE FOLLOWING SELECTION.

The Equal Pay Act prohibits pay discrimination because of sex. Men and women performing work in the same establishment under similar conditions must receive the same pay if their jobs require equal skill, effort, and responsibility. Differentials in pay based on a seniority or merit system, a system that measures earnings by quantity or quality of production, or any other factor than sex are permitted.

Employers may not reduce the wage rate of any employee in order to eliminate illegal differentials. Labor organizations are prohibited from causing or attempting to cause employers to violate the act.

The act was approved in 1963 as an amendment to the Fair Labor Standards Act and applies to most workers in both the public and private sectors, including executive, administrative, and professional employees and outside sales personnel.

The Labor Department officially interpreted the provisions of the act to apply to "wages," which includes all remuneration for employment. Thus, the act prohibits discrimination in all employment-related payments, including overtime, uniforms, travel, retirement, and other fringe benefits. The Supreme Court has upheld the position that jobs of men and women need be only "substantially equal"—not identical—for purposes of comparison under the law.

36. Which of the following groups of people are covered by the Fair Labor Standards Act?

   (1) Office workers

   (2) Office bookkeepers

   (3) Lawyers

   (4) All of the above

   (5) None of the above

37. The term *wages* includes which of the following?

   (1) Regular salary

   (2) Overtime

   (3) Fringe benefits

   (4) Working clothes

   (5) All of the above

38. According to the information in the passage, which of the following best explains why Paul and Nancy receive the same salary, even though their jobs have different titles?

   (1) Their jobs require equal expertise and responsibility.

   (2) They were both hired at the same time.

   (3) They work the same number of hours.

   (4) Nancy is better liked and received more overtime than Paul.

   (5) Paul had his salary decreased to eliminate illegal differences.

39. According to the provisions of the act, which of the following must be true in order for jobs to require equal pay for men and women?

   (1) The jobs must be exactly alike.

   (2) The jobs must be in the same level.

   (3) The jobs must be equal but not necessarily identical.

   (4) Salaries may not be based on seniority or merit.

   (5) Salary scales must be the same in the public and private sectors.

40. Which of the following statements is the most likely reason why this law was enacted?

   (1) People had been discriminated against on the basis of age.

   (2) Managers were having a difficult time attracting workers.

   (3) Wages were unequal because of differences in educational level.

   (4) Women were doing the same types of jobs as men but were receiving less pay.

   (5) People were being discriminated against on the basis of nationality.

practice test

41. During World War I, the Germans were pinned down in France, and millions of Germans were also stalemated on the eastern front in Russia. At the same time, the Germans had men fighting in Africa and also in the Far East.

According to the above facts, what was a main cause of Germany's defeat in World War I?

(1) The failure of the Schlieffen plan.

(2) The difficulties of bringing supplies to their armies.

(3) There was fighting on too many fronts.

(4) Russia's withdrawal in 1917.

(5) Hitler losing the support of his generals.

42. The French revolution had a great effect on the subsequent development of democracy in France, as expressed by the famous motto: Liberte, Egalite, Fraternite. What class of people benefited the most from this revolution?

(1) The first estate—clergy

(2) The second estate—nobles

(3) The third estate—common people

(4) Foreigners

(5) The elderly

ITEM 43 REFERS TO THE FOLLOWING EXCERPT.

Written in the Nineteenth Amendment to the U.S. Constitution are the following words:

"The right of citizens of the United States to vote shall not be denied or abridged by the United States or by any State on account of sex."

43. What was the name given to the group who fought for and demonstrated for the principle contained in this amendment?

(1) Whigs

(2) Tories

(3) Suffragettes

(4) Abolitionists

(5) Freedom-fighters

44. After WWII, Japan was occupied by the victorious Allied powers for seven years. A new constitution was established, and the country's economy was slowly rebuilt and modernized. Who was the Supreme Commander of this occupation?

(1) General Dwight D. Eisenhower

(2) Winston Churchill

(3) General Tojo Hidecki

(4) General Douglas MacArthur

(5) None of the above

45. The theory of the class struggle—conflicts between economic groups, the "haves" versus the "have-nots," the propertied "bourgeois" against the majority workers—is a part of which one of the following philosophies of government?

(1) Liberalism

(2) The enlightenment

(3) Communism

(4) Monarchism

(5) Republicanism

ITEMS 46 TO 48 REFER TO THE FOLLOWING GRAPH.

DEPOSITORS IN THE XYZ SAVINGS BANK

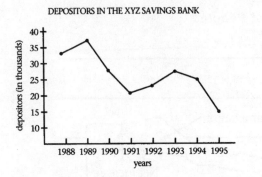

46. In which year did the XYZ Savings Bank have the greatest number of depositors?

(1) 1988

(2) 1989

(3) 1991

(4) 1992

(5) 1995

47. In 1994, the bank had approximately how many depositors?

(1) 3

(2) 30

(3) 35

(4) 25,000

(5) 35,000

48. Which of the following statements about the bank's depositors is FALSE?

(1) The number of depositors increased slightly in 1992.

(2) The lowest number of depositors is recorded in 1995.

(3) The number of depositors decreased slightly in 1993.

(4) The number of depositors continues to rise each year.

(5) The number of depositors varies from year to year.

ITEMS 49 AND 50 REFER TO THE FOLLOWING GRAPH.

Components of Population Change: 1960 to 1985

Millions of People

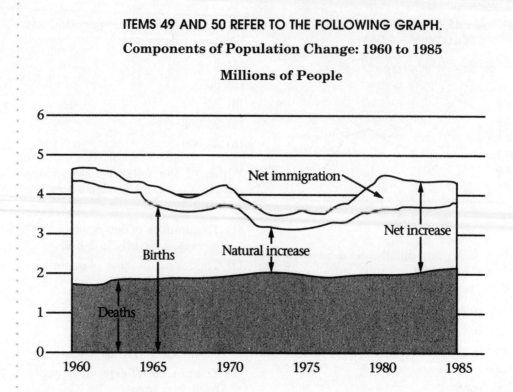

49. According to the chart, what outcomes could be supported in describing the United States population between 1960 and 1985?

   (1) The birth rate declined sharply in the 1970s.

   (2) Immigration has decreased considerably in the 1980s.

   (3) The rate of population growth will continue to decline.

   (4) The birth rate will soon become the highest ever recorded in the nation.

   (5) The death rate continues to decrease.

50. Based on the information recorded in the graph, what portion of the net population increase in the 1980s is due to immigration?

   (1) 4 percent

   (2) 12 percent

   (3) 16 percent

   (4) 25 percent

   (5) 45 percent

TEST 3: SCIENCE

80 Minutes • 50 Questions

Directions: The Science Test consists of multiple-choice questions intended to measure general concepts in life science, earth and space science, physics, and chemistry. Some of the questions are based on short readings. Others are based on graphs, charts, tables, or diagrams. For each question, study the information given and then answer the question or questions based upon it. Refer to the information as often as necessary in answering the questions. Record your answer in the Science Section of your answer sheet.

Q A physical change may alter the state of matter, but does not change its chemical composition. Which of the following is NOT a physical change?

(1) Boiling water
(2) Dissolving salt in water
(3) Shaving wood
(4) Rusting metal
(5) Breaking glass

① ② ③ ● ⑤

A When metal rusts, a new substance is formed. This is a chemical, not a physical, change. Therefore, answer space (4) should be marked on your answer sheet.

practice test

**ITEMS 1 TO 4 REFER TO THE
FOLLOWING INFORMATION.**

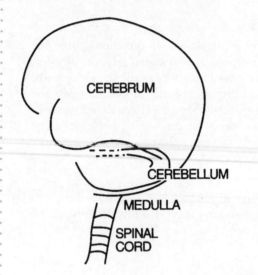

Part	Function
Cerebrum	memory, creativity, intelligence
Cerebellum	balance and coordinating controllable actions
Medulla	reflexes for the upper part of the body and control over heart and respiratory system
Spinal Cord	lower body reflexes

1. If the cerebellum of an eagle were destroyed, which of the following would the bird be unable to do?

   (1) Build a nest
   (2) Fly
   (3) Find food
   (4) Reproduce
   (5) Breathe

2. Which of the following does the cerebrum allow people to do?

   (1) Cough
   (2) Sneeze
   (3) Bite their nails
   (4) Take this test
   (5) Walk a tightrope

3. Which part of the brain increases a person's breathing and heart rate while she is running a race?

   (1) Cerebellum
   (2) Cerebellum and cerebrum
   (3) Spinal cord
   (4) Medulla
   (5) Spinal cord and cerebrum

4. How does the human brain differ from that of a cat?

   (1) A cat has a better spinal cord.
   (2) A human has a more developed cerebrum.
   (3) A human has a more developed cerebellum.
   (4) A cat has a more developed cerebellum.
   (5) A cat has a more developed cerebrum.

5. In 1997, scientists in Scotland performed the unprecedented feat of cloning "Dolly." What is meant by the term "cloning"?

   (1) Making a genetically exact copy of an individual
   (2) Making a test-tube baby
   (3) Creating an artificial intelligence
   (4) Preserving a person's DNA for posterity
   (5) Transplanting actual hair successfully

6. In 1979 a power-generating plant at Three Mile Island in Pennsylvania had an accident, which negatively affected the public's support of the nuclear energy industry. What happened?

   (1) There was a major meltdown.
   (2) Nothing happened.
   (3) It was switched from nuclear to coal capability.
   (4) A bad shipment of nuclear material was processed.
   (5) Radioactivity was released.

ITEMS 7 AND 8 REFER TO THE FOLLOWING TABLE.

BLIZZARD OF 1978

	Massachusetts	Rhode Island	New Hampshire	Maine	New Jersey
Deaths	73	26	0	0	0
Injured or Ill	4,324	232	28	3	0
Hospitalized	483	50	1	0	0
Houses Destroyed	301	0	13	22	3
Persons Sheltered	23,520	9,150	483	0	155

7. Which state suffered the greatest damage during the blizzard of 1978?

   (1) Rhode Island
   (2) New Hampshire
   (3) Massachusetts
   (4) Maine
   (5) New Jersey

8. How many people died in the blizzard of 1978?

   (1) 483
   (2) 232
   (3) 99
   (4) 26
   (5) 73

PERIODIC TABLE OF THE ELEMENTS

Atomic number

| 1 |
| H |
| 1.0079 |

Atomic mass

1A		2A
1 H 1.0080		4 Be 9.0122
3 Li 6.941		12 Mg 24.305
11 Na 22.9898		20 Ca 40.08
19 K 39.102		38 Sr 87.62
37 Rb 85.468		56 Ba 137.34
55 Cs 132.91		88 Ra (226)
87 Fr (223)		

Transition elements (d block)

3B	4B	5B	6B	7B	8B	8B	8B	1B	2B
21 Sc 44.96	22 Ti 47.90	23 V 50.94	24 Cr 51.996	25 Mn 54.94	26 Fe 55.85	27 Co 58.93	28 Ni 58.71	29 Cu 63.55	30 Zn 65.37
39 Y 88.91	40 Zr 91.22	41 Nb 92.91	42 Mo 95.94	43 Tc 98.91	44 Ru 101.07	45 Rh 102.91	46 Pd 106.4	47 Ag 107.87	48 Cd 112.4
	72 Hf 178.49	73 Ta 180.95	74 W 183.85	75 Re 186.2	76 Os 190.2	77 Ir 192.2	78 Pt 195.1	79 Au 196.97	80 Hg 200.59

Representative elements (p block)

3A	4A	5A	6A	7A	8A
					2 He 4.0026
5 B 10.81	6 C 12.011	7 N 14.007	8 O 15.9994	9 F 19.00	10 Ne 20.183
13 Al 26.98	14 Si 28.09	15 P 30.974	16 S 32.064	17 Cl 35.453	18 Ar 39.95
31 Ga 69.72	32 Ge 72.59	33 As 74.92	34 Se 78.96	35 Br 79.9	36 Kr 83.8
49 In 114.82	50 Sn 118.69	51 Sb 121.75	52 Te 127.6	53 I 126.9	54 Xe 131.3
81 Tl 204.37	82 Pb 207.2	83 Bi 208.98	84 Po (210)	85 At (210)	86 Rn (222)

57 La 138.91	58 Ce 140.12	59 Pr 140.91	60 Nd 144.24	61 Pm (147)	62 Sm 150.4	63 Eu 151.96	64 Gd 157.25	65 Tb 158.93	66 Dy 162.5	67 Ho 164.93	68 Er 167.26	69 Tm 168.93	70 Yb 173.04	71 Lu 174.97
89 Ac (227)	90 Th 232.04	91 Pa 231.04	92 U 238.03	93 Np 237.05	94 Pu (242)	95 Am (243)	96 Cm (247)	97 Bk (247)	98 Cf (247)	99 Es (254)	100 Fm (253)	101 Md (256)	102 No (254)	103 Lr (257)

Inner transition elements (f block)

9. The periodic table consists of horizontal rows called periods and vertical columns called groups. Those elements that have similar chemical properties appear in the same group. Which of the following elements is most similar to magnesium (Mg) in its chemical properties?

    (1) Sodium (Na)
    (2) Chlorine (Cl)
    (3) Potassium (K)
    (4) Calcium (Ca)
    (5) Zinc (Zn)

10. The atoms of different elements have different numbers of electrons and protons, corresponding to their atomic numbers. The number of electrons or protons in a neutral atom is called the atomic number of that element. Which of the following elements has the greatest number of electrons?

    (1) Argon (Ar)
    (2) Boron (B)
    (3) Cobalt (Co)
    (4) Phosphorus (P)
    (5) Fluorine (F)

11. The most reactive elements are the ones with only one electron or seven electrons in their outermost shells. The least reactive are the ones with eight electrons in their outermost shells. The group number suggests the number of electrons in the outermost shell of an atom. Which group contains the most reactive metals?

    (1) I A
    (2) III B
    (3) IV B
    (4) VII A
    (5) VIII A

12. The noble gases have eight electrons in their outermost shells. These elements tend not to react with other elements to form compounds. Which of the following elements belongs to the group of noble gases?

    (1) Oxygen (O)
    (2) Neon (Ne)
    (3) Sulfur (S)
    (4) Hydrogen (H)
    (5) Nitrogen (N)

13. One half of the moon's surface is always illuminated by the sun. Yet from the earth, the moon appears to change its shape as it goes through a cycle of phases. Which of the following explains why an observer on the earth sees the phases of the moon?

    (1) The moon revolves around the sun.
    (2) The moon rotates on its axis.
    (3) The earth revolves around the sun.
    (4) The moon revolves around the earth.
    (5) The moon can change its shape.

ITEM 14 REFERS TO THE DIAGRAM BELOW.

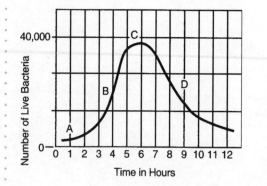

14. The illustration above depicts which one of the following?

(1) Seasons of the year

(2) Solar eclipse

(3) Lunar eclipse

(4) Sunspots

(5) The effect of tides

ITEMS 15 TO 19 REFER TO THE FOLLOWING EXPERIMENT.

Below is a graph describing the results of an experiment that was done by a biologist. He put live bacteria and growth medium (food for bacteria to live on) into a closed container. He then counted the number of live bacteria every half-hour for a 16-hour period.

15. Which of the following choices correctly describes the process by which the bacteria grew?

(1) Fission

(2) Sporing

(3) Vegetative propagation

(4) Meiosis

(5) Sexual reproduction

16. The bacteria used in the experiment reproduce every half-hour. If the experiment was started with 1 cell, how many would there be 4 hours later?

(1) 8

(2) 16

(3) 256

(4) 512

(5) 40,000

17. What is happening at point "B" on the graph?

(1) The temperature is increasing rapidly.

(2) The number of bacteria is increasing rapidly.

(3) The bacteria are getting larger.

(4) The number of bacteria is decreasing slowly.

(5) Cannot be determined from the information given.

18. Why did the number of live bacteria decrease at point "D"?

(1) The temperature decreased.

(2) The bacteria ran out of food.

(3) The bacteria got larger.

(4) High temperature killed all of the bacteria.

(5) The bacteria were poisoned by their own waste products.

19. Which of the following can be inferred from the results of this experiment?

(1) Bacteria can grow anywhere, anytime.

(2) Bacteria can be easily eliminated with cleaners.

(3) It takes a very long time for bacteria to grow.

(4) It is important to store leftover food correctly.

(5) Bacteria pose a very real threat to people.

ITEMS 20 TO 22 REFER TO THE DIAGRAM BELOW.

The diagram represents resistors R_1 and R_2, connected to a constant power source of 40 volts.

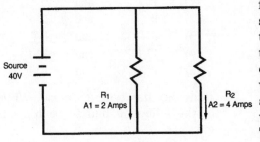

20. The voltage drop across R_1 is

(1) 10

(2) 12

(3) 15

(4) 40

(5) 50

21. The power (P = Volts × Current) supplied to the circuit, in watts, is

(1) 80

(2) 120

(3) 160

(4) 240

(5) 300

22. Stanley wants to increase the current in A2. Which of the following will achieve this result?

(1) Increase the resistance of R_2.

(2) Increase the resistance of R_1.

(3) Decrease the voltage of the source.

(4) Add another resistor.

(5) It can't be done.

ITEMS 23 TO 25 REFER TO THE FOLLOWING INFORMATION.

Microwave ovens use a principle of heating different from that employed by ordinary ovens. The key part of a microwave oven is its magnetron, which generates the microwaves that then go into the oven. Some of these energy waves hit the food directly, while others bounce around the oven until they find their way into the food. Sometimes the microwaves intersect, strengthening their effect. Sometimes they cancel each other out. Parts of the food may be heavily saturated with energy, while other parts may receive very little. In conventional cooking, you select the oven temperature. In microwave cooking, you select the power level. The walls of the microwave oven are made of metal, which helps the microwaves bounce off them. However, this turns to a disadvantage for the cook who uses metal cookware.

23. There are both advantages and disadvantages to microwave cooking. Based on the information given, which of the following is probably the greatest disadvantage of microwaving?

(1) Overcooked food

(2) Radioactive food

(3) Unevenly cooked food

(4) Expensive costs of preparing food

(5) Cold food

24. In a conventional oven, the temperature selection would be based upon degrees. In a microwave oven, the power selection would probably be based upon

(1) wattage.

(2) voltage.

(3) lumens.

(4) solar units.

(5) ohms.

25. What is the source of the microwaves in the oven?

(1) Reflected energy

(2) Convection currents

(3) The magnetron

(4) Short waves and bursts of energy

(5) The food itself

ITEMS 26 TO 28 REFER TO THE FOLLOWING INFORMATION.

Since each parent contributes one half of the genetic material to the offspring, the genes occur in pairs. Different forms of the same gene are called alleles. In human beings, multiple alleles determine blood type. These alleles are designated I^A, I^B, and i. The chart below indicates the possible combinations for each blood type.

Blood Type	Genotype
A	$I^A I^A$ or I^A i
B	$I^B I^B$ or I^B i
AB	$I^A I^B$
O	ii

26. John has type B blood. Which of the choices below could represent the genes of John's parents?

	Father		Mother
(1)	$I^A I^A$	and	ii
(2)	I^A i	and	I^A i
(3)	$I^A I^B$	and	ii
(4)	ii	and	ii
(5)	$I^A I^B$	and	$I^A I^A$

27. A person with type AB blood is sometimes called a universal recipient because he can receive blood from anyone. A person with type O blood is sometimes called a universal donor because he can give blood to anyone.

If Martha is a universal donor, what must have been the blood type of her parents?

	Father		Mother
(1)	$I^A I^A$	and	ii
(2)	ii	and	$I^B I^B$
(3)	ii	and	ii
(4)	$I^A I^A$	and	$I^A I^B$
(5)	$I^A I^B$	and	$I^A I^B$

28. Baby Jay has type AB blood. Which of the following had to be his parents?

	Father		Mother
(1)	$I^A I^A$	and	$I^A I^A$
(2)	I^A i	and	I^A i
(3)	$I^A I^B$	and	ii
(4)	I^A i	and	I^B i
(5)	I^B i	and	$I^B I^B$

ITEMS 29 AND 30 REFER TO THE FOLLOWING GRAPH.

The pH Scale

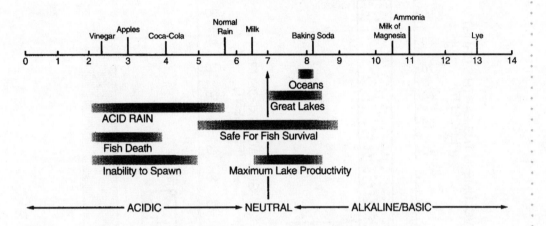

pH values of common acid and alkaline substances;
a lower value denotes a higher acid content.

29. According to the graph, which of the following best defines acid rain?

    (1) Precipitation having a pH less than normal rain

    (2) Precipitation having a pH between 6 and 7

    (3) Precipitation that has a pH greater than the pH of ocean water

    (4) Precipitation that always results in death to fish

    (5) Precipitation that results in maximum lake productivity

30. Which of the following best describes the pH of normal rain?

    (1) Extremely acidic

    (2) Slightly acidic

    (3) Neutral

    (4) Slightly alkaline

    (5) Extremely alkaline

ITEMS 31 TO 34 REFER TO THE FOLLOWING TWO GRAPHS.

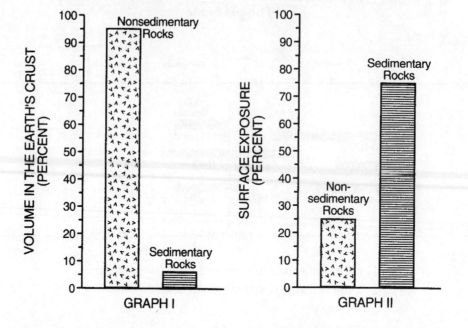

GRAPH I

GRAPH II

31. What do the two graphs indicate?

   (1) The arrangement of materials on the earth's surface

   (2) The advantage of sedimentary rocks

   (3) The contents of nonsedimentary rocks

   (4) The contents of the earth's core

   (5) The composition of the earth's crust

32. According to the graphs, approximately what percentage of the earth's crust is composed of sedimentary rock?

   (1) 5%

   (2) 25%

   (3) 45%

   (4) 75%

   (5) 95%

33. All of the rocks represented in graph I must contain which of the following?

   (1) Minerals

   (2) Fossils

   (3) Outcrops

   (4) Sediments

   (5) Shale

34. Which of the following statements can be inferred from the data shown on the graphs?

   (1) The crust of the earth is composed mostly of sedimentary rocks.

   (2) Rock outcrops on the earth's surface are chiefly of the nonsedimentary type.

   (3) Most nonsedimentary rocks are composed of the melted remains of sedimentary rocks.

   (4) Most sedimentary rock is found at or near the surface of the earth.

   (5) Most sedimentary rocks are found deep within the earth's core.

practice test

ITEMS 35 AND 36 REFER TO THE FOLLOWING INFORMATION.

Energy is needed to heat water. Our gas or electric bill indicates this at the end of each month. To heat 1 gram of water 1 Centigrade degree requires 1 calorie of energy.

35. How many calories are required to heat 200 grams of water for tea from 20°C to 100°C?

(1) 200

(2) 1,000

(3) 1,600

(4) 4,000

(5) 16,000

36. Suppose that you had enough fuel left in your camping heater to supply 180,000 calories of heat. If the water was supplied from a stream at 10°C, how many grams of water could be heated to boiling (100°C)?

(1) 200

(2) 800

(3) 1,000

(4) 2,000

(5) 20,000

37. Chemicals act like people. When they are put under stress, they tend to do anything they can to reduce that stress. When more chemicals are added to one side of the reaction below, then this excess stress will be used up when it reacts to form more chemicals on the other side of the reaction.

Chlorine is obtained from salt (sodium chloride) by the formula: Sodium Chloride <−> Sodium + Chlorine
If the concentration of sodium is increased in the reaction container, how will this affect the concentration of chlorine and salt produced?

(1) More chlorine and salt

(2) More chlorine and less salt

(3) Less chlorine and salt

(4) Less chlorine and more salt

(5) No change

ITEMS 38 TO 41 REFER TO THE FOLLOWING GRAPH.

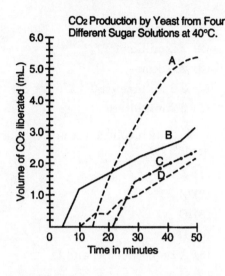

CO₂ Production by Yeast from Four Different Sugar Solutions at 40°C.

38. What does this graph measure?

(1) The O_2 produced by CO_2 in a yeast culture

(2) The waste products of sugar solutions infused with CO_2

(3) The CO_2 produced from yeast culture placed in a water solution of four different sugars of the same concentration

(4) The water produced from yeast culture placed in four different salt solutions

(5) The CO_2 produced from a yeast culture placed in a yeast solution of four different sugar solutions at 55°C

39. What was the volume of CO_2 liberated from solution B after 30 minutes?

   (1) 2.2 microns

   (2) 2.2 millimeters

   (3) 2.2 liters

   (4) 3.0 millimeters

   (5) 2.2 milliliters

40. From which solution was CO_2 liberated first?

   (1) A

   (2) B

   (3) C

   (4) D

   (5) A tie between C and D

41. Which of the following processes could this graph be recording?

   (1) Respiration

   (2) Circulation

   (3) Bread production

   (4) Photosynthesis

   (5) Candy production

ITEM 42 REFERS TO THE FOLLOWING DIAGRAM.

The diagram below shows the discharge measured at a point in a stream during a period of one year.

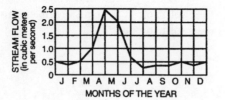

42. According to the diagram, when does the greatest change in stream flow occur?

   (1) January 1 to March 1

   (2) March 1 to May 1

   (3) May 1

   (4) May 1 to July 1

   (5) October 1 to December 1

ITEMS 43 TO 46 REFER TO THE FOLLOWING SELECTION.

It seems that not a season goes by without at least one diet book high on the best-seller list. Some diets advocated by these books are simply variations of a basic, safe 1,000- to 1,200-calorie balanced diet. But others may be downright dangerous, as they emphasize one food or food group and the elimination of others—in other words, they advocate diets that are unbalanced.

Some of these diets fraudulently claim that certain foods have the ability to "burn fat." No food can do that. Body fat is "burned" or gotten rid of only by using more energy than is supplied by the food you eat.

One extreme form of this type of diet—a liquid protein diet containing fewer than 400 calories a day—was linked to 17 deaths in 1977 and 1978. Scientists who studied the deaths found that the dieters had died of irregular heart rhythms and cardiac arrest.

The Food and Drug Administration now requires warning labels on weight-reduction products when more than 50 percent of the product's calories come from protein.

Other low-calorie liquid and powdered products have appeared on the market recently with a lower proportion of protein. But consumers should be aware that any diet of fewer than 800 calories a day is potentially dangerous and should be undertaken only under medical supervision.

43. Under which of the following conditions will body fat be burned?

    (1) When you stop exercising

    (2) When you eat a high-protein diet

    (3) When you eat certain foods

    (4) Only if you consume a high carbohydrate diet

    (5) When you use more calories than you consume

44. According to the reading, which of the following is the reason that liquid protein diets may be dangerous?

    (1) Ketones are burned.

    (2) Dieters may suffer cardiac arrest.

    (3) Carbohydrates are excreted.

    (4) Body fat is burned.

    (5) Fat deposits are broken down more quickly than carbohydrates.

45. According to this passage, a person on a diet of 600 calories a day could expect to

    (1) die from an irregular heart rhythm.

    (2) gain weight first and then lose weight slowly.

    (3) lose weight first and then gain it back.

    (4) lose a pound of fat each day.

    (5) lose weight fairly rapidly.

46. An average daily balanced diet for people who wish to lose weight should contain how many calories?

    (1) Between 400 and 800

    (2) Between 800 and 1,000

    (3) Between 1,000 and 1,200

    (4) Between 1,500 and 2,000

    (5) Between 2,000 and 3,000

ITEMS 47 TO 49 REFER TO THE FOLLOWING EXPERIMENT.

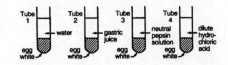

47. For the experiment to be valid, which of the following must be true?

    (1) All four test tubes must have varying temperatures.

    (2) The same person must handle the test tubes.

    (3) The substances must be added to the test tubes at precisely the same moment.

    (4) All four test tubes must be kept at a constant temperature.

    (5) The test tubes must be kept in the same position.

48. Which nutrient is being acted upon in this experiment?

    (1) Sugar

    (2) Starch

    (3) Protein

    (4) Fat

    (5) Liquid

49. In which test tube would the egg white dissolve most rapidly?

    (1) 1

    (2) 2

    (3) 3

    (4) 4

    (5) 1 and 2

50. Diets high in saturated fat and cholesterol have been linked to heart disease and a diet high in fat to some cancers. If you wish to cut down on saturated fats and cholesterol in your diet, which of the following foods should you avoid?

(1) Fish

(2) Poultry

(3) Dry beans and peas

(4) Cheese

(5) Spaghetti

TEST 4: LANGUAGE ARTS, READING

65 Minutes • 40 Questions

Directions: The Language Arts, Reading Test consists of multiple-choice questions based on a variety of excerpts from literary and nonfiction writings. Read each selection carefully and then answer the questions based upon it. You may refer to the selection as often as necessary to answer the questions. However, do not spend more time than necessary on any one item. Record your answers on the Language Arts, Reading Section of your answer sheet.

Q He died at eventide . . . I saw his breath beat quicker and quicker, pause, and then his little soul leapt like a star that travels in the night and left a world of darkness in its train. The day changed not . . . Only in the chamber of death writhed the world's most piteous thing—a childless mother.

The reader can infer that death has come to (a)n

- **(1)** old man.
- **(2)** favorite dog.
- **(3)** child.
- **(4)** mother.
- **(5)** soldier.   ① ② ● ④ ⑤

A The correct answer is "child"; therefore, you should blacken answer space (3) on your answer sheet.

ITEMS 1 TO 6 REFER TO THE FOLLOWING SELECTION.

What Is on Georgiana's Cheek?

Line The crimson hand, which at first had been strongly visible upon the marble paleness of Georgiana's cheek, now grew more faintly
(5) outlined. She remained not less pale than ever; but the birthmark, with every breath that came and went, lost somewhat of its former distinctness. Its presence had been
(10) awful; its departure was more awful still. Watch the stain of the rainbow fading out of the sky, and you will know how the mysterious symbol passed away.
(15) "By Heaven! it is well-nigh gone!" said Aylmer to himself, in almost irrepressible ecstasy. "I can scarcely trace it now. Success! Success! And now it is like the faintest
(20) rose color. The lightest flush of blood across her cheek would overcome it. But she is so pale!"

He drew aside the window curtain and suffered the light of natural day
(25) to fall into the room and rest upon her cheek. At the same time he heard a gross, hoarse chuckle, which he had long known as his servant Aminadab's expression of delight.
(30) "Ah, clod! ah, earthly mass!" cried Aylmer, laughing in a sort of frenzy. "You have served me well! Matter and spirit—earth and heaven—have both done their part in this! Laugh, thing of
(35) the senses! You have earned the right to laugh."

These exclamations broke Georgiana's sleep. She slowly unclosed her eyes and gazed into the mirror which
(40) her husband had arranged for that purpose. A faint smile flitted over her lips when she recognized how barely perceptible was now that crimson hand which had once blazed with such
(45) disastrous brilliancy as to scare away all their happiness. But then her eyes sought Aylmer's face with a trouble and anxiety that he could by no means account for.
(50) "My poor Aylmer!" murmured she.

"Poor? Nay, richest, happiest, most favored!" exclaimed he. "My peerless bride, it is successful! You are perfect!"

"My poor Aylmer," she repeated with
(55) a more than human tenderness, "you have aimed loftily; you have done nobly. Do not repent that with so high and pure a feeling, you have rejected the best the earth could offer. Aylmer,
(60) dearest Aylmer, I am dying!"

—from "The Birthmark"
by *Nathaniel Hawthorne*

1. What can we infer about Aylmer?

   (1) He does not love Georgiana.

   (2) He is trying to kill his wife.

   (3) He is disappointed at the result.

   (4) He has performed some operation on his wife.

   (5) He has caused his wife to commit suicide.

2. The birthmark is in the shape of a(n)

   (1) crimson hand.

   (2) pale rose.

   (3) rainbow.

   (4) butterfly.

   (5) all-over flush.

3. Which of the following statements correctly describes what happens to the mysterious symbol on Georgiana's cheek?

   (1) It does not change.

   (2) Its color deepens.

   (3) It begins to fade.

   (4) It is completely obliterated.

   (5) Its shape changes.

4. How does Aylmer regard Georgiana in the end of the passage?

   (1) Humorous

   (2) Flawless

   (3) Amusing

   (4) Unappreciative

   (5) Moody

5. What is the main idea of this selection?

   (1) Perfection cannot be achieved on Earth.

   (2) Birthmarks should be removed.

   (3) Leave well enough alone.

   (4) Beauty is in the eye of the beholder.

   (5) Love conquers all.

6. Sometimes, in the process of trying to help someone we love, we actually wind up hurting them instead. How does this possibility relate to this selection?

   (1) Aylmer was superstitious and performed some sort of magical rite on Georgiana's cheek.

   (2) He botched the operation because he loved his wife too much.

   (3) The crimson hand was a symbol of love, but Aylmer didn't see it.

   (4) Georgiana's eagerness to be beautiful cost her her life.

   (5) In trying to help Georgiana, Aylmer harmed her instead.

ITEMS 7 TO 12 REFER TO THE FOLLOWING POEM.

What Happened to Ozymandias?
Ozymandias

Line　I met a traveler from an antique land

Who said: "Two vast and trunkless legs of stone

Stand in the desert. Near them, on the sand,

Half sunk, a shattered visage lies, whose frown

(5)　And wrinkled lip, and sneer of cold command,

Tell that its sculptor well those passions read

Which yet survive, stamped on these lifeless things,

The hand that mocked them, and the heart that fed:

And on the pedestal these words appear:

(10)　'My name is Ozymandias, king of kings:

Look on my works, ye Mighty, and despair!'

Nothing beside remains. Round the decay

Of that colossal wreck, boundless and bare

The lone and level sands stretch far away."

—*Percy Bysshe Shelley*

practice test

7. Which of the following is Shelley NOT writing about in this poem?

   (1) The sin of pride

   (2) An ancient pharaoh or king

   (3) The healing process

   (4) A wrecked statue in the desert

   (5) A tale told by a tourist

8. Who can the reader assume Ozymandias was?

   (1) The kind and benevolent ruler

   (2) Alexander the Great

   (3) A sculptor of ancient Greece

   (4) A haughty king of ancient times

   (5) A traveler in the desert

9. What is the "shattered visage" the author writes about?

   (1) A broken promise

   (2) A torn sheet of papyrus

   (3) A shattered head

   (4) A smashed statue

   (5) None of the above

10. The repetition of sounds in "boundless and bare / The lone and level sands stretch far away." (lines 13 and 14) provide an example of which of the following?

   (1) Simile

   (2) Alliteration

   (3) Onomatopoeia

   (4) Personification

   (5) Metaphor

11. Which of the following best describes the meaning of this poem?

   (1) Time heals all wounds.

   (2) Here today, gone tomorrow.

   (3) The bigger they are, the harder they fall.

   (4) Even the mighty are mortal.

   (5) Pride goeth before a fall.

12. What does Shelley mean by "an antique land"?

   (1) A country from ancient times

   (2) A country with many old fallen sculptures

   (3) Egypt

   (4) Arabia's desert culture

   (5) Ozymandias

ITEMS 13 TO 18 REFER TO THE FOLLOWING SELECTION.

Who Are Binnie and Mrs. Teenie Thompson?

Line There was an insane youth of twenty, twice released from Dunning. He had a smooth tan face, overlaid with oil. His name was Binnie. Or *(5)* perhaps it was Bennie, or Benjamin. But his mother lovingly called him "Binnie." Binnie strode the halls, with huge eyes, direct and annoyed. He strode, and played "catch" with *(10)* a broken watch, which was attached to a long string wound around his left arm. There was no annoyance in his eyes when he spoke to Maud Martha, though, and none in his *(15)* nice voice. He was very fond of Maud Martha. Once, when she answered a rap on the door, there he was, and he pushed in before she could open her mouth. He had *(20)* on a new belt, he said. "My Uncle John gave it to me," he said. "So my pants won't fall down." He walked about the apartment, after closing the door with a careful sneer. *(25)* He touched things. He pulled a petal from a pink rose with savage anger, then kissed it with a tenderness that was more terrible than the anger; briskly he rapped on the *(30)* table, turned suddenly to stare at her, to see if she approved of what he was doing—she smiled uncertainly; he saw the big bed, fingered it, sat on it, got up, kicked it. He *(35)* opened a dresser drawer, took out a

ruler. "This is ni-ce—but I won't take it" (with firm decision, noble virtue). "I'll put it back." He spoke of his aunt, his Uncle John's wife
(40) Octavia. "She's ni-ce—you know, she can even call me, and I don't even get mad." With another careful sneer, he opened the door. He went out.

Mrs. Teenie Thompson. Fifty-three;
(45) and pepper whenever she talked of the North Shore people who had employed her as housemaid for ten years. "She went to huggin' and kissin' of me—course I got to receive
(50) it—I got to work for 'em. But they think they got me thinkin' they love me. Then I'm supposed to kill my silly self slavin' for 'em. To be worthy of their love. These old whi' folks.
(55) They jive you, honey. Well, I jive 'em just like they jive me."

—from "Neighbors"
by *Gwendolyn Brooks*

13. What was one of Binnie's favorite games?

   (1) Bouncing on beds

   (2) Snapping his belt

   (3) Knocking on doors and then hiding

   (4) Playing catch with his watch

   (5) Calling his Aunt Octavia and hanging up

14. How did Maud feel while Binnie was in her apartment?

   (1) Exhausted

   (2) Frightened

   (3) Happy

   (4) Annoyed

   (5) Flattered

15. Which of the following best describes the "North Shore people" Mrs. Teenie Thompson speaks about in lines 48–56?

   (1) Young

   (2) Southern

   (3) Rich

   (4) Affectionate

   (5) Poor

16. Why is the phrase describing Mrs. Teenie Thompson as "pepper whenever she spoke of the North Shore people who had employed her" especially effective?

   (1) It succinctly describes her anger at her employers.

   (2) It clearly describes her admiration for her employers.

   (3) It describes her love of her job.

   (4) It describes how she treats Binnie.

   (5) It explains her relationship with Binnie.

17. What is Dunning?

   (1) It is a jail from which Binnie was just released.

   (2) It is a well-known reformatory.

   (3) It represents the name of a nearby town.

   (4) It is the name of Binnie's uncle's home.

   (5) It is probably a mental institution.

18. How can Binnie's behavior best be described?

   (1) He is humorous, childish, and annoying.

   (2) He is restless and explosive.

   (3) He is violent but affectionate with his family and neighbors.

   (4) He is attention-seeking but helpful.

   (5) He relates well to everyone he meets.

practice test

ITEMS 19 TO 24 REFER TO THE FOLLOWING EXCERPT FROM A PLAY.

What Makes a Lady?

Line LIZA: But it was from you that I learnt really nice manners; and that is what makes one a lady, isn't it? You see it was so very difficult for
(5) me with the example of Professor Higgins always before me. I was brought up to be just like him, unable to control myself, and using bad language on the slightest provo-
(10) cation.

HIGGINS: Well!!

PICKERING: Oh, that's only his way, you know. He doesn't mean it.

LIZA: [*Continuing.*] It was just like
(15) learning to dance in the fashionable way: there was nothing more than that in it. But do you know what began my real education?

PICKERING: What?

(20) LIZA: [*Stopping her work for a moment.*] Your calling me Miss Doolittle that day when I first came to Wimpole Street. That was the beginning of self-respect for me. [*She*
(25) *resumes stitching.*] And there were a hundred little things you never noticed, because they came naturally to you. Things about standing up and taking off your hat and opening
(30) doors.

PICKERING: Oh, that was nothing.

LIZA: Yes: things that showed you thought and felt about me as if I were something better than a scul-
(35) lery-maid. You never took off your boots in the dining room when I was there.

PICKERING: You mustn't mind that. Higgins takes off his boots all
(40) over the place.

LIZA: I know. I am not blaming him. It is his way, isn't it? But it made such a difference to me that you didn't do it. I shall always be
(45) a flower girl to Professor Higgins, because he always treats me as a flower girl, and always will; but I know I can be a lady to you, because you always treat me as a
(50) lady, and always will.

PICKERING: Well, this is really very nice of you, Miss Doolittle.

LIZA: I should like you to call me Eliza, now, if you would.

(55) PICKERING: Thank you. Eliza, of course.

LIZA: And I should like Professor Higgins to call me Miss Doolittle.

HIGGINS: I'll see you damned first.

(60) MRS HIGGINS: Henry! Henry!

PICKERING: [*Laughing.*] Why don't you slang back at him? Don't stand it. It would do him a lot of good.

LIZA: I can't. I could have done it
(65) once; but now I can't go back to it. You told me, you know, that when a child is brought to a foreign country, it picks up the language in a few weeks, and forgets its own. Well,
(70) I am a child in your country. I have forgotten my own language, and can speak nothing but yours. That's the real breakoff with the corner of Tottenham Court Road. Leaving
(75) Wimpole Street finishes it.

PICKERING: [*Much alarmed.*] Oh! but you're coming back to Wimpole Street, aren't you? You'll forgive Higgins?

(80) HIGGINS: [*Rising.*] Forgive! Will she, by George! Let her go. Let her find out how she can get on without us. She will relapse into the gutter in three weeks without me at her
(85) elbow.

—from *Pygmalion* by *Bernard Shaw*. Used by permission of The Society of Authors on behalf of the Bernard Shaw Estate.

19. What effect has Pickering's behavior toward Liza had on her?

    (1) It taught her what it feels like to be a "lady."

    (2) It made her understand the meaning of good manners.

    (3) It taught her about kindness.

    (4) Choices (1), (2), and (3)

    (5) It made her feel humble.

20. By asking that Higgins call her "Miss Doolittle," what does Eliza indicate?

    (1) That Higgins has just arrived

    (2) The many injustices she felt from being a flower girl

    (3) Her admiration for Higgins

    (4) Her willingness to continue her education

    (5) Her displeasure that Higgins treats her like a maid

21. People sometimes say to youngsters they're trying to influence, "Do as I say, not as I do!" How is this advice related to the way Liza perceives Pickering?

    (1) It directly expresses her view of Pickering's message.

    (2) This expression has nothing to do with this selection.

    (3) It is the opposite of how she sees Pickering.

    (4) Liza sees Pickering as a nag who says similar things to her.

    (5) It suggests that Pickering sets a poor example with his actions.

22. Which of the following is true, according to this selection?

    (1) Liza has much to learn about manners.

    (2) Professor Higgins is bad-mannered and ill-tempered.

    (3) There is bad feeling between Pickering and Professor Higgins.

    (4) Professor Higgins thinks poorly of Pickering and Liza.

    (5) Liza is probably about to curse Professor Higgins.

23. What does Higgins mean in his last speech when he says, "She will relapse into the gutter"?

    (1) He admires Liza for her spunk.

    (2) Liza will lose all grace and manners.

    (3) Liza will become ill.

    (4) Liza's drinking problem will become more pronounced.

    (5) Liza will live in a shanty hut with the other street urchins.

24. If Liza were alive today, which of the following would she most likely endorse?

    (1) Free higher education for everyone

    (2) Giving everyone a patch of land to garden

    (3) Selling flowers at tourist attractions

    (4) Taking off your boots in the dining room

    (5) Referring to people only by their last names

practice test

ITEMS 25 TO 30 REFER TO THE FOLLOWING SELECTION.

A Colorful Childhood

Line After the war had ended, 6-year-old Roslyn and her mother relocated to Yokohama. They moved into a small European-style stucco house which
(5) served as the gate house to the former British Embassy residence in Japan. This main residence now housed the female social workers of the American Red Cross, and her mother, Ruth, who
(10) had been widowed during the war, had just been hired as the housekeeper. But the rest of the city had been leveled, with its people mostly living in improvised tin huts.

(15) Their neighborhood was called the "Bluff," a community of colorful English-style two-story stone residences perched on top of a hill overlooking the big harbor. Europeans had lived
(20) there for many decades.

There was an international cemetery nearby, where Roslyn's father was buried among the many other foreigners who had come to Japan and died
(25) there. The names and different styles of the tombstones and burial plots showed their diverse origins—Russian, French, English, even American, and many others representing various
(30) religions and backgrounds.

Roslyn's father had been a musician from Germany who had brought his young wife and baby daughter to live in Japan before World War II began.
(35) He had died soon after of natural causes. Roslyn remembered him well, however. He had been a gentle, attentive father, who had taught his violin students at their house.

(40) Roslyn's best friend was Minette, whose father was Japanese, her mother French. Because she had been born while her parents were visiting Hawaii, Minette was an American by
(45) nationality. Her other friend, Guy, had a Russian mother and French father.

Guy's mother supported them, while his father spent much time playing tennis and bullying Guy.

(50) All the children were multilingual, speaking Japanese to each other when playing, but usually some other language at home, according to their parents' nationality. Roslyn spoke Ger-
(55) man to her Mom, Japanese to her friends, and English in school. It seemed totally natural and effortless.

Three years later, Roslyn and Ruth boarded a freighter, the *President*
(60) *Grant*, and emigrated to the United States to join their relatives. The dozen or so passengers included a hunter who was bringing back some two thousand exotic animals and birds
(65) for the St. Louis Zoo. Roslyn spent the days playing with many of them, especially a soft little long-armed baby gibbon ape that swung himself happily around the ship, but liked most of all
(70) to sit on her ankle as she walked.

The trip across the Pacific to San Francisco took almost six weeks. Once the tiny ship survived a serious day-long storm. Waves dashed against the
(75) round porthole windows. As the ship was thrown about dangerously, unsecured items, including heavy metal drawers from under the bunk beds, were dislodged and flew around
(80) Roslyn's small cabin. Someone said an earthquake from the ocean floor had been detected. Everyone, both human and animal, was terrified and seasick and grateful when it ended.

—From *A Colorful Childhood*,
by S. Lenchiner, 2005.
Used by permission.

25. Which of the following is a TRUE statement according to this passage?

   (1) This story is about a large Japanese family.

   (2) Roslyn was an only child.

   (3) Roslyn's mother was a violinist.

   (4) Earthquakes happen regularly in Japan.

   (5) Everyone in Japan is Japanese.

26. What is the overall tone or mood of this story?

   (1) More or less neutral.

   (2) Extremely sad, because of the mention of war.

   (3) Hilariously funny.

   (4) Ironic and sarcastic.

   (5) Satiric.

27. What can you infer as to the reason the city of Yokohama was "leveled"?

   (1) There must have been a major earthquake.

   (2) Japan was modernizing its cities.

   (3) It had been bombed during the war.

   (4) Yokohama was putting in level one-family houses.

   (5) It was too full of hills for a city.

28. Which of the following is a FALSE statement?

   (1) Roslyn's mother worked for the American Red Cross.

   (2) Her father had died.

   (3) Crossing the Pacific took over a month.

   (4) The "Bluff" was a hill in Yokohama.

   (5) Foreigners rarely came to Japan.

29. Why didn't Roslyn and her friends speak just one language?

   (1) They couldn't all learn Japanese.

   (2) They went to different schools.

   (3) They did all speak just one language—English.

   (4) They were of different nationalities.

   (5) None of the above.

30. Why did the *President Grant* carry only a dozen passengers?

   (1) It was a very small vessel.

   (2) Because of all the wildlife on board, there was little room.

   (3) It was a freighter, which normally is meant mainly for cargo.

   (4) Because of all the noise, people didn't want to ride on it.

   (5) It was too luxurious and costly for most people.

ITEMS 31 TO 35 REFER TO THE FOLLOWING FILM REVIEW.

What Are the Effects of *Chocolat*?

Line The movie *Chocolat* is a delightful charmer, a treat for the eyes and soul.

A lovely mysterious young woman, *(5)* a single parent called Vianne Rocher (played by Juliette Binoche), one day in the winter of 1959, arrives in a sleepy French village. It is a typical little town where everyone *(10)* knows his place, and almost everyone behaves according to age-old rules. Her young daughter, Anouk (Victoire Thivisol), accompanies her. She has made arrangements to rent an empty *(15)* wreck of a store and miraculously turns it quickly into an elegant, inviting chocolate shop. Vianne immediately shocks the folks of the town by opening for business during Lent. *(20)* An unpardonable sin! And she befriends, one by one, the more

unusual but approachable citizens of the town. The mayor and local priest are shocked and feel threat-
(25) ened by her, and embark on a plan to sabotage the little shop and run Vianne out of town. But Vianne charms at least some of the villag-ers—the aroma of the chocolate being
(30) made into scrumptious concoctions, her warmth and caring, her open-ness and ability to respond to the desires and needs of the townsfolk. She gives out delicious samples, and
(35) listens to people's problems. But she refuses to attend church! And contrary to local custom wears her bright red shoes! A wandering vaga-bond (Johnny Depp) comes into
(40) town—an unwelcome intrusion into the "proper" village. A relationship and complications develop.

The movie, underneath the charm and humor of the story, deals with
(45) some serious issues—acceptance of "strange" or eccentric individuals, in-tolerance, cruelty, capacity for change, preconceived notions about who is a "good" person and who isn't. Its
(50) messages are there to be perceived by the viewer.

The acting is generally wonderful with great casting. Judi Dench plays an out-spoken, elderly and lonely grandmother;
(55) Alfred Molina, the self-righteous mayor and self-appointed keeper of the mor-als; Hugh O'Conor, the eager and am-bitious young priest who becomes the tool of the mayor; Lena Olin, the abused
(60) wife who is helped by Vianne to attain her independence; and, a brief appear-ance by Leslie Caron who plays a vil-lage matron.

The film was released in January
(65) 2001, runs 116 minutes, and has deli-cious cinematography by Roger Pratt. The script was written by Robert Nel-son Jacobs, who adapted the best-sell-ing book by Joanne Harris.
(70) See *Chocolat* with someone you love!

1/28/01

31. Where does the movie *Chocolat* take place?

    (1) In a chocolate factory
    (2) In the nineteenth century
    (3) In a French village
    (4) On a French farm
    (5) French Canada

32. How can you best describe Vianne?

    (1) She is a person who has a mind of her own.
    (2) She is a woman with poor taste in clothes.
    (3) She is clearly a troublemaker.
    (4) She is too friendly with the wrong people.
    (5) She must be fat from eating too much chocolate.

33. What is the reviewer's overall opin-ion of this movie?

    (1) That *Chocolat* is lacking in substance but fun anyway
    (2) That this is a romantic movie that can be enjoyed on many levels
    (3) That the movie is too long and rambling
    (4) That French villages make poor settings for movies
    (5) That Vianne should leave the village for her own sake and for the sake of the villagers

34. The title *Chocolat*

    (1) is a misspelling.
    (2) can be viewed as a metaphor for enjoyment and "doing your own thing."
    (3) shows that this is a light comedy.
    (4) comes from the name of the shop.
    (5) refers to the sweetness of Vianne.

35. Why is the village described as "sleepy"?

    (1) It has few shops and no night-life.

    (2) Everyone gets up late.

    (3) It is very small and dull.

    (4) All villages are sleepy.

    (5) Its inhabitants seem to be unwilling to change.

ITEMS 36 TO 40 REFER TO THE FOLLOWING DOCUMENT.

What Are the Responsibilities of Taking Out a Student Loan?

Line When you take out a student loan, you have certain responsibilities. Here are a few of them:

    When you sign a promissory note, *(5)* you're agreeing to repay the loan according to the terms of the note. The note is a binding legal document and states that you must repay the loan— even if you don't complete your educa- *(10)* tion (unless you were unable to complete your program of study because the school closed); aren't able to get a job after you complete the program; or are dissatisfied with, or don't *(15)* receive, the education you paid for. Think about what this obligation means before you take out a loan. If you don't repay your loan on time or according to the terms in your promis- *(20)* sory note, you may go into default, which has very serious consequences.

    You must make payments on your loan even if you don't receive a bill or repayment notice. Billing statements *(25)* are sent to you as a convenience, but you're obligated to make payments even if you don't receive any reminders.

    If you apply for a deferment, you *(30)* must continue to make payments until you are notified that the request has been granted. If you don't, you may end up in default. You should keep a copy of any request form you *(35)* submit, and you should document all contacts with the organization that holds your loan. You must notify the appropriate representative that manages your loan when you graduate, *(40)* withdraw from school, or drop below half-time status; change your name, address, or Social Security Number; or transfer to another school.

    If you borrow a Perkins Loan, your *(45)* loan will be managed by the school that lends you the money. If you borrow a Direct Loan, it will be managed by the Direct Loan Servicing Center. If you borrow a FFEL Program Loan, *(50)* your lender or its servicing agent will manage it. During your loan counseling session, you'll be given the name of the representative that manages your loan.

(55) If you default on your loan, the lender and the federal government may take action to recover the money and notify national credit bureaus of your default. This may affect your *(60)* credit rating for a long time. If you decide to return to school, you will not be able to receive any more federal student aid.

2000–2001 Financial Aid
The Student Guide
U.S. Department of Education

36. Which of the following represents the main message of this selection?

   (1) Getting a student loan is not a "big deal"—everyone should apply.

   (2) Colleges or schools issue all loans.

   (3) Taking out a student loan is a serious decision that should be thought through beforehand.

   (4) The author implies that people should be wary of loans and avoid them if possible.

   (5) It's better to get a loan through a bank than a college.

37. From this article, you can infer that a possible consequence of defaulting on your student loan is that

   (1) you could go into further debt.

   (2) you might have trouble buying a new car.

   (3) you will have to attend college less than half time.

   (4) you will have to drop out.

   (5) your college will fail you.

38. Where can you get a Perkins Loan?

   (1) Through a bank

   (2) Through your local credit union

   (3) Through the school you attend

   (4) Through a loan representative at Perkins

   (5) All of the above

39. You are studying medical technology at Southern State University in North Dakota after getting a $4,000 student loan. Midyear you decide that the courses are too hard and you're going to drop out. According to this article, what will happen now?

   (1) Since you only went to school half the year, you will just have to repay $2,000.

   (2) You won't have to be responsible for any part of the loan because you are no longer a student at Southern State.

   (3) You can probably use the unused portion of the loan at another school, so you needn't worry.

   (4) You will have to wait for a bill and then start repaying the loan.

   (5) You will notify your loan representative of your plans, and still be responsible for repaying the full amount of the loan according to the terms you had agreed to.

40. You have just made your third payment on a FFEL Program college loan and suddenly lose your job. What should you do now about the loan?

   (1) Just stop paying—they'll understand.

   (2) Call your loan representative and promise to start repaying your loan as soon as you find another job.

   (3) Use your charge card to put off paying.

   (4) Call your loan representative immediately and find out how to get a deferment on your loan.

   (5) Take out a bank loan so you can keep paying the college loan.

TEST 5: MATHEMATICS

90 Minutes • 50 Questions

Part 1—25 questions (a calculator is permitted): 45 minutes

Part 2—25 questions (a calculator is not permitted): 45 minutes

> **Directions:** The Mathematics Test consists of questions intended to measure general mathematics skills and problem-solving ability. The questions are based on short readings that often include a graph, chart, or figure. Work carefully, but do not spend too much time on any one question. Be sure you answer every question. You will not be penalized for incorrect answers.

Formulas you may need are given on page 712. Only some of the questions will require you to use a formula. Record your answers on the separate answer sheet. Be sure that all information is properly recorded.

There are three types of answers found on the answer sheet:

Type 1 is a regular format answer, which is the solution to a multiple-choice-type question. It requires shading in one of 5 bubble choices.

> **Q** Jill's drug store bill totals $8.68. How much change should she get if she pays with a $10.00 bill?
>
>   **(1)** $2.32
>   **(2)** $1.42
>   **(3)** $1.32
>   **(4)** $1.28
>   **(5)** $1.22
>
> ① ② ● ④ ⑤
>
> **A** The correct answer is "$1.32." Therefore, you should mark answer space (3) on your answer sheet.

Type 2 is an alternate format answer that is the solution to a Standard Grid "fill-in" type question. It requires shading in bubbles representing the actual numbers, including a decimal or division sign where applicable.

Type 3 is an alternate format answer that is the solution to a Coordinate Plane Grid problem. It requires shading in the bubble representing the correct coordinate of a graph.

For examples on how to record Type 2 and Type 3 answers, please refer to page 119.

FORMULAS

Description	Formula
AREA (*A*) of a:	
square	$A = s^2$; where s = side
rectangle	$A = lw$; where l = length, w = width
parallelogram	$A = bh$; where b = base, h = height
triangle	$A = \frac{1}{2}bh$; where b = base, h = height
circle	$A = \pi r^2$; where π = 3.14, r = radius
PERIMETER (*P*) of a:	
square	$P = 4s$; where s = side
rectangle	$P = 2l + 2w$; where l − length, w = width
triangle	$P = a + b + c$; where a, b, and c are the sides
Circumference (*C*) of a circle	$C = \pi d$; where π = 3.14, d = diameter
VOLUME (*V*) of a:	
cube	$V = s^3$; where s = side
rectangular container	$V = lwh$; where l = length, w = width, h = height
cylinder	$V = \pi r^2 h$; where π = 3.14, r = radius, h = height
square pyramid	Volume = $\frac{1}{3} \times$ (base edge)^2 $\times$ height
cone	Volume = $\frac{1}{3} \times \pi \times$ radius^2 $\times$ height; π is approximately equal to 3.14.
Pythagorean theorem	$c^2 = a^2 + b^2$; where c = hypotenuse, a and b are legs of a right triangle
distance (*d*) between two points in a plane	$d = \sqrt{(x_2 - x_1)^2 + (y_2 - y_1)^2}$; where (x_1, y_1) and (x_2, y_2) are two points in a plane
slope of a line (*m*)	$m = \dfrac{y_2 - y_1}{x_2 - x_1}$ where (x_1, y_1) and (x_2, y_2) are two points in a plane
trigonometric ratios	given an acute angle with measure x of a right triangle, $\sin x = \dfrac{\text{opposite}}{\text{hypotenuse}}$, $\cos x = \dfrac{\text{adjacent}}{\text{hypotenuse}}$, $\tan x = \dfrac{\text{opposite}}{\text{adjacent}}$
mean	mean = $\dfrac{x_1 + x_2 + \cdots + x_n}{n}$; where the x's are the values for which a mean is desired, and n = number of values in the series
median	median = the point in an ordered set of numbers at which half of the numbers are above and half of the numbers are below this value
simple interest (*i*)	$i = prt$; where p = principal, r = rate, t = time
distance (*d*) as function of rate and time	$d = rt$; where r = rate, t = time
total cost (*c*)	$c = nr$; where n = number of units, r = cost per unit

Part 1

You may now begin Part 1 of the Mathematics Test. You may use your calculator for this part. Bubble in the correct response to each question on Part 1 of your answer sheet.

1. A formula in physics, $D = A \times T^2$ relates the distance (D) traveled over a period of time (T). If A = 1, and D = 137, find T.

   (1) 3.7
   (2) 11.7
   (3) 13.2
   (4) 17.8
   (5) 68.5

2. Igor and Laura, standing at the foot (A) of a 1-mile-long hill, want to measure its height (BC) (see diagram). If the angle the hill makes with the ground is 20°, how many miles above the ground is the top (B)?

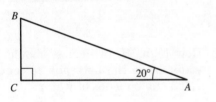

   (1) 0.27
   (2) 0.29
   (3) 0.34
   (4) 0.36
   (5) 0.94

3. Giant cement cubes in Salena, Italy, are stacked off-shore in the bay as a breakwater for ships. If the edge of each cube is 2.38 feet, find the volume, in cubic feet, of each one.

   (1) 1.5
   (2) 5.7
   (3) 7.14
   (4) 13.5
   (5) 14.28

4. In isosceles trapezoid *ABCD*, the side *AB* = 8.00, and m ∠ *A* = 15°. Find *h* to two decimal places (see diagram).

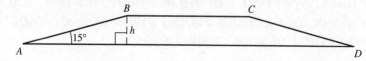

Mark your answer in the circles in the grid on your answer sheet.

ITEMS 5 AND 6 REFER TO THE FOLLOWING INFORMATION.

Al's Garage charges $25 per hour to service domestic cars and $30 per hour for foreign cars. Bob brought his 3-year-old Chevrolet to the garage for repairs. The worksheet for Bob's car shows that the following mechanics worked on Bob's car:

Carl for 5 hours 16 minutes
Anne for 3 hours 49 minutes
Ed for 37 minutes

5. What is the total time in hours for which Bob should be charged?

Mark your answer in the circles in the grid on your answer sheet.

6. If the bill for new parts totaled $84.25, what will Bob have to pay for parts and labor for this servicing?

(1) $158.25
(2) $242.50
(3) $326.75
(5) $375.25
(5) $459.50

ITEM 7 REFERS TO THE FOLLOWING PICTURE.

[Volume = 1,155 in³]

H

9

14

7. How high, *H*, in inches, should the water be in the fish tank to contain 1,155 cubic inches of water?

(1) $8\frac{1}{3}$

(2) $9\frac{1}{6}$

(3) $11\frac{1}{6}$

(4) $12\frac{1}{6}$

(5) $12\frac{5}{6}$

ITEM 8 REFERS TO THE FOLLOWING INFORMATION ABOUT THE SALE OF CAKES FROM B&B BAKERY ON WEDNESDAY.

Type of Cake	Selling Price ($/lb) to the Customer	Cost ($/lb) to the Baker	Amount (lbs) Sold
Apple Crumb	3.49	.97	25
Dutch Chocolate	3.99	1.06	50

8. What was the bakery's profit in dollars?

   (1) $87.25
   (2) $146.50
   (3) $199.50
   (4) $209.50
   (5) $286.75

9. Income tax in a certain state is figured at 2% of the first $1,000, 3% of the next $2,000, 4% of the next $3,000 and 5% thereafter. Find the tax on an income of $25,000.

   (1) $1,150
   (2) $1,015
   (3) $950
   (4) $200
   (5) $187

10. A small country has a population of 52,376 people in 2002. During the year 2003, the following statistics were recorded:

    Population growth factors
       Births   577
       Immigration   876
    Population decline factors
       Deaths   689
       Emigration   592

    What would be the new population in 2003?

    (1) 51,980
    (2) 52,204
    (3) 52,376
    (4) 52,548
    (5) 52,600

11. In a discount department store, a woman's suit was priced at $239. In the succeeding 3 weeks, it was discounted 3 times: first by 5%; then by 8%; and finally by 12%. What is the best approximation for the final sale price (in dollars)?

    (1) $79
    (2) $179
    (3) $184
    (4) $191
    (5) $225

12. Rose was designing an electrical circuit for her do-it-yourself project. In electrical theory, a formula used is:

$$I_1 = \frac{R_2}{R_1 + R_2} \times I_2$$

Find the value for I_1, if:
       $R_1 = 4$
       $R_2 = 4$
       $I_2 = 17$

Mark your answer in the circles in the grid on your answer sheet.

13. The top three batters for the Tigers, a Little League baseball team, had batting averages of 0.250, 0.273, and 0.302. What was their mean batting average?

Mark your answer in the circles in the grid on your answer sheet.

14. A real estate investor buys a house and lot for $44,000. He pays $1,250 to have it painted, $1,750 to fix the plumbing, and $1,000 for grading a driveway. At what price must he sell the property in order to make a 12% profit?

(1) $53,760

(2) $52,800

(3) $52,000

(4) $49,760

(5) $44,480

ITEMS 15 AND 16 REFER TO THE CHART BELOW.

Susanne's Cost of Preparing "Franks and Beans" at the Little League Ball Game on June 1, 2003

Food (package)	Cost($)	Portions/ package
Franks	1.75	8
Rolls	.83	10
Beans	.85	4

15. What was the cost of one dinner of franks and beans? (1 dinner is 1 frank, 1 roll, and 1 portion of beans.)

(1) $0.34

(2) $0.51

(3) $0.83

(4) $0.88

(5) $1.15

16. The cost of a dinner increased to $.58 in 2004. If Susanne sells a dinner for $2.50, how many dinners must she sell to be able to make at least a $500 profit?

(1) 199

(2) 200

(3) 261

(4) 290

(5) 301

ITEMS 17 AND 18 REFER TO THE GRID SHOWN.

17. Ben buys a rectangular parcel of land 4 km (km is a kilometer) by 8 km. On a graph paper, he marks off 1 km parallel lines across the length and width as shown:

If he builds his house at the center of the parcel, coordinates (0,0), what are the coordinates of the point farthest from his house in the Southeast (SE) quadrant, where he plans to erect a propane tank?

DO NOT MARK THE POINT ON THE GRAPH ABOVE.

Mark your answer on the coordinate plane grid on your answer sheet.

18. Ben decides to build a fence from the house to the tank. What is theapproximate length of the fence in kilometers?

    (1) 2.0

    (2) 2.4

    (3) 3.2

    (4) 4.5

    (5) 6.2

19. At the Apex company, five employees earn $15,000 per year, three employees earn $17,000 per year, and one employee earns $18,000 per year. What is the average yearly salary of these employees?

    (1) $17,000

    (2) $16,667

    (3) $16,448

    (4) $16,025

    (5) $16,000

20. Alice smokes 25 cigarettes each day and has finally found a reason to stop—to get healthier and in better physical shape. She also discovered that she had been spending a lot of money on her smoking habit.

    If cigarettes cost $4 per pack with 20 cigarettes in each pack, how long will it take her to save enough money to buy a $500 exercise bike?

    (1) 80 days

    (2) 100 days

    (3) 125 days

    (4) 156 days

    (5) 200 days

21. How much had she been spending each year for cigarettes? [1 year = 365 days]

    Mark your answer in the circles in the grid on your answer sheet.

22. Alice was making a salary of $18,000 per year. What percentage of her salary did she spend on buying cigarettes each year? Round off your answer to two decimal places.

    Mark your answer in the circles in the grid on your answer sheet.

    ITEMS 23 TO 25 REFER TO THE INFORMATION PROVIDED BY THE GRAPH BELOW.

    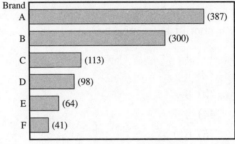

    CANS OF SOUP SOLD BY BRAND IN YEAR 2003 FROM SHOP4ALL SUPERMARKETS

    Number of cans (in thousands) sold

23. In 2003, approximately what percentage of all soup sold was made up of Brand A?

    (1) 30%

    (2) 33%

    (3) 39%

    (4) 42%

    (5) 54%

24. If the stock manager, Wanda, decided that only the top 3 most popular brands should be stocked in the year 2004, what percent of space would Brand B contain?

    (1) 15.0%

    (2) 30.0%

    (3) 32.5%

    (4) 37.5%

    (5) 47.5%

25. Wanda decides to arrange the cans of Brand B in a cube, held together with a stacking frame, as shown below:

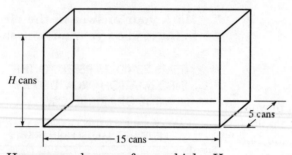

H cans

5 cans

15 cans

How many layers of cans high, H, should the stack be?

(1) 1

(2) 2

(3) 3

(4) 4

(5) 5

Part 2

You may not return to Part 1 of the Mathematics Test or use your calculator for this part. Fill in the correct response to each question on Part 2 of your answer sheet.

26. Louis had a shopping bag full of vegetables he just bought at the market containing the following: squash ($3\frac{1}{2}$ pounds), carrots ($2\frac{1}{3}$ pounds), and tomatoes ($1\frac{3}{4}$ pounds). How much did it weigh in pounds?

(1) $6\frac{1}{8}$

(2) $6\frac{5}{9}$

(3) $7\frac{1}{4}$

(4) $7\frac{9}{5}$

(5) $7\frac{7}{12}$

27. Samantha budgeted $35 for allowances to give to her 4 children. If each child received the same amount, how much did each get? Round off the answer to the nearest penny.

(1) $0.88

(2) $1.10

(3) $8.75

(4) $11.00

(5) $11.67

ITEM 28 REFERS TO THE FOLLOWING DIAGRAM OF A QUILTING PATTERN.

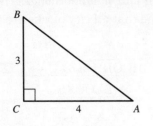

28. Find the sin A.

    (1) 0.6
    (2) 0.7
    (3) 0.8
    (4) 1.3
    (5) 1.7

29. How many pints of blood must be donated in order to supply 9,500 milliliters to the blood drive? (1 quart = 0.95 liters)

    (1) 18
    (2) 20
    (3) 22
    (4) 24
    (5) 26

30. In the movie set for *The Wizard of Oz,* the length of the Yellow Brick Road was 200 yards, and its width was 1.5 yards. How many square feet of yellow flooring material was necessary to cover the road?

    (1) 600
    (2) 1,000
    (3) 1,700
    (4) 2,700
    (5) 3,000

31. In a new car lot, $\frac{1}{4}$ of the cars were red and $\frac{3}{4}$ were green. At the end of the month, $\frac{1}{2}$ of the red cars were sold, and $\frac{1}{3}$ of the green ones were sold. What was the total fraction of cars sold?

Mark your answer in the circles in the grid on your answer sheet.

practice test

ITEMS 32 AND 33 REFER TO THE FOLLOWING GRAPHS.

The graphs below represent comparative land use in four neighborhoods. The area of each neighborhood is expressed in city blocks. Assume that all city blocks are the same size.

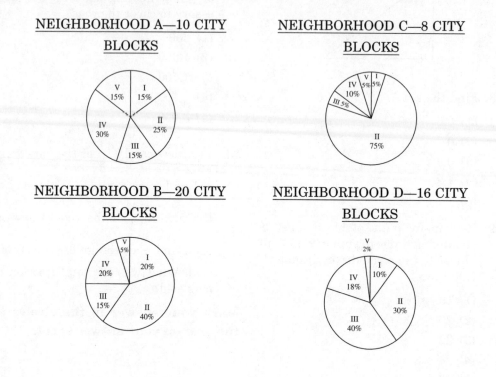

NEIGHBORHOOD A—10 CITY BLOCKS

NEIGHBORHOOD C—8 CITY BLOCKS

NEIGHBORHOOD B—20 CITY BLOCKS

NEIGHBORHOOD D—16 CITY BLOCKS

KEY:
   I – One- and two-family houses
  II – Apartment buildings
 III – Office buildings
 IV – Retail stores
  V – Factories and warehouses

32. Which two neighborhoods devote the same number of city blocks to residential use?

(1) A and C

(2) A and D

(3) B and C

(4) B and D

(5) C and D

33. Which one of the following types of buildings occupies the same amount of land area in Neighborhood B as the amount of land area occupied by retail stores in Neighborhood A?

(1) One- and two-family houses

(2) Apartment buildings

(3) Office buildings

(4) Retail stores

(5) Factories and warehouses

34. Two fences in a field meet at 120°. A cow is tethered at their intersection with a 15-foot rope, as shown in the figure below. Over how many square feet may the cow graze?

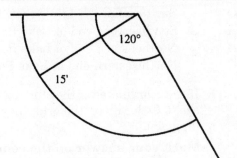

- **(1)** 50π
- **(2)** 75π
- **(3)** 80π
- **(4)** 85π
- **(5)** 90π

35. On January 1, 1983, Brian was hired to work at Company X for an annual salary of $15,000. On January 1st of each subsequent year, Brian received an $800 raise in his annual salary. Which of the following expressions represents his annual salary after receiving his raise on January 1, 1988?

- **(1)** 15,000 + 800 (6)
- **(2)** 15,000 (800) (6)
- **(3)** 15,000 (800 + 5)
- **(4)** 15,000 + 800 (5)
- **(5)** 15,000 (800 + 6)

ITEMS 36 AND 37 REFER TO THE FOLLOWING TABLE, DESCRIBING THE TRAIL THAT JOSH AND JUAN FOLLOWED USING THEIR COMPASS AS A GUIDE TO HIKE FROM THE STARTING FLAG TO THE LAKE.

Direction hiked	Distance (miles)	Point on the map	Special feature
		O	Starting flag
West	1	A	Southeastern end of Lake Po
North	3	B	Northeastern end of Lake Po
West	4	C	Northwestern end of Lake Po

36. How many miles would they save by canoeing from A to C, instead of walking from A to B to C?

(1) 1

(2) 2

(3) 3

(4) 4

(5) 5

37. If the coordinates of the starting flag are (0,0), locate on the grid, the ending point.

Mark your answer on the coordinate plane grid on your answer sheet.

ITEMS 38 TO 40 (ON THE NEXT PAGE) REFER TO THE FOLLOWING GRAPH.

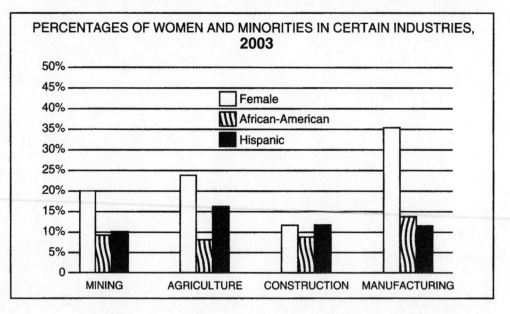

PERCENTAGES OF WOMEN AND MINORITIES IN CERTAIN INDUSTRIES, 2003

38. In which area was the percentage of male workers four times that of female workers?

   (1) Mining

   (2) Agriculture

   (3) Construction

   (4) Manufacturing

   (5) Not enough information is given.

39. If 733,000 miners were employed in all in 2003, about how many of them were Hispanic?

   (1) 2,000

   (2) 5,000

   (3) 12,000

   (4) 48,000

   (5) 73,000

40. What percentage of construction workers were neither Hispanic nor African-American?

   (1) 93.4%

   (2) 80%

   (3) 70%

   (4) 23.5%

   (5) 15%

41. In the game of baseball, the distance from the pitcher to the batter is 60 feet. A fastball was thrown at 90 miles per hour (132 feet per second). Approximately how many seconds will it take to reach the batter?

   (1) 0.45

   (2) 0.68

   (3) 1.00

   (4) 1.47

   (5) 2.2

ITEMS 42 AND 43 REFER TO THE FOLLOWING TABLE OF VARIOUS VALUES OF THE CONSUMERS PRICE INDEX (CPI) FROM 1920 THROUGH 2000.

Year	CPI
1920	$ 20.00
1980	82.40
1997	160.50
2000	172.20

Because of inflation, the value of money decreases over time. This is measured by the Consumer Price Index (CPI). For example, looking at the table above, an item in 1920 that cost $20.00 would cost $172.20 in 2000.

42. If a ticket to watch Babe Ruth play in a N.Y. Yankees baseball game in 1920 cost $5.00, how much should the same ticket cost in 2000?

   (1) $20.00

   (2) $43.05

   (3) $68.88

   (4) $86.66

   (5) $172.20

43. What percent of inflation occurred between 1920 and 2000?

   Mark your answer in the circles in the grid on your answer sheet.

ITEMS 44 TO 47 REFER TO THE DATA BELOW.

ATTENDANCE AT SPORTS EVENTS (IN MILLIONS)

Activity	1960	1965	1970	1974	1975	1976	1977	1978
Baseball, major leagues:								
Regular season	19.9	22.4	28.7	30.0	29.8	31.3	38.7	40.6
American League	9.2	8.9	12.1	13.0	13.2	14.7	19.6	20.5
National League	10.7	13.6	16.7	17.0	16.6	16.7	19.1	20.1
Basketball, professional,								
NBA	2.0	2.8	5.1	6.9	7.9	8.5	11.0	10.9
Football, collegiate	20.4	24.7	29.5	31.2	31.7	32.0	32.9	34.3
Football, professional,								
NFL	3.2	4.7	10.0	10.7	10.7	11.6	11.6	13.4
Horseracing	46.9	62.9	69.7	74.9	78.7	79.3	76.0	76.0
Greyhound racing	7.9	10.9	2.7	16.3	17.5	19.0	20.0	20.1
Hockey, NHL	2.4	2.8	6.0	8.6	9.5	9.1	8.6	8.5

44. In which year did attendance at American League baseball games first exceed attendance at National League games?

(1) 1960

(2) 1970

(3) 1975

(4) 1977

(5) 1978

45. Which sporting event was the most popular during 1965?

(1) Baseball

(2) Horseracing

(3) Football

(4) Hockey

(5) Not enough information is given.

46. In 1978, what percentage of the people who attended major league ball games (basketball, baseball, and football) went to baseball games?

(1) 17%

(2) 21%

(3) 63%

(4) 65%

(5) 71%

47. In 1977, which sporting activity netted the LEAST revenue?

(1) Hockey

(2) Football

(3) Greyhound racing

(4) Baseball

(5) Not enough information is given.

ITEMS 48 AND 49 REFER TO THE FOLLOWING INFORMATION.

MICHAEL'S MONTHLY BUDGET

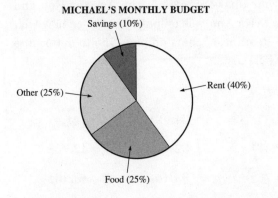

48. In 2000 Michael earned $1,600 per month, at the rate of $20.00 per hour. How many hours per week did he work? Assume 4 weeks = 1 month.

  (1) 100
  (2) 80
  (3) 60
  (4) 40
  (5) 20

49. If his rent increases by $160 per month, what will it be?

  (1) $560
  (2) $800
  (3) $1,000
  (4) $1,120
  (5) $2,400

50. As shown in the figure below, a cylindrical oil tank is one-third full. If 3 more gallons are added, the tank will be one-half full. What is the capacity of the tank?

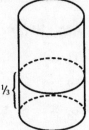

  (1) 15 gallons
  (2) 16 gallons
  (3) 17 gallons
  (4) 18 gallons
  (5) 19 gallons

ANSWER KEY AND EXPLANATIONS

After completing Practice Test 2, check your answers against the Answer Key and Explanations that follow. Next, turn to the Error Analysis on page 754 to see how well you did. Finally, go to the "Assessing Your Readiness" chart on page 755 to determine how prepared you are to take the actual GED tests.

Test 1. Language Arts, Writing—Part 1

1. (2)	11. (3)	21. (1)	31. (2)	41. (4)
2. (4)	12. (2)	22. (3)	32. (1)	42. (3)
3. (5)	13. (1)	23. (5)	33. (4)	43. (5)
4. (5)	14. (4)	24. (2)	34. (3)	44. (3)
5. (3)	15. (2)	25. (4)	35. (2)	45. (4)
6. (3)	16. (4)	26. (4)	36. (4)	46. (1)
7. (2)	17. (5)	27. (3)	37. (2)	47. (5)
8. (5)	18. (4)	28. (1)	38. (1)	48. (3)
9. (4)	19. (2)	29. (2)	39. (4)	49. (4)
10. (1)	20. (3)	30. (3)	40. (3)	50. (4)

1. **The correct answer is (2).** Since this sentence introduces the topic of the second paragraph, it should be moved to the beginning of paragraph B.

2. **The correct answer is (4).** The correct phrase becomes *he wants to know.*

3. **The correct answer is (5).** The phrase should read *what the company expects.*

4. **The correct answer is (5).** This is a run-on sentence that needs to be divided into two sentences. By putting a period after *interested,* and starting the next sentence with *Let him* we have two complete and correct new sentences.

5. **The correct answer is (3).** The newly rewritten sentence becomes *The nicer you look, the better you will be treated.*

6. **The correct answer is (3).** A comma is needed to separate the first two items in this list, as in *shined shoes, a pressed dress shirt.*

7. **The correct answer is (2).** The word *too* means also, and needs to be changed here to *to.*

8. **The correct answer is (5).** *Was* needs to be changed to *has* as in *has been practiced.*

9. **The correct answer is (4).** *Them* needs to be changed to *it,* because *it* here refers to *This informal support,* which is singular.

10. **The correct answer is (1).** The new sentence reads *When an illness or accident does occur, many studies show that such support helps prevent ill health and promotes recovery.*

11. **The correct answer is (3).** This sentence is useless and unnecessary here and should be deleted. It is

unnecesary because "mutual help" has already been explained in the previous discussion.

12. **The correct answer is (2).** These are not proper nouns or names, nor is this a title. Therefore, it is not correct to use capital letters for *socially and intellectually.*

13. **The correct answer is (1).** The newly rewritten sentence reads *The benefits of a shared identity and a sense of common purpose are often obtained by members in groups such as religious congregations, civic and fraternal organizations, and social clubs.*

14. **The correct answer is (4).** This is a run-on sentence, and the colon is not appropriate here. To make the correction, insert a period after "social change," and start the next word with a capital. This will turn the incorrect run-on sentence into two clear and correct sentences.

15. **The correct answer is (2).** The word *effects* is a noun, which cannot be used in this way. The correct word is *affects*, which is a verb meaning *to influence.*

16. **The correct answer is (4).** This is a run-on sentence, which is corrected by dividing it with a period after *waves,* and a new sentence starting with *They.*

17. **The correct answer is (5).** This sentence is correct as written.

18. **The correct answer is (4).** The newly rewritten sentence becomes *Inside the oven the waves bounce around, penetrating the food repeatedly.*

19. **The correct answer is (2).** The word *threw* is incorrect because it means to have tossed something. The correct word here is *through*, or *all the way into*, the food.

20. **The correct answer is (3).** The correct verb usage here is *To complete cooking of.*

21. **The correct answer is (1).** Sentence (3) starts a new idea and can be used to begin a new paragraph for greater clarity.

22. **The correct answer is (3).** The correct past tense plural form of the verb *to be* is *were.* The sentence refers to the members who *were* unable to attend.

23. **The correct answer is (5).** This is another run-on sentence. *Plan ahead* is a complete sentence and needs to be followed by a period. This results in two complete correct sentences.

24. **The correct answer is (2).** There is no need for quotation marks here, since *consumer agency* is not a quote, nor is it a title as used here.

25. **The correct answer is (4).** The sentence is talking about a particular kind of liability, as in *personal liability.* As used here *personal* is an adjective that modifies the noun, *liability.*

26. **The correct answer is (4).** This is a kind of written communication piece that is simply an outline of a talk. It is not necessary to divide this piece into paragraphs, since doing so doesn't improve clarity or separate distinct ideas. Therefore, the three sections should be combined.

27. **The correct answer is (3).** The word *know* is necessary for the second phrase to make sense, as in *know exactly what work will be done.*

28. **The correct answer is (1).** The newly written sentence reads *Because you could then refuse to pay the credit card company until possible problems with the job are corrected, pay by credit card when you can.*

29. **The correct answer is (2).** The comma after *contractor* needs to be changed to a colon to emphasize the list of situations that follow.

30. The correct answer is (3). The word *they're* is a contraction of *they are,* which is incorrect here. What is needed is *their,* which is a possessive meaning *belonging to them.*

31. The correct answer is (2). The comma here should be removed because it breaks up the thought, which is *It is easy to understand why many parents and adolescents find this such a difficult period to survive.*

32. The correct answer is (1). The rewritten sentence becomes *Even the most rebellious child often becomes appreciative, affectionate, and devoted once it is over.* Choice (5) would be correct also if there were a comma in the question, so that the sentence then would be *Even the most rebellious child, once it is over, often becomes appreciative, affectionate, and devoted.* However, since there is no comma after *child* in the original sentence, the only correct answer is choice (1).

33. The correct answer is (4). The correct word is *irritating,* which is an adjective referring to the noun, *behavior. Irritated* is an adverb, which can not be used to modify a noun.

34. The correct answer is (3). The complete verb is *to show poor judgment,* or as used here, *parents sometimes show poor judgment.*

35. The correct answer is (2). The tense of the first half of the sentence should match the second half. Also, this paragraph is written in the present tense, so the phrase should be *Adolescence is a trying period.*

36. The correct answer is (4). This sentence, which is the first of several dealing with parents and their imperfections, belongs in the next paragraph, which is paragraph C.

37. The correct answer is (2). This is a sentence fragment. By replacing the first three words with *Man has* this error is corrected.

38. The correct answer is (1). Proper names of places must be capitalized. Therefore, the name of the country, *egypt,* needs to be changed to *Egypt.* The word *pharaoh* is not capitalized here because, like the words *king* or *ruler,* it is not a proper name.

39. The correct answer is (4). The correct word here is *weight,* which refers to how heavy something is.

40. The correct answer is (3). The newly rewritten sentence reads *This was a very important development, since bread constituted the major part of a person's diet at that time.*

41. The correct answer is (4). As this sentence is written in the past tense, the last part of the sentence should read *was sold primarily to unwary travelers at the local inns.*

42. The correct answer is (3). Sentence (14) deals with another kind of bread, and belongs further up in the paragraph. Since sentence (11) mentions *the first two kinds* of bread, it seems logical to put this sentence directly above it. This change has the effect of making this paragraph flow more smoothly and clearly.

43. The correct answer is (5). The other verbs in this sentence, such as *weren't* and *was,* indicate that this is a sentence written in the past tense. Therefore, *local officials are serving* should be changed to *local officials served.*

44. The correct answer is (3). The word *courts* as used in this sentence is not a proper noun and should not be capitalized.

45. The correct answer is (4). The whole sentence refers to *a citizen.* So, the correct pronoun here is *he,* not *they.*

46. The correct answer is (1). The correct verb here is *To judge. Judging* is an adverb, which is incorrect here.

47. The correct answer is (5). The correct newly written sentence is *Depending upon the importance of the case being tried, the Athenian juries were very large, often consisting of 201, 401, 501, 1,001 or more men.*

48. The correct answer is (3). The comma here creates a comma splice, meaning that it breaks up a complete thought. It should be removed.

49. The correct answer is (4). The verb is needed, as in *was marked by.* The word *marked* used alone here is not a verb.

50. The correct answer is (4). Paragraph C begins the discussion of how juries were set up, with paragraph B giving more of the details. Therefore, in order to make the piece more understandable, paragraph B should come after paragraph C.

Language Arts, Writing—Part 2

SAMPLE ESSAY RESPONSE

According to surveys, 85 percent of American households regularly clip and redeem supermarket coupons and refund offers. These are usually found in local newspapers or in circulars delivered to households throughout the country, and are redeemable in the larger area stores. However, since it takes so much time and energy to do this, not to mention the discipline needed to organize the resulting paperwork, why do people do it at all?

For some, living on a tight budget makes it a necessity to save money on their purchases whenever possible. With double- and triple-value coupons, there can be an additional savings over regular retail prices. Other people dread hearing from a friend that "I got it cheaper than you did." The thought of paying more than you have to can be very disheartening, especially if someone you know took advantage of some deal that you also could have benefited from but failed to follow up on.

In general, many people see themselves as "smart shoppers" trying to get the most and best purchase for the least amount of money. Savvy consumers save substantial money on their weekly food shopping since this represents a major budget item. In addition, redeeming a refund offer on big-ticket items such as major appliances, entertainment accessories, or clothing can make significant savings as well.

Unless one has unlimited funds, the natural inclination of most people is to look out for bargains by using coupons and refund offers, thereby saving money that can be put aside and banked for a rainy day.

Test 2. Social Studies

1. (2)	11. (3)	21. (4)	31. (3)	41. (3)
2. (5)	12. (5)	22. (1)	32. (2)	42. (3)
3. (1)	13. (1)	23. (4)	33. (5)	43. (3)
4. (3)	14. (4)	24. (2)	34. (4)	44. (4)
5. (3)	15. (5)	25. (4)	35. (2)	45. (3)
6. (5)	16. (1)	26. (3)	36. (4)	46. (2)
7. (3)	17. (3)	27. (1)	37. (5)	47. (4)
8. (2)	18. (5)	28. (5)	38. (1)	48. (4)
9. (2)	19. (3)	29. (4)	39. (3)	49. (1)
10. (1)	20. (4)	30. (4)	40. (4)	50. (4)

1. **The correct answer is (2).** The last sentence of the article describes the farms as "run-down." The same sentence goes on to say that the temptation was great to leave the farm for the better economic possibilities of full family employment in the mills.

2. **The correct answer is (5).** The answer can be found in the third sentence: "whites . . . supplied the bulk of the labor for the textile mills and such others as required skilled operators, while a preponderance of blacks did the harder work of the mines." The subject of education does not come up at all in this selection.

3. **The correct answer is (1).** People were employed regardless of their educational level. We know that choice (2) is false because blacks "did the harder work of the mines." Choice (3) is false, as shown in such sentences as "Wages were low, at first far lower than wages paid in the Northern mills." Choice (4) is false, for conditions were static. Choice (5) is false because the article specifically says the South failed to attract immigrants.

4. **The correct answer is (3).** In the mills, whole families could work for money. Individual wages were low, but the combined income of all family members brought in far more than the subsistence farms.

5. **The correct answer is (3).** Since the article indicates all able-bodied people worked, we can infer that it was not economically practical to employ greater numbers of children.

6. **The correct answer is (5).** The only conclusion that can be drawn from the information given on the map is that Afghanistan has no access to the sea.

7. **The correct answer is (3).** Based on the fact that there is a wide variety of different languages and only 10 percent of the people are literate, it follows that Afghanistan is agriculturally, not technologically, based.

8. **The correct answer is (2).** Choices (1), (4), and (5) cannot be determined from this map. Indeed, the mountain lakes and streams of Afghanistan do provide fish, but the question requires that you answer on the basis of the map alone. As for choice (3), Kabul is far from the sea and is,

furthermore, not in Europe. By virtue of their proximity, we can assume that the climates of Afghanistan and Tajikistan are similar.

9. **The correct answer is (2).** Misrepresentation. The company exaggerates the strength of its socks.

10. **The correct answer is (1).** Meaningless claim. Cleer is guaranteed to last 40 percent longer than what?

11. **The correct answer is (3).** Bait and switch. The seller has no intention of selling the advertised product. Instead, the Simmonses are offered a higher priced model.

12. **The correct answer is (5).** Fictitious pricing. Television City overstated the list price to convince the buyer that the advertised price represented a savings.

13. **The correct answer is (1).** Meaningless claim. While the ad may seem to be an example of misrepresentation, there are no real facts here to be exaggerated. The first sentence in particular makes no sense. Why would CHATTERING TEDDY BEARS sold by *competitive companies* outsell other toys? This would make sense only if the CHATTERING TEDDY BEARS *sold by the company that is advertising* outsold other toys. Thus, we have what appears to be useful information that turns out to be meaningless on closer examination.

14. **The correct answer is (4).** France was eliminated as a power, thus vanishing from the map. Choice (1) makes no sense; if France defeated England, England should vanish from the map. Choice (2) is the same as choice (1); if Spain diverted its forces, it should have lost control of its land in America and thus vanished from the map. Choices (3) and (5) have nothing to do with the question.

15. **The correct answer is (5).** British Columbia, in the extreme north-

west portion of the map, has no shading, indicating it is not controlled by any country listed here.

16. **The correct answer is (1).** Louisiana is in the southern part of the area controlled by France.

17. **The correct answer is (3).** According to the map, the Mississippi River divides the land controlled by Spain from the land controlled by England. We can assume, therefore, they share control of the river.

18. **The correct answer is (5).** People recognize that cards make purchases, especially unplanned ones, easier. In addition, cards are relatively safe. Choices (1) and (2) are not true. Choice (3) is true but not sufficient reason to explain credit cards' enormous popularity. Choice (4) is not true.

19. **The correct answer is (3).** The approximate distance is 3,000 miles, which would be 3 times $1\frac{1}{2}$ inches on the map, or $4\frac{1}{2}$ inches.

20. **The correct answer is (4).** Britain, acting alone, under great odds, was the only country that had resisted an invasion by Hitler. If the British had given in, all of Europe would have been conquered.

21. **The correct answer is (4).** In 1957 the Soviets launched Sputnik, which had a very large payload, into space. However, in 1969, the United States accomplished an almost impossible feat—a precise landing on the moon with astronauts Neil Armstrong and Edwin Aldrin.

22. **The correct answer is (1).** This is a town meeting being held to determine the future status of the sewer services to be provided. It is an example of participatory government, wherein people are involved in solving community problems jointly with their elected officials.

answers practice test 2

23. **The correct answer is (4).** Adam Smith (1723–1790), the famous Scottish economist, promoted the idea of the *laissez-faire* economy. This philosophy states that it is best for governments *not* to manipulate the economy but to stick to a "hands off" policy. From the French, the term means to "leave alone."

24. **The correct answer is (2).** The barge's cargo is garbage, politely known as "solid waste." It is obvious that the garbage has nowhere to go; no one wants it. This has become a serious problem as landfills fill up and we all become aware of the dangers of ocean pollution and of air pollution from burning.

25. **The correct answer is (4).** NIMBY stands for "Not In My Back Yard." This is regrettably a common attitude toward the solution to many social and ecological problems. ACWA stands for "Administrative Careers With America," an examination for jobs with the federal government. IATA is the "International Association of Travel Agents." COCOM is the "Coordinating Committee on Multi-lateral Export Controls," which does not deal with exporting garbage. DoD is the "Department of Defense."

26. **The correct answer is (3).** Recycling appears to be the answer to the problem. Waste products that are recycled need not be disposed of at all.

27. **The correct answer is (1).** Unfortunately, the United States is the most wasteful nation on Earth. We consume the most and throw the most away.

28. **The correct answer is (5).** This is a timely topic that would be dealt with in a daily newspaper. Indeed, the event depicted did occur with respect to 3,100 tons of garbage from Islip, New York, in 1987. The garbage traveled for 6,000 miles over a period of 112 days and was rejected by three countries before it was finally returned and burned as a last resort.

29. **The correct answer is (4).** Denver is the headquarters for Region VIII, which includes Utah, where Salt Lake City is located.

30. **The correct answer is (4).** New York City is headquarters for Region II, which includes Puerto Rico.

31. **The correct answer is (3).** Region VII includes Iowa, Missouri, Kansas, and Nebraska.

32. **The correct answer is (2).** It has a great many people in need of government services.

33. **The correct answer is (5).** The next-to-last column shows the actual number of people in rural communities for each census year. The number continued to grow until 1940, then decreased in the period 1940–1970.

34. **The correct answer is (4).** The fourth column shows the total percentage of United States population living in urban areas for each census year. By 1940 more than 50 percent of the United States population was living in urban areas. Choice (1): Although the actual percentage of people living in rural areas decreased relative to the total population, 36 million people lived in rural areas in 1880, and 54 million in 1970. Choice (2): The percentage of people living in rural areas dropped from 55 percent in 1910, to 44 percent in 1940, and to 27 percent in 1970. Choice (3): By reading the third column, it can be seen that the number of people living in urban areas increased during the nineteenth century. Choice (5): The fifth column shows that the number of people living in rural areas increased from 1880 until 1940, then decreased between 1940 and 1970.

35. **The correct answer is (2).** The availability of factory and other industrial jobs in urban areas attracted farm workers as well as immigrants. Choice (1): Farm production had to increase to meet the needs of a growing urban population. Farm machinery freed rural workers for industrial employment. Choice (3): Immigration quotas were first imposed in the 1920s. Choice (4): Although transportation improved, this was not the most significant factor in urban development. Choice (5): A decreasing birth rate would not explain urban growth.

36. **The correct answer is (4).** The act covers all of the workers listed.

37. **The correct answer is (5).** "Wages" include regular salary, overtime, fringe benefits, and work clothes as stated in paragraph 4.

38. **The correct answer is (1).** Workers whose jobs require the same skill, effort, and responsibility must receive the same pay, as stated in the second sentence of paragraph 1.

39. **The correct answer is (3).** According to the Supreme Court ruling mentioned in the last sentence, jobs of men and women need not be identical, only "substantially equal," to qualify for equal pay.

40. **The correct answer is (4).** The purpose of the act was to prevent pay discrimination because of sex.

41. **The correct answer is (3).** The German army had diluted its strength by having to fight on too many fronts at the same time. They had miscalculated the respective strengths of their foes, and this led to their defeat in this war.

42. **The correct answer is (3).** The third estate, representing 97 percent of the people in France, benefited most, resulting in the rise of a middle class and of religious and personal freedoms and proportional taxation for all.

43. **The correct answer is (3).** In 1920 the Nineteenth Amendment to the U.S. Constitution was adopted. It had been vigorously championed by the suffragettes who fought for its passage throughout the nineteenth and early twentieth centuries.

44. **The correct answer is (4).** General Douglas MacArthur was the Supreme Commander. He helped establish political reforms that would be conducive to the successful functioning of new democratic institutions in postwar Japan.

45. **The correct answer is (3).** These concepts were expressed in the writings of Karl Marx (1818–1883), who developed the ideas underlying the revolutionary form of socialism known as communism.

46. **The correct answer is (2).** The highest point of the graph is 1989.

47. **The correct answer is (4).** Use your pencil or the edge of a piece of paper to see where the dot for 1994 meets the scale for number of depositors. There were approximately 25,000 depositors in 1994.

48. **The correct answer is (4).** The number of depositors has risen and fallen over the period shown, so choice (4) is false.

49. **The correct answer is (1).** The line representing births takes a dip in the 1970s with only a slight rise at the end of the decade. Choices (2), (3), (4), and (5) are unsupported. The immigration rate seems to have increased; there is no discernible increase or decrease overall during the period 1980–1985. The highest number of births appear in the earliest years shown on the chart, but there is no indication of an actual rate of births/thousand. The number of deaths shows a slight increase through the period.

50. **The correct answer is (4).** About 75 percent of the net increase is represented as a natural increase on the chart; the remaining 25 percent is represented as net immigration.

Test 3. Science

1. (2)	11. (1)	21. (4)	31. (5)	41. (3)
2. (4)	12. (2)	22. (2)	32. (1)	42. (2)
3. (4)	13. (4)	23. (3)	33. (1)	43. (5)
4. (2)	14. (3)	24. (1)	34. (4)	44. (2)
5. (1)	15. (1)	25. (3)	35. (5)	45. (5)
6. (5)	16. (3)	26. (3)	36. (4)	46. (3)
7. (3)	17. (2)	27. (3)	37. (4)	47. (4)
8. (3)	18. (5)	28. (4)	38. (3)	48. (3)
9. (4)	19. (4)	29. (1)	39. (5)	49. (2)
10. (3)	20. (4)	30. (2)	40. (2)	50. (4)

1. **The correct answer is (2).** The cerebellum controls balance, which is necessary for flight.

2. **The correct answer is (4).** Your cerebrum allows you to think.

3. **The correct answer is (4).** The medulla controls heart rate and respiration.

4. **The correct answer is (2).** A human has a more highly developed cerebrum.

5. **The correct answer is (1).** In 1997 Ian Wilmut and his colleagues at the Roslin Institute in Edinburgh, Scotland, made a genetic copy of an adult sheep called "Dolly," thus generating a whole new sheep. This is a very important development with regard to many areas of medical research.

6. **The correct answer is (5).** The first sentence refers to an "accident at the nuclear generating plant." We can assume radioactive material was released. Choice (4) is incorrect, for we have no way of knowing from the passage what caused the accident. Choice (1) is too extreme.

7. **The correct answer is (3).** Massachusetts has the highest number in all five categories.

8. **The correct answer is (3).** Total 73 (Massachusetts) and 26 (Rhode Island) to find this answer.

9. **The correct answer is (4).** Magnesium (Mg) and calcium (Ca) are both in Group IIA. Elements in the same group have similar chemical properties.

10. **The correct answer is (3).** Cobalt has an atomic number of 27, which means it has 27 electrons and 27 protons. This is more electrons than any other element listed.

11. **The correct answer is (1).** The elements in Group IA, the metals, have only one electron in their outermost shells. Therefore, they are the most reactive.

12. **The correct answer is (2).** The noble gases all belong to Group VIIIA. Neon is in Group VIIIA.

13. **The correct answer is (4).** As the moon changes its position in its orbit around the earth, different amounts of the illuminated side are visible from the earth.

14. **The correct answer is (3).** During a lunar eclipse, the shadow of the earth is cast upon the moon.

15. **The correct answer is (1).** Bacteria reproduce by a process called binary fission. One cell splits into two cells, then each of the two cells divides to form four cells, and so on . . . .

16. **The correct answer is (3).** Start with 1; a half hour later there are 2; 1 hour later there are 4; then 8, 16, 32, 64, 128, and then 256 at the end of 4 hours.

17. **The correct answer is (2).** The number of bacteria is increasing rapidly, as indicated by the sharply rising line on the graph.

18. **The correct answer is (5).** The bacteria, in a closed container, have no more room in which to live and are being poisoned by their own waste products.

19. **The correct answer is (4).** The bacteria flourished in a growth medium (food). In the same way, we can infer that incorrectly stored food provides a breeding ground for bacteria. While choice (5) is true, it cannot be inferred from this experiment.

20. **The correct answer is (4).** The voltage across each branch of a parallel circuit is the same. Since the source supplies 40 volts, the potential difference, voltage through R_1 is also 40 volts.

21. **The correct answer is (4).** The power is calculated by p = V × I = 40(volts) × 6(amp); p = 240 watts.

22. **The correct answer is (2).** The greater the resistance in R_1, the more current will be diverted to R_2.

23. **The correct answer is (3).** The uneven saturation of energy would probably result in unevenly cooked food.

24. **The correct answer is (1).** Electrical power in the home is measured in watts or kilowatts. As the degree is a measure of heat energy, the watt is a measure of electrical energy.

25. **The correct answer is (3).** The magnetron within the microwave oven generates the energy.

26. **The correct answer is (3).** To have type B blood, John must have received at least one I^B gene with no I^A gene.

27. **The correct answer is (3).** For type O blood, Martha had to receive a recessive gene (i) from each parent.

28. **The correct answer is (4).** To have type AB blood, a child must receive an I^A gene from one parent and an I^B gene from the other parent.

29. **The correct answer is (1).** According to the graph, the pH of acid rain is between 2 and 5.6. The pH of normal rain is indicated as 5.6. Therefore, the best definition of acid rain is precipitation having a pH less than that of normal rain.

30. **The correct answer is (2).** The pH of normal rain is approximately 5.6 on the scale. This is best described as slightly acidic.

31. **The correct answer is (5).** The two graphs indicate the composition of the earth's crust. They do not indicate how these materials are arranged, choice (1), nor the advantage of certain types of rocks, choice (2).

32. **The correct answer is (1).** Graph 1 shows that most of the earth's crust is composed of nonsedimentary rocks. According to this graph, sedimentary rocks make up 5% of the total crust.

33. **The correct answer is (1).** All rocks are composed of minerals.

34. **The correct answer is (4).** Graph 1 shows that sedimentary rocks make up a very small percentage of the total volume of the earth's crust. Graph 2 suggests that there is a lot of sedimentary rock exposed at the earth's surface. Using both graphs, it may be inferred that there is very little sedimentary rock, but that much of what is present is at the earth's surface.

35. **The correct answer is (5).** The temperature of the water must be

raised from 20°C to 100°C, or by 80 Centigrade degrees. It takes one calorie to raise one gram of water one Centigrade degree. It must take *more* calories to raise *200* grams of water *80* Centigrade degrees. 200 × 80 = 16,000 calories.

36. **The correct answer is (4).** This problem is similar to the previous one with the unknown being the amount of water instead of the amount of energy. Therefore, X grams × (100 − 10) Centigrade degrees = 180,000 calories. The result is 2,000 grams.

37. **The correct answer is (4).** More products on the right side of an equation indicate a greater chance of reactants on the right. Therefore, the more sodium, the more salt is produced, and the more chlorine is used up.

38. **The correct answer is (3).** As indicated on the top of the graph, this is a measurement of the CO_2 produced from yeast cultured in sugar solutions.

39. **The correct answer is (5).** Select the curve for solution B, the solid line. Then, draw a vertical line upward from 30 minutes until it intersects the curve. Now, draw a horizontal line to the left until it intersects the scale for column of CO_2 liberated. This will be at 2.2 ml. The abbreviation "ml" stands for "milliliters."

40. **The correct answer is (2).** The curve for solution B (the solid line) shows that CO_2 was liberated after about five minutes, well before any of the other solutions showed CO_2 production.

41. **The correct answer is (3).** Yeast is fermented to produce bread.

42. **The correct answer is (2).** On March 1, the discharge of the stream is 0.5 cubic meters per second. On May 1, the discharge has increased to 2.5 cubic meters per second. This represents a greater change in stream flow than occurred during any of the other periods listed.

43. **The correct answer is (5).** The passage states that body fat is burned "only by using more energy than is supplied by the food you eat."

44. **The correct answer is (2).** Scientists who studied the deaths of people on liquid protein diets found that "the dieters had died of irregular heart rhythms and cardiac arrest."

45. **The correct answer is (5).** While a diet of 600 calories a day may not be healthy, a person on such a diet will lose weight fairly rapidly.

46. **The correct answer is (3).** The second sentence indicates that a basic, safe diet consists of 1,000 to 1,200 calories per day.

47. **The correct answer is (4).** The test tubes must be kept at the same temperature for the experiment to be valid. Choice (2) is incorrect, for it would not matter who put the material into the tubes. Choice (3) is incorrect, as the experiment would be valid as long as time charts were kept. Choice (5) is incorrect, as it would not matter if the tubes were in different positions in the lab.

48. **The correct answer is (3).** The white of an egg is composed of albumen, which is a protein. Pepsin is an enzyme that digests proteins.

49. **The correct answer is (2).** Gastric juice is formed in the stomach. It contains the enzymes pepsin and rennin, hydrochloric acid, and water. Pepsin, in the presence of hydrochloric acid, digests proteins, of which egg white is an example.

50. **The correct answer is (4).** Milk and milk products such as cheese and yogurt (unless made from skim or low-fat milk) are high in saturated fat and cholesterol.

Test 4. Language Arts, Reading

1. (4)	11. (5)	21. (3)	31. (3)
2. (1)	12. (1)	22. (2)	32. (1)
3. (3)	13. (4)	23. (2)	33. (2)
4. (2)	14. (2)	24. (1)	34. (2)
5. (1)	15. (3)	25. (2)	35. (5)
6. (5)	16. (1)	26. (1)	36. (3)
7. (3)	17. (5)	27. (3)	37. (2)
8. (4)	18. (2)	28. (5)	38. (3)
9. (3)	19. (4)	29. (4)	39. (5)
10. (2)	20. (5)	30. (3)	40. (4)

1. **The correct answer is (4).** The key words, "Success! Success!" indicate that something has been attempted and completed. The fifth paragraph tells us that the "crimson hand which had once blazed" is now "barely perceptible," so we know that Aylmer has done something to try to remove it.

2. **The correct answer is (1).** The first sentence describes the birthmark as a "crimson hand."

3. **The correct answer is (3).** Again, the first sentence tells us the birthmark is beginning to fade. The fifth paragraph, however, informs us the mark never completely vanishes.

4. **The correct answer is (2).** In the seventh paragraph, Aylmer describes his wife as "perfect." The word "flawless"—without flaws or faults—means "perfect."

5. **The correct answer is (1).** By trying to perfect his wife, Aylmer destroyed her. Perfection cannot be achieved by man, the author is saying.

6. **The correct answer is (5).** Aylmer's eagerness to help Georgiana toward physical perfection costs her her life.

7. **The correct answer is (3).** The first two lines of the poem state that this story was told by a traveler, or tourist, and describe the wrecked statue—"two vast and trunkless legs"—so choices (4) and (5) are incorrect. Lines 10 and 11 suggest feelings of excessive pride in an ancient king or pharaoh. However, since there is no mention of the "healing process," choice (3) is the correct answer.

8. **The correct answer is (4).** The phrase "sneer of cold command" and the inscription on the base of the statue describe a proud king. The statue, destroyed by the passage of time, lies in an "ancient land." This tells us Ozymandias lived long ago.

9. **The correct answer is (3).** A visage is a face. The shattered visage in this poem is part of a shattered head.

10. **The correct answer is (2).** The repetition of the initial sound in *b*oundless and *b*are, *l*one and *l*evel, *s*ands and *s*tretch is an example of alliteration.

11. **The correct answer is (5).** The point of the poem is that Ozymandias was evidently an important person

in his time but most certainly was not a nice individual—"sneer of cold command" . . . "hand that mocked them"—and was hated by his subjects, including the sculptor. This haughty person has left no fond memories, no legacy. Because of his pride, he has fallen and has been totally forgotten.

12. **The correct answer is (1).** Shelley means that this was an ancient country—one that existed long ago.

13. **The correct answer is (4).** The first paragraph describes how he "played catch with a broken watch."

14. **The correct answer is (2).** Binnie "sneers" and shows "savage anger" in Maud's apartment. She smiles at him "uncertainly," indicating that she is frightened of him.

15. **The correct answer is (3).** The North Shore people are best described as rich, as they have been able to afford a housemaid for ten years. Although they hug and kiss her, (4) is a poor choice, since their show of affection is solely designed to get her to work harder for them.

16. **The correct answer is (1).** "Pepper" is biting and sharp, best describing her anger at the North Shore people who employ her. The two paragraphs from the same work included here describe two persons who may well be neighbors. The two paragraphs, however, do not in any way discuss the relationship between the subjects of the two separate descriptions.

17. **The correct answer is (5).** Since the author describes Binnie as "insane," Dunning is probably a mental institution of some kind. The story doesn't indicate that he committed any crimes, so there is no reason to assume that Dunning is a jail or reformatory.

18. **The correct answer is (2).** The description of Binnie wandering the hallways, twirling his watch, and

touching Maud Martha's belongings suggests that he is restless. His unexpected "savage anger" with the flower, and his statement ". . . and I don't even get mad" with his aunt Octavia, suggest that he is probably angry and explosive much of the time.

19. **The correct answer is (4).** The piece suggests that Pickering treated Liza kindly and gave her feelings of self-respect. She says that she felt as if he "always treated me as a lady." She states that she learned manners from his example. Therefore, the first three are all correct, and choice (4) is the correct answer.

20. **The correct answer is (5).** Liza is indicating her displeasure at the way Professor Higgins treats her. She insists on the formality of "Miss Doolittle" to put distance between them.

21. **The correct answer is (3).** Since Pickering did the opposite, choice (3) is correct. He taught Liza by the example of his behavior, not his words, the meaning of being well-mannered.

22. **The correct answer is (2).** The description of Professor Higgins's behavior by Liza and by Pickering, and his outburst during this scene, suggest that he loses his temper easily and that he has bad manners.

23. **The correct answer is (2).** The gutter is often associated with a fall from income, grace, or manners. Higgins believes that Liza will regress to her former ill-mannered ways without his help and assistance.

24. **The correct answer is (1).** Liza has climbed the social ladder only through Higgins's help. She would welcome free higher education to give more people a chance to move up in the world.

25. **The correct answer is (2).** The first and fourth paragraphs tell you that the family originally consisted

of Roslyn and her mother and father, making her an only child.

26. **The correct answer is (1).** This selection is neither sad, funny, sarcastic, nor satiric in tone or mood. The author presents the facts about Roslyn and her life in Japan in a matter-of-fact way, and while sad and funny incidents are mentioned, the overall tone is neutral.

27. **The correct answer is (3).** The first line states that this story took place immediately "after the war," so you can safely infer that "leveled" refers to the effects of the bombing that the Allies inflicted on Japan during World War II. When a place is "leveled" it means that everything—buildings, houses, factories, schools, and other buildings—are knocked down.

28. **The correct answer is (5).** The question calls for a *false* or untrue statement as being the correct answer. The presence of a neighborhood of European-style houses, as well as an international cemetery, suggest that there were a sizable number of foreigners who visited or lived in Japan. The other answer choices are all true statements.

29. **The correct answer is (4).** The fifth and sixth paragraphs tell you that the children came from homes of different nationalities and that they spoke English in school and Japanese when playing with each other. Since they lived in a multicultural environment, they would need to speak different languages.

30. **The correct answer is (3).** The second to last paragraph states that the ship was a *freighter*, a ship meant to carry *freight*, or cargo, in this case the wildlife. It was probably not equipped to carry more people, so choice (3) is the best answer. There is no evidence given that it was small, noisy, or more luxurious than other ships.

31. **The correct answer is (3).** This is clearly stated in the second line of this selection.

32. **The correct answer is (1).** Vianne moves to an unknown place, opens a business, dresses as she pleases, and generally is able to function with or without the approval of other people. This suggests that she has a mind and will of her own.

33. **The correct answer is (2).** Clearly, the reviewer likes the charm and fun of this movie. But, in paragraph two, she mentions that the film tackles some more serious topics also. Therefore, choice (2) is the correct answer.

34. **The correct answer is (2).** *Chocolat* also seems to be referring to things other than chocolate—enjoyment, love, seduction, fun. Therefore, it can be seen as a metaphor. *Chocolat* is not a misspelling. It is the French word for "chocolate."

35. **The correct answer is (5).** We aren't told how many shops the village has or when people rise in the morning. The author seems to be describing the tendency of its inhabitants to stick to tradition and "age-old rules." That's what makes it sleepy.

36. **The correct answer is (3).** The whole point of this selection is that a loan becomes a serious legal obligation. It doesn't say not to take one or where to find one. It does say that it is indeed a "big deal" to take on the responsibility of a student loan.

37. **The correct answer is (2).** The last paragraph states that if you default on the loan, the lender may notify the national credit bureaus. If this happens, and you were subsequently to apply for a car loan, you might be unable to get one.

38. **The correct answer is (3).** Lines 44–46 state that Perkins Loans are

managed and lent by the school attended.

39. The correct answer is (5). The first paragraph states that the loan must be repaid, even if you drop out. Also, the third paragraph states that you must notify your loan representative if you drop out of a school program.

40. The correct answer is (4). Again, the piece states that the loan representative must be called. Choice (3) is partly wrong—the terms are set by the lender, not the borrower. Choices (1) and (2) would create more difficulties and are not suggested by the reading passage.

Test 5. Mathematics

1. (2)	11. (3)	21. (1825)	31. (3/8)	41. (1)
2. (3)	12. (8.5)	22. (10.14)	32. (5)	42. (2)
3. (4)	13. (.275)	23. (3)	33. (3)	43. (761)
4. (2.07)	14. (1)	24. (4)	34. (2)	44. (4)
5. (9.7)	15. (2)	25. (4)	35. (4)	45. (2)
6. (3)	16. (3)	26. (5)	36. (2)	46. (3)
7. (2)	17. (4, −2)	27. (3)	37. (−5, 3)	47. (5)
8. (4)	18. (4)	28. (1)	38. (1)	48. (5)
9. (1)	19. (5)	29. (2)	39. (5)	49. (2)
10. (4)	20. (2)	30. (4)	40. (2)	50. (4)

Note: The word ⒞⒜⒧⒞⒰⒧⒜⒯⒪⒭ indicates that you should enter the following on your calculator.

1. The correct answer is (2). Substitute the given values into the equation.

$$D = A \times T^2$$

$$137 = 1 \times T^2 = T^2$$

To find T, take the square root of both sides: $\sqrt{137} = T$

⒞⒜⒧⒞⒰⒧⒜⒯⒪⒭ 137 shift x^2 = [Answer: 11.7046; rounded to **11.7**]

2. The correct answer is (3). Find the Trigonometric Ratios on the Formula page. The function that combines angle A (20°), BC, and AB (1 mile) is the

$$\sin x = \frac{\text{opposite}}{\text{hypotenuse}}$$

$$\sin A = \frac{BC}{AB} \text{ (equation 1)}$$

[CALCULATOR] Make sure that the calculator reads degrees "DEG" in the display window on top. If it doesn't, press: mode 4

Substitute values from the problem into (1): $\sin 20° = \dfrac{BC}{1} = BC$ (equation 2)

[CALCULATOR] 20 sin   [Answer: BC = 0.3420; rounded to **0.34** miles]

3. **The correct answer is (4).** The Volume of a cube from the Formula page is, Volume = side^3; V = 2.38^3

[CALCULATOR] 2.38 × 2.38 × 2.38 =

[Answer: V = 13.4812; rounded to **13.5** cubic feet]

4. Alternate form: **2 . 0 7 __**

From the Formula page, the Trigonometric Ratio that relates, $15°$, h, and AB (8.00) is $\sin x = \dfrac{\text{opposite}}{\text{hypotenuse}}$.

$\sin 15° = \dfrac{h}{AB} = \dfrac{h}{8}$; Solving for h,

$h = 8 \times \sin 15°$

[CALCULATOR] 8 × 15 sin = [Answer: 2.0705; rounded to **2.07**]

5. Alternate form: **9 . 7 __ __**

Add the hours for each of the mechanics:

5 hr 16 min
3 hr 49 min
   37 min
8 hr 102 min

(102 min = 102/60 hours = 1.7 hours)
8 hr + 1.7 hr = **9.7 hr**

                  or alternatively,

[CALCULATOR] 5 + 16 ÷ 60 + 3 + 49 ÷ 60 + 37 ÷ 60 = [Answer: **9.7**]

6. **The correct answer is (3).** The charge of labor on a *domestic car* is $25 per hour.

$\dfrac{25 \text{ dollars}}{\text{hour}} \times 9.7 \text{ hours} = 242.50 \text{ dollars}$

Add the cost of parts to get total charges:
$242.50 + $84.25 = **$326.75**

                  or alternatively,

[CALCULATOR] 25 × 9.7 + 84.25 = [Answer: **326.75**]

answers practice test 2

7. The correct answer is (2). See Formula page for the *volume of a rectangular-solid*.

Sketch the tank:

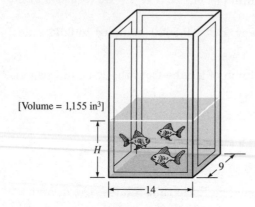

[Volume = 1,155 in³]

Volume = length × width × height
Let H be the height of the tank
1,155 = 14 × 9 × H;

Solve for H by dividing both sides by 14 × 9

$$H = \frac{1155}{(14 \times 9)}$$

⌨ CALCULATOR   1,155 ÷ (14 × 9) = [Answer: 9.1666 . . .] But since

0.1666. . . = $\frac{1}{6}$, the answer can be also written, **9 1/6** inches high.

Hint: Recall some **common decimal/fraction equivalents**:

$\frac{1}{2}$ = 0.5; $\frac{1}{3}$ = 0.333. . .; $\frac{1}{4}$ = 0.25; $\frac{1}{5}$ = 0.20; $\frac{1}{6}$ = 0.166. . .; $\frac{1}{8}$ = 0.125

8. The correct answer is (4). Profit = Amount Sold × (selling price − cost)
{let S = Selling Price; C = Cost; N = Amount (lbs) sold; P = Profit}

P = N × (S − C)

⌨ CALCULATOR   For Apple: P = 25 × (3.49 − .97) = [Answer: $63]

⌨ CALCULATOR   For Chocolate: P = 50 × (3.99 − 1.06) =

[Answer: $146.50]

Total Profit = $63 + $146.50 = **$209.50**

Note: Here, the calculator display indicates that the answer is 209.5, so *just add a zero* (0) making it $209.50. We recall that 2 decimals are required when discussing dollars and cents. When a zero is added, the value of the number remains unchanged.

9. **The correct answer is (1).** 2% of $\$1000 = \$1000 \times .02 = \$20$

3% of $\$2000 = \$2000 \times .03 = \$60$

4% of $\$3000 = \$3000 \times .04 = \$120$

5% of $(\$25{,}000 - \$6000) = 5\%$ of $\$19{,}000 = .05 \times \$19{,}000 = \$950$
Total tax $= \$20 + \$60 + \$120 + \$950 = \$1150$

10. **The correct answer is (4).** Let P {2002} be the population in the year 2002.

P{2003} = P{2002} + Growth factors − Decline factors

`CALCULATOR`   P{2003} = 52,376 + 577 + 876 − 689 − 592 =

[Answer: **52,548**]

11. **The correct answer is (3).** Each time the suit is discounted,
New price = Old price − (% discounted) × (Old price)

First: $239 - 0.05 \times 239 = $ (answer: 227.05)

Second: $227.05 - 0.08 \times 227.05 = $ (answer: 208.886)

Third: $208.886 - 0.12 \times 208.886 = $ (answer: 183.81968)

The final selling price, rounded, is **$184**.

12. In this problem, just substitute the number values for the letters:

$I_1 = \dfrac{4}{4+4} \times 17 = \mathbf{8.5}$
Alternate form: **8 . 5** __ __

13. Alternate form: **. 2 7 5** __
To find the mean, add the three batting averages and divide by 3.

0.250
0.273
<u>0.302</u>
0.825

To find the average, divide by the number of players, 3:
`CALCULATOR` $0.825 \div 3 = $ [Answer: **0.275**]

14. The correct answer is (1). Add the cost of the house, driveway, painting, and plumbing.

$44,000 + $1,250 + $1,750 + $1,000 = $48,000

If he wants to make a 12% profit when reselling the house, he should increase the total cost by 12% to find the new selling price.

12% of $48,000 = $5,760

$48,000 + $5,760 = **$53,760**

15. The correct answer is (2). Add up the cost for each serving of food.

Cost/Serving = Cost ($/package) ÷ portions/package

Franks: 1.75 ÷ 8 = .21875 (rounded to $.22)

Rolls: 83 ÷ 10 = .083 (rounded to $.08)

Beans: .85 ÷ 4 = .2125 (rounded to $.21)

Add them to get: Total = **$.51** per dinner

16. The correct answer is (3).

Profit = Number of dinners × sales/dinner − Number of dinners × cost/dinner

(Let P = profit; N = No. of dinners; S = sales/dinner; C = cost/dinner)

$$P = N \times S - N \times C =$$
$$P = N \times (S - C)$$
$$500 = N \times (2.50 - 0.58), \quad N = \frac{500}{(2.50 - .58)}$$

CALCULATOR   500 ÷ (2.50 − .58) = [Answer: 260.4166 or she must sell MORE than 260, namely **261** meals to make "*at least $500*"]

17. Alternate form, Coordinate Plane Grid: **(4, −2)**
Sketch the graph. The Southeast (SE) quadrant is at the bottom right.
(4, −2) is *farthest away* from the origin (0,0) in the SE quadrant.

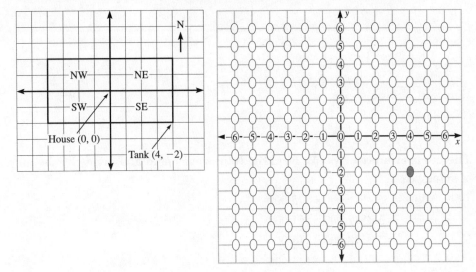

18. The correct answer is (4). Refer to the Formula page to find the *distance between points* for the two locations, the house (0,0) and the tank (4, −2).

Sketch it.

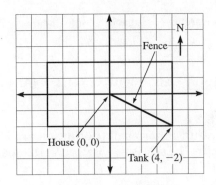

$$d = \sqrt{(x_2 - x_1)^2 + (y_2 - y_1)^2}$$
$$= \sqrt{(4-0)^2 + (-2-0)^2}$$
$$= \sqrt{16+4} = \sqrt{20}$$

20 SHIFT x^2 [Answer: 4.4721; rounded to **4.5 km**]
An alternative method to solve this problem is to use the Pythagorean theorem.

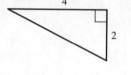

Here, $\sqrt{4^2 + 2^2} \approx$ **4.5**

19. **The correct answer is (5).** Find the total wages paid and divide by the number of employees:

Total wages:
$$5 \times \$15,000 = \$75,000$$
$$3 \times \$17,000 = \$51,000$$
$$1 \times \$18,000 = \underline{\$18,000}$$
$$\$144,000$$

Number of employees = 5 + 3 + 1 = 9
Average wage = $144,000 ÷ 9 = $16,000

20. **The correct answer is (2).** Express the answer in units of [days to save up for the bike] or **[days/bike]**

$$\frac{1 \text{ day}}{25 \text{ cigarettes}} \times \frac{20 \text{ cigarettes}}{\text{pack}} \times \frac{1 \text{ pack}}{4 \text{ dollars}} \times \frac{500 \text{ dollars}}{\text{bike}} =$$

CALCULATOR   20 × 500 ÷ 25 ÷ 4 = [Answer: **100** days to buy a bike]

21. Alternate form: **1 8 2 5 __**
Express the final result in terms of **[dollars/year]**
Recall: 20 cigarettes/1 pack is *equivalent to* 1/20 packs/cigarette), so,

$$\frac{4 \text{ dollars}}{\text{pack}} \times \frac{1 \text{ pack}}{20 \text{ cigarettes}} \times \frac{25 \text{ cigarettes}}{\text{day}} \times \frac{365 \text{ days}}{\text{year}} =$$

CALCULATOR   4 × 25 × 365 ÷ 20 = [Answer: **1825** dollars/year]

22. Alternate form: **1 0 . 1 4**

$$\text{Percentage} = \frac{\text{the part}}{\text{the whole}} \times 100$$

$$\text{Percentage} = \frac{1825 \text{ dollars}}{18,000 \text{ dollars}} \times 100 = 10.14\%$$

CALCULATOR   1825 ÷ 18000 × 100 = [Answer: 10.1388; rounded to **10.14%**]

23. **The correct answer is (3).** Sum total of cans sold = 387 + 300 + 113 + 98 + 64 + 41 = 1003

$$\text{Percent} = \frac{\text{cans of A sold}}{(\text{sum total of cans sold})} \times 100$$

$$\text{Percent of A} = \frac{387}{1003} \times 100$$

[C][A][L][C][U][L][A][T][O][R]   387 ÷ 1003 × 100 = [Answer: 38.58425; rounded to **39%**]

24. **The correct answer is (4).** $\text{Percent} = \dfrac{\text{cans of B sold}}{\text{sum of A + B + C}} \times 100 = \dfrac{300}{800} \times 100 = \textbf{37.5\%}$

25. **The correct answer is (4).** From the Formula page, the volume of a rectangular solid is:

V = L × W × H

Substituting, 300 = 15 × 5 × H = 75 × H

Solve for H, by dividing both sides by 75.

[C][A][L][C][U][L][A][T][O][R]   300 ÷ 75 = [Answer: **4 cans**]

4 layers of cans must be stacked, one on top of the other, to hold 300 cans.

answers

practice test 2

Part 2

26. The correct answer is (5). Add the individual amounts. Add the whole number separately from the fractions.

     S: 3

     C: 2

     T: 1

Total: 6

$$\frac{1}{2} = \frac{6}{12} \quad (\text{LCD} = 4 \times 3 = 12)$$

$$\frac{1}{3} = \frac{4}{12}$$

$$\frac{3}{4} = \frac{9}{12}$$

$$= \frac{19}{12} = 1\frac{7}{12}$$

Combine the results: $6 + 1 + \dfrac{7}{12} = 7\dfrac{7}{12}$ pounds of veggies.

27. The correct answer is (3). Divide $35.00 by 4:

$$
\begin{array}{r}
8.75 \\
4{\overline{\smash{\big)}\,35.00}} \\
\underline{32} \\
30 \\
\underline{28} \\
20 \\
\underline{20}
\end{array}
$$

or $ **8.75** is given to each child.

28. The correct answer is (1). From the Formula page, the Trigonometric ratio for

$$\sin A = \frac{\text{opposite}}{\text{hypotenuse}} = \frac{3}{AB}$$

use the Pythagorean theorem to find AB:

$$3^2 + 4^2 = AB^2 = 25$$

$$AB = \sqrt{25} = 5$$

Therefore, $\sin A = \dfrac{3}{AB} = \dfrac{3}{5} = \mathbf{0.6}$

29. The correct answer is (2). Convert the units from milliliters to pints.

$$9500 \text{ milliliters} \times \frac{1 \text{ liter}}{1000 \text{ milliliters}} \times \frac{1 \text{ quart}}{.95 \text{ liters}} \times \frac{2 \text{ pints}}{\text{quart}} =$$

$$\frac{9500 \times 2}{1000 \times 0.95} = \frac{9500^{10} \times 2}{950_1} = \textbf{20 pints}$$

30. The correct answer is (4). Change the dimensions to what is asked for . . . feet. Therefore,

200 yards × 1.5 yards becomes

600 feet × 4.5 feet when we multiply each yard by 3 to get feet.

"Square feet" tells you that you are looking for the area of the Yellow Brick Road. From the Formula page, area of a rectangle = length × width.

Therefore, the area of the road is

600 × 4.5 = **2700 square feet.**

31. Alternate Form: **3 / 8 __ __**

Total fraction of cars = sum of the fractions sold for each color car

$$\text{Red: } \frac{1}{2} \times \frac{1}{4} = \frac{1}{8} = \frac{3}{24}$$

$$\text{Green: } \frac{1}{3} \times \frac{3}{4} = \frac{3}{12} = \frac{6}{24}$$

$$\frac{9}{24} = \frac{3}{8}$$

$\dfrac{3}{8}$ of his cars were sold.

32. The correct answer is (5). Residential use includes sectors I and II, one-and two-family houses and apartment buildings. Neighborhoods C and D both devote 6.4 blocks to residential use: C = 80% of 8 and D = 40% of 16. A and B devote 4 and 12 blocks, respectively.

33. The correct answer is (3). Retail stores occupy 3 blocks (30% of 10) in Neighborhood A. Office buildings occupy 3 blocks (15% of 20) in Neighborhood B. In Neighborhood B, one- and two-family houses occupy 4 blocks, apartment houses 8 blocks, retail 4 blocks, and factories 1 block.

34. The correct answer is (2).

Area of sector
$$= \frac{120}{360} \cdot \pi \cdot 15^2$$
$$= \frac{1}{3} \cdot \pi \cdot 15 \cdot 15$$
$$= 75\pi$$

35. The correct answer is (4). List the years and add:

1983:	$15,000
1984:	$800
1985:	800
1986:	800
1987:	800
1988:	800
Total:	**$15,000 + 800(5)**

36. The correct answer is (2). Try to visualize the problem by making a sketch of the trail.

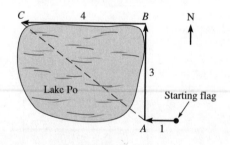

The distance saved = (AB + BC) − AC = (3 + 4) − AC

To find AC, remember the *familiar* right triangles: 3-4-5; AC = 5

Therefore, the distance saved is 7 − 5 = 2 miles

If you didn't remember the 3-4-5 right triangle relationship, you could have used the Pythagorean theorem, to find the hypotenuse (*AC*):

$$AB^2 + BC^2 = AC^2; \quad 3^2 + 4^2 = AC^2; \quad 9 + 16 = AC^2$$
$$AC = \sqrt{25} = 5$$

37. Alternate form, Coordinate Plane Grid: [Answer:**(−5, 3)**]

From the sketch in the answer to question 36, if the START is at the origin, (0,0), then the ending point (*E*) is (−5,3). On the coordinate grid answer sheet, the answer is:

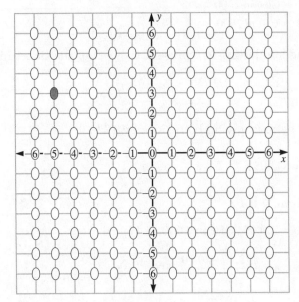

38. The correct answer is (1). If female workers made up about 20% of mining workers, the remaining 80% were male. 80% is four times 20%.

39. The correct answer is (5). The graph indicates that about 10% of miners were Hispanic.

733,000 × 10% = 73,300, or about 73,000

40. The correct answer is (2). Add the percentages first to find how many construction workers *were* Hispanic or African-American. The percentages are around 12 and 8 percent, for a total of 20%. Then the percentage of workers who were *neither* is 100% − 20%, or 80%.

41. The correct answer is (1). Multiply the units so that *[feet]* units divide out and the final result is in units of *[seconds]*.

Hint:

$\dfrac{132 \text{ feet}}{1 \text{ second}}$ is equivalent to $\dfrac{1 \text{ second}}{132 \text{ feet}}$. Therefore,

$\dfrac{1 \text{ second}}{132 \text{ feet}} \times 60 \text{ feet} = 0.45 \text{ seconds}$

Another way of solving this problem is by recalling the formula:

rate × time = distance; $132 \times t = 60$;

$t = \dfrac{60}{132} = 0.45$ seconds

42. The correct answer is (2). Costs for different years are proportional to the CPI of the respective years.

Make a ratio of corresponding pieces of information:

$$\frac{\text{Cost in 1920}}{\text{CPI in 1920}} = \frac{\text{Cost in 2000}}{\text{CPI in 2000}}$$

Substituting and letting X represent the cost of the ticket in 2000,

$$\frac{5.00}{20.00} = \frac{1}{4} = \frac{X}{172.20}$$

Solve for X by multiplying both sides by 172.20:

$$X = \frac{172.20}{4} = \$43.05$$

43. Alternate form: <u>**7**</u> <u>**6**</u> <u>**1**</u> / __ __

CPI in 1920 = 20.00; CPI in 2000 = 172.20

$$\text{The \% difference} = \frac{172.20 - 20.00}{20.00} \times 100$$

$$\frac{15220}{20} = 761\%$$

[Answer: **761**]

44. The correct answer is (4). Look across the chart on the two baseball league lines. The first time that the American League overtook the attendance figures was in 1977 when the American League = 19.6 million and National League = 19.1.

45. The correct answer is (2). The most popular sporting event in 1965 can be found by looking down the column for 1965. The greatest attendance was 62.9 million, for horseracing.

46. The correct answer is (3).
40.6 million—baseball, regular season
10.9 million—basketball, NBA
<u>13.4 million</u>—football, NFL
64.9 million—Total

$$\text{\% baseball} = \frac{40.6}{64.9} \times 100 = 62.56, \text{ [rounded to 63\%]}$$

$$= \textbf{63\%}$$

47. The correct answer is (5). The chart, *Attendance at Sports Events*, does not mention any data on cash revenues but only on attendance at events.

48. **The correct answer is (5).** Divide like terms to get the final result in terms of "*[$] / [month]*" units.

Let T represent the number of hours per week that Michael worked.

$$\frac{\$20}{hour} \times \frac{T \ hours}{week} \times \frac{4 \ weeks}{month} = \frac{\$1600}{month}$$

$20 \times T \times 4 = 1600; \ 80 \times T = 1600$

Divide both sides by 80:

$$T = \frac{1600}{80} = 20 \frac{hours}{week}$$

49. **The correct answer is (2).** His original rent is 40% of $1600.

Original Rent = 0.40 × 1600 = 640

New Rent = Original Rent + 160 = 640 + 160 = $800

50. **The correct answer is(4).** Let C = the capacity in gallons.

Then $\frac{1}{3}C + 3 = \frac{1}{2}C$

Multiplying through by 6, we obtain $2C + 18 = 3C$ or $C = 18$

ERROR ANALYSIS FOR PRACTICE TEST 2

Circle the number of each question you answered incorrectly. Count the number of circles in each content area and write the total number missed in the column headed "Number Incorrect." A large number of incorrect responses in a particular area indicates the need for further study in that area.

SUBJECT AREA	QUESTIONS	NUMBER INCORRECT
TEST 1. LANGUAGE ARTS, WRITING	50	
Sentence Structure	4, 5, 10, 13, 16, 18, 23, 27, 28, 32, 34, 37, 40, 47, 48	
Usage	2, 3, 8, 9, 17, 20, 22, 25, 33, 35, 41, 43, 45, 46, 49	
Mechanics	6, 7, 12, 14, 15, 19, 24, 29, 30, 31, 38, 39, 44	
Organization	1, 11, 21, 26, 36, 42, 50	
TEST 2. SOCIAL STUDIES	50	
History	1, 2, 3, 4, 5, 6, 7, 8, 14, 15, 16, 17, 18, 20, 21, 23, 41, 42, 43, 44, 45	
Economics	9, 10, 11, 12, 13, 36, 37, 38, 39, 40, 46, 47, 48	
Geography	19, 29, 30, 31, 32, 49, 50	
Civics and Government	22, 24, 25, 26, 27, 28, 33, 34, 35	
TEST 3. SCIENCE	50	
Life Science	1, 2, 3, 4, 5, 15, 16, 17, 18, 19, 26, 27, 28, 43, 44, 45, 46, 47, 48, 49, 50	
Chemistry	9, 10, 11, 12, 37, 38, 39, 40, 41	
Physics	6, 20, 21, 22, 23, 24, 25, 35, 36	
Earth and Space Science	7, 8, 13, 14, 29, 30, 31, 32, 33, 34, 42	
TEST 4. LANGUAGE ARTS, READING	40	
Drama and Poetry	7, 8, 9, 10, 11, 12, 19, 20, 21, 22, 23, 24	
Literary Readings	1, 2, 3, 4, 5, 6, 13, 14, 15, 16, 17, 18, 25, 26, 27, 28, 29, 30	
Nonfiction	31, 32, 33, 34, 35	
Business Readings	36, 37, 38, 39, 40	
TEST 5. MATHEMATICS	50	
Measurement and Geometry	2, 3, 4, 9, 11, 14, 17, 26, 30, 34, 37, 38, 39, 40, 42, 48, 50	
Algebra	7, 8, 10, 12, 16, 18, 25, 28, 35, 36, 41, 43	
Number Standards and Operations	1, 5, 6, 15, 20, 21, 22, 27, 29, 31	
Data Analysis	13, 19, 23, 24, 32, 33, 44, 45, 46, 47, 49	

ASSESSING YOUR READINESS

Now that you have devoted a good deal of time and effort to your GED study, you should be better prepared to apply for a date to take the GED. However, do not rush into this big step. Plot your scores from the sample test you just completed on the table below.

	Ready	Probably Ready	Possibly Ready	Not Yet Ready
Language Arts, Writing	38–50	26–37	18–25	0–17
Essay	4	3	2	1
Social Studies	38–50	26–37	18–25	0–17
Science	38–50	26–37	18–25	0–17
Language Arts, Reading	30–40	21–29	14–20	0–13
Mathematics	38–50	26–37	18–25	0–17

If all your scores are in the "Ready" column, you are probably well prepared for the actual GED test. You can therefore go ahead and sign up for the exam. If you have scores in the "Probably Ready" column, consult the Error Analysis table on page 775, and direct your study toward your area of weakness. "Probably Ready" is most likely good enough for passing and getting a GED diploma, but why take chances?

If any of your scores still fall into the lower categories, go back to the relevant chapters and study some more before tackling the last practice GED test in this book. For example, if your chief weakness lies in essay writing, practice by writing some more essays, either on topics suggested on pages 243–244 or on topics of your own choosing. Then, try the last practice test.

Practice Test 3

DIRECTIONS FOR TAKING THE PRACTICE TEST

Directions: The GED Practice Test has five separate tests: Language Arts, Writing; Social Studies; Science; Language Arts, Reading; and Mathematics.

1 Read and follow the directions given at the start of each test.

2 Stick to the time limits.

3 Enter your answers on the tear-out Answer Sheets provided on pages 759–763.

4 When you have completed the entire test, compare your answers with the correct answers given in the Answer Key and Explanations at the end of this practice test.

5 Use the Error Analysis Chart following each practice test to see where you are weak and where you are strong.

6 Don't forget to consult the "Assessing Your Readiness" section to gauge how close you are to mastering the GED tests.

practice test 3

ANSWER SHEET PRACTICE TEST 3

Correct answers for this test begin on page 838.

Test 1. Language Arts, Writing—Part 1

1. ①②③④⑤	11. ①②③④⑤	21. ①②③④⑤	31. ①②③④⑤	41. ①②③④⑤
2. ①②③④⑤	12. ①②③④⑤	22. ①②③④⑤	32. ①②③④⑤	42. ①②③④⑤
3. ①②③④⑤	13. ①②③④⑤	23. ①②③④⑤	33. ①②③④⑤	43. ①②③④⑤
4. ①②③④⑤	14. ①②③④⑤	24. ①②③④⑤	34. ①②③④⑤	44. ①②③④⑤
5. ①②③④⑤	15. ①②③④⑤	25. ①②③④⑤	35. ①②③④⑤	45. ①②③④⑤
6. ①②③④⑤	16. ①②③④⑤	26. ①②③④⑤	36. ①②③④⑤	46. ①②③④⑤
7. ①②③④⑤	17. ①②③④⑤	27. ①②③④⑤	37. ①②③④⑤	47. ①②③④⑤
8. ①②③④⑤	18. ①②③④⑤	28. ①②③④⑤	38. ①②③④⑤	48. ①②③④⑤
9. ①②③④⑤	19. ①②③④⑤	29. ①②③④⑤	39. ①②③④⑤	49. ①②③④⑤
10. ①②③④⑤	20. ①②③④⑤	30. ①②③④⑤	40. ①②③④⑤	50. ①②③④⑤

Test 2. Social Studies

1. ①②③④⑤	11. ①②③④⑤	21. ①②③④⑤	31. ①②③④⑤	41. ①②③④⑤
2. ①②③④⑤	12. ①②③④⑤	22. ①②③④⑤	32. ①②③④⑤	42. ①②③④⑤
3. ①②③④⑤	13. ①②③④⑤	23. ①②③④⑤	33. ①②③④⑤	43. ①②③④⑤
4. ①②③④⑤	14. ①②③④⑤	24. ①②③④⑤	34. ①②③④⑤	44. ①②③④⑤
5. ①②③④⑤	15. ①②③④⑤	25. ①②③④⑤	35. ①②③④⑤	45. ①②③④⑤
6. ①②③④⑤	16. ①②③④⑤	26. ①②③④⑤	36. ①②③④⑤	46. ①②③④⑤
7. ①②③④⑤	17. ①②③④⑤	27. ①②③④⑤	37. ①②③④⑤	47. ①②③④⑤
8. ①②③④⑤	18. ①②③④⑤	28. ①②③④⑤	38. ①②③④⑤	48. ①②③④⑤
9. ①②③④⑤	19. ①②③④⑤	29. ①②③④⑤	39. ①②③④⑤	49. ①②③④⑤
10. ①②③④⑤	20. ①②③④⑤	30. ①②③④⑤	40. ①②③④⑤	50. ①②③④⑤

Test 3. Science

1. ①②③④⑤	11. ①②③④⑤	21. ①②③④⑤	31. ①②③④⑤	41. ①②③④⑤
2. ①②③④⑤	12. ①②③④⑤	22. ①②③④⑤	32. ①②③④⑤	42. ①②③④⑤
3. ①②③④⑤	13. ①②③④⑤	23. ①②③④⑤	33. ①②③④⑤	43. ①②③④⑤
4. ①②③④⑤	14. ①②③④⑤	24. ①②③④⑤	34. ①②③④⑤	44. ①②③④⑤
5. ①②③④⑤	15. ①②③④⑤	25. ①②③④⑤	35. ①②③④⑤	45. ①②③④⑤
6. ①②③④⑤	16. ①②③④⑤	26. ①②③④⑤	36. ①②③④⑤	46. ①②③④⑤
7. ①②③④⑤	17. ①②③④⑤	27. ①②③④⑤	37. ①②③④⑤	47. ①②③④⑤
8. ①②③④⑤	18. ①②③④⑤	28. ①②③④⑤	38. ①②③④⑤	48. ①②③④⑤
9. ①②③④⑤	19. ①②③④⑤	29. ①②③④⑤	39. ①②③④⑤	49. ①②③④⑤
10. ①②③④⑤	20. ①②③④⑤	30. ①②③④⑤	40. ①②③④⑤	50. ①②③④⑤

answer sheet

Test 4. Language Arts, Reading

1. ①②③④⑤   11. ①②③④⑤   21. ①②③④⑤   31. ①②③④⑤
2. ①②③④⑤   12. ①②③④⑤   22. ①②③④⑤   32. ①②③④⑤
3. ①②③④⑤   13. ①②③④⑤   23. ①②③④⑤   33. ①②③④⑤
4. ①②③④⑤   14. ①②③④⑤   24. ①②③④⑤   34. ①②③④⑤
5. ①②③④⑤   15. ①②③④⑤   25. ①②③④⑤   35. ①②③④⑤
6. ①②③④⑤   16. ①②③④⑤   26. ①②③④⑤   36. ①②③④⑤
7. ①②③④⑤   17. ①②③④⑤   27. ①②③④⑤   37. ①②③④⑤
8. ①②③④⑤   18. ①②③④⑤   28. ①②③④⑤   38. ①②③④⑤
9. ①②③④⑤   19. ①②③④⑤   29. ①②③④⑤   39. ①②③④⑤
10. ①②③④⑤   20. ①②③④⑤   30. ①②③④⑤   40. ①②③④⑤

Test 5. Mathematics—Part 1

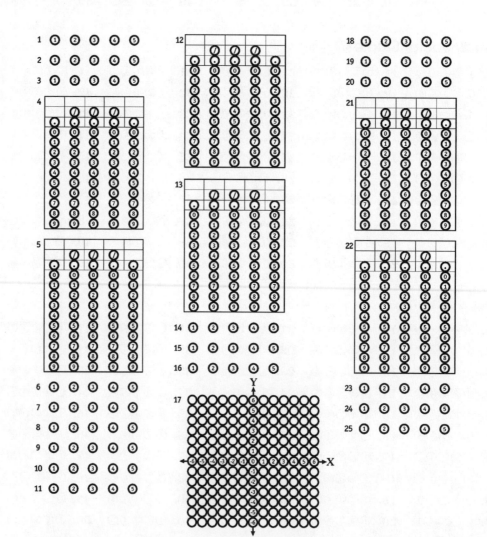

Test 5. Mathematics—Part 2

26 ① ② ③ ④ ⑤   38 ① ② ③ ④ ⑤
27 ① ② ③ ④ ⑤   39 ① ② ③ ④ ⑤
28 ① ② ③ ④ ⑤   40 ① ② ③ ④ ⑤
29 ① ② ③ ④ ⑤   41 ① ② ③ ④ ⑤
30 ① ② ③ ④ ⑤   42 ① ② ③ ④ ⑤

31 [grid-in answer grid]   43 [grid-in answer grid]

32 ① ② ③ ④ ⑤   44 ① ② ③ ④ ⑤
33 ① ② ③ ④ ⑤   45 ① ② ③ ④ ⑤
34 ① ② ③ ④ ⑤   46 ① ② ③ ④ ⑤
35 ① ② ③ ④ ⑤   47 ① ② ③ ④ ⑤
36 ① ② ③ ④ ⑤   48 ① ② ③ ④ ⑤
                              49 ① ② ③ ④ ⑤
37 [coordinate grid grid-in]   50 ① ② ③ ④ ⑤

ANSWER SHEET PRACTICE TEST 3

Language Arts, Writing—Part 2 Essay Test

_____

_____

_____

_____

_____

_____

_____

_____

_____

_____

_____

_____

_____

_____

_____

_____

_____

_____

_____

_____

Language Arts, Writing—Part 2 Essay Test (continued)

_____

_____

_____

_____

_____

_____

_____

_____

_____

_____

_____

_____

_____

_____

_____

_____

_____

answer sheet

TEST 1: LANGUAGE ARTS, WRITING

This test has two parts. Part 1 measures your ability to recognize errors in written material. Part 2 tests your ability to write a short essay.

Part 1. Recognizing and Correcting Errors

75 Minutes • 50 Questions

Directions: The Language Arts, Writing Test consists of several written passages with numbered sentences and lettered paragraphs. Some of the sentences contain errors in sentence structure, usage, or mechanics. There will also be a few errors of organization that will require moving a sentence or paragraph, or deleting or replacing a sentence. Read each passage carefully first, then answer the questions that follow. For each question, choose the answer that will correct an error and result in the most effective writing. The best answer must be consistent with the meaning and tone of the passage. Record your answers in the Language Arts, Writing Section of the answer sheet.

Q Often their are two equally effective ways to solve a problem.
What correction should be made to this sentence?

   (1) replace <u>their</u> with <u>there</u>
   (2) change <u>are</u> to <u>is</u>
   (3) change <u>two</u> to <u>too</u>
   (4) insert a comma after <u>equally</u>
   (5) no change is necessary

                                           ● ② ③ ④ ⑤

A In this example, the word <u>their</u>, which means "belonging to them," is incorrectly substituted for the word <u>there</u>. To indicate this correction, mark answer space (1) on your answer sheet.

ITEMS 1 TO 8 REFER TO THE FOLLOWING PASSAGE.

The 2000 Census

A

(1) Every ten years, the United States Census Bureau conducts a census that give us a lot of information about our country. (2) The last census was April 1, 2000, by more than 285,000 census takers. (3) A short questionnaire was delivered to each household. (4) It asked questions about seven subjects: name, sex, age, relationship, Hispanic origin, race, and housing tenure (whether your home is owned or rented). (5) A small sampling of households received a longer questionnaire; that asked about 27 additional subjects, such as education, ancestry, employment, and disability. (6) What are some of the things the results tell us?

B

(7) They told us that the total population on the date of the census was 281,421,906 people. (8) Of these, 50.9 percent are women, and 49.1 percent, male. (9) There are more than 4 million people over the age of 85, and more than 72 million under the age of eighteen. (10) The median age of people in the United States is 35.3 years. (11) Racially and cultural, we are a multiracial and multiethnic society. (12) Approximately 77 percent of the population classifies itself as white, over 12 percent as black, and more than 12 percent as Hispanic or Latino. (13) Of this latter group, the majority, or more than 20 million, are Mexican-Americans.

C

(14) Household patterns have shown changes in recent years. (15) For example, women head almost 13 million households, with more than 7 million of these having children under the age of 18 years. (16) More than 27 million people live alone, 54 million people live with their husbands or wives, and over 4 million people are institutionalized.

D

(17) The census is important to our nation as highways and telephone lines. (18) Federal dollars supporting schools, employment services, housing assistance, highway construction, hospital services, programs for the elderly, and more are distributed on the basis of census figures.

1. Sentence (1): **Every ten years, the United States Census Bureau conducts a census that give us a lot of information about our country.**

   What correction should be made to this sentence?

   (1) change census to Census
   (2) insert a comma after Bureau
   (3) change conducts to conduct
   (4) change give to gives
   (5) remove the comma

2. Sentence (2): **The last census was April 1, 2000, by more than 285,000 census takers.**

   What correction should be made to sentence (2)?

   (1) change was to was conducted on
   (2) change census takers to census-takers
   (3) change over to more than
   (4) delete the comma after 2000
   (5) insert in the United States after The last census

3. Sentence (5): **A small sampling of households received a <u>longer questionnaire; that asked</u> about 27 additional subjects, such as education, ancestry, employment, and disability**.

Which of the following is the best way to write the underlined portion of this sentence? If you think that the original is best, pick option (1).

(1) longer questionnaire; which asked

(2) longer questionnaire that asked

(3) longer questionnaire that ask

(4) longer questionnaire. That asked

(5) longest questionnaire; that asked

4. Sentence (6): **What are some of the things the results tell us?**

What revision should you make to sentence (6) in order to improve the organization of this selection?

(1) move it after sentence (3)

(2) move it to the beginning of paragraph A

(3) move it to the beginning of paragraph B

(4) move it to the end of paragraph B

(5) no revision is necessary

5. Sentence (7): **They told us that the total population on the date of the census was 281,421,906 people.**

What correction should be made to this sentence?

(1) put a comma after <u>us</u>

(2) change <u>told</u> to <u>spoke</u>

(3) change <u>on the date</u> to <u>on this date</u>

(4) change <u>was</u> to <u>were</u>

(5) change <u>They told us</u> to <u>They tell us</u>

6. Sentence (11): **Racially and cultural, we are a multiracial and multiethnic society.**

What correction should be made to this sentence?

(1) change <u>Racially</u> to <u>Racial</u>

(2) change <u>cultural</u> to <u>culturally</u>

(3) change <u>multiracial</u> to <u>multiracial</u>

(4) change <u>society</u> to <u>societies</u>

(5) no correction is necessary

7. Sentence (17): **The <u>census is important</u> to our nation as highways and telephone lines.**

Which of the following choices is the best way to write the underlined portion of this sentence? If you think the original is best, pick option (1).

(1) The census is important

(2) The census, is important

(3) The census, important

(4) The census is as important

(5) The census is important,

8. Sentence (18): **Federal dollars supporting schools, employment services, housing assistance, highway construction, hospital services, programs for the elderly, and more are distributed on the basis of census figures.**

If you began this sentence with the words <u>On the basis of census figures,</u> the next words would be

(1) programs for

(2) and more

(3) federal dollars

(4) are distributed

(5) dollars for

ITEMS 9 TO 15 REFER TO THE FOLLOWING BUSINESS MEMO.

Business Memo

From: Mr. George Grace, Jr.
To: All Sales Managers for Grace Bros. Department Store
Re: New Sales Targets for Spring 2004

A

(1) Instead of attaining our projected 10% increase in sales for this quarter, our sales have declined by 15%. (2) This represents a net drop of 25% from our expected target. (3) This is very disappointed, so we must try to improve our output for the next quarter. (4) Our goal is to increase sales by 30%, thus attaining a net growth of 5% over two quarters.

B

(5) We must all pitching in. (6) Grace Bros. management persons must do the following: Beginning in two weeks, and staffed by a reduced crew of salespersons, management will keep the store open two extra hours each day. (7) The store will open one hour earlier in the morning and stay open one hour longer in the evening. (8) Extra advertising will announce this change. (9) Also, new accounting procedures of sales will result in smaller inventory and thus less waste and more profits.

C

(10) Sales personnel will hopefully help make the atmosphere at Grace Bros. more upbeat. (11) Coffee, tea, and cake will be served throughout the day. (12) Each salesperson will make his/her sales station more attractive. (13) Customers will be surveyed as to their special needs and requirements their spending habits will be categorized and inserted into a computerized spreadsheet.

D

(14) If we surpass our new goal of a 30% increase in sales for the next quarter, the sales staff will get a bonus. (15) The department, showing the most improvement, in sales will get a special bonus.

E

(16) Let's work together this quarter to make Grace Brothers the most popular and successful department store in the city!

9. Sentence (3): **This is very disappointed, so we must try to improve our output for the next quarter.**

Which of the following is the best way to write the underlined portion of this sentence? If you think the above is the best way to write the sentence, choose option (1).

(1) disappointed, so we
(2) disappointment, so we
(3) disappoint, so we
(4) disappointed. And, so we
(5) disappointing, so we

10. Sentence (5): **We must all pitching in.**

What correction should be made to this sentence?

(1) change pitching to pitched
(2) change must to should
(3) change pitching in to pitcher
(4) change pitching to pitch
(5) no correction is necessary

11. Sentence (6): **Grace Bros. management persons must do the following: Beginning in two weeks and staffed by a reduced crew of salespersons, management will keep the store open two extra hours each day.**

What correction should be made to this sentence?

(1) change Beginning to beginning
(2) change management to Management
(3) capitalize salespersons and management
(4) change staffed to staffing
(5) remove the comma

12. Sentence (9): **Also, new accounting procedures of sales will result in smaller inventory and thus less waste and more profits.**

If you rewrote this sentence beginning with Smaller inventory and thus less waste and more profits, the next word(s) should be

(1) procedures of sales
(2) and sales
(3) will result from
(4) new accounting procedures
(5) will resulting in

13. Sentence (13): **Customers will be surveyed as to their special needs and requirements their spending habits will be categorized and inserted into a computerized spreadsheet.**

Which of the following is the best way to write the underlined portion of this sentence? If you think the original is best, choose option (1).

(1) and requirements their
(2) and requirements. Their
(3) requirements and there
(4) and requiring their
(5) and requirements. There

14. Sentence (15): **The department, showing the most improvement, in sales will get a special bonus.**

What correction should be made to this sentence?

(1) change department to Department
(2) remove both commas
(3) remove the first comma
(4) change special to especially
(5) no correction is necessary

15. Which revision would improve the organization of the text of this memo?

   (1) combine paragraphs A and B

   (2) move paragraph D before paragraph A

   (3) put sentence (1) at the end of paragraph A

   (4) move paragraph E to the end of paragraph D

   (5) combine paragraphs C, D, and E

ITEMS 16 TO 22 REFER TO THE FOLLOWING ARTICLE.

Starting a Business

A

(1) Sometimes the job market is so poor that it's impossible to finding work. (2) You ask around, you scour the want ads, you call up employment agencies, you confer with your friends and relatives, but in the end you are still jobless. (3) What should you do in such a situation? (4) This might be the time to show your creativity and start a business of your own.

B

(5) In order to go about accomplishing this, you needs to look at two things. (6) First, what kinds of work or services are possibly needed in your community that are not currently being provided by others? (7) Second, what are the skills and services you might be able to offer that would be of use to people and lead to income for you? (8) For example: could you provide day-care for children, do odd jobs, repair appliances; are you good at housekeeping; do you know how to paint or do repairs to a house; do you know how to read directions and assemble things; are you good with cars? (9) It might be good to "problem solve" with a friend or two in the same boat, paper and pencil in hand, and jot down the ideas that will inevitably coming.

C

(10) Many young people their own successful business in this way. (11) One young woman started a "home secretary" service for elderly people who need help in doing their bills, balancing checkbooks, and answering letters. (12) A young man living in a small City has a thriving business as a daily caregiver for the pets of working or traveling business people. (13) Another invested in a couple of lawn mowers and cares for the yards of several dozen neighbors. (14) In the winter, he converts the mowers into snowplows.

16. Sentence (1): **Sometimes the job market is so poor that it's <u>impossible to finding work.</u>**

Which of the following is the best way to write the underlined portion of this sentence? If you think that the original is best, choose option (1).

   (1) impossible to finding work

   (2) impossible to finds work

   (3) impossible for to finding work

   (4) impossible to find working

   (5) impossible to find work

17. Sentence (5): **In order to go about accomplishing this, you needs to look at two things.**

What correction should be made to this sentence?

   (1) change <u>accomplishing this,</u> to <u>accomplish this,</u>

   (2) change <u>two things</u> to <u>things, too</u>

   (3) change the comma to a colon

   (4) change <u>you needs</u> to <u>you need</u>

   (5) change <u>to go about</u> to <u>to getting to</u>

18. Sentence (9): **It might be good to "problem solve" with a friend or two in the same boat, paper and pencil in hand, and jot down the ideas that will inevitably coming.**

    What correction should be made to this sentence?

    (1) change jot down to jotting down
    (2) change inevitably coming to inevitably come
    (3) change good to to good for
    (4) change a friend or two to two friends
    (5) no correction is needed

19. Sentence (10): **Many young people their own successful business in this way.**

    Which of the following is the best way to write the underlined portion of this sentence? If you think the original is the best, choose option (1).

    (1) people their own
    (2) people starts their own
    (3) people have started their own
    (4) people had starting their own
    (5) people starting their own

20. Sentence (12): **A young man living in a small City has a thriving business as a daily caregiver for the pets of working or traveling business people.**

    What correction should be made to this sentence?

    (1) put a comma after business
    (2) change caregiver to care-giver
    (3) change pets to pet's
    (4) change small City to small city
    (5) put a colon after thriving business

21. Sentence (13): **Another invested in a couple of lawn mowers and cares for the yards of several dozen neighbors.**

    If you rewrote this sentence beginning with Another cares for the lawns of several dozen neighbors, the next words would be

    (1) after investing
    (2) invested in
    (3) lawn mowers
    (4) in a
    (5) couple of

22. In order to improve the clarity of *"Starting a Business,"* which of the following choices would make the best closing line to follow sentence (14)?

    (1) Some businesses make money, and some don't.
    (2) A large number of businesses fail each year.
    (3) As these examples show, a person who is resourceful can often create a job where none existed before.
    (4) How would you start a business?
    (5) Everyone has some useful skills and abilities.

    ITEMS 23 TO 29 REFER TO THE ARTICLE BELOW.

    The Importance of Sales Workers

    A

    (1) The success of any small retail establishment depends largely on it's sales staff. (2) Courteous and efficient service from behind the counter or on the sales floor does much to build a store's reputation, as well as please customers with the kind of personal attention no longer offered by large stores.

B

(3) Weather selling furniture, electrical appliances, or clothing, a sales worker's primary job is to interest customers in the merchandise. (4) Describing the product's construction, demonstrating its use, and showing various models and colors. (5) For expensive "big ticket" items, special knowledge or skills are needed. (6) Personal computer sales workers, for example, must have sufficient up-to-date knowledge of electronics to explain to customers the features of various brands and models and the meaning of manufacturer specifications.

C

(7) In addition to selling, most retail sales workers make out sales checks, receive cash payments, and give change and receipts. (8) Most stores have now installed point-of-sale terminals that register sales, adjusting inventory figures, and perform simple calculations. (9) This equipment increases workers' productivity it enables them to provide better customer service. (10) Sales persons also handles returns and exchanges of merchandise and keep their work areas neat. (11) In addition, retail workers may help stack shelves or racks, mark price tags, take inventory, and prepare displays. (12) However, where standard articles such as food, hardware, linens, or housewares are sold, sales workers often do little more than take payments and wrap purchases.

23. Sentence (1): **The success of any retail establishment depends largely on it's sales staff.**

Which of the following is the best way to write the underlined portion of this sentence? If you feel the original way is best, pick option (1).

(1) on it's sales staff.
(2) on it's selling staff.
(3) on its sales staff.
(4) on its selling.
(5) upon it's sales staff.

24. Sentence (3): **Weather selling furniture, electrical appliances, or clothing, a sales worker's primary job is to interest customers in the merchandise.**

What correction should be made to this sentence?

(1) change Weather to Whether
(2) delete the comma after appliances
(3) change interest customers to interest customer's
(4) change primary job to prime job
(5) change sales worker's to sales' worker's

25. Sentence (4): **Describing the product's construction, demonstrating its use, and showing various models and colors.**

What correction should be made to this sentence?

(1) change product's construction to products construction
(2) change showing to show
(3) insert done at the end of the sentence
(4) change demonstrating its use to demonstrate its use
(5) insert This is done by before Describing

26. Sentence (7): **In addition to selling, most retail sales workers make out sales checks, receive cash payments, and give change and receipts.**

    Which of the following sentences would make a good substitute for this sentence in order to clarify paragraph C?

    (1) Most sales people are no longer given commissions on their sales.

    (2) Sales persons need to stand on their feet for up to eight hours a day.

    (3) Computer sales go up every year since they have become an integral part of life.

    (4) Much depends on the size of the store.

    (5) None of the above

27. Sentence (8): **Most stores now have installed point-of-sale terminals that register sales, adjusting inventory figures, and perform simple calculations.**

    Which of the following is the best way to write the underlined portion of sentence (8)? If you think that the original is best, pick option (1).

    (1) register sales, adjusting
    (2) registered sales, adjusting
    (3) register sales, adjust
    (4) register sales: adjusting
    (5) registering sales, adjusting

28. Sentence (9): **This equipment increases workers' productivity it enables them to provide better customer service.**

    What correction should be made to this sentence?

    (1) change enables them to enabling them

    (2) change productivity it enables to productivity. It enables

    (3) insert a comma after productivity

    (4) change increases to increasing

    (5) change workers' to workers

29. Sentence (10): **Sales persons also handles returns and exchanges of merchandise and keep their work areas neat.**

    Which of the following is the best way to write the underlined portion of this sentence? If you think that the original is best, choose option (1).

    (1) also handles returns
    (2) handling returns also
    (3) also handling returns
    (4) also handle returns
    (5) also handles returnings

ITEMS 30 TO 36 REFER TO THE FOLLOWING PASSAGE.

Becoming a Construction Inspector

A

(1) To become a construction or building inspector, several years of experience as a construction contractor, supervisor, or craft worker are generally required. (2) Most employers also required an applicant to have a high school diploma. (3) High school preparation should include courses in drafting, algebra, geometry, and english. (4) During the first couple of weeks on the job, they need to learn about inspection techniques, codes, and regulations.

B

(5) Workers who want to become inspectors should have a thorough knowledge of construction materials and practices, in either a general area like structural or heavy construction, or in a specialized area such as electrical or plumbing systems, reinforced concrete, or structural steel. (6) Construction and building inspectors usually receive most of their training on the job. (7) They begin by inspecting less complex types of construction, such as residential buildings, then gradually the difficulty of their assignments. (8) A significant number of construction and building inspectors have recent experience as carpenters, electricians, plumbers, or pipefitters.

C

(9) Many employers prefer inspectors who have graduated from an apprenticeship program, and have studied engineering or architecture for at least two years, inspectors might have a degree from a community or junior college, with courses in construction technology, blueprint reading, mathematics, and building inspection.

D

(10) Construction building inspectors must be in good physical condition in order to walk and climb about construction cites. (11) They must also have a motor vehicle operator's license. (12) In addition, federal, state, and many local governments usually require that inspectors pass a civil service examination.

---

30. Sentence (2): **Most employers also required an applicant to have a high school diploma.**

What correction should be made to this sentence?

(1) change <u>employers</u> to <u>employees</u>

(2) insert <u>are</u> between <u>also</u> and <u>required</u>

(3) change <u>required</u> to <u>require</u>

(4) change <u>to have</u> to <u>having</u>

(5) No correction is necessary.

31. Sentence (3): **High school preparation should include courses in drafting, algebra, geometry, and english.**

What correction should be made to this sentence?

(1) capitalize <u>drafting</u>, <u>algebra</u>, <u>geometry</u>, and <u>english</u>

(2) change <u>include</u> to <u>have included</u>

(3) capitalize <u>geometry</u> and <u>english</u>

(4) capitalize <u>English</u>

(5) No correction is necessary.

32. Sentence (4): **During the first couple of weeks on the job, they need to learn about inspection techniques, codes, and regulations.**

What revision should be made to sentence (4) to improve the organization of paragraph A?

(1) move sentence (4) to the beginning of paragraph A

(2) move sentence (4) to follow sentence (7)

(3) move sentence (4) to follow sentence (2)

(4) move sentence (4) to follow sentence (1)

(5) No revision is necessary.

33. Sentence (6): **Construction and building inspectors usually receive most of their training on the job.**

If you rewrote sentence (6) beginning with Usually, most training of construction and building inspectors, the next word(s) should be

(1) is received

(2) they

(3) and

(4) receive most

(5) on

34. Sentence (7): **They begin by inspecting less complex types of construction, such as residential buildings, then gradually the difficulty of their assignments.**

What correction should be made to sentence (7)?

(1) remove the comma after construction

(2) insert is increased after assignments

(3) change buildings to building

(4) insert increasing after assignments

(5) change begin by inspecting to begin to inspect

35. Sentence (9): **Many employers prefer inspectors who have graduated from an apprenticeship program and have studied engineering or architecture for at least two years, inspectors might have a degree from a community or junior college with courses in construction technology, blueprint reading, mathematics, and building inspection.**

Which of the following is the best way to write the underlined portion of this sentence? If you think the original is the best way to write the sentence, choose option (1).

(1) two years, inspectors

(2) two years even though, inspectors

(3) two years. Inspectors

(4) two years, Inspectors

(5) two years inspectors

36. Sentence (10): **Construction building inspectors must be in good physical condition in order to walk and climb about construction cites.**

Which of the following is the best way to write the underlined portion of this sentence? If you think the original is the best way to write the sentence, choose option (1).

(1) about construction cites

(2) on construct cites

(3) around construction cites

(4) around constructing

(5) around construction sites

ITEMS 37 TO 43 REFER TO THE ARTICLE BELOW.

Physical Fitness for Kids

A

(1) Physical fitness activities begin with play early in life, starting with random arm and leg movements in infancy. (2) As the baby gets older, we have all observed how active and physical most healthy children. (3) Jumping, climbing, running, and movement of all sorts are as natural to young children as breathing. (4) When children reach school age, physical movement usually become more controlled, and they then need the guidance of parents, teachers, and coaches in selecting individual and team play activities for physical and emotional development. (5) Besides helping to build physical fitness and a sense of physical power, play is a child's outlet for expressing joy, frustration, anger, or pride. (6) Group play and sports encourage growth in emotional stability and maturity and offer that good feeling of belonging. (7) The ability to win or lose gracefully and to take pride in the success of others are added values learned through these activities who also provide lessons in honesty, cooperation, teamwork, tolerance, and consideration for others. (8) Parent's and teacher's know that when students are in good health, they get better grades in school, gaining in self-esteem and self-confidence.

B

(9) All these are important reasons for schools to provide physical fitness programs for all students—kindergarten through high school and college? (10) Schools and parents need to take an active interest and, where possible, work together in creating physical education programs in which all students, whatever their capabilities or special needs, can take part. (11) These programs help students understand the connection between exercise, diet, rest, and relaxation and all other aspects of health. (12) Well-planned physical education programs help children establish lifelong patterns of wholesome and rewarding physical activities.

37. Sentence (2): **As the baby gets older, we have all observed how active and physical most healthy children.**

What correction should be made to this sentence?

(1) remove the comma
(2) add the word <u>are</u> after <u>children</u>
(3) change <u>observed</u> to <u>seen</u>
(4) change <u>gets</u> to <u>get</u>
(5) change <u>the baby</u> to <u>baby</u>

38. Sentence (4): **When children reach school age, physical movement usually <u>become more controlled, and</u> they then need the guidance of parents, teachers, and coaches in selecting individual and team play activities for physical and emotional development.**

Which of the following is the best way to write the underlined portion of this sentence? If you think the original is the best way to write the sentence, choose option (1).

(1) become more controlled, and
(2) become more controlled. And
(3) becomes more controlled, and
(4) becoming more controlled, and
(5) being more controlled, and

39. Sentence (5): **Besides helping to build physical fitness and a sense of physical power, play is a child's outlet for expressing joy, frustration, anger, or pride.**

What revision should be made to sentence (5) in order to improve the organization of this reading passage?

(1) begin a new paragraph with sentence (5)

(2) move sentence (5) to the beginning of paragraph A

(3) move sentence (5) to the beginning of paragraph B

(4) delete sentence (5)

(5) no revision is needed

40. Sentence (7): **The ability to win or lose gracefully and to take pride in the success of others are added values learned through these activities who also provide lessons in honesty, cooperation, teamwork, tolerance, and consideration for others.**

What correction should be made to sentence (7)?

(1) change take pride to taking pride

(2) change gracefully to gracefull

(3) change are added to is added

(4) change who also provide to , which also provide

(5) no correction is needed

41. Sentence (8): **Parent's and teacher's know that when students are in good health, they get better grades in school, gaining in self-esteem and self-confidence.**

Which of the following is the best way to write the underlined portion of this sentence? If you think that the original is best, choose option (1).

(1) Parent's and teacher's know

(2) Parent's and Teacher's know

(3) Parent's and teacher's: know

(4) Parents' and teachers' know

(5) Parents and teachers know

42. Sentence (9): **All these are important reasons for schools to provide physical fitness programs for all students—kindergarten through high school and college?**

What correction should be made to this sentence?

(1) change schools to school

(2) change programs to programming

(3) change the dash to a comma

(4) change college? to college.

(5) put a comma after reasons

43. Sentence (12): **Well-planned physical education programs help children establish lifelong patterns of wholesome and rewarding physical activities.**

If you rewrote this sentence, starting with Children establish lifelong patterns of wholesome and rewarding physical activities the next word should be

(1) well-planned

(2) with

(3) programs

(4) help

(5) education

ITEMS 44 TO 50 REFER TO THE FOLLOWING PIECE.

How to Protect Your Privacy

A

(1) In this age of computers and the Internet, it is more important than ever to take steps to protect your privacy. (2) The three main areas of concern is charge cards, telephones, and the Internet. (3) As a general rule, in order to preserve your privacy, don't say information that isn't necessary for the particular situation.

B

(4) Concerning charge cards, watch them closely. (5) Only give people your credit card, charge card, debit card, or bank account number if you're using that account to pay for a purchase or applying for credit. (6) It isn't necessary to give that type of information for any other reason. (7) Don't allow your credit record to be checked except for legitimate reasons. (8) A lender or employer can check your credit record. (9) However, it's illegal for a business to check your record unless you're seeking financing. (10) You should also screen your telephone calls carefully.

C

(11) You can use an answering machine to listen to a caller; and decide whether you want to pick up. (12) Keep your phone number private. (13) You can buy a service to block others from using Caller ID to see your name and the number you're calling from. (14) But be aware that this blocking may not work with every type of number you call.

D

(15) Never give anyone your online password. (16) Con artists may try to trick you into providing your password by pretending to be your online service provider in order to use your access at your expense. (17) Your service provider already has your password, and no one else should need it.

44. Sentence (2): **The three main areas of concern is charge cards, telephones, and the Internet.**
What correction should be made to this sentence?

(1) change <u>concern</u> to <u>concerns</u>

(2) change <u>of</u> to <u>for</u>

(3) change <u>is</u> to <u>are</u>

(4) replace the commas with semicolons

(5) no correction is necessary

45. Sentence (3): **As a general rule, in order to preserve your privacy, don't say information that isn't necessary for the particular situation.**

What correction should be made to this sentence?

(1) change <u>say</u> to <u>provide</u>

(2) remove the comma after <u>rule</u>

(3) change <u>don't</u> to <u>do not</u>

(4) change <u>don't say</u> to <u>giving</u>

(5) delete <u>As a general rule</u>

46. Sentence (5): **Only give people your credit card, charge card, debit card, or bank account number if you're using that account to pay for a purchase or applying for credit.**

Which of the following is the best way to rewrite the underlined portion of this sentence? If you think the original is the best way to write the sentence, choose option (1).

(1) or applying for credit.

(2) or apply for credit.

(3) application for credit.

(4) or credit application.

(5) or are applying for credit.

47. Sentence (9): **However, it's illegal for a business to check your record unless you're seeking financing.**

If you rewrite sentence (9) beginning with However, unless you're seeking financing, the next words would be

(1) for a business

(2) check your record

(3) illegal for

(4) it's illegal

(5) record your business

48. Sentence (10): **You should also screen your telephone calls carefully.**

Which revision should be made to sentence (10)?

(1) move sentence (10) to the beginning of paragraph B

(2) move sentence (10) to the beginning of paragraph C

(3) move sentence (10) to the end of paragraph C

(4) delete sentence (10)

(5) no revision is necessary

49. Sentence (11): **You can use an answering machine to listen to a caller; and decide whether you want to pick up.**

What correction should be made to this sentence?

(1) change you want to you wanting

(2) change to listen to for listen

(3) change answering machine to Answering Machine

(4) change an to the

(5) change caller; and decide to caller and decide

50. Which sentence below would be the most effective if inserted before sentence (15)?

(1) Your computer requires special safeguards, so beware.

(2) What are online passwords for?

(3) This is definitely the age of computers.

(4) Apply for a password immediately.

(5) It is worthwhile to get an unlisted telephone number.

Part 2. Essay Test

45 Minutes • 1 Essay

Directions: This part of the GED is designed to find out how well you write. You will be given one question that asks you to either explain something or present an opinion on an issue. In constructing your answer for this part of the exam, you should think of your own observations and experiences, and take the following steps:

1 Before you begin to write your answer, read the directions and the question carefully.

2 Think of what you wish to say and plan your essay in detail before you begin to write.

3 Use the blank pages in the test booklet (or scrap paper provided for you) to make notes for planning your essay.

4 Write your essay neatly on the separate answer sheet.

5 Carefully read over what you have written and make any changes that will improve your work.

6 Check your paragraphing, sentence structure, spelling, punctuation, capitalization, and language usage, and correct any errors.

You will have 45 minutes to write a response to the question you are given. Write clearly with a ballpoint pen so the evaluators can read what you have written. Any notes you make on the blank pages or scratch paper will not be included in your evaluation.

Your essay will be scored by at least two trained readers who will evaluate the paper according to its overall impact. They will be concerned with how clearly you make your main points, how thoroughly your ideas are supported, and how effective and correct your writing is throughout the entire composition. You will receive no credit for writing on a topic other than the one assigned.

Sample Topic

Computers have certainly been responsible for many changes in the world. Some of these changes have made our lives better, while others, more difficult.

Write a composition of about 250 words describing the effect of computers on modern life. You may describe the positive effects, the negative effects, or both. Be as specific as possible, and use examples from your own experience to support your view.

TEST 2: SOCIAL STUDIES

70 Minutes • 50 Questions

Directions: The Social Studies Test consists of multiple-choice questions intended to measure your knowledge of general concepts in history, economics, geography, and civics and government. The questions are based on reading passages, maps, graphs, charts, and cartoons. For each question, first study the information given and then answer the question about it. You may refer to the readings or graphs as often as necessary in order to answer the questions. Record your answers in the Social Studies Section of your answer sheet.

Q Which medium most regularly presents opinions and interpretations of the news?

    (1) National television news programs

    (2) Local television news programs

    (3) Newspaper editorial pages

    (4) Teletype news agency reports

    (5) Radio news broadcasts

                                   ① ② ● ④ ⑤

A The correct answer is "newspaper editorial pages." Therefore, you should mark answer space (3) on your answer sheet.

practice test

ITEM 1 REFERS TO THE FOLLOWING GRAPH.

Working Women with Children, By Age of Children

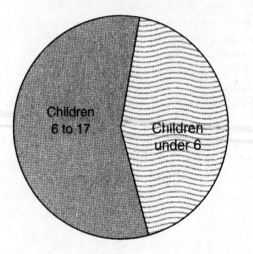

1. Which of the following conclusions is supported by the graph below?

   (1) Only women with children work.

   (2) Most working women have children.

   (3) Slightly more than half of all women in the workforce have children ages 6 to 17.

   (4) Slightly less than half of women in the workforce with children have children under the age of 6.

   (5) Half of all children are under the age of 6.

S 2 TO 5 REFER TO THE FOLLOWING SELECTION.

Although the poll takers are most widely known for their political surveys, the greatest part of their work is on behalf of American businesses. There are three kinds of commercial surveys. One is public relations research, such as that done for banks, which finds out how the public feels about a company. Another is employee-attitude research, which learns from rank-and-file workers how they really feel about their jobs and their bosses, and which can avert strikes by getting to the bottom of grievances quickly. The third, and probably most spectacular, is marketing research, the testing of public receptivity to new products and designs. The investment a company must make for a new product is enormous—$10,000,000 to $20,000,000, for instance, for just one new product.

Through surveys, a company can discover in advance what objections the public has to competing products, and whether it really wants or needs a new one. These surveys are actually a new set of signals permitting better communications between business and the general public—letting them talk to each other. Such communication is vital in a complex society. Without it, we would have not only tremendous waste but also the industrial anarchy of countless new, unwanted products appearing and disappearing.

2. According to the passage, polls can benefit industry by

   (1) reducing waste.

   (2) establishing fair prices.

   (3) strengthening people's faith in business.

   (4) saving small businesses.

   (5) serving as a new form of advertising.

3. What method is used to develop the ideas in this selection?

   (1) Cause and effect

   (2) Contrast

   (3) Examples

   (4) Anecdotes

   (5) Vivid description

4. Which is NOT mentioned as an area in which polls have been conducted?

   (1) New products

   (2) New designs

   (3) Employee attitudes

   (4) Labor-management relationships

   (5) Family relationships

5. Which of the following best describes the use of surveys for business purposes?

(1) Overrated

(2) Too widely used

(3) Often deceptive

(4) Necessary

(5) Costly

ITEMS 6 TO 9 REFER TO THE FOLLOWING SELECTION.

The stock market collapse began in October 1929 when banks in Great Britain raised their interest rates to 6½ percent in order to bring home needed capital that had been attracted to the United States by the speculation for high profits. As a result, many European holdings were thrown on the market, and the prices of stocks began to fall. Frightened by declining stock prices and no longer able to borrow at will, American speculators also began to unload. Frantic selling followed, and the value of stocks listed on the New York Stock Exchange plummeted from $87,000,000,000 to $55,000,000,000, or about 37 percent. This, however, was only the beginning. Despite repeated assurances from high government and financial authorities that prosperity was just around the corner, nine similar declines to new low levels were recorded during the next three years. By the first of March, 1933, all stocks listed on the New York Stock Exchange were worth only about $19,000,000,000.

It was soon apparent that a period of unparalleled depression had begun. The prices of goods dropped sharply; foreign trade fell off; factories curtailed production or, frequently, simply closed their doors; real estate values (but not mortgages) declined; new construction practically stopped; banks failed. Worst of all, wages were cut drastically and unemployment began to mount. By the end of 1930, about six or seven million workers were out of jobs; two years later, the number had doubled. The United States was not alone in its distress. It was soon visible to all that whatever seriously affected one great nation would eventually affect the world.

6. Which of the following statements is best supported by evidence presented in this selection?

(1) All governments are corrupt.

(2) All great nations are tied together by economics.

(3) When many people lose their jobs, unemployment develops.

(4) The Depression could have been avoided by clever people.

(5) If America was ruled by a dictator, the stock market crash would not have happened.

7. Which of the following is a hypothesis supported by this selection?

(1) Inflation goes hand-in-hand with unemployment.

(2) Mortgage rates drop during a depression.

(3) Land values go up when real estate declines.

(4) Unemployment rises when prices drop.

(5) Government can prevent a depression by assuring people.

8. Which of the following occurred when the Depression began?

(1) Factories decreased output.

(2) Foreign trade increased.

(3) Confidence was restored.

(4) Prices of goods increased.

(5) Wages were unaffected.

9. According to the information in the passage, what set off the stock market collapse?

    (1) England tried to bring more money into the country.

    (2) America attempted to correct a foreign trade imbalance.

    (3) Wages were cut sharply and unemployment rose.

    (4) American stockholders were frightened.

    (5) Mortgages dropped quickly; real estate prices fell off.

ITEMS 10 AND 11 REFER TO THE FOLLOWING INFORMATION.

The Constitution provides for a separation of power between federal and state governments and a system of checks and balances to regulate the three branches of government. The three most important powers of government are lodged mainly in three separate branches: the legislative branch has the power to make laws, the executive branch has the power to enforce laws, and the judicial branch has the power to interpret laws.

10. Which of the following statements best explains the reason for the system of checks and balances?

    (1) It allows the government to use checks to pay bills.

    (2) It allows the president to choose the best possible advisers.

    (3) It permits congressional committees to conduct investigations.

    (4) It diffuses power so that no one branch of government becomes too strong.

    (5) It gives the United States greater stature as leader of the free world.

11. Which of the following is an example of the system of checks and balances in action?

    (1) The Bill of Rights guarantees freedom of speech.

    (2) States are responsible for the health and safety of their citizens.

    (3) The president vetoes legislation passed by Congress.

    (4) The vice president takes over if the president is unable to fulfill the duties of his office.

    (5) Members of Congress are free from arrest for anything said on the floor of Congress.

ITEMS 12 TO 15 REFER TO THE FOLLOWING SELECTION.

Genocide is the systematic destruction and eradication of a racial, political, or cultural group. Its aim is total annihilation of that group, of its history, and of all memories of it. Genocide is not a new concept. Over the ages, groups in power have tried to eliminate peoples weaker than themselves. While genocide in practice involves the cooperation of many, it is usually the idea of one strong leader.

Carthage was established in 850 BCE at a sheltered point on the Gulf of Tunis. Because of its strategic location and fine harbor, the colony grew to be the center of Phoenician trade. Carthage became one of the largest and richest cities of ancient times, with a population estimated at more than 1,000,000.

In time, the ambitions of Carthage collided with those of other nations. It was with Rome that the great struggle occurred in a series of three long and bitter wars extending intermittently from 264 BCE to 146 BCE with the Romans finally victorious. Because their leaders insisted that Carthage must be destroyed if the Romans were ever to have peace, the Romans killed or enslaved the Carthaginians, burned their city, and plowed under the site.

It has been said that in the long run only religion, art, and wisdom ensure immortality. The Carthaginians apparently were more successful at trade than at any of these, for there are few traces of their civilization today.

12. According to the information in the passage, which of the following is an example of genocide?

    (1) Carthage had a population estimated at more than 1,000,000.

    (2) The wars lasted more than 100 years and the Romans were victorious.

    (3) The Romans killed or enslaved the Carthaginians, burned their city, and plowed under the site.

    (4) The ambitions of Carthage collided with those of other nations.

    (5) The Phoenicians were very successful at trade.

13. According to the passage, which of the following statements shows that the Romans were successful in their genocide?

    (1) The Romans needed to destroy Carthage in order to have peace.

    (2) There are few traces of the civilization of Carthage remaining today.

    (3) Carthage was one of the largest and richest cities of ancient times.

    (4) Carthage was established about 850 BCE

    (5) Traces of Roman civilization may be found throughout northern Africa.

14. According to the passage, which of the following ensures immortality?

    (1) Great wealth

    (2) Celebrated victories

    (3) Harsh laws

    (4) Sound economy

    (5) Fine art

15. According to the passage, why did the Romans want to conquer Carthage?

    (1) They were jealous because Carthage was such a wealthy city.

    (2) They objected to the religion of the Carthaginians.

    (3) They feared the strength of the Carthaginians.

    (4) They wanted to take over Phoenician trade.

    (5) They had traditionally hated the Carthaginians.

ITEMS 16 TO 19 REFER TO THE FOLLOWING SPEAKERS.

Economists *A, B, C, D,* and *E* represent five points of view on what each believes the relationship of big business and government should be.

Economist A: As this nation has industrialized, much business has grown so large that only the federal government is capable of regulating it. The government must protect the consumer against trusts, for, after all, the government exists to help the individuals do what they cannot do by themselves.

Economist B: This country's amazing economic growth rests upon private enterprise, which should be allowed to function freely. The government's role should be only to provide an economic climate conducive to the development of business.

Economist C: Major industry has become so large that the individual citizen is at the mercy of the big corporations. The only way to solve the problem is for the government to assume ownership of the nation's basic industries.

Economist D: Ours is a market economy where the consumer is king. Leave business alone, and it will provide consumers with what they want at the cheapest prices possible.

Economist E: Combinations in business are not necessarily an evil, but government must regulate their diverse activities to assure the welfare of various economic groups.

16. Which economist would be considered a socialist?

(1) A

(2) B

(3) C

(4) D

(5) E

17. Which economist is most likely to favor such measures as the Truth in Packaging Act and the Truth in Lending Act?

(1) A

(2) B

(3) C

(4) D

(5) E

18. Which economist best represents the policies followed by the United States government during the period of great economic growth experienced through most of the nineteenth century?

(1) A

(2) B

(3) C

(4) D

(5) E

19. According to the theory of *laissez-faire* economics advocated by Economist D, prices should be determined chiefly by

(1) government regulations.

(2) supply and demand.

(3) leaders of business and industry.

(4) negotiations between labor and management.

(5) lobbyists working for a variety of special interest groups.

ITEM 20 REFERS TO THE FOLLOWING QUOTATION.

"To whom does this land belong? I believe it belongs to me. If you asked me for a piece of it I would not give it. I cannot spare it and I like it very much. . . I hope you will listen to me."

20. This quotation most likely represents the point of view of a member of which of the following groups?

(1) A European immigrant in the 1890s

(2) A civil rights advocate in the 1960s

(3) A professional worker in the 1980s

(4) A Native American in the 1860s

(5) A southern sharecropper during Reconstruction

ITEMS 21 TO 25 REFER TO THE FOLLOWING INFORMATION.

Taxes are classified according to the way they are paid and the way they relate to the taxpayer's income. Listed below are five types of taxation and a brief description of how each works.

1. **Negative income taxes**   federal payments to families with income below a stipulated level

2. **Value-added taxes**   added at each stage of the processing of a raw material or the production and distribution of a commodity

3. **Progressive taxes**   based on the taxpayer's income; the more he earns, the more he is required to pay

4. **Regressive taxes**   take a higher percentage of income from the poor than the rich

5. **Surtax**   a tax on a tax

Each of the following statements describes one type of taxation. Choose the category in which the taxation described would most likely occur. The categories may be used more than once in the set of items but no one question has more than one best answer.

21. Taxes are paid on all tobacco products at each step in the production process, including harvesting, drying, processing, and the finished cigarettes, pipe tobacco, etc. These taxes are best described as

    (1) negative income taxes.
    (2) value-added taxes.
    (3) progressive taxes.
    (4) regressive taxes.
    (5) surtaxes.

22. Below is a table of tax rates.

Income	Tax
$0−6,000	0%
6,001−16,000	15%
16,001−28,000	25%
28,001−60,000	30%

    The tax shown on the table above is best described as

    (1) negative income tax.
    (2) value added tax.
    (3) progressive tax.
    (4) regressive tax.
    (5) surtax.

23. The federal government has determined that it requires $9,000 a year to support a family of four. The Dittmeir family, made up of a father, mother, and two children, earns a total of $8,500 per year. The federal government gives the family $500 per year. This payment is an example of

    (1) negative income tax.
    (2) value added tax.
    (3) progressive tax.
    (4) regressive tax.
    (5) surtax.

24. If a man earns $200 a month, and he buys $50 worth of goods upon which there is a 10% tax, that tax takes 2½% of his income for that month. Another man, who earns $1,000 a month, may buy the same goods at $50. He will pay only ½ of 1% of his income in taxes.

    Which type of tax is illustrated by this example?

    (1) Negative income tax
    (2) Value added tax
    (3) Progressive tax
    (4) Regressive tax
    (5) Surtax

25. The federal government needs an additional 1 million dollars of income for this fiscal year. To raise the money, the government adds 4¢ a gallon to the 15¢ a gallon gasoline tax. This tax is an example of

(1) negative income tax.

(2) value-added tax.

(3) progressive tax.

(4) regressive tax.

(5) surtax.

ITEMS 26 TO 28 REFER TO THE FOLLOWING BILL.

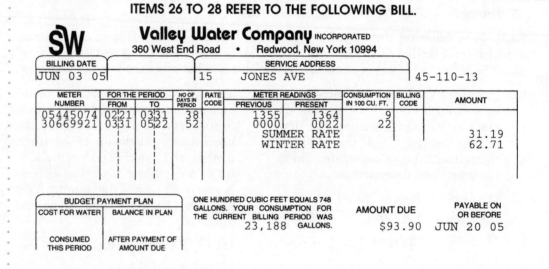

26. Based on this bill, how many gallons of water were used from February 21 to March 31?

(1) 1,364

(2) 6,732

(3) 16,456

(4) 28,424

(5) It cannot be determined from the information given.

27. How much does 100 cubic feet of water cost in the winter given the fact that the winter rate ends on March 31?

(1) $1.42

(2) $1.46

(3) $3.02

(4) $3.47

(5) $6.97

28. Based on an average cost, how much did each gallon of water cost?

(1) $.004

(2) $.01

(3) $.40

(4) $1.29

(5) $3.12

ITEM 29 REFERS TO THE FOLLOWING PASSAGE.

New England merchants sold lumber, meat, and fish in the West Indies in exchange for molasses and money. The molasses was distilled into rum. The rum was then sold in Africa in exchange for slaves and gold. The merchants also sold raw materials in England. They used the money they earned to buy finished goods from England. This was called the "Triangular Trade."

29. Which of the following statements best explains one of the reasons for the establishment of the "Triangular Trade," according to the information presented in the paragraph?

   (1) New England colonists used rum as a medicine.

   (2) Slaves were needed to run factories in England.

   (3) England needed a market for the goods it manufactured.

   (4) The people in the West Indies paid high wages to their slaves.

   (5) African nations had a well-developed merchant marine fleet.

ITEMS 30 TO 34 REFER TO THE FOLLOWING SELECTION.

The events of the period from 1920 to 1930 in the United States have been consolidated by historians into a special area of study. The era of the 1920s lends itself to study as a unit in regard to the pervading temperament and interests of the decade. The twenties have been called the "Jazz Age," the age of flappers, Lindbergh, and frivolous nonsense. The 1920s, however, had a serious side, as well, that reflected the needs and short-comings of a nation that was trying to adjust to the aftermath of a world war.

Historical and literary works of this period are abundant. Some of the major themes of these works on the 1920s dealt with the Red Scare, immigration, urbanization, the farmer, and the change in morals in the United States. In general, the 1920s was a period in which the United States was transformed from a rural nation into a world power with far-reaching responsibilities. The historiographical and popular writings, both contemporary and modern, suggest that the era of the twenties was overwhelmed by the pressures of the new machine age. Thus, the 1920s represented a period of transition, a reaction to the coming of the modern American way of life.

30. Based on the information in the article, which of the following statements best describes the 1920s?

   (1) It was a time of frivolous nonsense.

   (2) It was marked by depression and hard times.

   (3) There was great change.

   (4) Many great works were produced, especially movies.

   (5) There were many great inventions.

31. What prominent feature of life in the 1920s is not mentioned at all in the article?

   (1) The urbanization of America

   (2) Prohibition

   (3) Frivolity and nonsense

   (4) Rise of America to world status

   (5) Prolific writing

32. Based on the passage, what do the terms "Jazz Age" and "flappers" represent?

    (1) Fads of the 1920s
    (2) The names of political parties of the 1920s
    (3) Terms used before 1900
    (4) An omen of things yet to come
    (5) Immigrants who arrived during the 1920s

33. Which of the following statements best explains the reasons why historians treat the 1920s as a special area of study?

    (1) There were a great many literary and historical works produced.
    (2) The United States transformed from a rural to an industrial nation.
    (3) It had a mood all its own.
    (4) It was the first machine age.
    (5) The 1920s were a great deal like the present age.

34. Which of the following statements can be inferred based on the information in the article?

    (1) 1920–1930 was a period of great happiness.
    (2) The "Jazz Age" was a unique era in American life.
    (3) The twenties represented an era of unparalleled change.
    (4) There were no Communists in the twenties.
    (5) Historians group eras on the basis of different characteristics.

ITEM 35 REFERS TO THE FOLLOWING CARTOON.

35. What does the cartoonist see happening when inflation increases very rapidly?

  (1) Unskilled workers will not know how to sail a ship.
  (2) Unskilled workers will be unlikely to survive.
  (3) Skilled workers will have a better captain.
  (4) The seas will be very rough for all workers.
  (5) Skilled workers will be better able to compensate for the ravages of inflation than unskilled workers.

ITEMS 36 TO 40 REFER TO THE FOLLOWING PASSAGE.

Many organizations have established group meal programs for the elderly, who might not otherwise eat properly because they cannot afford to buy proper food or do not know what foods make up a balanced diet. Often the elderly are not physically able to shop or prepare meals. Many, because of loneliness and isolation, may decide it is too much trouble to prepare a meal to eat alone. One of the most important aspects of the group meal program is the companionship it provides, which reduces loneliness.

The Older Americans Act provides for a national nutrition program for the elderly and authorizes the federal government to pay up to 90 percent of the cost, with state and local governments paying at least 10 percent. The states allocate these funds to local sponsoring agencies, called grantees, that employ persons to operate the nutrition projects. In 1975, there were more than 4,200 sites in the federal program, providing almost a quarter of a million meals each day to older Americans.

Since participation in the federal program does not meet all the nutritional needs of the elderly, many senior centers and other publicly and privately funded agencies also provide low-cost meals.

36. Which of the following titles best expresses the main idea of this article?

  (1) "Feeding Americans"
  (2) "Providing an Adequate Diet for the Elderly"
  (3) "Eating Well and Keeping Fit"
  (4) "The Loneliness of the Aged"
  (5) "Meals: Nutritious and Inexpensive"

37. According to the article, how many meals are served every day to the elderly with the support of the federal government?

  (1) 2,500
  (2) 4,000
  (3) 100,000
  (4) 250,000
  (5) 2,500,000

38. Which of the following does the author feel the elderly should be guaranteed?

  (1) Financial support
  (2) Mental stimulation
  (3) Psychological assistance
  (4) Adequate exercise
  (5) Proper nutrition

practice test

39. According to the information presented in the article, which of the following statements is the most likely explanation for the large number of elderly who participate in the nutrition program?

   (1) Today, many elderly people are living on their own.

   (2) There are few supermarkets near elderly people.

   (3) The elderly enjoy eating by themselves.

   (4) These centers are near public transportation.

   (5) Older Americans enjoy cooking for themselves.

40. Which of the following statements is best supported by evidence presented in this article?

   (1) There are adequate federal resources to support the nutrition program.

   (2) The nutrition program was designed only to feed the elderly.

   (3) The program satisfies an elderly person's total daily nutritional needs.

   (4) Some elderly people suffer as much from isolation as from inadequate nutrition.

   (5) The program needs to be extended to meet the needs of younger Americans.

ITEMS 41 AND 42 REFER TO THE FOLLOWING MAP.

Hazardous Waste Sites—2001

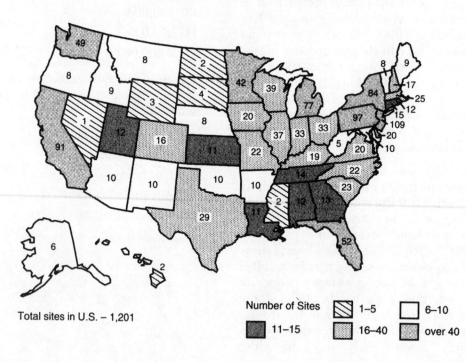

Total sites in U.S. – 1,201

Number of Sites   ▨ 1–5   ☐ 6–10
▩ 11–15   ▨ 16–40   ▨ over 40

41. Based on this map, in which of the following states are residents LEAST likely to be exposed to toxic wastes?

(1) Nevada

(2) Texas

(3) California

(4) Florida

(5) Missouri

42. According to this map, an administrator allocating funding to the clean-up of hazardous waste sites would probably choose which area in order to improve the environment of the greatest number of people?

(1) Maine, Vermont, New Hampshire

(2) New York, New Jersey, Pennsylvania

(3) Washington and Oregon

(4) Georgia, Alabama, Florida

(5) Texas and Oklahoma

43. The Colonists wrote these words in 1776:

"The history of the present King of Great Britain is a history of repeated injuries and usurpations, all having in direct object the establishment of an absolute Tyranny over these States. To prove this, let Facts be submitted to a candid world."

Why would these words be written?

(1) To justify a revolution against the king

(2) To thank the king for ruling fairly

(3) To send an ambassador to meet with the king

(4) To set up an American Constitution

(5) To force the king to abdicate

44. Sulfur dioxide emissions from industrial plants combine with water in the atmosphere to form a poisonous rain or snow. What is this called?

(1) Water pollution

(2) Air pollution

(3) Sulfur pollution

(4) Acid rain

(5) Industrial accidents

ITEM 45 REFERS TO THE CHART BELOW.

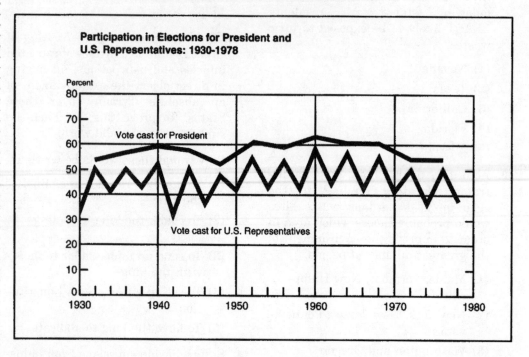

Participation in Elections for President and
U.S. Representatives: 1930-1978

45. The chart shown above pictures the behavior of American voters in national elections from the 1930s through the 1970s. Based on this information, what could the student of American history conclude?

  (1) The end of World War II discouraged voters' interest in the 1948 presidential election.

  (2) Candidates for the House of Representatives receive fewer votes in "off-year" elections.

  (3) Candidates for president receive a higher number of votes in "off-year" elections.

  (4) President Eisenhower's popularity drew the highest number of voters to the polls during the time period 1930–1977.

  (5) Domestic dissension over the Vietnamese Conflict encouraged intense voter participation in the 1966 presidential election.

46. Since 1948, when the United Nations established the state of Israel, there has been much conflict between the Israelis and the Arabs. Where is Israel located?

  (1) Europe

  (2) Asia

  (3) Africa

  (4) Far East

  (5) East Indies

ITEM 47 REFERS TO THE FOLLOWING EXCERPT.

The following is taken from the first amendment of the Bill of Rights, which consists of the first ten amendments to the U.S. Constitution.

"Congress shall make no law respecting an establishment of religion, or prohibiting the free exercise thereof; or abridging the freedom of speech, or of the press; or the right of the people peaceable to assemble, and to petition the Government for a redress of grievances."

47. This important amendment is often referred to by which one of the following names?

   (1) Freedom of speech
   (2) Freedom of the press
   (3) Peaceful assembly
   (4) Establishment clause
   (5) Grievances clause

48. Although it seems that the sun rises in the eastern part of the country and sets in the western part, in what direction does the earth actually rotate?

   (1) West to east
   (2) East to west
   (3) North to south
   (4) South to north
   (5) It doesn't rotate at all.

49. During the Renaissance period in Italy, which of the following was the famous writer who wrote a book describing the state of man and how he can gain political power—a book that has served as an inspiration for many leaders until the present day?

   (1) Sforza
   (2) Medici
   (3) Shakespeare
   (4) Erasmus
   (5) Machiavelli

50. What natural boundaries played an important role in the United States in adopting "isolationist" policies for much of its past?

   (1) Atlantic and Pacific Oceans
   (2) Atlantic and Antarctic Oceans
   (3) Atlantic and Indian Oceans
   (4) Pacific Ocean and the Gulf of Mexico
   (5) Pacific Ocean and the Great Lakes

practice test

TEST 3: SCIENCE

80 Minutes • 50 Questions

Directions: The Science Test consists of multiple-choice questions intended to measure general concepts in life science, earth and space science, physics, and chemistry. Some of the questions are based on short readings. Others are based on graphs, charts, tables, or diagrams. For each question, study the information given and then answer the question or questions based upon it. Refer to the information as often as necessary in answering the questions. Record your answer in the Science Section of your answer sheet.

Q A physical change may alter the state of matter, but does not change its chemical composition. Which of the following is NOT a physical change?

(1) Boiling water
(2) Dissolving salt in water
(3) Shaving wood
(4) Rusting metal
(5) Breaking glass

① ② ③ ● ⑤

A When metal rusts, a new substance is formed. This is a chemical, not a physical, change. Therefore, answer space (4) should be marked on your answer sheet.

ITEMS 1 TO 4 REFER TO THE FOLLOWING SCHEMATIC DIAGRAM.

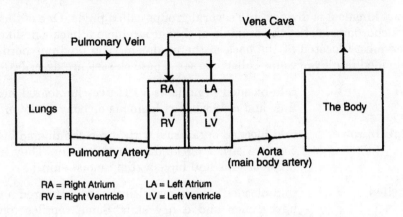

RA = Right Atrium   LA = Left Atrium
RV = Right Ventricle   LV = Left Ventricle

The above diagram indicates how blood circulates in the human body.

1. According to the diagram, in which direction do arteries carry blood?

    (1) To the heart

    (2) Away from the heart

    (3) Both to and from the heart

    (4) Only to the body

    (5) Between the body and lungs

2. To which of the following does the left ventricle pump blood?

    (1) The pulmonary artery

    (2) The vena cava

    (3) The pulmonary vein

    (4) The left atrium

    (5) All parts of the body

3. The blood found in the pulmonary vein has just left the lungs. Which of the following statements is true about this blood?

    (1) It is rich in iron.

    (2) It is poor in oxygen.

    (3) It is rich in oxygen.

    (4) It has no blood cells.

    (5) It lacks the ability to fight germs.

4. Which of the following sequences shows the actual flow of blood?

    (1) Lungs, the heart, right atrium, right ventricle

    (2) The body, the lungs, vena cava, aorta

    (3) Vena cava, right atrium, left ventricle, aorta

    (4) Right ventricle, pulmonary artery, lungs, pulmonary vein

    (5) Right ventricle, right atrium, vena cava, the lungs

ITEMS 5 AND 6 REFER TO THE FOLLOWING INFORMATION.

The animal kingdom is divided into several groups called phyla. One of these phyla is called the chordates. All of the animals of this group have a backbone-like structure and a nerve cord located at the back of the organism. The phylum chordata can be further divided into five groups called classes. These classes are described as follows:

1. Fish	cold-blooded organisms with two-chambered hearts, gills, fins, and either a cartilaginous or bony skeleton.
2. Amphibians	cold-blooded organisms with three-chambered hearts. They can live either on land or in the water. They have either lungs or gills and have a slimy moist skin.
3. Reptiles	cold-blooded organisms with three-chambered hearts. They have lungs and a dry skin. Some reptiles have a four-chambered heart.
4. Birds	warm-blooded organisms with four-chambered hearts. They all have lungs and are covered with feathers.
5. Mammals	warm-blooded organisms with four-chambered hearts. They nourish their young with milk. They all have lungs.

Each of the following items describes a class of vertebrates that refers to one of the five classes listed above. For each item, choose the one class that best describes the animal. Each of the classes above may be used more than once in the following set of items.

5. This cold-blooded animal is greatly feared. It has a cartilaginous skeleton, gill openings, and a mouth on its underside. It has been known to attack man. This animal belongs to which of the following classes?

   (1) Fish
   (2) Amphibians
   (3) Reptiles
   (4) Birds
   (5) Mammals

6. Ancient scientists thought that these animals simply came from the mud. This was because there were none of these animals in the water one day, and on the next day, there were thousands of them. A few weeks later the water was clear again, and those animals that were left alive were living on the land. These animals belonged to which of the following classes?

   (1) Fish
   (2) Amphibians
   (3) Reptiles
   (4) Birds
   (5) Mammals

ITEMS 7 AND 8 REFER TO THE FOLLOWING INFORMATION.

NORMAL TEMPERATURE DURING JANUARY FOR SELECTED CITIES

	Maximum	Minimum
San Francisco, CA	55	42
Los Angeles, CA	67	48
Phoenix, AZ	65	39
Denver, CO	43	16
Miami, FL	75	59
Atlanta, GA	51	33
Chicago, IL	29	14
New Orleans, LA	62	43
Boston, MA	36	23
St. Paul, MN	20	2
New York City, NY	37	26
Portland, OR	44	34
Philadelphia, PA	39	24
Houston, TX	62	41

7. As a travel agent, Sam uses the chart above to advise his clients about weather conditions in the cities they plan to visit. Based on this temperature chart and the travel plans that follow, which of Sam's clients can expect to experience the widest range of temperatures on the trip scheduled?

   (1) Pat, who will spend the week of January 12 in New York, Chicago, and Denver

   (2) Julie, who will spend the first two weeks of January in Miami, Atlanta, and New Orleans

   (3) Joe, who will tour New Orleans, Phoenix, and Houston the last week of January

   (4) Mike, whose travel plans include visits to Phoenix, Los Angeles, and San Francisco in mid-January

   (5) Sue, who will make a trip to Portland, San Francisco, and Denver at the end of January

8. Which of the five travelers would be most likely to experience the coldest weather on the trip planned?

   (1) Pat
   (2) Julie
   (3) Joe
   (4) Mike
   (5) Sue

9. When Charles turned on the radio on Labor Day, the announcer was talking about a deep tropical depression 50 miles east of the Bahamas. The announcer was most likely referring to conditions that would generate

   (1) spreading of the seabed.
   (2) a tornado.
   (3) mineral deposits.
   (4) continental shelf.
   (5) a hurricane.

**ITEM 10 REFERS TO THIS
DIAGRAM OF A ROCK.**

10. Which description most nearly represents the process by which the rock shown here was formed?

(1) Magma is intruded into a sill or a dike.

(2) Batholiths become exposed as a mountain is worn away.

(3) Volcanic ash piles up on the ground and forms rock when squeezed together.

(4) Gravel and other large particles settle out of water and eventually become cemented together.

(5) Heat and pressure have transformed sediments into a new kind of rock.

ITEM 11 REFERS TO THE FOLLOWING GRAPH.

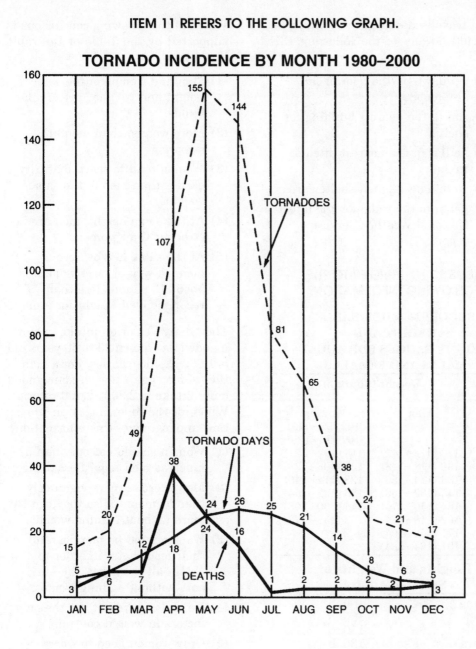

TORNADO INCIDENCE BY MONTH 1980–2000

11. Which of the following conclusions is supported by the graph?

   (1) The greatest number of tornadoes and the greatest number of tornado deaths occur in the same month.

   (2) Although tornadoes can occur in any month, the greatest number of tornadoes occurs in May.

   (3) Fall tornadoes result in more tornado deaths than spring tornadoes.

   (4) Winter tornadoes tend to be more severe than spring or summer tornadoes.

   (5) There are more than 700 tornado deaths each year.

12. If a traveler does sight a tornado, he should do any of the following EXCEPT

  (1) get down on the floor of the automobile.

  (2) run to the nearest building for shelter.

  (3) lie flat in the nearest ditch or ravine.

  (4) go to a designated shelter area.

  (5) listen to the radio for the latest National Weather Service report.

ITEMS 13 TO 15 REFER TO THE FOLLOWING INFORMATION.

SUGGESTED DESIRABLE WEIGHT AND HEIGHT RANGES FOR ADULT MALES AND FEMALES

Height (inches)	Weight (pounds)	
	Men	**Women**
58		102 (92–119)
60		107 (96–125)
62	123 (112–141)	113 (102–131)
64	130 (118–148)	120 (108–138)
66	136 (124–156)	128 (114–146)
68	145 (132–166)	136 (122–154)
70	154 (140–174)	144 (130–163)
72	162 (148–184)	152 (138–173)
74	171 (156–194)	
76	181 (164–204)	

Heights and Weights of Selected Adults

Jane	64"	150 lb
Jeff	72"	165 lb
Bill	68"	130 lb
Sara	68"	130 lb
Paul	66"	156 lb

13. Based on the Table of Desirable Weights, which of the following adults should gain some weight?

  (1) Jane

  (2) Jeff

  (3) Bill

  (4) Sara

  (5) Paul

14. Which of the following conclusions is supported by the Table of Desirable Weights?

  (1) Men and women of the same height and weight have similar builds.

  (2) More women than men are overweight.

  (3) Women tend to reach maturity earlier than men of the same weight.

  (4) At the same height, men are stronger than women.

  (5) At the same height, recommended weight for a woman is about 10 pounds less than recommended weight for a man.

15. The daily calorie intake recommended for women 23 to 50 years old is 1,600–2,400 calories. For a man of the same age, the recommended daily intake is 2,300–2,700 calories. Which of the following is an important application of this information?

  (1) Women should eat only half as much as men regardless of size.

  (2) Men exercise more vigorously than women and so they can eat more without gaining weight.

  (3) Women must be more careful in their food choice in order to obtain all the necessary nutrients without gaining weight.

  (4) Height and weight are the only factors in weight control.

  (5) Only women need to worry about weight control.

Jane can push with a force of 40 newtons. A graph describing her ability to do work is shown below.

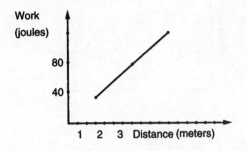

The amount of force necessary to move an object along a flat surface is:

W(work) = F(force) × D(distance)

16. If Jane pushes a block with a horizontal force of 40 newtons, at a constant speed of 2 meters per second, then how much work, in joules, is done on the block in 6 seconds?

    (1) 80
    (2) 120
    (3) 240
    (4) 480
    (5) 500

**ITEMS 17 TO 20 REFER TO THE
FOLLOWING ARTICLE.**

A knowledge of the spine can help in understanding the hows and whys of backache.

The spine is made up of thirty-three or thirty-four vertebrae (bones), the total depending on whether an individual has four or five vertebrae in the coccyx (tailbone), a normal variation. The vertebrae are separated and cushioned by oval pads called discs. For medical diagnostic purposes, the vertebrae are divided into five sections: the cervical(neck) region, containing seven vertebrae; the thoracic or dorsal (mid-back) region, containing twelve vertebrae; the lumbar (lower back) region, containing five vertebrae; the sacrum (back of the pelvis), which is one bone; and the coccyx (tailbone), with its four or five vertebrae. The most flexible regions—the neck and lower back—are the sites of most back problems.

Physicians often talk about vertebrae and discs with letter and number designations that are abbreviations for the section of the back and distance from the top of the spine. For example, the second vertebra down in the lumbar area is called L2.

Each disc is designated by the vertebrae above and below it. For instance, the L2-L3 disc is between the L2 and L3 vertebrae. The T12-L1 disc is between the lowest thoracic vertebra and the highest lumbar vertebra. Discs under heavy mechanical stress, and thus the ones most likely to cause problems, are C5-C6, L3-L4, and L5-S1. Nerves in and around the spine are designated in the same manner as the vertebrae.

The back also contains ligaments, thick strong strands of tissue that attach one bone to another, and tendons, which are structures similar to ligaments but which attach muscles to bones.

The ligaments attached to the spine may rupture if the back flexes suddenly. This can be a source of localized pain for long periods. The remedy for a ruptured spinal ligament is usually surgery.

17. Most back problems seem to occur in which area of the spine?

    (1) Neck and lower back
    (2) Fused areas
    (3) Tailbone
    (4) Mid-back
    (5) Pelvic region

18. The back contains which of the following parts?

    I. Ligaments
   II. Tendons
  III. Bones
  IV. Vertebrae
   V. Discs
  VI. Nerves

  (1) I, II, and IV only

  (2) II, III, V, and VI only

  (3) I, II, and III only

  (4) II, IV, V, and VI only

  (5) I, II, III, IV, V, and VI

19. What is the function of the discs?

  (1) To separate the five regions of the spine

  (2) To provide a means for numbering the vertebrae

  (3) To attach muscles to bones

  (4) To separate and cushion the vertebrae

  (5) To make up for variations in the number of vertebrae

20. If you twist suddenly and experience a sharp pain in your back, you may have torn a

  (1) vertebra.

  (2) ligament.

  (3) coccyx.

  (4) sacra.

  (5) dorsal bone.

21. If line *A* in the diagram below represents a population of hawks in a community, then what would most likely be represented by line *B*?

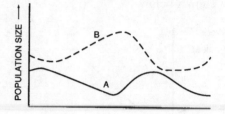

  (1) The dominant trees in that community

  (2) A population with which the hawks have a mutualistic relationship

  (3) Variations in the numbers of producers in that community

  (4) A population on which the hawks prey

  (5) A population of hawk parasites

22. Occasionally hospitals have outbreaks of staphylococcus bacteria infections, which resist treatment with antibiotics that were once effective. What is the most acceptable explanation for this condition?

  (1) Due to selective forces, new staphylococcus strains have become more abundant.

  (2) Newer antibiotics are weaker than those used in the past.

  (3) Laboratory strains of staphylococcus have been weakened.

  (4) Patients have become less susceptible to bacterial infection.

  (5) Staphylococci are weakened by age.

ITEMS 23 TO 25 REFER TO THE FOLLOWING PASSAGE.

Scientists now know that even the densest matter is mostly made up of empty space with particles so utterly small that they have never been seen or photographed. These particles have been demonstrated by mathematical physicists in a series of ingeniously designed experiments. Experiments conducted by Sir Ernest Rutherford in 1911 first revealed the basic structure of the atom. Additional experiments by Moseley, Bohr, Fermi, Millikan, Compton, Urey, and many others have added to our understanding of atomic structure. Groups of atoms make molecules. Matter is composed of molecules whose average diameter is about $\frac{1}{125}$ millionth of an inch. Five million average-sized atoms placed in a row would fit across the period at the end of this sentence. Although indivisible by ordinary chemical means, atoms are now known to be composed of a nucleus with protons (positively charged particles), neutrons (electrically neutral particles), and electrons (negatively charged particles) which revolve at incredible speed around the atomic nucleus.

23. According to the passage, atoms are composed of which of the following particles?
    I. Protons
    II. Neutrons
    III. Electrons
    IV. Molecules

    (1) I and II only
    (2) II only
    (3) IV only
    (4) I, II, and III only
    (5) I, II, III, and IV

24. Which of the following best describes the relationship between atoms and molecules?

    (1) An atom is $\frac{1}{125}$ millionth the size of a molecule.
    (2) Atoms revolve around the nucleus of a molecule.
    (3) Molecules are made up of groups of atoms.
    (4) Atoms may be broken down into molecules.
    (5) Molecules are much smaller than atoms.

25. Which of the following reasons best explains why atoms have never been seen?

    (1) They are too small to be seen.
    (2) They revolve too quickly to be seen.
    (3) They are mostly empty space.
    (4) They do not really exist.
    (5) They are indivisible by ordinary chemical means.

ITEMS 26 TO 28 REFER TO THE FOLLOWING INFORMATION.

Medical assistance should generally be given only by properly trained persons. However, you may find yourself in a situation where immediate assistance is unavailable, and you may have to help the injured victims. In these cases, remember these basic first aid rules:

Unless absolutely necessary because of the danger of fire or other hazard, avoid moving the injured person. If he must be moved, get help and try not to change the position in which he was found. If possible, cover him with coats or blankets to keep him warm.

Never lift a victim by holding him under the shoulders (armpits) and knees.

If a victim appears to have a broken back or broken neck, and you bend him forward or sit him up, you may cut his spinal cord and paralyze him permanently. Such a victim should only be lifted on a rigid board or lying on his stomach with the head supported. In turning such a victim over, be sure not to double him, let his neck fall forward, or twist his head.

Control excessive bleeding with thick cloth pads, as clean as possible, applied with pressure by hand.

Cover burns with clean cloths to reduce the pain. Apply no ointments.

Do not offer the injured anything to drink.

If the injured person does not seem to be breathing, attempt to revive breathing by administering "artificial respiration."

26. Jimmy dashed into the burning house and saw his grandfather lying on the floor, a wooden beam across his back. According to the basic first aid rules, what should Jimmy do with his injured grandfather?

    (1) Move him out of the house without changing his position.
    (2) Sit him up and drag him out of the house.
    (3) Put him over his shoulder and carry him out of the house.
    (4) Make him stand and walk out of the house.
    (5) Leave him where he is.

27. Bleeding should usually be stopped by

    (1) applying a bandage to the wound.
    (2) waiting for it to stop on its own.
    (3) administering artificial respiration.
    (4) a doctor.
    (5) applying pressure to the wound.

28. Why does the author believe that everyone should know proper first aid?

    (1) No doctor may be available.
    (2) The victim may experience compounded injuries if he is improperly treated at the scene of the accident.
    (3) The victim might die if he is not attended to.
    (4) Choices (1), (2), and (3)
    (5) Choices (1) and (3) only

29. If a doctor describes his patient as dehydrated, he is saying that the person

    (1) has a contagious disease.
    (2) needs insulin.
    (3) cannot manufacture chlorophyll.
    (4) has lost a great deal of water.
    (5) has just been inoculated.

ITEMS 30 TO 32 REFER TO THE FOLLOWING INFORMATION.

The number of protons remains the same for an atom of a given element, but the number of neutrons may vary. When this happens, we have two different varieties of the same element, or two isotopes of the element. One isotope is heavier than the other, but chemically they behave the same way. Isotopes of the same element have the same atomic number but different atomic mass.

30. Based on the information above, which is true of isotopes of an element?

    (1) They have the same number of protons but a different number of electrons.
    (2) They have the same atomic number but different atomic weight.
    (3) They have more protons than electrons.
    (4) They react more readily to form compounds.
    (5) They are exactly alike.

31. Which pair of atoms represents different isotopes of the same element?

    (1) $^{12}_{6}$ C and $^{13}_{6}$ C

    (2) $^{12}_{6}$ C and $^{12}_{7}$ C

    (3) $^{12}_{6}$ C and $^{13}_{7}$ C

    (4) $^{14}_{7}$ N and $^{14}_{8}$ N

    (5) $^{235}_{92}$ U and $^{235}_{93}$ Np

32. In one half-life, half of a radioactive mass disintegrates. Strontium 90 has a half-life of 20 years. A sample originally weighing 8 grams, at the end of 40 years, will weigh

    (1) 1 gram.

    (2) 2 grams.

    (3) 4 grams.

    (4) 16 grams.

    (5) 32 grams.

ITEMS 33 AND 34 REFER TO THE FOLLOWING PASSAGE.

For the past six or seven years, a group of scientists has been attempting to make fortunes by breeding "bugs"—microorganisms that will manufacture valuable chemicals and drugs. This budding industry is called genetic engineering, and out of this young program, at least one company has induced a lowly bacterium to manufacture human interferon, a rare and costly substance that fights virus infections by "splicing" human genes into their natural hereditary material. But there are dangers in this activity, including the accidental development of a mutant bacterium that may change the whole life pattern on Earth. There are also legal questions about whether a living organism can be patented and what new products can be marketed from living matter. The Congressional agency that oversees these new developments says that it will be about seven years before any new product developed by genetic engineering will be allowed to be placed on the market.

33. Which of the following possibilities is one of the potential problems of genetic engineering?

    (1) An oversupply of bacteria

    (2) Dangerous mutations

    (3) Overpopulation

    (4) Excess food

    (5) Too many engineers

34. Human interferon can be used to fight viral infections. This means that interferon may be helpful in curing

    (1) diseases that are responsible for deformities.

    (2) diseases that are genetic in origin.

    (3) problems related to psychological stress.

    (4) the common cold.

    (5) diseases caused by drugs and alcohol.

practice test

ITEMS 35 TO 38 REFER TO THE FOLLOWING INFORMATION.

Listed below are five types of chemical reactions and brief descriptions of the characteristics of each reaction.

1. Combination reaction	two or more substances combine to form a more complex substance
2. Decomposition reaction	a substance is broken down to form two or more simpler substances, often accomplished by the addition of heat
3. Single replacement reaction	one element of a compound is replaced by another element
4. Double replacement reaction	two compounds react by exchanging their positive ions, often producing a solid that is called a precipitate
5. Atomic fission	the nucleus of an atom of a heavy element is split to release energy and two lighter elements

Each of the following items describes a chemical reaction that may be classified as one of the types of chemical reactions defined above. For each item, choose the category that best describes the reaction given. Each of the categories above *may* be used more than once in the following set of items.

35. Sulfur reacts with oxygen to form sulfur dioxide, a common cause of air pollution:

$$S + O_2 \rightarrow SO_2$$

This reaction may be classified as

(1) a combination reaction.
(2) a decomposition reaction.
(3) single replacement reaction.
(4) double replacement reaction.
(5) atomic fission.

36. Neutrons penetrate the nuclei of uranium^{235} to form barium and krypton plus an enormous amount of energy.

This reaction may be classified as

(1) a combination reaction.
(2) a decomposition reaction.
(3) single replacement reaction.
(4) double replacement reaction.
(5) atomic fission.

37. Magnesium hydroxide neutralizes hydrochloric acid in the stomach by forming magnesium chloride and water:

$$Mg(OH)_2 + 2HCl \rightarrow MgCl_2 + 2H_2O$$

This reaction is an example of

(1) a combination reaction.
(2) a decomposition reaction.
(3) single replacement reaction.
(4) double replacement reaction.
(5) atomic fission.

38. Sodium reacts with chloride to yield sodium chloride (salt):

$$2Na + Cl_2 \rightarrow 2NaCl$$

This reaction may be classified as

(1) a combination reaction.

(2) a decomposition reaction.

(3) single replacement reaction.

(4) double replacement reaction.

(5) atomic fission.

ITEM 39 REFERS TO THE FOLLOWING GRAPH.

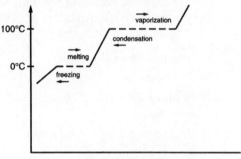

Heating/Cooling Curve for Water

39. The Heating/Cooling Curve describes the two special temperatures at which the phases of water change. When water boils, each gram gains an amount of heat equal to the heat of which of the following?

(1) Fusion

(2) Vaporization

(3) Sublimination

(4) Reaction

(5) Molecules

40. The force necessary to move a mass is equal to its mass times its acceleration. Two blocks are to be moved along a flat surface:

Block	Mass	Acceleration
1	2 kg	3 m/sec^2
2	4 kg	6 m/sec^2

Compared to block 1, the force necessary to move block 2 is

(1) one half as much.

(2) the same.

(3) twice as much.

(4) three times as much.

(5) four times as much.

ITEMS 41 TO 43 REFER TO THE FOLLOWING INFORMATION.

SARSAT—Search and Rescue Satellite Aided Tracking—is a project designed to demonstrate the use of satellites to save lives by reducing the time required to locate and rescue air and maritime distress victims.

This system can be used for regional or global coverage and will be able to locate the distress site within 1 to 3 miles. When the system is fully operational, it will be capable of detecting and locating 200−300 distress signals at a time.

Satellites were used to track a Japanese adventurer while he trekked by dogsled across the Greenland ice cap to the North Pole. They tracked a number of sailboats during a European race in 1979 and tracked both the successful and unsuccessful "Double Eagle" transatlantic balloon flights.

41. SARSAT can pinpoint the locations of disaster victims to within a range of how many miles?

(1) $\frac{1}{2}$ to 1 mile

(2) 1 to 3 miles

(3) 5 to 10 miles

(4) 100 to 150 miles

(5) 200 to 300 miles

42. Who is most likely to benefit from SARSAT?

I. Victims of plane crashes
II. Victims of accidents at sea
III. Victims of disasters in space
IV. Lost or injured explorers

(1) I and III only

(2) II and III only

(3) I, II, and III only

(4) I, II, and IV only

(5) I, II, III, and IV

43. What are the advantages of SARSAT to air rescue efforts?

(1) Saves time and increases accuracy

(2) Saves time and reduces cost

(3) Saves time and is easy to use

(4) Increases accuracy and reduces cost

(5) Always works

ITEMS 44 TO 46 REFER TO THE FOLLOWING PASSAGE.

Genetic material is now known to be deoxyribonucleic acid (DNA). The two general functions of DNA are (1) to replicate for the propagation of life and (2) to serve as a template for protein synthesis. It is this second function that we shall outline here. The initial step is the assemblage of messenger ribonucleic acid (m-RNA) by DNA. This process is known as transcription. The m-RNA then acts as a complement of the genetic code in the DNA molecule that assembled it. The m-RNA then directs the assembly of a protein from an available pool of protein building blocks, amino acids. This process is known as translation. Therefore, we can summarize protein synthesis as transcription and translation. A second kind of RNA, known as transfer ribonucleic acid (t-RNA), is responsible for directing the correct amino acid to its correct place in the amino acid sequence that is to become the protein.

44. Based on the information in the passage, which of the following is true?

(1) DNA is directly responsible for the synthesis of a protein.

(2) m-RNA makes DNA.

(3) Transcription follows translation.

(4) Proteins are assemblages of amino acids.

(5) None of the above

45. This article describes a portion of the knowledge scientists now possess concerning DNA and RNA. Based on this description, which of the following can we infer scientists are able to do?

(1) Synthesize new proteins

(2) Cure cancer

(3) Replace defective genetic material

(4) Create exact reproductions of people

(5) Create models of DNA and RNA

46. Conductors are materials through which electrons can flow freely. Most metals make good electrical conductors, but of all, silver is the best. Next to silver, copper is a good conductor, with aluminum following closely behind.

Which of the following best explains why copper is the metal most widely used in electrical wiring?

(1) It is the best conductor of electricity.

(2) It has a high resistance to electricity.

(3) It is cheaper than aluminum.

(4) It is a better conductor than aluminum and cheaper than silver.

(5) It is the most flexible metal.

47. In 2000 the human genome project was completed, marking a milestone in our scientific understanding of genetics. The project was related to genes

(1) in the human cell nucleus.

(2) in the human chromosome.

(3) in DNA.

(4) controlling cancer.

(5) determining sex-linked traits.

48. The main fuels used today in the engines of automobiles, diesels, and planes are fossil fuels. These fuels are

(1) found in the air.

(2) created by engineers.

(3) found in the earth's crust.

(4) obsolete.

(5) None of the above

49. What is the unique problem associated with using uranium in nuclear power plants that generate energy?

(1) Uranium destroys the ozone layer.

(2) Nuclear power causes global warming.

(3) Too much energy causes smog.

(4) Uranium releases radioactivity.

(5) Nuclear energy uses up important resources.

50. A physicist would be most likely to study which one of the following?

(1) The creation of better plant fertilizers

(2) The makeup of rocks on the moon

(3) Cures for cancer

(4) The ways to produce copper compounds

(5) The collision of particles

practice test

TEST 4: LANGUAGE ARTS, READING

65 Minutes • 40 Questions

Directions: The Language Arts, Reading Test consists of multiple-choice questions based on a variety of excerpts from literary and nonfiction writings. Read each selection carefully and then answer the questions based upon it. Do not spend more time than necessary on any one item. Record your answers in the Language Arts, Reading Section of your answer sheet.

Q   He died at eventide . . . I saw his breath beat quicker and quicker, pause, and then his little soul leapt like a star that travels in the night and left a world of darkness in its train. The day changed not . . . Only in the chamber of death writhed the world's most piteous thing—a childless mother.

The reader can infer that death has come to a(n)

(1) old man.
(2) favorite dog.
(3) child.
(4) mother.
(5) soldier.

① ② ● ④ ⑤

A   The correct answer is "child"; therefore, you should blacken answer space (3) on your answer sheet.

ITEMS 1 TO 6 REFER TO THE FOLLOWING EXCERPT FROM A PLAY.

What Happened to the Manuscript?

Line *LOVBORG*: To you I can tell the truth, Hedda.

HEDDA: The truth?

LOVBORG: First promise me—
(5) give me your word—that what I now confide to you Thea shall never know.

HEDDA: I give you my word.

LOVBORG: Good. Then let me tell
(10) you that what I said just now was untrue.

HEDDA: About the manuscript?

LOVBORG: Yes. I have not torn it to pieces—nor thrown it into the
(15) fiord.

HEDDA: No, n—But—where is it then?

LOVBORG: I have destroyed it none the less—utterly destroyed it,
(20) Hedda!

HEDDA: I don't understand.

LOVBORG: Thea said that what I had done seemed to her like a child-murder.

(25) *HEDDA*: Yes, so she said.

LOVBORG: But to kill this child— that is not the worst thing a father can do to it.

HEDDA: Not the worst?

(30) *LOVBORG*: No. I wanted to spare Thea from hearing the worst.

HEDDA: Then what is the worst?

LOVBORG: Suppose now, Hedda, that a man—in the small hours of
(35) the morning—came home to his child's mother after a night of riot and debauchery, and said: "Lis- ten—I have been here and there—in this place and that. And I have
(40) taken our child with me—to this place and to that. And I have lost the child—utterly lost it. The devil knows into what hands it may have fallen—who may have had their
(45) clutches on it."

HEDDA: Well—but when all is said and done, you know—this was only a book—

LOVBORG: Thea's pure soul was
(50) in that book.

HEDDA: Yes, so I understand.

LOVBORG: And you can under- stand, too, that for her and me together no future is possible.

(55) *HEDDA*: What path do you mean to take then?

LOVBORG: None. I will only try to make an end of it all—the sooner the better.

(60) *HEDDA* (*a step nearer him*): Eilert Lovborg—listen to me. Will you not try to—to do it beautifully?

LOVBORG: Beautifully? (*Smiling*) With vine-leaves in my hair, as you
(65) used to dream in the old days—?

HEDDA: No, no. I have lost my faith in the vine-leaves. But beauti- fully nevertheless! For once in a way!—Good-bye! You must go now—
(70) and do not come here any more.

LOVBORG: Good-bye, Mrs. Tesman. And give George Tesman my love. (*He is on the point of going.*)

(75) *HEDDA*: No, wait! I must give you a memento to take with you. (*She goes to the writing-table, opens the drawer and takes out a pistol.*)

LOVBORG (*looks at her*): This? Is
(80) this the memento?

HEDDA (*nodding slowly*): Do you recognize it? It was aimed at you once.

LOVBORG: You should have used
(85) it then.

HEDDA: Take it—and do you use it now.

LOVBORG (*puts the pistol in his breast pocket*): Thanks!

(90) *HEDDA*: And beautifully, Eilert Lovborg. Promise me that! (*Hedda listens for a moment at the door. Then she goes up to the writing- table, takes out the packet of
(95) manuscript, peeps under the cover,*

draws a few of the sheets half out, and looks at them. Next she goes over and seats herself in the arm-chair beside the stove, with the (100) *packet in her lap. Presently she opens the stove door, and then the packet.)*

    HEDDA (throws one of the quires into the fire and whispers to her- (105) *self):* Now I am burning your child, Thea!—Burning it, curly-locks! *(Throwing one or two more quires into the stove)* Your child and Eilert Lovborg's. *(Throws the rest in)* I am (110) burning—I am burning your child.
    —Hedda Gabler, by Henrik Ibsen

1. What is the general mood of this scene?

    (1) It is emotionally charged.

    (2) It is full of beauty.

    (3) It expresses strong love and friendship.

    (4) It is emotionally neutral.

    (5) It is comic.

2. Lovborg compares his manuscript to

    (1) a child.

    (2) vine-leaves.

    (3) a memento.

    (4) his soul.

    (5) his best friend.

3. When Hedda says, "Will you try to—to do it beautifully?" what does she mean?

    (1) She is urging Lovborg to kill Thea.

    (2) She wants Lovborg to write a better manuscript next time.

    (3) She wants Lovborg to commit suicide in a beautiful way.

    (4) She wants Lovborg to dress more colorfully and wear vine-leaves on his head.

    (5) She is urging Lovborg to return to Thea.

4. The reader can tell from its use in the play that the word "quires" refers to

    (1) a book.

    (2) pistol cases.

    (3) an entire manuscript.

    (4) children.

    (5) sheets of paper.

5. From this scene, what can we infer about Hedda's character?

    (1) She is a loving and giving person who knows how to respond to a friend in need.

    (2) She is open and truthful, and says what she thinks.

    (3) She is deceitful and destructive, even toward her friends.

    (4) She tends to respond in a highly emotional way in any crisis.

    (5) She does thoughtless things that hurt people, but she doesn't mean to.

6. "With friends like these, who needs enemies?" How can we relate this saying to the situation in this scene?

    (1) Thea and Lovborg are lovers who have no enemies.

    (2) Hedda is an enemy in the guise of a friend to Lovborg.

    (3) Hedda is a loving friend to Lovborg and helps him to see his situation more clearly.

    (4) With an enemy like Hedda, Lovborg will need many friends.

    (5) The saying has no relationship to the scene, whatsoever.

ITEMS 7 TO 12 REFER TO THE FOLLOWING SELECTION.

What Is the Man Doing in the Yukon?

Line Day had broken cold and gray, exceed-ingly cold and gray, when the man turned aside from the main Yukon trail and climbed the high earth bank,
(5) where a dim and little-traveled trail led eastward through the fat spruce timberland. It was nine o'clock. There was no sun or hint of sun, though there was not a cloud in the sky. It
(10) was a clear day, and yet there seemed an intangible pall over the face of things, a subtle gloom that made the day dark, and that was due to the ab-sence of sun.
(15) But all this—the mysterious, far-reaching hairline trail, the absence of sun from the sky, the tremendous cold, and the strangeness and weirdness of it all—made no impression on the
(20) man. It was not because he was long used to it. He was a newcomer to the land, a cheechako, and this was his first winter. The trouble with him was that he was without imagination.
(25) That there should be anything more to it than that was a thought that never entered his head.

As he turned to go, he spat specula-tively. There was a sharp, explosive
(30) crackle that startled him. He spat again. And again, in the air, before it could fall to the snow, the spittle crackled. He knew that at fifty below spittle crackled in the snow, but his
(35) spittle had crackled in the air. Un-doubtedly it was colder than fifty be-low—how much colder he did not know.

At the man's heels trotted a dog, a
(40) big native husky, the proper wolf dog, gray-coated and without any visible or temperamental difference from its brother, the wild wolf. The animal was depressed by the tremendous cold. It
(45) knew that it was not time for travel-ing. Its instinct told it a truer tale than was told to the man by the man's judgment.

—Adapted from *To Build a Fire,*
by Jack London

7. What words does the author use to emphasize the extreme cold?

(1) The "spittle crackling"

(2) The "subtle gloom" and "little traveled trail"

(3) The absence of sun

(4) "The strangeness and weirdness of it all"

(5) "The mysterious, far-reaching hairline trail"

8. The mood of the story is clearly and successfully established in the first sentence with the words

(1) "main Yukon trail," "high earth bank."

(2) "led Eastward," "fat spruce timberland."

(3) "cold and gray," "dim."

(4) "man turned aside," "led Eastward."

(5) "Day had broken," "little-traveled trail."

9. Which of the following can be in-ferred from the selection?

(1) The man is jealous of the dog.

(2) The man is unusually percep-tive and wise.

(3) It is impossible to build a fire.

(4) The dog is wiser than the man.

(5) The extreme cold will kill them both.

10. What is the temperature of the Yukon in the story?

(1) −30 degrees

(2) −10 degrees

(3) 0 degrees

(4) −65 degrees

(5) −50 degrees

11. Of the following possible choices, which is the one most likely to be true?

(1) The traveler will surely die from the cold.

(2) The man has a serious but unstated reason for setting out on this journey.

(3) The man is a casual weekend camper.

(4) The man must be a fresh-air fanatic to be out in such cold weather.

(5) The man is familiar with the Yukon and clearly knows what he is doing.

12. What is unusual about the author's description of the dog?

(1) He infers that he is really a wolf.

(2) It is strange that he can survive such cold temperatures.

(3) It is unlikely that the dog would walk behind the man instead of leading the way.

(4) It is strange that the dog doesn't run home.

(5) He writes about him as having human capabilities.

ITEMS 13 TO 18 REFER TO THE FOLLOWING POEM.

Do Good Fences Make Good Neighbors?

Line   Something there is that doesn't love a wall,
That sends the frozen-ground-swell under it,
The work of hunters is another thing:
I have come after them and made repair
(5)   Where they have left not one stone on a stone,
But they would have the rabbit out of hiding,
The gaps I mean,
No one has seen them made or heard them made,
But at spring mending-time we find them there.
(10)   I let my neighbor know beyond the hill;
And on a day we meet to walk the line
And set the wall between us once again.
There is where we do not need the wall:
He is all pine and I am apple orchard.
(15)   My apple trees will never get across
And eat the cones under his pine, I tell him.
He only says, "Good fences make good neighbours."
Spring is the mischief in me, and I wonder
If I could put a notion in his head:
(20)   "*Why* do they make good neighbors?
Before I built a wall I'd ask to know
What I was walling in or walling out,
Something there is that doesn't love a wall,
That wants it down."
(25)   I see him there
Bringing a stone grasped firmly by the top

In each hand, like an old stone savage armed.
He moves in darkness as it seems to me,
He says again, "Good fences make good neighbours."

—Reprinted from *The Poetry of Robert Frost,*
edited by Edward Connery Lathem,
by permission of Henry Holt and Company, Inc.

13. According to the author, which of the following destroys walls?

(1) Hunters and farmers

(2) Hunters and nature

(3) Orchards and bad weather

(4) Rabbits and hunters

(5) His neighbor and animals

14. The neighbor would agree most closely with which one of the following opinions?

(1) "Something there is that doesn't love a wall."

(2) "He is all pine and I am apple orchard."

(3) "*Why* do they make good neighbors?"

(4) "Good fences make good neighbors."

(5) "He moves in darkness, it seems to me."

15. The speaker feels that

(1) walls are necessary to keep hunters from the cows.

(2) walls are important to isolate apple orchards from pine trees.

(3) walls help neighbors stay close.

(4) it is important to keep fences well repaired.

(5) walls between people are unnecessary.

16. Of the choices below, which one best defines the sentence: "He moves in darkness as it seems to me"?

(1) Night is falling and they still have a lot of wall to repair.

(2) His neighbor has a vision problem.

(3) His neighbor has never questioned the importance of walls.

(4) Good neighbors are made slowly, over the years.

(5) Acts of kindness are usually not rewarded.

17. What is the tone of this poem?

(1) Resigned yet questioning

(2) Angry and despairing

(3) Hopeful and eager

(4) Proud and haughty

(5) Nonchalant

18. According to this poem, how has the speaker tried to influence his neighbor to let the fence fall?

(1) With threats

(2) By letting hunters come through

(3) By planting an apple orchard and a pine forest

(4) With humor and logic

(5) With silence and stones

ITEMS 19 TO 23 REFER TO THE FOLLOWING BIOGRAPHY.

Who Were Elizabeth Barrett and Robert Browning?

Line The letter that began the most famous courtship of the nineteenth century opened, "I love your verses with all my heart, dear Miss
(5) Barrett." The writer, Robert Browning, was a young poet and playwright, respected in close literary circles, writing to a woman six years his senior, an invalid, and
(10) a poet of national and international fame. It must have delighted him that Elizabeth Barrett had recognized his own genius, that intense poetic heart of his that she
(15) had likened to a pomegranate, mentioning it and him by name in a poem of her own. To suggest that Browning's first letter to Elizabeth Barrett was spurred by the slightest
(20) notion of self-aggrandizement would be to misunderstand the caliber of the man and to misrepresent the relation these two poets had to each other and to their times. Easy
(25) enough to misrepresent. Their courtship, their secret marriage, their fifteen years in Italy, were exceptional—even by the rigorous standards of their own time.
(30) Browning, introducing himself to Miss Barrett in that first letter, found his prose soaring ahead of his intentions: "In this addressing myself to you—your own self, and
(35) for the first time, my feeling rises altogether," he told her. Then leaving literary allusions and Victorian propriety in his wake, Robert Browning dared to express
(40) his feelings: "I do, as I say, love these verses with all my heart—and I love you too."

One might say, at that very moment, as he wrote those words,
(45) he fell in love.

"I thank you, dear Mr. Browning, from the bottom of my heart," Elizabeth Barrett answered on the very next day, January 11, 1845,
(50) beginning a correspondence that would last for twenty months. The two would write each other 573 letters during that time—574 if we include the one Elizabeth asked him
(55) to burn. The last word was Elizabeth's, written on a Friday night, September 18, 1846, on the eve of their journey to Italy.

The letters confirm that the one
(60) myth about the Brownings that was absolutely true was the most romantic one—the drama of their courtship. Robert Browning fell in love with an invalid poet, wrote to
(65) her, visited. Their love took her from the couch she hardly ever left, down the stairs of the house on Wimpole Street, to the drawing room, to a walk in the park, and
(70) then to Italy—a climate that would support their art and her health.

—From *Dared and Done, The Marriage of Elizabeth Barrett and Robert Browning*, by Julia Markus. Used by permission.

19. Which of the following choices best represents the main idea of this selection?

(1) Life in Victorian times was dull.

(2) The courtship of Robert and Elizabeth was quite famous.

(3) It is often hard to meet a famous poet.

(4) Sometimes you have to write many letters before you can make progress in a relationship.

(5) Poets often write excellent letters.

20. The events described took place in the

(1) American colonies.

(2) late nineteenth century.

(3) mid-1840s.

(4) mid-eighteenth century.

(5) middle ages.

21. According to this selection, which of the following statements is true?

(1) It was considered unusual in Victorian times for people to openly express their feelings.

(2) Both Robert and Elizabeth were well-known poets in Victorian England.

(3) Elizabeth was deeply offended by Robert's expressions of love.

(4) Elizabeth was a far less emotional person than Robert.

(5) It is unlikely that Robert really was serious in his intentions toward Elizabeth.

22. Why was it surprising for Robert Browning to have fallen in love with Elizabeth Barrett?

(1) Elizabeth was famous and Robert was unknown.

(2) She was an invalid and rarely left her room.

(3) Elizabeth was quite a few years older than Robert.

(4) He had never met her but only knew her through her poetry.

(5) All of the above

23. Currently, Robert Browning is considered a very great poet, while Elizabeth Browning is far less admired. In the context of this biography, why is this ironic?

(1) It is ironic because nowadays no one reads poetry anymore.

(2) It was unusual for women to write in Victorian times.

(3) It is ironic that famous poets could be considered "stars" at that time, but not anymore.

(4) The irony, according to the story, is that the reverse was true then.

(5) The irony is that two poets could live together harmoniously, either then or now.

ITEMS 24 TO 28 REFER TO THE FOLLOWING BUSINESS DOCUMENT.

What Does This Company Employee Have to Know?

EMPLOYEE HANDBOOK
(EXCERPTS)

SECTION 3.1 Expense Accounts:

(a) It is important to hand in Expense Account Form 2X394 and relevant receipts within two weeks of the incurred expense(s).

(b) These forms are to be filled out for all work-related expenses by company representatives, sales personnel, administrative personnel, and others.

(c) Reimbursements will be made directly to you in the case of out-of-pocket expenses within 3 to 4 weeks.

(d) Those using company-issued credit cards will be expected to hand in those receipts as well.

(e) Examples of work-related expenses might be: taking a prospective or active client to lunch or dinner; taking taxi cabs or public transportation to reach clients; expenses for car rentals; airline fares; hotel expenses when staying out of town overnight.

SECTION 4.8 Client Lists:

(a) All prospective and potential clients' names are to be kept on file, both on the appropriate company computer file, and on office lists under "C."

(b) These files are to include date of contact, outcome of contact, and possibilities for future sales.

(c) As clients are contacted in the future, these files must be regularly updated.

SECTION 6.1 Transportation:

(a) A limited number of Lee Company cars are available for the use of employees. These are located in "B" lot and are in the care of garage personnel.

(b) Form 3Y24 must be completed for use of these cars, with careful attention to times and dates of use, names of prospective clients, and reasons for use.

(c) Careful note of mileage data, both going in and out, must be made.

(d) For employees ranked below administration level, the signature of your supervisor must be obtained first, and handed in to the garage personnel along with Form 3Y24.

(e) In case a car is needed and all company cars are already in use, then arrangements may be made for a car rental through the McMillan Company, which has a contract with this company.

Excerpts from *Lee Company Employee Handbook,* Lenox, Maine
9/23/02

24. According to this handbook, what is an "expense account"?

    (1) The weekly fee for an employee's cab

    (2) Car insurance

    (3) A list of job-related expenses that an employee incurs

    (4) Lunch bills for clerks and administrative personnel

    (5) The company rent bill

25. In using a company car, the employee must remember to

    (1) check the tires.

    (2) make note of mileage information before leaving and after returning the car.

    (3) check with the McMillan Company first.

    (4) go to "C" lot.

    (5) ask the client first, and submit Form 2X394.

26. Which of the following is a true statement?

    (1) Only administrators in Lee Company may use company cars.

    (2) All client lists must be submitted to the supervisor.

    (3) Clients may use company cars if their names are in appropriate computer files.

    (4) No credit cards can be used.

    (5) If you take a client out to dinner, you have to hand in Form 2X394 along with the receipts.

27. From the information given, it is reasonable to assume that

    (1) Lee Company must be a good-sized firm.

    (2) this company sells client lists.

    (3) this company has many expenses.

    (4) this firm manufactures computers.

    (5) this company owns only a small number of cars.

28. What is the most likely business for Lee Company to be in, judging by the handbook?

    (1) They do scientific research for a university.

    (2) They're obviously a minor family-owned business.

    (3) They manufacture Jeeps for the government.

    (4) They probably sell a service or product to the public.

    (5) They're a nonprofit company offering consumer information.

ITEMS 29 TO 34 REFER TO THE FOLLOWING STORY.

What Is the Young Girl Feeling?

Line What a surprise this was to me, that I longed to be back in the place that I came from, that I longed to sleep in a bed I had
(5) outgrown, that I longed to be with people whose smallest, most natural gesture would call up in me such a rage that I longed to see them all dead at my feet. Oh, I had
(10) imagined that with my one swift act—leaving home and coming to this new place—I could leave behind me, as if it were an old garment never to be worn again, my sad
(15) thoughts, my sad feelings, and my discontent with life in general as it presented itself to me. In the past, the thought of being in my present situation had been a comfort,

(20) but now I did not even have this to look forward to, and so I lay down on my bed and dreamt I was eating a bowl of pink mullet and green figs cooked in coconut *(25)* milk, and it had been cooked by my grandmother, which was why the taste of it pleased me so, for she was the person I liked best in all the world and those were the *(30)* things I liked best to eat also. The room in which I lay was a small room just off the kitchen—the maid's room. I was used to a small room, but this was a different sort of *(35)* small room. The ceiling was very high and the walls went all the way up to the ceiling, enclosing the room like a box—a box in which cargo traveling a long way *(40)* should be shipped. But I was not cargo. I was only an unhappy young woman living in a maid's room, and I was not even the maid. I was the young girl who watches *(45)* over the children and goes to school at night. How nice everyone was to me, though, saying that I should regard them as my family and make myself at home. I believed *(50)* them to be sincere, for I knew that such a thing would not be said to a member of their real family. After all, aren't family the people who become the millstone *(55)* around your life's neck?

—From *Lucy*, by *Jamaica Kinkaid*.
Used by permission.

29. Many people have said, "absence makes the heart grow fonder." How can this saying be compared to the feelings expressed in this story?

  (1) The author seems to really miss the home she previously despised, much to her surprise.

  (2) The young woman is just an unhappy person who has no heart.

  (3) The author misses her home but has not grown fonder of her family.

  (4) The author was a murderer at heart and needed to get away.

  (5) The girl misses only her grandmother's cooking but is not fond of anyone at home.

30. What does the story suggest about the young woman's employment?

  (1) That she has a job as a servant

  (2) That she is overworked

  (3) That she is probably an *au pair* in a new home

  (4) That she is treated badly by her employers

  (5) That she is doubtlessly on her way back home

31. The narrator in all probability

  (1) comes from a neighboring town.

  (2) is really a farm girl.

  (3) will never adjust to her new life.

  (4) hates her employers.

  (5) comes from another culture.

32. Which of the following choices best describes the young girl's feelings about her family back home?

  (1) Her feelings are totally negative.

  (2) They are definitely mixed, which is very typical.

  (3) Her feelings show that she was abused by them.

  (4) They show that she will be a bitter person her entire life.

  (5) They will never change.

33. What does the story suggest about the narrator?

(1) That she is spiteful and lazy

(2) That she doesn't enjoy life and is ungrateful

(3) That she doesn't trust anyone because of the hard life she has lived

(4) That she is thoughtful about life as well as studious

(5) That she has a very big appetite but doesn't know how to cook

34. When she describes family as being "the people who become a millstone around your life's neck," what does the young woman mean?

(1) She is just making a joke.

(2) She means that responsibility is hard.

(3) She means that family is a burden your entire life.

(4) She doesn't know what she means.

(5) She views family as an evil that must be punished.

ITEMS 35 TO 40 REFER TO THE FOLLOWING SHORT STORY.

Why Is Granddad Going Away?

Line Petey hadn't really believed that Dad would be doing it—sending Granddad away.

(5) But here was the blanket that Dad had that day bought for him, and in the morning he'd be going away.

"Now, isn't that a fine blanket!" said the old man, smoothing it over his knees. "And isn't your father a kind

(10) man to be giving the old fellow a blanket like that to go away with? It cost something, it did—look at the wool of it! And warm it will be on cold winter nights. There'll be few blankets there

(15) the equal of this one!"

It was like Granddad to be saying that. He was trying to make it easier. He'd pretended all along that he

wanted to go away to the great brick

(20) building—the government place.

"Oh, yes, it's a fine blanket," said Petey, and got up and went into the house. He wasn't the kind to cry, and besides, he was too old for that.

(25) He'd just come in to fetch Granddad's fiddle.

It was the last night they'd be having together. There wasn't any need to say, "Play all the old tunes."

(30) Granddad tuned up for a minute, and then said, "This is one you'll like to remember."

They didn't hear the two people coming down the gully path. Dad had

(35) one arm around the girl with the hard, bright face like a doll's. Dad didn't say anything, but the girl came forward and spoke to Granddad prettily: "I won't be here when you leave

(40) in the morning, so I came over to say good-by."

"It's kind of you," said Granddad, with his eyes cast down. "And will you look at this," he said "the fine

(45) blanket my son has given me to go away with!"

"Yes," she said, "it's a fine blanket." She felt of the wool and repeated in surprise, "A fine blanket—I'll say it

(50) is!" She turned to Dad and said to him coldly, "That blanket really cost something."

He cleared his throat and defended himself: "I wanted him to have the

(55) best. . . ."

The girl stood here, still intent on the blanket.

"It's double, too," she said, as if accusing Dad.

(60) The boy went suddenly into the house. He was looking for something. He could hear that girl scolding Dad, and Dad becoming angry in his slow way. And now she was suddenly going

(65) away in a huff. . . . As Petey came out, she turned and called back, "All the

same, he doesn't need a double blanket!" And she ran off up the gully path.

(70) "Oh, she's right," said the boy coldly. "Here, Dad"—and he held out a pair of scissors. "Cut the blanket in two."

"Yes," said the boy harshly, "a single blanket's enough for an old man (75) when he's sent away. We'll save the other half, Dad; it will come in handy later."

"Now, what do you mean by that?" asked Dad.

(80) "I mean," said the boy slowly, "that I'll give it to you, Dad—when you're old and I'm sending you—away."

There was a silence. But Granddad understood, for he put out a hand and (85) laid it on Dad's shoulder. And he heard Granddad whisper, "It's all right, son—I knew you didn't mean it . . ." And then Petey cried.

But it didn't matter—because they (90) were all three crying together.

—"The Blanket," *Floyd Dell*

35. What is the predominant symbol in this story?

(1) The fiddle

(2) The blanket

(3) The scissors

(4) The young boy

(5) The old man

36. How can you best state the theme?

(1) When money is scarce, one should not buy expensive items like a blanket.

(2) The old man got exactly his due.

(3) Unintentionally, we all do cruel things at times.

(4) It can be difficult having old people around when one is planning to marry.

(5) Things have changed greatly over the past fifty years.

37. What is the author saying about old age and the difference between generations?

(1) There is an enormous difference between the three generations.

(2) Old age is a golden time.

(3) It is better to be young than old.

(4) There is no real "generation gap" because we will all be old some day.

(5) The old are very poorly treated as a general rule.

38. The overall tone of this story is

(1) melancholy.

(2) cheerful.

(3) uplifting.

(4) cruel.

(5) sarcastic.

39. What do the scissors represent?

(1) Getting away from an unpleasant duty

(2) Cutting the bonds of love, duty, and respect

(3) Cutting loose from whatever is holding you back

(4) Cutting away dead weight

(5) Assuming new freedom

40. Which of the following best describes Granddad's attitude?

(1) Considerate and understanding

(2) Resentful toward his son's fiancée

(3) Anxious and worried

(4) Bitter but resigned

(5) Angry and humiliated

TEST 5: MATHEMATICS

90 Minutes • 50 Questions

Part 1—25 questions (a calculator is permitted): 45 minutes

Part 2—25 questions (a calculator is not permitted): 45 minutes

Directions: The Mathematics Test consists of questions intended to measure general mathematics skills and problem-solving ability. The questions are based on short readings that often include a graph, chart, or figure. Work carefully, but do not spend too much time on any one question. Be sure you answer every question. You will not be penalized for incorrect answers.

Formulas you may need are given on page 826. Only some of the questions will require you to use a formula. Record your answers on the separate answer sheet. Be sure that all information is properly recorded.

There are three types of answers found on the answer sheet:

Type 1 is a regular format answer which is the solution to a multiple-choice-type question. It requires shading in one of 5 bubble choices.

Q   Jill's drug store bill totals $8.68. How much change should she get if she pays with a $10.00 bill?

   (1) $2.32
   (2) $1.42
   (3) $1.32
   (4) $1.28
   (5) $1.22   ① ② ● ④ ⑤

A   The correct answer is "$1.32." Therefore, you should mark answer space (3) on your answer sheet.

Type 2 is an alternate format answer that is the solution to a Standard Grid "fill-in" type question. It requires shading in bubbles representing the actual numbers, including a decimal or division sign where applicable.

Type 3 is an alternate format answer that is the solution to a Coordinate Plane Grid problem. It requires shading in the bubble representing the correct coordinate of a graph.

For examples of how to record Type 2 and Type 3, refer to page 119.

FORMULAS

Description	Formula
AREA (A) of a:	
square	$A = s^2$; where s = side
rectangle	$A = lw$; where l = length, w = width
parallelogram	$A = bh$; where b = base, h = height
triangle	$A = \frac{1}{2}bh$; where b = base, h = height
circle	$A = \pi r^2$; where $\pi = 3.14$, r = radius
PERIMETER (P) of a:	
square	$P = 4s$; where s = side
rectangle	$P = 2l + 2w$; where l = length, w = width
triangle	$P = a + b + c$; where a, b, and c are the sides
Circumference (C) of a circle	$C = \pi d$; where $\pi = 3.14$, d = diameter
VOLUME (V) of a:	
cube	$V = s^3$; where s = side
rectangular container	$V = lwh$; where l = length, w = width, h = height
cylinder	$V = \pi r^2 h$; where $\pi = 3.14$, r = radius, h = height
square pyramid	Volume $= \frac{1}{3} \times (\text{base edge})^2 \times \text{height}$
cone	Volume $= \frac{1}{3} \times \pi \times \text{radius}^2 \times \text{height}$; π is approximately equal to 3.14.
Pythagorean theorem	$c^2 = a^2 + b^2$; where c = hypotenuse, a and b are legs of a right triangle
distance (d) between two points in a plane	$d = \sqrt{(x_2 - x_1)^2 + (y_2 - y_1)^2}$; where (x_1, y_1) and (x_2, y_2) are two points in a plane
slope of a line (m)	$m = \dfrac{y_2 - y_1}{x_2 - x_1}$ where (x_1, y_1) and (x_2, y_2) are two points in a plane
trigonometric ratios	given an acute angle with measure x of a right triangle, $\sin x = \dfrac{\text{opposite}}{\text{hypotenuse}}$, $\cos x = \dfrac{\text{adjacent}}{\text{hypotenuse}}$, $\tan x = \dfrac{\text{opposite}}{\text{adjacent}}$
mean	mean $= \dfrac{x_1 + x_2 + \cdots + x_n}{n}$; where the x's are the values for which a mean is desired, and n = number of values in the series
median	median = the point in an ordered set of numbers at which half of the numbers are above and half of the numbers are below this value
simple interest (i)	$i = prt$; where p = principal, r = rate, t = time
distance (d) as function of rate and time	$d = rt$; where r = rate, t = time
total cost (c)	$c = nr$; where n = number of units, r = cost per unit

Part 1

You may now begin Part 1 of the Mathematics Test. You may use your calculator for this part. Bubble in the correct response to each question on Part 1 of your answer sheet.

1. The city bought salt to spread over icy roads during the cold season. It used $\frac{1}{3}$ of the salt before January 1st, and $\frac{2}{5}$ after January 1st. Express the total amount used as a decimal.

   (1) 0.25
   (2) 0.27
   (3) 0.28
   (4) 0.38
   (5) 0.73

   ITEM 2 REFERS TO THE FOLLOWING RIGHT TRIANGLE.

   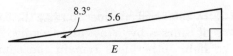

2. Find the value for E.

   (1) 0.81
   (2) 0.82
   (3) 3.88
   (4) 4.65
   (5) 5.54

3. Jessica needs $4\frac{2}{3}$ yards of material to complete sewing her outfit. At $12.85 per yard, what was the cost in dollars?

   (1) $12.57
   (2) $51.40
   (3) $52.07
   (4) $59.97
   (5) $65.00

4. Mary looks out the window and sees that the outdoor temperature is 12° Centigrade. She wants to convert Centigrade to Fahrenheit temperature so that Mark, who is not familiar with the metric system, will understand.

   The conversion formula is:

   $$F = \frac{9}{5}C + 32$$

   What is the Fahrenheit temperature?

   Mark your answer in the circles in the grid on your answer sheet.

5. Christopher took out a bank loan to mortgage his home. He paid $95,321.58 in the first 10 years. 85% of his mortgage went toward interest. How much interest did he pay? Round your answer to the nearest whole dollar amount.

   Mark your answer in the circles in the grid on your answer sheet.

6. Tony earned $1,000 in $3\frac{1}{2}$ years. If he invests $2,000, what rate (percent) of interest must his money earn each year?

   (1) 1.6%
   (2) 3.5%
   (3) 7.0%
   (4) 14.3%
   (5) 16.0%

7. Jim loaded parcels at the Express Motor Company for 3 hours on Thursday night, 4 hours on Friday night, and 8 hours on Saturday, for a pay rate of $7.00 an hour. On Monday and Tuesday he worked the usual 4 hours each afternoon in the college bookstore at $4.50 an hour. How much did Jim earn in the past week?

(1) $123
(2) $130
(3) $141
(4) $175
(5) $540

8. A packer for a knitting yarn company must organize his work so the boxes with the greatest weight are placed in the bottom of the shipping crate and lighter boxes are placed on the top. Five boxes must be packed for the next shipment. The boxes have the following weights:

   Yarn D—216 ounces
   Yarn E—5.7 pounds
   Yarn F—35 pounds
   Yarn G—77.4 ounces
   Yarn H—10.3 pounds

Which of the following sequences correctly lists the order in which boxes should be packed?

(1) E, H, F, G, D
(2) G, E, H, D, F
(3) D, G, F, H, E
(4) F, D, H, E, G
(5) F, D, G, H, E

ITEMS 9 TO 11 REFER TO THE FOLLOWING ESTIMATE OF COLLEGE COSTS FOR ERIC AT NORTH STATE UNIVERSITY (NSU).

Expenses	Cost in 2002	Cost in 2003
Course	$55/credit	?
College Fees	430/year	?
Other (books, supplies, etc.)	100	?

9. Eric decides to get his associate's degree in two years taking 30 credits each year. How much will he have to pay in 2002 to attend NSU?

(1) $530
(2) $1,750
(3) $2,080
(4) $2,180
(5) $2,220

10. In 2003 NSU decides to raise the cost of courses by 3.75% and fees by 8%. If his other fees remain the same, how much will Eric be paying in 2003?

(1) $2,276
(2) $1,750
(3) $2,080
(4) $2,180
(5) $2,220

11. What was the percent increase in college costs for 2003 over 2002?

(1) 1.0%
(2) 4.0%
(3) 4.2%
(4) 4.4%
(5) 5.0%

12. The area of a wheel is 2.25 square feet. What is the radius of the wheel in feet? Give the answer to two decimal places.

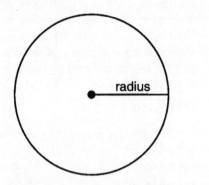

Mark your answer in the circles in the grid on your answer sheet.

13. In 1900, the wage rate in a certain trade was $1.60 an hour for a 40-hour week and $1\frac{1}{2}$ times the base pay for overtime. How much did an employee who worked 48 hours in a week earn?

Mark your answer in the circles in the grid on your answer sheet.

ITEMS 14 AND 15 REFER TO THE FOLLOWING INFORMATION.

June Hansen made a series of deposits and withdrawals from her checking account during the month of September. They were:

September 2	$375 deposit
September 6	$150 withdrawal
September 10	$35 withdrawal
September 12	$42 deposit
September 19	$140 withdrawal
September 26	$28 withdrawal

14. According to Hansen's August statement, she started the month of September with a balance of $257. What was her checkbook balance on October 1?

(1) $165

(2) $185

(3) $321

(4) $331

(5) $465

15. On December 1, Hansen had a balance of $421 and wrote a check for $193.47. How much money must she deposit in order to bring her checkbook balance to a total of $600?

(1) $127.59

(2) $362.41

(3) $372.47

(4) $500.00

(5) $627.59

16. Two cars leave the same location at 2:00 p.m. If one car travels north at the rate of 20 m.p.h. and the other travels east at the rate of 40 m.p.h., how many miles apart are the two cars at 4:00 p.m.?

(1) 34.6

(2) 44.7

(3) 89.4

(4) 120

(5) 6.3

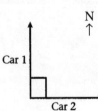

17. If right triangle <u>ABC</u> is plotted on a large graph, and $\overline{AB}$ is drawn along the *x*-axis, and coordinate point B is (40, 0), then what are the coordinates of point A?

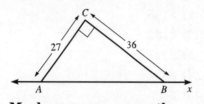

Mark your answer on the coordinate plane grid on your answer sheet.

ITEMS 18 AND 19 ARE BASED ON THE HEIGHT AND WEIGHT CHART FOR THE REDWOOD HS BASKETBALL TEAM.

Player	Height	Weight(lbs)
Joe	5 ft 11 in	186
Keith	6 ft 4 in	248
Neal	6 ft	199
Sal	6 ft 6 in	256
George	6 ft 1 in	195

18. The average height of the team is

   (1) 6 feet.

   (2) 6 feet 1 inch.

   (3) 6 feet 2 inches.

   (4) 6 feet 3 inches.

   (5) 6 feet 4 inches.

19. If Joe were traded, how heavy would his replacement have to be in order to bring the team's average weight to 230 lbs?

   (1) 224 lbs

   (2) 239 lbs

   (3) 242 lbs

   (4) 248 lbs

   (5) 252 lbs

20. A car dealer advertises two different payment plans for a new car. If the buyer pays cash, the car costs $5,700. If the buyer pays on the installment plan, he pays 20% of the cash cost as a down payment, and then $200 a month for 24 months. How much more money must a buyer pay on the installment plan than on the cash plan?

   (1) $1,140

   (2) $1,000

   (3) $520

   (4) $480

   (5) $240

21. If a distance estimated at 150 feet is really 146.3 feet, find the percent of error in this estimate. (Record the answer to the nearest *tenth*.)

Mark your answer in the circles in the grid on your answer sheet.

22. Between 7 a.m. and 7:19 a.m., how many degrees does the minute hand of a clock move?

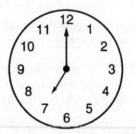

Mark your answer in the circles in the grid on your answer sheet.

ITEMS 23 AND 24 REFER TO THE FOLLOWING GRAPH.

DANIELLA'S SURVEY OF BURGER-MEAL PRICES IN LAKEWOOD

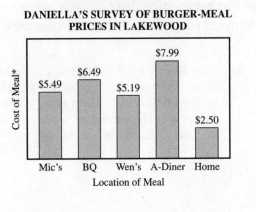

*Note: A meal consists of 1/4 pound of meat, small fries, 8 oz soda, and a salad.

23. What's the average cost of eating a meal outside of her home?

(1) $5.03

(2) $5.53

(3) $6.00

(4) $6.29

(5) $6.49

24. If Daniella ate ten burger-meals last month at home instead of at Wen's, how much did she save?

(1) $2.69

(2) $10.69

(3) $25.00

(4) $26.90

(5) $36.90

ITEM 25 REFERS TO THE FOLLOWING INFORMATION COMPARING TWO SIMILAR MODEL REFRIGERATORS.

Brand	Cost ($)	Dimensions (inch)		
		Width	**Height**	**Length**
1. Kenmore	1,000	33	31	65
2. GE	1,100	31	31	67

25. Anne wanted to choose the best value between the two refrigerators listed above. She was concerned about two factors: cost and size. Which brand had the *least* cost/volume ratio, and what was the ratio?

(1) Kenmore: .015

(2) Kenmore: .017

(3) GE: .015

(4) GE: .017

(5) Both are identical: .015

Part 2

You may not return to Part 1 of the Mathematics Test or use your calculator for this part. Fill in the correct response to each question on Part 2 of your answer sheet.

26. Sara bought 2.65 pounds of meat at $4.25 per pound. How much did she pay in dollars?

(1) $29.15

(2) $24.00

(3) $14.85

(4) $11.26

(5) $1.13

27. The Martin family surveyed their TV viewing habits and found that they watched $\frac{1}{4}$ of their shows before 6 p.m., and that of those, $\frac{2}{3}$ included explicitly violent images. What fraction of all the shows they watched were seen before 6 p.m. and had violent images?

(1) $\frac{1}{6}$

(2) $\frac{1}{3}$

(3) $\frac{3}{8}$

(4) $\frac{2}{3}$

(5) $\frac{11}{12}$

28. The Red River was tested for pollution. Its contents included 1/12th-part PCBs and 2/5th-part algae. What was the combined fraction containing both PCBs and algae?

(1) $\frac{3}{60}$

(2) $\frac{3}{17}$

(3) $\frac{29}{60}$

(4) $\frac{31}{60}$

(5) $\frac{3}{4}$

29. In the year 2525, an archaeologist found a cornerstone in Chicago with the following date:

M C M L X I X

In Roman numerals it represents which number?

(1) 964

(2) 1131

(3) 1931

(4) 1969

(5) 2509

30. A box for playing cards has the dimensions

$$L = 3 \text{ inches}$$
$$W = 2 \text{ inches}$$
$$\text{Thickness} = \frac{1}{2} \text{ inch}$$

If each card measures 3 inches × 2 inches and has a thickness of $\frac{1}{100}$ inch, how many cards can fit into the box?

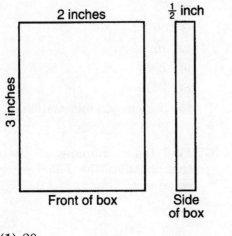

Front of box

Side of box

2 inches

½ inch

3 inches

(1) 20
(2) 30
(3) 40
(4) 50
(5) 100

31. The baker cut a $1\frac{1}{3}$-pound slice from a $3\frac{1}{2}$-pound piece of chocolate cake.

How many pounds were left? Express the answer as an improper fraction.

Mark your answer in the circles in the grid on your answer sheet.

32. Jack's allowance is $30 per month. In April, Jack sponsored two friends in a walkathon for a total contribution of $7.50. What percent of Jack's April allowance does this contribution represent?

(1) 7.5%
(2) 10%
(3) 20%
(4) 25%
(5) 30%

33. A 10-foot high cylinder is full of radioactive liquid waste. If the diameter of the cylinder is 1 foot, how many cubic feet of liquid can it contain?

(1) 1π
(2) 1.5π
(3) 2π
(4) 2.5π
(5) 3π

practice test

ITEMS 34 TO 36 REFER TO THE INFORMATION PROVIDED BY THE GRAPHS BELOW.

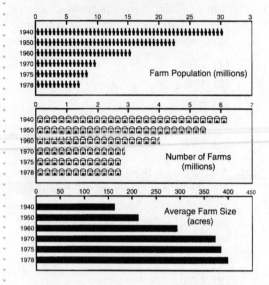

34. Which of the following statements is true about the changes in farming between 1940 and 1978?

   (1) Farm population, number of farms, and average farm size all increased.

   (2) Farm population and number of farms have increased but average farm size decreased.

   (3) Farm population and number of farms decreased, but average farm size increased.

   (4) Farm population decreased, but the number of farms and average farm size increased.

   (5) Farm population, number of farms, and average farm size all decreased.

35. The average population on each farm during 1975 was most nearly

   (1) 1

   (2) 2

   (3) 3

   (4) 4

   (5) Not enough information is given.

36. The percent of increase in average farm size from 1940 to 1978 is most nearly

   (1) 50%

   (2) 75%

   (3) 100%

   (4) 150%

   (5) Not enough information is given.

37. Find the coordinates of the point that satisfies the following set of equations:

$$x - y = 3$$
$$y = 2x$$

Mark your answer on the coordinate plane grid on your answer sheet.

ITEMS 38 TO 41 REFER TO THE CHART BELOW.

Cigarette Smoking

Percentage of students who reported smoking cigarettes daily in the previous 30 days by grade and gender, selected years 1980–1998

	1980	1985	1990	1991	1992	1993	1994	1995	1996	1997
12th-graders: Total	21.3	19.5	19.5	18.5	17.2	19.0	19.4	21.6	22.2	24.6
Male	18.5	17.8	17.8	18.8	17.2	19.4	20.4	21.7	22.2	24.8
Female	23.5	20.6	20.6	17.9	16.7	18.2	18.1	20.8	21.8	23.6

Source: Monitoring the Future Study conducted by the University of Michigan under a grant from the National Institute on Drug Abuse.

38. In what year did males first begin to smoke more than females?

(1) 1990

(2) 1991

(3) 1994

(4) 1996

(5) 1997

39. What was the average percentage of smokers between 1994 and 1997?

(1) 21.01%

(2) 21.17%

(3) 21.95%

(4) 22.28%

(5) 22.80%

40. What was the median percentage of smokers from 1990 through 1997?

(1) 17.80%

(2) 19.00%

(3) 19.45%

(4) 20.23%

(5) 20.25%

41. Between the years 1994 through 1997, the data does not support which of the following statements?

A. The percentage of males who smoked increased.

B. The percentage of females who smoked increased.

C. The percentage of males who smoked was greater than females who smoked.

D. The difference between the percentage of males and females who smoked was less than 2.4.

E. Most students smoke.

(1) A

(2) B

(3) C

(4) D

(5) E

42. In one year at James Madison Elementary School, twice as many boys were registered for kindergarten as girls. If 90 children attended kindergarten that year, how many pupils were boys and how many were girls?

(1) 20 boys and 70 girls

(2) 30 boys and 60 girls

(3) 45 boys and 45 girls

(4) 60 boys and 30 girls

(5) 75 boys and 15 girls

43. A rectangular swimming pool is to be filled with water to a depth of 10 feet. If the pool is 30 feet long by 20 feet wide, how many cubic feet of water will be needed to fill the pool?

Mark your answer in the circles in the grid on your answer sheet.

44. If the following numbers are arranged in order from the least to the greatest, what will be their correct order?

I. $\dfrac{9}{13}$

II. $\dfrac{13}{9}$

III. 70%

IV. $\dfrac{1}{.70}$

(1) II, I, III, IV

(2) III, II, I, IV

(3) III, IV, I, II

(4) II, IV, III, I

(5) I, III, IV, II

45. A radio has a sale price of $42.50, which is 15% off the regular price. Which of the following is equal to the regular price of the radio?

(1) $42.50 × .15

(2) $42.50 ÷ .15

(3) $42.50 + .15

(4) $42.50 × .85

(5) $42.50 ÷ .85

ITEMS 46 AND 47 REFER TO THE FOLLOWING CHART, REPRESENTING VOTES CAST FOR MAYOR FROM THE 250 ELIGIBLE VOTERS IN THE LOCAL ELECTION IN EASTCHESTER, KANSAS.

Candidates	Number
A	25
B	75
C	125
No vote	25

46. In drawing a pie chart to represent these results, how many degrees should be used to draw each of the four sectors representing A, B, C, and No Vote, respectively?

(1) 30, 90, 170, 30

(2) 36, 108, 180, 36

(3) 36, 36, 108, 180

(4) 25, 75, 235, 25

(5) None of the above

47. What was the mean number of voters who voted for a particular candidate?

(1) 25

(2) 50

(3) 56

(4) 60

(5) 75

**ITEMS 48 TO 50 REFER TO THE
INFORMATION BELOW.**

**THE CHURCHILL FAMILY'S MONTHLY
BUDGET CHART**

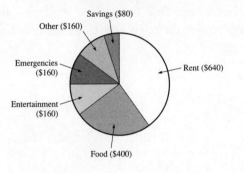

**ITEM 50 REFERS TO THE FOLLOWING
INFORMATION AND PIE CHART.**

Ron and his wife, Steffi, are expecting
their third child. They plan to get a bigger rental apartment for $860 per month.
All items in the old budget will remain
the same except for the following:

Budget Item	New Amount (Anticipated)
Food	$500
Rent	$860
Other	$240

50. How much more per month will Ron
have to earn on a second job to enable them to afford their new expenses?

(1) $160

(2) $400

(3) $1,360

(4) $1,600

(5) $2,000

48. Ron and Steffi Churchill have two
children. Ron is the only wage earner
in the family. What percentage of
their budget is allocated for "entertainment" and "emergencies" combined?

(1) 20%

(2) 35%

(3) 50%

(4) 65%

(5) 85%

49. Ron gives a $300 birthday party for
his 90-year-old mother. How much of
his "emergency" money would be
needed to supplement the use of his
"entertainment" money to pay for the
party?

(1) $10

(2) $40

(3) $80

(4) $140

(5) $160

ANSWER KEY AND EXPLANATIONS

After completing Practice Test 3, check your answers against the Answer Key and Explanations
that follow. Next, turn to the Error Analysis on page 867 to see how well you did. Finally, go to the "Assessing Your Readiness" chart on page 868 to determine how prepared you are to take the actual GED tests.

Test 1: Language Arts, Writing—Part 1

1. (4)	11. (1)	21. (1)	31. (4)	41. (5)
2. (1)	12. (3)	22. (3)	32. (2)	42. (4)
3. (2)	13. (2)	23. (3)	33. (1)	43. (2)
4. (3)	14. (2)	24. (1)	34. (2)	44. (3)
5. (5)	15. (4)	25. (5)	35. (3)	45. (1)
6. (2)	16. (5)	26. (5)	36. (5)	46. (5)
7. (4)	17. (4)	27. (3)	37. (2)	47. (4)
8. (3)	18. (2)	28. (2)	38. (3)	48. (2)
9. (5)	19. (3)	29. (4)	39. (1)	49. (5)
10. (4)	20. (4)	30. (3)	40. (4)	50. (1)

1. **The correct answer is (4).** The word *gives* is correct because it modifies the *United States Census Bureau*, which is singular.

2. **The correct answer is (1).** In order for the sentence to make sense, the verb *was* needs to be followed with *conducted*.

3. **The correct answer is (2).** The semicolon breaks up the complete thought, which is *A small sampling of households received a longer questionnaire that asked.* . . . A comma is not needed either.

4. **The correct answer is (3).** This sentence seems to introduce a new topic that is continued in paragraph B. Therefore, it makes a better beginning for this paragraph than an ending for the first paragraph.

5. **The correct answer is (5).** Since the sentences before and after sentence (7) are in the present tense,

this one should be also. Therefore, *told* should be changed to *tell*.

6. **The correct answer is (2).** *Racially* needs to be balanced with *culturally*. These words must be in this form because they are adverbs.

7. **The correct answer is (4).** The census is being compared in importance to highways and telephone lines, so the word *as* needs to be inserted after *is*, as in *The census is as important.* . . .

8. **The correct answer is (3).** The complete rewritten sentence would read: *On the basis of census figures, federal dollars supporting schools, employment services, housing assistance, highway construction, hospital services, programs for the elderly, and more are distributed.*

9. **The correct answer is (5).** *Disappointed* needs to be changed to the

present tense. The resulting phrase is *This is very disappointing*.

10. **The correct answer is (4).** The correct phrase is to *pitch in*, meaning that everyone must participate in the common effort.

11. **The correct answer is (1).** The first letter of the word coming after a colon should not be capitalized.

12. **The correct answer is (3).** The new sentence would read *Smaller inventory and thus less waste and more profits will result from new accounting procedures of sales.*

13. **The correct answer is (2).** Sentence (3) is a run-on sentence that needs to be divided with a period after *requirements*. The word *Their* is now capitalized because it begins a new sentence.

14. **The correct answer is (2).** The comma after *department* needs to be removed because it breaks up a complete thought, as in *The department showing the most improvement*. The second one also needs to be deleted because it also breaks up the meaning, as in *the most improvement in sales.*

15. **The correct answer is (4).** Since paragraph E just continues the theme expressed in paragraph D, it is better to combine these two paragraphs.

16. **The correct answer is (5).** The correct verb form here is *to find,* as in, *it's impossible to find.*

17. **The correct answer is (4).** The correct verb to use with *you* is *need*, not *needs*.

18. **The correct answer is (2).** The expression is *that will inevitably come.*

19. **The correct answer is (3).** This is a sentence fragment that needs a verb between *Many young people* and *their own successful business in this way* to explain what happened. In-

serting *have started* allows this sentence to make sense.

20. **The correct answer is (4).** The word *City*, as it is used here, is not part of a proper noun and therefore should not be capitalized.

21. **The correct answer is (1).** The newly rewritten sentence reads: *Another cares for the lawns of several dozen neighbors after investing in a couple of lawn mowers.*

22. **The correct answer is (3).** A good concluding sentence ties together the thoughts expressed just above. Here, choice (3) draws the conclusion from the examples given that a resourceful or clever person can sometimes use his abilities to make a job for himself, which is the point of this article. The other choices given are irrelevant ideas that do not relate clearly to this selection.

23. **The correct answer is (3).** The correct word is *its,* which is the possessive referring to *retail establishment*. The words *it's* means *it is,* which would be incorrect here.

24. **The correct answer is (1).** The correct spelling here is *whether,* meaning *if* or *when*.

25. **The correct answer is (5).** This is a sentence fragment, meaning it isn't a full sentence. In order to make it correct, the words *This is done by* should be inserted in the beginning.

26. **The correct answer is (5).** There is no need to substitute any of these choices for sentence (7), which is a good introductory sentence for this paragraph.

27. **The correct answer is (3).** The word *adjusting* needs to be changed to *adjust* in order to balance *register* and *perform*.

28. **The correct answer is (2).** This is a run-on sentence, meaning it has too many sections, is confusing, and needs to be turned into two sentences.

answers practice test 3

By putting a period after *productivity* and starting the next sentence with *It,* you have two correct sentences.

29. The correct answer is (4). The word *handles* would be used for *person,* not *persons,* which is plural. The word *handle* is correct, as in *Sales persons also handle.*

30. The correct answer is (3). The context suggests that this sentence should be written in the present tense, as in *Most employers also require.*

31. The correct answer is (4). *English* is the name of a language. Therefore, it must be capitalized.

32. The correct answer is (2). This sentence doesn't belong in the first paragraph, which deals with the preparation involved in becoming a construction inspector. It should be moved after sentence (7), which discusses the training of a construction inspector once he's on the job.

33. The correct answer is (1). The newly written sentence would read *Usually, most training of construction and building inspectors is received on the job.*

34. The correct answer is (2). The lack of a present perfect verb ending to this sentence makes it a sentence fragment. *Is increased* at the end turns it into a complete correct sentence.

35. The correct answer is (3). This is a run-on sentence that needs to be converted into two sentences. By putting a period after *two years* and starting a new sentence with *Inspectors,* it is corrected.

36. The correct answer is (5). The correct word here is *sites,* which refers to places. The word *cites* is pronounced the same way, but is the verb meaning to quote, or summon.

37. The correct answer is (2). This is a sentence fragment, meaning it isn't a complete sentence. In order to be correct the word *are* must be added after *most healthy children.*

38. The correct answer is (3). The word *becomes,* which is the singular present tense form of "to become," must be used in this sentence, as in *becomes more controlled,* because it modifies *physical movement.*

39. The correct answer is (1). This sentence begins a whole new part consisting of four sentences all dealing with the important and beneficial outcomes of exercise. It should therefore begin a new paragraph to emphasize the ideas presented.

40. The correct answer is (4). The word *who* is only used when referring to people and should not be used here. *Which* is more appropriate here, because it refers to *these activities.*

41. The correct answer is (5). The plural of "parent" is *parents,* and the plural of "teacher" is *teachers.* The *'s* is a possessive and should not be used here.

42. The correct answer is (4). There is no reason to put a question mark at the end of this sentence, since it is not asking a question. The question mark needs to be changed to a period.

43. The correct answer is (2). The new sentence would read *Children establish life-long patterns of wholesome and rewarding physical activities with well-planned physical education programs.*

44. The correct answer is (3). The singular form of the verb "to be" should not be used here, since the sentence lists three *areas of concern.* The correct plural form is *are.*

45. The correct answer is (1). The sentence is talking about the act of giving information, not speaking. The word *provide* is a correct substitute for *say.*

46. **The correct answer is (5).** *Are applying* is correct because it needs to balance *are,* as in *you're using* at the other end of the sentence.

47. **The correct answer is (4).** The correctly rewritten sentence reads: *However, unless you're seeking financing it's illegal for a business to check your record.*

48. **The correct answer is (2).** This sentence is better placed as a topic sentence for this paragraph, which it can introduce. Sentence (10) and the following paragraph both deal with privacy as related to telephone use.

49. **The correct answer is (5).** The semicolon creates confusion here and is unnecessary since the word *and* already connects the two parts of the sentence.

50. **The correct answer is (1).** Since the final paragraph refers to the computer, this would make the best topic sentence. The other choices are examples of sentences that are irrelevant to this paragraph.

Language Arts, Writing—Part 2

SAMPLE ESSAY RESPONSE

The presence of computers is evident everywhere—in government offices, stores, banks, hospitals, the military, cars, businesses, libraries, schools, homes, and work settings. It is easy to see that computers have changed life for everyone. It is not easy to remember how we all functioned before they became part of modern existence.

The most important positive aspect of all this is the fast dissemination of information. Today, anyone sitting at a computer has a personal unlimited library and research tool to work with that is able to access most human knowledge. This is true whether the person is in a remote village in a third-world country or in a modern world-class capital. Computers can empower people with knowledge and understanding of the world around them. Also, many tedious and time-consuming tasks are routinely and more efficiently now done on computer, cutting costs for businesses and increasing the productivity of employees. Just a few examples include record keeping, billing, tracking of inventories, and cost accounting.

Computers do have a drawback, however. Since they are relied on so heavily, they do have the potential of intruding in people's lives or invading their privacy. Personal information that used to be private can now be accessed by anyone. There is little about our lives that is truly private any more—it's all out there on computers.

Nonetheless, it is clear that we are in an unstoppable computer revolution that is far more positive than negative in its effects on everyone's lives.

Test 2: Social Studies

1. (4)	11. (3)	21. (2)	31. (2)	41. (1)
2. (1)	12. (3)	22. (3)	32. (1)	42. (2)
3. (3)	13. (2)	23. (1)	33. (3)	43. (1)
4. (5)	14. (5)	24. (4)	34. (5)	44. (4)
5. (4)	15. (4)	25. (5)	35. (5)	45. (2)
6. (2)	16. (3)	26. (2)	36. (2)	46. (2)
7. (4)	17. (1)	27. (5)	37. (4)	47. (4)
8. (1)	18. (2)	28. (1)	38. (5)	48. (1)
9. (1)	19. (2)	29. (3)	39. (1)	49. (5)
10. (4)	20. (4)	30. (3)	40. (4)	50. (1)

1. **The correct answer is (4).** The pie graph shows slightly less than half of working women with children having children under the age of 6. There is no support for choices (1), (2), or (5). Choice (3) ignores the fact that this graph refers only to working women *with children* and not to all working women.

2. **The correct answer is (1).** By knowing in advance what the public is willing to buy, business saves itself a lot of time and money.

3. **The correct answer is (3).** Each of the kinds of surveys is highlighted by an example.

4. **The correct answer is (5).** The selection does not refer to family relationships.

5. **The correct answer is (4).** The reader is left with the impression that surveys help businesses and are therefore necessary.

6. **The correct answer is (2).** All nations that need to trade with each other are tied together by economics. Whatever drastically affects one affects its trading partners in some way.

7. **The correct answer is (4).** When prices drop, it is generally because of the availability of too many goods. When this happens, factories stop producing, and workers are laid off.

8. **The correct answer is (1).** As stated in the second sentence of paragraph 2, factories produced less or closed down when the Depression began.

9. **The correct answer is (1).** The first sentence states that the collapse began when Great Britain raised its interest rates "to bring home needed capital."

10. **The correct answer is (4).** The system of checks and balances is intended to prevent any one branch of government from gaining too much power.

11. **The correct answer is (3).** Only Congress can pass legislation. The president has the power to veto legislation of which he does not approve. Congress, in turn, can override a presidential veto by a two-thirds majority. This is the only example provided that illustrates how two branches of government can be checked and balanced by each other.

12. **The correct answer is (3).** Genocide occurred when the Romans killed the Carthaginians and destroyed their city.

13. **The correct answer is (2).** As defined in paragraph 1, the aim of genocide is the destruction of a racial, political, or cultural group. Proof that the Romans were successful in destroying the Carthaginians is that few traces of their civilization remain.

14. **The correct answer is (5).** As stated in the last paragraph, immortality is ensured by art, religion, and wisdom.

15. **The correct answer is (4).** As stated in paragraph 2, Carthage was the center of Phoenician trade. The Romans destroyed the Carthaginians because they wished to take over this profitable trade, and they feared this would never be possible if the Carthaginians were allowed to survive.

16. **The correct answer is (3).** Economist C expresses the socialist's point of view because this economist wants the government to assume ownership of basic industries.

17. **The correct answer is (1).** Economist A is concerned with government protection of the consumer. The Truth in Packaging Act, which outlaws deceptive containers, and the Truth in Lending Act, which requires retailers and lenders to provide consumers with the true cost of credit, are both intended to protect the consumer.

18. **The correct answer is (2).** Economist B advocates the free private enterprise system, which was the policy of the U.S. government during most of the nineteenth century.

19. **The correct answer is (2).** *Laissez-faire* economics calls for the removal of government intervention in the

answers practice test 3

marketplace. Without government regulation, the law of supply and demand will determine what is produced and how much people will pay.

20. **The correct answer is (4).** The concept of land was central to the Native Americans but totally different from the European concept, which allowed for purchase, payment, and deeds. The confiscation of land took place throughout the United States until the Native Americans were confined to limited areas called reservations. The words quoted were spoken by a Native American during treaty talks in South Dakota in 1866.

21. **The correct answer is (2).** Taxes added at each stage of processing are value-added taxes.

22. **The correct answer is (3).** The table shows that the more a person earns, the more he is required to pay. For example, the person who earns $16,500 would pay 25 percent of his income in taxes, while the person who earns $6,500 would pay only 15 percent in taxes. This is an example of a progressive tax.

23. **The correct answer is (1).** Since the Dittmeirs earn less than the stipulated level of income ($9,000 in this case), the federal government provides payments to increase their family income. This is an example of a negative income tax.

24. **The correct answer is (4).** A tax that takes a higher percentage of income from the poor than from the rich is a regressive tax.

25. **The correct answer is (5).** A tax added to an existing tax is a surtax.

26. **The correct answer is (2).** The bill says 900 cubic feet of water were used from February 21 to March 21 and that 100 cubic feet of water equals 748 gallons. Multiply $9 \times 748 = 6,732$ gallons.

27. **The correct answer is (5).** 900 cubic feet were used during the win-ter period. The cost for the water was $62.71. Divide 62.71 by 9; the answer is $6.97.

28. **The correct answer is (1).** The total amount of water consumed was 23,188 gallons. The total bill was $93.90. Divide $93.90 by 23,188 to get an average cost of $.004 per gallon. (Round numbers to $94 and 23,000 gallons.)

29. **The correct answer is (3).** The only reason mentioned in the choices that would explain England's involvement in the "Triangular Trade" is choice (3).

30. **The correct answer is (3).** The 1920s was a time of transition or change. (See last sentence of the passage.)

31. **The correct answer is (2).** The Eighteenth Amendment to the Constitution became effective on January 16, 1920. The amendment prohibited the manufacture, sale, and transportation of alcoholic beverages. Prohibition unwittingly contributed to defiance of the law, illicit behavior of many sorts, and the rise of organized crime.

32. **The correct answer is (1).** Jazz and flappers (people who adopted a certain style of clothing and distinctive mannerisms) were considered, at the time, fads of the 1920s.

33. **The correct answer is (3).** The second sentence speaks of the era's "pervading temperament."

34. **The correct answer is (5).** The second sentence explains how historians classified the era, implying there are other methods of classification. There is nothing to suggest the twenties were unique, choice (2), or that the changes that marked the period were unparalleled, choice (3). Choice (1) is contradicted by sentence 4. The second paragraph indicates a "Red Scare," referring to Communists, so choice (4) is also incorrect.

35. **The correct answer is (5).** Skilled workers, as represented by the smoothly sailing ship, are not foundering under the "winds" of inflation. The unskilled workers, in contrast, are in danger of capsizing.

36. **The correct answer is (2).** The entire passage deals with nutrition programs for the elderly.

37. **The correct answer is (4).** The text states "nearly a quarter of a million," which is 250,000.

38. **The correct answer is (5).** The passage deals only with nutrition for the elderly.

39. **The correct answer is (1).** It is most likely that more elderly are living on their own, causing the problems described in the article.

40. **The correct answer is (4).** The article states that some of the nutritional problems the elderly experience are directly related to loneliness and isolation.

41. **The correct answer is (1).** Of the states mentioned, Nevada has only one waste site, and the others have significantly more.

42. **The correct answer is (2).** All three of these states have the shading that indicates "over 40" sites per state. In addition, these are three of the most densely populated states in the nation.

43. **The correct answer is (1).** These words, from the Declaration of Independence, list grievances against the King of England. They were written to justify the American Revolution.

44. **The correct answer is (4).** Acid rain, spawned over the high smokestacks of the industrial Midwest, regularly falls in the forests, lakes, and streams of the Northeast, causing devastating ecological damage to wildlife and forests.

45. **The correct answer is (2).** "Off-year elections," that is, years spaced midway between presidential contests, show a consistently lower level of voter participation. Choice (3) is incorrect because presidential candidates do not run in "off years." Choices (1) and (5) are not supported by the graph. Choice (4) makes no sense at all. Eisenhower was elected president in 1952 and 1956.

46. **The correct answer is (2).** Israel is located in the part of the world called the Middle East, which is in the southwestern part of Asia.

47. **The correct answer is (4).** The "establishment clause," among other protections, provides that the United States government cannot establish an official religion for the country. There was a great fear about this issue due to the religious persecution in Europe under which the colonists had often suffered.

48. **The correct answer is (1).** The sun does not move appreciably; however, since the earth rotates from west to east, the western part of a country "sees" the sun later than the east. Therefore, for example, New York time is 3 hours earlier than California time.

49. **The correct answer is (5).** Niccolo Machiavelli (1469–1527) wrote *The Prince,* a book describing how a successful leader must be as "strong as a lion" and "as cunning as a fox."

50. **The correct answer is (1).** Before the advent of fast airplanes and rockets, the two oceans (Atlantic and Pacific) presented significant barriers to any threats of invasion. These bodies of water also contributed to the feeling in the United States that it was located far from the concerns and troubles in the rest of the world, thereby helping create an isolationist feeling.

Test 3. Science

1. (2)	11. (2)	21. (4)	31. (1)	41. (2)
2. (5)	12. (1)	22. (1)	32. (2)	42. (4)
3. (3)	13. (3)	23. (4)	33. (2)	43. (1)
4. (4)	14. (5)	24. (3)	34. (4)	44. (4)
5. (1)	15. (3)	25. (1)	35. (1)	45. (5)
6. (2)	16. (4)	26. (1)	36. (5)	46. (4)
7. (2)	17. (1)	27. (5)	37. (4)	47. (1)
8. (1)	18. (5)	28. (4)	38. (1)	48. (3)
9. (5)	19. (4)	29. (4)	39. (2)	49. (4)
10. (4)	20. (2)	30. (2)	40. (5)	50. (5)

1. **The correct answer is (2).** Arteries carry blood away from the heart.

2. **The correct answer is (5).** The left ventricle pumps blood into the aorta, which distributes blood throughout the body.

3. **The correct answer is (3).** Blood goes to the lungs to pick up oxygen. The oxygen-rich blood then returns to the heart for distribution throughout the body.

4. **The correct answer is (4).** This is the only correct sequence according to the diagram.

5. **The correct answer is (1).** The animal described is a shark, which belongs to the class of fish. The clue words are cold-blooded, cartilaginous skeleton, and gill openings.

6. **The correct answer is (2).** Frogs have "two lives." The young tadpoles have gills and live in the water, while the adult frogs have lungs and most species can live on land or in water. Animals that can live both on land and in water are amphibians.

7. **The correct answer is (2).** Find the difference between the lowest and highest temperatures expected for the cities named for each traveler. Julie will experience temperatures ranging from a low of 33° in Atlanta to a high of 75° in Miami.

This is a range of 42°, which is the widest range of the five scheduled trips.

8. **The correct answer is (1).** Pat will experience temperatures ranging from 14° in Chicago to 43° in Denver. These are the coldest low and high expected for the trips shown.

9. **The correct answer is (5).** The announcer is referring to a hurricane, a common weather pattern in the Caribbean during late summer.

10. **The correct answer is (4).** Gravel and other large particles have settled out of water and have become cemented together. Choices (1), (2), and (3) refer to igneous rocks; choice (5) refers to metamorphic rocks.

11. **The correct answer is (2).** 155 tornadoes occurred in May as indicated by the highest point on the dotted line representing tornadoes. Choice (1) is incorrect because the greatest number of tornado deaths occurs in April, not May. Choice (3) is incorrect because there are fewer tornado deaths in fall than in spring. Choice (4) is not covered by the information in the graph. Choice (5) is incorrect because the graph shows a total of more than 700 tornadoes, not deaths, for the 27-year period from 1980–200.

12. The correct answer is (1). Act promptly when you sight a tornado. Go into a designated shelter area as soon as the weather reports warn you. If there is no designated shelter, seek out a building and hide in an interior hallway, closet, or bathroom on as low a floor as possible. Do not stay in your automobile, but lie flat in a ditch or ravine with your head covered.

13. The correct answer is (3). Desirable weight for a man 5'8" (68") is 145. At 130, Bill is underweight.

14. The correct answer is (5). Look at the weight columns for men and women. In almost every case, the desirable weight for men is 10 pounds more than the desirable weight for women of the same height. This is the only conclusion that is supported by the information provided by the table.

15. The correct answer is (3). It is easier to obtain all the necessary nutrients on a higher-calorie diet. Therefore, women must choose their foods more carefully than men if they are to get all the necessary nutrients without gaining weight.

16. The correct answer is (4). The work done is W = F × D, but the distance is not given. However, D = R(rate) × T(time), or D = 2(m/sec) × 6(sec) = 12 m. Substituting, we get: W = F × D, W = 40 × 1.2 = 480 joules.

17. The correct answer is (1). As stated in the last sentence of paragraph 2, most back problems occur in the neck and lower back.

18. The correct answer is (5). The back contains ligaments, tendons, bones, vertebrae, discs, and nerves.

19. The correct answer is (4). As stated in the second sentence of paragraph 2, "The vertebrae are separated and cushioned by oval pads called discs."

20. The correct answer is (2). The last paragraph states that the ligaments may rupture (tear) if the back flexes suddenly.

21. The correct answer is (4). When the population of hawks increases, the population of its prey decreases and vice versa.

22. The correct answer is (1). Because of the absence of competition from antibiotic-sensitive strains, the antibiotic-resistant strains have become more prevalent. This is an example of natural selection.

23. The correct answer is (4). The last sentence states that atoms are composed of protons, neutrons, and electrons. Molecules are groups of atoms.

24. The correct answer is (3). The fifth sentence says, "Groups of atoms make molecules."

25. The correct answer is (1). The first sentence states that matter is made up of "particles so utterly small that they have never been seen."

26. The correct answer is (1). The second paragraph advises against moving an injured person "unless absolutely necessary because of the danger of fire. . . ."

27. The correct answer is (5). Paragraph 5 recommends that you control excessive bleeding by applying pressure.

28. The correct answer is (4). Everyone should know the basic rules of first aid for all of the reasons given.

29. The correct answer is (4). To dehydrate something is to deprive it of water.

30. The correct answer is (2). Isotopes have a different number of neutrons. The number of protons is the same, so the atomic number is the same. However, one isotope has more neutrons than the other, so their atomic weights will vary.

31. The correct answer is (1). Isotopes have the same atomic number (the lower number to the left of the chemical symbol) and different atomic masses (the upper number to the left of the symbol). 12_6C and 13_6C represent isotopes of carbon.

32. The correct answer is (2). One-half of the strontium 90 will disintegrate every 20 years.

$$8 \text{ grams} \times \frac{1}{2} = 4 \text{ grams}$$

(after 20 years)

$$4 \text{ grams} \times \frac{1}{2} = 2 \text{ grams}$$

(after 40 years)

33. The correct answer is (2). As stated in the passage, one of the dangers of genetic engineering is "the accidental development of a mutant bacterium that may change the whole life pattern on Earth."

34. The correct answer is (4). Since the common cold is a virus, interferon might be helpful in curing it.

35. The correct answer is (1). Two substances (sulfur + oxygen) combine to form a more complex substance (sulfur dioxide). This is an example of a combination reaction.

36. The correct answer is (5). Splitting the nucleus of a heavy element to release enormous amounts of energy is an example of atomic fission.

37. The correct answer is (4). Two compounds exchange ions as the magnesium combines with the chlorine and the hydrogen with the oxygen in this double replacement reaction.

38. The correct answer is (1). Two substances (sodium + chlorine) combine to form a more complex substance (sodium chloride). This is a combination reaction.

39. The correct answer is (2). As indicated on the graph, when water reaches the boiling point, it changes to vapor.

40. The correct answer is (5). Since force = m × a, multiply the mass by the acceleration for each block:

Block	Mass	×	Accel.	=	Force
1	2		3		6
2	4		6		24

Therefore, the second block requires 4 times as much force as the first.

41. The correct answer is (2). As stated in paragraph 2, the system will be able to locate the distress site within 1 to 3 miles.

42. The correct answer is (4). Paragraph 1 mentions air and maritime (sea) distress victims. Paragraph 3 mentions tracking a Japanese adventurer.

43. The correct answer is (1). Paragraph 1 states that SARSAT reduces the time needed to locate victims. Paragraph 2 mentions the accuracy with which SARSAT can locate distress sites. There is no mention of cost, ease of use, or reliability.

44. The correct answer is (4). DNA mediates protein synthesis through m-RNA, which it makes; therefore answer choices (1) and (2) are incorrect. Transcription leads to translation, so choice (3) is incorrect. Translation is defined as the process of assembling a protein from amino acids; therefore, choice (4) is correct.

45. The correct answer is (5). From the passage, all we can assume is that scientists can create models of DNA and RNA to study.

46. The correct answer is (4). Copper is the metal most widely used in electrical wiring because it is almost as good a conductor of electricity as silver and considerably less expensive.

47. The correct answer is (1). Scientists from the private company, Celera Genomics, announced the completion of the "human genome" project. This achievement provides us with a virtual road map to an estimated 95 percent of all the genes in the human body. This knowledge may help us to understand how our bodies work and to find cures for many diseases.

48. **The correct answer is (3).** Fossil fuels are naturally existing, organic, and carbon-containing fuels that are found in the earth.

49. **The correct answer is (4).** There are many problems associated with

generating nuclear energy. However, uranium is unique in that it is the only fuel that is radioactive. Exposure to excess radioactivity may cause cancer.

50. **The correct answer is (5).** One of the areas that interest physicists is motion and forces. The other choices would be studied by botanists, geologists, biologists, and chemists, respectively.

Test 4. Language Arts, Reading

1. (1)	11. (2)	21. (1)	31. (5)
2. (1)	12. (5)	22. (5)	32. (2)
3. (3)	13. (2)	23. (4)	33. (4)
4. (5)	14. (4)	24. (3)	34. (3)
5. (3)	15. (5)	25. (2)	35. (2)
6. (2)	16. (3)	26. (5)	36. (3)
7. (1)	17. (1)	27. (1)	37. (4)
8. (3)	18. (4)	28. (4)	38. (1)
9. (4)	19. (2)	29. (1)	39. (2)
10. (4)	20. (3)	30. (3)	40. (1)

1. **The correct answer is (1).** This is a scene between a man in deep personal trouble and his calculating friend. It expresses desperation and suicidal feelings. This makes it an emotionally charged scene.

2. **The correct answer is (1).** In lines 22–24, Lovborg states that Thea thinks destroying the manuscript is "like a child-murder." In other words, the manuscript is compared to a child.

3. **The correct answer is (3).** In line 58, Lovborg says he will make an end of it. In line 62, Hedda asks him to "do it beautifully," meaning to commit suicide in a beautiful way.

4. **The correct answer is (5).** In the last twenty-one lines, the directions state that Hedda takes out a packet

of manuscript and begins to throw it in the fire one or two quires at a time. From this information, you can infer that quires are sheets of paper.

5. **The correct answer is (3).** Lovborg comes trustingly to Hedda, desperate and on the point of suicide. He has lost his precious manuscript. She not only has this manuscript in her possession, but also hands him a pistol to use for killing himself. She is obviously a deceitful and vicious person.

6. **The correct answer is (2).** The saying refers to friends who may at times act like real enemies. That is certainly the case here, with Hedda's betrayal of Lovborg. An enemy could

not have harmed Lovborg more seriously than his supposed friend has done.

7. **The correct answer is (1).** The fact that the spittle crackles before it hits the ground indicates that the temperature is colder than 50 below zero.

8. **The correct answer is (3).** Both halves of choice (3) establish the frigid, forbidding Yukon, "exceedingly cold and gray."

9. **The correct answer is (4).** The final sentences tell us the dog knew "it was no time for traveling." "Its instinct told it a truer tale than was told to the man by the man's judgment."

10. **The correct answer is (4).** See lines 35–38. The only choice lower than 50 below is 65° below.

11. **The correct answer is (2).** Choice (2) is the most likely. The man is probably on a serious errand that brought him out into this cold and unfamiliar territory. We can't say that he will necessarily die, since he might possibly be near his destination. It's unlikely that he's a camper or fresh-air fanatic. The story says that he is a newcomer, so choice (5) is also incorrect.

12. **The correct answer is (5).** The author describes the dog as "depressed" and says it "knew that it was not time for traveling." It is usually assumed that animals are not capable of having these kinds of ideas or feelings.

13. **The correct answer is (2).** The first two lines explain how nature destroys walls. The second two discuss the way hunters scatter the rocks.

14. **The correct answer is (4).** He only says, "Good fences make good neighbors." The neighbor seems to feel that fences are necessary to establish clear boundaries in order for neighbors to get along well.

15. **The correct answer is (5).** The speaker questions the necessity of walls. "*Why* do they make good neighbors?" he wonders.

16. **The correct answer is (3).** The neighbor never questions why they need a wall between them, although apple orchards and pine trees naturally separate their land.

17. **The correct answer is (1).** Although the speaker is resigned to not changing the neighbor's mind, he still questions the validity of walls.

18. **The correct answer is (4).** The speaker uses logic with his neighbor by pointing out that the wall doesn't seem to serve any useful purpose. He also uses humor, as in the line "My apple trees will never get across and eat the cones under his pines, I tell him." Therefore, choice (4) is the correct answer.

19. **The correct answer is (2).** The whole piece is about how these two writers first met, so choice (2) is the correct answer.

20. **The correct answer is (3).** The second-to-last paragraph tells us when all of this took place. It began with the first letters in January 1845, which places these events in the mid-1840s. By "eighteenth century" is meant the 1700s, and the "middle ages" refers to the fifth through the fifteenth centuries.

21. **The correct answer is (1).** The last several lines of the first paragraph tell us the answer to this question. "Then leaving literary allusions and Victorian propriety in his wake, Robert Browning dared to express his feelings." This tells us that it was not proper in Victorian times to be so open with others. Choice (2) is incorrect since only Elizabeth was well known at the time, not Robert, who was only "respected in close literary circles" but not famous yet.

22. **The correct answer is (5).** This is the correct answer, since all of these

circumstances existed and made the relationship highly unusual and unexpected.

23. **The correct answer is (4).** The irony lies in the fact that, at that time, Elizabeth was world-famous and Robert was considered her "gifted" husband, while now, it is the other way around. Some of the other choices may have a grain of truth but do not represent the true irony referenced in the question.

24. **The correct answer is (3).** You can infer from Section 3.1 that it is a list of expenses that an employee incurs in doing her job for the company. This might involve travel and meal expenses when going out of town on behalf of the company.

25. **The correct answer is (2).** Section 6.1, part (c), states that you must list the mileage information for the car you are borrowing. This must be done before leaving with the car and when returning it to the lot.

26. **The correct answer is (5).** This requirement is stated in the first sentence of Section 3.1. Part (e) gives this as an example of a work-related expense.

27. **The correct answer is (1).** A company that has so many types of employees, company cars, and parking lots must be fairly large. There is no evidence for any of the other choices given.

28. **The correct answer is (4).** Judging by their emphasis on dealing with possible clients, such as expense accounts for their employees, they must be selling either a product or a service to the public. Therefore, choice (4) is the only reasonable choice.

29. **The correct answer is (1).** The entire selection is an expression of the girl's homesickness after having left her home and family behind. She is puzzled by these unexpected feelings.

30. **The correct answer is (3).** The duties she describes, as well as her going to school, describe a typical *au pair* situation. An *au pair* is usually a young person from another country who comes to live with a family, helps out in the home and with the children, goes to school, and thereby has an opportunity to become familiar with another country.

31. **The correct answer is (5).** Her expressed feelings of strangeness in being in a regular room and her longing for her grandmother's dishes, which were certainly unusual from the perspective of traditional American tastes in food, suggest that the girl comes from another part of the world and a different culture.

32. **The correct answer is (2).** The girl admits her negative feelings about her family, but she also is feeling miserable because she misses them, which suggests that she loves them. Thus, her feelings toward her family are very mixed, as is true for most of us.

33. **The correct answer is (4).** She goes to school at night, which shows us that she is studious. Also, her many concerns and feelings suggest that she is a serious thinker as well.

34. **The correct answer is (3).** She seems to mean two things. First, she implies that a family is forever part of a person's life and feelings. Also, she views her family as a great burden. While she is talking about an emotional burden, she compares this to the physical burden of having a great stone about your neck.

35. **The correct answer is (2).** A blanket is a symbol of warmth, comfort, and home. Obviously, the symbol is being used here in an ironic manner, as that is what is being denied to Granddad.

36. **The correct answer is (3).** The father did not really mean to be cruel, as evidenced by the ending, which shows his love for his father.

37. The correct answer is (4). Petey's line about saving the other half of the blanket for *his* father when he sends *him* away tells us this.

38. The correct answer is (1). This is a melancholy, sad story, as we feel the sad music and lonely times bred by misunderstanding and conflict.

39. The correct answer is (2). By offering to cut the blanket, Petey is saying that if that is the way you, Dad, treat your father, you can expect me to treat you that way, too.

40. The correct answer is (1). We must understand that Granddad is not being sarcastic in what he says; he honestly attempts to see his son's point of view.

Test 5. Mathematics

1. (5)	11. (4)	21. (2.5)	31. (13/6)	41. (5)
2. (5)	12. (.85)	22. (114)	32. (4)	42. (4)
3. (4)	13. (83.20)	23. (4)	33. (4)	43. (6000)
4. (53.6)	14. (3)	24. (4)	34. (3)	44. (5)
5. (81023)	15. (3)	25. (1)	35. (3)	45. (5)
6. (4)	16. (3)	26. (4)	36. (4)	46. (2)
7. (3)	17. (−5, 0)	27. (1)	37. (−3, −6)	47. (5)
8. (4)	18. (3)	28. (3)	38. (2)	48. (1)
9. (4)	19. (5)	29. (4)	39. (3)	49. (4)
10. (1)	20. (5)	30. (4)	40. (3)	50. (2)

Note: The word CALCULATOR **indicates that you should enter the following in your calculator.**

1. The correct answer is (5).

The amount used $= \dfrac{1}{3} + \dfrac{2}{5}$

CALCULATOR $1 \div 3 + 2 \div 5 =$ [Answer: 7.333; rounded to **0.73**]

An alternative method is to add the fractions and *then* use the calculator.

$$\frac{1}{3} + \frac{2}{5} = \frac{5}{15} + \frac{6}{15} = \frac{11}{15}$$

CALCULATOR $11 \div 15 =$ [Answer: .7333; rounded to **.73**]

2. **The correct answer is (5).** From the Formula page, use the Trigonometry Ratio, which relates an angle (8.3°) with the side adjacent it (E), and the hypotenuse (5.6).

$$\cos 8.3° = \frac{E}{5.6}$$

Multiply both sides by 5.6 to find E:

$$E = 5.6 \times \cos 8.3°$$

Check that the calculator shows "DEG" in the display window. If not, press:

CALCULATOR mode 4

CALCULATOR 5.6 × 8.3 cos = [Answer: 5.5413; rounded to **5.54**]

3. **The correct answer is (4).** Check the units:

$$\text{Cost} = \frac{12.85 \text{ dollars}}{\cancel{\text{yards}}} \times 4\frac{2}{3} \ \cancel{\text{yards}} =$$

CALCULATOR 12.85 × (4 + 2 ÷ 3) = [Answer: 59.9666; rounded to **$59.97**]

4. Alternate form: <u>5</u> <u>3</u> . <u>6</u> __

Solve for F using the temperature conversion formula.

$$F = \frac{9}{5}C + 32$$

Substitute 12 for C:

$$F = \frac{9}{5} \times 12 + 32$$

CALCULATOR 9 ÷ 5 × 12 + 32 = [Answer: F = **53.6°** Fahrenheit]

One way of writing the answer to this Alternate Form question is:.

Another way of writing the correct answer is:

5. Alternate Form: **8 1 0 2 3**

Interest = 85% "of" principle; $I = 0.85 \times \$95,321.58$

CALCULATOR $.85 \times 95321.58 =$ [Answer: \$81023.343; rounded to **\$81023**]

6. **The correct answer is (4).** From the Formula page,

$$\text{Interest} = P \times R \times T$$
$$1000 = 2000 \times R \times 3.5$$
$$\frac{1000}{2000 \times 3.5} = R$$

CALCULATOR $R = 1000 \div (2000 \times 3.5) =$ [Answer: 0.1428; rounded to .143]

The question asks for rate as a *percent*, so multiply the answer by 100.

$R \times 100 = .143 \times 100 = \textbf{14.3\%}$

7. **The correct answer is (3).** Look at each job separately to find the total number of hours worked at each rate of pay. On the first job, Jim worked $3 + 4 + 8 = 15$ hours at \$7.00; hence, the first part: 7×15 represents job one. Find the same information for job two: the total hours worked is $4 + 4 = 8$. The rate of pay is 4.50 per hour; hence, 4.5×8.

CALCULATOR $7 \times 15 + 4.5 \times 8 =$ [Answer: earnings are **\$141**]

8. The correct answer is (4). The packer needs to convert the weight of each box to the same units in order to compare them and arrange them from heavier to lighter.

D	216 ounces $= \dfrac{216}{16} =$	13.5 pounds
E	5.7 pounds	
F	35 pounds	
G	77.4 ounces $= \dfrac{77.4}{16} =$	4.8 pounds
H	10.3 pounds	

Rank them from heavy to light: F(35), D(13.5), H(10.3), E(5.7), G(4.8)

9. The correct answer is (4).

$$\text{Cost of courses per year} = \frac{\$55}{\text{credit}} \times \frac{30 \text{ credits}}{\text{year}} = \$1,650 \text{ per year}$$

$$\text{Cost of college} = \text{Cost of courses} + \text{College fees} + \text{Other}$$
$$= 1,650 + 430 + 100 = \$2,180$$

10. The correct answer is (1).

$$\text{Courses} = 1650 + 0.0375 \times 1650 = 1,711.875$$
$$\text{Fees} = 430 + 0.08 \times 430 = 464.40$$
$$\text{Other} = 100.00$$
$$\text{Total} = 2,276.275$$
$$\text{(rounded to } \mathbf{\$2,276})$$

11. The correct answer is (4).

$$\text{Percent Change} = \frac{\text{Costs in 2003} - \text{Costs in 2002}}{\text{Cost in 2002}} \times 100$$

CALCULATOR $(2276 - 2180) \div 2180 \times 100 =$ [Answer: 4.4036; rounded **4.4%**]

12. Alternate form: $\underline{.\,\mathbf{8}\,\mathbf{5}\,\_\,\_}$

The area of a circle, from the Formula page, is

$A = \pi r^2$, or substituting 2.25 for A, and dividing both sides by π,

$r^2 = \dfrac{2.25}{\pi}$, and taking the square root of both sides,

$$r = \sqrt{\frac{2.25}{\pi}}$$

CALCULATOR $(2.25 \div \text{SHIFT EXP}) \text{ SHIFT } X^2 =$ [Answer: 0.8462; rounded to **0.85**]

13. Alternate form: $\underline{8}\ \underline{3}\ .\ \underline{2}\ \underline{0}$

Total salary = Regular salary + Overtime salary; Total − Regular = Overtime

Hours overtime: 48 − 40 = 8

Salary for 8 hours overtime:

1.5 × \$1.60 × 8 = \$19.20

Salary for 40 hours regular time:

1.60 × 40 = \$64.00

Total salary = \$64.00 + 19.20 = \$83.20

[Answer: **83.20**]

14. The correct answer is (3). Balance the checkbook by adding deposits and subtracting withdrawals. From the given information:

		Deposits (+)	Withdrawals (−)
9/1	Balance	\$257	
9/2	Deposit	375	
9/6	Withdrawal		\$150
9/10	Withdrawal		35
9/12	Deposit	42	
9/19	Withdrawal		140
9/26	Withdrawal		28
	Totals	\$674	\$353
10/1	Balance \$674		
	− 353 = \$321		

Using a calculator, ADD the "balance" and "deposits"; and SUBTRACT the "withdrawals":

C A L C U L A T O R   257 + 375 − 150 − 35 + 42 − 140 − 28 = [Answer: **\$321**]

15. The correct answer is (3). We already know the balance on Dec. 1 is \$421. Subtracting a check for \$193.47 would leave her with: \$421 − \$193.47 = \$227.53. To get the balance up to \$600.00 she would need the difference, or \$600.00 − \$227.53 = \$372.47.

C A L C U L A T O R   600 − (421 − 193.47) = [Answer **\$372.47**]

16. **The correct answer is (3).** Car 1 traveling north, in 2 hours, goes:

    $20 \times 2 = 40$ miles

    Car 2 traveling east, in 2 hours, goes: $40 \times 2 = 80$ miles

    The graphic representation looks like:

    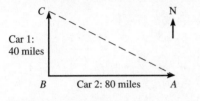

    The distance (AC) by the Pythagorean theorem is:

    $AC^2 = 40^2 + 80^2$
    Taking the square root of both sides,

    $AC = \sqrt{40^2 + 80^2}$

    $\boxed{\text{CALCULATOR}}$ $(40\,\text{X}^2 + 80\,\text{X}^2)$ shift $\text{X}^2 =$
    [Answer: 89.4427; rounded to **89.4** miles]

17. Alternate Form, Coordinate Plane Grid: **(−5,0)**

    Use the Pythagorean theorem from the Formula page:

    $AB^2 = AC^2 + BC^2$

    Substituting values,

    $AB^2 = 27^2 + 36^2$

    $\boxed{\text{CALCULATOR}}$ $27\,\text{X}^2 + 36\,\text{X}^2 = [AB^2 = 2025]$

    To find AB, take the square root of this result:

    $\boxed{\text{CALCULATOR}}$ 2025 SHIFT $\text{X}^2 = 45$

    You are not finished yet. You must find the coordinates of point A.

Points A and B both lie on the *x*-axis and therefore they both have the same value for *y*: $y = 0$. But point B is 45 units to the right of point A. Therefore, the *x* value for the coordinate of point A is at $40 - 45 = -5$, five units to the left of the origin (0,0).

The point lies at the coordinates, **(−5,0)**.

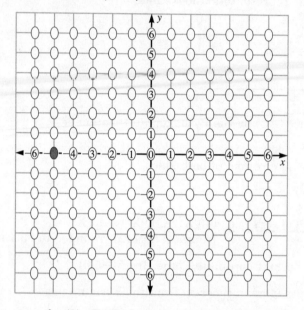

18. **The correct answer is (3).** To find the average height, add the heights and divide by 5:

```
    5' 11"
    6'  1"
    6'
    6'  6"
    6'  4"
   29' 22" = 30' 10" (since 12" = 1')
```

$$
\begin{array}{r}
6' 2" \\
5\overline{)30' 10"}
\end{array}
$$

19. **The correct answer is (5).**

The average weight of team $= \dfrac{\text{sum of the weights}}{5}$

Eliminating Joe's weight and substituting X for his replacement's weight,

$$230 = \frac{X + 248 + 199 + 256 + 195}{5}$$

$$5 \times 230 = X + 898$$

Solving for X,

CALCULATOR $5 \times 230 - 898 =$ [Answer: X is **252 lbs**]

20. **The correct answer is (5).** Installment Plan

    20% down payment = $5,700 × .20 = $1,140

    $200 per month for 24 months = $200 × 24 = $4,800

    Total cost = $1,140 + $4,800 = $5,940

    $5,940 − $5,700 = $240

    🄲🄰🄻🄲🄤🄻🄰🄣🄾🄡 .20 × 5,700 + 200 × 24 − 5,700 = [Answer: **$240**]

21. Alternate form: **2** . **5** __ __

    There was an error of 150 ft − 146.3 ft = 3.7 ft.

    The percent of error is the error divided by the actual distance, $\frac{3.7}{146.3} \times 100$

    🄲🄰🄻🄲🄤🄻🄰🄣🄾🄡 3.7 ÷ 146.3 × 100 = [Answer: 2.5290; rounded to **2.5**]

22. Alternate form: **1 1 4** __ __ __

    In 19 minutes, the minute hand covers $\frac{19}{60}$ of the full circle (360°)

    🄲🄰🄻🄲🄤🄻🄰🄣🄾🄡 360 × 19 ÷ 60 = [Answer: **114°**]

23. **The correct answer is (4).**

    $\text{Average Cost} = \dfrac{\text{Sum of the cost of meals NOT at home}}{4}$

    🄲🄰🄻🄲🄤🄻🄰🄣🄾🄡 (5.49 + 6.49 + 5.19 + 7.99) ÷ 4 = [Answer: **$6.29**]

24. **The correct answer is (4).** Subtract the cost of eating 10 times at home from the cost at Wen's.

    $$\begin{aligned}
    \text{Cost at Wen's} &= 10 \times 5.19 = \ \ 51.90 \\
    \text{Cost at home} &= 10 \times 2.50 = \ \ 25.00 \\
    \text{The difference} &= 51.90 - 25.00 = \$26.90
    \end{aligned}$$

25. The correct answer is (1). From the Formula page, the volume of a rectangular solid is length × width × height.

On the table, calculate the respective values for Volume and for Cost/Volume.

| Brand | Cost ($) | Dimensions (inch) | | | Volume (in³) | Ratio |
		Length	Width	Height	[l × w × h]	[Cost/Volume]
1. Kenmore	1000	33	31	65	66495	$1000/V_1$ = **.015**
2. GE	1100	31	31	67	64387	$1100/V_2$ = .017

The best value for Anne was the Kenmore, which has a cost to volume ratio of .015. (The lesser the ratio, the lesser the cost and the greater the volume. Both factors were important to Anne's choice.)

PART 2

26. The correct answer is (4). The units of the answer must be in dollars; therefore, multiply and cancel similar units.

$$2.65 \ \text{pounds} \times \frac{4.25 \ \text{dollars}}{\text{pound}} = \text{dollars}$$

$$2.65 \times 4.25 \ \text{dollars}$$

$$
\begin{array}{r}
2.65 \\
\times \ \ 4.25 \\
\hline
1325 \\
530 \\
1060 \\
\hline
112625
\end{array}
$$

4 decimals in answer: $11.2625; rounded to **$11.26**

27. The correct answer is (1).

$$\frac{2}{3} \ \text{of} \ \frac{1}{4} \ \text{means:} \ \frac{\cancel{2}^1}{3} \times \frac{1}{\cancel{4}_2} = \frac{1 \times 1}{3 \times 2} = \frac{1}{6}$$

28. The correct answer is (3). The fraction of PCBs *combined* with algae refers to the fraction of PCB + fraction of algae = $\frac{1}{12} + \frac{2}{5} = \frac{5}{60} + \frac{24}{60} = \frac{29}{60}$

29. The correct answer is (4). In Roman numerals:

M	=	1000
CM	=	900
L	=	50
X	=	10
IX	=	9
Total		**1969**

30. The correct answer is (4). The important factor is the thickness of the box and of the card. Dividing $\frac{1}{2}$ by $\left(\frac{1}{100}\right)$, we get the number of cards/box = **50 cards.**

31. Alternate form: <u>1</u> <u>3</u> <u>/6</u> __

Subtract the two fractions. First rewrite each as an improper fraction:

$$3\frac{1}{2} = \frac{7}{2} = \frac{21}{6}$$

$$-1\frac{1}{3} = -\frac{4}{3} = -\frac{8}{6}$$

$$\frac{13}{6}$$

32. The correct answer is (4). Set up a proportion:

$$\frac{\text{amount contributed}}{\text{total allowance}} = \frac{x}{100\%}$$

$$\frac{7.50}{30.00} = \frac{x}{100}$$

$$30x = 750$$

$$x = 25\%$$

33. The correct answer is (4). From the Formula page, $V = \pi r^2 h$. Substituting,

$$V = \pi \times \left(\frac{1}{2}\right)^2 \times 10$$

(Remember that the radius is half the diameter, $\frac{1}{2}$ of 1 foot $= \frac{1}{2}$ foot.)

$$V = \pi \times \frac{1}{4} \times 10$$

$$V = 2.5\pi$$

34. The correct answer is (3). Look at the three graphs. They show that

- Farm Population *decreased* from 30 million in 1940 to 8 million in 1978

- Number of Farms *decreased* from 6.2 million in 1940 to 2.8 million in 1978

- Average Farm Size *increased* from 160 acres in 1940 to 400 acres in 1978

35. The correct answer is (3). To find the population per farm in 1975, find the total farm population for 1975 on the first graph and number of farms on the second graph.

$$\text{Average population per farm} = \frac{\text{farm population}}{\text{number of farms}}$$

$$= \frac{8 \text{ million}}{2.8 \text{ million}} = 2.86; \text{ rounded to } \mathbf{3} \text{ people per farm}$$

36. The correct answer is (4). Percent of increase is found by dividing amount of increase by original size and multiplying by 100.

Average farm size in 1940 = 160 acres

Average farm size in 1978 = 400 acres

Amount of increase = 400 − 160 = 240 acres

$$\frac{240}{160} = 1.5 \times 100 = \mathbf{150\%}$$

37. Alternate form, Coordinate Plane Grid: **(−3, −6)**

$x - y = 3$ (equation 1)

$y = 2x$ (equation 2)

Substitute $2x$ for y in Equation (1):

$x - (2x) = 3$; combine all like terms.

$-x = 3$; multiply both sides by (-1).

$x = -3$

Substitute -3 for x in Equation (2),

$(6)y = 2(-3) = -6$
The answer is $(x,y) = $ **(−3,−6)**

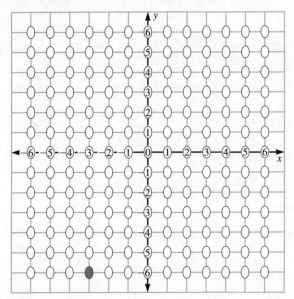

38. The correct answer is (2). Look at line 2 (male) and line 3 (female). The first time the data indicates that boys smoked at a greater rate than girls was in **1991**. (see 18.8 > 17.9)

39. The correct answer is (3). Definition of the "average" is the sum of all the values divided by the number of values.

Here, the sum $= \dfrac{(19.4 + 21.6 + 22.2 + 24.6)}{4} = \dfrac{87.8}{4} = $ **21.95**

40. The correct answer is (3). The median refers to the middle number or the average of the two middle numbers if the total is even.

Here there are 8 numbers between 1990 and 1997:

19.5   18.5   17.2   19.0   19.4   21.6   22.2   24.6

In increasing order, the first 5 numbers are (the middle numbers are 4th and 5th):

17.2   18.5   19.0   19.4   19.5

And the average of the two middle numbers are: $\dfrac{19.0 + 19.4}{2} = \mathbf{19.2}$

41. The correct answer is (5). Read the question *carefully*. Note that the question asks which statement is *false*. (Where does the data *not* support the statement?) Also, remember to ONLY look at the information contained during the time period, *1994–1997*.

Line 1 shows that about 20% smoked; so about 80% *did not* smoke. Therefore, most students *do not* smoke. Statement E is incorrect.

42. The correct answer is (4). Let the unknown number of girls be represented by x.

x girls + $2x$ boys = 90 pupils total

$$3x = 90$$
$$x = 30 \text{ (number of girls)}$$
$$2x = 60 \text{ (number of boys)}$$

30 girls + 60 boys total **90 pupils**

43. Use the Formula page. For volume of a rectangular container, $V = L \times W \times H$. Substituting, $V = 30 \times 20 \times 10 = 6000$.

Alternate Form: 6̲ 0̲ 0̲ 0̲ __

44. The correct answer is (5).

$$\frac{9}{13} = 13\overline{)9.00}$$

$$\begin{array}{r} .69 \\ 13\overline{)9.00} \\ \underline{78} \\ 120 \\ \underline{117} \end{array}$$

$$\begin{array}{r} 1.44 \\ \frac{13}{9} = 9\overline{)13.00} \\ \underline{9} \\ 40 \\ \underline{36} \\ 40 \\ \underline{36} \end{array}$$

70% = .7

$$\frac{1}{.70} = \frac{1}{.7} = \frac{10}{7} = 7\overline{)10.00}$$

$$\begin{array}{r} 1.42 \\ 7\overline{)10.00} \\ \underline{7} \\ 30 \\ \underline{28} \\ 20 \end{array}$$

Correct order is $\frac{9}{13}$, 70%, $\frac{1}{.70}$, $\frac{13}{9}$ or **I, III, IV, II.**

45. The correct answer is (5). $42.50 is 15% off the regular price. Therefore, $42.50 is 85% of the regular price (100% − 15% = 85%). If $42.50 = .85 × regular price, then regular price = $42.50 ÷ .85.

46. The correct answer is (2). Divide each voting result by the total eligible voters, 250, to get fractions for each. Then multiply each result by 360° to get the number of degrees for each sector. It is easy to organize your work in a chart form as follows:

Candidates	Number	Fraction	Sector size (degrees)
A	25	25/250 = 1/10	1/10 × 360 = **36**
B	75	75/250 = 3/10	3/10 × 360 = **108**
C	125	125/250 = 1/2	1/2 × 360 = **180**
No vote	25	25/250 = 1/10	1/10 × 360 = **36**

47. The correct answer is (5). Find the mean (M) *for those who voted* for A, B, or C:

$$M = \frac{A + B + C}{3} = \frac{25 + 75 + 125}{3} = \frac{225}{3} = 75$$

48. The correct answer is (1).

$$\text{Percentage Spent} = \frac{\text{Entertainment + Emergencies}}{\text{Total Budget}} \times 100$$

The total budget is the sum of all items in the pie chart:

$$\text{Total Budget} = 640 + 80 + 160 + 160 + 160 + 400 = 1600$$

$$\text{Percentage Spent} = \frac{(160 + 160)}{1600} \times 100 = \textbf{20\%}$$

49. The correct answer is (4).

Cost of Party − Entertainment money = Over-spending on the party

$$\$300 - \$160 = \textbf{\$140}$$

50. The correct answer is (2). For each item that has changed, the added amount is: New costs − Old costs:

Budget Item	New Amount (Anticipated)	Additional Spending
Food	$500	500 − 400 = 100
Rent	860	860 − 640 = 220
Other	240	240 − 160 = 80

Total additional earnings required: **$400**

ERROR ANALYSIS FOR PRACTICE TEST 3

Circle the number of each question you answered incorrectly. Count the number of circles in each content area and write the total number missed in the column headed "Number Incorrect." A large number of incorrect responses in a particular area indicates the need for further study in that area.

SUBJECT AREA	QUESTIONS	NUMBER INCORRECT
TEST 1. LANGUAGE ARTS, WRITING	50	
Sentence Structure	2, 7, 8, 12, 13, 19, 21, 25, 28, 33, 34, 35, 37, 43, 47	
Usage	1, 5, 9, 10, 16, 17, 18, 27, 29, 30, 38, 40, 44, 45, 46	
Mechanics	3, 6, 11, 14, 20, 23, 24, 31, 36, 41, 42, 49	
Organization	4, 15, 22, 26, 32, 39, 48, 50	
TEST 2: SOCIAL STUDIES	50	
History	6, 7, 8, 9, 12, 13, 14, 15, 20, 29, 30, 31, 32, 33, 34, 43, 45, 49	
Economics	1, 16, 17, 18, 19, 21, 22, 23, 24, 25, 26, 27, 28, 35	
Geography	41, 42, 46, 48, 50	
Civics and Government	2, 3, 4, 5, 10, 11, 36, 37, 38, 39, 40, 44, 47	
TEST 3: SCIENCE	50	
Life Science	1, 2, 3, 4, 5, 6, 13, 14, 15, 17, 18, 19, 20, 22, 26, 27, 28, 29, 33, 34, 44, 45, 47	
Chemistry	23, 24, 25, 35, 36, 37, 38, 39	
Physics	16, 30, 31, 32, 40, 46, 48, 49, 50	
Earth and Space Science	7, 8, 9, 10, 11, 12, 21, 41, 42, 43	
TEST 4: LANGUAGE ARTS, READING	40	
Drama and Poetry	1, 2, 3, 4, 5, 6, 13, 14, 15, 16, 17, 18	
Literary Readings	7, 8, 9, 10, 11, 12, 29, 30, 31, 32, 33, 34, 35, 36, 37, 38, 39, 40	
Nonfiction	19, 20, 21, 22, 23	
Business Readings	24, 25, 26, 27, 28	
TEST 5: MATHEMATICS	50	
Measurement and Geometry	2, 3, 5, 6, 7, 10, 13, 20, 21, 22, 25, 30, 33, 36, 48	
Algebra	4, 12, 16, 19, 37, 42, 43, 45, 49, 50	
Number Standards and Operations	1, 8, 11, 15, 17, 26, 27, 28, 29, 31, 32, 44, 46	
Data Analysis	9, 14, 18, 23, 24, 34, 35, 38, 39, 40, 41, 47	

ASSESSING YOUR READINESS

Plot your scores on the final GED practice test on the table below.

	Ready	Probably Ready	Possibly Ready	Not Yet Ready
Language Arts, Writing	38–50	26–37	18–25	0–17
Essay	4	3	2	1
Social Studies	38–50	26–37	18–25	0–17
Science	38–50	26–37	18–25	0–17
Language Arts, Reading	30–40	21–29	14–20	0–13
Mathematics	38–50	26–37	18–25	0–17

If all of your scores indicate that you are "Ready" or "Probably Ready," you should feel very good about yourself and your ability to succeed. Take the exam. Get your diploma.

If some of your scores fall into the "Possibly Ready" category, especially at the higher end of the range, you can safely give it a try. You are quite likely to pass. And keep in mind that a failure on a GED exam or a part of the exam is not a failure for life. You can put in some more study time and try again. If your chances look reasonable, go for it.

If, on the other hand, you are "Not Yet Ready" in any category, do not put yourself into a position of certain failure, discouragement, and loss of confidence. There is no upper age limit for earning a GED diploma. Make yourself ready and try later.

If you have really followed through on all the text and exercises in this book and are still falling down in one area, you may have to look for help elsewhere. A full-fledged GED preparation program may not be necessary. You may be able to pick up a night high school or adult education course in a particular subject that will give you just what you need. Or you might ask a teacher or librarian for a recommendation to a book targeting your area of weakness. After some more study, try one or more of the sample exams again. Of course, you will do better the second time around on the same exam, but you will know which questions are easier because you have developed greater insight and understanding of the subject matter and the methods for figuring out and choosing the answers.

By now you should have a real feeling for the GED exam and for what is required of you. Unless you are seriously deficient in one specific subject, you should be ready to try and to succeed. We wish you good luck on your exam and in your career as a high school graduate.

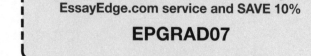

Thomson Peterson's
Book Satisfaction Survey

Give Us Your Feedback

Thank you for choosing Thomson Peterson's as your source for personalized solutions for your education and career achievement. Please take a few minutes to answer the following questions. Your answers will go a long way in helping us to produce the most user-friendly and comprehensive resources to meet your individual needs.

When completed, please tear out this page and mail it to us at:

Publishing Department
Thomson Peterson's
2000 Lenox Drive
Lawrenceville, NJ 08648

You can also complete this survey online at **www.petersons.com/booksurvey.**

1. **What is the ISBN of the book you have purchased? (The ISBN can be found on the book's back cover in the lower right-hand corner.)** _____

2. **Where did you purchase this book?**
   ❏ Retailer, such as Barnes & Noble
   ❏ Online reseller, such as Amazon.com
   ❏ Petersons.com or Thomson Learning Bookstore
   ❏ Other (please specify) _____

3. **If you purchased this book on Petersons.com or through the Thomson Learning Bookstore, please rate the following aspects of your online purchasing experience on a scale of 4 to 1 (4 = Excellent and 1 = Poor).**

	4	3	2	1
Comprehensiveness of Peterson's Online Bookstore page	❏	❏	❏	❏
Overall online customer experience	❏	❏	❏	❏

4. **Which category best describes you?**
   ❏ High school student
   ❏ Parent of high school student
   ❏ College student
   ❏ Graduate/professional student
   ❏ Returning adult student
   ❏ Teacher
   ❏ Counselor
   ❏ Working professional/military
   ❏ Other (please specify) _____

5. **Rate your overall satisfaction with this book.**

Extremely Satisfied	Satisfied	Not Satisfied
❏	❏	❏

6. **Rate each of the following aspects of this book on a scale of 4 to 1 (4 = Excellent and 1 = Poor).**

	4	3	2	1
Comprehensiveness of the information	❑	❑	❑	❑
Accuracy of the information	❑	❑	❑	❑
Usability	❑	❑	❑	❑
Cover design	❑	❑	❑	❑
Book layout	❑	❑	❑	❑
Special features (e.g., CD, flashcards, charts, etc.)	❑	❑	❑	❑
Value for the money	❑	❑	❑	❑

7. **This book was recommended by:**
   - ❑ Guidance counselor
   - ❑ Parent/guardian
   - ❑ Family member/relative
   - ❑ Friend
   - ❑ Teacher
   - ❑ Not recommended by anyone—I found the book on my own
   - ❑ Other (please specify) _____

8. **Would you recommend this book to others?**

Yes	Not Sure	No
❑	❑	❑

9. **Please provide any additional comments.**

_____

_____

_____

_____

_____

Remember, you can tear out this page and mail it to us at:

Publishing Department
Thomson Peterson's
2000 Lenox Drive
Lawrenceville, NJ 08648

or you can complete the survey online at **www.petersons.com/booksurvey.**

Your feedback is important to us at Thomson Peterson's, and we thank you for your time!

If you would like us to keep in touch with you about new products and services, please include your e-mail here: _____